Child Abuse, Domestic Violence, and Animal Abuse

Child Abuse, Domestic Violence, and Animal Abuse

Linking the Circles
of Compassion for
Prevention and Intervention

edited by Frank R. Ascione and Phil Arkow

Purdue University Press

West Lafayette, Indiana

03 02 01 00 99   5 4 3 2 1

⊗™ The paper used in this book meets the minimum requirements of American National Standard for Information Sciences Permanence of Paper for Printed Library Materials, ANSI Z39.48-1992.

Printed in the United States of America

𝄢 This project was made possible by the assistance of the Latham Foundation, a unique nonprofit organization devoted to promoting respect for all life through education. The Latham Foundation welcomes joint ventures with other organizations or individuals who share Latham's commitment to respecting all life.

Library of Congress Cataloging-in-Publication Data

Child abuse, domestic violence, and animal abuse : linking the
   circles of compassion for prevention and intervention / edited by
   Frank R. Ascione and Phil Arkow.
       p.   cm.
   Includes bibliographical references and index.
   ISBN 1-55753-142-0 (cloth : alk. paper). — ISBN 1-55753-143-9
(pbk. : alk. paper)
   1. Animal welfare—Moral and ethical aspects.   2. Violence.
3. Cruelty.   4. Child abuse.   5. Family violence.   I. Ascione,
Frank R.   II. Arkow, Phil.
HV4712.C32   1999
362.82′927′0973—dc21   98-48878
                                                       CIP

Dedicated to Hugh H. Tebault, Sr.
President, The Latham Foundation, 1952–98

Our task must be to free ourselves from this prison by widening our circle of compassion to embrace all living creatures and the whole of nature in its beauty.

—Albert Einstein,
New York Post, November 28, 1972

Contents

Foreword

UNTIL RECENTLY, the less fortunate members of society were cared for, if at all, by religious institutions and extended families. Today's elaborate network of universal education, hospitals, and nonprofit charities are relatively new phenomena.

The proliferation of many organizations that have assumed tasks for the care and well-being of the victims of today's social problems has led to, at best, a specialization among the professionals involved and, at worst, a balkanization of perspectives. Paradoxically, specialization, although holding undeniable benefits for so many disciplines, also has its down side. For example, child protection workers today often need to be reminded that the origin of their work was in the animal protection movement. Spouse abuse and child abuse have traditionally been examined as separate issues; distinct service delivery systems have developed to address them, and practitioners frequently fail to recognize the direct and important relationships between the two.

It is easy to lose sight of the broader picture. It is easy to overlook the fact that child abuse, animal abuse, and domestic violence are directly related as different manifestations of the common denominator of family violence.

This book is part of the Latham Foundation's ongoing effort to reacquaint professionals engaged in the prevention of animal abuse, child abuse, and domestic violence with this common denominator. This effort is based upon three axioms:

1. Animals, particularly companion animals but to a lesser extent farm animals, are important members of the family.
2. Cowardly acts of aggression against vulnerable members of the family are matters of power and control. Whether the victims have two legs or four seems to be as much a matter of opportunity as anything else.
3. Acts of aggression against any member of a family endanger all in the household and put others in the community at risk as well. Only recently have researchers begun to take a serious look at the long-term impacts of animal abuse perpetrated by or witnessed by children.

There is but one word and meaning for cruelty. The abatement of cruelty is dramatically enhanced by direct cooperation between responsible human and animal welfare agencies.

—Hugh H. Tebault, Sr.
Director Emeritus, The Latham Foundation

Preface

THAT WE LIVE in a society increasingly prone to violence is nothing new. Nor should it surprise anyone that institutions formerly perceived as safe havens—home, school, offices—are often sites of violent behavior. As statistics soar regarding handgun deaths, community and family violence rates, drug deals gone sour, and disgruntled employees opening fire on their supervisors, a shell-shocked public wrings its hands in helpless horror and questions what the world is coming to.

The world has come to this: an angered husband in Ohio intimidated his wife by biting off the head of the family kitten to warn her what he can do to her. A 13-year-old boy in New York bludgeoned a 4-year-old to death; at the age of 9 he had choked his neighbor's cat to death with a garden hose clamp. Two youths in Utah videotaped themselves shooting a trapped cat with arrows and stomping it to death. A teenager in Mississippi, after beating his dog with clubs, dousing her with lighter fluid, setting her on fire, and writing in his diary about relishing the sound of her howls, stabbed his mother to death and went on a rampage at his high school where he killed two students and wounded seven others.

Behind each of these and many other gruesome incidents described in this book and elsewhere is a jumble of twisted emotions and warped values: unbridled anger, steely vengeance, cold-hearted retribution, false bravado, and a dozen other motivations. These forces confound those who would devise strategies to curb America's shameful rates of violence: psychologists, educators, social workers, probation officers, police, judges, lawmakers, animal protection personnel, and others.

Animal protection personnel???

In considering the full spectrum of family violence, it has become apparent to an increasing number of professionals in a diverse array of fields that companion animals are significant, albeit often-forgotten, members of today's concept of "family." A well-cared-for pet may easily outlast the length of the parents' marriage. More households have pets than have children. Americans spend more money on pet food than they do on baby food. Emotional attachments to our pets often run so high that protocols are in place regarding rescue of pets from disaster areas and for the therapeutic use of animals in institutional and clinical settings. The nuclear family may be disappearing, but pets seem to be here to stay.

The scientific community and caseworkers in several disciplines are finding that the cycle of violence often begins with violence toward animals. Abuse directed against animals is indisputably linked to child maltreatment and domestic violence. Society has traditionally compartmentalized these acts of violence and those agencies charged with their prevention. But evidence is mounting that violent acts are not separate and distinct, but rather have common origins and influences. Perhaps a more integrated, collaborative approach is indicated. Why not pool resources and work together?

Hence, the relation between the maltreatment of nonhuman animals and interpersonal violence is receiving renewed attention. The potential confluence of animal abuse with child maltreatment and domestic violence is encapsulated in a diagram of interlocking circles, illustrating how each form can occur independently or in combination with each other (see figure 1).

Anecdotal and empirical data reveal that animals are killed or harmed to frighten and control battered partners and sexually abused children, in acts of "interspecies sexual assault," and by children modeling aggressive behaviors and rehearsing their own suicides. Children in dysfunctional environments often witness displays of animal abuse, which compounds their other trauma and psychological maltreatment. Witnessing the abuse of their mother and their pet may compromise children's psychological adjustment, increase their propensity for interpersonal violence (via observational learning and/or identification with the aggressor), and increase the likelihood of their subsequently abusing animals as a symptom of their distress (Ascione, Weber, & Wood 1997; Ascione 1998).

Our ability to comprehend fully the relationship of animal abuse to other forms of family violence is currently limited by the absence of systematic data collection, but this much we can state unequivocally: those who are seeking innovative intervention and prevention strategies to reduce family violence might consider a

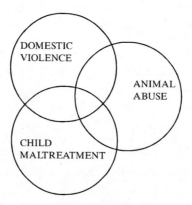

Figure 1. The Interlocking Circles of Domestic Violence, Animal Abuse, and Child Maltreatment

whole new paradigm that incorporates animals as members of the family because the old strategies are clearly not working.

Violence directed against animals is often a coercion device and an early indicator of violence that may escalate in range and severity against other victims. Conversely, animal-based interventions can create healing environments that offer violence-prone individuals opportunities to express nurturance and empathy. Prevention programs can be enhanced by including the network of community animal protection personnel who have traditionally been excluded largely because human service personnel do not yet know that animal abuse falls within the continuum of family violence.

In this regard, we are at a stage analogous to the era prior to the publication of a landmark article in the *Journal of the American Medical Association* that established the "battered child syndrome" as a definable pathology with recognizable symptoms. Dr. C. Henry Kempe and his colleagues (1962) awakened the medical and human services communities not only to the fact that child abuse exists, but that it is a serious public health problem requiring a coordinated, interdisciplinary response. Similarly, Lenore Walker's (1979) description of the "battered woman" set in motion a national initiative to recognize spousal or partner abuse as a significant public health concern.

It was against this backdrop that the Latham Foundation began to look at animal abuse in a new way. Latham, which was founded in 1918 to promulgate animal-based education initiatives to inspire a more peaceful world, recognized that traditional societal and legal sanctions against "cruelty to animals" needed to be updated into a new paradigm more consonant with today's criminal justice and social services systems. One of Latham's hallmarks has been to encourage multiple viewpoints and engage in open discussion of admittedly troubling social issues, and this initiative was no exception.

In the 1980s, the Latham Foundation began publishing articles, and in 1995 produced a video and a training manual, *Breaking the Cycles of Violence,* that began to redefine animal abuse not as an isolated incident with only an animal victim, but rather as an under-recognized component of family violence with serious implications for multiple victims and for society. Experts in a wide range of disciplines began to think in similar terms. Articles, conferences, and initiatives launched by the Humane Society of the United States and the American Humane Association began to encourage violence prevention personnel to look for animal abuse in their community radar screens. Helen Munro's (1996, 1998) definition of the "battered pet" and publication of descriptive animal care and condition scales that offer quantifiable assessments of nonaccidental injuries and risk factors (Patronek 1998) brought the animal protection field to par with its child protection and domestic violence counterparts. The accession of the battered pet syndrome to the list of recognized diagnoses will advance the fields of veterinary medicine, animal welfare, social services, and violence prevention, will help legitimize the efforts of those attempting to intervene legally on behalf of animals, and will provide a broader perspective and attract more community resources to the battle against family violence.

This book is the next stage in this evolution. Latham invited internationally respected authorities to write original essays about what is often called "The Link" between animal abuse, child abuse and domestic violence. We encouraged, by design, a multidisciplinary focus, joining social workers, lawyers, prosecutors, veterinarians, animal shelter workers, child protection caseworkers, and domestic violence administrators to discuss a common topic. We fully anticipated that some contributors would write from research-based perspectives; others would describe interventions with unbridled enthusiasm. We also felt that the most dramatic way to illustrate "The Link" would be to invite its victims to tell their first-person accounts, knowing full well that they could not withstand peer review but that they, more than anyone, could describe animal abuse in violent households.

Thus, this book was born of diversity. We have attempted to approach The Link and its multiple perspectives in a systematic fashion. We have offered a forum for the researchers with their studies, the philosophers with their dreams, the program leaders with their strategies, and the survivors with their remarkable courage to speak out.

Our book begins with a series of essays that set the stage and redefine animal abuse. In *Evolutions*, four chapters describe the societal, historical, and legal origins of these three violence prevention fields and their linkages over time.

We then present *Connections*, three parts with essays written by child protection, domestic violence prevention, and animal protection officials who explain why The Link is important for their constituencies. They share a common recommendation: that despite apparent programmatic differences, philosophically the three fields should be linked more closely for more integrated, comprehensive, and effective solutions.

The section on *Legislative and Legal Contexts* examines how these connections may be effected within the legal system. We present perspectives from legislators, prosecutors, and law enforcement officers who describe the challenges and opportunities of uniting the three fields.

Many encouraging programs have begun to emerge in which populations at risk of victimization or violence perpetration are placed in animal-based healing environments. In some communities, animal protection agencies are collaborating with human services organizations in innovative coalitions for which federal funding may be available. Our section on *Applications* describes 10 of these programs in action with hopes that they will inspire readers to create others.

Finally, in *Conclusions*, Scott McVay provides a powerful, philosophical essay encouraging readers to look differently at the question of violence in America to achieve systemic change. The editors then present a series of recommendations to help effect this change.

This book is designed to be provocative, interdisciplinary, of interest to both academicians and workers in the "trenches," groundbreaking and uplifting. We hope to raise more questions than we answer. For example:

- How can we redefine family violence to include animal abuse? More importantly, how can we end it?
- How can we integrate animal protection agencies into community prevention teams to reduce violence?
- What data do we need to gather, and how can these data be compiled?
- What strategies can women's safehouses, child protective services, and animal shelters implement to cross-train workers in one field to recognize suspected maltreatment in another discipline and report it to appropriate authorities?
- What legislative and prosecutorial initiatives can we undertake that integrate the best aspects of child protection, animal protection, and domestic violence laws and enforcement procedures?
- Can we describe stereotypical pathologies that provide diagnostic criteria for objective assessment of the extent of animal maltreatment, the degree of risk, and the need for intervention?

Collaborative, multidisciplinary approaches clearly open new horizons in the areas of understanding and reducing aggression toward humans and other animals. Recognizing and achieving our common goals remain challenging and daunting— but not impossible—tasks.

This book would not have been possible without the persistence and fortitude of key individuals who helped inspire us and guide this project. To all the contributors, our sincere thanks for your patience, insights, and courage. We thank the Latham Foundation's President Emeritus Hugh Tebault and Director of Communications Judy Johns for shepherding this book past many obstacles. And we would be sorely remiss to not offer special acknowledgments to our wives and families (children and pets), for whom our many nights and weekends lost to this project may not have seemed as humane or family-oriented as our philosophy should espouse; we earnestly hope the book now in your hands is testimony to our love, our vision, and our hope for more peaceful tomorrows.

REFERENCES

Ascione, F. R. 1998. Battered women's reports of their partners' and their children's cruelty to animals. *Journal of Emotional Abuse* 1(1):119–33.

Ascione, F. R., C. V. Weber, and D. S. Wood. 1997. The abuse of animals and domestic violence: A national survey of shelters for women who are battered. *Society & Animals* 5(3):205–18.

Kempe, C. H., F. N. Silverman, B. F. Steele, W. Droegemueller, and H. K. Silver. 1962. The battered child syndrome. *Journal of the American Medical Association* 181:17–24.

Munro, H. 1996. Battered pets. *Irish Veterinary Journal* 49(12):712–13.

Munro, H. 1998. The battered pet syndrome. In P. Olson, ed., *Recognizing & Reporting Animal Abuse: A Veterinarian's Guide,* 76–81. Englewood, Colo.: American Humane Association.

Patronek, G. 1998. Issues and guidelines for veterinarians in recognizing, reporting, and assessing animal neglect and abuse. In P. Olson, ed., *Recognizing & Reporting Animal Abuse: A Veterinarian's Guide,* 25–39. Englewood, Colo.: American Humane Association.

Walker, L. E. 1979. *The Battered Woman.* New York: Harper & Row.

Introduction

And the God with a billion faces asked,
Where is the animal? The child?
Do they prosper as I had hoped?
Are they cherished as individuals?

For certainly everyone must know
They are My special creation
They are the stars, the universes and the galaxies
They are My future.
—Patricia Olson

Animal Cruelty and Societal Violence
A Brief Look Back from the Front
Randall Lockwood

THE CONTRIBUTORS to this volume reflect an impressive diversity of interests and activities, but they are joined by their common recognition of the significance of the connections between cruelty to animals and many forms of violence against human victims. I am fortunate to have met and worked with many of these people. I consider them to be true pioneers, introducing the rest of society to new ideas, new opportunities, and unique challenges. For many of these people, their efforts to educate the public and professionals to the importance of these concepts was driven by a strong sense of frustration at the status quo. Quite simply, animal abuse was not taken seriously as a significant problem in itself or as an indicator or predictor of the potential for other violence by the perpetrators of animal cruelty.

My own earliest writings on this subject were in response to the lack of awareness of animal cruelty among child protection professionals (DeViney, Dickert, & Lockwood 1983) and the widespread concern among local humane societies and animal care and control agencies that serious animal cruelty cases were rarely being prosecuted, or were resulting in minimal punishment (Lockwood & Hodge 1986). For many of us, an even greater concern was that those who were not directly involved in animal protection seemed tolerant of or disinterested in animal cruelty.

A decade ago, stories of animal cruelty and human violence were not a significant part of popular culture and did not attract major media attention. That has changed dramatically. As I write this, much of our time at the Humane Society of the United States (HSUS) is being devoted to widespread media interest in the prosecution of two 18 year-olds in Fairfield, Iowa, for beating 16 cats to death at an animal shelter. The case has attracted world-wide attention and, according to *People* magazine reporters, more mail than almost any other story they have covered (Jewel & Sandler 1997). This is not an isolated event. Several other recent stories of high-profile violent acts have drawn attention to the perpetrators' early histories of animal cruelty. These have included coverage of 16-year-old Luke Woodham, convicted of the killing of his mother and two students in Pearl, Mississippi, who had described the torture and killing of his own dog; and the international coverage of the killing and beheading of a student in Kobe, Japan, by a 14-year-old boy with a lengthy history of animal cruelty. Even coverage of the spree killer Andrew Cunanan, responsible for the murder of designer Gianni Versace and four other men, made the connection. An interview with Cunanan's roommate drew attention to the fact that a "foreshadowing clue" was Cunanan's practice of going to tide pools to catch crabs and burn their eyes out (ABC News 1997).

Does this heightened media interest accurately reflect concern about these connections among the general public? This seems to be the case. A December 1996 survey of more than 1,000 representative U.S. households (Penn & Schoen Associates 1997) indicated a high level of public interest and concern about animal cruelty. Of those surveyed, 81 percent favored strengthening laws against cruelty to animals and 71 percent favored making some forms of animal cruelty a felony offense. In addition, 80 percent favored having social workers, animal welfare workers, and law enforcement officials share information on cases of animal abuse to help identify potential problems of child abuse. Eighty-three percent favored having teachers, social workers, animal welfare workers and law-enforcement officials share information on juveniles who abuse animals as a way to help identify violent criminals.

People are willing to translate these concerns into action. Nearly 75 percent of the respondents said that they would be more likely to support a political candidate who supports tougher animal cruelty laws. As of August 1998, 21 states have made some forms of animal cruelty subject to felony-level penalties (not including dog fighting, which is already a felony in 43 states). Most of these changes have been introduced in the last 10 years.

The public offered a variety of reasons why animal cruelty should be taken seriously. The largest number (32%) indicated that tougher laws against animal cruelty should be supported because such behavior was an indicator of violence in the home. Another 30 percent responded that cruelty was simply wrong and that defenseless animals should not be subjected to such treatment, and 17 percent responded that the most important argument was that such acts provided an indicator of juveniles who were at risk of becoming involved in other violent crimes. Ironically, such strong opinions were not necessarily the result of direct personal experience with animal cruelty. Only 16 percent of respondents had witnessed anyone intentionally inflict pain or suffering on an animal during the last five years.

Because this represented the first such survey of public attitudes toward animal cruelty, we do not know whether such strong support represents a significant increase in public concern over the last decade. The only previous surveys exploring similar attitudes were Kellert's surveys of American attitudes toward animals conducted between 1974 and 1980 (Kellert 1989). In these surveys he attempted to characterize the prevalence of various attitudes. The concerns expressed above come closest to describing the "moralistic" attitude, which was defined as having an emphasis on proper human conduct toward the nonhuman world, most strongly associated with opposition to inflicting pain, harm, or suffering. Members of humane and environmental groups scored high on this scale, as did women and those with a high degree of education. Overall, Kellert reported that only 20 percent of the American population in his surveys was strongly oriented to the moralistic attitude. Thus it is possible that the differences seen in these surveys conducted nearly 20 years apart may reflect a true shift in the proportion of the population holding strong moralistic concerns about the treatment of animals.

What has produced this apparent cultural shift? Many factors may be responsible:

Stronger scientific support for the connection between animal cruelty and violence against humans. These connections have slowly attracted mainstream scientific interest and there has been a gradual growth in academic and scientific support for these concepts (Lockwood & Ascione 1997). Much of this literature existed well before 1980, but appeared to have had little impact on public opinion or policy until the last decade. This research did, however, have some effect on professional sensitivity to these issues. Two indicators of this change are the inclusion of animal cruelty into the diagnostic criteria for Conduct Disorder (American Psychiatric Association 1994) and the widespread distribution of material on this connection to the law-enforcement community by the International Association of Chiefs of Police (Lockwood 1989).

Overall growth of the animal welfare, animal protection, and animal rights movements. Some of the societal shift in concern about animal abuse may be attributed to the overall growth of animal advocacy as a social movement. Even among those who may reject many of the concerns of animal rights or animal protection, opposition to the intentional infliction of pain and suffering may represent one piece of the message that they can accept without conflict. Ironically, some animal rights advocates view giving too much attention to the connections between violence against animals and humans as undermining efforts to view animal abuse as an evil that stands alone, regardless of the implications for the treatment of people.

Specific campaigns of animal advocacy groups. During the last decade there have been major campaigns by several national animal protection and animal advocacy organizations to educate the public and professionals to the connections between animal cruelty and other forms of violence. These have included well-crafted campaigns, publications, and workshops conducted by the Humane Society of the United States, American Humane, the Latham Foundation, and others, as well as efforts by local humane societies including the Washington Humane Society, Michigan Humane Society, and Toledo Humane Society. Such efforts have created a climate where the public has clearly been sensitized to the problem of animal abuse and to its relevance to the larger issues of crime and violence in society.

Societal concern about violence. Public interest in and awareness of this issue is a natural corollary of the much greater concern about violence in society. Concerns about the proliferation of crime, family violence, and other forms of antisocial behavior are, in a sense, the new environmental movement as society seeks to locate, prevent, and correct the sources of "social toxicity" in our world. Attention to animal cruelty offers possible tools for the early identification of victims and perpetrators of this toxicity.

Practical validity. The many essays in this volume illustrate another reason for growing public recognition of the violence connections—attention to these connections works! It helps professionals confronting violence do their jobs better. Law-enforcement officers benefit by taking the actions of animal abusers seriously, social workers and other mental health professionals get useful information by paying attention to the treatment of animals in the home, therapists seeking interventions that will build empathy and diffuse violence see the benefits of fostering compassion for animals.

All of these factors, and perhaps others we will come to appreciate later on, have created a climate of unprecedented concern about animal cruelty and human violence. Social change proceeds when society at large changes its attitudes toward the level of injustice and harm it will tolerate. Although we still seem to be immersed in a culture of violence, there are indicators that a large segment of society is moving away from that violence. Animals continue to be used, exploited, and harmed in many ways that society regards as acceptable. But that tolerance is undergoing change, and growing outrage at intentional harm is an important step in that change.

Public concern about animal cruelty shows interesting parallels to attitudes toward another form of violence, namely corporal punishment. Most children in the United States experience spanking and other legal forms of corporal punishment by their parents, but the numbers are beginning to change. In the 1950s, 99 percent of parents used spanking; in 1975 this was 97 percent, and in 1985 this was about 90 percent. A more recent survey indicated that 84 percent of Americans agreed that it is sometimes necessary to give a child a good hard spanking (Straus 1994). Although the prevalence is still high, society seems to be slowly changing, as well as making adjustments in its thinking about when such actions are justified (e.g., increasingly turning away from use of corporal punishment on young infants). Similar trends could be described in changing public attitudes toward violence against women, such as the "zero-tolerance" approach to domestic violence cases now being adopted by many law-enforcement agencies.

Although we are far from achieving a violence-free society, I am optimistic about these trends. Attention to animal cruelty and human violence has helped society to recognize first of all that animal abuse *is* family violence. Animals are a part of our lives and our families and their victimization affects other family members as well. Also, this connection has helped us move away from blaming the victims of violence for their victimization, because it is often easier to see animal victims as truly innocent, thus placing the spotlight on the problems of the abuser.

The contributors to this volume, and their many colleagues, have made significant progress in the last decade. How can we secure the ground we have gained? First, we must significantly expand the research in this area. The field is rich with unasked and unanswered questions (Arluke & Lockwood 1997; Lockwood & Ascione 1997). Second, we must improve our assessment and documentation of the ways in which attending to these connections improves our ability to do our jobs better, whether as social workers, therapists, law enforcement officers, educators or others. Third, we must be careful to not oversell the importance of these ideas. Identifying the victims and perpetrators of animal cruelty is a valuable tool, but it is not a panacea for the elimination of violence. Finally, we must be prepared to work within the limits of existing systems. For example, as we strive to have animal cruelty taken more seriously by law-enforcement agencies and the courts, we must recognize that the criminal justice system is already seriously overburdened and we must seek ways of working with them to relieve these burdens through creative use of diversion programs, community service projects, or other alternatives to prosecution or incarceration of offenders.

Despite the advances made by animal protection and animal rights activists, the legal status of animals has remained essentially unchanged since the introduction of animal welfare reforms more than a century ago (Favre & Tsang 1993). It is unlikely that we will soon see the same kind of revolutionary change in the legal status of animals that affected the treatment of women and children during that period. What we are seeing, however, is a significant advance in the enforcement of existing laws protecting animals, and greater recognition of the significance of animal cruelty in the much broader universe of antisocial and criminal behavior. That is an important step on the path to a truly humane society.

REFERENCES

ABC News. 1997. The Roommate Who Saw the Other Side of Cunanan. *PrimeTime Live* July 30.

American Psychiatric Association. 1994. Conduct Disorder 312.8, 85–91. *Diagnostic and statistical manual of mental disorders.* Washington D.C.: American Psychiatric Association.

Arluke, A., and R. Lockwood. 1997. Understanding cruelty to animals. *Society and Animals* (5):3:183–93.

DeViney, L., J. Dickert, and R. Lockwood. 1983. The care of pets within child abusing families. *International Journal for the Study of Animal Problems* 4(4):321–336.

Favre, D., and V. Tsang. 1993. The development of anti-cruelty laws during the 1800's. *Detroit College of Law Review* 1:1–35.

Jewel, D., and B. Sandler. 1997. Mischief or Murder? *People* November 24.

Kellert, S. R. 1989. Perception of Animals in America. In R. J. Hoage, ed., *Perceptions of animals in American culture.* Washington, D.C.: Smithsonian Institution Press, 5–24.

Lockwood, R. 1989. *Cruelty to animals and human violence.* Training Key No. 392. Arlington, Va.: International Association of Chiefs of Police.

Lockwood, R., and F. R. Ascione (editors). 1997. *Cruelty to animals and interpersonal violence: Readings in research and application.* W. Lafayette, Ind.: Purdue University Press.

Lockwood, R., and G. R. Hodge. 1986. The tangled web of animal abuse. *The Humane Society News* 31(3):10–15.

Penn & Schoen Associates. 1997. "Americans Support Tougher Laws, Enforcement, Tracking of Animal Abuse." Press Release March 3, 1997, The Humane Society of the United States, Washington, D.C.

Straus, M. A. 1994. *Beating the devil out of them: Corporal punishment in American families.* Jossey-Bass, San Francisco, Calif.: Lexington Books.

Protecting Children
and Animals from Abuse
A Trans-Species Concept of Caring
James Garbarino

ALTHOUGH MY professional career has been spent seeking to improve the quality of life for children, I come from a family of avowed and unabashed animal lovers. From my childhood, I recall clearly that the greatest outrage arose in my parents and siblings from stories of cruelty to animals. When the cowboys and Indians battled on television or in the movies, it was for the wounded *horses* that the greatest sympathy was reserved. In fact, in the household of my childhood it was accepted practice to root for the animals whenever they were in conflict with humans.

I have found many expressions of this heritage in my own life as an adult. For many years my first social interactions each day have been with the animals who have lived as part of my household. The tone of these interactions sets the stage for the rest of my day. Rising before other humans in the household, I encountered the canine. For a decade this meant Abby—her head resting patiently on the side of the bed, with tail wagging, generally assuming the attitude of adoration for which dogs in general and Labs in particular are known and regarded. Now it is Mac, another yellow Lab. Indeed, among the many social relationships in which I have been involved as an adult human, my relationships with Abby and Mac have been the most simply positive. I bring the historical and contemporary nature of my relationships with animals to my understanding of what we can and should mean when we speak of "humane treatment"—of children and animals.

In this I am not alone. Josephine Donovan (1990) dedicated her analysis of "Animal Rights and Feminist Theory" "to my great dog Rooney . . . whose life led me to appreciate the nobility and dignity of animals." This is particularly interesting and important in the present context, because in her article Donovan recounts the fact that one of the contributions of feminist theory to the formulation of animal rights is the assertion that it is from their capacity to *feel* that the rights of animals derive. As outlined by psychologist Carol Gilligan (1982), this orientation to feelings stands in sharp contrast to conventional masculine thinking, which sees the origins of animal rights either in the ability to think or in the use they serve in the human community. I begin my analysis on precisely this issue, that any genuine understanding of the rights of children and animals must arise out of empathy. *We (and they) feel. Therefore we are entitled.*

TRANS-SPECIES KINSHIP

When Desmond Morris (1967) referred to the human race as "the naked ape," he acknowledged an important though clearly controversial thread in our civilization, namely the recognition of kinship between people and animals. The theological implications of acknowledging this kinship have long been a battleground. In the nineteenth century it pitted evolutionists against creationists in a knock-down drag-out fight that continues today in the back waters of academic discourse as well as in the town halls and boards of education in some of our more "fundamentalist" communities. What are the boundaries of our identity as humans versus that of "other" animals? To be "we" or not to be "we." That is the question.

In the latter part of the twentieth century the arena for this debate is found in the more radical propositions of the "animal rights" movement. Listen to Carl Sagan (1977) ask *the* fundamental question of research on the social and psychological competence, the emotional, mental, and linguistic processes of the apes: "If they are 'only' animals, if they are beasts which abstract not, then my comparison is a piece of sentimental foolishness . . . but I think it is certainly worthwhile to raise the question: Why, exactly, all over the civilized world, in virtually every major city, are apes in prison?" Anyone who wishes to explore this question in dramatic visual depth need only view the film *Greystoke: The Legend of Tarzan and the Apes.* Having done so, simply visit a zoo and sit before the apes with open eyes, open mind, and open heart. Or, have breakfast some morning with me and Mac.

But how far can we take this kinship? And what does it imply for the coordination of child welfare and animal welfare programs and policies? There are scientific, philosophical, and logistical dimensions to this question. Modern science tells us that the linguistic and intellectual abilities of some animals are quite impressive—reaching the operational level of young children in some cases. Clearly, there are some animals who are functionally "superior" to some humans—at least in some respects. As Sagan put it: "How far will chimpanzees have to go in demonstrating their abilities to reason, feel, and communicate before we define killing one as murder, before missionaries will seek to convert them?" I do not want to walk the well documented path of those over the centuries who have sought to establish the ability of dolphins to analyze or gorillas to learn to use language. Others have done a good job of that. Rather, I want to consider briefly a series of issues that arise in my mind as I contemplate efforts to link child protection and the protection of animals.

Child welfare and animal welfare ought to be natural collaborators, even if in practice there have been historical wedges driven between these two caring communities. Certainly the more we postulate the need for a general ethic of caring the more we can see a natural collaboration. What is more, the repeatedly documented correlation between child maltreatment and the abuse and neglect of animals (Ascione 1993) warrants a synchronicity of effort. The fact is that professionals who uncover one sort of abuse in a household should be on special alert for the other. Thus, child protection investigators should be trained to be on the lookout for animal abuse—both as a condition bolstering their concern for the children and as a step in the direction of cost effectiveness by forwarding their observations to animal protection professionals. The reverse is true for animal protection officers as well, that is, using the occasion of investigating animal abuse as an opportunity to do an assessment of the quality of care for any children cohabiting with the animals in question. This sort of coordination ought to be a matter of elementary human policy at the highest community and state levels. Rather than closing ourselves off to the suffering of beings beyond our professional or institutional mission, we should at the very least conceptualize a generic empathy for the victimized as part of our core missions.

IS A UNITARY APPROACH TO CHILDREN AND ANIMALS WISE?

Despite the obvious need for a generic approach to protecting the vulnerable, we should consider the possible limits of this approach. Perhaps we can restate this question in the following way: Is it wise to have unbounded empathy? Certainly empathy is one of the foundations upon which to build morality in general, and a morality of child and animal protection in particular. *When we open ourselves to the feelings of abuse we create a prima facie case for protection.* Conceptual discussions of "aggression" or "punishment" may result in an abstract conclusion that children need discipline, that punishment is an acceptable strategy, and that under stress parents may engage in aggression. But look at a child who has been beaten or burned and the feelings create a powerful moral mandate. We reserve a special brand of judgment for those who inflict or profit from such violence to children.

But can we say the same of animals? Who can bear to look at a fox mutilated in a trap? Obviously the fox hunter can. Is he just an insensitive clod or a sadistic maniac? How is he different from the person who can tolerate or even enjoy being witness to or perpetrator of the suffering of an abused child? It is easy enough to see the similarities—unless you have known a hunter who cares for his children with gentleness and compassion.

Popular culture sometimes struggles with this issue. One recent example was to be found in the film *Powder,* in which a rather odd young man possesses the capacity for *imposing* empathy on others. At one point in the film he confronts a deer hunter by transmitting a wounded deer's feelings to the hunter. The hunter—regretfully and with reluctance to abandon a way of life—disposes of his rifle collection and abandons hunting immediately. Who (other than a masochist who actually enjoys pain) could do otherwise? This, of course, is behind the oft repeated insight that if fish could scream there would be far fewer among us who would cast a baited hook into the water. I know that as I have expanded the boundaries of my own empathy there came a point where I could imagine the screaming of fish—and then ceased to be able to cast that baited hook.

CAN WE ACCOMMODATE "HUMAN RIGHTS" AND AN "ETHIC OF CARING"?

In practice, this issue of unlimited empathy is not a matter of much concern in most situations, most of the time. The more common problem, it would seem, is not too much empathy, but too little. Dealing with the most obvious cases of child and animal abuse and neglect already strains our response capacities to, and beyond, the breaking point. Some of us, however, recognize that the foundation for *child* protection is *childhood* protection, because child maltreatment is at least in part a social indicator, that is, an indicator of deficiencies in the supportive quality of the social environment. Thus, by examining the values and policies that either support or undermine quality of care for children (childhood protection) we understand better the factors that generate the need for child protection among vulnerable families. This analysis leads to a focus on "social toxicity" in the community and the larger society (Garbarino 1995). Similarly, we can make progress in animal protection by focusing on the foundation for animal protection in the larger issue of the very concept of an ethic of caring for nonhuman life forms. This is where the animal rights movement intersects with animal protection.

Indeed, those of us who have worked with the most victimized among the human population (i.e., the most horribly abused who become perpetrators of heinous violence and end up in prison), see the loss of human dignity as the principal precipitator of "bestial" violence. I find this in my interviews with boys incarcerated for murder (Gabarino 1999). Psychiatrist James Gilligan (1996) worked with men in the Massachusetts prison system for a long period and from his experience learned that shame based upon denial of basic human rights is the engine that drives the violence machine. A rights-based culture is a culture that has a chance of establishing the reservoirs of self-worth and positive identity that promote high standards of care for children—and animals. An ethic of caring is the goal if we are to build the foundation for both child and animal welfare and protection. But how do we sort out the difficult issues we face as human beings who rely upon nonhuman species of various types for our livelihoods and how do we reconcile our fundamental moral loyalty to our own species in our dealings (from a position of power) with other species?

Perhaps Albert Schweitzer offered some clues decades ago when he propounded the view that the farmer plowing his field to raise food who thereby kills thousands of flowers is doing God's work, while if that same man gratuitously kills even one flower along the road on his way home that evening he has committed a sin. This focus on necessity and instrumentality is a clue, but only that. Human wants create gratuitous suffering and destruction for animals when animals are valued solely on the basis of instrumentality. To wit, the following cases, which to my mind represent stark differences in their moral foundations:

- When my son was six years old he was bitten by a raccoon in the forest of northern New York State. There was a chance that the raccoon was rabid. To rule out rabies, it was necessary to submit the animal's brain to analysis, which meant that the raccoon had to die.
- It has been reported that in order to test the toxicity of new cosmetics before they are placed on the market for human use, they are applied to the eyelids of rabbits. By all accounts, the result is excruciating for the rabbits and effective as a pretest for human use.

In seeking an ethic of caring for nonhuman life forms I am looking for a system that consistently generates the "right" answers for these two situations, which seem on the surface to bear a distinct similarity. Sacrificing the raccoon to save the life of my son was the right answer. Sacrificing the rabbits so that a new shade of eye makeup is available is the wrong answer. What moral framework generates the decision to sacrifice the raccoon but not the rabbits? That is what I seek, and what we need.

I have no delusions that this search is easy or unambiguous. Many a vegetarian would quickly argue that the line should be drawn at the sacrifice of sentient beings for human consumption. And yet, there are very few among us—even among vegetarians—who would accept an absolute equivalence between human and animal lives. Put another way, while there is real debate about whether throwing a cat in the fire is fundamentally different from tossing live lobsters into a pot of boiling water, who would dispute the moral distinction between killing and eating a child versus a beloved dog? Few would—at least in principle.

But if a ship were sinking at sea, who would approve of saving a dog, a cat, or a chimp over any human being? (My mother, for one, if the person in question had shown himself or herself to be morally inadequate.) And, who could approve of a policy that rationed food in favor of the pets of the rich in place of the children of the poor? Who indeed. A look at the economic realities of life for poor children around the world and rich pets in every country tells us that this policy exists de facto.

Is there no way out of this quandary? The answer, I think, is "not absolutely." There is only dialogue in social, cultural, and historical context. There is no absolute definition of child maltreatment, only a series of tentative negotiated settlements in which science and society reach an accommodation about how much risk is acceptable, how much pain is necessary, and how far to push the limits of essential empathy (Garbarino, Guttmann, & Seeley 1986). Is the circumcision of baby boys physical abuse? Is the use of nude children in artistic photographs sexual abuse? Is the teasing of children psychological abuse? Is abortion child abuse? It depends. It depends. It depends.

It depends upon how and to whom we apply the concept of rights, how far we extend the ethic of caring, and what we learn about the consequences of these actions for development. Is abortion the killing of a child or a discretionary medical procedure? Is the slaughter of cows to make hamburgers murder or business? Most of us struggle to negotiate a path through this maze of contradictions and compromises.

The same is true of the lines between the standards applied in protecting children and animals. We seek an expansion of caring, the progressive application of an ethic of caring that conveys respect within the terms available to us in our culture—both our local culture, and what the cultures of the larger world have to offer.

I believe we would do well to seek an ever-expanding ethic of caring, in part because dignity, respect, and caring knit together a social fabric that clothes all who are dependent upon the powerful. Desmond Morris (1967) observed, "The viciousness with which children are subjected to persecution is a measure of the weight of dominant pressures imposed on their persecutors." This seems true when we examine the socioeconomic and demographic correlates of child maltreatment.

But by the same token, the cruelty with which animals are treated seems a measure of the cultural foundations for cruelty in general. We know there is some empirical connection developmentally—cruelty to animals bears some correlation with subsequent cruelty to children (Ascione 1993). I hear it often in my interviews with boys who have committed acts of lethal violence.

In principle and in fact, when we say that someone is treating a child "like a dog" we tell a great deal about the person and the culture from which they come. Linking our animal protection efforts to a general ethic of caring for nonhuman life forms is, I think, a powerful strategy for elevating the quality of care for both animals and children.

Opening our eyes and hearts to the rights of animals to dignity and caring (even when we accept their use as instrumentalities under carefully controlled and evaluated conditions to meet the needs and improve the welfare of human beings) is one foundation for establishing the minimum standards of care for children. Animal protection and child welfare are natural partners.

REFERENCES

Ascione, F. 1993. Children who are cruel to animals: A review of research and implications for developmental psychopathology. *Anthozoös* 6:226–47.
Donovan, J. 1990. Animal rights and feminist theory. *Signs: Journal of Women in Culture and Society* 12:350–75.
Garbarino, J. 1999. *Lost boys: Why our sons turn violent and how we can save them.* New York: The Free Press.

Garbarino, J. 1995. *Raising children in a socially toxic environment.* San Francisco: Jossey-Bass.

Garbarino, J., E. Guttmann, and J. Seeley. 1986. *The psychologically battered child.* San Francisco: Jossey-Bass.

Gilligan, C. 1982. *In a different voice.* Cambridge, Mass.: Harvard University Press.

Gilligan, J. 1996. *Violence.* New York: G. P. Putnam.

Morris, D. 1967. *The naked ape.* New York: McGraw-Hill.

Sagan, C. 1977. *The dragons of Eden.* New York: Ballantine Books.

Evolutions

Until he extends the circle of his compassion to all living things, man will not himself find peace.

—Albert Schweitzer, *The Philosophy of Civilization*

The Evolution of Animal Welfare as a Human Welfare Concern

Phil Arkow

> If [man] is not to stifle his human feelings, he must practice kindness towards animals, for he who is cruel to animals becomes hard also in his dealings with men. We can judge the heart of a man by his treatment of animals.
>
> —Immanuel Kant (1724–1804), *Lectures on Ethics*

WE ARE COMING full circle. In the nineteenth century, newly organized Societies for the Prevention of Cruelty to Animals (SPCAs) intuitively believed there was a link between animal abuse and other forms of community violence. They were founded on the premise that persons who harmed animals would escalate their violent acts to include vulnerable humans. Concurrent campaigns against alcoholism, the lack of social controls, and increases in community violence simultaneously spawned intertwined movements for women's rights, child welfare, and the prevention of cruelty to animals (ten Bensel 1984; Lansbury 1985). Many of the earliest SPCAs were chartered for, or later assumed responsibility for, the prevention of cruelty to children as well.

A fortuitous confluence of factors in 1874 resulted in the first child abuse case, the successful and highly publicized prosecution of the "Little Mary Ellen" incident, which was brought forth by an animal protection group, the American SPCA. Costin (1991) has identified the factors that inspired organized attention to child abuse:

- widespread and often lurid publicity by a newly emerging press;
- revelation of "cracks in the system" that indicated widespread dereliction of responsibility on the part of private charities and public relief;
- the contemporaneous presence of other, more encompassing social movements such as women's rights;
- the emergence of a system of "judicial patriarchy," which gave courts new powers; and
- a perceived link with the SPCA due to new Darwinian thought that lessened the distance between humans and other animals.

Following the success of this case, fledgling animal protection organizations began pursuing the prevention of child abuse with the same zeal with which they attacked animal cruelty. On the national level, the American Humane Association was formed in 1877 and today remains the federation of both animal welfare and child protection organizations.

Implicit in this construct was the unbridled belief that children were particularly impressionable and that "humane education," that is, inculcating schoolchildren with the value of kindness toward animals, would inspire them toward prosocial behaviors. "Just so soon and so far as we pour into all our schools the songs, the poems and literature of mercy toward these lower creatures, just so soon and so far shall we reach the roots not only of cruelty, but of crime," said George T. Angell (1884), who founded the Massachusetts SPCA in 1868 and who is generally acknowledged as the pioneer of humane education interventions. Natural history textbooks of the era echoed this sentiment. For example, a lack of knowledge about animal life "often leads to cruel treatment of animals, and a consequent loss in the refinement of one's nature; for, one who is cruel to a cat or a dog, a bird or a fish, will be cruel to his fellow-man, and such cruelty dulls all those finer feelings which make a true gentleman or lady" (Johnson 1900).

The animal protection movement of that time, however, was more concerned with how animal abuse demeaned, degraded, and defiled human society than it was with the pain experienced by the animals or the violation of any rights the animals may have had. Courts were uncomfortable with basing criminal laws solely upon the welfare of animals. Consequently, animal protection laws were enacted widely but primarily upon the justification that witnessing acts of cruelty dulled individuals' humanitarian feelings. From the outset, animal cruelty laws were enacted primarily for human welfare: to protect humanity rather than the animals. French law adopted this philosophy so literally that animal abuse was a crime only when the act occurred in public so as to affect human observers (Wolfson 1996).

The investigation and prosecution of animal abuse is constrained by the legal doctrine that animals lack "standing," that is, they are defined by the law as chattel property and, as such, cannot represent their own interests in a court of law. The rationale for these laws is based on the protection of the owner's investment, not surprising given the importance of animals to early agricultural societies (Paul 1986). It is a fundamental premise of property law that property cannot itself have rights against human owners and that, as property, animals are objects of the exercise of human property rights (Francione 1996).

In today's *zeitgeist*, "pet ownership" is now being increasingly thought of as "animal companionship" as a result of the restricted range of human-animal interactions brought about by urbanization and suburbanization. An increasing number of Americans consider pets as part of their families and are fully receptive to arguments and advocacy on behalf of a raised moral status for animals (Loew 1993).

Research today is beginning to define and elucidate the role of animal welfare in human welfare concerns. Frustration with the failure of existing interventions to stem a rising tide of community violence has led the humane movement to re-examine animal abuse as a key indicator in the etiology of antisocial behaviors and as an overlooked component within the fuller context of family violence. This renewed interest is focused on four key areas:

1. Acts of animal abuse perpetrated by children:
   Aggressive acts against animals are an early diagnostic indicator of future psychopathology, which, if unrecognized and untreated, may escalate in range and severity against other victims (Kellert & Felthous 1985; Lockwood & Hodge 1986).
2. Acts of animal abuse witnessed by children:
   Exposure to animal abuse desensitizes impressionable children to violence (Ascione 1993). This desensitization may come through individual traumatic acts against animal companions, or through cultural conditioning such as hunting (Clifton 1997).
3. Acts of animal abuse in the context of domestic violence:
   Animals living in violent households become victims of abuse themselves. Batterers also know that hurting a pet is a way of hurting and coercing another person. Animal abuse may coerce, control, and intimidate battered women and their children to remain in, or be silent about, abusive situations (Ascione 1996; Arkow 1996; Firmani 1997).
4. Redefining animal abuse as part of the continuum of family violence:
   Animal abuse should be considered an indicator of other problems in dysfunctional and violent households (Arkow 1995).

Many humane organizations, which had divested themselves of their child protection roles when this function became a mandated service of government, are again recognizing their responsibilities to vulnerable human members of the family. By returning to their roots, these organizations are broadening their missions and creating innovative opportunities to help break the intergenerational cycles of violence.

HISTORY OF PROTECTION EFFORTS

Organizations for the prevention of abuse to children, animals, and women are relatively recent phenomena (Bross 1990). It is even more novel to elevate children, animals, and women out of the status of chattel property into another class with certain rights and who deserve more in life than to be battered.

In the pre-industrial age, abandoned and unwanted children were either fostered out or cared for by church institutions, relatives, or orphanages, usually with no judicial examination of their cases. Juvenile correction systems subjected children to the same punishments as adults. The first juvenile court, with a premise that children were less able than adults to grasp the long-term consequences of their actions and thus were less strictly responsible, was not created until 1899 in Cook County, Illinois.

Women's rights before the industrialized era were limited to the "rule of thumb," the humane standard under English Common Law that a man could beat his wife provided that the stick were no thicker than his thumb. Proponents of women's rights today are still frustrated by a judicial system that often clings to an unwritten code that says a man's home is his castle and what happens there should stay there. In some states a man who strikes his wife is guilty of only a misdemeanor but if he attacks a stranger he commits a felony.

Animal protection organizations have existed only since 1824 when reformers in England formed what became the Royal SPCA. This idea spread to Germany, France, Austria, Norway, and Russia before taking root in the United States immediately after the Civil War. Defining animal abuse as a social problem had distinct elements of class struggle. The growing concern for animal welfare during this period was accompanied and propelled by a tremendous increase in the popularity of pets, which spread downward from the aristocracy to the new urban middle class (Serpell 1986). Humane organizations defined cruelty as a disturbing propensity of rural and working-class citizens. The investigation and prosecution of abuse was further legitimized by raising public health and economic issues: abused animals produced unwholesome meat and the destruction of overworked horses was economically wasteful (Kete 1994; Ritvo 1987).

Rapid industrialization and urbanization in the nineteenth century resulted in a social upheaval that left no area of Western life untouched. Reformers in many countries addressed a variety of social injustices—child labor, debtors' prisons, slavery, women's suffrage, and animal welfare. Victorian-era reform movements that focused on such goals as temperance, women's rights, child protection, and animal welfare were the nineteenth century's strategies to prevent family violence: harm to one vulnerable family member was seen as harm to others. The resulting philanthropic and legislative energies legitimized society's right to cross the sanctified threshold of the home whose members were clearly in trouble. The prevention of family violence became a mainstream societal concern, although ascribing "rights" to victims was then, and remains today, problematic and politically volatile.

Calling animal abuse socially unacceptable behavior has a long history. North America has the distinction of having the world's oldest laws prohibiting animal abuse, dating to 1641 with Liberties Nos. 92 and 93 of the Massachusetts Bay Colony (Leavitt & Halverson 1990). Despite this tradition, however, enforcement of animal protection laws today generally is sporadic, legal terminologies and interpretations differ widely across jurisdictional lines, and serious sanctions are rarely imposed upon those convicted. Animal protection organizations frequently are isolated from other social service agencies and there are few programmatic protocols to connect human and humane services.

RENEWED INTEREST IN "THE LINK"

Although the motivations and symptomatology of child abuse have long been studied (Lynch 1985), it was not until recently that Kellert and Felthous (1985, 1122–24) identified a typology of nine motivations for cruelty to animals.
These motivations are:

1. to control an animal;
2. to retaliate against an animal;
3. to retaliate against another person;
4. to satisfy a prejudice against a species or breed;
5. to express aggression through an animal;
6. to enhance one's own aggressiveness;
7. to shock people for amusement;
8. to displace hostility from a person to an animal;
9. to perform nonspecific sadism.

Not unlike child abusers and spouse batterers, animal abusers frequently exhibit more than one motivation. They objectify their victims and treat them as property. There may be a strong leader-follower relationship between the abuser and the victim. The victim is often physically weaker and unable to defend itself against the perpetrator. Abusers expect an unusually high, and often unattainable, level of performance from victims. They believe physical punishment to be necessary and appropriate. They rarely empathize with the victim's feelings. They repeat abuse generation after generation. As with other episodes of family violence, acts of animal abuse take place within a constellation of dysfunctional psychopathologies and harmful households. It is rare to see cases of severe animal abuse and neglect in which other problems are not also extant.

Walker (1980) and Hutton (1983) found numerous instances where cases being handled by SPCAs were also known to child protective services, suggesting that information gained from SPCA investigations could act as an external reflection of similar phenomena among the human members of the family. But these agencies were not sharing data. DeViney, Dickert, and Lockwood (1983) found abuse of pets had occurred in 60 percent of child-abusing families. In 1987 the *Diagnostic and Statistical Manual of Mental Disorders* (DSM-III-R) (American Psychiatric Association 1987) first included cruelty to animals as a diagnostic criterion for Conduct Disorder, "a persistent pattern of conduct in which the basic rights of others and major age-appropriate societal norms or rules are violated."

The American Humane Association (1991, 1992) convened leaders in child protection and animal protection at two summit meetings. The Latham Foundation (1995) published a training manual and video and has already published more than 60 articles in its newsletter to help child protection, domestic violence prevention, and animal protection personnel recognize and report each others' forms of abuse.

The American Humane Association (1995) followed with a guide, training work-shops and a "Campaign against Violence" to help animal control officers and humane investigators recognize and report suspected child abuse. The Humane Society of the United States conducted workshops and a "First Strike" campaign for grassroots groups launching interdisciplinary coalitions to prevent violence.

These animal protection activities may remind child protection leaders of their field in the 1960s. It is hard to imagine that as recently as the 1950s, abused children were routinely labeled "accident-prone" (Lynch 1985). The identification of the "battered child syndrome" as a medical pathology (Kempe et al. 1962) was instrumental in defining child abuse as a public health problem. This led to a monumental paradigm shift in which federal grants were made available to states that enacted mandatory child abuse reporting laws. Within five years, all 50 states imposed systems of mandated reporting and county child protective services. This national standard may be one of the most rapid and widespread responses in American history to a health and social services problem.

The concept of "battered" women seems to have passed into accepted usage through Walker's seminal *The Battered Woman* (1979). A variety of health care responses were subsequently initiated by nurses, emergency room personnel, gynecologists, and physicians, including diagnostic, assessment, and documentation interventions.

Similar to the premise that the "battered child syndrome" and the "battered woman syndrome" were legitimate medical pathologies worthy of the attention of health officials, veterinarians are now attempting to identify the diagnostic features of what Munro (1996) first called "battered pets" (see Munro, "The Battered Pet: Signs and Symptoms," this volume). Veterinary involvement in animal abuse interventions has been discussed for several years (Arkow 1992, 1994; Phillips 1994; California Veterinary Medical Board 1996) and was given impetus when the American Veterinary Medical Association (1996) made it policy for veterinarians to report suspected animal cruelty, abuse, or neglect to appropriate authorities. Veterinarians in West Virginia, Idaho, Minnesota, Arizona, and California are either required to report suspected animal abuse or are exempted from civil and criminal liability if they do so in good faith; Colorado is the only state in which veterinarians are specifically mandated to report suspected child abuse (Arkow 1994; Reisman & Adams 1996). Maine has a protocol whereby the Department of Human Services (child protection) and the Department of Agriculture (animal welfare) cross-report allegations of suspected abuse or neglect to each other. Humane agents in Florida and Ohio still retain century-old statutory authority to investigate cruelty to children and to remove maltreated children into protective custody (Arkow 1995). A training manual has been published to assist veterinarians in recognizing and reporting suspected abuse (Olson 1998). California added humane officers to its list of mandated child abuse reporters in 1994, bringing the humane movement, in that state at least, back full circle to its historical roots.

A SYMBIOTIC APPROACH TO THE PREVENTION OF FAMILY VIOLENCE

Symbiosis is the relationship that occurs when two dissimilar organisms live together for mutual benefit. The term generally describes two species that each gain a survival edge in cohabiting an ecosystem. Recent studies of the therapeutic benefits of companion animals have described pets and people as symbionts in the modern urban environment (Arkow 1985).

Organizations are living, evolving organisms as well, a macrocosm of the entities within them. Community caregiving agencies, whether shelters for battered pets, shelters for battered women, or protection programs for abused and neglected children, cannot exist in isolation, nor do they fit nature's roles of parasites, predators, or prey. They must function symbiotically to survive. They exist to benefit the societal ecosystem and they, in turn, are improved. And they are most effective when they work in concert with one another.

Animal abuse, spouse abuse, and child abuse have traditionally been examined as separate issues. Distinct service delivery systems have developed to address them, and practitioners have often missed their coexistence within their caseloads (McKay 1994). The suggestion that animal welfarists encounter child abuse and domestic violence often comes as a surprise to those who are not familiar with the range of troubled families encountered regularly by animal control officers, humane investigators, and veterinarians. Effective animal care and control organizations investigate thousands of reports of suspected animal abuse and neglect each year and often are the first community agencies to visit troubled households. Many cases of deliberate and aggressive acts of violence against animals involve youths. These include

- abusive males harming or killing animals, or forcing battered partners to perform acts of bestiality to coerce and intimidate female partners and their children;
- adolescents torturing animals as initiation rites to enter gangs;
- day care providers killing or threatening to kill resident pets to coerce children into sexual abuse and to remain silent about these abuses;
- religious cults practicing animal sacrifices in rituals that involve children;
- children attending dogfights and cockfights; and
- children killing their animals before a dominant adult can do so, or as a way of rehearsing their own suicides.

While investigating an animal welfare complaint, humane society, SPCA or animal control officers may observe children wearing inadequate clothes or experiencing insufficient nutrition or housing. Officers may observe children locked in a closet or with suspicious bruises, burn marks, behaviors, or fractures, conditions that would automatically trigger a report were the officer a mandated reporter. Animal protection officers likewise visit homes where domestic violence has occurred.

Similarly, though it would appear at first glance that caseworkers in child protection and domestic violence have little occasion to become involved with animal welfare, numerous scenarios prove otherwise. Animal cruelty is so common for unattached "children without a conscience" that family pets are "endangered species" in these households (Magid & McKelvey 1987). For example, a child protective services caseworker

- making a home visit, observes pets with inadequate food, water, or shelter, or dead;
- visiting a farm home, observes livestock near starvation;
- removing children into protective custody, must leave family pets behind (the welfare of these animals is in jeopardy and the children may have emotional attachments to their pets);
- cannot enter a home because of an aggressive, protective dog; or,
- conducting an assessment, learns the child loves animals but has had pets killed by dominant adults (Robin et al. 1984).

Likewise, domestic violence workers encounter

- women seeking refuge who deferred leaving abusive homes because there was no one to care for the animals in their absence;
- women on emergency hotlines who say their batterers will kill the pets if they leave;
- women who arrive at the safehouse with pets in the car;
- women who describe consistent patterns where animals are abused in order to coerce or control them, or to force the children into sexual abuse or silence; or
- an extremely high turnover of pets, suggesting families who have difficulty making and sustaining long-term relationships.

The linkages between domestic violence and animal abuse are surprisingly common. Of women with pets seeking safehouse services, 71 percent reported their male partner had threatened to hurt or kill or had hurt or killed pets; 32 percent reported their children had hurt or killed pets; and 18 percent reported that concern for their animals' welfare had prevented them from coming to the shelter sooner (Ascione 1996). A subsequent study (Ascione, Weber, & Wood 1997) reported that in 85 percent of women's shelters surveyed nationally, women who come into the shelters reveal incidents of pet abuse and in 63 percent of these shelters the children talk about pet abuse incidents; but only 27 percent of the shelters include questions about pets in the intake interview.

THE CHALLENGES OF CROSS-REPORTING

Until recently, there have been few incentives to inspire professionals from one field to cross-report other forms of family violence to colleagues outside their own domains. Even if they are willing to expand their horizons, many professionals' humanitarian interests collide with legal responsibilities, organizational constraints and economic necessities. Reasons why practitioners in one discipline may be reluctant to report other suspected abuse include

- inadequate training in recognizing and evaluating other forms of abuse and neglect;
- fear of litigation;
- unwillingness to breach client confidentialities;
- inadequate resources to handle existing priorities;
- absence of protocols establishing cross-reporting policies and procedures;
- fear of economic reprisal;
- inconsistent definitions of abuse and neglect across professional boundaries;
- absence of an organization to which suspicions of abuse may be reported;
- lack of faith in the capabilities of the organization to which a report is made;
- reluctance to involve the government in a family matter;
- perception that the abuse is not serious enough to warrant an investigation; and
- no desire to become involved.

This reluctance is exacerbated by public ambivalence about family violence. Though most Americans would agree that children are worthy of protection, the Department of Health and Human Services reported (Riechmann 1996) that between 1986 and 1993 abuse and neglect of America's young increased 98 percent and the estimated number of seriously injured children quadrupled, while program cutbacks during this period resulted in the percentage of reported cases that were investigated decreasing from 44 percent to 28 percent. A new "backlash" movement is attempting to restrict the powers of child protection agencies to remove children into protective custody. Critics describe the child protection system as a self-serving industry comprised of hysterical witch-hunters and bleeding-heart zealots who trample the rights of innocent citizens (Shapiro 1993). Many people consider juvenile offenders no longer part of a privileged class of children, but rather as a generation without moral compunction and incapable of empathy, a subculture with what one police official described as "no hope, no fear, no rules, and no life expectancy" (Gest 1996).

Societal ambivalence about domestic violence is also widespread. Many of the estimated 1,800 hotlines, outreach centers, and shelters for women who are battered were overwhelmed with record demands for services following the O. J. Simpson criminal trial. Yet domestic violence and child abuse programs receive less than 1 percent of all grant dollars (Greene 1995) and jurors and philanthropists often blame women who are battered for not leaving abusive relationships (Hancock 1995).

Animal abuse is generally not regarded as a serious crime in the criminal justice system. Arluke and Luke (1997) identified four factors that create widespread indifference among police, prosecutors, and judges:

- Society in general attributes less value to animals than to people.
- Serious human issues eclipse other concerns and reduce perceptions concerning their prevalence and seriousness.
- Because only a small fraction of animal cruelty cases reach the courts or the press, it is easy to presume that animal abuse is rare.
- Incidents of animal abuse are viewed as isolated crimes having no relationship to human interpersonal violence.

Meanwhile, the status of animals is confused, complex, and subject to what Francione (1996) called "moral schizophrenia." Some animals are doted upon and spared no expense by their caregivers. Others are abandoned by society to be euthanized in animal shelters. Some are highly prized symbols and economic investments. Some are objects of admiration. Others are trophies of hunting. And some wind up on someone's dinner plate.

COMMON DENOMINATORS FOR THE THREE DOMAINS

Violence has been a chronic problem in America (Courtwright 1996) and its causes and manifestations are complex; many interrelated environmental, psychological and biological risk and protective factors have been cited (Ascione 1993; Hays, Roberts, & Solway 1981). No one theory or combination of variables predicts which individuals will commit violent acts or which interventions will prevent these acts initially or reduce the incidence of repeated offenses. Nevertheless, a synergistic, symbiotic response holds great promise.

The three domains have occasionally focused more on internecine squabbling than on the common goal of preventing violence. Advocates for women who are battered have called child welfare workers insensitive to women's concerns and too quick to remove children from violent homes. Child abuse investigators have accused domestic violence programs of blocking their investigations (McKay 1994). Domestic violence leaders have lamented that there are more shelters for homeless animals than for women who are battered. Legislators have inherited this myopia as well: Colorado legislators once defeated a bill that would have restricted dogs from riding untethered in the backs of pickup trucks because there was no similar provision for children and they did not want their constituents to think they favored dogs over children. On the other hand, in 1996 the Oklahoma legislature increased penalties for spousal abuse by adding this provision to a bill that prohibited bear wrestling and horse tripping. Police in Massachusetts recently were unable to file charges against a couple for leaving their two young children unattended in a hot car, but were able to rescue the children by charging the couple with animal cruelty because there was a dog in the car as well.

Rather than look at differences, agencies within the three domains should concentrate on their commonalties in philosophical orientation, operational structures, and community challenges. These include inadequate data, inconsistent programming, common case management techniques, inadequate resources, common target populations, and common perpetrators.

Inadequate data. Sensational media accounts of children living in squalor, spousal abuse involving a celebrity, and egregious aggression against animals capture public interest. Yet it is difficult for each discipline to determine whether rates of maltreatment are rising or if reporting systems are merely improving. There is a critical need for better data systems to help us understand the manifestations of family violence.

Inconsistent programming. Though the 1974 Child Abuse Prevention and Treatment Act set federal uniform operating standards for the identification and management of child maltreatment cases, individual states continue to maintain their own definitions, investigative procedures, services, and monitoring systems. Companion animal protection is left to an uncoordinated patchwork of several thousand autonomous local organizations working under 50 state statutes and uncounted community ordinances. Domestic violence prevention is receiving some federal attention through the 1994 Violence Against Women Act that enhances interdisciplinary cooperation, but programs are sporadic and exist largely at the local level. Meanwhile, each domain experiences serious gaps in services in rural areas and high dependency on unpredictable whims of community support.

Common case management techniques. The process of case management is similar, whether the complaint of maltreatment involves children, animals, or women (figure 1). Reports are investigated and determined to be invalid, marginal, or substantiated; outcomes may include foster care, referrals, or legal action. One significant difference is that the goal in child protection is to restore the family, while the goal in animal protection is to remove the animal from the family. The domestic violence field struggles with the paradox that most remedies involve removing the victim, rather than the batterer, from the household (McKay 1994).

Inadequate resources. Neither domain has achieved an adequate income stream or public support to address comprehensively the many challenges facing violence prevention. Sayres (1996) estimated that after 130 years of activity, animal welfare groups receive only 1 percent of all charitable contributions and count only 2 percent of Americans as members. Support for child protection and domestic violence prevention undoubtedly follow similar patterns. Interventions that integrate the strengths of all three domains might achieve more effective utilization of scant resources and greater political potency.

Common target populations. More people today have pets than children (see Lagoni, Butler, & Olson, "Why the Link Is Important to Animal Care, Animal Control, and Veterinary Personnel," this volume). Companion animals are members of the family. More than 58 percent of all households, and more than 70 percent of households

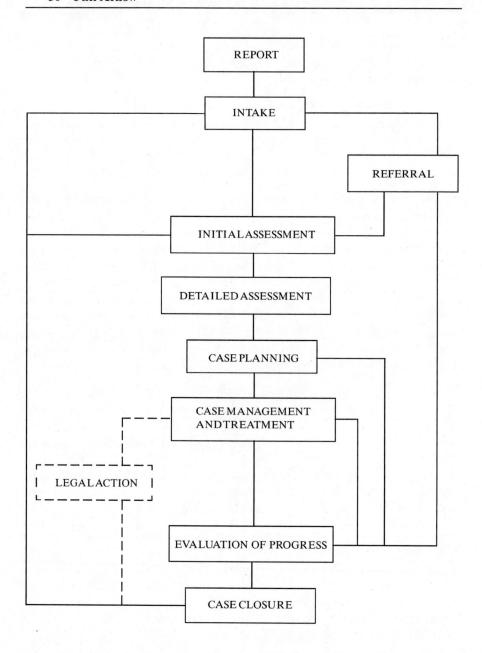

Figure 1. Model of Case Management for Cruelty, Abuse, and Neglect

with children under age six and 78 percent of households with children over age six, have pets (American Veterinary Medical Association 1997). Acts of aggression against vulnerable members of the family are matters of power and control; whether the victim has two legs or four seems to be as much a matter of opportunity as anything else. These acts of aggression endanger all in the household and put others in the community at risk as well.

Common perpetrators. Investigators in each domain frequently are dealing with the same perpetrators but rarely exchange information or coordinate efforts.

DIRECTIONS FOR THE FUTURE

Numerous interagency interventions are now sensitizing the field of violence prevention to these commonalties. Additional strategies should include identification of physical and behavioral pathologies indicative of "battered pets"; recodification of the taxonomy of animal cruelty; inclusion of animal protection organizations in community coalitions against violence; refinement of organizational protocols; financial incentives to initiate multi-agency interventions; and additional research.

Identification of physical and behavioral pathologies indicative of "battered pets." In the pre-Kempe era, not only were physicians unaware of what to look for, they did not know that child abuse was a diagnostic possibility (Munro 1996, 1998). Veterinarians are in an analogous situation today. Lack of attention to animal cruelty issues does not appear to be a result of rejection of its significance, but rather a result of either unfamiliarity with the linkage or competition with other concerns (Arluke & Lockwood 1997). An urgent need is the development of a diagnostic matrix where patient histories, results of physical examinations, and laboratory findings are assessed to determine objective physiological and behavioral indicators of animal abuse and to guide veterinarians to appropriate reporting and treatment responses. The American Academy of Pediatrics' Committee on Child Abuse and Neglect (Krugman et al. 1991) has designed a model to help physicians make the decision to report sexual abuse of children; this may serve as a framework for similar protocols in veterinary medicine. The Tufts University School of Veterinary Medicine has developed Animal Care and Condition Scales to assess dogs' body conditions, weather and environmental risks, and physical care in this regard (Patronek 1998).

Recodification of the taxonomy of animal cruelty. All states have statutes that prohibit cruelty to animals but broad standards leave interpretation of the law to the discretion of individual investigators, prosecutors, and judges. Meanwhile, public perception of cruelty frequently varies widely from legal definitions. Rowan (1993) has written that "cruelty" as a term has lost its utility because it describes many behaviors and requires the accuser to make a value judgment regarding the perpetrator's motivations. Is swatting a fly or spanking a dog cruelty? Rowan proposes a new taxonomy, based in part upon the child protection model, that avoids potential contentiousness over such lexicological issues. In Rowan's scheme, cruelty should be reserved for a small subset of cases in which the perpetrator gains satisfaction from causing harm. "Abuse" would define careless or unintentional maltreatment where the perpetrator gains satisfaction from dominance over the animal. "Neglect" would define passive maltreatment or the absence of satisfaction (see Rowan, "Cruelty and Abuse to Animals: A Typology," this volume). Odendaal (1994) has further proposed that ethological attributes—the behavior of a creature in response to its environment—rather than clinical findings are more appropriate criteria for defining animal welfare and maltreatment. Beirne (1997) has further argued that the crime of "bestiality" should be reclassified as "interspecies sexual assault" because it is similar to the sexual assault of women and children.

Inclusion of animal protection organizations in community coalitions against violence. To stretch limited community resources, animal care and control agencies can play key roles in identifying abusive households and providing resources and therapeutic interventions. Examples of such interdisciplinary collaborations include

- community task forces that cross-report incidents of family violence (as in Colorado Springs, Colorado, Toledo, Ohio, Detroit, Michigan, and San Francisco, California);
- animal welfare agencies that provide foster care for animals belonging to human victims of violence (as in Colorado Springs, Colorado, Escondido, California, West Lafayette, Indiana, Provo, Utah, Ft. Lauderdale, Florida, and San Mateo, California);
- targeted interventions that teach at-risk children nonviolent responses through animal-centered behavioral training (as at Wisconsin Humane Society, Milwaukee, Wisconsin; Green Chimneys, Brewster, New York; and Miami-Dade Community College, Miami, Florida).

Refinement of organizational protocols. An organization that initiates interdisciplinary programming must plan for budgetary, legal, risk management, and programmatic considerations. For example, Ascione, Weber, & Wood (1997) identified the following issues that an animal shelter will confront should it provide foster care for pets of battered women:

- When the woman leaves the safehouse, what will she do with the animals if she no longer has a home to which she may return?
- If the woman is abusive herself, or has a history of substance abuse, may the animal shelter deem her unfit to care for the animals?
- Does the animal shelter have an obligation to reveal the whereabouts of the animals to the woman's batterer, or to release the animals to him? Is this issue affected by communal-property laws?
- May the woman and her children visit the animals while in foster care?

Financial incentives to initiate multi-agency interventions. Federal funding for training and demonstration projects that integrate animal protection into child protection and domestic violence prevention programs will expedite the recognition of animal abuse as a problem of public health and safety and as a risk factor for family violence. The COPS program (see Jorgensen and Maloney, "Animal Abuse and the Victims of Domestic Violence," this volume) may be one such vehicle for this funding. Mandating the reporting of animal abuse and adding animal care and control professionals to the list of mandated reporters of child abuse will be key steps in multidisciplinary communications and coordination.

Additional research. More comprehensive and reliable information is needed about the incidence, prevalence, epidemiology, and etiology of animal abuse and its relationship to other forms of family violence. Data about animal abuse should be regularly and systematically collected by domestic violence and child protection caseworkers and vice versa. Research is needed to understand the attachments toward companion animals held by children in violent households. Grassroots coalitions for the prevention of family violence need to be evaluated to determine their effectiveness and to expedite their replication elsewhere.

CONCLUSION

Frequently, animal care and control personnel are first on the scene to a dysfunctional or abusive household where child protection or domestic violence intervention would also be appropriate, but lacking training in the recognition of child abuse or domestic violence, they do not know whom to call for help. Similarly, child protection caseworkers encounter suspected animal abuse and domestic violence but lack training in its recognition or reporting procedures. Domestic violence officials frequently learn of incidents of child abuse or animal abuse and of women whose own safety is severely compromised by concern for the welfare of their children and animals. The three fields are inextricably linked.

But consistently and curiously absent from statistics about community and family violence—from the FBI down to the local police department—are figures about aggression against the nonhuman members of our families. Animal abuse has been overlooked by the field of violence prevention.

It is easy to say that violence begets violence and that each act of violence numbs us a little more as individuals and as a society. Our knowledge of the extent of violence, the consequences of abusive home environments, and the dynamics of the intergenerational transmission of violence is still limited (Widom 1989). Yet we know intuitively, if not empirically, that many little boys in abusive households are at risk of becoming abusers and even more little girls in those families are at risk of becoming victims. If there are several children in an abusive home, the cycle of violence may create three or four new dysfunctional households in the next generation, thereby perpetuating the problem exponentially. But running through these kids' lives are two constants: each of them has the potential to act out rage against animals; and each of them also has the potential of having his or her anger mediated by the calming, nurturing influence of animals. For as yet unknown reasons, some children in violent households seek solace in their pets and become kinder and more compassionate individuals.

The time is ripe for community animal care and control professionals to take their rightful place at the table of social service agencies. The problems of family violence are far too many for any one discipline to solve alone. Traditional compartmentalized interventions are clearly not working. By working symbiotically, more effective use of resources can be made and each domain can improve conditions for its constituency.

Walker (1980) was perhaps the first to recommend that social workers should reach out to veterinarians and SPCAs in coordinated referrals and educational programs to teach abused children proper pet care and positive caregiving models. She encouraged social workers to include pets within the family system and to record observations of family members' interactions with their pets.

Today, leaders in the three domains are beginning to work together. They acknowledge the challenges that confront them and the opportunities that link their philosophies and programming. They recognize that interdisciplinary involvement may help resolve critical public health and safety problems.

The Behavioral Science Unit of the FBI, one of the many agencies studying these links, believes that animal abuse is not a harmless venting of emotion by a healthy individual. Animal abuse is a warning sign that the individual is not mentally healthy and needs some sort of intervention. Abusing animals does not dissipate violent emotions; rather, it may fuel them (Lockwood & Church 1996).

We must not wait to pursue this cooperation. Animal abuse must be examined as a serious human problem (Lockwood & Hodge 1986). When animals are abused, people are at risk, and when people are abused, animals are at risk.

REFERENCES

American Humane Association. 1991. *Report on the Summit on Violence towards children and animals, November 1–3, 1991.* Englewood, Colo.: American Humane Association.

American Humane Association. 1992. *Protecting children and animals: Agenda for a non-violent future.* Englewood, Colo.: American Humane Association.

American Humane Association. 1995. *A training guide for recognizing and reporting child abuse for animal control officers and humane investigators.* Englewood, Colo.: American Humane Association.

American Psychiatric Association. 1987. *Diagnostic and statistical manual of mental disorders*, 3rd ed., rev. Washington, D.C.: American Psychiatric Association.

American Veterinary Medical Association. 1996. Veterinarians should (must?) report animal abuse. *Journal of the American Veterinary Medical Association* 208(2):175.

American Veterinary Medical Association. 1997. *U.S. pet ownership & demographics sourcebook*. Schaumburg, Ill.: American Veterinary Medical Association.

Angell, G. T. 1884. Speech, February 14. Quoted in J. Wynne-Tyson, 1990, *The extended circle: An anthology of humane thought*. London: Sphere Books.

Arkow, P. 1985. The humane society and the human-companion animal bond: Reflections on the broken bond. *Veterinary Clinics of North America: Small Animal Practice* 15(2):455–66.

Arkow, P. 1992. The correlations between cruelty to animals and child abuse and the implications for veterinary medicine. *Canadian Veterinary Journal* 33:518–21.

Arkow, P. 1994. Child abuse, animal abuse, and the veterinarian. *Journal of the American Veterinary Medical Association* 204(7):1004–7.

Arkow, P. 1995. *Breaking the cycles of violence: A practical guide*. Alameda, Calif.: Latham Foundation.

Arkow, P. 1996. The relationship between animal abuse and other forms of family violence. *Family Violence & Sexual Assault Bulletin* 12(1–2):29–34.

Arluke, A., and R. Lockwood. 1997. Guest editors' introduction: Understanding cruelty to animals. *Society & Animals* 5(3):183–93.

Arluke, A., and C. Luke. 1997. Physical cruelty toward animals in Massachusetts, 1975–1996. *Society & Animals* 5(3):195–204.

Ascione, F. R. 1993. Children who are cruel to animals: A review of research and implications for developmental psychopathology. *Anthrozoös* 6(4):226–47.

Ascione, F. R. 1996. Domestic violence and cruelty to animals. *Latham Letter* 1(16):1–16.

Ascione, F. R., C. V. Weber, and D. S. Wood. 1997. The abuse of animals and domestic violence: A national survey of shelters for women who are battered. *Society & Animals* 5 (3): 205–18.

Beirne, P. 1997. Rethinking bestiality: Towards a concept of interspecies sexual assault. *Theoretical Criminology* 1(3):317–40.

Bross, D. 1990. Law and the abuse of children. *Currents in Modern Thought—Child Abuse and Society's Response,* June, 473–88.

California Veterinary Medical Board. 1996. Reporting of suspected instances of child abuse. *News & Views* 15(1):15.

Clifton, M. 1997. Grisly crimes spotlight control, keeping, and the missing link. *Animal People* 6(6):18.

Costin, L. B. 1991. Unraveling the Mary Ellen legend: Origins of the "cruelty" movement. *Social Service Review* 65(2):203–23.

Courtwright, D. T. 1996. Violence in America. *American Heritage,* September, 37–51.

DeViney, E., J. Dickert, and R. Lockwood. 1983. The care of pets within child abusing families. *International Journal for the Study of Animal Problems* 4:321–29.

Firmani, D. 1997. Helping preserve the human-animal bond. *Animal Sheltering* 20(1):15–18.

Francione, G. 1996. Animals as property. *Animal Law* 2:i–vi.

Gest, T. 1996. Crime time bomb. *U.S. News & World Report,* March 25, 28–36.

Greene, E. 1995. Family violence overburdens charities. *Chronicle of Philanthropy* 24(7):1–16.

Hancock, L. 1995. Why batterers so often go free. *Newsweek,* October 16, 61.

Hays, J. R., T. K. Roberts, and K. S. Solway. 1981. *Violence and the violent individual.* New York: Spectrum.

Hutton, J. S. 1983. Animal abuse as a diagnostic approach in social work: A pilot study. In A. H. Katcher and A. M. Beck, eds., *New Perspectives on Our Lives with Companion Animals,* 444–47. Philadelphia: University of Pennsylvania Press.

Johnson, I. T. 1900. *Young people's natural history: A popular story of animals, birds, reptiles, fishes and insects, describing their structure, habits, instincts and dwellings, with thrilling stories of adventure and amusing anecdotes of wild and tame animals.* Chicago: A. B. Kuhlman.

Kellert, S. R., and A. R. Felthous. 1985. Childhood cruelty toward animals among criminals and noncriminals. *Human Relations* 38:1113–29.

Kempe, C. H., Silverman, F., Steele, B., et al. 1962. The battered child syndrome. *Journal of the American Medical Association* 181 (July 7):17–24.

Kete, K. 1994. *The beast in the boudoir: Petkeeping in nineteenth-century Paris.* Berkeley: University of California Press.

Krugman, R., J. A. Bays, D. Chadwick, et al. 1991. Guidelines for the evaluation of sexual abuse of children. *Pediatrics* 87:257.

Lansbury, C. 1985. *The old brown dog: Women, workers and vivisection in Edwardian England.* Madison: University of Wisconsin Press.

Latham Foundation. 1995. *Breaking the cycles of violence.* Alameda, Calif.: Latham Foundation.

Leavitt, E. S., and D. Halverson. 1990. The evolution of anti-cruelty laws in the United States. In Animal Welfare Institute, *Animals and Their Legal Rights,* 4th edition. Washington, D.C.: Animal Welfare Institute.

Lockwood, R., and A. Church. 1996. Deadly serious: An FBI perspective on animal cruelty. *HSUS News,* Fall, 27–30.

Lockwood, R., and G. R. Hodge. 1986. The tangled web of animal abuse: The links between cruelty to animals and human violence. *The Humane Society News,* Summer, 10–15.

Loew, F. M. 1993. The moral status of animals and U.S. public policy. *Animal Policy Report* 7(2) (August):1–2.

Lynch, M. A. 1985. Child abuse before Kempe: An historical literature review. *Child Abuse & Neglect* 9:7–15.

Magid, K., and C. A. McKelvey. 1987. *High risk: Children without a conscience.* New York: Bantam Books.

McKay, M. M. 1994. The link between domestic violence and child abuse: Assessment and treatment considerations. *Child Welfare* 73(1):29–39.

Munro, H. 1996. Battered pets. *Irish Veterinary Journal* 49(12):712–13.

Munro, H. 1998. The battered pet syndrome. In P. Olson, ed., *Recognizing & reporting animal abuse: A veterinarian's guide.* Englewood, Colo.: American Humane Association.

Odendaal, J. S. J. 1994. Veterinary ethology and animal welfare. International Office of Epizootics. *Scientific and Technical Review: Animal Welfare and Veterinary Services* 13(1):261–75.

Olson, P. 1998. *Recognizing & reporting animal abuse: A veterinarian's guide.* Englewood, Colo: American Humane Association.

Patronek, G. 1998. Issues and guidelines for veterinarians in recognizing, reporting and assessing animal neglect and abuse. In P. Olson, ed., *Recognizing & reporting animal abuse: A veterinarian's guide.* Englewood, Colo.: American Humane Association.

Paul, P. 1986. Some origins of laws and legal codes regarding animals. *Community Animal Control,* January–February, 13–23.

Phillips, T. 1994. Cruelty: To report or not to report? *Large Animal Veterinarian* 49(4):34.

Reisman, R., and C. A. Adams. 1996. Should vets tell? *Animal Watch,* Summer, 19–21.

Riechmann, D. 1996. Study finds big rise in child abuse. *Philadelphia Inquirer,* September 19, A-2.

Ritvo, H. 1987. *The animal estate: The English and other creatures in the Victorian age.* Cambridge: Harvard University Press.

Robin, M., R. W. ten Bensel, J. Quigley, and R. K. Anderson. 1984. Abused children and their pets. In R. K. Anderson, B. L. Hart, and L. A. Hart, eds., *The pet connection: Its influence on our health and quality of life,* 111–18. Minneapolis: University of Minnesota Center to Study Human-Animal Relationships and Environments.

Rowan, A. 1993. Cruelty to animals. *Anthrozoös* 6:218–20.

Sayres, E. 1996. Promoting unity in the humane community. Presentation to NoKills in 1996 Conference, Englewood, Colorado, September 8.

Serpell, J. 1986. *In the company of animals.* New York: Basil Blackwell.

Shapiro, L. 1993. Rush to judgment. *Newsweek,* April 19, 54–60.

ten Bensel, R. W. 1984. Historical perspectives of human values for animals and vulnerable people. In R. K. Anderson, B. L. Hart, and L. A. Hart, eds., *The pet connection: Its influence on our health and quality of life,* 2–14. Minneapolis: University of Minnesota Center to Study Human-Animal Relationships and Environments.

Walker, J. R. 1980. A study on the relationship of child abuse and pet abuse. Unpublished professional project, University of Pennsylvania School of Social Work, Philadelphia.

Walker, L. 1979. *The battered woman.* New York: Harper and Row.

Widom, C. S. 1989. Does violence beget violence? A critical examination of the literature. *Psychological Bulletin* 106:3–28.

Wolfson, D. J. 1996. Beyond the law: Agribusiness and the systemic abuse of animals raised for food or food production. *Animal Law* 2:123–54.

Working Out the Beast
An Alternative History
of Western Humaneness
James A. Serpell

Sometimes men have held the anthropomorphic view that animals and men are very much alike, with the same emotions and similar mental powers. . . . At other times men have held stubbornly to the anthropocentric opinion that this is a man's world and that an unbridgeable chasm yawns between the human race and other species. Among Europeans, Christianity has encouraged this anthropocentric attitude.

—Dix Harwood, Love for Animals and How it Developed in Great Britain, 1928

INTRODUCTION

MOST HISTORICAL ACCOUNTS of the growth of public sympathy for the plight of non-human animals (henceforth referred to as "animals") depict it as a relatively recent phenomenon associated with the great social reform movements of the eighteenth and nineteenth centuries (Harwood 1928; Ritvo 1987; Ryder 1991; Thomas 1983; Turner 1980). These surveys clearly document a significant softening of attitudes toward the treatment of animals during this period, particularly among the emerging urban middle classes, and they tend to give the impression that kindness or compassion toward animals is a strictly modern and largely Western invention. Less than three hundred years ago, for example, animal-loving England was described by one foreign visitor as "a hell for horses," and the centuries of European history prior to about 1700 seem to offer little more than a bleak vista of ongoing callousness and cruelty toward animals, receding forever into an increasingly brutal, savage, and Hobbesian past (Harwood 1928). Or, as one recent article put it, "despite references to kindly treatment of animals in the Bible, among the ancient Greeks, and in some early ecclesiastical writings, little concern existed among the general populace toward this issue prior to the modern era" (Kellert & Felthous 1985).

For the founders of the humane movement during the nineteenth century, this historical change in attitudes regarding animal suffering was a clear sign of social progress toward the goal of moral enlightenment. Cruelty to animals was, in their view, a symptom of the fundamentally brutal nature of most humans. As far as many educated Victorians were concerned, children—especially male children—were innately cruel and heartless and needed to be carefully socialized and "improved" through exposure to morally uplifting activities and pastimes. Also ripe for moral uplift were the working classes who were widely regarded as a dangerous and disorderly rabble, governed by "brute" passions and addicted to vicious "blood sports" such as bull-baiting and cock-fighting (Ritvo 1987).

At the same time, sensational travelers' tales of "primitive savages" living wild, animal-like existences in remote outposts of the Empire helped to fuel the Victorian middle classes' sense of beleaguered cultural superiority. Even Charles Darwin had reservations about the humanity of some of the peoples he encountered on his famous *Beagle* voyage. Referring to the native people of Tierra del Fuego, he confessed to his journal that he "could not have believed how wide was the difference between savage and civilized man; it is greater than between a wild and domesticated animal, inasmuch as in man there is a greater power of improvement." For Darwin and his contemporaries, "civilization" was a process clearly analogous to animal taming or domestication. It could only be achieved and maintained through the active suppression of mankind's original, savage or beastlike character, and the simultaneous cultivation of domesticity, gentility, and self-control. While the poet Tennyson exhorted his readers to "move upwards, working out the beast," nineteenth-century humanitarians used humane education—the attempt to inculcate compassion and concern for animals and other vulnerable groups—as a key weapon of social control against what they saw as the bestial and disruptive elements of Victorian society (Ritvo 1987).

Notwithstanding the demands of political correctness, these progressionist ideas about the origins of cruelty and kindness to animals are still firmly imbedded in our culture. They form the basis of most of our anticruelty laws and they are implicit in many of our humane education programs and initiatives. Inadvertently, they have also given rise to the notion that cruelty to animals, or at least indifference to their welfare, is essentially the bottom line, and that humaneness is a sort of luxury that can only be afforded by those individuals and cultures who are fortunate enough to have the time and resources to squander on such refinements. The aim of the present chapter is to challenge these long-established ideas and perceptions by re-examining the history of humaneness from a somewhat wider perspective. According to this alternative account, the association of humaneness with "civilization" is based on erroneous beliefs about the ethics (or lack of ethics) of preliterate and "precivilized" peoples, and on a strictly limited, Eurocentric history of the treatment of animals. I argue, instead, that the virtual exclusion of animals from the sphere of moral consideration that typified pre-eighteenth century Europe was the exception rather than the rule, and that the changes in attitude that occurred after this represented a sort of reversion to pre-existing moral values following a temporary, and in many ways aberrant, episode of extreme anthropocentrism.

IN THE BEGINNING

Until about 11,000 years ago, humans throughout the world lived entirely by hunting, fishing, and foraging for wild foods. The term "hunter-gatherer" has been coined to describe cultures of this type, and it is generally accepted that this was the original, ancestral lifestyle of all modern humans. We can only guess at the length of time our hominid forebears lived by hunting and gathering, but even the most conservative estimates suggest that variations on this subsistence theme have been around for at least 500,000 years (Mithen 1996). Anthropologists and archaeologists are understandably cautious about using living or recent hunter-gatherers as a source of insight concerning the attitudes and beliefs of our pre-agricultural ancestors. Among the very few that still survive, most living hunter-gatherers have been more or less acculturated by their more aggressive agricultural neighbors and nearly all of them have been substantially marginalized economically. Nevertheless, as surviving exemplars of a particular—and once universal—mode of economic subsistence, recent hunter-gatherers can hardly be ignored as a reference point, particularly when the same ideological themes are shared by many otherwise ethnically diverse populations. One of these shared themes concerns the perception and treatment of animals.

A remarkable degree of consistency in attitudes and beliefs about animals exists among hunter-gatherer societies as far apart as Siberia, Amazonia, or the Kalahari region of southern Africa. Briefly summarized, these beliefs include the notion that animals are fully rational, sentient, and intelligent beings in no way inferior to humans, and that the bodies of animals, like those of people, are animated by noncorporeal spirits or "souls" that survive the body after death. Although it is recognized that certain skills are needed in order to be a good hunter, it is also believed that no amount of skill or ingenuity will succeed if the animal quarry is unwilling to submit to being killed. Game animals must therefore be treated at all times with proper respect and consideration in order to earn their goodwill. Failure to treat the animal respectfully may cause either the animal's spirit, or that of its spiritual guardian, to demand some form of posthumous restitution. Types of spiritual retribution that may result from disrespectful behavior include the infliction of illness, injury, madness, or death on the hunter or other members of his family or clan, or loss of success in future hunting (Speck 1977; Martin 1978; Campbell 1984; Nelson 1986; Guenther 1988; Wenzel 1991). As Ingold (1994:15) has observed, "The hunter hopes that by being good to animals, they in turn will be good to him. But by the same token, the animals have the power to withhold if any attempt is made to coerce what they are not, of their own volition, prepared to provide. . . . Animals thus maltreated will desert the hunter, or even cause him ill fortune."

Not surprisingly, these beliefs about animals and the consequences of treating them improperly tend to generate considerable anxiety: anxiety that is expressed and relieved through the performance of strict and elaborate hunting rules and rituals. In many cultures, for example, the actual act of killing an animal is performed in a prescribed way, often accompanied by spoken apologies or excuses, and in a manner that avoids unnecessary cruelty. A wounded animal must be tracked and pursued, for days if necessary, rather than being allowed to die in vain, and once dead, its carcass must be treated in a morally appropriate fashion: skinned and butchered appropriately, scrupulously shared with other members of the group, and consumed entirely so that no edible or usable remains are wasted. Any parts that cannot be used must be disposed of in the correct ceremonial manner appropriate to the species; for instance, among certain Native American groups, unused beaver remains were carefully wrapped up together and placed in the nearest river or stream.

Specific dietary taboos are also widespread. In general, these arise from the notion that each hunter has a special spiritual affinity with certain animal species, and is therefore forbidden to kill them or eat their flesh. Often this sense of affinity is derived from the contents of dreams or visions induced by fasting, dancing, sleep deprivation, or the consumption of psychoactive drugs. The object of these vision quests is to obtain the goodwill of the animal spirits; an essential prerequisite for good health and successful hunting. In addition to dietary fasting, sexual abstinence and other forms of self-denial (or even self-mutilation) are also commonly practiced in order to win the animals' sympathy (Hallowell 1926; Benedict 1929; Speck 1977; Martin 1978; Campbell 1984; Nelson 1986; Wenzel 1991; Ingold 1994). Although, in theory, anybody can gain access to the spirit world by these means, certain individuals, often known as shamans, are believed to possess a special talent for communicating with animal or guardian spirits. In many hunter-gatherer societies, the shaman thus fulfills the same sort of role as a medium or priest by interceding with the supernatural powers on behalf of the rest of the community (Eliade 1964).

All of this emphasis on maintaining correct and respectful relations with animals and nature, and particularly the prohibitions against waste, have led some anthropologists to describe hunter-gatherers as "resource managers" who have developed a "conservation ethic" that inhibits them from overexploiting their natural resources. Referring to the Koyukon of central Alaska, for example, the anthropologist Richard Nelson (1986:211) states that

> Strong sanctions apply to killing animals or plants and leaving them unused. Meat is carefully butchered and stored where it will not spoil . . . and fullest possible use is made of it to avoid offending the animal's spirit. . . . Koyukon hunters go to great lengths to avoid losing wounded game. If a shot animal escapes, it is doggedly pursued, every effort is made to retrieve it, and if it is not found the hunter is genuinely upset. Most animal meat and organs are utilized, and disposal of the parts considered unusable is carried out in special, respectful ways. . . . Among the

Koyukon, reverence for nature, which is strongly manifested in both religion and personality, is unquestionably related to conscious limitation of use.

In reality, however, the explicit reason given for avoiding wasteful use of animal products is the fear of causing the animal offense and thereby provoking its spiritual retaliation. This may or may not include the disappearance of game, but it also carries the more immediate personal threat of disease, injury, or death if ritual codes of conduct—some of which appear to have no obvious relation to resource conservation—are violated. It may therefore be more accurate to say that hunter-gatherers have evolved an *ethic of respect* for animals based on the belief that they share many of the morally relevant characteristics of persons. Killing animals needlessly, disrespectfully, or in a manner likely to cause unnecessary suffering is thus morally equivalent to murder, a sin that must be expiated and atoned for in order to avoid supernatural punishment.

So what happened to this highly developed ethic of respect for animals? Why do we see so few traces of it among the cultures (including our own) that gradually displaced subsistence hunter-gatherers from all but the most marginal corners of the globe? Probably because such an egalitarian moral ideology was incompatible with the successful exploitation of domestic, as opposed to wild, animals. Subsistence hunters need to understand and identify with the animals they depend on for food. An insensitive hunter is a bad hunter; a good hunter is one who learns to "think like" his prey, to empathize with it. Such a high level of personal identification almost inevitably leads to the animals being perceived as near equals or even kinsmen, not to mention the attendant moral conflicts associated with hunting and devouring those "kin." Conversely, a hunter does not ordinarily interact with his prey socially and, except at the moment of the animal's death, he exercises little or no control over it. The animal remains an independent being with a mind of its own, and it is possible for the hunter to convince himself that, if the animal allowed itself to be killed, it did so of its own free will. It would require a supreme feat of self-deception for a farmer or herdsman to reach a similar conclusion. The domestic animal is almost totally dependent for survival on its human custodian. It has no free will, as such. Moreover, because they live together in what is, to some extent, a combined social group, it is not unusual for farmers and herdsmen to establish social bonds with their animals and vice versa. The moral dilemma is, therefore, far more intense for the farmer than the hunter, because killing or harming the animal in this context effectively constitutes a gross betrayal of trust (Serpell 1996).

Farmers, herdsmen, and others who benefit from the exploitation of domestic species have dealt with this ethical dilemma using a variety of coping strategies (see Serpell 1996). Perhaps the most pervasive and durable was the idea that humans are both morally separate from, and superior to, all other animals. As Ingold (1994, 16) has recently observed, the ideological difference between hunters and herdsmen primarily involves a shift from human-animal relations based on *trust* to those based on *domination:*

> In the world of the hunter, animals, too, are supposed to care, to the extent of laying down their lives for humans by allowing themselves to be taken. They retain, however, full control over their own destiny. Under pastoralism, that control has been relinquished to humans. It is the herdsman who makes life-or-death decisions concerning what are now 'his' animals. . . . He sacrifices them; they do not sacrifice themselves to him. They are cared for but they are not themselves empowered to care. Like dependents in the household of a patriarch, their status is that of jural minors, subject to the authority of their human master. In short, the relationship of pastoral care, quite unlike that of the hunter towards animals, is founded on a principle not of trust but of domination.

LAMBS OF GOD

The advent of agriculture and animal husbandry roughly 11,000 years ago thus produced a dramatic shift in the balance of power between humans and the animals they depended on for food. From being independent coequals or superiors, animals became slaves and subordinates, increasingly dependent on people for care and protection. This shift in power relations was reflected in religious belief systems that became progressively more and more hierarchical throughout the ancient world. Just as humans became dominant over their domestic livestock, the original animal guardian spirits were elevated to the status of zoomorphic gods with increasingly awesome powers over human lives and livelihoods. Initially, the jurisdiction of these godlike entities was probably confined to the species they represented: bull gods to regulate the husbandry and slaughter of cattle, ram gods presiding over sheep, and so on. Over time, however, the connections between these gods and their animal progenitors became increasingly tenuous, and the gods themselves became correspondingly anthropomorphic in appearance and behavior. During this metamorphosis, they first acquired human heads or torsos before eventually becoming fully humanoid. Long after this, however, many retained the ability to transform themselves into animals when occasion demanded. The "major" gods also became fewer in number and associated in more general ways with aspects of the agricultural cycle: the sun, the rain, soil fertility, seasonal changes, and so on (Schwabe 1994). Perhaps reflecting the potentially devastating ecological uncertainties of rising populations and seasonal agricultural production, this new generation of deities was also viewed as capricious and spiteful, ready to dole out drought, famine, and pestilence on a seemingly arbitrary basis. In response to these perceived threats, wholesale animal sacrifice was widely practiced during this period. In theory, these sacrifices represented a way of nourishing the gods and atoning for any grievances they may have had. In practice, they also provided people with a method of exonerating themselves from the guilt associated with slaughtering and consuming their animal dependents.

In all of the ancient agrarian civilizations—Greece, Egypt, Mesopotamia, Assyria, and India—the killing of food animals in a nonsacrificial manner was considered a crime, morally equivalent to manslaughter. Only those properly versed in the sacred mysteries were allowed to sacrifice animals, and only the blood or small portions of the animals typically were reserved for the gods. The rest of the meat was either returned to the animal's owner or redistributed to the populace at large. Because the consumption of unsacrificed meat was also considered taboo, the priests who performed these sacrifices tended to exercise relatively exclusive control over meat production, slaughter, and distribution. Surviving accounts of sacrificial rituals indicate that ideally the animal was supposed to approach the altar willingly, without coercion, and that it was often encouraged to nod its head as if assenting to its own slaughter. Following the sacrifice, the priests who performed the act sometimes whispered apologies in the animal's ear, and it was not uncommon for the sacrificial knife to be "punished" by being destroyed. In many cases, the sacrificial animal was also pampered and nurtured for a period of time before being killed, as if to compensate it for its untimely demise. All of these features of animal sacrifice, including the specialized role of the priesthood, appear specially designed to evade individual responsibility for the animal's death. First, the animal is blamed for giving its assent, then the knife is blamed as the instrument of slaughter, then the priests are culpable as the agents of death, and finally the gods are ultimately responsible for demanding the sacrifice in the first place. The whole performance resembles an elaborate exercise in blame shifting (Serpell 1996).

Direct evidence of ambivalence regarding the ethics of animal sacrifice can also be discerned in early literature. In the earliest religious text from India, the *Rig Veda,* the oldest sections are primarily devoted to describing how, when, and where animal sacrifice should be performed. It is apparent that during this period, religious slaughter was a ubiquitous and extremely frequent occurrence that preceded almost any endeavor for which the outcome was uncertain. Later sections, however, thought to date from around 800 B.C.E., categorically reject sacrifice and advocate the practice of *ahimsa* (noninjury) toward all living things, an idea that subsequently became integral to the philosophies of three major, contemporary Indian religions: Buddhism, Jainism, and the yogic branches of Hinduism. It seems that the civilization of India underwent some sort of revolution in attitudes to the treatment of animals at about this time in its history, and one recent authority has suggested that this was a moral reaction to the excessive use of sacrifice in the earlier period (Jacobson 1994).

Evidence of similar concerns are also apparent in classical Greek literature from about 500 B.C.E. Although it is not known whether the new ideas were locally generated or the result of cultural transmission from the East, it is clear that the Pythagorean and Orphic schools of Greek philosophy believed in the characteristically eastern concept of metempsychosis or reincarnation—the idea that the soul or spirit is eternally reborn after death in different bodies, including those of animals. According to most accounts, Pythagoras and his followers were not only opposed to animal sacrifice for this reason, but also advocated a vegetarian diet. Opposition to religious slaughter and vegetarian advocacy continued to recur as themes in classical philosophical literature until at least the third century A.D. (Sorabji 1993; Spencer 1993). In contrast to the situation in India, however, their influence was counterbalanced and ultimately overwhelmed by Aristotle's (384–322 B.C.E.) hierarchical and purposeful account of nature as an ascending ladder (*Scala Naturae*) of living creatures, each created by a "Supreme Being" to serve as food or labor for those higher up the scale. Aristotle based his hierarchy on differences in the supposed rationality or reasoning ability of different organisms. In his view, humans, by virtue of their superior powers of reason, were entitled to use less rational beings for food or other purposes, and no duty of respect was owed to them since, in effect, they only existed in order to be used. This essentially human-centered worldview represented a radical departure from all previous ideas concerning humanity's place in nature. Whereas all previous philosophies had accorded animals at least some degree of respect, as well as acknowledging the inherent moral culpability associated with killing and eating them, Aristotle's proposal effectively provided its adherents with a license to use or abuse other life forms with a clear conscience (Clutton-Brock 1995).

THE CHRISTIAN TRADITION

Around the beginning of the fourth century A.D., Aristotle's ideas were incorporated into Christian tradition. In a discussion of the biblical commandment, "Thou shalt not kill," St. Augustine (A.D. 354–430) stated that people should not make the mistake of applying this rule to "irrational living things, whether flying, swimming, walking, or crawling, because they are not associated in a community with us by *reason*, since it is not given to them to have *reason* in common with us. Hence it is by a very just ordinance of the Creator that their life and death is subordinated to our use" (quoted in Sorabji 1993).

Augustine's views were later consolidated and refined by the medieval Dominican scholar Thomas Aquinas (A.D. 1225–1274), who not only denied rationality to animals but also immortality. Like Aristotle, on whose works he drew heavily, Aquinas believed that only the reasoning part of the soul survived the body after death. Because animals lacked the power of reason, their souls therefore perished along with their bodies. This apparently simple conclusion had far-reaching implications. By denying animals an afterlife, Aquinas rescued Christians from the otherwise alarming prospect of encountering the vengeful spirits of their hapless animal victims somewhere in the hereafter. It therefore reinforced the notion that humans had no reason to feel morally concerned about the treatment of other species. As if to emphasize this point, Aquinas also reinterpreted Old Testament passages that appeared to advocate kindness toward animals: "If in Holy Scripture there are found some injunctions forbidding the infliction of some cruelty towards brute animals . . . this is either for removing a man's mind from exercising cruelty towards other men, lest anyone, from exercising cruelty upon brutes, should go on hence to human beings; or because the injury inflicted on animals turns to a temporal loss for some man." In other words, according to Aquinas, people had no direct moral duties toward animals at all. Wanton cruelty should be avoided, but only for economic reasons or because it might encourage cruelty to fellow humans; not because of the suffering inflicted on the animals themselves. Animals had no moral rights because "only a person, that is, a being possessed of reason and self-control, can be the subject of rights and duties." Aquinas also sanctioned Aristotelian physics and astronomy, according to which the Sun and the planets revolved around the Earth, which was conveniently fixed in the middle of a finite Universe. By doing so, he placed humans on a pinnacle at the very center of creation and endowed them with the freedom to exercise total dominion over every other living thing (Serpell 1996).

Aquinas's *Summa Theologiae* soon became one of the most important and influential works of Christian theology. It had a profound impact on European thought and philosophy, and, as a guide to how Christians ought—or ought not—to behave, it was virtually unchallenged until the growth of Renaissance skepticism toward the end of the sixteenth century. Even now, the Catholic Church's position on the status and treatment of animals remains essentially the same as that proposed by Aquinas more than 700 years ago.

The longevity of Aquinas's ideas owes a great deal to the writings of the brilliant French philosopher René Descartes, whose famous dualist view of human nature reinforced the Thomist doctrine by creating an absolute, unbridgeable gap between humans and other animals. Descartes, a deeply religious man, was disturbed by the skeptic critiques of philosophers, such as Montaigne, who openly attacked the notion of excluding animals from moral consideration. He countered by arguing that only humans are capable of rational thought, and that this characteristic not only endows us with immortal souls but also makes us fundamentally different from all other life forms, which are essentially no different from complex machines (Serpell 1996). Although he probably never intended it so, Descartes's theory also lead to the denial of feelings or "sentience" to animals. It therefore helped to create a moral climate in which established forms of animal abuse, such as "canned" hunts and animal-baiting and fighting could flourish, as well as promoting the newly fashionable pursuit of vivisection. Public displays of the vivisector's art—performed at a time when there were no anaesthetic or analgesic agents available to dull the victim's pain—were commonplace throughout Europe during this period, and they eventually became one of the main focuses of humanitarian criticism from the beginning of the eighteenth century onward (Maehle 1994).

The progress of this new enlightenment sensitivity to animal suffering has been amply documented elsewhere, and need not be reiterated here (see, e.g., Harwood 1928; Thomas 1983; Maehle 1994). The point that is worth re-emphasizing, however, is that the extreme anthropocentrism of medieval and early modern Christianity apparently provoked a moral backlash, in some ways similar to the vegetarian backlash prompted by the excesses of sacrifice and meat-eating some 2,000 years earlier.

CONCLUSIONS

Nineteenth-century humanitarians promulgated a distorted history of humaneness according to which the growth of sympathetic feelings for animals was a mark of civilization—a sign that middle-class Victorians and their successors had risen above, and brought under control, a world of nature that included their own potentially "brutish" animality. Although no longer explicit, this *kind-cruel, tame-wild, civilized-uncivilized* metaphor still carries considerable rhetorical force within the humane movement, as well as informing many of its policies. The main conclusion of this chapter is that this particular account of why people are kind or abusive toward animals is largely erroneous.

Humaneness is not a modern phenomenon. It is an ancient human characteristic with its roots buried somewhere in our hunting and gathering past. Precisely how ancient is largely a matter of guesswork because values and belief systems leave few traces in the archaeological record. Given the overwhelming prominence of animal images in Paleolithic cave art, however, it appears likely that ritual concerns about the ethical aspects of animal exploitation were already widespread at least 30,000 years ago (Lewis-Williams & Dowson 1989; Mithen 1996), some 19,000 years before the dawn of agriculture, and some 28,000 years before the birth of Christ. If so, it seems reasonable to claim that humaneness is a "natural" human propensity that needs to be actively suppressed or denied in order to engage in acts of animal abuse or cruelty. This claim is certainly borne out by the history of post-Neolithic Europe where successive religious ideologies pushed animals closer and closer to the limits of moral concern, while simultaneously providing people with an assortment of ethical justifications for ignoring their suffering. Official Christianity, at least in its medieval and early modern form, represented the most extreme and exaggerated exemplar of this trend.

Does it really matter if our histories of humaneness are distorted or erroneous? What difference does it make in the long run? First and foremost, it makes a difference to how we should deal with animal abuse and cruelty in the modern context. Our beliefs concerning the origins of cruel or abusive treatment of animals determine our strategies for overcoming these problems, so it is obviously helpful if our beliefs approximate reality. If we assume, as did the Victorians, that animal abuse is a manifestation of savage and primitive "animal" instincts lurking beneath the civilized veneer of modern life, we may limit ourselves to fighting an apparent rearguard action against biological or socioeconomic forces beyond our control. If, on the other hand, we begin with the premise that humans possess a natural propensity to include animals within their sphere of moral concern but are sometimes discouraged from doing so by cultural or ideological factors, then the prospects for real improvements in the treatment of animals seem more attainable.

Above all, this alternative history suggests that we should focus more of our energies on trying to understand the reasons why—and the processes by which—these natural humane tendencies become suppressed or corrupted during development. Our culture has a 700-year history of condoning and even promoting widespread and systematic animal abuse—a tradition that still thrives in a number of socially accepted practices such as factory farming, sport hunting, rodeos, rattlesnake roundups, and so on. As long as such activities are considered normal or even "fun," it will be difficult to resurrect the sort of ethic of respect for animals so typical of our hunting and gathering forebears. On the other hand, our culture's peculiarly anthropocentric worldview appears to be highly atypical, and it is probably therefore vulnerable to being overturned by more humane, zoophilic, and ecocentric moral philosophies. The last three hundred years has seen a gradual but accelerating change in attitudes to the treatment of animals and the natural world, and this trend seems certain to continue for the foreseeable future. Who knows? A hundred years from now, the anthropocentrism of medieval and early modern Europe may seem like a brief and destructive hiccup in the ideological history of our species.

REFERENCES

Benedict, R. F. 1929. The concept of the guardian spirit in North America. *Memoirs of the American Anthropological Association,* 29:3–93.

Campbell, J. 1984. *The way of the animal powers.* London: Times Books.

Clutton-Brock, J. 1995. Aristotle, the Scale of Nature, and modern attitudes to animals. *Social Research* 62:421–40.

Eliade, M. 1964. *Shamanism: Archaic techniques of ecstacy,* trans. W. R. Trask. New York: Routledge.

Guenther, M. 1988. Animals in Bushman thought, myth and art. In T. Ingold, D. Riches, and J. Woodburn, eds., *Hunters and gatherers 2: Property, power and ideology,* 192–202. Oxford: Berg.

Hallowell, A. I. 1926. Bear ceremonialism in the Northern Hemisphere. *American Anthropologist* 28(1):1–175.

Harwood, D. 1928. *Love for animals and how it developed in Great Britain.* New York: Columbia University Press.

Ingold, T. 1994. From trust to domination: an alternative history of human-animal relations. In A. Manning and J. A. Serpell, eds., *Animals and human society: Changing perspectives,* 1–22. London: Routledge.

Jacobson, K. A. 1994. The institutionalization of the ethics of "non-injury" toward all "beings" in ancient India. *Environmental Ethics* 16:287–301.

Kellert, S. R., and A. R. Felthous. 1985. Childhood cruelty to animals among criminals and non-criminals. *Human Relations* 38:1113–29.

Lewis-Williams, D., and T. Dowson. 1989. *Images of power: Understanding Bushman rock art.* Johannesburg: Southern Book Publishers.

Martin, C. 1978. *The keepers of the game.* Berkeley: University of California Press.

Maehle, A-H. 1994. Cruelty and kindness to the "brute creation": Stability and change in the ethics of the man-animal relationship, 1600–1850. In A. Manning and J. A. Serpell, eds., *Animals and human society: Changing perspectives,* 81–105. London: Routledge.

Mithen, S. 1996. *The prehistory of the mind.* London: Thames & Hudson.

Nelson, R. K. 1986. A conservation ethic and environment: The Koyukon of Alaska. In N. M. Williams and E. S. Hunn, eds., *Resource managers: North American and Australian hunter-gatherers,* 211–28. Canberra: Institute of Aboriginal Studies.

Ritvo, H. 1987. *The animal estate.* Cambridge, Mass.: Harvard University Press.

Ryder, R. D. 1989. *Animal revolution: Changing attitudes towards speciesism.* Oxford: Basil Blackwell.

Schwabe, C. 1994. Animals in the ancient world. In A. Manning & J. A. Serpell, eds., *Animals and human society: Changing perspectives,* 36–58. London: Routledge.

Serpell, J. A. 1996. *In the company of animals,* 2nd edition. Cambridge: Cambridge University Press.

Sorabji, R. 1993. *Animal minds and human morality: The origins of the western debate.* Ithaca, N.Y.: Cornell University Press.

Speck, F. G. 1977. *Naskapi,* 3rd edition. Norman: University of Oklahoma Press.

Spencer, C. 1993. *The heretic's feast: A history of vegetarianism.* London: Fourth Estate.

Thomas, K. 1983. *Man and the natural world: Changing attitudes in England 1500–1800.* London: Allen Lane.

Turner, J. 1980. *Reckoning with the beast: Animals, pain and humanity in the Victorian mind.* Baltimore: Johns Hopkins University Press.

Wenzel, G. 1991. *Animal rights, human rights: Ecology, economy and ideology in the Canadian Arctic.* London: Belhaven Press.

The Abuse of Animals and Human Interpersonal Violence
Making the Connection

Frank R. Ascione

> Unlike sadness, anger is energizing, even exhilarating.
> —Daniel Goleman, *Emotional Intelligence,* 1995, 59

IT HAS BEEN described as a quiet, suburban community similar to so many others across our nation. But on October 1, 1997, Pearl, Mississippi, became associated with a murderous rampage that shocked the world. At this writing, the alleged killer, Luke Woodham, 16 years of age, was awaiting trial in a case involving the murder of his mother and two high school students and the injury of seven other students at Pearl High School in one single, extended "episode."[1]

Sometime prior to this mayhem, Luke had allegedly written in his diary about the torture and killing of his own dog, Sparkle (Morello 1997). After being beaten with clubs, Sparkle was doused with lighter fluid, set on fire, and thrown into a pond. The diary entries include: "I'll never forget the sound of her breaking under my might." "I will never forget the howl she made. . . . It sounded almost human. We laughed and hit her more" (Hewitt, Harms, & Stewart 1997).

Sparkle's killing was witnessed by an adult neighbor. The incident was never reported to the police or animal control (Officer Billy Barr, Animal Control, Pearl Police Department, personal communication, October 27, 1997). Was this an omen ignored, a portent that could have prompted intervention and prevented the human tragedy on October 1?

OVERVIEW

In this chapter, I use a broad brush to summarize past and current research that examines the relations between the abuse of animals (companion, domesticated,

Andrew Vachss was kind enough to review an earlier version of this paper. I thank him for his thoughtful suggestions.

wild, and stray) and various forms of human interpersonal violence. At the outset, I emphasize that this is a *relation* and not necessarily a causal one. Animal abuse does not inevitably lead to interpersonal violence but we must come to a better understanding of the circumstances in which it does—for the sake of both animals and people.

When presenting information on this topic, I am often confronted with the criticism, "but animal abuse doesn't *cause* child abuse or domestic violence—why should we pay attention to it?" First of all, although it is true that animal abuse may not cause violence to people, it may make it more likely. For example, abusing animals may desensitize the perpetrator to suffering in general and reduce his or her capacity to empathize with a potential victim, human or animal. In a climate of pervasive terror, the roots of human empathy may wither and die, or fail to develop at all. Second, the same underlying factors, such as domestic violence or exposure to violent models, may give rise to abuse of both animals and humans. Animal abuse is significant because it is one of the earliest emerging symptoms of Conduct Disorder in children (Frick et al. 1993) and thus could serve as an early warning sign or red flag for a child in need of mental health attention. And we know that early intervention is critical in the prevention and reduction of aggression and violence in childhood and adolescence. When children engage in animal abuse and there are no negative consequences, their threshold for being interpersonally violent may be lowered.

In an earlier paper (Ascione 1993, 228), I defined cruel treatment or abuse of animals as "socially unacceptable behavior that intentionally causes unnecessary pain, suffering, or distress to and/or death of an animal." Thus, I have excluded socially and culturally sanctioned activities that harm animals, for example, certain agricultural practices, hunting and trapping, rodeos, and laboratory research—topics that are worthy of attention in their own right. Animal maltreatment can include physical abuse and neglect, including acts of commission and omission, and sexual abuse that may involve bestiality. Defining animal abuse is further complicated by our differing attitudes toward members of different species and the continuum of severity that can range from teasing to torture. The forms of human interpersonal violence I address range from aggression in homes where there are child abuse and neglect and domestic violence between siblings or adult partners to aggression in neighborhoods and communities.

The conceptual model I enlist is ecological theory (Bronfenbrenner & Morris 1997). Ecological theory examines individual human development within nested contexts that extend from face-to-face family relationships (with parents, siblings, pets) and relations with peers and adults in school settings, neighborhoods, and churches to institutions such as social welfare, mass media, law enforcement, animal welfare, and human and veterinary health care. The model also includes the societal and cultural elements of beliefs and practices in which human development is embedded.

The welfare of animals may be relevant in an ecological framework. We may consider companion animals as symbiotic members of human families, stray animals as participants in neighborhood and community ecosystems, and societal views about our treatment of farm animals and wildlife as part of our cultural environment.

The reciprocal influences among contexts may move from the individual to the societal (as when an individual incident of animal abuse—like the Pasado case in Washington State)—galvanizes a community to make legislative change; see Fox's essay, "Treating Serious Animal Abuse as Serious Crime," in this volume) or from the broader community to the level of the individual (for example, as when the accumulation of research on the diagnostic significance of cruelty to animals filters to the individual therapist assessing a client for propensity toward violence).

With specific regard to animal abuse, we have recently witnessed increasing research and policy attention at each of these ecological levels. For example, at the level of the individual, since 1987 (American Psychiatric Association 1987, 1994), the psychiatric and psychological communities have considered physical cruelty to animals as symptomatic of antisocial mental disorder in youth and adults. At the level of interpersonal relations, there is mounting evidence that animal abuse is often thematic in families and communities scarred by child abuse and neglect and violence between intimate adult partners and toward the elderly (Lockwood & Ascione 1997). At the social welfare level, animal abuse is beginning to be considered a human public health issue that should be included as a topic in curricula for the training of veterinarians and human health care professionals (Ascione & Barnard 1998). One recent example of change at the cultural level has been the move to make animal abuse a more serious criminal offense in a number of states in the United States (American Humane Association 1996).

The ecological model also suggests that disturbances in the relations between the levels can prevent effective interventions. These disturbances or gaps can occur at any level of the model. For example, at the level of the individual, the failure to report the killing of Sparkle to authorities precluded any significant law enforcement or mental health response to psychological stressors Luke Woodham may have been experiencing. Even when animal abuse is reported, effective intervention may not ensue. As an example, in 1991, near Salt Lake City, two adolescents trapped a cat, shot it with arrows, and stomped the animal to death. The boys videotaped their assault so they could relive the incident and share it with friends. The boys were apprehended and were charged and found guilty of misdemeanor cruelty to animals. The judicial response was to fine one of the youths $100 (the other youth had left the court's jurisdiction). When I asked the judge if he was going to refer the young man for assessment and counseling, he responded by saying that social services personnel were too busy to consider such a case, since "it was only a cat." Disturbances can also occur at a societal and cultural level. Witness the division in the community of Fairfield, Iowa where, on March 7, 1997, three young men broke into an animal sanctuary and bludgeoned 16 cats to death, injuring many others (Associated Press 1997). The boys were convicted of misdemeanors, "after the jury concluded the strays were worth no more than $31.25 each." Community response ranged from minimizing the event ("boys will be boys") to depicting these young men as future Ted Bundys. If society is so confused about the significance of this incident, one can only wonder about the boys' appraisal of their own acts.

In contrast, when the interrelations between levels are acknowledged and strengthened, both animals and humans can benefit. For example, churches conduct a blessing of the animals (often, on the feast of St. Francis of Assisi) to call attention to the value and sanctity of all life. And humane education programs heighten children's (and their parents') attention to why animal maltreatment is wrong and what to do about it. Humane education includes "instilling, reinforcing, and enhancing young people's knowledge, attitudes, and behavior toward the kind, compassionate, and responsible treatment" of humans and animals (Ascione 1997b). The methods of humane education range from classroom visits by animal welfare professionals to literature programs and year-long curricula.

RESEARCH HIGHLIGHTS

Although the past two decades have seen a resurgence of research interest in the associations between how animals are treated and how people treat each other, the associations have been acknowledged for centuries. The artist William Hogarth (Shesgreen 1973, plates 77–79) and philosopher John Locke (Axtell 1968) called our attention to it in the 1700s; early psychiatric writings by Pinel (1809) in the 1800s (Berrios 1996) and Krafft-Ebing (1906) and Ferenczi (1916) in the early 1900s, and fictional treatments by Edgar Allan Poe (*The Black Cat*) and William Golding (*Lord of the Flies*) illustrate the ways that animal abuse might presage human violence.

One of the first research studies on the topic of animal abuse was conducted by Fernando Tapia (1971), who provided detailed case illustrations of antisocial children referred to a clinic, in part, for their abuse of animals. Tapia anticipated current research in this domain by highlighting the often violent and abusive homes from which these children came. Tapia followed up some of these children (Rigdon & Tapia 1977) and found that the persistence of animal abuse was evident two to nine years later. This prospective research was buttressed by a series of retrospective studies by Alan Felthous (1980) and his colleagues (Kellert & Felthous 1985; Felthous & Yudowitz 1977) on adult criminals and psychiatric patients. Currently violent adults often reported childhood and adolescent histories of severe animal torture and killing and these results have been substantiated in a recent study of South African prisoners (Schiff, Louw, & Ascione in preparation).[2] Federal Bureau of Investigation research by Ressler, Burgess, and Douglas (1988) also found substantial rates (in some cases, over 50%) of severe animal abuse in childhood and adolescence in a sample of serial sexual homicide perpetrators. These men also admitted to engaging in bestiality as well as physical animal abuse, behaviors that may overlap. Current work by one of my students, Monique Frazier (1997), has also found high rates (37%) of bestiality and sexual abuse of animals in a sample of sexually violent juvenile offenders. The suspicion in some of this research is that animal abuse may be a form of rehearsal for human-directed violence.

A landmark study was conducted by DeViney, Dickert, and Lockwood (1983) with families meeting legal criteria for child abuse and neglect, all of whom had family pets. They discovered that 60 percent of these families also abused or neglected companion animals. In a recent study (Ascione 1998) of women who are battered and seek shelter at a safehouse, I found that pet ownership was common (74%) and threats to or actual harm and killing of animals by partners were prevalent (71%). Thirty-two percent of the women with children reported that their children were also abusive toward animals (comparable to DeViney, Dickert, and Lockwood's 1993 finding that 26% of children in abusive households were cruel to animals). Social learning theory would suggest that violent homes may provide a training ground for animal abuse by exposing children to adult models of such behavior. Claudia Weber and I have since replicated and extended the study of women who are battered with a larger sample of 101 women and have found similar results. We also discovered that 62 percent of women who were battered indicated their children had witnessed animal abuse (Ascione et al. 1997a). I will return to this issue when discussing institutional responses to human abuse of animals.

Research in this area has been fostered, in part, by the inclusion of animal abuse among the symptoms of Conduct Disorder, the youthful equivalent of Antisocial Personality Disorder, in recent revisions (III-R, IV) of the *Diagnostic and Statistical Manual of Mental Disorders* (American Psychiatric Association 1987, 1994) and the *International Classification of Mental and Behavioural Disorders* (ICD-10; World Health Organization 1996). These changes and continued diagnostic evolution should prompt more formal efforts by clinicians to take note of histories of animal abuse when evaluating clients. Because cruelty to animals was not specifically mentioned in diagnostic protocols prior to 1987, research conducted and published prior to that date might not include reference to the abuse of animals. Thus, the reader is cautioned that failure to address animal abuse in clinical case histories may not mean such abuse was absent, but rather that no one asked about it.

Another dilemma in this area of research is that information about animal abuse is most often derived from self reports by the potential perpetrators of such acts. Although in some cases we have corroborating evidence—the videotape in the Salt Lake City case, the physical evidence in Fairfield, Iowa, women and children's agreement on witnessing animal abuse in domestic violence—often we do not. Parents participating in developmental research or seeking mental health services for their children may be asked to report on their children's cruelty to animals but we know that animals may be abused secretively and such acts may not come to the attention of parents. In other cases, animal abuse may not be witnessed by adults but adults may *hear* about it, as in the case of teachers who are told about children's acts of violence toward animals. Children's sexual abuse of animals is only beginning to be acknowledged, much less assessed. Therefore, it is important that we solicit information from as many sources as feasible when assessing histories and current patterns of animal abuse.

MOTIVATIONS FOR CHILD AND ADOLESCENT ABUSE OF ANIMALS

> We are tested, and sometimes we fail. The maltreated child cries, "I hurt." Unheard or unheeded, that cry becomes prophesy.
>
> —Andrew Vachss, *Another Chance to Get it Right* 1993, 21

Beyond seeing adults do it, what factors might prompt young people to abuse animals? In our work with troubled children and families, some of which is reported in Ascione, Thompson, and Black (1997), we have explored the varied motivations that may underlie animal abuse. Obviously, with very young children, animal abuse may be a byproduct of the curiosity and exploration common to this age group. In essence, this may be normative as is abusive behavior fostered by peer reinforcement and goading in older children. In such cases, humane education by parents and other adults about animal suffering will probably be effective in reducing or eliminating such behavior. In other cases, however, the motivations may be more disconcerting and ominous. There have been reports that animal abuse may be included as part of initiation rites in youth gangs (Carolyn Andersen, Third District Juvenile Court, Utah, personal communication, May 1995) and children may be forced to abuse animals by adults who abuse children. In one case, I learned that a child was photographed in the act of animal abuse and the adult child abuser then used this photo to threaten the child into compliance and silence.

Youthful sex offenders have admitted to engaging in animal abuse and bestiality to "elevate" their mood state when bored or depressed. The psychological mechanism of identification with the aggressor suggests that when a child is victimized, he or she may seek out a more vulnerable victim to victimize including younger children or pets—powerlessness is frightening and demoralizing, and, unfortunately, exerting control over another can restore a sense of self-efficacy. Children who are victims of sexual abuse may reenact their victimization by abusing animals in an almost ritualized, stereotypical pattern reminiscent of posttraumatic play. In one case study, we discovered that a young child would agitate the family cat until the animal began to seriously scratch the child's arms—at which time the child would smile. Such self-injurious behavior is not uncommon in abused children; the use of an animal as an implement of self-injury is. Finally, children may abuse the pet of a sibling or peer as a form of emotional or psychological maltreatment. The motivations listed here are not exhaustive. I refer the reader to a manual written by Phil Arkow (1995) for the Latham Foundation for a listing of other motivations including those more common for adult perpetrators of animal abuse.

Understanding motivations for animal abuse will facilitate diagnosis, prevention, and intervention efforts in a number of ways. For example, when we read about John Steinbeck's character Lennie Small killing animals in *Of Mice and Men,* we know that his developmental retardation mitigated his culpability. Contrast this with serial killer Arthur Gary Bishop, executed for the abduction, torture, and killing of five young boys. After his first human murder, he admitted to obtaining a number of puppies, torturing and killing them to relive the excitement of his first human kill (Hickey 1991). Culpability and responsibility must clearly play a part in our judgments of the significance of animal abuse. I recall a story told by an American POW in Vietnam who adopted a pet bird that he kept in his cell. He described how his captors took note of his affection for the bird and how he killed it before his captors could torment the animal. Motivations and intentions are critically important in our judgments of the meaning of animal abuse.

INSTITUTIONAL RESPONSE TO ANIMAL ABUSE

Studying the past decade reveals increased systemic attention to the overlaps between child abuse and neglect, domestic violence, community violence, and animal abuse. The extent of these overlaps is as yet unclear because few studies examine all areas of maltreatment. I have begun to focus my research efforts on the overlaps between domestic violence and the abuse of animals because we have found such a high co-occurrence of these forms of violence in the samples we have studied. Ascione, Weber, and Wood (1997) recently surveyed U.S. shelters for women who are battered and discovered that the overlap is acknowledged by the majority (83.3%) of shelter directors, yet fewer than 28 percent systematically query clients about animal abuse. This raises important policy questions as some women may delay seeking shelter at a safehouse because they have no place to put their pets, fearing to leave them home as possible prey for their batterer. At a recent Humane Society of the United States (HSUS) "First Strike" symposium (September 1997), a full day was set aside to examine issues of animal welfare and safety, bringing together professionals in veterinary medicine, animal welfare, and human services. One product that has already emerged from this meeting is a brochure for women who are battered, entitled "Making the Connection: Protecting Your Pet from Domestic Violence." It provides information and guidance about pet-related issues if a woman is thinking of seeking out-of-home shelter. In November 1997, I was invited to present my research on animal abuse and domestic violence to the Utah Governor's Cabinet Council on Domestic Violence. The response to my presentation and the cabinet's discussion of the issue was so positive that, as of January 1998, all domestic violence case intake forms used by Utah police, crisis centers, and shelters for women who are battered will include a question about animal abuse and killing by batterers (Brandy Farmer, Utah Attorney General's Office, personal communication, November 6, 1997). Collaborative efforts such as these may serve to increase societal and cultural attention to the significance of animal maltreatment and to design effective prevention and intervention programs for individuals and families caught in the web of interpersonal violence. The Latham Foundation, the Geraldine R. Dodge Foundation, the American Humane Association, HSUS, and other organizations have been at the forefront of enabling such collaborative approaches.

These collaborative approaches will confront a number of challenges (Ascione, Weber, & Wood 1997). Domestic violence professionals will need to examine animal abuse as a potential indicator of dangerousness or lethality in a batterer and determine if animal abuse predicts escalation of violence in homes with domestic violence. Animal welfare should be incorporated into safety plans for women who must remain at home with their violent partner and for those who decide to leave. A batterer's history of animal abuse may be useful information in obtaining protective orders and could be used to document emotional abuse of children who witness pets being harmed. For example, due to legislative action in Utah in 1997, domestic violence is a more serious offense if children witness such violence. Human shelters must also be willing to address women and children's grief over separation from or loss of their beloved pets and the possibility that women have been forced to engage in bestiality.

Animal welfare organizations that shelter pets for women who leave their homes will confront issues of workplace safety, confidentiality of records, and economic factors if they board animals for these women. Leaving a batterer can be the most dangerous time for a woman and the batterer may try to locate boarded pets to retaliate against or coerce his partner to return home. More careful screening of adopters may be necessary, because some batterers may adopt shelter animals to give to their partners as gifts or as extortion tools. Programs are also needed that address the concerns of women in rural areas whose needs may include the welfare of farm animals and livestock, which can be the target of a batterer's wrath or subject to neglect. Veterinary training would also be enhanced by providing information on the forms of and connections between human and animal abuse and guidelines for reporting suspected abuse.

Child welfare professionals should be alerted to the significance of animal abuse, both when children are exposed to it and when children perform it themselves (in San Diego, social workers who investigate families for child abuse and neglect are now required to report on the condition and treatment of animals in these homes, a model that could be adopted nationally). Children in homes where there is animal abuse may be more prone to develop animal phobias and may display inappropriate sexual behavior with animals. These diagnostic signs should prompt immediate and early intervention.

FUTURE DIRECTIONS

Finally, I would suggest that the links between animal abuse and interpersonal violence are ripe for research at all ecological levels, from the individual to society and culture. We need to learn more about individual children's responses to growing up in frightening environments, why some succumb to violence themselves and why others are somehow buffered. Why do some children vent their anger on animals and others care for animals as a respite from the abuse that surrounds them? We need to learn how women in jeopardy can be enabled to seek safety for themselves, their children, and their beloved pets. We need to reexamine the taboo subject of bestiality as it relates to child abuse and the abuse of women. And we need to study the responses of animal and human welfare agencies to this renewed emphasis on animal maltreatment.

Some specific questions include the following.

We know that animal abuse is reported frequently by women who enter shelters for women who are battered. How common is animal abuse in cases where battered women remain at home?

There are numerous programs for the prevention and reduction of violence by children (e.g., Slaby et al. 1995). There are also programs for preventing juvenile fire setting (Wooden & Berkey 1984), a behavior that shares numerous characteristics with animal abuse. Can these programs be adapted to include animal abuse issues?

Concern over media effects on children has now extended to examining content on the Internet. Although much has been written about the impact of violence in television cartoons and news on children, I know of no research that has examined this new form of media. Children may gain access to depictions of animal abuse and bestiality using benign search words like "animal," "pet," or "beast." And we wonder "how a child or adolescent got the idea to do *that*" to another child or animal. George Gerbner (1995) has reviewed the prevalence of animal abuse in televised media and emphasized the desensitizing role it may play in children's development. This area is also in need of further study.

Yearly national estimates of child abuse and neglect are available and have helped us gauge the extent of this problem and the efforts to ameliorate it. Can a similar reporting system be developed for animal abuse?

Studies are needed to directly *assess the overlaps in child abuse and neglect, domestic violence, and animal abuse.* As shown in figure 1, all three forms of abuse may occur separately, or two or more may overlap. Speculating about the extent of the overlaps is no longer sufficient.

Resources are becoming available to aid researchers and field practitioners in these efforts. I have also mentioned *Breaking the Cycles of Violence,* the cross-training manual and its accompanying video produced by the Latham Foundation (Arkow 1995). A compilation of research papers on this topic, *Cruelty to Animals and Interpersonal Violence: Readings in Research and Application,* has recently been published (Lockwood & Ascione 1997). Patricia Olson (1998) has edited a veteri-

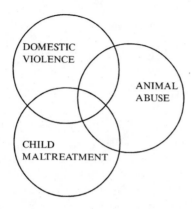

Figure 1. The Overlapping Domains of Animal Abuse, Domestic Violence, and Child Maltreatment

narian's guide to preventing, recognizing, and verifying animal abuse. It is clear that the types of abuse humans experience—physical, sexual, emotional, and neglectful—are frequently shared by our nonhuman companions and other animals. A better understanding of the factors leading to abuse, of humans and of animals, may help transform landscapes of terror into safer havens.

NOTES

1. Luke Woodham was convicted and sentenced to three life sentences, July 12, 1998.
2. Andrew Vachss (personal communication, December 1997) notes, "Significantly, many hyper-violent children report terror and rage and helplessness at the 'execution' of a beloved pet by a parent."

REFERENCES

American Humane Association. 1996. *Cruelty statutes: United States and Canada.* Englewood, Colo.: American Humane Association.
American Psychiatric Association. 1987. *Diagnostic and statistical manual of mental disorders,* 3rd edition, revised. Washington, D.C.: American Psychiatric Association.
American Psychiatric Association. 1994. *Diagnostic and statistical manual of mental disorders,* 4th edition. Washington, D.C.: American Psychiatric Association. Author.
Arkow, P. 1995. *Breaking the cycles of violence.* Alameda, Calif.: Latham Foundation.

Ascione, F. R. 1993. Children who are cruel to animals: A review of research and implications for developmental psychopathology. *Anthrozoös* 6:226–47.

Ascione, F. R. 1997a. Final Report: Animal welfare and domestic violence (Geraldine R. Dodge Foundation). Logan, Utah: Department of Psychology, Utah State University.

Ascione, F. R. 1997b. Humane education research? Evaluating efforts to encourage children's kindness and caring toward animals. *Genetic, Social, and General Psychology Monographs* 123(1):57–77.

Ascione, F. R. 1998. Battered women's reports of their partners' and their children's cruelty to animals. *Journal of Emotional Abuse* 1(1):119–33.

Ascione, F. R., and Barnard, S. 1998. The link between animal abuse and violence to humans: Why veterinarians should care. In P. Olson (ed.), *Recognizing and reporting animal abuse: A veterinarian's guide.* Englewood, Colo.: American Humane Association.

Ascione, F. R., T. M. Thompson, and T. Black. 1997. Childhood cruelty to animals: Assessing cruelty dimensions and motivations. *Anthrozoös* 10(4). 170–177.

Ascione, F. R., C. V. Weber, and D. S. Wood. 1997. The abuse of animals and domestic violence: A national survey of shelters for women who are battered. *Society and Animals* 5(3):205–18.

Associated Press. 1997. Teens who killed cats guilty of misdemeanors. *Salt Lake Tribune* November 8, A4.

Axtell, J. L. 1968. *The educational writings of John Locke.* Cambridge: Cambridge University Press.

Berrios, G. E. 1996. *The history of mental symptoms.* Cambridge: Cambridge University.

Bronfenbrenner, U., and P. A. Morris. 1997. The ecology of developmental processes. In W. Damon, ed., *Handbook of child psychology,* 5th ed., 1:993–1028. New York: Wiley.

DeViney, E., J. Dickert, and R. Lockwood. (1983). The care of pets within child abusing families. *International Journal for the Study of Animal Problems* 4:321–29.

Felthous, A. R. 1980. Aggression against cats, dogs and people. *Child Psychiatry and Human Development* 10:169–77.

Felthous, A. R., and B. Yudowitz. 1977. Approaching a comparative typology of assaultive female offenders. *Psychiatry* 40:270–76.

Ferenczi, S. 1916. *Sex in psycho-analysis.* Boston: Gorham Press.

Frazier, M. R. 1997. Physically and sexually violent juvenile offenders: A comparative study of victimization history variables. Ph.D. diss., Utah State University, Logan.

Frick, P. J., B. B. Lahey, R. Loeber, L. Tannenbaum, Y. Van Horn, and M. A. G. Christ. 1993. Oppositional defiant disorder and conduct disorder: A meta-analytic review of factor analyses and cross-validation in a clinic sample. *Clinical Psychology Review* 13:319–40.

Gerbner, G. 1995. *Animal-issues in the media: A groundbreaking report.* Commissioned by the Ark Trust. Englewood, Colo.: American Humane Association.

Goleman, D. 1995. *Emotional intelligence.* New York: Bantam Books.

Hewitt, B., J. Harms, and R. Stewart. 1997. The avenger. *People* November 3:122.

Hickey, E. W. 1991. *Serial murderers and their victims.* Belmont, Calif.: Wadsworth.

Kellert, S. R., and A. R. Felthous. 1985. Childhood cruelty toward animals among criminals and noncriminals. *Human Relations* 38:1113–29.

Krafft-Ebing, R. V. 1906. *Psychopathia sexualis,* revised edition, 1934. Brooklyn: Physicians and Surgeons Book Company.

Lockwood, R., and F. R. Ascione, eds. 1997. *Cruelty to animals and interpersonal violence: Readings in research and application.* West Lafayette, Ind.: Purdue University Press.

Morello, C. 1997. Did occult turn misfits into murderers? *USA Today* October 21:4A.

Olson, P., ed. 1998. *Recognizing & reporting animal abuse: A veterinarian's guide.* Englewood, Colo.: American Humane Association.

Pinel, P. 1809. *Traité médico-philosophique de la aliénation mentale,* 2nd edition. Paris: Brosson.

Ressler, R. K., A. W. Burgess, and J. E. Douglas. 1988. *Sexual homicide: Patterns and motives.* Lexington, Mass.: Lexington Books.

Rigdon, J. D., and F. Tapia. 1977. Children who are cruel to animals—A follow-up study. *Journal of Operational Psychology* 8:27–36.

Schiff, K., Louw, D., and Ascione, F. R. (in preparation). Childhood cruelty to animals in a sample of aggressive and non-aggressive South African criminals.

Shesgreen, S., ed. 1973. *Engravings by Hogarth.* New York: Dover Publications.

Slaby, R. G., W. C. Roedell, D. Arezzo, and K. Hendrix. 1995. *Early violence prevention: Tools for teachers of young children.* Washington, D.C.: National Association for the Education of Young Children.

Tapia, F. 1971. Children who are cruel to animals. *Child Psychiatry and Human Development* 2:70–77.

Vachss, A. 1993. *Another chance to get it right.* Milwaukie, Oreg.: Dark Horse.

Wooden, W. S., and M. L. Berkey. 1984 *Children and arson: America's middle class nightmare.* New York: Plenum Press.

World Health Organization. 1996. *International classification of mental and behavioural disorders* (ICD-10). Cambridge: Cambridge University Press.

Another Weapon for Combating Family Violence
Prevention of Animal Abuse
Charlotte A. Lacroix

If the United States is to rid society of family violence, then violent acts against animals in the home is conduct that cannot be tolerated. In fact, such conduct merits judicial attention and community resources equal to that devoted to acts of violence toward humans. An aggressive, national response to abusive treatment of animals is not a distortion of priorities but rather a recognition that the solution to a violent society does not lie in the characterization of the victims but in the characteristics of the offenders.

The protection of animals furthers several human interests including the preservation and promotion of societal morals and the protection of the general welfare of society (Francione 1995). Specifically, anticruelty laws foster the moral principle that nonhuman animals should be treated humanely, provided adequate food and shelter, and not subjected to needless pain.

These protective laws have been enacted to prevent humans from acting cruelly toward one another. It would behoove judges, prosecutors, and other legal professionals who deal with family violence cases on a daily basis to acknowledge this purpose and include animal anticruelty statutes among their arsenals in combating family violence.

FAMILY VIOLENCE: A MULTIVICTIM APPROACH

Violence exhibited by one family member against another rarely involves a single act of abuse against one type of victim. In fact, where there is one form of family violence, there are likely to be others. A multivictim approach to understanding family violence focuses on the similarities between the different forms of family violence. For example, the abuse usually results from perpetrators' misuse of power and control over their victims; the psychological and sociocultural factors that lead to the violence are often the same regardless of the type of victim; and the psycho-

An earlier version of this essay appeared in *Animal Law* 4 (1998).

logical effects and symptoms experienced by victims of family violence are similar (American Psychological Association 1996).

Studying the similarities among victims and the relationships among various forms of family violence including a close examination of the occurrence correlation between abused spouses, children, and pets, will lay the foundation for a comprehensive solution to family violence. Such an examination is necessary to justify a departure from the current approach to dealing with family violence, which consists of victim-specific remedies that focus on protecting one victim while failing to identify and protect other family members who also may be at risk.

Historically, the law has treated child abuse and spousal abuse as two separate, distinct, and unrelated offenses. Evidence of their concurrence has had little influence on the judicial decisions that have emanated from these cases (Dohrn 1995; Enos 1996). Yet, there are a number of studies that indicate that domestic violence and child abuse are linked within families, and that either form of abuse can be a strong predictor of the other (McKay 1994; Sigler 1989). This linkage lends support to the proposition that prosecutors, judges, and law makers should seriously consider this correlation in their decisions, which ultimately will impact how family violence is understood and remedied in our society (Cahn 1991).

The numerous research studies supporting the occurrence correlation between spousal abuse and child abuse leave little doubt that children raised in homes where their mothers are beaten have an increased risk of being physically abused by the batterer. One study, which involved 1,000 battered women, found that child abuse was present in 70 percent of the families in which there was spousal abuse. These findings have been corroborated in studies examining abused children. For example, a 1986 study of abused children found that about 60 percent of their mothers were also victims of family violence. In some instances, violence against the child has also been perpetrated by the battered spouse. Several studies have found that battered women are more likely to abuse their children as compared to women who are not abused (Cahn 1991).

In addition to suffering from physical abuse, children who witness violence toward their mothers often suffer from emotional, behavioral, and psychological problems. These other forms of abuse may have a profound and lasting effect on the child's ability to cope with the normal stages of development. Studies have shown that the children who observe parental violence are more aggressive and behave differently than children raised in nonviolent households (Cahn 1991).

FAMILY PETS ARE VICTIMS OF FAMILY VIOLENCE

The shared characteristics of women and children as victims of family violence can easily be extended to family pets. Victims of family violence share common traits. For example, women, children, and animals have historical status under the law as property, which means their rights under the law have been superseded by the conflicting rights of their abusers. Unlike women and children who have had their rights increased by reform movements, animals continue to be the losers when their interests are weighed against the possessory, use, and enjoyment interests of their owners. Women, children, and family pets share the results of their abusers' misuse of power and control. And they share economic dependence, strong emotional bonds, and a enduring sense of loyalty to their abusers.

With close to 60 percent of all American households owning pets (Gehrke 1997), it follows that these pets should be considered among the vulnerable victims of family violence. To those of us who are pet owners, it seems intuitive that pets should be regarded as family members. Results from one study designed to determine the role of pets in the family system revealed that 87 percent of the respondents considered their pet to be a member of the family (Hutton 1983).

Multiple surveys focusing on the relationship between pet owners and their pets have corroborated this finding, including data that 79 percent of owners celebrate their pets' birthdays, 33 percent of pet owners who are away from home talk to their pets on the phone or through the answering machine, and 62 percent of pet owners sign letters or cards from themselves and their pets (American Animal Hospital Association 1995; Albert & Bulcroft 1988).

The multivictim approach to understanding the dynamics of family violence is incomplete unless all potential victims are identified. Increasing the pool of potential victims is likely to increase the probability of identifying families at risk and to enhance early intervention. Given the weight of evidence indicating that people have "human-like" relationships with their pets, it would be an act of ignorance not to include family pets among this pool of potential victims.

ANIMAL ABUSE LINKED TO VIOLENCE TOWARD PEOPLE

Until recently, the theory that violence against animals may be associated with violence against people has been overlooked by law-enforcement agencies, legislators, officers of the court, and social services agencies (Ritter 1996). The correlation between spousal abuse and child abuse, where either can be an indicator of the other, sets a strong precedent for the intuition that abuse of the family pet may also be a predictor of other forms of family violence. Several reports support the link between animal abuse and violence toward people.

There is ample evidence to suggest that individuals who engage in acts of animal cruelty have a greater probability of committing acts of violence against people as compared to individuals who have no history of committing acts of violence against animals (Ritter 1996; Arkow 1995; Lockwood & Hodge 1986). Early evidence that supports this correlation has come from single anecdotal case histories of serial and mass murders. Such criminals include Albert DeSalvo, also known as the "Boston Strangler," who in his youth trapped dogs and cats in crates and shot arrows at them through the boxes; Ted Bundy, who was executed in 1989, spent much of his childhood torturing animals; and, serial killer Jeffrey Dahmer impaled frogs and staked cats to trees in his backyard during his youth.

Evidence derived from empirical research studies has indicated that this correlation is more than a random coincidence. One of the first studies in this area was conducted by Hellman and Blackman (1966), who looked at the life histories of 84 prison inmates. The results showed that 75 percent of the inmates charged with committing a violent crime also had a history of cruelty to animals, fire-setting, and bed-wetting. Other research conducted by Felthous and Kellert (1985) supported this correlation. Their study consisted of a survey among three groups of men: noncriminals, aggressive criminals, and nonaggressive criminals. Of the aggressive criminals, 25 percent reported five or more childhood acts of cruelty toward animals, compared to 6 percent of the nonaggressive criminals, and zero in the sample of noncriminals. This study also shed light on some of the motives for animal abuse, including (1) a need to control the animal's behavior, (2) retaliation either against the animal or other individuals, (3) fear and hatred of the animal, and (4) a need to visualize the impact it had on others who witnessed the cruelty.

In spite of this evidence, the association between childhood cruelty to animals and future violent acts against people remains a matter of debate (Miller & Knutson 1997). Certainly not all children who harm animals will grow up to be violent criminals (Widom 1989). It is common for children to go through a developmental phase during which time they injure animals in the process of learning about themselves and exploring their world. When these acts are coupled with proper role modeling from parents and guardians, these children learn about the consequences of their behavior and develop empathy and compassion for animals (Finch 1989). But children who grow up in violent, abusive or negligent families learn that aggressive behavior is a means of solving problems and getting obedience and compliance (Loar 1996).

Similarly, whether the abuse of a companion animal in a household is directly related to the risk of child abuse in the same household is an area of research that is largely uncharted and in need of more investigation. Three studies address this correlation and raise the suspicion that these two forms of violence are directly linked.

A 1980 pilot study conducted in England found evidence suggesting that children are at risk of abuse or neglect in households that abuse their family pet (Hutton 1983). The results indicated that of the 23 families that had a history of animal abuse, 83 percent had been identified by human social service agencies as having children at risk of abuse or neglect. Based on these findings, Hutton concluded that the evaluation of companion animals in the family might be a useful diagnostic tool for social workers in their investigations of alleged child abuse. A similar study comparing records of a Pennsylvania county's society for prevention of cruelty to animals with those of the same county's youth social services agency found that the behavior patterns toward one's children were similar to those toward one's pets (Walker 1980).

DeViney, Dickert, and Lockwood (1983) reported the results of a study that surveyed the treatment of animals in 53 pet-owning families in which child abuse had occurred. In 60 percent of these families, at least one family member had abused the family pet; of the families in which physical child abuse had occurred, 88 percent also had animals that had been abused.

It is not difficult to imagine that a similar link exists in families that have battered partners. The literature on domestic violence is filled with anecdotal reports of incidents of cruelty to family pets where partner battering occurs (Adams 1994).

Three studies support the anecdotal findings. In a survey of 38 women seeking shelter from their batterers, Ascione (1998) found that of the 74 percent of women who reported either currently or recently owning pets, 71 percent reported that the batterer had threatened to hurt or kill their pets(s) or had actually hurt or killed their pet(s).

The Community Coalition Against Violence in La Crosse, Wisconsin (Quinlisk 1994), showed that 80 percent of the battered partners who had family pets reported violence toward the animals. The Colorado Springs, Colorado, Center for Prevention of Domestic Violence survey reported that 23 percent of the battered women who sought refuge in the shelter reported animal cruelty (Arkow 1994).

THE NEED FOR MORE RESEARCH

Studies documenting the correlation between animal abuse and family violence are subject to the similar criticisms of studies that look at whether abused children grow up to be abusive parents (Widom 1989). First, the retrospective nature of some of these studies may lead to distorted findings in that the information sought out may have been forgotten or inaccurately recollected or the information may be provided by someone who has only second-hand knowledge. Second, few studies define animal abuse and they lack direct evidence of the severity, frequency, or chronicity of the alleged abuse. Finally, few studies use control groups, which are necessary to assess the independent effects on individuals who abuse animals.

Although these criticisms should cause us to scrutinize the correlation of animal abuse to other forms of violence, they should not be viewed as invalidating these research efforts. Rather, the studies and their problems should provide the foundation and impetus for further research in this area.

PREVENTION OF ANIMAL CRUELTY

Improving the detection of violence against animals is likely to enhance society's detection of violence toward other family members. Including the prevention of animal cruelty among the current methods used to combat family violence transforms what is currently a victim specific solution to one that is comprehensive and superior to the current approach because it is based on the acknowledgment that acts of violence against family members do not occur in a vacuum. It forces us to focus on the repetitive nature of the violent acts and enhances our detection of the perpetrator's chronic violent behavior. The benefits arising from a comprehensive approach to the analysis and resolution of family violence can only be maximized when each victim receives adequate protection under our laws. Working toward a comprehensive solution will reduce incidents of family violence and increase the seriousness with which our society perceives animal abuse.

Preventing animal cruelty is primarily addressed through educational campaigns conducted by local and national humane societies and by anticruelty laws enacted by state governments. This current scheme fails to provide adequate protection because the type of educational information and the form in which it is disseminated varies greatly among the regions of the country, and the laws as written are ineffective deterrents. The detection and prosecution of animal cruelty offenses would be significantly enhanced by drafting clearer, stricter, and enforceable animal cruelty laws, mandating the reporting of animal abuse, developing a national consensus on the criteria for animal cruelty, and maintaining central reporting registries.

THE BASICS OF ANTICRUELTY STATUTES

All 50 states have enacted criminal laws primarily designed to punish individuals who commit acts of cruelty against animals (Leavitt 1990). Most state anticruelty laws are comprised of six elements: (1) the types of animals protected, (2) the types of acts prohibited or duties imposed, (3) the mental culpability required to impose liability, (4) the defenses to liabilities, (5) certain activities exempted from the law, and (6) the penalty for each offense. Although the specifics of each element may differ significantly among the states, common trends exist.

The first element to address in assessing whether an offense of animal cruelty has been committed is to determine whether the animal is covered by the statute. Most states define "animal" to include all nonhuman vertebrates. Some states, however, have a narrower definition of "animal" such that certain living creatures may be excluded, such as, fowl, livestock, insects, and pests.[1] Other states fail to provide definitions altogether, leaving it up to the courts to infer which species are covered by the statute.

The second question involves assessing whether the act, failure to act, or neglect falls within the scope of the statute. Generally these statutes protect against three forms of cruelty. The most common type of statute is one that prohibits the willful, deliberate, or intentional commission of certain acts, which often include beating, torturing, or mutilation. The second most frequently encountered statute imposes a duty on animal owners or their custodians to provide food, water, and adequate shelter. The third type of cruelty prohibited by statute is the participation in, the witnessing of, the aiding in, or in any way engaging in the furtherance of any fight between animals.

In most states, the third component of the offense requires that the prohibited act, omission, or neglect be performed with a state of mind that indicates a high degree of culpability. For there to be a conviction, states usually require that the act of cruelty be committed maliciously, willfully, intentionally, knowingly, or recklessly.[2] A few of the modern statutes have lowered the degree of culpability required to that of ordinary negligence or criminal negligence, which has the effect of increasing the likelihood of a conviction.[3]

The fourth and fifth elements, defenses and exempted activities, both bar a conviction for animal cruelty. Defendants have been excused where their acts of cruelty were committed to protect humans, protect property, or were incidental to the disciplining or training of animals. In addition, where the offense charged has been one of neglect or failure to provide proper veterinary care, defendants' limited finances and inability to pay for proper care has been put forth as a defense.

Exempted activities are deemed by society to be necessary or justifiable practices that outweigh the interests of the animals and serve to promote the general public welfare. Activities that usually qualify as exceptions include animal research; veterinary and animal husbandry practices such as dehorning, castration, and tail docking; hunting; trapping; and slaughtering of animals for human consumption.[4]

Finally, violations of anticruelty statutes in most states are categorized as misdemeanors. Within the last decade, however, at least 15 states have upgraded the penalty for intentional cruelty offenses to a felony crime.[5] Still other states have supplemented their prison and fine penalties with sentences that focus on the rehabilitation of offenders by requiring psychiatric, psychological, or behavioral counseling.[6] Some states also may require that the mistreated animal be surrendered to the local SPCA and the offender be prohibited from future ownership, custody, or control of any pet or companion animal.[7]

STRICTER LAWS AND CONSISTENT ENFORCEMENT

Current anticruelty statutes fail to provide adequate protection for animals and have had little, if any, deterrent effect (Francione 1995; Favre & Loring 1983, 9.1–9.25). There are two fundamental reasons why these laws have been ineffective in protecting animals: first, the primary goals of these laws have not been to protect animals; and second, legal professionals have been reluctant to legislate and enforce these laws.

A brief analysis of the legal theory behind the origin of state anticruelty statutes leads us to conclude that the primary focus of such laws has not been the protection of animals. State animal cruelty statutes are criminal laws, not civil laws. The main objective of civil laws under the tort system is to compensate victims for any wrongs they have suffered due to the actions of the wrongdoer. In contrast, the purpose of criminal laws under the criminal legal system is (1) to punish perpetrators for what a human society considers to be dangerous and undesirable behavior, (2) to protect the same human society from such perpetrators, and (3) to deter similar activities in the future. Because animals are property and have no legal standing or rights under the U.S. legal system, the protections animals receive from these statutes are secondary to the threefold goals of the criminal justice system and are limited because they are weighed against the owners' interests in the possession, use, and enjoyment of their animals. Therefore, because these laws were primarily enacted to protect humans from other humans with an intent to minimally interfere with owners' property rights, it should be no surprise that these laws have proved relatively ineffective at protecting animals from acts of cruelty and neglect.

Historically, legislators, prosecutors, and the courts have been disinterested in legislating and enforcing such laws, for several reasons. First, the attitude of society, policy makers, and legislators toward animals and their welfare has resulted in minimal activity in this legislative arena. Second, the difficulty in defining and agreeing on what is abusive treatment has lead to difficulties in the interpretation and subsequent enforcement of these statutes. Third, the penalties imposed by anticruelty statutes are generally misdemeanors, which are not prosecuted aggressively because they have little plea-bargain value and compete with felony offenses for limited time and resources. Finally, enforcement has been plagued by a lack of funding, manpower, and confusion resulting from states delegating the authority to enforce such laws to humane organizations.

Most of the anticruelty statutes have remained largely unchanged since their enactment in the mid-1800s. This absence of legislative activity may be a result of prioritization of political agendas, which has left concern for animal welfare close to the bottom of the list. Currently, animals have no independent legal status and are no more than chattel subject to the laws of personal property. In a society faced with epidemic proportions of crime, poverty, and violence, a clogged court system, and politicians aggressively competing to stay in office, it is not difficult to imagine why legislators have been reluctant to limit animal owners' property rights.

DEFINITIONS OF ANIMAL CRUELTY

Determining what acts are prohibited has caused great difficulties in the application of animal cruelty laws. A majority of the states define cruelty with such vague and ambiguous language that unless the alleged act or omission is extreme and outrageous it is unlikely that it will violate the statute.

Throughout the statutes, cruelty is commonly referred to as the "needless" mutilation, "unjustifiable" infliction of injuries, failure to provide "proper" sustenance, and infliction of "unnecessary" pain and suffering.[8] Some states continue to use definitions, in some cases over 100 years old, that inadequately represent contemporary uses of animals and society's attitude toward their welfare. For example, referring to cruelty as overdriving, overloading, and overworking an animal may have been effective in protecting draft horses but such specifications provide little protection for companion animals today.[9] The use of such imprecise and outdated terms with little additional statutory guidance has left law enforcement officials, prosecutors, and judges confused as to what acts fall within the scope of the statute. As a result, enforcement of anticruelty laws has been inconsistent and unpredictable.

Another problem is the sole focus on the acts of the offender: no statute refers to cruelty from the perspective of the injuries suffered by the animal. At this point in time, there is no medical profile for animal abuse analogous to the battered child syndrome model (Kempe et al. 1962) that could provide physical symptoms from which to make a diagnosis of animal abuse. Although a "battered animal syndrome" is not essential to improving anticruelty laws, it would help to distinguish accidents from incidents of abuse (see Munro, "The Battered Pet: Signs and Symptoms," this volume).

Redefining what constitutes cruelty is essential. Before animal cruelty charges or convictions can be considered relevant evidence of conduct that places other family members at risk, the statutes must reflect a clear and current understanding of what is meant by cruel treatment.

State legislators should also redraft their laws to differentiate among the different forms of animal cruelty and impose corresponding penalties to reflect the severity of the offense. Laws should distinguish between violent acts of abuse, mistreatment, and neglect. These crimes are generally distinguishable in the degree of pain and suffering they cause to the animal as well as the requisite level of criminal culpability. Oregon's legislature adopted such changes in 1995. Its anticruelty statute now distinguishes between animal abuse and neglect, and depending on the culpability of the offender, separates the offenses into Class A and B misdemeanors.[10] Upgrading animal cruelty crimes to felonies will increase the gravity of the offense in the eyes of judges and prosecutors, who will respond by devoting more time and consideration to these cases. Provisions that require counseling for offenders and protections for animals may stop the violence before it escalates and affects other family members.

ENFORCEMENT OF ANIMAL CRUELTY LAWS

It is in the purview of state and local officials to enforce anticruelty laws. Recognizing that resources are limited, however, many legislatures have authorized nonprofit SPCAs or humane societies or municipal animal control agencies to aid in the enforcement of these laws.[11] Depending on the state, these organizations may be granted the authority to intervene and prevent the commission of acts of cruelty, take custody of mistreated animals with or without a warrant, make arrests with or without a warrant, and carry weapons (Leavitt 1990).

This delegation of authority has been problematic in at least two ways. First, the lack of state funding has left these organizations with limited resources to hire and train investigators needed to respond to allegations of animal cruelty. Although these organizations generally obtain nonprofit and tax-exempt status, which aids them in procuring the donations to fund their activities, this is usually not enough. Second, most states have no programs to train humane officers in identifying and investigating animal cruelty cases, which has left the training to the humane societies. The variation in quality and degree of training has resulted in inconsistent and unpredictable enforcement of these statutes.

MANDATING THE REPORTING OF ANIMAL ABUSE

Mandated reporting, common in the context of child abuse, maximizes the identification of abuse cases by people who come into contact with children as part of their occupational duties (Levine 1993). This affirmative duty is usually imposed on teachers, day care providers, counselors, doctors, and health care workers. As long as there is a reasonable cause to suspect that there is child abuse and the report is made in good faith, the law will grant the reporter immunity from liability.

Although every state mandates the reporting of child abuse, only Minnesota and West Virginia mandate the reporting of animal abuse.[12] Similar laws must be adopted by every state before any significant progress can be made in reducing the incidence of animal abuse and family violence. Such laws would also provide needed data to quantify the animal cruelty problem.

In considering mandating the reporting of animal abuse, one should be cognizant of the criticisms directed at child abuse reporting laws (Kalichman 1993). The general vagueness of child abuse reporting laws has left mandated reporters confused about what types of maltreatment are reportable and the level of certainty that must be reached before reporting is required. Mandated reporters often lack the training to recognize child abuse and understand their responsibilities under the statute. The utility of such statutes has been questioned because child protective agencies are so limited in resources that many reports are not investigated.

In spite of these problems, most critics have not called for the repeal of reporting laws, but rather that the laws be redrafted to increase the accuracy of reporting. This continued faith in the value of child reporting laws supports the undertaking of analogous reporting laws to protect animals.

Cross-reporting is a multidisciplinary approach to reporting incidents of child and animal abuse. Under this scheme, social workers are trained to recognize and report animal abuse they encounter during their investigations of child abuse. Similarly, humane officers are trained to recognize and report child abuse they encounter during their investigations. Implementation of such programs would lead to a better understanding of the etiology of such acts and ultimately result in more effective solutions.

Cross-reporting also expands the pool of trained personnel, which enhances early detection of family violence and subsequently improves the success of intervention. The recognition that the prevention of child abuse can be improved by mandating cross-reporting is evidenced by California's 1993 amendment to its Child Abuse and Neglect Reporting Act, which mandates that animal control officers and humane society officers report known or suspected instances of child abuse to child protective agencies.[13]

NATIONAL CRITERIA AND REPORTING REGISTRY

Differences among the states' numerous definitions of animal cruelty and the standards that must be met for a conviction compromise nationwide efforts to prevent animal abuse and relate it to other forms of family violence. A serious commitment to the prevention of animal abuse is likely to require a general consensus among the states and the national humane organizations as to what constitutes animal cruelty. A general consensus could be achieved in one of two ways: federal legislation or nationwide cooperation among the states.

There is no companion animal analog to the Child Abuse Prevention and Treatment Act of 1974 (CAPTA).[14] Federal statutes that deal with the protection of animals only address specific sectors of the animal industry and fail to take a comprehensive approach to the cruel treatment of animals (Cohen 1995).[15] It would be possible to tailor federal legislation to provide national standards for defining animal abuse and to set up a national registry to monitor the incidence of animal abuse, either by enacting an independent law pursuant to Congress's taxing and spending power or by amending a federal law already in existence.

Under the spending clause, the federal government could provide federal assistance to states that implement programs for the reporting and prosecution of animal abuse cases. Such a law could look very similar to CAPTA. CAPTA was passed in 1974 and provides federal funding to states that establish child abuse programs aimed at identifying and preventing child abuse and neglect. The act provides a model definition for child abuse and neglect and sets the standard for state mandatory reporting laws, which states have to adopt in order to receive federal child protection funds (Kalichman 1993). Such a proposal is likely to attract a significant amount of criticism given the current political trend to downsize government. As with addressing so many other social problems, the issue will be whether to spend resources now and focus on prevention or spend a lot more money later trying to cure an epidemic.

Alternatively, the federal government could provide funding for states that implement programs of identification, prevention, and treatment of animal abuse and neglect by amending an existing federal law. For example, the Victims of Child

Abuse Act of 1990 (42 U.S.C. §§ 13001 et seq.) provides grants to states that develop and implement multidisciplinary child abuse investigation and prosecution programs that increase the reporting of child abuse. Although unlikely to have been contemplated during the legislative sessions which preceded the enactment of this act, it could be argued that cross-reporting and strengthening animal cruelty laws are multidisciplinary approaches to preventing child abuse, which qualify for federal funding.

In lieu of a federal law that would provide an incentive for states to adopt a uniform scheme to prevent animal abuse, a nationwide plan could be achieved through cooperation among the states. Coordination of such an undertaking would not be easy, but could be facilitated by the participation of the national humane organizations that have already become leaders in this area, including the American Humane Association, Humane Society of the United States, and the Latham Foundation. Specifically, these organizations could draft model laws, provide standards for training investigators, set up regional registries to record reports of abuse, and use their influence to persuade state legislators to redraft their animal cruelty laws.

PREVENTION OF CHILD ABUSE THROUGH THE PREVENTION OF ANIMAL ABUSE

In 1874, a social worker sought the assistance of the Society for the Prevention of Cruelty to Animals (SPCA) in the removal of a child from the custody of her abusive foster parents. This led to the earliest documented conviction for child abuse and the establishment of the first society for the protection of cruelty to children (Costin, Karger, & Stoesz 1996).

It seems ironic that laws protecting animals preceded laws protecting children. This paradox may be indicative of a society that has a lower tolerance for animal abuse than for child abuse (Boat 1995). Society's increased sensitivity to incidents of animal abuse and its correlations with child abuse should be a basis for cooperation between child protection agencies and humane organizations. The detection and treatment of abusive individuals could be enhanced through interagency collaboration and the sharing of evidence between child abuse and animal abuse proceedings.

The advantage of such cooperation is that more perpetrators can be identified without increasing the number of investigators. Although child protection workers and animal welfare officers work with different victims, the parallelism in their duties facilitates their cross-cooperation.

Each state has child protective agencies that employ social workers to investigate allegations of child abuse or neglect. If the investigation leads the social worker to conclude that the child should be removed from the household, a complaint is filed with the juvenile court requesting that the state take legal custody of the child.

The court then evaluates the state's case and makes a determination as to the parents' fitness and what custodial arrangement is in the best interest of the child.

Although animal humane officers help different victims, their methods of investigating abuse and neglect are very similar. Humane officers receive complaints, assess which allegations require visits, work with the owners to correct the problem, secure warrants for the removal of the animal, and maintain records on their cases (Arkow 1995; Walker 1980). In fact, humane officers may have a better opportunity to monitor the status of a child who has been abused. This is because animal welfare cases often result in greater supervision requirements than child welfare cases, and the animal welfare worker may be the only person checking on the welfare of abused victims in the home (Loar 1994). Several communities around the country have instituted cooperative cross-reporting programs, recognizing that social workers and humane officers are in a position to share information and help each other in reducing violence in the home.

PROVING CHILD ABUSE WITH EVIDENCE OF ANIMAL ABUSE

Each state provides two avenues for the adjudication of child abuse cases. Depending on numerous factors, including the weight of the evidence against the perpetrator and the severity of the abuse at issue, the petitioning party may seek the protection of either the civil or criminal laws. Although the decision of whether to pursue civil or criminal sanctions remains debatable, there is a tendency to favor the civil process.

The use of criminal courts to adjudicate cases of child abuse has been criticized because of the higher level of proof required to get a conviction, the difficulty in proving the perpetrator had the requisite level of intent for the offense, and courts' failure to adequately address family rehabilitation once a conviction has been obtained. In contrast, the use of juvenile and family courts has been preferred because a lower standard of proof is required to prove the elements of the offense and the remedial measures implemented by these courts focus on rehabilitation of the perpetrators and provide better protections for the victimized children (Kramer 1994).

Regardless of whether child abuse actions are pursued criminally or civilly, the judicial process is usually plagued with evidentiary problems. The evidence available to prove the offense is often solely circumstantial because child abusers typically commit their acts of violence within the privacy of their homes with no witnesses. Furthermore, abused children rarely testify on their behalf because attorneys or family members fear that such testimony will corroborate the perpetrator's story, further endanger the children, or have serious adverse psychological effects.

Circumstantial evidence often comes in the form of expert medical testimony, testimony from investigators or social workers, proof of prior abuse or neglect of siblings, and hearsay statements (Kramer 1994). Such circumstantial evidence often falls short of establishing a prima facie case of abuse, that is, that the injury was nonaccidental and caused by the accused. Additionally, a case brought in criminal court based solely on circumstantial evidence is frequently doomed because the petitioners must prove their case beyond a reasonable doubt.

Given the circumstantial nature of the evidence in child abuse cases, petitioners must stack their cases with sufficient evidence such that the trier of fact can make the necessary inferences to support an allegation of child abuse. Some jurisdictions have facilitated the stacking of circumstantial evidence by relaxing their rules of evidence or allowing evidence of prior misconduct, where such misconduct was the prior abuse of the victim's sibling.[16] Some courts have admitted such evidence as exceptions to the character evidence rule. Others have focused on balancing the interests between the parties and have concluded that such evidence's probative value along with the need to protect the children outweighs any prejudicial effect on the accused (Kramer 1994).

By allowing evidence of prior abuse of a sibling, courts are recognizing that there is a correlation between the prior abuse of a sibling and the current abuse of the victim. The use of such evidence in building a case against an alleged child abuser therefore serves as a precedent for the admission of other forms of similar evidence. Such similar evidence would include prior abuse of other family members, specifically family pets.

Fearing they will lose the case and thus further endanger victims of child abuse, many petitioners are reluctant to pursue allegations of child abuse because of the lack of direct evidence and insufficient circumstantial evidence to support their allegations. These evidentiary difficulties may be overcome by presenting sufficient circumstantial evidence such that the trier of fact may infer the child was abused and the accused was responsible for the abuse. Increasing the sources of circumstantial evidence by including among the admissible evidence prior acts or convictions of animal abuse would increase the number of child abuse cases brought before the courts and result in greater protections for abused children.

In addition to using evidence of animal abuse in the adjudication phase of civil or criminal child abuse cases, the use of such evidence in child custody hearings would be further instrumental in protecting abused children. Child custody hearings are a forum from which a judge determines where and with whom a child should reside and under what conditions such custody arrangement should take place. Such custodial decision making is necessary in civil child abuse and protection hearings to determine the disposition of an abused or neglected child, and in private custody hearings to resolve custody disputes between separating or divorcing parents.

Civil child protection proceedings usually consist of an adjudicatory hearing and a dispositional hearing. During the adjudicatory hearing, the child protection agency presents evidence against the parents who have been charged with child abuse, in an attempt to prove that children have been mistreated and that the mistreatment was caused by the parents. Depending on the jurisdiction, the agency will have to prove the parents' mistreatment either by a preponderance of the evidence or by clear and convincing evidence.

Once the state has met its burden of proving child abuse or neglect in the adjudication proceeding, it will assert jurisdiction over the child and a dispositional hearing will follow where a judge will determine whether the child should remain with the parent(s) or the state should be granted custody of the child. The dispositional hearing is necessary to determine which custody arrangement is in the best interest of the child and which arrangement will best assist ultimate family reunification. Where the judge determines that the parents are unfit because of abuse or neglect, it is well settled that the state can deny parents custody if the well-being of the child requires it. But, where the judge allows the child to remain with the parent(s), the judge may order the parent(s) to submit to psychological therapy and participate in parent training classes, and may order periodic reports to the court in an effort to monitor parental rehabilitation and cooperation (Kramer 1994).

Child custody hearings are also necessary when separating or divorcing parents cannot agree on issues such as with whom the child will live or who will have primary care. Where there is an unresolved custody dispute, a judge will determine a custody arrangement that is in the best interest of the child. Before awarding child custody, judges will consider many factors which often includes evaluations from psychiatrists, social workers and health professionals. Additionally, some states require that judges take into consideration evidence of family violence (Guggenheim, Lowe, & Curtis 1996).

Although many factors are taken into consideration during both forms of child custody hearings, none look at whether there is evidence of animal abuse in the family. Yet, the accuracy in weighing the risk of future violence in custody determinations may well be enhanced by considering all forms of family violence, including abusive acts toward family pets.

Several states have recognized that domestic violence and custody decision making are interrelated and should affect child custody determinations. In response to this recognition, some states have gone so far as to statutorily mandate that where there is evidence of domestic violence, it should be considered as a factor in custodial decisions.[17] By analogy, if acts of violence against other humans committed by a parent and witnessed by a child are relevant in assessing the child's best interests, it follows that acts of violence against family pets are equally relevant, particularly in those states where courts must consider past violent acts or abusive conduct when determining custody arrangements.[18] Both forms of violence are evidence that the parent has a propensity for violent and abusive behavior, which may be directly correlated with the safety of the child's environment, and could aid juvenile court judges in assessing the dangerousness of the adult's behavior (Jordon 1991). Second, the recognition of the harmful effects suffered by children who witness family violence has resulted in the use of such evidence to influence the outcome of child custody decisions (Cahn 1991; Widom 1989). Similarly, the history of acts of violence toward animals may be helpful in measuring the amount of violence to which a child is exposed in the household.

In some respects, the evidentiary value of acts of animal abuse has advantages over the use of prior acts of family violence. First, evidence of animal abuse may be detected more easily, thus prompting a report. Abused animals are more likely to be detected than abused children because animals commonly go outdoors. Furthermore, unattended and neglected animals have a tendency to become a nuisance, which may also prompt a reporting. This is in contrast to family violence that usually occurs in the privacy of the home. Second, violent acts against animals are not accorded the same privacy protection that shield most intimate family disputes. Third, animal abuse does not invite the frequent argument that the battered spouse failed to mitigate her abuse by failing to leave. Animals, like children, are entirely dependent on their caretakers and cannot be blamed for allowing the abuse to continue.

Because judges have broad discretion in custody cases to decide the weight to accord each factor, it is unlikely that the inclusion of evidence of animal abuse as an additional factor would lead to absurd results. If the only evidence of violence is that of animal cruelty, removal of a child is unlikely because custodial decision making does not rely on any one factor.

A custodial decision can only be made in the best interest of the child when proper weight is accorded to the different forms of family violence that a child witnesses. Evidence of parental violence directed toward animals should be used to make better decisions, thus enhancing the protection afforded to children. Legislation and court decisions should accept evidence of animal abuse as probative in determining whether a child's welfare is at risk. Judges, lawyers, and legal scholars should heighten their understanding of family violence and strive to improve the mechanisms by which human and nonhuman members of the family may best be protected.

CONCLUSION

Family violence has plagued this country and despite of the efforts of many different protective agencies, it continues to be an epidemic. Although the problem is not clearly understood and there are no obvious solutions, it appears that success in abating family violence lies in a multidisciplinary approach. It is not enough to look at a single victim. Often the violence extends to other members of the family, who will remain unidentified and unprotected unless protective agencies work together.

Family pets, often considered by their owners to be members of the family, can suffer the same terrible injuries as other victims of family violence. The evidence correlating child abuse, spousal abuse, and animal abuse strongly supports the inclusion of animals among the victims of family violence. As laws are drafted to protect children, spouses, and the elderly from abuse, care should be taken not to overlook how animal abuse is related to these forms of violence.

By strengthening animal cruelty laws, mandating the reporting of animal abuse, establishing clear guidelines for recognizing abuse, and setting up regional reporting registries, we can better understand and prevent animal abuse. Preventing animal abuse can then benefit other victims of family violence. Specifically, detection of child abusers and effective intervention can be enhanced through interagency cooperation and the sharing of evidence. Only if we resist the temptation to prioritize the victims, can the prevention of animal abuse become another weapon for combating family violence.

NOTES

1. See, for example, Hawaii Rev. Stat. §§ 711-1109 (excluding insects, vermin, or other pests; Iowa Code § 717B (excluding livestock); and Louisiana Rev. Stat. Ann. § 102.1 (excluding fowl).

2. See, for example, Hawaii Rev. Stat. § 711-1109(requiring intentionally, knowingly, or recklessness) and Okla. Stat. 21 § 1685(requiring willfully or maliciously).

3. See, for example, Idaho Code §§ 25-3502 (requiring negligence for certain acts); Louisiana Rev. Stat. Ann. § 102.1 (requiring intentionality or with criminal negligence); and New Hampshire Rev. Stat. Ann. § 644:8 (requiring negligence for certain acts).

4. See, for example, Alaska Stat. § 11.61.140; Maryland Code Ann. art. 27 § 59; South Carolina Code Ann. § 47-1-40.

5. See, for example, Florida Stat. Ann. § 828.12; New Hampshire Rev. Stat. Ann. § 644:8; Oklahoma Stat. Ann. 21 § 1685. The other states that have felony animal anticruelty statutes are California, Delaware, Louisiana, Maine, Michigan, Missouri, Montana, Oregon, Pennsylvania, Rhode Island, Washington, and Wisconsin.

6. See, for example, Minn. Stat. §343.21; Utah Code Ann. § 76-9-301; West Virginia Code § 61-8-19; Colorado Rev. Stat. § 19-2-918.5.

7. See, for example, Massachusetts Gen. Laws Ann. 272 § 77; Minnesota Stat. §343.21.

8. See, for example, California Penal Code § 597.

9. See, for example, New Jersey Stat. Ann.§ 4:22–17.

10. Oregon Rev. Stat. §§167.315–30.

11. For example, California Civ. Code § 607f. (a); Pennsylvania Stat. Ann. 3 §456.4.

12. Both Minnesota and West Virginia impose a duty on veterinarians to report known or suspected cases of animal abuse (Minnesota Stat. Ann.§ 346.37(e); West Virginia Code § 7-10-4a). Idaho Code § 25-3514A provides veterinarians with immunity from criminal and civil liability without imposing an affirmative duty.

13. California Penal Code § 11166. Similarly, Colorado's Child Abuse and Neglect Statute includes veterinarians among the health professionals who are required to report known or suspected cases of child abuse or neglect. Colorado Rev. Stat. Ann.. § 19-3-304.

14. Child Abuse Prevention and Treatment Act, Pub. L. No. 93-247 (1974) (current version at 42 U.S.C.S. §§ 5101 et seq.)

15. See Animal Welfare Act, 7 U.S.C. §§ 2131-2159 (providing guidelines for the humane treatment, care, and transportation of animals by dealers, exhibitors, and researchers); Horse Pro-

tection Act, 7 U.S.C. §§ 1821-1831 (prohibiting the showing, exhibition, or selling of lame horses); Humane Slaughter Act, 7 U.S.C. §§ 1901-1906 (providing for humane guidelines in the slaughtering of livestock and the handling of livestock in connection with slaughter); Twenty-Eight Hour Law, 49 U.S.C. § 80502 (requiring transportation companies (excluding truckers) to follow guidelines in transporting cattle, sheep, and swine).

16. See New Jersey Stat. Ann. § 9:6-8.46, providing that "proof of the abuse or neglect of one child shall be admissible evidence on the issue of the abuse or neglect of any other child."

17. For example, Minnesota Stat. § 518.17 (2); Oregon Rev. Stat. § 107.137(1).

18. For example, 23 Pennsylvania Cons. Stat. Ann. § 5303.

REFERENCES

Adams, C. 1994. Bringing peace home: A feminist philosophical perspective on the abuse of women, children, and pet animals. *Hypatia* 9:63.

Albert, A., and K. Bulcroft. 1988. Pets, families and the life course. *Journal of Marriage and Family* (50):543, 550.

American Animal Hospital Association. 1995. *The 1995 American animal hospital report: A study of the companion animal veterinary services market.* Denver, Colo.: American Animal Hospital Association.

American Psychological Association. 1996. *Violence and the family, report of the American Psychological Association presidential task force on violence and the family.* Washington, D.C.: American Psychological Association.

Arkow, P. 1994. Animal abuse and domestic violence: Intake statistics tell a sad story. *Latham Letter* (Spring), 17.

Arkow, P. 1995. *Breaking the cycles of violence.* Alameda, Calif.: Latham Foundation.

Ascione, F. R. 1998. Battered women's reports of their partners' and their children's cruelty to animals. *Journal of Emotional Abuse* 1(1):119-33.

Boat, B. 1995. The relationship between violence to children and violence to animals: An ignored link? *Journal of Interpersonal Violence* 10(4):229-35.

Cahn, N. R. 1991. Civil images of battered women: The impact of domestic violence on child custody decisions. *Vanderbilt Law Review* (44):1041, 1093-94.

Cohen, H. 1995. Federal animal protection statutes. *Animal Law* 1:143.

Costin, L. B., H. J. Karger, and D. Stoesz. 1996. *The politics of child abuse in America.* New York: Oxford University Press.

DeViney, E., J. Dickert, and R. Lockwood. 1983. The care of pets within child abusing families. *International Journal for the Study of Animal Problems* 4:321-29.

Dohrn, B. 1995. Domestic violence, child abuse, and the law; Bad mothers, good mothers, and the state: Children on the margins. *University of Chicago Law School Roundtable* (2)1.

Enos, V. P. 1996. Prosecuting battered mothers: State laws' failure to protect battered women and abused children. *Harvard Women's Law Journal* (19):229, 251-52.

Favre, D. S., and M. Loring. 1983. *Animal law* 9.1-9.25. Greenwood Press.

Felthous, A. R., and S. R. Kellert. 1985. Childhood cruelty toward animals among criminals and noncriminals. *Human Relations* 38:1113.

Finch, P. A. 1989. *Breaking the cycle of abuse.* Washington, D.C.: Humane Society of the United States.

Francione, G. L. 1995. *Animals, property, and the law.* Philadelphia: Temple University Press.

Gehrke, B.C. 1997. Results of AVMA survey of U.S. pet-owning households on companion animal ownership. *Journal of the American Veterinary Medical Association* 211:169.

Guggenheim, M., A.D. Lowe, and D. Curtis. 1996. *The rights of families.* Carbondale: Southern Illinois University Press.

Hellman, D. S., and N. Blackman. 1966. Enuresis, firesetting and cruelty to animals: A triad predictive of animal crime. *American Journal of Psychiatry* 122:1431.

Hutton, J. S. 1983. Animal abuse as a diagnostic approach in social work: A pilot study. In A. H. Katcher, and A. M. Beck, eds., *New perspectives on our lives with companion animals.* Philadelphia: University of Pennsylvania Press.

Jordon, L. 1991. Bless the beasts and the children. *CHAIN Letter* 4:6 (Marin Human Society, Novato, Calif.).

Kalichman, S. C. 1993. *Mandated reporting of suspected child abuse: ethics, law, and policy.* Washington, D.C.: American Psychological Association.

Kempe, C. H., et. al. 1962. The battered-child syndrome. *Journal of the American Medical Association* 181:17–24.

Kramer, D. T. 1994. *Legal rights of children,* 2nd edition. Colorado Springs, Colo.: Shepard's/McGraw-Hill.

Leavitt, E. 1990. *Animals and their rights: A survey of American laws from 1641 to 1990,* 4th edition. Washington, D.C.: Animal Welfare Institute.

Levine, M. 1993. A therapeutic jurisprudence analysis of mandated reporting of child maltreatment. *New York Law School Journal of Human Rights* 10:717–19.

Loar, L. 1994. Congratulations . . . and welcome! *CHAIN Letter* 7:9 (Marin Humane Society, Novato, Calif.).

Loar, L. 1996. I likes the policeman that arrested that dog. *Latham Letter* (Spring), 2.

Lockwood, R., and G. Hodge. 1986. The tangled web of animal abuse: The links between cruelty to animals and human violence. *Humane Society of the United States News* (Summer).

McKay, M. M. 1994. The link between domestic violence and child abuse: Assessment and treatment considerations. *Child Welfare* 73:29.

Miller, K. S., and J. F. Knutson. 1997. Reports of severe physical punishment and exposure to animal cruelty by inmates convicted of felonies and by university students. *Child Abuse & Neglect* 21:79.

Quinlisk, A. 1994 *1994/95 survey results.* La Crosse, Wis.: Domestic Violence Intervention Project.

Ritter, A. W. 1996. The cycle of violence often begins with violence toward animals. *The Prosecutor* 30:31.

Sigler, R. T. 1989. *Domestic violence in context: An assessment of community attitudes.* New York: Lexington Books.

Walker, J. R. 1980. A study on the relationship of child abuse and pet abuse. Unpublished professional project, University of Pennsylvania School of Social Work, Philadelphia.

Widom, C. S. 1989. Does violence beget violence? A critical examination of the literature. *Psychological Bulletin* 106:3–28.

Connections—Child Abuse

A writer in the *Home Journal* suggested a way to improve the prevention-of-cruelty movement by extending its protection to "miserable children (animals, we might call them,)" so evident in the streets of New York. "Let there be a lawful interference; in short, let us have a legally constituted and organized Society for the Prevention of Cruelty to Children."

—Lela B. Costin, citing Zulma Steele, *Angel in Top Hat,* 1942

Abuse of Children and Abuse of Animals
Using the Links to Inform Child Assessment and Protection
Barbara W. Boat

I saw a child brought in, carried in a horse blanket, at the sight of which men wept aloud, and I heard the story of Mary Ellen told again, that stirred the soul of a city and roused the conscience of a world that had forgotten; and, as I looked, I knew I was where the first chapter of the children's rights was being written.

—Jacob Riis, Police Reporter, New York City, 1874

THE LINKS between violence to children and violence to animals have received implicit acknowledgment throughout the history of movements to address both forms of abuse, but the practical utilization of these links has been largely ignored in the field of child abuse and neglect (Boat 1995).

Awareness of the links often appears to simmer just below the surface for many professionals. Child protection workers, law enforcement officers, teachers, social workers, physicians, nurses, child advocates, judges, youth workers, and therapists will exclaim, "I never thought of that before!" when they first "hear" about and "see" the links. Then, inevitably, they will offer spontaneous relevant anecdotes from their own experiences that illustrate the connection. A psychiatrist said, "That reminds me of my patient who is a Vietnam vet. He said that he went through hell in the war and can deal with that. But what he cannot deal with is his father killing his dog when he was a kid." A teacher wondered, "You know, as a child I was so terrified of my father. He never laid a hand on me—didn't even yell at me. But he was harsh and mean to our pets. I must have known that if he could do that to the animals, he could do that to me." A child advocate recalled, "Last year I was working with a 12-year-old boy who told me his divorced mother abandoned his dog on a country road, saying that she had to do that because the boy's father would not give her enough money to keep the dog." A judge described a teen in her courtroom testifying that her father threatened to kill her dog if she would not have sex with him.

As we increase our awareness and acknowledge the potential links among animal abuse prevention and child abuse prevention, animal protection and child protection, and early interventions, we can forge exciting new connections that will enhance the safety of both children and animals. In this chapter I discuss the several roles that awareness of violence to animals can play in the field of child protection and assessment.

CRUELTY TO ANIMALS AND RISK ASSESSMENT

Risk for the Child to Be Abused or Neglected

The evidence continues to mount that where animals are abused people are abused and vice versa (Arkow 1995). Higher rates of animal abuse by parental figures have been found in substantiated cases of child physical abuse than in the general population (DeViney, Dickert, and Lockwood 1983). Abused animals were found in 88 percent of the homes of 57 families with pets where child physical abuse had been substantiated. Two-thirds of the pets were abused by fathers; a disconcerting one-third of pet abuse was perpetrated by the children. Furthermore, persons, including children, living in homes where pets were abused were 10 times more likely to have been bitten or attacked by the abused pet.

Our awareness of the child abuse-animal abuse connection is being heightened in regard to domestic violence settings. Witnessing domestic violence is considered a priori psychological maltreatment of the child and the statistics for risk of abuse are sobering. In a national survey of over 6,000 U.S. families, researchers found that 50 percent of men who frequently assaulted their wives also frequently abused their children (Straus and Gelles 1990). Many men who resort to violence to control women can enhance their control by harming or killing family animals or by threatening to do so. Persons who counsel battered women report that dogs and cats have been stabbed, shot, hanged, and otherwise mutilated by abusive spouses. Sometimes the animals simply disappear or die mysteriously. Recent surveys of violence to animals witnessed by women seeking refuge in shelters for battered women define the extent of the problem (Ascione 1998). In a study of 38 battered women who were consecutive intakes in a shelter, 71 percent who owned pets reported that their violent partners had threatened or actually harmed their pets. Equally disturbing is that 32 percent of the women reported that their children were perpetrating abusive acts against the pets as well. For some women, concern over their pets' welfare delayed them from seeking shelter sooner for themselves and their children, prolonging exposure to the risk environment.

Questions about animal-focused violence or threats of violence can be included in standard assessments made during child protection investigations and by intake workers at safehouses for battered women. Questions may include several suggested by Ascione (1998):

- "Do you have any pets?" or "Have you had any pets in the past year?"
- "Has your partner (or anyone else) threatened to harm your pet or actually harmed your pet?"
- "Has your child harmed your pet?"
- "Do you worry about your pets' safety?"
- "Did concern about your pets' safety keep you from seeking shelter sooner?"

Such questions can alert us to the extent that violence to animals may be perpetrated or witnessed in the child's environment. Killing, maiming, or torturing animals may correlate with potential for dangerous acts. The inclusion of animal abuse as one of the lethality markers is being evaluated in several settings. For example, Randall Lockwood of the Humane Society of the U.S. cites the experience of Nashville, Tennessee, a city that had among the highest domestic violence homicides in the nation when a policy was instituted on domestic violence calls to obtain information on three possible lethality indicators: brandishing a weapon or threatening with a weapon, threatened suicide by batterer, and abuse of pets in the family. Batterers meeting any of these lethality criteria were remanded to special programs. Domestic violence fatalities decreased from 30 to 6 within one year of instituting this new policy, while at the same time numbers of cases increased from 12,000 to 18,000, Lockwood says (1997).

Asking a child about pets when the child is seen in medical, school, or investigatory settings can provide a window into a child's home life and illuminate risks that might otherwise go undetected. For example, when we are concerned that children may live in an abusive or traumatizing environment, we can ask specific questions of children and caregivers about the existence and treatment of pets. Some potentially useful questions include:

- Do you have pets or other animals at your house?
- What kind? What are their names?
- Who takes care of _____?
- Does anyone hurt _____? Or, does _____ ever get hurt? How? By whom?
- How is _____ disciplined (trained, taught to be good, etc.)?
- Have you ever lost a pet or animal you really cared about? What happened?
- Do you ever worry about something bad happening to your pet or animal?

Questions such as these can be a stepping-stone to talking about more personal topics. Frequently, children will disclose what happens to their pets before talking about themselves. For example, a 10-year-old boy of upper-middle-class parents whom the boy described as "arguing a lot" (police had recently responded to a domestic violence call involving attempted choking) frequently witnessed his father "being mean" to one of their cats, throwing it down the stairs and kicking it when it came near. This was his mother's cat. He then went on to reveal fears he had for his and his mother's safety when his father was in "one of his bad moods."

We also can ask older children or caregivers questions like, "How many pets have you had?" and "What happened to them?" In some family settings where domestic violence occurs, pets seldom reach the age of two years. Reports by children of frequent pet turnovers or loss of pets may "red flag" a chaotic household where the safety of the children is also compromised.

Reports to children's social services agencies of suspected abuse or neglect of children that include maltreatment of animals should be viewed as a serious cause for concern. In a recent fatality case review, a protective services worker followed up on a call from a neighbor who witnessed a three-year-old boy being severely beaten by his father. The neighbor also reported that the father had killed a cat in the presence of his family by slamming the cat against a wall. The protective services worker investigated the family and wrote in her report that the father denied mistreating his son but he did admit to killing the cat because it "peed on the rug." The worker dismissed the act of killing the cat by noting that the incident had happened over a month ago. No further interventions were offered to the child and family. Two months later the boy died of a cerebral hemorrhage inflicted by his father.

Finally, awareness of treatment of pets has been suggested as important for investigators of "failure to thrive" children, but with an unusual twist. This term is applied to children whose growth is significantly less than the developmental norms established for a child's age and sex. According to the National Center for the Prosecution of Child Abuse (1995), criminal culpability depends on the investigators' showing that a child's failure to thrive was due to intentional, knowing, reckless, or criminally negligent acts or omissions of caregivers. In documenting intentional neglect, investigators are advised to note if there are pets and if so to document the presence of pet food. In some cases there will be food for parents, older children, and family dogs, but none for the victim. Of course, it may be that a pet is malnourished as well.

Risk for the Child to Be Cruel or Abusive to Others

Data on adults document a relationship between patterns of chronic interpersonal aggression and childhood histories of animal cruelty (Kellert & Felthous 1985; Arkow 1996). Physical cruelty to animals was first listed as a symptom indicative of Conduct Disorder in 1987 in the *Diagnostic and Statistical Manual of Mental Disorders* (DSM-III-R). In the DSM-IV (1994), cruelty to animals has an even more prominent position. A diagnosis of Conduct Disorder is highly concerning, as it is considered to be a more intractable problem, affecting between 2 percent and 8 percent of children. It is multigenerational and results in destructive acts that harm society. Therefore, early detection affords greater opportunities for intervention. It is significant that hurting animals is considered one of the earliest reported symptoms, appearing at a mean age of about six years (Frick et al. 1993).

The etiology and expression of cruel behaviors in children is not well understood (Ascione, Thompson, & Black 1995). Indeed, "cruelty" is a difficult concept to define, whether the cruelty involves behaviors toward children or animals. One reason for our difficulty is that perceptions of humane treatment to both children and animals have varied—and continue to vary—historically and culturally. One hundred years ago in the United States, very young children worked in sweatshops and horses were driven until they collapsed. Neither were protected by law. Even today, when we have many more protections in place for children and animals, we still struggle with what constitutes "cruel" physical punishment. Today, as in the past, the monetary value of an animal determines the extent to which cruelty is perceived and punished. In the hierarchy of importance, cruelty to horses is subject to the largest fine, followed by cruelty to dogs, and finally to cats. In a case of two boys setting fire to a cat, the public defender sought to have the charges dismissed, citing a ruling that animal cruelty laws applied only to "socially useful" animals and that cats did not meet this criterion.

People also have personal hierarchies of value of different kinds of animals. Ascione (1994) reports a case where two teenaged boys in Utah caught a six-month-old kitten in a leg-hold trap, shot arrows into the kitten and then stomped it to death, laughing and joking while they videotaped the entire event. The tape was later confiscated. During the court hearing, the juvenile judge was asked if he would recommend further evaluation or counseling for the boys. He responded, "No. Not just for killing a cat." The mother of one of the boys was confused about the uproar her son's behavior created. She protested that he was not a cruel child because he had never mistreated his dog.

The reasons behind children's cruel behavior to animals are complex and multidetermined (Ascione 1994). For example, in young children lack of modeling and monitoring appropriate behaviors with animals can lead to cruel interactions including hitting with objects, poking, choking, stepping on, kicking, and restraining (e.g., tying up or putting in a box). Peer reinforcement for "showing off" or "daring" may result in collective cruel acts to an animal that would not occur if the child were alone. Tying a cat to a railroad track can win peer approval, enhance personal aggressiveness and be an exciting and elating feat to a group of children. Children may identify with the aggressor in settings where animals have been hurt or killed to frighten or coerce the child, or they may imitate punitive actions of adults. The child's cruelty can reflect a desire to control and inflict pain, have the quality of repetitious post-traumatic play reenactment or be a displacement of hostility onto animals. Ascione describes an unusual motive for a child's cruel behavior toward a cat where the child, as a means of self-mutilation, provoked the cat to severely scratch her arms. Killing animals also may signal great distress on the part of the child and a possible wish to die, according to Gil (1994). She cites cases where children hurt or killed animals and also evidenced suicidal behaviors.

Definitions of cruel behaviors are undergoing refinement. Rowan (1993) has suggested the model shown in table 1.

Table 1. A Proposed Model for New Cruelty-to-Animals Terminology

Description	Perpetrator's Motivation	Animal Suffers?	Society's Attitude
Cruelty	Satisfaction from suffering	Always	Condemns
Abuse	Satisfaction from dominance	Usually	Condemns
Neglect	No satisfaction derived	Usually	Condemns
Use	Justified by personal or societal gains	Sometimes. Attempts made to minimize	Approves if justified or suffering minimized

It is very important that we assess the possible motivations of children when animal cruelty is perpetrated in order to offer the most effective interventions. It is not uncommon for our professional judgment to be clouded when confronted with children who are cruel to animals. Recently, a colleague described two youths who doused a kitten with lighter fluid and set it on fire. The kitten ran under a car and the car blew up. This professional said he had worked with children who had perpetrated extreme violence, even murdered other children, but this was, without exception, the "worst" case of cruelty he had ever seen. He felt angry and defeated by the boys' behavior and apparent lack of remorse. When he evaluated one of the boys, however, he discovered a profoundly chaotic childhood. The mother said the boy was sometimes whipped too hard by his father; the father had also severely physically abused the mother and was charged with domestic violence seven times during the 12-year marriage, charges that were always dropped. When asked about family pets, the boy reported there had been 15 dogs, as well as many rabbits, hamsters, birds, and turtles. He did not know what had happened to the pets. They just "ran away, I guess." They never had a cat because his father hated cats. However, the boy did identify two dogs that were special to him and a source of comfort when he was feeling stressed.

THE BOAT INVENTORY ON ANIMAL-RELATED EXPERIENCES

Although anecdotes abound, to date we have not systematically gathered information about a wide range of experiences with animals. The Boat Inventory on Animal-Related Experiences (BIARE) was developed to elicit information about a wide range of events to determine if animal-related trauma, cruelty, or support are part of the child's, adolescent's, or adult's history (see my appendix after this essay). Areas explored include

- pet ownership history;
- experiencing animals as a source of support;

- loss of animals;
- cruelty to animals;
- killing of animals;
- animals used to coerce or control a person;
- sexual interactions with animals; and
- animal-related fears.

In addition, optional background information forms are included as well as questions for sexual abuse victims and offenders. The inventory is meant to be used as a screening and information-gathering instrument. It has not been standardized or normed. Users may opt to ask any of the questions that appear relevant to a particular case. I strongly recommend reading the questions aloud to the respondent.

The inventory has been piloted in a study exploring traumatic experiences and post-traumatic stress disorder (PTSD) symptoms in female and male veterans (Baker et al. 1998) as well as a preliminary study on screening for trauma indicators in 35 psychiatrically hospitalized adolescents (Boat, Baker, & McConville 1996). In the latter study, the responses of a 14-year-old boy provided information that the hospital staff believe was shared because of structured questioning. One area discussed during the interview with this teen was the loss of his favorite dog whom he believed was "made really mean" by a neighbor who would hit the dog with garden tools whenever the dog went into his yard. In response to inventory questions, the boy described an undiminished sense of loss since the age of eight and undiminished anger at the person responsible for the loss. "I *still* hate him!" he said vehemently.

When the same teenager was questioned about ever having hurt or tortured an animal, he replied, with a slight smile, that he had put his sister's cat in the microwave. The cat died two days later and he had a friend drive over the cat's body with his truck so the death would appear accidental. Why did he choose the cat? "I hate cats, the way they act—all cocky. Like they rule the world. They just piss me off." He also had hanged the family's cocker spaniel over the upstairs railing by its leash and collar because it "peed on my bed." Later, again in response to specific questions on the inventory, the boy acknowledged that he had witnessed a friend "butt-fucking his dog." All of this was new and highly concerning information to the hospital staff.

ENHANCING DETECTION OF CHILD ABUSE AND NEGLECT

The potential for broadening coverage for children by linking child and animal maltreatment is one of the most exciting outcomes of our heightened awareness (American Humane Association 1993). "Cross-coverage" and "cross-training" programs promote interactions among law enforcement, protective services, and animal welfare agencies to detect and prevent violence in mutual environments where children and animals co-exist. In such programs, if an animal control officer determines that an animal is suffering, the officer also checks on how the children are doing. Child protective services workers reciprocate by noting the condition of animals when they investigate a case. Even where the connection is not formalized, professionals *are* cooperating. In one state, a sheriff's deputy responding to a domestic violence call noticed that three pit bulls were chained in the front yard. He became suspicious and returned with an animal control officer and a search warrant. Behind the house the officers found the bodies of 3 dogs, 30 live pit bulls in cages, 10 of them puppies, and a pit bull fighting ring. They also confiscated videotapes of the dog fights. Social Services later investigated the welfare of the children living in this setting.

Expansion of mandated reporting of child abuse and neglect to include veterinarians and animal control officers is another potential form of cross-coverage. Many veterinarians and animal control officers go into people's homes to care for animals and thus have access to observing the adults and children. Veterinarians are aware of the types of injuries that can result from animal abuse (American Humane Association 1998). They also report observing bruises on some women who bring their pets for treatment.

The importance of mandated reporting in the protection and early intervention for children cannot be underestimated. For example, animal control officers entered a home where numerous turtles were kept in cages and pens. Four children lived among the cages and a toddler was observed poking her fingers into the turtle feces and then putting her fingers in her mouth. The risk for the child contracting salmonellosis was substantial and these children benefitted from an animal control officer who recognized that they, as well as the turtles, needed help. Because animal control officers are trained investigators who thoroughly document their observations, their reports can be very useful to child protection agencies.

Animal control officers also can be instrumental in helping parents recognize the seriousness of a child's cruel acts, as demonstrated when a 10-year-old boy tied a dog's legs and mouth and strung the dog over a barn rafter where its body was discovered two weeks later. The boy's parents dismissed the behavior until an animal control officer urged them to be very concerned and to seek help.

ANIMAL WELFARE AND CHILD WELFARE ADVOCACY

Another compelling link between animal abuse and child abuse is our lower tolerance for cruelty and damage to animals than for cruelty and damage to children. Incidents of concerned public response to reports of severe cruelty to animals or to heroic efforts displayed by animals are frequently described in the news. For example, when news media reported that a mother cat in New York had entered a burning building five times to retrieve her kittens, offers to adopt the kittens poured in from all over the country.

We seem more able to identify with the vulnerability of animals than the vulnerability of humans. In California, a mountain lion attacked and killed a female jogger. The lion left one cub; the woman left two young children. By September 1994, $22,000 had been donated to support the orphaned cub now residing in a local zoo. Only $9,000 had been donated to the grieving family.

Professionals, knowingly and unknowingly, utilize this link. A pediatrician, subpoenaed to court to testify in a case of physical abuse, was describing the severity of the injuries that had been inflicted upon the young child by his stepfather. She noted the extreme choking, bruising, and battering that had occurred, but the judge appeared unmoved. Frustrated and wanting to convey the desperateness of the child's plight, she asked the judge to imagine someone choking and battering a very young puppy in a similar manner. She later was told that the animal image immediately evoked an empathic response that led to more severe restrictions on the offender. In another example, a prosecutor described a case where a woman had tried to protect a dog from being shot and was, herself, shot, but not killed. The prosecutor said she had no difficulty winning the case because the woman's actions were targeted at saving an animal. If there had been no animal involved, questions of the woman's motives and her role in provoking the shooting would have been raised.

ASSESSING LOSS AND TRAUMA

In the mental health arena, we often ask children about loss of significant persons in their environment, including parents, siblings, and grandparents, as well as teachers and friends. But we frequently overlook the loss of pets or possible traumatic experiences related to animals in the lives of children, adults, and the elderly. Questions need to tap not only the loss, but how the loss occurred and the severity of the loss experience both at the time it occurred and currently. My colleagues and I have developed a survey (Boat, Baker, & Abrahamson 1996) consisting of 14 questions about potentially traumatic experiences, including loss of a favorite animal and being frightened by an animal. Because trauma is in the eye of the beholder, we are interested in not only whether an event occurred, but the age(s) and a rating of the "badness" of the event both when the event happened and currently. The pet- and animal-related questions are as follows:

Have you or your family ever had a pet?   Y N
If *yes*, have you lost a pet that you really cared about (e.g., died, was killed or taken away)?   Y N
    If *yes*, how old were you? (*circle all that apply*):
        1. Under age 6   2. 6–12 years   3. Teenager   4. Adult
    How bad was it (or the *worst* event) for you?
        1. Not bad   2. Somewhat bad   3. Very bad
    How much does it (or the *worst* event) bother you now?
    1. Not at all   2. Somewhat   3. A lot
Was someone ever violent or abusive toward the pet?   Y N

If *yes,* how old were you? (*circle all that apply*):
    1. Under age 6   2. 6–12 years   3. Teenager   4. Adult
How bad was it (or the *worst* event) for you?
    1. Not bad   2. Somewhat bad   3. Very bad
How much does it (or the *worst* event) bother you now?
    1. Not at all   2. Somewhat   3. A lot
Have you ever been badly frightened or attacked by an animal?   Y N
  If *yes,* how old were you? (*circle all that apply*):
    1. Under age 6   2. 6–12 years   3. Teenager   4. Adult
How bad was it (or the *worst* event) for you?
    1. Not bad   2. Somewhat bad   3. Very bad
How much does it (or the *worst* event) bother you now?
    1. Not at all   2. Somewhat   3. A lot

We have surveyed several different populations about animal loss experiences. The samples included incarcerated sex offenders, juvenile sex offenders, male and female veterans, and adolescents on a psychiatry inpatient unit, for a total of 311 respondents. We noted the following trends:

1. Ownership of a pet as a child ranged from 82 to 100 percent.
2. Loss of a pet they really cared about was a common experience, ranging from 68 to 83 percent in the various samples.
3. The loss of a pet was rated as "very difficult" (on a three-point scale) by 60 to 71 percent of respondents.
4. Turning to a pet as a source of comfort in a stressful time ranged in frequency from 34 to 100 percent of respondents in the samples, with the lowest number endorsed by male veterans and the highest by male juvenile sex offenders.

Among 35 adolescents hospitalized in an inpatient psychiatry adolescent unit, losing a favorite pet was endorsed by more than two-thirds of our sample, was rated among the top six trauma events in frequency, and was perceived to be as "bad" as being verbally or emotionally abused by a parent or as having a parent who was physically violent. Reasons given for pet loss often were not benign, for example, "Someone stomped on my cat's head," or, "My grandmother gave my dog away when I was at school."

Loss of significant animal companions as a common and frequently difficult event for children is a reaction noted by other researchers (Brown, Richards, & Wilson 1996), supporting the consideration that we assess for animal-related experiences and incorporate this knowledge when planning interventions.

SUMMARY

Enhancing our awareness and knowledge about the relationships between violence to animals and violence to children provides a unique opportunity to enhance our services to both. Certainly, cross-coverage by child and animal welfare professionals has the potential to detect neglectful and abusive settings. Mandated reporting of animal abuse and child abuse by veterinarians and animal control officers is consistent with a focus on prevention and early intervention. Systematic questioning and observations of children and caregivers can become part of the professional's repertoire in assessing the existence and impact of experiences such as loss of a favorite pet, witnessed or perpetrated animal cruelty, as well as the supportive roles that animals play in the lives of children, adolescents, adults, and the elderly. Finally, by being aware of the links, we will continue to collect data to inform creative interventions and programs to reduce violence in the lives of both children and animals.

REFERENCES

American Humane Association. 1998. *Recognizing and reporting animal abuse: A veterinarian's guide.* Englewood, Colo.: American Humane Association.

American Humane Association. 1993. *A training guide for recognizing and reporting child abuse.* Englewood, Colo.: American Humane Association.

American Psychiatric Association. 1987. *Diagnostic and statistical manual of mental disorders,* 3rd edition, revised. Washington, D.C.: American Psychiatric Association.

American Psychiatric Association. 1994. *Diagnostic and statistical manual of mental disorders,* 4th edition. Washington, D.C.: American Psychiatric Association.

Arkow, P. 1995. *Breaking the cycles of violence: A practical guide.* Alameda, Calif.: Latham Foundation.

Arkow, P. 1996. The relationships between animal abuse and other forms of family violence. *Family Violence and Sexual Assault Bulletin* 1(1–2):29–34.

Ascione, F. R. 1994. Hurting children/hurting animals: Current research linking these forms of maltreatment and implications for prevention and intervention. Paper presented at the Conference on Preventing Violence in Society Through Humane Education, Ramat Gan, Israel.

Ascione, F. R. 1998. Battered women's reports of their partners and their children's cruelty to animals. *Journal of Emotional Abuse* 1(1):119–33.

Ascione, F. R., T. M. Thompson, and T. Black. 1995. Childhood cruelty to animals: Assessing cruelty dimensions and motivations. Paper presented at the 7th International Conference on Human-Animal Interactions, Geneva, Switzerland (September).

Baker, D. G., B. W. Boat, H. T. Grinvalsky, and T. D. Geracioti. 1998. Interpersonal trauma and animal-related experiences in female and male military veterans: Implications for program development. *Military Medicine* 163:20–26.

Boat, B. W. 1995. The relationship between violence to children and violence to animals: An ignored link? *Journal of Interpersonal Violence* 10:229–35.

Boat, B. W., D. Baker, and S. Abrahamson. 1996. The Childhood Trust Events Survey. Department of Psychiatry, University of Cincinnati, Cincinnati.

Boat, B. W., D. Baker, and B. McConville. 1996. Comparison of frequency of traumatic events reported by psychiatrically hospitalized adolescents and documented in the chart: A preliminary study. Unpublished manuscript, Department of Psychiatry, University of Cincinnati, Cincinnati.

Brown, B. H., H. C. Richards, and C. A. Wilson. 1996. Pet bonding and pet bereavement among adolescents. *Journal of Counseling and Development* 74:505–9.

DeViney, E., J. Dickert, and R. Lockwood. 1983. The care of pets within child abusing families. *International Journal for the Study of Animal Problems* 4:321–29.

Frick, P. J., B. B. Lahey, R. Loeber, L. Tannenbaum, Y. Van Horn, M. A. G. Christ, E. L. Hart, and K. Hanson. 1993. Oppositional defiant disorder and conduct disorder: A meta-analytic review of factor analyses and cross-validation in a clinic sample. *Clinical Psychology Review* 13:319–40.

Gil, E. 1994. Children and animals: A clinician's view. *Animals' Agenda* 14:20.

Kellert, S. R., and A. R. Felthous. 1985. Childhood cruelty toward animals among criminals and noncriminals. *Human Relations* 38:1113–29.

Lockwood, R. 1997. The dynamics of animal cruelty and the psychology of abuse. Presentation at The Tangled Web of Abuse Conference, Greenville, S.C.

National Center for the Prosecution of Child Abuse. 1995. *Update,* 8:10. Alexandria, Va.: American Prosecutors Research Institute.

Rowan, A. N. 1993. Cruelty to animals. *Anthrozoös* 6:218–20.

Straus, M. A., and R. J. Gelles, eds. 1990. *Physical violence in American families.* New Brunswick, N.J.: Transaction Publishers.

APPENDIX: BOAT INVENTORY ON ANIMAL-RELATED EXPERIENCES

"These questions are about some of your experiences with animals and include things you may have heard about, seen, or done yourself. Although some of the questions are of a personal nature, please answer them if you can."

Ownership

1. Have you or your family ever had any pets?   Y N

   If yes, what kind(s)? (read types below and circle all that apply)

   How many?   How many?

   a. dog(s) _____

   b. cat(s) _____   f. turtles, snakes, lizards, insects, etc.   _____

   c. bird(s) _____   g. rabbits, hamsters, mice, guinea pigs, gerbils _____

   d. fish _____   h. wild animals (describe) _____

   e. horse(s) _____

   How old were you when you or your family owned any animals or pets? (circle all that apply)

   a. under 6   b. 6–12 years   c. teenager   d. adult

2. Do you have a pet or pets now?   Y N

If yes, what kind(s)? (read types and circle all that apply)

How many?   How many?
a. dog(s)   _____
b. cat(s)   _____   f. turtles, snakes, lizards, insects, etc.   _____
c. bird(s)   _____   g. rabbits, hamsters, mice, guinea pigs, gerbils   _____
d. fish   _____   h. wild animals (describe) _____
e. horse(s) _____

3. Of your animals, do you—or *did* you—have a favorite?   Y N

   Which one? _____

   Why? _____

Support

"Sometimes pets or other animals are special sources of support in times of stress."

4. Has there ever been difficult or stressful times when a pet or animal was a
source of comfort for you—even if you did not own the animal?   Y N

   How old were you? (circle all that apply)
        a. under 6   b. 6–12 years   c. teenager   d. adult

   What kind of pet or animal gave you support? _____

   How did the pet or animal give you support? _____

   _____

5. Are there times when it has been easier to talk to animals than to people?   Y N

   If yes, how often does/did this happen? (please circle)
        a. just a little   b. somewhat   c. a lot

6. Did you ever have a favorite stuffed toy animal?   Y N

   Do you still have it?   Y N

Loss

"Sometimes people lose animals that are special."

7. Have you ever lost an animal you really cared about? (For example, the animal
was given away, ran away, died or was somehow killed?)   Y N

   If yes, what kind of animal? _____

If your pet died, was the death:
  a. natural (old age, illness, euthanized)   b. accidental (hit by car)
  c. deliberate (strangled, drowned)   d. cruel or violent (pet was
                                                  tortured)

What happened? _____
_____
_____

Was the death or loss used to punish you or make you do something?   Y N

How difficult was the loss for you?
  a. not at all difficult   b. somewhat difficult   c. very difficult

How much does it bother you now?
  a. not at all   b. somewhat   c. a lot

How did people react / what did they tell you after you lost your pet?
  a. supportive   b. said it was your fault   c. punished you
  d. other _____

How old were you?
  a. under age 6   b. 6–12 years   c. teenager   d. adult

Was any person responsible for you losing the animal?   Y N

If yes, how do you feel now about what that person did? (please circle)
  a. upset at first, but no longer   b. still somewhat upset   c. still *very* angry

8. Have you ever worried about bad things happening to an animal you really
cared about?   Y N

  What were your worries? _____
  _____

Cruelty or Killing

"Sometimes people do mean things to animals, deliberately hurting, torturing or kill-ing them in a cruel way."

9. Have you *heard* about people deliberately hurting, torturing or killing
an animal?   Y N

  What did you hear? _____
  _____

10. Did you ever *see* anyone deliberately hurt, torture or kill a pet or animal
in a cruel way?   Y N

If yes, who? (please circle)
- a. friend or acquaintance
- b. family member or relative
- c. stranger
- d. other (who?) _____

What kind of animal(s)? (read types below and circle all that apply)
How many?   How many?
- a. dog(s) _____
- b. cat(s) _____   f. turtles, snakes, lizards, insects, etc.
- c. bird(s) _____   g. rabbits, hamsters, mice, guinea pigs, gerbils _____
- d. fish _____   h. wild animals (describe) _____
- e. horse(s) _____

How did they hurt, torture or kill the animal(s)? (circle all that apply)
- a. drowned
- b. hit, beat, kicked
- c. stoned
- d. shot (BB gun, bow & arrow)
- e. strangled
- f. stabbed
- g. burned
- h. starved or neglected
- i. trapped
- j. had sex with it
- k. other (describe) _____

What happened afterwards? _____
_____

How old were you when you saw this happen? (circle all that apply)
- a. under 6   b. 6–12 years   c. teenager   d. adult

11. Have *you* ever deliberately hurt, tortured or killed a pet or animal in a cruel way?   Y N

If yes, what kind? (circle all that apply)
How many?   How many?
- a. dog(s) _____
- b. cat(s) _____   f. turtles, snakes, lizards, insects, etc.
- c. bird(s) _____   g. rabbits, hamsters, mice, guinea pigs, gerbils _____
- d. fish _____   h. wild animals (describe) _____
- e. horse(s) _____

What did you do to hurt, torture or kill the pet or animal? (circle all that apply)
- a. drowned
- b. hit, beat, kicked
- c. stoned
- d. shot (BB gun, bow & arrow)
- e. strangled
- f. stabbed
- g. burned
- h. starved or neglected
- i. trapped
- j. had sex with it
- k. other (describe) _____

What happened afterwards? _____

_____

How old were you? (circle all that apply)
    a. under 6   b. 6–12 years   c. teenager   d. adult

Were you alone when you did this?   Y N

12. Have you ever *seen* anyone give animals any drugs (alcohol, pot, etc.)?   Y N

Describe: _____

_____

Have *you* ever given animals any drugs (alcohol, pot, etc.)?   Y N
    Describe: _____

_____

Have you ever *seen* animals being made to fight (pit bulls, cocks, etc.)?   Y N
    Describe: _____

_____

Have *you* ever made animals fight?   Y N
    Describe: _____

_____

Coercion or Control

"Sometimes people make children or adults do mean things to animals, trying to control people with threats or actually hurting an animal, (e.g. If you tell, I'll kill your dog)."

13. Have you ever *seen* or *heard* about someone doing this?   Y N

    What have you seen or heard? _____

_____

14. Has anyone ever threatened you this way?   Y N

    If yes, what happened? _____

_____

Who did this? (circle)
    a. friend or acquaintance   c. stranger
    b. family member or relative   d. other (who?) _____

How old were you? (circle all that apply)
    a. under 6   b. 6–12 years   c. teenager   d. adult

Sexual Interactions

"Sometimes animals are used by people in sexual ways."

15. Have you ever *heard* about people being sexual with animals?   Y N

    What did you hear? _____

    _____

16. Have you ever *seen* others do sex acts or sexual touching with animals?   Y N

    If yes, what kind(s) of animals?_____

    Please describe what you saw: _____

    _____

    Where did you see this? _____

    Who did this? (circle)
        a. friend or acquaintance   c. stranger
        b. family member or relative   d. other (who?) _____

    How old were you? (circle all that apply)
        a. under 6   b. 6–12 years   c. teenager   d. adult

17. Have *you* ever done sex acts or sexual touching with animals?   Y N

    If yes, what kind of animals? _____

    Please describe what you did or were made to do: _____

    _____

    Who made you do this? (if applicable)
        a. friend or acquaintance   c. stranger
        b. family member or relative   d. other (who?) _____

    How old were you? (circle all that apply)
        a. under 6   b. 6–12 years   c. teenager   d. adult

Fears

"Some people are afraid of some animals."

18. Have you ever been really frightened by an animal (eg. chased or bitten)?   Y N

    If yes, what kind of animal? _____

What did the animal do? _____

_____

How old were you?
      a. under 6   b. 6–12 years   c. teenager   d. adult

Were you hurt?   Y N
     If yes, how were you hurt or injured? _____

_____

Are you still afraid of the kind of animal that frightened you?   Y N

"Roadkill"

"Seeing roadkill (dead animals by the side of the road) bothers some people."

19. Does seeing "roadkill" bother you?   Y N

    If yes, how much? (please circle)
          a. just a little   b. somewhat   c. a lot

    What about the "roadkill" bothers you? _____

_____

Movies, TV

"Seeing animals portrayed as hurt or mistreated bothers some people."

20. Does seeing movies or TV shows where animals are hurt or mistreated
bother you?   Y N

    If yes, how much? (please circle)
          a. just a little   b. somewhat   c. a lot

Taking Animal Abuse Seriously
A Human Services Perspective
Suzanne Barnard

ANIMALS, ESPECIALLY PETS, can get caught up in the cycle of family violence. Women and children are sometimes intimidated into silence about sexual or other abuses through threats made toward a favorite pet. Pets are sometimes hurt or killed to punish a child for something he or she has done. An abused child might act out aggression and frustration on an animal that is perceived to be more vulnerable. In many cases, the animal is just the last victim in a chain of abuse that filters down from the strongest family member to the weakest. At the same time, research on the relational issues between violence to children and animals has begun to show disturbing correlations between early childhood cruelty to animals and later juvenile delinquency or adult aggressive criminal behavior to humans. For these reasons, it is becoming increasingly important for human services professionals to take animal abuse seriously and to recognize it as a possible indicator of serious family dysfunction.

Human services professionals can contribute to the growing body of knowledge about the shared roots of violence by understanding the parallel nature of the historical development of the two professional fields, by contributing to the data needed to influence more research, analysis, and policy issues in the area of violence to children and animals, and by sharing expertise on the nature of human behavior.

THE EVOLUTION OF REPORTING LAWS

The laws regarding the reporting and treatment of child abuse and animal cruelty came into existence independently of each other. It has only been over the last 20 years that professionals in the two fields have begun to study the possible correlations between the two.

The animal protection movement began in England in the 1820s. Not long after that, it spread throughout Europe, reaching the United States in 1866 and Canada in 1869. Following a famous 1874 case in which an abused child was removed from the foster parents who had injured her, the American Society for the Prevention of Cruelty to Children was founded, and in 1878 the American Humane Association founded its Children's Division to ensure adequate protection of children from abuse and neglect.

The line between abuse and discipline was never clearly drawn, and courts were reluctant to become involved in family matters except when presented with the most abhorrent circumstances. That began to change in 1962 with the publication of Dr. C. Henry Kempe's landmark study, "The Battered Child Syndrome," which appeared in the *Journal of the American Medical Association* in July of that year (Kempe et al. 1962). For the first time, a prestigious medical journal had set forth a scientific framework within which child abuse and neglect could be addressed.

Shortly after that study, model statutes dealing with child abuse and child abuse reporting were prepared on the presumption that when parents or caretakers are unwilling or unable to protect children, the government must intervene to keep children safe. In 1963, the National Center on Child Abuse and Neglect put forth its proposed statute, followed in 1965 by two more, one from the American Medical Association and one from the Program of State Governments. With these prestigious entities leading the debate, virtually every state in the union had passed laws by 1966 requiring physicians to report suspected child abuse.

Once these laws were enacted, a process ensued in which the categories of professionals required to report were expanded to include such individuals as nurses, dentists, social workers, teachers, day care providers, and others in professions that worked with children. The definition of child abuse was subsequently broadened to include such conduct as emotional maltreatment, malnourishment, sexual abuse, and exploitation (Besharov 1990; Kalichman 1993).

In 1974, the Federal Government became involved in the prevention of child abuse with the passage of the Child Abuse Prevention and Treatment Act (CAPTA; Public Law 93-247). For the first time, there was a unified source for the funding of research and demonstration projects. There was also a centralized system for incident reporting and data collection and dissemination. Mechanisms were put in place to assist states and municipalities in implementing programs and interagency and interdisciplinary task forces were organized to oversee and assist with the work of public child protection agencies.

CAPTA also contained a working definition of child abuse and neglect: "The physical or mental injury, sexual abuse, negligent treatment, or maltreatment of a child under the age of 18 by a person who is responsible for the child's welfare under circumstances which indicate the child's health or welfare is harmed or threatened thereby as determined in accordance with regulations prescribed."

While the federal act attempted to bring unity to the process of defining child abuse, individual states have continued to utilize significantly different definitions of such types of conduct as maltreatment, emotional maltreatment, educational neglect, medical neglect, abandonment, and dependency. These differences may reflect varying community norms or simply local politics. It is safe to say that despite all efforts to move toward uniform standards of child protection, that goal has yet to be realized. With the advent of government intervention in requiring child protection reporting, society began a rapid path toward aggressively dealing with child abuse and neglect. Reporting requirements helped to broaden the identification of maltreated children and to designate agencies specifically required to prevent or investigate and manage maltreatment cases. A different path was taken regarding cruelty to animals, so that violence to children and violence to animals came to be viewed as separate issues by most of U.S. society.

Laws forbidding cruelty to animals date back to the Body of Liberties passed by the Puritans of the Massachusetts Bay Colony in 1641. Between 1828, when New York State passed the first anticruelty to animals statute, and 1913, when Arizona enacted its statute, every state and the District of Columbia enacted some form of law forbidding mistreatment of animals.

As in the case of child abuse laws, animal mistreatment definitions are not uniform and enforcement and penalty procedures—even the definitions of the type of animal to be protected—vary from state to state. The definitions of animal cruelty have never been as well-defined as those pertaining to child abuse. Although work is underway to create better definitions of animal cruelty based on child protection models, the animal welfare field still struggles, at times, to put in place the same types of reporting and protection systems that have evolved in the child protection arena.

Unlike the child abuse scenario, where the responsibility for the protection of children moved from the community to a government agency, the major responsibility for the protection of animals is still largely perceived to lie within the purview of the community. Although this can be viewed as a positive outcome for animals when a community rallies to defend "those who cannot defend themselves," it does create confusion about the best action to take when animals are deliberately harmed because of malicious acts or because caretakers are unwilling or unable to care for their pets properly. For example, in Colorado, veterinarians are mandated reporters of suspected child abuse yet they are not required to report suspected cruelty to animals.

CROSS-TRAINING

The need for cooperation between child abuse protection workers and animal welfare workers is demonstrated by the fact that 50 percent of all pet owners are parents of children. That means that when animal protection workers are investigating cruelty to animals, there are likely to be juveniles in the household.

By working in concert with animal protection professionals, the protection of children can be increased in several ways. The animal protection worker may be the first or the only individual to have access to an abusive family environment. If child abuse or neglect is occurring, the presence of an animal welfare worker may be useful not only for observation and intervention but for later legal testimony if children must be removed and placed in protective custody. In cases where animal cruelty is confirmed, the ability to provide observations of pet behavior and family history of animal care can also add to evidence in those situations where physical proof of child abuse is limited (Barnard et al. 1995).

Cross-training also enables each field to contribute to the growing data on the correlation between animal-directed violence and human cruelty. Every case involving the two types of violence should be noted and made available to those developing academic or clinical research on the subject. But this is not always easy to accomplish. Obstacles to this type of collaborative approach include

- confidentiality laws that forbid the release of information concerning identification of youthful perpetrators or victims of child abuse;
- turf and funding issues;
- public perceptions that violence to one population is more significant than violence to the other (e.g., lower tolerance for animal abuse than for child abuse); and
- lack of consistent definitions of what constitutes animal "cruelty."

Finding creative solutions to the obstacles preventing the collection of valuable information must be the first priority in any collaboration. Denver District Attorney William Ritter (1996) suggested that special flags or tracking numbers be attached to criminal cases where animal cruelty is in evidence. He also indicated that information regarding animal cruelty could be used in sentencing and parole decisions for convicted perpetrators. This type of knowledge, as it expands, can provide valuable data upon which other legislative and judicial decisions can comfortably be reached.

Another important use of this data is education of the public. Although much of what comes to light through the national media tends toward the sensational (e.g., the killing and torturing of animals), it nonetheless creates a more receptive public willing to consider the more scientific information on the subject. Heightened public awareness from the stories in the popular press can give human service or animal protective workers a starting point in the discussion of the need to observe, report, and intervene in animal cruelty cases.

STRENGTHENING LEGISLATION

In any situation in which there is an effort to get the government to enact new legislation or change existing policies, the formation of effective coalitions is essential. Therefore, when working on cases involving multiple forms of abuse, the human services professional should be attuned to individuals and agencies that share common goals, and should seek out and enlist the support of those entities when there is need for public action.

Many communities are already starting to form coalitions to bring recognition to the importance of collaboration between human service and animal welfare agencies. In Mobile, Alabama, the newly formed Quad-Alliance Against Violence, which was established to bring attention to all forms of family violence and to bring about the strengthening of animal and child maltreatment laws, has members from the child welfare, domestic violence, and animal welfare communities. In Colorado Springs, Colorado, the Domestic Violence Enhanced Response Team (DVERT), which was formed for immediate response to potentially lethal domestic violence situations, has members of the local humane society as part of its secondary response team. The primary response team includes a police officer, detective, deputy district attorney, and victim advocate (see Jorgensen and Maloney, "Animal Abuse and the Victims of Domestic Violence," in this volume).

As municipalities and states attempt to grapple with the growing concern over cruelty to animals, the legislative process gives another opportunity to the concerned human services professional. With documentation of cases, data collected, and research performed, testimony at legislative hearings can help persuade those in power to enact laws to protect animals and to require cross-training and cross-reporting. Such testimony also provides valuable and inexpensive publicity to educate the public (Rosenthal 1996).

A team approach using testimony from a social worker, a psychologist, a humane investigator, a veterinarian, and a district attorney has been very successful in Colorado in moving along passage of a bill that calls for increased financial penalties and mental health treatment for juvenile or adult perpetrators convicted of animal cruelty. The combination of professionals from human services and animal welfare backgrounds who provided testimony in support of the bill helped the mostly skeptical legislators eventually understand that "taking animal abuse seriously" is a concern of many professions and not just part of an "animal lovers" agenda.

CHILD PROTECTIVE SERVICES AND ANIMAL CRUELTY

The risk of nonintervention is perhaps best highlighted by the media-sensationalized cases of Ted Bundy, Albert DeSalvo (the Boston Strangler), David Berkowitz (Son of Sam), and Jeffrey Dahmer. All had committed incidents of cruelty to animals in their childhoods. In addition, studies have linked childhood histories of cruelty to animals to aggressive male prison inmates, to convicted child molesters, to assaultive women offenders, to sexual homicide perpetrators, and to rapists (Ascione 1993). The very clear bottom line is that in households where there is cruelty to animals, other forms of cruelty are likely.

It is reasonable to assume from the foregoing rogues' gallery that children who are cruel to animals early on might grow up to be cruel to other humans. If there is an innate barrier against inflicting pain on other human beings, can it be said that inflicting pain on animals is a step toward breaking down that barrier?

Bill Ritter, the district attorney of Denver, testified in 1997 before the Colorado State Legislature in support of a bill strengthening Colorado's animal cruelty laws.

He said: "Cruelty to animals is one of those things that when you see them on a juvenile's record, we are usually reading the record, and the person is now being held for, or convicted of, an act of violence. It is a predictor of violent behavior, and as good a predictor as I have seen."

Those sentiments were echoed by Art Walsh, a former juvenile referee in Colorado Springs, who commented upon his observations from the bench: "In sentencing juvenile offenders, we received a pre-sentence investigative report that contained a social history. If we saw evidence of animal cruelty in that history, we invariably knew we were dealing with a more disturbed individual with a less likely chance of rehabilitation."

Colorado State Representative Ken Gordon of Denver, commenting in support of tougher animal cruelty laws, said, "It is my sense that these people who start with animal cruelty are actually more likely to be sociopaths than other criminals."

The earlier there is intervention in antisocial, deviant, or dangerous behavior, the greater the probability that the intervention will be successful. The above-mentioned professionals from the legislative, executive, and judicial branches all recognize the importance of animal cruelty as an indicator of other emotional problems or the potential for later violence.

Consider also that the two groups who go into households to investigate acts of cruelty are animal welfare workers and child protection workers. It is inevitable that workers in each discipline will be exposed to evidence of abuse in the other. It makes sense, then, that each profession should understand how to recognize and report suspected animal or child abuse.

Even though statistics on child abuse show increases, these may be due in part to increases in reporting. A great deal of child abuse—animal cruelty as well—goes unreported. The problems are too large for any one entity or discipline to tackle single-handedly. Because of the evidence supporting a correlation between cruelty to animals and other forms of family violence, child protection investigators should be prepared and educated to notice and report parallel problems.

More importantly, the histories, comments, and research suggest that we can no longer view violence as an isolated or compartmentalized phenomenon. Animal cruelty is part of a larger human problem of violence in general, and its study may provide valuable clues toward root causes of cruelty to both humans and animals.

Some state governmental agencies have begun to realize the connections between forms of abuse. For example, the Maine Department of Human Services *Child and Family Services Manual* noted in 1982 that violence targeted against one population may be indicative of abuse or neglect aimed at another population. The manual commented that although laws for the protection of children and animal welfare laws originated independently of one another, they bear similarities. Maine treats child abuse reports from its humane officers exactly as it would treat reports from protective services workers or law enforcement officials. Likewise, social workers and law enforcement personnel are required to report to humane officers acts of animal cruelty they may encounter (Arkow 1995:40).

Similarly, some local governments have begun to show concern with the link between child abuse, domestic violence, and cruelty to animals. The county of San Diego, California, requires any social worker of San Diego County to report any observed or reasonably suspected instance of animal cruelty or neglect to the County Department of Animal Control as part of the Penal Code and the San Diego County Code (SDCC 62.601[c]).

Despite all of the legal protections that exist, there is no guarantee that an animal protection worker will be alerted in all cases of cruelty, or that a protective services worker will be notified in all cases of child abuse. For this reason, those working in the related fields of animal cruelty and child abuse must consider whether they have a moral obligation to cooperate and pool their limited resources to meet the overwhelming need for their services.

The patterns of abuse and cruelty to animals described here strongly suggest that the animal cruelty–child abuse link is the next frontier in the campaign against violence. The subject can be seen as a broadening of the child abuse reporting field, or a continuing extension of the need to make child protection services stronger. These trends are demonstrated in the revised version of the mental health manual, the *Diagnostic and Statistical Manual-IV* (American Psychiatric Association 1994), which includes cruelty to animals as a criterion for Conduct Disorder (312.8):

> A. A repetitive and persistent pattern of behavior in which the basic rights of others or major age-appropriate societal norms or rules are violated, as manifested by three more of the following criteria in the past 12 months, with at least one criteria present in the past 6 months:
> Aggression to people and animals.
> (4) Has been physically cruel to people;
> (5) Has been physically cruel to animals.

The existence of a diagnostic norm for behavior patterns that include physical cruelty to both man and animal is yet another indicator that the time has come for society to recognize that cruelty to animals is part of a continuum of violence that includes child abuse and domestic violence.

Finally, there is a cost-benefit advantage to involving professionals in both the child protection and animal protection fields. Earlier and shared intervention will bring a greater likelihood of success in the prevention of family violence. This preventive medicine can lessen the necessity for costly treatment down the road.

As research continues and a base of statistical evidence emerges, the link between these forms of violence is certain to strengthen. As this occurs, and as the economic benefits of early intervention become apparent, one can anticipate legislative action leading to more and tighter reporting requirements.

Beyond legislative action, however, it is imperative that public attitudes toward both animal abuse and child abuse be continually shaped through education (American Humane Association 1996). All citizens, not just law enforcement or social services personnel, need to be awakened to the far-reaching impact of cruelty to animals and its link to violence against humans. By combining solid statistical evidence with heightened public concern and improved collaboration between animal and child protection, true benefits can be achieved that take us all a step closer toward eliminating violence in our society.

REFERENCES

American Humane Association. 1996. *Addressing violence through public awareness: A guide to reaching the media with your message.* Englewood, Colo.: American Humane Association.

American Psychiatric Association. 1994. *Diagnostic and statistical manual of mental disorders,* 4th edition. Washington, D.C.: American Psychiatric Association.

Arkow, P. 1995. *Breaking the cycles of violence: A practical guide.* Alameda, Calif.: Latham Foundation.

Ascione, F. R. 1993. Children who are cruel to animals: A review of research and implications for developmental psychopathology. *Anthrozoös* 6(4):226–47.

Barnard, S., Parry, C., Edwards, M., Muslim, E., and Kaufmann, M. 1995. *A training guide for recognizing and reporting child abuse for animal control officers and humane investigators.* Englewood, Colo.: American Humane Association.

Besharov, D. J. 1990. *Recognizing child abuse: A guide for the concerned.* New York: Free Press.

Kalichman, S. C. 1993. *Mandated reporting of suspected child abuse: Ethics, law, and policy.* Washington, D.C.: American Psychological Association.

Kempe, C. H., F. N. Silverman, B. F. Steele, W. Droegemuller, and H. K. Silver. 1962. The battered child syndrome. *Journal of the American Medical Association* 181:17–24.

Ritter, A. W. 1996. The cycle of violence often begins with violence toward animals. *The Prosecutor* 30(1, January–February):31–33.

Rosenthal, C. 1996. *Protecting animals from violence through legislative activism: A citizen's guide: Growing up humane in a violent world: A parent's guide: What you should know before changing your anti-cruelty laws.* Englewood, Colo.: American Humane Association.

The Link's Direct Connection to Child Protective Services

Robert P. Hall

CHILD ABUSE, along with other forms of domestic violence, is a serious health and social service problem in our society. It is at, or near, the top of the public agenda in the criminal justice, public health, juvenile justice, and social services fields. It even appeals to the philanthropic sector, with United Way donors demonstrating support through their designated gifts for organizations preventing family violence, especially child abuse.

At the same time, the problem of child abuse in this nation appears to be getting no better. In 1991, the United States Advisory Board on Child Abuse and Neglect reported that the status of the child abuse problem in this nation was "a national emergency." More recently, that body called it "a national disgrace." The numbers of new cases being reported to child protective services agencies are not declining significantly. More importantly, the numbers of serious and substantiated cases, that is, those cases requiring active child protective services interventions, are showing increases.

It also appears that the formal system that our nation has put into place to protect children—the child protective services agencies each state has instituted—is in crisis. Almost half of these agencies are operating under some degree of court order. Each year, the survey of child protective services agencies conducted by the National Committee to Prevent Child Abuse (NCPCA) reports that many individual state systems are experiencing increases in caseloads, but decreases in resources.

This essay explores the origins of this system in an older, but definitely related and still relevant, public service system. It further considers how a re-emerging link between the issues dealt with by child protection and animal protection could assist the younger system. It will also suggest ways that the productive use of this link could lead to a meaningful improvement in efforts to reduce violence in this country.

A VIEW OF THE BEGINNING

Most professionals in the animal and child protection fields are aware that the formal child protection system in this country traces its origins to the celebrated

109

"Mary Ellen" case of 1871 and the decision of the American Society for the Prevention of Cruelty to Animals (ASPCA) in New York City to undertake her defense. This case, in which an animal protection organization used one of its customary interventionary processes (court petition) to obtain the removal of an abused child, is often considered to be the first formally investigated child abuse case in this country. Even by today's standards, the reported details of the case would warrant a formal intervention were it to come to the attention of any of the nation's child protective services systems.

The significance of the Mary Ellen case has become the subject of some debate, but it is important in that the stated basis for action on the part of Henry Bergh of the ASPCA was an ill-defined minimum standard of protection to which both animals and children are entitled. According to Bergh, once this standard had been compromised, society had a right and a responsibility to act. This clearly became the basis for both the powers and the responsibilities that the states have given to their child protective services systems.

It can also be argued that the response in this case established a precedent. Bergh's successful petition was to remove Mary Ellen from the dangerous home in which she was living. This was achieved and a more successful placement was found. This beginning, based on the animal welfare model, led to a service model that probably relied heavily upon placement rather than treatment and fostered the unfortunate misconception that child protective services workers even today are "child snatchers" bent on removing children from homes and giving them to strangers.

The core model of both child protection and animal protection can be characterized as one of *investigation* (assessing a reported or observed situation in which a child or animal is at risk), *impoundment* (removing a child or animal in actual danger from the dangerous situation and placing the child or animal in one of greater safety), *enforcement* (using the criminal justice system to punish those who put the child or animal at risk), and *adoption or placement* (placing the child or animal in a more permanent and presumably more functional home). Children's services used gentler language, calling their places of impoundment "orphanages." The basic models for the interventionary care of children and animals at risk were astonishingly parallel, even to the most casual observers. Such models remained in use well into this century and, for animals, are still the basis for services in most communities even today.

Voluntary organizations committed to child protection—the all-public child protective services agencies are surprisingly modern—freely acknowledged their origins in the animal protective community. Beginning in 1873, Societies for the Prevention of Cruelty to Children sprang up in a number of states including New York, Massachusetts, and Delaware. What is less clear is whether or not these organizations and their leaders recognized the scientific link between the abuse of animals and the abuse of children and its implications for their work. It is unlikely that there was any forum for such study or recognition. Because both systems have tended to be crisis-driven, even more so in their early years, there would have been no reason to consider such matters, as the model was so basic and its successes (in both fields) were at least minimally acceptable.

DIVERGENCE

The parallels between the two systems began to exhibit divergence during the early years of the twentieth century, when child protection increasingly became a matter involving the government sector. Although animal protection and animal control were matters of law in most communities, the agencies who did the actual work of investigation and impoundment were private, voluntary organizations.

As child protection agencies became governmental entities, the child protection field gained a degree of sophistication. It became clear that the old system of impoundment and outplacement of children was neither feasible nor desirable in all cases.

The child protective services system began to include treatment options, attempting to modify parental behaviors to assure safe homes. This treatment most often took the form of traditional counseling or psychotherapy, assuming that the maltreatment of children was a rare and clinically abnormal behavior.

These early efforts in the 1950s and early 1960s enjoyed mixed success. Child protective services caseloads in this period were relatively small and the intake systems were fairly passive. By 1967, however, every state in the nation had passed a child protection law and the size of the caseloads began to increase. This led to a period of development in the child abuse treatment field, with more innovative and less traditional approaches being taken. Perhaps the most significant of these was Parents Anonymous, which began in California in 1970 under the leadership of Leonard L. Lieber, a psychiatric social worker who had worked in the child protective services system. Unlike other support group programs, Parents Anonymous gladly accepted public funding and entered into strong relationships with the public welfare system. As a result, Parents Anonymous spread across the country. It became a valuable treatment resource for many state child protective services systems and their client families.

Other developments included additional support group-type programs (such as Parents United International), specialized parent education programs (e.g., the Nurturing Programs of Family Development), and home visiting programs using paraprofessional companion counselors (e.g., parent aides, Family Outreach). Most of these programs took a humanistic approach to therapy and education, resisting the traditional temptation to "client-ize" the participating families and respecting them as partners in the programs. Perhaps as a result, these programs had considerable success, especially in redirecting parental aggression, not previously experienced in the child protection field.

Moreover, most of these programs recognized the cyclical nature of child abuse and neglect and offered services to both parents and children (as opposed to the older, more traditional programs that clearly targeted parents). Parents Anonymous, Parents United, and Family Development all promoted services to both parents and children; Parents United added help for adults who were abused as children.

All of this clearly differentiated the models being used by the child protection field from those being used by the animal protection field. The latter continued to rely upon the impoundment and outplacement model, with, of course, the additional recourse of euthanasia. And in most cases, this was still work being done by private, voluntary entities, albeit with occasional public funding. By contrast, the public child protective services system and its increasingly diverse private partners were growing a wide range of interventionary resources.

A further divergence between the two systems began to develop in the 1970s. As program services for child protection became more innovative and less traditional, interest grew in developing programs aimed at the prevention of child abuse, rather than its treatment. Many of these programs resembled the models already developed for treatment services, especially home and hospital visiting services aimed at new, particularly first-time, parents. This development drew elements of the child protection field away from the formal child protective services system and toward partnerships with other agencies, especially the public health services system.

One area of commonality between the animal and child protection fields comes in this prevention field. This is partly because prevention by its very nature is typically a voluntary endeavor. This is so even in the child protection field, where the leadership of the prevention movement has usually rested with the private entities, for example, the NCPCA. There is, however, an even more programmatic aspect to this commonality.

Advocates for both animals and children have relied upon the education of children and training of those who work with them to impart basic concepts, such as respect, safety, and so on. Animal advocates call their programs "humane education" and promote respect for other species. Child advocates call their programs "prevention education." Initially, these programs taught personal safety; more recently, they have emphasized respect for self, other family members, and neighbors. These programs, which are usually sponsored by voluntary organizations, offer useful and immediate opportunities to build upon the linkages between the animal and child protection fields.

CURRENT SITUATION

The public child protective services systems continue to respond to growing numbers of reports. Virtually all authorities agree that these cases are becoming increasingly difficult, requiring complex responses.

Most recently in the 1980s the child protective services systems have emphasized family preservation programs, such as Homebuilders. Although there are some questions about the efficacy of these programs, the basic commitment to keeping families together remains.

At the same time, the child protective services systems are confronting external pressures that affect both the families whom they serve and their own capacity to deliver programming. An example of the former is welfare reform, which is causing stress on families due to diminishing benefits. These are precisely the types of stresses that historically lead to incidents of child abuse. The latter examples include health care reform, where changes in payment patterns are affecting treatment plans. This is affecting the ability of the child protection community to offer services to families at risk, especially traditional therapeutic services over reasonable periods of time.

This is in contrast to the animal protection field, which is relatively exempt from these pressures but definitely subject to influences from the overall economy, which affects charitable giving (still the life blood of many animal welfare organizations). Animal protection agencies are dealing primarily with the serious problem of over-population and are increasingly emphasizing low-cost spay-and-neuter programs as a solution.

A disturbing trend in recent years has been the emergence, fortunately rare, of public information campaigns that promote rivalry among the fields. Examples include efforts by the child care field to claim that domestic animals are afforded more space than children in care (clearly a classic case of apples and oranges) and claims by certain child advocates that crimes against children result in more lenient punishments than crimes against animals (generally untrue). Domestic violence officials have lamented that there are more shelters in the United States for homeless animals than for battered women. These attempts to create rivalry where there are historically and clinically viable linkages are unfortunate and counterproductive and ought to be discouraged.

A somewhat less disturbing but equally challenging phenomenon in both fields is an emerging tendency toward radicalization. On the animal side, one can witness the development of organizations such as People for the Ethical Treatment of Animals (PETA), whose stated purpose is the promotion of animal rights rather than animal welfare. In many cases, the goals of these organizations are well beyond those of the traditional animal protection organizations. Indeed, the animal rights groups are often quick to criticize the older animal protection organizations and to chide them for perceived limitations of scope.

This radicalization is less prevalent on the children's side but it is growing. The National Committee on Children's Rights, for example, has been critical of what they perceive to be major compromises made by the mainstream child protection community on the drafting of the latest Child Abuse Prevention and Treatment Act. This type of radicalization is worth noting, because it has mobilized considerable resources among animal advocates and may well do the same among supporters of children's causes.

RECOGNIZING AND DEFINING THE RELATIONSHIP

The child protection field has become increasingly aware that the categorical problem of child abuse intervention is but a part of the overall problem of family dysfunction. The relationship between child abuse and neglect and alcoholism and other chemical dependencies, for example, has been recognized formally in recent years and addressed through two series of Comprehensive Emergency Services grants by the National Center on Child Abuse and Neglect (1991 and 1994). The quest for permanency planning, assuring that abused children do not "drift" through the foster care system, is older. But it clearly demonstrates the problems faced by child protective services agencies.

If children are to be maintained in stable homes, preferably their homes of origin, then their families have to be supported and assisted with far more than the threat of investigation. This has led to renewed interest in family support services, ranging from the older parent support and /or education programs to newer, more complex, resources. Some of these are delivered through other institutions with which the families are active, such as child care programs and schools.

This broadening of the child protective services field has resulted not only from this clinical awareness of the broader problems faced by families but also from changes in the federal funding streams available for child protection work. As categorical funding diminishes, public child welfare agencies are able to put into place broader systems of family support and preservation that are, it is hoped, more flexible and better able to respond to assessed family needs. As part of this process, many child protective services agencies are renaming themselves to emphasize their broader role, "family services" agency, for example. The negative side of this, unfortunately, is an expanding bureaucracy that is not always able to mobilize effectively the voluntary sector, whose strengths are on the much-needed prevention side.

Moreover, as the child protection field becomes increasingly aware of the relationship between violence against children and other social problems such as substance abuse and poverty, it is now beginning to understand the relationship between violence against children and other forms of violence. These include violence against spouses or partners, violence against the elderly, and violence against domestic pets. (To date, the prevention of elder abuse has not reached the same level of system development, reporting, or research as other forms of family violence.)

Child protection specialists in the subarea of sexual abuse have long argued that children witnessing sexual violence were themselves being victimized. This argument has been transferred to the broader child protection community, where it is now agreed that children witnessing any form of violence, even if they are not the intended targets, are in fact being victimized. For one thing, this victimization, even if it is unintentional, appears to put the offended children fully into the "cycle" of abuse and make them at risk of actually perpetrating (or even accepting victimization by) the witnessed behavior later in their lives. For another, it is known that active violence against children can be accompanied by other forms of family violence. For example, sexual abuse is well known to be reinforced by threats of violence against pets or even other parents. More broadly, it is realistic to assume that the same risk factors which put children at risk can put other family members at risk as well. A dysfunctional family rarely limits its dysfunctional activity to one category. Men at risk of resorting to violence due to the disinhibiting influence of alcohol, for example, are as likely to lash out at their spouses as they are at their children or even their pets.

It is therefore more appropriate to consider defining part of the problem faced by child protective services agencies not as violence against children but rather as violence itself. In this, the child protective services field can find a common bond with the animal protective services field and with the domestic violence field. To a certain extent, things are coming full circle. Henry Bergh must have wondered what would have happened had Mary Ellen's cruel stepparents had access to a puppy or a kitten.

Of course, recognition of this commonality does not in and of itself fully address the problem from a service delivery point of view. But it provides some key areas of discussion and suggests some ways in which the child protective services field might receive some much-needed help.

LINKING FOR IMPROVEMENT

There are a number of ways in which the link between animal abuse and child abuse can be utilized to improve this nation's efforts at child protection. These may be categorized into three broad areas: broadening the community, building public support, and mobilizing the voluntary sector.

BROADENING THE COMMUNITY

Any discussion of the current state of the child protective services agencies will invariably include the issue of staffing. Child protective services agencies are usually understaffed, resulting in inadequate resources for investigation and undesirable ratios of cases to workers. Involving workers from other disciplines, including animal protection, adult (elderly) protection, and so on, simply makes good sense and expands the personnel resources available to each. Although it does not necessarily mean that significantly more work will be done, it does help to assure that fewer cases will "fall through the cracks" or be overlooked. This is because both the animal protection system and the child protection system rely heavily upon third-party reporting for the identification of cases.

Many animals and children suffer serious and even life-threatening maltreatment simply because their cases do not come to the attention of the authorities. For the most part, the child protection system relies upon other professionals (especially educators and, to an unfortunately lesser extent, medical providers) to make quality reports. Prevention education and training programs typically include encouragement and instructions for mandated reporters (who may, in some states may be virtually everyone).

Therefore, it would be extremely helpful if other persons who have access to the homes of potentially dysfunctional families, such as animal protection officers, were trained and encouraged to report situations in which children were also at risk. Animal protection officers are typically uniformed and endowed with constabulary powers, so they are often able to obtain access more easily than other service deliverers. Their investigations could easily be expanded to include other family members in need and this information could, in this technological age, be efficiently transmitted to child protection authorities.

The obvious benefit of such cross-involvement has led to cross-training of animal and child protection workers. Although it is too early to assess the impact of this training, it is clear that this is a potentially monumental step in adding to the precious human resources available for the investigation of actual and potential violence against our most helpless family members. Properly trained, animal protection workers do more than report suspicions; they present information obtained from their own investigations, thus enabling child abuse investigators to make crucial decisions based upon hard evidence.

Beyond reporting and investigation, there is also potential benefit from combining efforts in the closely related area of prevention or humane education. Earlier child abuse prevention education programs such as "Red Flag, Green Flag" and "Good Touch, Bad Touch" basically taught safety skills. More recent efforts have gone beyond this to include consideration of communication styles, problem-solving skills, and the development of respect for self, peers, family members, and others. A good example of this is "Developing Nurturing Skills," a comprehensive family life education program validated and promoted by Family Development Resources.

This type of program actually has much in common with humane education programs, which teach respect for other species, habitats, and so on. Efforts ought to be made to develop comprehensive prevention education programs that include consistent discussions of respect for self, peers, family members, neighbors, and other species. These school-based programs would necessarily include prevention training components for counselors, teachers, and other school personnel.

BUILDING PUBLIC SUPPORT

It is important to go beyond the field professionals to see why the link between violence against animals and violence against children is so important to both fields, especially the latter. There is little doubt that the public ostensibly supports both animal and child protection efforts. They have voiced their support for child protection activities, especially child abuse prevention, in nationwide public opinion polls and in surveys conducted by federated funding organizations (e.g., United Way).

But it is unclear what this support has meant in terms of tangible help. For example, the public will generally be quick to call for improvements in child protective services; a study of the letters to the editor in any major newspaper following a highly publicized incident of child abuse will confirm this. But it is by no means certain that this same public would support increased taxation to pay for these improvements. Unfortunately, the voluntary sector, usually more creative than the government agencies, has been unable to capitalize upon the public's support for child abuse prevention. The same pollster (Harris, on behalf of NCPCA) that confirms the public's support concluded that, although the vast majority—as many as 90 percent—of Americans put child abuse prevention at the top of the social service agenda, only a tiny minority—less than a quarter—can identify a child abuse prevention organization with which they can become involved.

This contrasts unfavorably with other causes, such as disaster relief (Salvation Army, Red Cross) or single parenting (Big Brothers/Big Sisters, Parents Without Partners), with which most Americans can quickly and accurately identify the corresponding voluntary organizations. This even contrasts with the animal protection movement, where most people can at least identify a "humane society" or "SPCA" but are unfamiliar with the national organizations. Relatively few persons are aware that the 120-year-old national organization—the American Humane Association—has both animal protection and child protection divisions.

It would be helpful to the child protection community—public and private—to be able to build upon this raw goodwill and, in the tradition of the animal protection community, to be able to channel it into productive support. At a minimum, this ought to include generating private funds for program services that can keep at-risk families from becoming involved in the overburdened public protective services system and mobilizing volunteers for appropriate participation in targeted prevention services. More ideally, it ought to include the kinds of citizen activism and advocacy that have enjoyed such success on the animal side, for example, the animal protection (and animal rights) communities' generally successful onslaught against the fur industry.

This is no mean feat in efforts to reduce violence and protect children. In 1995, the U.S. House of Representatives quietly repealed the Child Abuse Prevention and Treatment Act. The public response was virtually nonexistent, requiring both intensive and extensive organizing and lobbying efforts by the child protection community's leadership to reintroduce this act in the Senate. This can be contrasted with the public outcry over the more popular Head Start program during the Nixon administration. Child abuse prevention and child protection need this support.

MOBILIZING THE VOLUNTARY SECTOR

This leads to a related but even broader benefit that the child protection community can use. The animal protection community has relied heavily, even totally in many cases, upon the voluntary sector, deploying private funds and volunteer personnel often to remarkable lengths and with great success.

The child protection community, by contrast, has been segmented. The public child protection services systems are public agencies with tax dollars. Their private sector contractors are more complex, adding to their government grants and contracts funds generated on the private side (e.g., United Way allocations). There is, however, little doubt that public funding is driving the programs.

It would be useful to recognize the links not only between animal abuse and child abuse but also between animal protection and child protection. That is, the child protection community would do well to emulate at least part of the voluntary character of the animal protection community, turning to the private sector for both financial and personnel resources to develop and sustain family support services that will prevent children and parents from becoming involved with the already and forever overburdened child protective services system. Children's Trust Funds and other structured mechanisms that support child abuse prevention and other child welfare services beyond the provisions of government funding are an excellent start in this direction.

Ideally, this would mean not only the utilization of volunteers in program services but also their involvement in leadership situations, as is the case in the animal protection community. This would require some much-needed clarification of the respective roles of the public and private sectors (e.g., the steering and rowing analogy), but it is apparent that the expansion of the resource pool is good for children and families. It is probable that leaving child protection totally in the hands of state bureaucrats does little to build public confidence in the system and this undermines both public support for it and, more importantly, public cooperation (e.g., reporting).

CONCLUSIONS

There is a clear relationship between the problems of animal abuse and child abuse. They are both forms of domestic violence. Households in which one is extant are likely to be households in which the other is either likely or also extant.

The child protection movement in this country grew out of the animal protection movement and, for a number of years, took similar forms. It can be argued that today's child protection system, although in many ways necessarily more sophisticated than its predecessor, could benefit from revisiting the old relationship. Recognizing that animal abuse and child abuse are two forms of a larger problem helps field professionals to define, identify and respond to the problem more accurately. Moreover, cross-training these field professionals improves investigations of abuse and provides more information on which to base interventions.

Also, studying the character of the animal protection community could help the child protection community to gain more meaningful and tangible public support. This support can be translated into resources that will both improve services and prevent unnecessary involvement with the protective services system. This, in turn, will protect children and strengthen families, the core unit of our society. And this will improve the quality of life for everyone.

READING LIST

There are several sources for basic information on child abuse, the child protective services system, and child abuse prevention programs.

The National Committee to Prevent Child Abuse, 332 South Michigan Avenue, Chicago, Illinois 60604, has an extensive publications program. *It Shouldn't Hurt to Be a Child* and *An Approach to Preventing Child Abuse* are affordable booklets that explain the premises of the child abuse prevention movement and its goals.

The American Humane Association, 63 Inverness Drive East, Englewood, Colorado 80112, also offers a range of publications. Their work emphasizes the role of the child protective services system.

Parents Anonymous, 675 West Foothill Blvd., No. 202, Claremont, California 91711, has a smaller publications program. The book *Hope for the Children* by Patte Wheat explains the history of the program. This organization has experienced significant transition over the years and its history has been rewritten several times, occasionally de-emphasizing the role of its professional founder Leonard L. Lieber in favor of more grassroots origins.

Family Development Resources, 3160 Pinebrook Road, Park City, Utah 84098, is another important source for information. *A Handbook for Understanding Child Abuse and Neglect* by Stephen J. Bavolek, Ph.D., is an excellent overview of the problem of child abuse. The organization publishes and disseminates a series of comprehensive and innovative family life education curricula that would be appropriate in any American community. The Nurturing Programs for Parents and Children are interventionary family life skills programs for group and home use for various age groups; and Developing Nurturing Skills is a school-based comprehensive prevention program.

"I'll Only Help You If You Have Two Legs"

or, Why Human Service Professionals Should Pay Attention to Cases Involving Cruelty to Animals

Lynn Loar

IN 1992, 12-YEAR-OLD Eric Smith killed a neighbor's cat. He was made to apologize and do some yard work for the wronged neighbor. In 1993, Eric Smith killed a four-year-old boy. He was convicted of second-degree murder for that offense the following year.

Shortly after Eric Smith's trial, I attended a workshop given by the child psychiatrist affiliated with Yale University who testified on the child's behalf at his trial. I was impressed by the psychiatrist's compassionate yet objective assessment of the boy. At the end of the workshop he took questions, and I asked if anyone had bothered to report the killing of the cat to their local humane society or municipal animal control agency. He replied that although that had not been done, consequences had been imposed on the child, namely the apology and yard work. I responded that the consequences addressed the property damage the neighbor experienced in the loss of his cat, but not the boy's taking the life of a sentient creature. Indeed, had the crime been reported, the child would likely have been required to undergo counseling and to have supervision when around defenseless living creatures. The psychiatrist replied that nothing more than the restitution and apologizing were done and he agreed that something important had been missed.

The response of this prominent and competent psychiatrist demonstrates the lack of awareness of the significance of cruelty to animals common among both human service professionals and the general public. Sensitive, thoughtful, and caring people seem rarely, if ever, to have considered the problem of cruelty to animals and its ramifications for human interaction. This blind spot allows inchoate behaviors in individuals to be ignored until they progress to the point of intractability, and contributes to society's high tolerance for cruel and violent acts.

The purpose of this essay is to describe the role of animal cruelty and neglect in the development of a perpetrator and to suggest how opposing values of empathy and compassion can be instilled through humane interventions. It is my hope that an appreciation of the role of animal maltreatment in dangerous human behavior will lead to earlier identification of people at risk, improve prognosis through timely and effective intervention, and contribute to a more humane society by raising awareness of the prevalence and ramifications of our high tolerance of inhumane behavior.

HISTORICAL OVERVIEW

Many social service providers are familiar with the story of May Ellen Wilson, a severely battered and neglected eight-year-old girl, whose case was one of the first child welfare matters heard in a court in the United States. On her behalf Henry Bergh, the founder (1866) and president of the American Society for the Prevention of Cruelty to Animals (ASPCA), and the ASPCA's lawyer, Elbridge Gery, filed a *habeas corpus* petition in Superior Court in New York in April, 1874, to remove her from inhumane circumstances. Although they were acting as private citizens, their prominence in the humane movement led to the myth that they asked the court to declare her an animal to qualify her for protection under statutes designed to protect animals from abuse. Bergh and Gerry succeeded not only in protecting Mary Ellen Wilson but in launching the first Society for the Prevention of Cruelty to Children which held its inaugural meeting the ASPCA's office in December, 1874.

The Mary Ellen case occurred decades after the first animal welfare legislation was introduced, 15 years after the publication of Charles Darwin's *The Origin of Species,* 10 years after the abolition of slavery, and 45 years before women got the right to vote, in an era when livestock, slaves, women, and children were all chattel valued for their abilities to work and bring income into a household.[1] A leading moral question in the second half of the nineteenth century was to what extent sentient creatures could be owned, used, and disposed of and to what extent ownership and usage should be prohibited (in the case of slaves) or restricted (in the cases of women, children, and animals).

It is important to realize that the definition of property is not fixed or absolute but changes over time and across cultures. For example, chattel in nineteenth-century America included most humans (i.e., women, children, African Americans of both genders) as well as livestock. In the twentieth century, however, living chattel is a status restricted to animals. But in any discussion of the role of animal abuse in human problems, it must be remembered that at one time both animals and people were owned property, and that the problems and vulnerability inherent in that status may still intrude. Moreover, because animals are the only group of living creatures currently considered ownable property in our society, the quality of their care and the attitudes of their owners reveal much about the dynamics of power and the owner's capacity for kindness. In addition, and of great interest to the social service professional, people are often much more candid in their discussions of animal maltreatment than of familial abuse because in their view the animals are merely disposable property not worthy of consideration. Thus, propensity for and refinement of dangerous behaviors are often practiced without much secrecy and described with little inhibition if the interviewer only asks. People likely fail to recognize that the step from ignoring the cries of a beaten animal to child abuse is a small one.

However, as John Locke (1705) pointed out in *Some Thoughts Concerning Education,* butchers were not permitted to serve on juries hearing capital cases because it was felt that their judgment was impaired by their daily practice of taking life. Indeed the foundation for cruel or compassionate behavior to animals and humans alike is laid in childhood:

> One thing I have frequently observed in Children, that when they have got Possession of any poor Creature, they are apt to use it ill: They often *torment,* and treat very roughly young Birds, Butterflies, and such other poor Animals which fall into their Hands, and that with a seeming kind of Pleasure. This I think should be watched in them, and if they incline to any such *Cruelty,* they should be taught the contrary Usage. For the Custom of Tormenting and Killing of Beasts, will, by Degrees, harden their Minds even towards Men; and they who delight in the Suffering and Destruction of inferiour Creatures, will not be apt to be very compassionate, or benign to those of their own kind. (Locke 1705, 116)

Over the years, humane societies and SPCAs have maintained an interest in problems affecting animals and people, and many still include in their mission statements the goal of helping animals and children. Common origins and goals notwithstanding, few human service professionals show an interest in cases involving animal abuse, report animal cruelty or neglect when they come across it, or work cooperatively with humane societies or animal control officers. The goal of this essay is to recommend such work to human service professionals with the aims of providing more comprehensive assistance to any sentient creature in distress, improving case outcomes through collaboration, increasing treatment opportunities through humane education and therapy programs, and identifying potentially serious and violent offenders who, as children, typically torture and kill animals.

OBSERVE PROBLEMATIC BEHAVIORS, NOT THE NUMBER OF LEGS OF THE VICTIM

Unfortunately, most parents spank their children as part of routine discipline, especially when their children are toddlers (Straus 1994). What makes the "terrible twos" so terrible and so apt to elicit abusive behaviors is the confluence of a number of trying and seemingly contradictory factors:

1. The child is highly mobile and relentlessly energetic, and thus needs constant supervision.
2. The child is noisy and argumentative, his or her first and favorite words being "no," "why?" and "mine."
3. Power struggles and tantrums erupt over eating and other matters of self-regulation.
4. And, the child is not yet toilet trained.

This combination of strength (the child's energy, noise, and resistance) and weakness (still in diapers) too often pushes parents beyond their limits. Throughout childhood, this mixture of oppositional, noisy and messy behaviors puts children at risk of maltreatment by their parents and other providers of care.

Animal abuse tends to be triggered by the same behaviors as child abuse. A cute puppy is also a busy and energetic puppy in need of supervision and activity. Animals bark and howl, especially when ignored or left alone too much. They may also be destructive, chewing, digging, and jumping on furniture or people. Housebreaking problems are common. They are also common triggers of abuse.

Elder abuse and abuse of the disabled stem from the same provocations. Supervision is often required even though an adult is involved. Limited activity leads to boredom, frustration, and irritating behaviors. Frustrated, ill and uncomfortable people may also be noisy, may complain, and may criticize their caregivers. Incontinence is often the last straw that brings on abuse.

Thus, regardless of the age or number of legs of the potential victim, the same behaviors put them at risk: the need for constant supervision, the level of activity, noise (crying, whining, barking, complaining), resistant or destructive behaviors (eating forbidden things, refusing to eat, chewing treasured objects), and toileting accidents. These are normal, if trying, behaviors. Problems stem from the limitations of the parents or other caregivers in meeting these demands. Intervention needs to address the potential for neglect or danger resulting from the limitations of the person in charge and not forfeit a sense of urgency just because of the category of the victim (animal, child, person with a disability, elder).

The physical, behavioral, and emotional indicators of physical abuse also tend to be the same for people and animals: inadequately explained injuries, withdrawn or aggressive behavior, self-destructive behavior (head-banging, creating sores, etc.), hypervigilance, extreme fear or anxiety, toileting accidents, wariness of physical contact, antisocial behavior, drastic behavioral change in the presence of the caregiver, and running away. Across ages and species, the emotional reactions are also consistent: fear, obsequiousness or cowering, depression, failure to grow or heal, hyperactivity, apathy, aggressive or bizarre behavior, unprovoked yelling or crying, and self-defeating actions (Loar & Weakland 1994).

Neglect—the failure to provide minimally adequate food, shelter, clothing (for people), medical care, and supervision—poses a great and serious threat to all dependent living creatures. Unable to ensure their own safety, hygiene, or dietary needs they suffer and are frightened when those they depend upon fail them. Attempts to meet their own needs can create dangerous situations such as digging or climbing out of a fenced yard and getting run over by a passing car; eating poisonous substances when hungry or unsupervised; or falling and injuring oneself in an attempt to find food, activity, and companionship or to get to a bathroom.

The behavioral indicators evidenced by neglected animals, children, the disabled, and the elderly also have much in common: being dirty or hungry; lacking appropriate food, shelter, bedding, and (for humans) clothes; being tired or despondent; having chronic untreated medical problems; showing fearfulness or learned helplessness; engaging in sucking, rocking, head banging, and other regressive and self-destructive behaviors; and begging for or stealing food.

In sum, then, all dependent living creatures have basic physical and affiliative needs, and the expression of these needs demands patience and protective responses by adults providing care and supervision. Risks to potential victims increase when demands are high or resources and skills of the caregiver are low. Assessments should, therefore, concentrate on the capabilities of and demands on the parent or other caregiver and secondarily consider attitudes that would reduce adequacy such as disposability ("it's only an animal"), minimization or rationalization ("she is a child or retarded or demented and won't understand"), and justification ("he deliberately provoked me by wetting the bed or carpet"). Ignoring the cruelty or neglect of an animal by a pet owner not only allows the maltreatment of that animal and additional animals the person may acquire to continue unchecked but also puts at risk humans exhibiting comparable behaviors and making similar demands on the caregiver.

RESPOND TO VIOLENT OR NEGLIGENT BEHAVIORS REGARDLESS OF THE AGE OR NUMBER OF LEGS OF THE VICTIM

Dangerous or negligent behaviors by people in positions of power or responsibility are a menacing problem and should be the focus of attention, irrespective of the victim. Indeed, because endangering behaviors can compromise the safety of all potential victims, removing a victim may only cause the targets to rotate, thereby increasing the risk for other potential victims in the family or area. It is as much a combination of bad luck, bad timing, proximity, and availability as individual characteristics that determine the hierarchy and likelihood of victimization.

The behavioral cues of the abusive or negligent caregiver are similar whether the one at risk is an animal, a child, an elder, or a person with a disability. These similar behaviors threaten all vulnerable creatures who happen to be in the presence of a potentially menacing individual. Such indicators include a history of abuse or neglect in the caregiver's own childhood; the use of harsh discipline or rigid or inappropriate rules; lack of knowledge about developmentally appropriate norms and the need for flexible rules; description of the animal, child, disabled person, or elder as big, powerful, demanding, and challenging; judgmental interpretation and cruel treatment of problematic behaviors; abuse of alcohol or drugs; overuse of or inappropriate use of medication or physical restraints to control or punish; and restricting access to the outside or to other people.

The emotional context will likely include harshness; blaming and belittling; being cold and rejecting; failing to support, encourage, or express positive values; being inconsistent and unpredictable; being uninterested in or trivializing the problems; and failing to recognize the victim as a separate being with worthy wants, needs, and interests. In essence, the parent or caregiver fails to regard the other as separate and to respond to his or her plight or vulnerability with compassion and empathy.

Negligent homes tend to be filthy, chaotic, unsanitary, and unsafe. They may not contain nutritious food for any resident, regardless of age or species. The family is apt to be isolated from relatives and neighbors and cut off from the environment, draping curtains over windows during the day, perhaps, or rarely venturing outside.

ROLES ANIMALS PLAY IN CASES OF CHILD ABUSE AND NEGLECT

Parents and caregivers may abuse or threaten to abuse an animal in order to control a child. Common examples include exacting compliance with a rule or goal by maltreating or threatening the welfare of an animal. Rooms get cleaned or noise is kept down because a child wants to spare a beloved pet. Children also report that parents threaten to kill or dispose of their pet if the child tells an outsider of the abuse in the home.

The child's role in this situation can vary. She or he may go to bed having a pet and wake up the next morning only to find it gone. The child may never be told what happened. Fear of the harm that came to the animal and fear of the uncertainty and unpredictability of the parent elicit frightened and insecure compliance.

A child may also be forced to watch while the animal is harmed. Children who grow up with domestic violence indicate that watching one parent harm the other while being powerless to stop the abuse is at least as deleterious as being the victim oneself. Because the child's only nonviolent and loving relationship may well be with the pet, being a spectator as the animal comes to harm must surely be as devastating to the child as observing domestic violence.

Being forced to participate in the abuse of the pet is sometimes a parental requirement, one that likely puts the child on the road to becoming a perpetrator. The San Francisco Department of Animal Care and Control intervened recently when a father made his 18-month-old son watch while he beat their pit bull puppy with a chain. The father then ordered the toddler to beat the dog with the chain and said he would beat his son with the chain if the boy did not beat the dog. The father's expressed purpose was to "toughen both of them up." Maintaining tenderness for the dog would have put the boy at risk of substantial harm from his father. Having no realistic choice, he made the transition from victim to perpetrator and achieved safety and approval from his father in so doing. It would not be surprising at all if this boy repeated this behavior in other situations in an attempt to sort out his many and conflicting feelings and reactions.

Children who repeat abusive behaviors are often referred to by mental health professionals as "abuse-reactive." That is, they react to the abuse they themselves have experienced by re-enacting it with others, often those they can easily victimize, usually smaller children and animals. Few children can maintain their sympathetic view of animals, younger siblings, and other small children in the face of pressure to act like the violent parent. Defiance of the parent and compassion for the victim would put them at risk of immediate harm from the dangerous parent. Safety lies in identifying with and behaving like the aggressive parent (Miller 1983).

As a result, abuse-reactive children often torture or kill animals in an attempt to gain mastery over their own experience and to understand the parent's hurtful behavior. By taking on the parent's role in a situation of the child's creation, children can explore the position of power not yet theirs in reality. This is not exceptional behavior: children routinely play house to learn about the workings of their family. In these games, the roles of mother and father are sought after by participating children because these are the positions of power. Just as children repeat parental shortcomings and foibles in games of house, they also repeat child abuse, animal abuse and domestic violence if that is what they have recently observed and are troubled by.

Children who both love their pet and fear that a parent may harm it live with stress, fear, and uncertainty. Waiting for the other shoe to drop is too much for some children to tolerate, especially if the parent has killed pets in the past. At times these children may kill the family pet themselves in an attempt to pre-empt the parent and ensure that at least the animal would die at the hands of someone who loved it. This euthanasia, however benignly motivated, gives children another burden to carry, one that all too often is too heavy. Thus, children will describe how they could not stand waiting for the parent to kill this beloved pet as they had killed others that were loved, and so took matters into their own hands. These children tearfully recount gently killing the animal so that it would not feel fear or pain. Then the children shift gears, change facial expression and tone, and add defiantly, "and I didn't care about that dog anyway." The pain of the hopeless situation, the animal's inevitable death, and the child's role as agent are overwhelming. To cope, children close off this tender and sympathetic part of themselves and take refuge in the relatively easier role of aggressor.

Another reason extremely troubled children may torture or kill animals is to experiment with the taking of a life. The aggression in this act is obvious, and stories like Eric Smith's where the animal's death prefigured a homicide are relatively well known (Lockwood & Hodge 1986; Lockwood 1989). The child may also be rehearsing suicide, a possibility clinicians often overlook (Schwartz 1992). Especially in work with teenagers, who can implode as readily as explode, this potential for refining suicidal skills through taking the life of animals must be watched for.

Animals also often play an important role in cases of sexual abuse. Parents, other adults, or older children having sex with minors typically groom and isolate their child victim in order to maintain their access and prevent the child's disclosure to an outsider. Child victims are encouraged to keep the sexual relationship a secret lest something bad befall them or their families. Typical threats and inducements include such comments as: "I love you in a special way that others would misunderstand"; "If you tell, I'll get arrested and go to jail, and I pay the rent so the family will become homeless"; "Nobody will believe you"; "Mommy will blame you and never hug you again"; "If you keep this secret and let me continue having sex with you, I will spare your younger sister"; "If you tell, I will hurt you or your mother"; and, "If you tell, I will kill your pet." As molested children usually feel estranged from the nonoffending parent for his or her failure to protect the child from harm, and cut off from people in general because of the need to keep the secret, their only carefree, physically affectionate and nonsexual relationship may well be with their pet. Thus, the pet, alive, may provide a safe haven for the child and his or her relational and tactile needs. Saving oneself at the expense of the beloved pet's life is a choice few children are prepared to make. As a result, threatening the animal's welfare is an effective way to buy a child's silence.

In neglectful households, neither the animal's lesser needs nor the child's greater needs for physical and emotional care get met. The message that neglect conveys to children is that they do not matter. Their cries and wants are ignored by the people they depend upon for life and nurturance. Neglect is thus devastating emotionally as well as physically to a child. The neglected child who has a pet matters to another living creature. They may both be hungry and scared, but they are less lonely because they have each other. The child is caring and cared for by the animal. The pet may substantially mitigate the emotional devastation of physically or psychologically absent parents.

An animal may serve as a barometer for families needing help because its requirements are more straightforward than the subtleties of bonding between parent and child, which require a trained eye to assess. Additionally, the plight of the animal may be more readily observed by neighbors, both because the animal goes outside unclothed so that starvation and injuries are visible and because it may howl and disrupt the quiet of the neighborhood when harmed or neglected. Moreover, people are more willing to report the maltreatment or neglect of an animal than of a child. With children, people tend to want to avoid interfering in someone else's family and may wonder what the child did to provoke the parent. Indeed, the role of the animal in troubled families may be to elicit intervention.

ROLES ANIMALS PLAY IN CASES OF ELDER ABUSE
AND NEGLECT

As people age, they gradually become weaker. In the absence of injury or accident, this progression may be slow and gradual, such that slippage is easily ignored both by the elder and by friends and family members who visit occasionally. At some point, however, the elder is no longer able to do some things necessary for minimally adequate standards both for himself or herself and for the pet. As with neglected children, the inadequate care of the animal may be what brings attention and intervention. The elder may not venture outdoors, so no one notices poor hygiene and loss of weight. No one visits so odors of human and animal waste throughout the house are unknown. Eventually a neighbor or passer-by sees an animal in need of assistance and the reported animal neglect reveals an elderly person in the same predicament as the animal.

Elders are victims of abuse in much the same way that children are, and animals play comparable roles in their families. There is, though, one aspect of elder abuse cases not common in child abuse cases, namely, economic abuse. An adult caring for an aged and infirm parent may, unfortunately, be more motivated by financial gain, such as the opportunity to take over or sell the parent's house. Thus, elders have reported to animal control officers how their adult children moved in with them nominally to provide care and assistance. They really wanted the parent's house or other material reward and consequently maltreated the parent's pet, gave it away, or banished it to the yard in order to coerce the parent into giving up the house or bank account. For elders living alone, the pet is an important companion and probably their only source of physical affection. Hearing their former companion howl outside under their bedroom window devastates them and forces them to yield to their children's request.

Although this behavior is repugnant and sympathy naturally goes to the elder being deprived of the companion animal, it must not be viewed out of context. In all likelihood, the frail elder now the object of concern was a cruel and harsh parent who taught the child precisely these techniques in his or her formative years. The saying, "what goes around comes around," aptly summarizes the transmission of values and behaviors from one generation to the next.

Effective intervention must therefore begin with an assessment of the histories, abilities and shortcomings of those in positions of responsibility and include the consideration of all potential victims regardless of their legal status. Failure to take this comprehensive approach may result in intervention that protects a victim from additional abuse or neglect, but stops short of addressing the endangering behavior pattern and thus leaves other potential victims at risk of harm, both presently and in generations to come. The following section discusses collaborative efforts that are interdisciplinary in nature and intergenerational in focus.

COLLABORATIVE RESPONSES TO ABUSE AND NEGLECT

Collaborative responses ensure greater safety for all living creatures at risk in a given situation. Animal control officers ask police officers to accompany them if they believe a situation is dangerous or involves more than crimes against animals. In 1991, the San Francisco Department of Animal Care and Control (SFACC) proposed a combined emergency response with the Juvenile Division of the San Francisco Police Department, a unit with special expertise in interviewing children and assessing danger to them. Whenever SFACC receives a call about an animal in a setting where children are also present, they respond with a juvenile officer so that adequate assessments are made and appropriate protective measures taken. Staff of both agencies receive training in cross-reporting, collaborating on responses, and common problems and risk factors.

In 1993, the Humane Coalition Against Violence, the advocacy and training program of the San Francisco Child Abuse Council and the San Francisco Department of Animal Care and Control, sponsored legislation in California (SB 665) that in 1994 added fire fighters, state humane officers, and animal control officers to the list of mandated reporters of child abuse. The dual purposes of this legislation were to require the reporting of dangerous situations and to provide the immunity given to mandated reporters. The Humane Coalition Against Violence is currently working to add state humane officers and animal control officers to the mandated reporters of elder abuse. Officers receive three to four hours of training in identifying and cross-reporting abuse and neglect of children, the elderly, and the disabled through training programs offered by the State Humane Association of California. For other states seeking to add these professionals to their reporting laws, it would be expeditious to amend the child abuse and elder abuse reporting statutes simultaneously.

Following the passage of SB 665, the San Diego Humane Society and SPCA and the San Diego County Department of Animal Care and Control met with their local Department of Social Services to discuss cross-reporting. They offered to provide training to the social workers in the human services departments to identify and report at-risk animals. There is now a Memorandum of Understanding in San Diego County requiring all state humane and animal control officers and all child and adult protective services workers to make appropriate reports whenever they learn about an endangered or neglected child, elder, person with a disability, or animal.

Such collaborative efforts can also improve safety in ongoing cases. Social workers typically visit families on their caseloads once each month. Animal control and state humane officers frequently implement orders permitting them to make unannounced home visits either to monitor the care of an animal or to make sure an animal has not been brought into a home where forbidden. These officers will readily coordinate their visits with those of the social worker so the family is seen at appropriately spaced intervals by people aware of all areas of concern in the family.

Frequently, cases protecting animals move through the legal system more quickly than do those protecting humans. Because an animal is property, it can be removed when endangered more readily than can a child or elder. Issues of bonding and attachment do not come up in the disposition of animal welfare cases, only the adequacy of care provided. Thus, in a few weeks or months there may be a factual finding by a court of a person's inability to care for an animal, and a sentence forbidding that person to acquire an animal for a period of three years and authorizing the local municipal animal control agency or humane society to make unannounced home visits during that time to make sure no animals have been acquired. This disposition by a court would surely strengthen the upcoming case of child abuse or elder abuse. If a person has been found by a criminal court to be unable to care for a dog or cat, his or her ability to have full responsibility for a child or elder must surely warrant close scrutiny.

Standards of care are often clearer and better for animals than for children, the disabled, or the elderly. Requirements for the operation of kennels are often more stringent than those for child care facilities or nursing homes. As an illustration of this point, kennels in California are to be inspected annually and must provide clean quarters and clean and nutritious food and water in appropriate amounts; animals must have current immunizations to be admitted. Day care facilities are inspected every three years and are not required to provide any sort of nourishment; children need not be immunized or disease-free to attend. In 1991, Governor Pete Wilson proposed abolishing inspection of child care facilities altogether in order to save the state money spent on the inspectors' salaries. Assemblywoman Jackie Speier responded by holding a press conference in which she compared the already inadequate standards for child care facilities with the far superior kennel requirements. The following Sunday, the *San Francisco Chronicle* ran a political cartoon in its editorial section comparing the inspection procedures, printed below. Governor Wilson promptly dropped his proposal to terminate inspection of child care facilities.

In San Diego and in four Bay Area counties (San Mateo, San Francisco, Marin, and Sonoma), collaboratives have developed between animal shelters and battered women's shelters. Similar programs exist in Loudoun County, Virginia, and Colorado Springs, Colorado (see Jorgensen and Maloney, "Animal Abuse and the Victims of Domestic Violence," in this volume). Studies (Adams 1995; Ascione 1997) have shown that many women will not enter a shelter if they must leave their pet(s) behind. Risk to the animal would surely increase when the batterer was faced with the departure of his partner. Now, in these five California counties people who answer the phone at the programs for battered women ask about the presence and potential safety of animals in the home. They also ask the woman if anyone else would give the animal food, water, and exercise were she to leave. If other options are not available, the phone counselor lets the caller know about the "Safe Pets Pro-

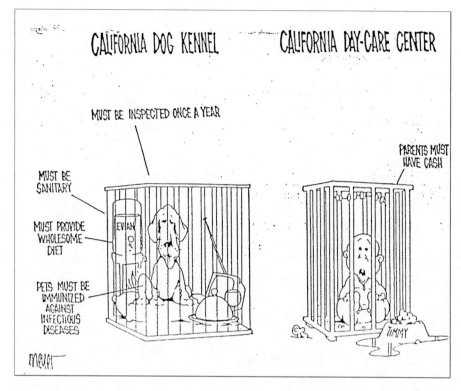

Figure 1. This *San Francisco Chronicle* cartoon targets inadequate regulation of child-care facilities. Reprinted with permission.

gram" (as it is called in the Bay Area), which will provide up to two weeks of shelter for the animal at no charge. Thus, the mother and her children can enter the battered women's program and have some time to come up with an alternative for the animal without having to worry about its immediate safety and care.

Humane collaborations offer innovative treatment opportunities to break the cycle of abuse and neglect so that inhumane attitudes and behaviors are not passed to the next generation. Perhaps the most well-known and established of these is Green Chimneys, a program in upstate New York that provides residential treatment and education through an onsite school and a wildlife rehabilitation program (see Ross, "Green Chimneys: We Give Troubled Children the Gift of Giving," in this volume). The children grow in discipline, responsibility, and compassion by taking on the care of injured animals. Away from the turbulent inner city, free from urban pressures to survive and conquer, they can explore gentle and nurturing sides of their personalities. However, these children return home after a year or two at Green Chimneys with little opportunity to stay connected with their new-found interest in and empathy for the natural world.

Lacking the resources of Green Chimneys, and desiring to teach alternatives to families in their own communities, a number of smaller therapeutic programs have been started at humane societies in the past decade. These community-based programs seek to integrate humane values into the daily fabric of the lives of at-risk children and their families by planting a seed that will blossom into life-long non-violent interests and principles. One of the most innovative programs is the Garden Project designed and implemented by Carol Rathmann, the shelter manager of the Humane Society of Sonoma County, California (Rathmann & Loar 1994; see Rathmann, "Forget Me Not Farm: Teaching Gentleness with Gardens and Animals," in this volume).

The San Francisco Department of Animal Care and Control (SFACC) sponsors a program to teach gentleness and compassion to inner-city children and their parents. Lacking the space and resources of the Humane Society of Sonoma County and dealing with urban poverty and its sequelae, its program is smaller and organized differently. The gardening component is provided by SLUG, the San Francisco League of Urban Gardeners.

Lack of transportation keeps many children from taking advantage of opportunities available in the city. Therefore, participating programs host a series of visits from SFACC. Staff and parents join the children to learn about animal care and behavior. For many of the adults, this is their first opportunity to handle gentle animals and develop an interest in them. Typically, their prior exposure has been only to vicious and maltreated dogs in housing projects.

The inner-city program uses uniformed officers rather than volunteers to take advantage of the opportunity to teach people who may have had bad experiences with the police that people in uniform can be caring and compassionate. One four-year-old boy remarked to his social worker, "I liked the policeman who arrested that dog!" as the animal control officer completed a class on understanding a dog's body language (Loar 1996). The class is also an opportunity for the officers to do preventive work and let the community see them in a positive light.

Social worker Susan Phillips explained how the officer's visits had allowed her to teach coping skills that might prevent molestation to young children in a housing project in the most dangerous part of San Francisco: "The visits gave many of the inner-city children living here their first chance to interact with animals and learn about touching and being touched in a friendly and non-threatening manner. Through this program, the children learned about the habits and natural habitats, the likes and dislikes of other creatures, and, most importantly, they learned respect for life. Because of this program, we were able to introduce the concepts of personal boundaries, good touch and bad touch, to very young children in a manner that made sense to them" (Loar 1996).

Although it is advisable to keep groups small, with children of similar ages and abilities, gardening and animal care are activities that appeal to all ages and can be enjoyed by people with disabilities and various levels of skill and strength. Thus, it is possible to include parents and guardians in the activities with their children, and teach humane behaviors, discipline, and nonviolent methods of behavior management while immersed in pastimes that the adults enjoy as much as their children do. Often, adults who experienced severe deprivation or abuse in their childhoods resent the care and attention their children get in therapeutic programs, and undermine or prevent the child's participation as a result. These programs offer resources to all, and nurture and support the parents along with their children.

These humane collaborations target specific populations or problems and tailor interventions and resources to meet their unique needs. They stand in contrast to the more commonplace humane education programs involving a humane educator going into a school to teach basic concepts of animal care, responsible pet ownership, respect for and kindness to animals, and the like. Children undoubtedly enjoy the appearance of an animal in their classroom along with a break from routine teaching, but the efficacy of these programs is questionable (Ascione 1997). Children are given occasional classroom presentations on a variety of topics including the dangers of drug and alcohol abuse, HIV prevention and safe sex, personal safety, and abuse prevention, with very limited benefit. That a one-hour presentation about humane education a few times in a child's academic career would have lasting impact seems unlikely, especially because so many of today's high school graduates have failed to master the basics of reading, writing, and arithmetic that are presumably stressed throughout 12 years of education (K. Savesky, Executive Director, Peninsula Humane Society, San Mateo, Calif., personal communication, 1996). These humane educational programs in all likelihood represent simply a pleasant interlude in the normal academic day for most children.

As with all one-size-fits-all approaches, those most in need of the information may be least able to absorb it in an academic setting (Loar 1994). Troubled and troublesome children who pose a threat to animals may also be poor students prone to behavior problems at school. Thus, they may gain little benefit from any information presented in a traditional classroom setting. Moreover, the appearance of the animal may itself be sufficiently provocative to cause the child to act up and be sent to the principal's office, missing the presentation altogether. This is not to say that lengthy and elaborate programs need to be developed to reach at-risk youth, but rather that strategically focused and concentrated efforts directed to children at risk, individually or in small groups, outside the classroom would be more likely to make an impression. One such example is a single session intervention for children visiting an incarcerated parent designed by the San Francisco Child Abuse Council and implemented by volunteers from the Marin Humane Society.

Marin County, immediately north of San Francisco, is home to San Quentin State Prison, a large and forbidding prison built in 1852 and containing several thousand inmates including those on California's death row. Visiting is permitted at the prison and there are two visiting rooms, one for the condemned and one for the general prison population. Being admitted for a visit is often a slow and intimidating process, especially on holidays and weekends when many people come to see a friend or relative. Because few of the families whose relatives are serving time in San Quentin live in affluent Marin County, most visitors travel considerable distances to get to the prison. Between the stress of the journey and the anxiety about a prison visit, people are typically irritated when faced with a wait of an hour or two at the prison gate. Children, scared, hungry, and tired, often become antsy, running around and creating a commotion. This is something the guards simply cannot tolerate. It is unfortunately common for a mother to smack her young son at this juncture and say, "You'd better stop that or you'll end up spending your life in prison just like your father, that son of a bitch!" Given the setting and the child's arousal, this sort of comment makes an indelible impression. Moreover, if this comment is repeated on monthly visits for the several years the father is serving time, it may become a self-fulfilling prophecy and is certainly the most career counseling many of these children receive.

California state law requires that there be a hospitality house at the gate of each state prison to assist visitors. These are rarely more than trailers, but they do give people access to a coffee pot and a bathroom. The prisons refuse to admit people wearing sexually provocative garb or denim, olive green, or tan (clothing that would resemble the inmates' or the guards'), so the hospitality houses lend clothing to those inappropriately dressed, featuring some of the most extraordinary polyester clothing that would under no circumstances be mistaken for government-issued garments. They also offer drop-in child care so that children who are not permitted inside the prison, who do not want to go, or who want to leave the visit early have some place safe to wait.

Due to the minimal staffing at the hospitality house and the inability to predict how many children will show up on any given day and how old they will be, no planned activities or interventions are available. Snacks are provided, usually things children can eat with their fingers. The Marin Humane Society has a volunteer with a trained therapy dog making Saturday visits to San Quentin, arriving just after snack time. The children's fingers being sticky, the dog runs to them immediately, wags its tail, and licks them enthusiastically. The volunteer takes Polaroid pictures of this to give the children and remarks, "As you know, dogs are excellent judges of human nature; he came right to you—tell me the good the dog saw in you so readily." The children focus on their strengths and have tangible proof of their goodness in the photo of the dog licking them. Thus, the children can tell a different story about what they learned about themselves on the prison visit.

CONCLUSION

Therapeutic and enrichment programs using gardens and animal care have the potential to break the cycle of abuse and deprivation in ways that traditional therapy does not. Many people referred to counseling have had bad experiences with people in authority—their parents, teachers, and representatives of "the system," among others. Thus, new information mediated by teachers or therapists will be tainted because of its source, no matter how useful the information is on its face. Few people, however, have had bad past experiences with flowers or baby goats. Thus, they can introduce concepts of gentleness, nurturance, and responsibility in fresh and appealing ways.

Additionally, because gardening and caring for animals are activities appropriate to people of all ages, parents and their children can work enjoyably together without coercion or abuse. Both generations learn that kindness and positive rewards work better when teaching an animal to come when called than hitting in response to noncompliance. An animal attendant can explain how hitting would only teach the animal to fear the person's hand without triggering the parents' defensive retort that they were hit as children and it did not do them any harm.

These activities can become life-long hobbies that introduce otherwise isolated families to people with similar interests and greater personal resources. Thus, through their participation in an enjoyable activity, humane and altruistic values and actions are encouraged and reinforced, especially if they are shared by a nurturing community of fellow gardeners or dog walkers. These attributes, moreover, are introduced and incorporated into the fabric of people's lives without putting them at odds with their family or community.

NOTE

1. *Chattel* and *cattle* are derived from the same Latin root, *capitale,* literally concerning the *caput,* or head, as in the number of head of livestock owned. In the antebellum era, chattel was divided into two categories, real and personal, the former referring to inanimate property and the latter to owned live property, slaves, for example (see Partridge 1983, 84).

REFERENCES

Adams, C. 1995. Woman-battering and harm to animals. In C. Adams and J. Donovan, eds., *Women and animals,* 55–84. Durham, N.C.: Duke University Press.

Ascione, F. R. 1997. Humane education research: Evaluating efforts to encourage children's kindness and caring toward animals. *Genetic, Social, and General Psychology Monographs* 123(1):57–77.

Ascione, F. R. 1998. Battered women's reports of their partners' and their children's cruelty to animals. *Journal of Emotional Abuse* 1(1): 119–33.

Loar, L. 1994. The limits of education. *CHAIN* (summer), 6–7.

Loar, L. 1996. "I liked the policeman who arrested that dog!" *The Latham Letter* (spring), 1–8.

Loar, L., and J. H. Weakland. 1994. *Working with families in shelters: A practical guide for counselors and child care staff.* Alameda, Calif.: Latham Foundation.

Locke, J. 1989 [1705]. *Some thoughts concerning education by John Locke.* Edited with introduction, notes, and critical apparatus by John W. and Jean S. Yolton. 5th ed. Oxford: Clarendon Press.

Lockwood, R. 1989. Cruelty to animals and human violence. *Training Key,* no. 392. Arlington, Va.: International Association of Chiefs of Police.

Lockwood, R., and G. Hodge. 1986. The tangled web of animal abuse: The links between cruelty to animals and human violence. *Humane Society News* (summer).

Miller, A. 1983. *For your own good: Hidden cruelty in childrearing and the roots of violence.* New York: Farrar, Straus & Giroux.

Partridge, E. 1983. *Origins: A short etymological dictionary of modern English.* New York: Greenwich House.

Rathmann, C., and L. Loar. 1994. A humane garden of children, plants, and animals grows in Sonoma County, California. *The Latham Letter* (spring), 6–9.

Schwartz, D. 1992. The abuse of power and the need for control. Speech given at the "Breaking the Cycle of Child and Animal Abuse" conference sponsored by the Humane Society of the United States and the Humane Coalition Against Violence, Sacramento, Calif., August 10.

Straus, M. A. 1994. *Beating the devil out of them: Corporal punishment in American families.* New York: Lexington Books.

First-Person Account
Cruelty to Animals, Cruelty to Children
Anonymous

I GREW UP in a house (not a home) that was characterized by anger, fear, and sadness. I am the oldest and illegitimate son of a woman consumed with anger, fear, and sadness related to years of incest that occurred with her mother's knowledge and tacit approval. My father was a rage-a-holic who suffered severe physical and emotional abuse, and perhaps incest as well. The forced marriage was ideal in some ways; my mother needed a strong, angry man who would avenge her anger ("Let's you and him fight!"), and my father needed someone he could defend, the circumstances of which could justify the unleashing of years of stored, murderous wrath.

Although my mother says I "ran away from home" at age two and a half (not *wandered* away, but *ran* away), the first clear memory I have involving animal cruelty occurred when I was six years old. My father secured employment as a laborer on a small farm in New England (he had been born and raised on a farm, and loved farm work). I vaguely remember his thirst for hunting and his love of guns and hunting dogs. Occasionally he would trap animals.

In those days, woodchucks (groundhogs) were perennial pests that could be found virtually everywhere. On a warm spring evening my father allowed me to accompany him as he checked some traps he had set in a pasture. I remember the excitement of being allowed to go along (a rarely granted privilege), the .22 rifle, and Dixie, a springer spaniel.

The first trap had been pulled down into the burrow by a woodchuck. My father grabbed the chain and dragged the victim out into the open. Dixie was prancing and barking, my father's respirations were loud and rapid. The little creature was writhing and tugging in a desperate effort to free a front leg firmly clutched by the metal teeth. As I watched, I became overwhelmed with the pain, terror, and helplessness I imagined it must feel. My father sicced the dog on the woodchuck, which valiantly tried to defend itself against the overwhelming odds. I asked my father to let it go, but he continued to encourage the dog to harass the animal. I began to cry and plead with him to let it go. I can still see the look of rage on his face as he began to scream at me. "You God-damned sissy. If you can't take it, go back to the house! Get out of here!" I ran as fast as I could, tears clouding my vision and the pain of my shame and humiliation feeling so great I thought I would die.

When I got to the house, my mother asked what happened. She was not sympathetic, but allowed me to go to my room. A short time later I heard my father talking to her in the kitchen. "I'll never take that spleeny kid anywhere with me again. The God-damned sissy will never amount to anything."

A second poignant event occurred when I was about 12. I don't remember why he decided to kill my cat, but I do remember him telling my mother that the next time he went to visit his parents he was going to kill it. I knew he would take me with him, just as I knew I would have to witness the death. As the time drew close I first asked and then pleaded with him to shoot the cat. When he replied, "I'm not going to waste a bullet on a God-damned cat," I knew he would kill it by hand—probably by breaking its neck.

My grandparents lived at the end of an old, seldom-used dirt road, several miles from town. As we climbed the last hill, my father stopped the car, got out, and opened the trunk. I thought, "Maybe he will shoot it after all." But instead of a gun, he took out a tire iron. Holding the cat by the back legs flat against a huge pine tree, he struck it on the back of the neck, shattering its tiny spine. He threw the body into the woods and climbed back into the car without saying a word. I did not shed a visible tear, but I could feel him gloating.

The last vivid incident occurred when I was 16. We had gone to get a Christmas tree he had cut earlier in the day and dragged to a spot along the road to be picked up later. Close to where he left the tree was a large pile of discarded brush from a logging operation conducted in the area the year before. As we approached, a startled snowshoe rabbit darted into the brush pile. In an instant my father turned into a predator. He cocked his shotgun (he always had a gun with him), and his body became slightly bent forward. His breath came in gasps, and he was oblivious to everything in the environment except that rabbit. He tried everything he had ever learned in an effort to force the rabbit into the open, but without success. He even began to take apart the brush pile until he realized he had neither the time nor the energy to complete so great a task. His rage at not catching the rabbit was, of course, displaced onto myself and my sisters.

My father was only violent in the woods and in the house. At work and on the street he was a chinner-and-grinner-type good ole boy. At his funeral an acquaintance remarked to me: "Yup, everybody loved old Johnny." My parents, their parents, and other family members were adept at maintaining family secrets. They had the accumulated expertise of at least three generations of perpetrators.

My mother dominated my father in every aspect of his life. She allowed him to hunt and kill because she derived a vicarious sense of power, revenge, and security from his aggression. She allowed him to be violent with his children, as she was violent. There is no such thing as an unexpressed emotion, and both had decades of wrath they needed to shed. She pulled hair, slapped, pinched, washed our mouths out with soap, and beat us with ropes, switches, belts, razor straps, or whatever weapon she had close at hand. He beat me with his fist, the back of his hand, belts, sticks, and other objects. The last time he beat me I was 16 years old. He took me to the woodshed and struck me with a one-by-four-inch hardwood board until he was tired. That was the last beating I ever received. I vowed to myself on that occasion that it would never happen again—no matter what I had to do to protect myself.

Physical and emotional abuse were multiple daily experiences during my teen years. My mother often played "Let's you and him fight!" although he needed no real encouragement. On those occasions he usually hit me in the face while trying not to hit my glasses, because glasses cost money to fix. The results were often bloody noses and what he liked to call "split lips." He often drew blood after being goaded by my mother. I can clearly remember her saying, "You can hit him without making him bleed." Then she would initiate Game Two: "I've got you now you son-of-a-bitch," and she would castrate him with a well-honed tongue. I think this was a "maintenance run," a check to assure herself that she still had total control over that awesome fury. And she did. He NEVER stood up to HER or answered back! Sometimes I wished I was a rabbit. For them it was over in a matter of minutes.

They could have put on a wonderful performance for talk show hosts as representatives of some backlash movement: typical, ideal, indignant, wounded parents who have been inexplicably accused of sordid horrid acts by a son they loved so deeply and for whom so many sacrifices were made.

Connections—Domestic Violence

A spaniel, a woman
and a walnut tree:
the more they're beaten
the better they be.

—Old English proverb

Animal Abuse and the Victims of Domestic Violence

Star Jorgensen and Lisa Maloney

Man can no longer live for himself alone. We must realize that all life is valuable and that we are united to all life. From this knowledge comes our spiritual relationship with the universe.

—Albert Schweitzer

DOMESTIC VIOLENCE, or spousal abuse or partner abuse, is usually described as any physical or psychological harm experienced by one person from another with whom an intimate relationship is shared. An increasing number of agencies are beginning to recognize that this violence often encompasses the physical and emotional abuse of children and household pets.

Providing adequate, and sometimes life-saving, assistance for the victims of domestic violence is the goal of many domestic violence prevention organizations. This requires an awareness of the many dynamics of abuse. The effects of domestic violence are amplified when animals are being abused, particularly with the knowledge of, or in front of, the children. For many victims, the first opportunity to tell their story in a safe and understanding environment comes when they seek help and refuge at a domestic violence prevention organization. As their story unfolds, many victims reveal abuse of animals as part of their histories. Victims and the professionals who work with them may be unaware of the importance animal abuse has in the abuse scenario. A growing number of studies are beginning to reveal the significance of this critical link (Arkow 1996).

Case Study

A victim entered the domestic violence center seeking a restraining order; she had been beaten the previous evening and had several bruises on her face and upper torso. The crucial factor in her deciding to seek help was that the abuser had hit her oldest child who had tried to intervene when an argument began. The victim noted on the checklist that household animals had also been abused. Upon further inquiry by the case manager, the victim stated the fight had begun when the children's new puppy soiled the carpet and the perpetrator had yelled at and kicked the puppy, picked it up and threw it against the wall. The perpetrator became verbally and physically abusive toward the victim and the child who was trying to protect the puppy.

Domestic violence professionals throughout the United States hear similar stories of abuse to animals and children as part of the power and control dynamics of the abuser. This composite of behaviors, violence toward animals and children, has been recognized within the domestic violence scenario only within the last couple of decades. Although American laws to protect animals date back to 1641 (Animal Welfare Institute 1990) and the first child abuse laws were passed in 1875 in New York State, today it is widely believed that child abuse and animal abuse are drastically underreported. A growing number of professionals are becoming aware of, and documenting, this relationship of abuse involving animals and children within the domestic violence context.

The direct forms of animal abuse are hands-on assaults from which the animal victim may receive bodily harm. These are physical, aggressive actions. Examples include pushing, slapping, kicking, striking with an object, and sexual assault. These are done to let the human victim know the capabilities of the abuser and what may be in store if the human victim does not conform to the wishes of the abuser. Control, intimidation, or retaliation are the goals intended. Certainly, this form of abuse has a profound effect if carried out in front of, or with the knowledge of, the children. It will also have a similar effect on the family pet.

Examples of direct animal abuse recorded at the Center for Prevention of Domestic Violence in Colorado Springs, Colorado, include

- kicking the dog or cat;
- throwing the dog or cat across the room or into objects;
- shooting the animal with a pellet gun;
- taking the animal into a field and shooting it with the human victim present;
- breaking the pet's legs or neck;
- hanging the family pet;
- cutting the cat's ears with scissors and burning its tail; and
- putting the dog in the corner and tying weights to it.

Indirect animal abuse may be less obvious, as there is no bodily contact. Yet this still has the capability of controlling and intimidating all victims involved. As with direct abuse, victims are profoundly affected. Examples of indirect abuse that we have noted include

- abandonment of the family pet;
- neglecting to feed and water farm animals;

- threatening to take the family pet away if the victim doesn't comply;
- taking pets to be euthanized to retaliate against the human victim;
- threatening to kill and cook the pet rabbit;
- mysterious disappearances of pets;
- intentionally overfeeding fish; and
- making a severely asthmatic woman live in a house with long-haired cats.

THE IMPACT OF ANIMAL ABUSE ON CHILDREN

Boys stone a frog in sport, but the frog dies in earnest.
—Poet Bion, 100 b.c.

Children and animals in a household have special relationships and they are profoundly affected by the abuse they experience and witness. The physical and behavioral indicators of abuse and neglect may apply to both children and animal victims. These similarities are striking, and include

- risk of being injured by the abuser;
- unexplained bruises, welts, fractures, or lacerations;
- changes in behavior such as relapses in training, regressive behavior;
- failure to thrive, withdrawal, and passivity;
- hostility and aggressiveness toward humans and animals;
- fear or distrust of the abuser or others similar to that person; and
- running away from home.

Children are at risk of repeating the abuse they experienced. Retrospective research studies (Felthous & Yudowitz 1977; Felthous 1980; Kellert & Felthous 1985; Tingle et al. 1986; Ressler et al. 1986; Felthous & Kellert 1987; Ressler, Burgess, & Douglas 1988) generally support the anecdotal claims (Lockwood & Hodge 1986; Lockwood 1987; Goleman 1991; Siino 1994) that many criminals who have been violent toward people share a common history of brutal parental punishment and cruelty to animals. Many serial killers and mass murderers were abused as children and have a history of abusive acts toward animals. DeViney, Dickert, and Lockwood (1983) looked at families being treated by the New Jersey Division of Youth and Family Services for incidents of child abuse. In 88 percent of the cases, animal abuse had also occurred. Like charity, pathology begins at home (White & Shapiro 1994).

We must emphasize that not all children who abuse animals will grow up to become mass murderers, nor do all children who are abused become abusers themselves. It is becoming apparent, however, that many persons who abuse animals were themselves abused as children.

Professionals working in domestic violence prevention, child protection agencies, and humane societies are beginning to recognize the connection between violence toward animals and violence toward humans. Boat (1995) has identified key reasons why this link is important.

GATHERING DATA

As awareness of the relationship between animal abuse and domestic violence increases, the need for development of identification methods and education programs becomes necessary. In February 1993 a conference—"Family Violence: Children in Jeopardy"—was presented by the Domestic Violence Coalition in Colorado Springs, Colorado. Phil Arkow, then Education and Publicity Director for the Humane Society of the Pikes Peak Region, gave a presentation entitled, "The Advantages of Cooperation Between Humane and Human Service Agencies." This became the impetus for the development of a protocol at the Center for Prevention of Domestic Violence to identify abuse toward animals and its role in the cycle of domestic violence.

By mid-1993, Star Jorgensen, then Advocacy Case Manager at the Center, developed a system to document abuse reported by clients utilizing the Center's services. At that time, intake forms had questions relating to incidence of child abuse and animal abuse, although no procedures were in place to record the answers statistically. Case managers reported child abuse to the El Paso County Department of Human Services, yet there was no follow-up for information gathered about animal abuse.

A Domestic Violence Checklist was developed to accompany intake forms with the following categories related to animals: (1) abuser threatened to harm animals and (2) abuser injured or killed pets. This was in addition to a question about animal abuse on the client intake form. A procedure was developed to gather statistics and comments in all three of the Center's programs: Advocacy, Safehouse, and MOVE (Men Overcoming Violent Encounters).

In the Advocacy program, clients are given assistance with obtaining restraining orders, finding counseling and community referrals, and crisis intervention. Most clients are walk-ins who have recently experienced a battering incident. For many clients the visit is less than one hour long. Clients are tracked for three and six months after their visit to the Center.

Clients in the Safehouse remain longer (up to six weeks) and will be assisted in developing long-range plans. Clients and their children are afforded a safe atmosphere during this process. Women and their children are required to participate in their own support groups. After they leave the Safehouse they are tracked for two weeks, one month, and two months.

Case managers and volunteers in Advocacy and the Safehouse were asked to record cases of clients who marked "yes" to animal abuse on the intake forms and to request and document detailed information. MOVE therapists and case managers were also asked to gather information. The statistics relating to animal abuse were gathered from the three programs and added to the Center's monthly statistics and later added to the annual data.

Case Manager Lisa Maloney took over responsibilities for documentation of animal abuse when Star Jorgensen left the Center. In 1996, the format on the intake forms and checklists was modified to better represent the categories. Previously, intake forms included a statement that asked if any animal abuse had occurred. It was found that although many clients marked "no" on the forms, during their interviews many admitted that their partner had kicked or hit their pet in the past and that there had been animal abuse involved. The wording on the questionnaire was changed to read: "Has an animal you care about ever been hurt?" This elicited more responses from clients, which strengthened the correlation between animal abuse and domestic violence.

For the advocacy statistics there are now three categories: (1) animals injured, (2) animals killed, and (3) animals threatened. Adding the "threatened" category recognized that threatening to hurt or kill an animal was another method utilized by perpetrators to gain psychological control over their victims. Separating the questions into three categories would make the statistics more precise. Comments and data continue to be collected monthly from client intake forms and interviews regarding the specific incidents of animal abuse. Survey results for 1993 to 1996 are presented as table 1.

THE ROLES OF DOMESTIC VIOLENCE PERSONNEL

"I am scared when I see my kitten with blood on his neck. I think he [my dad] did it."
—Tony, age 5

"The church people said my cat was evil because he jumped at my legs—they took him away. My mom got a 101 Dalmatians dog for us—his name was Ice, but we had to give him away when we came to the Safehouse. I miss him because he listens to me."
—Tina, age 8

Perpetrator treatment providers play an important role in lessening domestic violence and they must be educated to the relationship between spousal, child, and animal abuse. Procedures must be developed for identification during intake, and abusers must be questioned and held accountable for their actions. Interviews with perpetrator treatment providers indicate there is a low awareness of this correlation and reluctance to introduce the subject as part of the therapy. According to the *Diagnostic and Statistical Manual of Mental Disorders* (American Psychiatric Association 1994, 95–91) the diagnostic features of Conduct Disorder include being physically cruel to animals, people, and performing other acts of aggression toward people or animals. Addressing the issue of child abuse and animal abuse in perpetrator treatment is indicated.

Safehouse case managers play a special role in the dynamics of domestic vio-

Table 1. Animal Abuse Statistics, Center for Prevention of Domestic Violence, Colorado Springs, Colorado. Of note is the low incidence of animal abuse reported in the MOVE program. Many participants are in denial that they are abusers and they will not or do not volunteer information about abuse of children or animals.

	1993 (June–December)	1994	1995	1996	Total
Advocacy					
Total Intakes	1,175	2,238	2,103	1,748	7,264
Animals Threatened	n.a.	n.a.	n.a.	23	23
Animals Abused	124	265	241	181	811
Animals Killed	4	3	11	18	36
% Threatened, Abused, or Killed	10.9	12.0	12.0	12.7	12.0
Safehouse					
Total Intakes	122	247	238	203	810
Animals Abused	29	31	30	36	126
Animals Killed	unknown	unknown	unknown	unknown	unknown
% Abused or Killed	23.8	12.6	12.6	17.8	15.5
MOVE					
Total Intakes	189	411	435	319	1,354
Animals Abused	1	unknown	11	1	13
Animals Killed	unknown	unknown	unknown	unknown	unknown
% Abused or Killed	0.5	unknown	2.5	0.3	0.9

lence and the safety of victims. Many victims of abuse are reluctant to leave an abusive situation for fear of leaving the family pets behind. The safehouse at the Center for Prevention of Domestic Violence has an agreement with the Humane Society of the Pikes Peak Region to have pets boarded for up to 10 days at no cost to victims who seek shelter in the safehouse; the costs of longer stays are negotiated with the victims.

Programs for children at the safehouse include a field trip to the Humane Society and visits by the Humane Society's Petmobile to the safehouse. According to the children's case manager, the children eagerly visit the Humane Society to see the animals. The children are excited prior to the arrival of the Petmobile, yet hesitate to approach and play with the pets once they arrive. Humane Society volunteers have suggested that the children may be afraid to interact in a home-like atmosphere with an animal that reminds them of the pet they saw abused or left behind.

Case Study

A woman entered the safehouse one evening, and her little dog was taken in by a case manager as the Humane Society was closed for the evening. While in the home, the case manager noticed the dog reacted fearfully to certain objects, later found out to be objects used to beat the dog. It was later determined the dog had been also been abused by having been chained up just out of reach of its food and water dishes and within sight of two hound dogs who had access to their food and water.

THE DVERT PROGRAM

The DVERT (Domestic Violence Enhanced Response Team) program was initiated in 1996. It seeks to identify individuals who pose a significant risk to their past or present intimate partners. Individuals who are selected as appropriate for DVERT action will benefit from an enhanced response to any future abusive incidents.

The DVERT response team includes a Colorado Springs Police Department detective, a deputy district attorney, a caseworker from the Department of Human Services, a Colorado Springs Police Department Rotation officer, an El Paso County Sheriff's deputy, a Woodland Park Detective, a CASA court appointed special advocate supervisor and a victim advocate from the Center for Prevention of Domestic Violence. The team is on call 24 hours a day and responds to all calls involving an identified DVERT client's address where a patrol officer has determined there is probable cause that a new violation has been committed. The purpose of the team is to assist the patrol officer in the investigation of the offense, containment of the perpetrator, and providing support services for the victim. The DVERT protocol is presented in figure 1.

When cases involving children, elders, at-risk adults, military personnel, or animal abuse are indicated, a secondary response team made up of individuals with special expertise in these areas is called out. Such agencies include the El Paso County Department of Human Services, the Humane Society of the Pikes Peak Region, and the Senior Victim Assistance Team. Cases are staffed on a weekly basis to bring these agencies together to develop a plan to help with family intervention.

The Humane Society response protocol is presented in figure 2. Humane Society procedures note that, "Through combined efforts, we can hopefully stop a situation from escalating into a lethal one. An offender may abuse pets and children prior to, or in conjunction with, abuse of a spouse. One type of violent behavior can be an indicator of other violent acts."

Five Humane Society employees are designated to respond to calls for assistance from the DVERT team on a 24-hour basis. The procedure notes that when the Humane Society communications center or answering service receives a call from the Police Department requesting a member of DVERT to assist at the scene of a

DOMESTIC VIOLENCE

DVERT Protocol

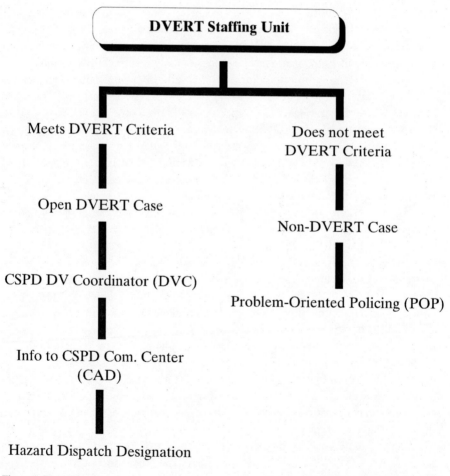

Figure 1. DVERT protocol

ENHANCED RESPONSE TEAM

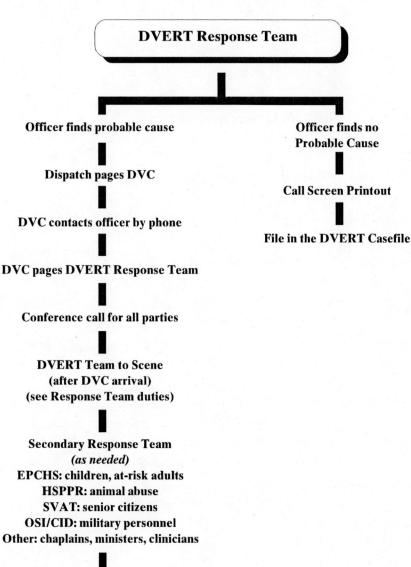

DVERT Response Team

Officer finds probable cause

Dispatch pages DVC

DVC contacts officer by phone

DVC pages DVERT Response Team

Conference call for all parties

DVERT Team to Scene
(after DVC arrival)
(see Response Team duties)

Secondary Response Team
(as needed)
EPCHS: children, at-risk adults
HSPPR: animal abuse
SVAT: senior citizens
OSI/CID: military personnel
Other: chaplains, ministers, clinicians

Clear scene

Follow-up activity

Officer finds no
Probable Cause

Call Screen Printout

File in the DVERT Casefile

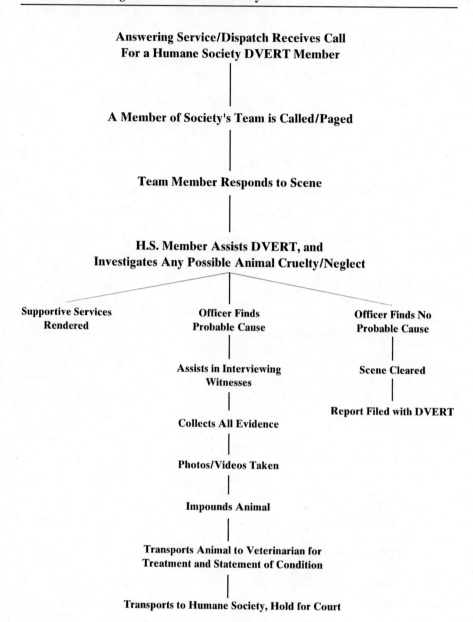

Figure 2. Protocol for Humane Society DVERT Team

possible offense, this call is considered a priority and will receive immediate response. The Humane Society's services in these cases includes

- investigation of cruelty or neglect;
- safekeeping of victims' animals;
- removing animals that are hampering investigations;
- referring suspected cases of domestic violence or child abuse to other appropriate agencies; and
- miscellaneous supportive services to DVERT.

Numerous cross-training initiatives have been implemented, such as training conferences and having humane officers ride along with Police Department domestic violence officers.

An interagency referral form (figure 3) has been designed to aid agencies in identifying individuals believed to be potential candidates for DVERT. The reasons for this referral are detailed.

Though the DVERT program is in its infancy, it has received national recognition for its early success. In December 1996 DVERT received the National League of Cities' 1996 Award for Excellence in Community Policing, and in 1997 was awarded a $516,000 federal grant from under the Department of Justice's COPS (Community Oriented Policing Services) program (see the editors' note at the end of this essay).

Case Study

A woman had left her abusive husband and was not allowed to take her elderly pet with her. The pet died shortly after she left. A few months later, the woman awoke to find her pet's frozen body hanging in a tree outside her residence. The body had been doused with gasoline and set afire.

GUIDELINES FOR ORGANIZATIONS

Organizations that work with victims and perpetrators of abuse are of major importance in the identification, documentation, and prevention of abuse to animals. One of the challenges of documenting animal abuse is that persons gathering the data need to recognize the importance of this type of information given by clients. Professionals who work with victims need to be able to help clients protect themselves, their children, and their animals from further abuse. Likewise, perpetrator treatment providers need to learn to encourage their clients to disclose abuse, and to develop methods to include the prevention of animal abuse in their treatment programs. We offer the following recommendations.

DOMESTIC VIOLENCE
Enhanced Response Team

DVERT Referral Form

DVERT Case Number:

Referring Person
Name:
Agency:
Phone:
Date:

Offender
Name/AKA (Last, First, Middle) Jr., Sr., 3rd

Date of Birth: Month   Day   Year

Social Security #:

Race/Sex:

Address:
                                        Apt#
City/State/Zip:

Phone: (h)   (w)

Name of Employer:
Relationship with Victim:

Victim
Name/AKA/Maiden Name (Last, First, Middle):

Date of Birth: Month   Day   Year

Social Security #:

Race/Sex:

Address:
                                        Apt#
City/State/Zip:

Phone: (h)   (w)

Children (Names and DOB's):

Please give detailed responses to the areas below:

1. History of Relationship:

2. Prior domestic violence arrests/child abuse (where?/when?):

3. List exact statements for threats of violence:

4. What were victim's actions after threats? (check one or more):

___ Restraining order   ___ Move out   ___ Change phone number
___ Inform neighbors   ___ Refusal to go to a safe place
___ Other (describe)

5. Recent losses (job, family, death, etc.):

6. List all injuries from this offender:

___ Medical care needed
___ Where and when

7. Abuse of others (children, elders, pets):

8. Access to weapons:

9. Stalking behavior (check one or more):

___ Violation of Restraining Order
___ Peeping, driving by
___ Harassment
___ Criminal trespass/burglary
___ Threat of death or physical harm
___ Leaving objects
___ Unexpected appearances
___ Other (describe):

C:\My Documents\FORMS\DVERT REFERRAL FORM.doc
REV: 11/12/98
DVERT 13

Figure 3. DVERT Referral Form

Develop educational training and outreach programs. Educate all personnel working with victims. This is the most important part; it is the foundation of your efforts. The success of these programs will be greatly affected by the cooperative efforts of personnel. If case managers and therapists who work with victims and perpetrators are oblivious to or minimize the impact of animal abuse in domestic violence, any methods you develop will be inadequate and ineffective. Utilize the resources available to educate and encourage professionals to take a proactive stance. These might include posters that educate how domestic violence and animal abuse are interrelated, such as the American Humane Association's Campaign Against Violence (1996) or special training programs (Smith 1995). Identify appropriate organizations in your community and develop programs for presentations at in-services, seminars, and conferences.

Develop methods to gather data. If a checklist is already in use, add questions regarding animal abuse. Most organizations have to record client data as part of their accountability programs. Using simple checklists will alert personnel working with victims or perpetrators to ask for more information about animal abuse. This information can be integrated into an existing format.

Develop programs for perpetrator treatment providers. Our data seem to indicate that perpetrators' abuse of animals needs to be addressed as part of their treatment programs. Treatment providers must include awareness of child abuse and animal abuse within their treatment plans whether or not this abuse has been indicated by clients. Like child abuse, sexual abuse, and partner abuse, animal abuse may not be admitted by perpetrators until they have been in treatment for a long time. It is important that perpetrator treatment providers become knowledgeable about the various forms of animal abuse as part of the cycle of violence and develop methods to address this early in their treatment.

SUMMARY

The human spirit is not dead: it lives on in secret. It has come to believe that compassion, in which all ethics must take root, can only attain its full breadth and depth if it embraces all living creatures and does not limit itself to mankind.
—Albert Schweitzer, Nobel Peace Prize Address

The challenge to educate professionals in domestic violence prevention, child protection agencies, and animal protection organizations is before us. Professionals who are dedicated to reducing violence against women, children, and animals need to develop community-wide prevention programs. It is our hope that the continued gathering and sharing of data and methods will enable us to predict and prevent domestic violence and animal abuse.

REFERENCES

American Humane Association. 1996. *Campaign against violence* (posters, public service announcements, training manuals). Englewood, Colo.: American Humane Association.

American Psychiatric Association. 1994. *Diagnostic and statistical manual of mental disorders,* 4th edition. Washington, D.C.: American Psychiatric Association.

Animal Welfare Institute. 1990. *Animals and their legal rights: A survey of American laws from 1641 to 1990,* 4th ed. Washington, D.C.: Animal Welfare Institute.

Arkow, P. 1996. The relationships between animal abuse and other forms of family violence. *Family Violence & Sexual Assault Bulletin* 12(1–2):29–34.

Boat, B. W. 1995. The relationship between violence to children and violence to animals: An ignored link? *Journal of Interpersonal Violence* 10(4):229–35.

DeViney, E., J. Dickert, and R. Lockwood. 1983. The care of pets within child abusing families. *International Journal for the Study of Animal Problems* 4:321–29.

Felthous, A. R. 1980. Aggression against cats, dogs and people. *Child Psychiatry and Human Development* 10:169–77.

Felthous, A. R., and S. R. Kellert. 1987. Childhood cruelty to animals and later aggression against people: A review. *American Journal of Psychiatry* 144:710–17.

Felthous, A. R., and B. Yudowitz. 1977. Approaching a comparative typology of assaultive female offenders. *Psychiatry* 40:270–76.

Goleman, D. 1991. Clues to a dark nurturing ground for one serial killer. *New York Times* August 7, A8.

Kellert, S. R., and A. R. Felthous. 1985. Childhood cruelty toward animals among criminals and noncriminals. *Human Relations* 38(12):1113–29.

Lockwood, R. 1987. Animal cruelty: No small matter. *Police Product News,* July.

Lockwood, R., and G. R. Hodge. 1986. The tangled web of animal abuse: The links between cruelty to animals and human violence. *The HSUS News* (summer), 10–15.

Ressler, R. K., A. W. Burgess, and J. E. Douglas. 1988. *Sexual homicide: Patterns and motives.* Lexington, Mass.: Lexington Books.

Ressler, R. K., A. W. Burgess, C. R. Hartman, J. E. Douglas, and A. McCormack. 1986. Murderers who rape and mutilate. *Journal of Interpersonal Violence* 1(3):273–87.

Siino, B. S. 1994. A shared cry: The abuse of animals is the first step toward the abuse of children. *Dog Fancy,* August, 47–51.

Smith, C. 1995. Animal cruelty and the link to other violent crimes. *Latham Letter* 16(1):1–8.

Tingle, D., G. W. Barnard, L. Robbins, G. Newman, and D. Hutchinson. 1986. Childhood and adolescent characteristics of pedophiles and rapists. *International Journal of Law and Psychiatry* 9:103–16.

White, K., and K. Shapiro. 1994. The culture of violence: The animal connection. *The Animals' Agenda,* March–April, 18–23.

Editor's Note:
Federal Funding Available under COPS Program

The DVERT program in Colorado Springs, Colorado, was awarded a $516,000 federal grant for its innovative approach in linking several community agencies—including the child protection service and humane society—in a coordinated response to domestic violence and having an emergency response team where a high potential for lethality is indicated.

Under the 1994 Crime Act, the U.S. Department of Justice implemented several initiatives through the COPS program—Community Oriented Policing Services. Community policing is a philosophy that promotes and supports organizational strategies to address the causes and reduce the fear of crime and social disorder through problem-solving tactics and community-police partnerships. The initiatives included efforts directed against gangs and youth firearms violence, hiring more officers for community policing, innovative community problem-solving partnerships, and training former soldiers for community policing.

One component of the COPS program for which grant money is available is Community Policing to Combat Domestic Violence. These grants provide law enforcement agencies with a unique opportunity to execute well-planned, innovative strategies employing community policing to combat domestic violence. There is no local match requirement for this program. Grant applications are submitted under one of three categories:

1. domestic violence training with a community oriented policing philosophy;
2. problem solving and community based programs; community policing partnerships and problem solving initiatives focusing on domestic violence; or
3. changing police organizations to be more responsive to domestic violence.

Initial projects were funded for a one-year period. Additional resources may be obtained for up to two additional years. Grant funds must be used to supplement, and not supplant, state or local funds that otherwise would be devoted to law enforcement.

All state, local, Indian Tribal, and other public and private law enforcement agencies which are committed to using community policing to address domestic violence are eligible to apply. Police departments are encouraged to partner with nonprofit, nongovernmental victim service programs, domestic violence shelters, or community service groups. This partnership must be described in a memorandum of understanding signed by both parties as part of the application.

Policing agencies must have an exemplary community policing plan which demonstrates that they:

1. have been practicing community policing for at least two years;
2. are currently training officers in community policing; and
3. have implemented an organizational style that is participatory, value-based, result-oriented, decentralized, and focused on innovative leadership and effectiveness.

An award under the Community Policing to Combat Domestic Violence Program does not affect the eligibility of an agency to apply to other COPS programs.

For additional information, or to contact the grant advisor for your state, contact:

U.S. Department of Justice
Office of Community Oriented Policing Services
1100 Vermont Avenue, NW, Washington, D.C. 20530
(202) 514-2058 or (800) 421-6770
www.usdoj.gov/cops

For information about the DVERT program, contact:

Colorado Springs Police Department Operations Center
705 S. Nevada Ave.
Colorado Springs, Colo. 80903
(719) 444-7813

Humane Society of the Pikes Peak Region
633 S. 8th St.
Colorado Springs, Colo. 80905
(719) 473-1741

Center for Prevention of Domestic Violence
P.O. Box 2662
Colorado Springs, Colo. 80901
(719) 633-1462

Resistance to The Link at a Domestic Violence Shelter

Anne Grant

A CASE HISTORY

SEVEN-YEAR-OLD "Charlie" has been tormenting his sister's cat. He is a gentle, sensitive child who sometimes writes in a notebook about his feelings.

Three years ago, after their parents separated, his sister "Kay," then 3, started having nightmares and wetting the bed. She complained of stomach aches and resisted going to her father's home for the three days and two nights the judge had ordered. She and Charlie said their father had given her a "bad touch."

At the hospital, the doctor found "positive signs of abrasions on hymen, vaginal areas." Though these were consistent with digital penetration, he reported his findings were not conclusive. The father hired a psychologist who testified in court that the mother was emotionally unstable and needed counseling to resolve her feelings of inadequacy and help her to "perceive [her husband] as less abusive."

After the parents separated, the mother testified in court that her husband had driven her in his Porsche at speeds over 110 miles an hour yelling, "I'm in control now! How does it feel?" She told how he choked and kicked her.

Unable to keep paying an attorney, the mother tried to plead the children's cause in court, only to become numb and flustered. With his lawyer and psychologist arguing for him, the father insisted that his estranged wife had a history of nervous disorder. But he assured the court he was willing to care for her if only she would come back to him. Surely he should not be kept from seeing his children, and they should not continue in counseling. Ruling in the father's favor, the judge allowed him unsupervised visits with Charlie and Kay, including a week's vacation at the father's country home.

Later, the children laughed nervously to tell how he taught them to burrow through the cat's fur in search of its little red penis. Their mother increasingly had to stop Charlie from tormenting the cat.

Charlie, Kay, and their mother had once lived at a shelter for victims of domestic violence. There the mother learned that cruelty to animals is a warning sign of a potential batterer. She recalled how her husband had taken delight in shooting at neighborhood cats from a third floor window and trying to poison dogs who got into the garbage. Looking back, she could see how readily she isolated those disturbing instances of animal abuse as if they bore no relevance for the family.

When she was six, Kay said her father gave her a bad touch through her clothing. More articulate than the last time, both children told how he had held her on his lap and scratched her crotch, afterward giving her a quarter but refusing to give one to Charlie. The children noticed how he used gifts to reward and punish them. That year they refused to go to his home for Christmas even though he warned they would get no gifts unless they came.

This time another judge issued a temporary restraining order to keep their father away while the children were evaluated for sexual abuse. Kay was first to talk to the counselor.

Soon after that, Kay complained about what Charlie was doing to her cat. Showing their mother, Kay stretched the cat up and used his front paw to stroke his penis. Charlie seemed embarrassed by his mother's disapproval.

When she raised the money for Charlie's evaluation, he seemed relieved to talk about the uncomfortable things that had been done to him. Their mother wished she had overcome her own feelings of denial and recognized the clues earlier. If only she had not been so focused on Kay that she missed the evidence of Charlie's struggle.

Though he is still a sensitive child, Charlie has not stopped tormenting the cat. He squeezes him, trying to force the cat to dance and to obey his wishes. With the cat, he becomes almost as controlling as his father.

The last time his mother heard the cat cry out, she ran in from the next room, grabbed Charlie by the shoulders and screamed in his face to stop. "Mommy, you're acting like Daddy now," Charlie said with disdain.

She admits it: "I terrorized him, and he called me on it." She says the only thing that helps is forbidding Charlie to touch the cat without her permission—supervised visitation.

If we view this true story as the court does, in fragmented legal motions, we may miss the larger picture and the ultimate hope for healing. Though she was distraught over the apparent sexual abuse of her daughter, this mother did not minimize the sexual abuse of a cat. But if she had expressed too much dismay at what Charlie did to the cat, the boy might not have been able to talk about it to the counselor.

Abused children often practice doing to younger children the upsetting things that have been done to them. We are finally beginning to notice the ways they also practice on pets. And we are discovering the help pets can offer when they are respected as an integral part of the family.

A CONFESSION

Until recently I was no animal lover. My parents gave me a kitten for my fifth birthday and a puppy when I turned 10, but I failed to connect emotionally with them. I was protected from the burden of feeding them or burying them. I did not have to see their bodies after the kitten got tangled in the fan of our refrigerator and the puppy died under the wheels of a car. I never saw them being buried and remember only a perfunctory sense of loss. As a dutiful daughter who strove to please, I followed along, hardly aware of my own feelings. I cannot remember ever thinking about my pets' feelings.

For a while, the book *Bambi* made a difference. When neighbors went hunting, I tramped through the forest behind them making a racket to warn the deer away. But after a harrowing experience finding my way home through the woods, I gave up that cause. By the time I turned 16, I had read about Annie Oakley, learned to shoot, and got my own hunting license because the image seemed so cool. I must have felt some ambivalence, for I was secretly relieved when the wildlife stayed out of my scope.

At the time our children were born, my inner conflicts had grown into full-blown depression. Thankfully, my feminist husband urged me to talk about my feelings and to venture into the women's movement. I soon threw myself into trying to change the world and the way it raised girls and boys. With such a compelling goal, who had time for animals?

My husband saw to it that our two sons had pets, small, manageable ones like fish, gerbils, and Peruvian guinea pigs. The boys played with their friends' dogs and tended the neighbor's horse and goat.

When they moved home from college, they did not come alone. One brought a boa constrictor, an iguana, a Jackson chameleon, lizards and toads of all varieties, and a bounding puppy who soon got a companion. Both dogs grew so fast and frolicked so irrepressibly that no barrier could restrain them.

I was not pleased. Exhausted by 60-hour weeks running a shelter for battered women and their children, I preferred working late to coming home where the dog hair flew. I could not sink wearily into a kitchen chair without a wet nose nuzzling its way under my arm. Their longing eyes and exuberant energy overwhelmed me.

Inevitably late trying to leave home in the morning, I would impatiently circle the dogs, desperately searching for my notebooks, my keys, my briefcase. Move, dog! Out of my way!

Our son would herd them into his room and gently tell me, "They have feelings, Mom."

"So do I!" I shot back.

Then our younger son, the largest member of the family, six-feet-four, 220 pounds of honed muscle, brought home a purring piece of Angora fluff tucked in his jacket. My kind of pet.

ENVISIONING A LINK

I was in the midst of this conversion experience when Rhode Island educator Pearl Salotto asked me to speak at a conference she was planning on the link connecting animal abuse with child abuse and domestic violence. Intellectually, I understood The Link, but emotionally it was a stretch.

Adults in counseling have told me of lifelong anguish over cruelties they witnessed as children against pets they loved. Abusers often terrorize family members and maintain control over the family by threatening or torturing animals. One woman knew her abuser was serious after he killed her prize horse.

Donna Ferrato's astonishing photographs, taken with permission as she settled into abusers' homes for her book, *Living with the Enemy*, include a series showing a man named Garth beating his wife, Lisa. Their three-year-old son cried hysterically beside their swimming pool as Garth gripped Lisa in a bear hug and dragged her into their elegant house to search for his cocaine pipe.

After Lisa and their son left home, Garth lingered on "with a pet boa constrictor and a pet ferret kept in adjacent glass boxes in the same bathroom where he had beaten Lisa. The ferret was forced to live in a state of constant anxiety next to the eye of the ever-hungry snake."

Batterers exult in devising mind games and terror. They can turn memories into powerful symbols and use them to buttress their control. One man could calmly scoop his wife's goldfish, Sparkle, from its bowl and deftly slice it with a knife. Months later at a party, jealous of another man's attentions to her, he had only to smile and say amiably over the buffet, "Hey, honey, remember Sparkle?" No one but she would recognize his threat. When she suddenly trembled and felt nauseous, other guests puzzled over her bizarre behavior and admired her attentive husband.

More than once, callers to our domestic violence hotline decided not to come to the shelter for fear of what might be done to their pets while they were away. Batterers often punish their escaping families by destroying any treasures left behind—shredding photos, cutting clothes, taking a chain saw to the furniture, killing pets. One shelter resident went home to feed her cats only to be beaten and hospitalized by her batterer, who had waited, knowing she would not abandon the animals.

WORKING WITH ANIMAL ADVOCATES

So I could see a win-win situation in linking up with animal advocates. For reasons of health and household order, pets could not stay at the shelter. But perhaps the Animal Rescue League would develop a list of safe homes willing to keep pets while women and children stayed at our shelter. When I inquired further, I found some of their people so ready to help that they offered to work on getting the necessary inoculations for pets that needed them.

I began to see other ways we could benefit from The Link, such as the cross-training of professionals and other specialists. Animal control officers, veterinarians, child protection workers and volunteers in those fields are in an ideal position to pick up clues to woman and child abuse if they are trained to see the signs.

In some areas, animal control officers can gain fast access to homes where animal abuse is suspected. If it is possible to jail a batterer because of animal abuse, that will protect the entire family.

Battered women may seek help for abused animals before they acknowledge that they themselves are becoming victims. Veterinarians and their staff need to recognize the signs of domestic violence.

They need to know, just as nurses and doctors do, that they should not report suspected domestic violence to the police unless there is an immediate emergency. Instead they should develop a supportive relationship with the victim. It helps if posters about domestic violence with hotline numbers are visible in waiting rooms and rest room stalls. Professionals who care for animals can establish an office protocol that family abuse is taken seriously and kept confidential by the staff. Their demeanor will show an emotionally or physically battered woman that she is not stupid or worthless, as her abuser tells her. These professionals can help by documenting evidence of abuse including verbatim conversations and photographs, then being willing to testify in court.

These are important messages to communicate to suspected victims:

- "I am concerned about your safety."
- "You don't deserve to be treated this way."
- "You're not alone. You can call the domestic violence hotline at any time to discuss what's happening." The national hotline at 1-800-799-SAFE (7233) will provide local numbers.

Simply encouraging a victim to go to a shelter is not enough, because leaving an abuser is very dangerous. Of the four women killed daily in this country by their husbands or boyfriends, most die when they are trying to escape.

A battered woman and her children need to work out a safety plan with the shelter hotline. They need a support system of people they can trust. That's why the most important step is not to call the police when there is not immediate emergency, but to build a supportive, affirming relationship with the victims. Cross-training is important for shelter staff, who can gain important information during an intake interview by asking whether new guests have witnessed animal abuse or are worried about their pets. Staff can alert humane and animal control officers to rescue the pets and get them to safe foster care. Officers on site may even find evidence to arrest the abuser. Shelter support groups are a good place to discuss animal abuse as a warning sign of a potential batterer.

Animal trainers also may provide a valuable service. Working with shelter staff, they may be able to develop responsible guard dog programs for women being stalked or threatened.

RESISTANCE TO THE LINK

It seems like a natural alliance, this linking of the movements against woman abuse, child abuse, and animal abuse. So why did I meet so much resistance when I first spoke about The Link at the shelter I had directed for more than seven years?

For one thing, the board and staff were exhausted. Staff at the shelter so often work at a fevered pitch, simply responding to crises on the hotline and in the house. All the more reason, I thought, to seek help from animal specialists and volunteers who care about the links between animals and people.

For some board members, this seemed like a whole new direction, far afield from our immediate priorities of helping families in their urgent quest for safe homes and jobs.

There also seemed to be a deeper, philosophical resistance. Many advocates for battered women are not inclined to spend their limited time, energy, and resources helping animals. Some have prejudices or other priorities, like those I confessed in my own story.

Advocates for battered women may resist animal rights activists and child protection workers, who sometimes have their own prejudice against women. For example, the latter group tends to prefer the term "spouse abuse" to "woman abuse." This gender neutrality minimizes the specific history of violence against women by men.

As women have achieved greater equality with men, they have faced virulent backlash. The first women entering male preserves—from military schools and boot camps to trade unions and professions—have been accused of "castrating" or "emasculating" men. Reprisals, often in the form of sexual assaults, have been vicious and without remorse.

Domineering men typically see their violence against women as a form of discipline, almost a divine duty, just as they are expected to master animals and take charge of their environment. The long history of men's violence against women and animals has been enshrined in such scurrilous wisdom as the Old English proverb, "A spaniel, a woman and a walnut tree, the more they're beaten the better they be."

Reporters Kim Ode and Paul McEnroe, writing in the *Minneapolis Star-Tribune,* identified similar sentiments from other cultures:

- From Italy: "As both a good horse and a bad horse heed the spur, so both a good woman and a bad woman need the stick."
- From China: "A bride received into the home is like a horse that you have just bought; you break her in by continually mounting her and continually beating her."
- From Nigeria: "A woman is like a horse: he who can drive her is her master."
- And from our own Ben Franklin's wisdom on women: "Love well, whip well."

The same assumptions may sink indelibly into young women on horseback, who sense more than a linguistic connection between the bridles used to control horses and the brides they are expected to become. A thousand years ago, the word "bride" could refer not only to a woman at her marriage, but also to a "bonnet-string," a "bridle," or a "rein."

According to the *Oxford English Dictionary* the ancient word, *bridelope*, the oldest known Teutonic name for a wedding, signifies the "bridal run" or "gallop" by which a bride was led to her new home. The groom's role, whether in charge of a woman or a horse, was to feed, curry, and train.

That sentiment prevails among some young military men who saw no harm done when their drill instructors were accused of sexually assaulting women recruits. Women are like farm animals, one said: they need to be tamed. No woman who is called "bitch" makes the mistake of thinking she is a man's best friend.

Child protection workers have been known to suggest that women abuse children more frequently than men do, failing to compare the vastly unequal expectations placed on mothers and fathers. Too often those intent on protecting children do not recognize classic signs that mothers also are trapped by abuse, not only from men, but from police, courts, welfare, schools, and other controlling systems.

Yes, there are "battered men," and we always must be ready to help them. But statistically there may be far more batterers with a compelling sense of male entitlement who see themselves as victims. O. J. Simpson insisted he was a victim and denied ever having hit Nicole even when 911 tapes, hotline records, DNA, bloody footprints, and the testimony of his closest friend said otherwise.

It galls many advocates for battered women and their children when they sense that police responses are more swift and court penalties more stiff against animal abusers than against woman and child abusers. The reality is that animal abuse prosecutions are relatively rare, convictions are very difficult to obtain, and most incidents are classified as misdemeanors with relatively light punishments, just like domestic violence. (Part of the legal strategy for regarding these crimes as misdemeanors is that felonies take much longer to prosecute.)

It may seem callous to women's advocates that there are thousands more shelters for abused animals than for abused women and children. The difference in numbers is understandable, however, given the 100-year head start in the animal protection movement and the high price of housing, food, plumbing, utilities, security systems, insurance, and professional staff required for human shelters. The cost is far higher and the risk far greater to operate shelters for battered women than for animals.

Rather than seeing animal advocates as the enemy, competing for scarce funds and justice, we need to envision the kind of alliance urged by the Latham Foundation. The battered women's movement has much to gain from this link.

NEW POSSIBILITIES

As advocates for battered women expand our sensitivity to animals, we can use this new vision to help children express their fears in new ways. Children who resist saying anything disloyal against their parents often are relieved to tell stories where animals take the place of people.

One fine example of this is *Barely Bearable,* written and illustrated by children "whose lives have been touched by violence." The book is edited by Barb Gartland and Bette Hurley, formerly of the Domestic Violence Center of Manitowoc, Wisconsin:

> Once upon a time there was a large and growly bear who married a monkey. The monkey was so dumb that the bear had to tell her what to do, where to go, who to talk to, what to say and everything else.
>
> They had three children . . . a bird, a bee and a mouse.
>
> The bird took care of everyone. She tried to keep the house clean enough, the kids quiet enough, and the bear happy enough.
>
> The bee bugged everyone. He was always in trouble at home, at school and everywhere. No one liked the bee.
>
> The mouse was always afraid. She hid, she cried, and she peed her pants. No one noticed the mouse.
>
> One day the monkey had an idea of her own. She wanted to bake cookies for everyone.
>
> This made the bear very mad. He screamed and yelled and broke everything in the house. He had to hit the monkey over and over because she wouldn't shut up.
>
> The noise and the fighting continued all day and all night. No one could sleep.
>
> The bird wished she could fly far away from the noise.
>
> The bee wished he could sting the bear a million times.
>
> The mouse wished she was invisible.
>
> But then the bus came and they all went to school.

Pearl Salotto helped me think about animals in new ways when she invited me to Rhode Island's first interdisciplinary conference devoted to The Link in 1995. There I heard Florida veterinarian Dick Dillman tell about companion animal programs. He described a tough, streetwise young man who made excuses to stay behind while the rest of his group went on a trip. Returning unexpectedly, Dick found the boy secretly cradling a rabbit, stroking it, and gently murmuring, "Nice bunny, nice bunny." Kids forced to maintain a defensive posture need safe places to practice their tenderness.

I saw Dick's video of city children happily conquering their fear and learning to love a bull named Bumper. I began to imagine the values animals could bring to our shelter.

Pearl's pet-inspired values development program and her "Kids' Kindness Network" suggested to me the ways that children who experience domestic violence could talk about what it means to live in a home that feels safe. They could benefit from activities like planting trees, knowing that their tree would one day provide a safe nesting place for baby birds. I began to envision a shelter-based children's program called the RAK Pack, where children who witnessed irrational acts of terror could plan their own "random acts of kindness."

After our shelter staff began discussing our links with animals, one volunteer observed how television violence upset her dog. We had not given much thought to the ways animals suffer in the presence of human battering, nor to the ways in which dogs who show unconditional love might help to heal victims of abuse who have been made to feel unlovable.

Sara Wye, our clinical therapist, had a dog named Sheba, a fierce-looking, 70-pound, tan and black German shepherd with a rottweiler mask. In her counseling, Sara already had seen many human connections with animals.

"If there is cruelty in childhood, it is often associated with animals," Sara said, describing someone who had been taught to kill animals as a child. "Now, whenever that person is angry, he struggles with wanting to hurt the very animal he cares most about."

Sara started bringing Sheba to work, watching children nervously approach the dog and discover how gentle she was. Simply by being herself, Sheba helped them practice overcoming their fear.

A large 12-year-old boy threw a tantrum in the dining room that put the staff on full alert. Seizing a knife, he held everyone at bay. Suddenly Sheba walked in and broke the tension. Like a parent who knows some problems cannot be confronted head-on, she produced the perfect distraction. In a moment of grace, the boy turned to her and forgot his rage.

Once we had a "wild child," a problem known to staff at many shelters. Without the language to describe her devastation, this four-year-old would run up and down the halls screaming, throwing her weight against anyone who tried to restrain her. Only Sheba could break through her panic, stop the child in her tracks, lick her tears and her runny nose, and soothe her aching soul.

When I left the shelter I still had not convinced the board that we needed this link with animals. But Sheba gradually brought a change from within. On Wednesdays she would lie in Sara's doorway, safely leashed to the filing cabinet, well away from anyone with allergies or dog-phobias. She loved watching the hallway traffic and delighted in the attention she got whenever someone stopped to say hello. She was a therapeutic agent, and it was not only the children who responded to her. Many of the women who had to leave pets behind saw her and grieved their own losses. It was something they needed to do, and Sheba helped them do it.

A FINAL THOUGHT

There may be deep personal and philosophical differences among activists in these movements devoted to ending animal abuse, child abuse, and woman abuse. But we are profoundly interconnected. And we are most likely to achieve our goals as we learn to work at them together.

Animal Abuse and Family Violence

Jane Ann Quinlisk

Young ladies, never put yourselves in the power or under the control of young men who treat their animals badly, for if you become their wives, they will abuse you.

—A warning issued by the Church of Jesus Christ of Latter Day Saints church leader George Q. Cannon in the 1890s.

MY FIRST DAY as a newly hired, freshly graduated, starry-eyed counselor at the local battered women's shelter almost made me run home crying. Not because of the black eyes and bruises that shadowed the women's faces. Not even because of the haunted looks in the small children's eyes. No, I was prepared for that (as much as one can be); after all, I had seen worse at my best friend's home. What I wasn't prepared for were the pictures my first client brought to show me, apologetically, to explain why she had to return home. The pictures were of her "loving" husband cutting her beloved dog's ears off with a pair of garden shears. He had sent the ears along, too, but her mother thankfully neglected to forward them.

As I started ranting about calling the police and animal shelter, my client calmed me down and with tears in her eyes, explained that in her county there was no humane society, and that the local sheriff was her husband's cousin, and that if she went home she could take care of the dog and the other animals on the farm and thank you very much for all the help but couldn't I please understand that it was best that she just go back? I felt horrified and helpless because I had no answers for her in my rattled brain. She returned home and we never heard from her again. Her face and those pictures still turn up in my nightmares.

Twelve years and thousands of stories later, I am no longer as shockable. Today I would have some better answers for her.

SURVEY RESULTS

After the La Crosse Community Coalition Against Violence (CCAV) held our first "Tangled Web: The Connection between Domestic Violence, Child Abuse, and Animal Cruelty" conference, our curiosity was roused and we created a survey asking about this connection. We sent a sample survey to our local domestic abuse shelter to distribute to clients. The survey was given to 17 women. This survey was then refined and a revised survey was sent to domestic violence programs statewide. Fifty-five additional completed surveys were received from 11 programs. This survey was completely anonymous and based on self-reports. It was not meant to be a scientific survey but rather a qualitative sampling of what women in our state were experiencing. Several of the program staff expressed some amazement about the survey content but none of the actual respondents indicated any surprise. In fact, the general consensus appeared to be surprise that no one had ever asked about it before.

Of the 72 total respondents, 10 (14%) reported having no animals in their homes. Thirteen (18%) had pets but indicated there was no violence directed toward the animals. There were 49 (68%) who reported that they had pets and there was violence toward the animals. In the homes where pets were present but there was no reported violence, some of the comments by the women were troubling. One reported that threats to give the bird away were used as a punishment and to control the family's behavior. One woman reported having asthma aggravated by cats but her husband insisted on keeping his cats in the house. Two other women reported threats to kill or give pets away if he didn't get what he wanted.

Of the 49 surveys where both animals and violence were present, 11 homes had only dogs, 5 only cats, 2 only birds, 1 had turtles, and 30 had multiple types of animals. Livestock included dairy cows, pigs, beef cattle, sheep, goats, turkeys, and rabbits. The types of abuse indicated by the surveys included kicking in 30 cases, hitting or punching in 24 instances, mutilation in 3 reports, and killing in 11 cases. Also common were neglecting food or water (13), neglecting proper shelter (10), and refusing needed veterinary care (13).

Women indicated that this abuse had been committed in their presence in 43 (88%) cases. They also indicated that their children had witnessed abuse to the animals in 37 (76%) cases.

Unfortunately, but not surprisingly, women indicated that of the children witnessing violence toward animals, 20 (54%) copied similar behaviors. Of these, 14 abused pets, 2 abused livestock, and in 4 cases the violence was directed toward wild animals. The good news is that two mothers stated that because of the abuse their children had witnessed, the children had become animal lovers and were very protective and loving toward pets.

In 1997, the same survey was sent out to a smaller number of area domestic violence agencies, resulting in 32 returned surveys. The results were very similar. No animals were present in three (9%) of the homes while six (19%) had pets but indicated no violence toward the animals. The remaining 23 (72%) homes indicated there was animal abuse.

Of these 23 homes, companion animals were involved in all but three cases. These three reported abuse to dairy cows. The kinds of abuse included kicking

(48%), hitting or punching (39%), mutilation (9%), killing (17%), and one (4%) incident of sexual abuse. Neglecting to provide food or water was present in 35 percent of the cases, neglecting to provide proper shelter in 17 percent, and refusing proper veterinary care in 35 percent of the cases.

Women witnessed the animal abuse in 65 percent of the cases and the children were present 43 percent of the time. Similar behavior perpetrated by the children was observed toward pets (39%) and livestock (9%).

Some of the comments by women were:

He killed the ferret just to scare us.
He beheaded the parakeet because she was singing.
He fed the dog gunpowder in hamburger to make it mean.
My cat throws up every time he yells at her.
The cows are so afraid of him they won't come in the barn when he's there even to get milked.
He made the dog do a sex act on him.
He said that if I left, he would only feed & milk "his half" of the herd.
It amused him to torture the cats.
Because I was late getting home he put my cat in the microwave. The cat died later that night. I left the next day and never went back.

THE EFFECTS ON CHILDREN

The surveys turned up both expected and unexpected results. Expected was the fact that animal abuse was done in front of the children in 43 percent of the surveys and that similar behavior was noted by the mothers in 57 percent of those cases. (These are mothers admitting their children have abused animals.) Although most of the cases involved children abusing companion animals, there were also several reports involving livestock and wild animals. The reported abuse ranged from excessive teasing and taunting to mutilation and sexual perversion. Although it is now widely accepted that children witnessing domestic violence frequently grow up to become either perpetrators or victims of violence in their adult relationships according to their gender, these findings would seem to indicate a further continuance of animal cruelty as well.

The indication that witnessing violence perpetrates further violence surprises no one reading this, but how are we to explain it when the opposite happens? Several women indicated that their children became protective and caring animal lovers because of the abuse they had witnessed. We need to figure out how to facilitate this positive response to the violence we have not yet figured out how to end.

This small survey did not ask about the ages, gender, extent of the abuse (both witnessed and perpetrated), and whether children abused animals alone or in groups. Obviously, this information would tell us a lot more about how witnessing abuse affects children. We don't yet know what makes some kids become abusive and others more compassionate toward animals.

MEN AND ANIMALS

As a corollary to the shelter surveys of women, the CCAV also did a small sample of male participants in the local abuser treatment program. More than 80 percent of the respondents had been court-ordered to attend this program. Of the men surveyed, over 50 percent said they were hunters and owned guns or rifles. All denied abusing animals as adults—even those who admitted spousal assault. However, approximately one-third admitted threatening to give away family pets. About 15 percent acknowledged some childhood participation in animal cruelty. Over 30 percent stated that parental threats to their childhood pets had been used to control their behavior.

Over 50 percent stated they currently had pets, but several denied feeling any sadness or sense of loss when an animal died. Others were outraged that we "dared to question" their love of animals and said that animal cruelty and domestic violence have nothing to do with each other. One man said he loved his dogs and would never, ever hurt them, and if his wife would just obey him like the dogs did, they wouldn't have a problem.

SOME CASE HISTORIES

Mary J. shot her husband as he entered their trailer, in fact blew the top of his head off. Why? Not because he hit her. He did. Not because he was mean to the children. He was. Not because he had isolated her from family and friends in a small trailer miles from anything. He had. No, she killed him because he told her he was going to bring home another puppy for her to hold down while he had intercourse with the animal.

Although known as the Dairy State, Wisconsin's dairy farms have declined in number and are facing difficult economic times. Over the past few years we have heard several particularly horrifying stories involving beating cows to death. One woman with two small boys reported that her husband walked into the house from the barn one night, hands and chest covered with blood, and announced to her and the children that they better do everything the way he said. One of the cows wouldn't do what he wanted and now she was dead—from the beating. He told his family, "That's what happens when you disobey me!"

Another woman called and wanted to know if it was normal for people to bite animals. Why was she asking? She just found out her new husband thought it was just fine to bite cows and, in fact, found it to be sexually stimulating. A check with several state sexual abuse authorities indicated that they had never heard of this one

Michael is a first-grader currently residing in a treatment foster home. This picture was part of a class assignment to draw an idea for a book the student would like to write. It could be about any topic. The picture shows Michael with a smile on his face, standing over a man wearing a frown. Next to the body are a grave and tombstone. The words are: "I see a man shoot a animal. I shoot a man. He is dayd [dead]."

before and had no advice for this woman (except "run away"). He was later convicted of domestic battery.

WHY DOESN'T SHE LEAVE?

Anyone who works in the domestic violence field hears this question a lot, often from well-meaning people trying to understand the dynamics of abuse. Our usual response is to explain the cycle of violence, the power and control wheel, and the generational factors. Upon closer look in our own community, members of the Community Coalition Against Violence realized from stories of local women seeking help that at least once a month the practical issues of pet welfare arise. This is not to say the other issues are not present; they usually are. But sometimes the actual decision-making factor of whether she leaves at that moment is as simple as what happens to the animals. If she calls us for help, we need to have options for her that include the safety of the animals. We have no way of knowing how many women stay in dangerous situations because of fear for their animals.

A quick telephone check of some Wisconsin domestic abuse shelters indicated that although most of the larger metropolitan programs routinely screen for animal welfare concerns, many of the smaller rural programs do not. In fact, several of the small programs said things like, "What a good idea!" and "I'll bring this up at our next staff meeting."

Several of the larger programs indicated they have arrangements with their local animal shelters and sometimes veterinarians or boarding kennels to provide housing for the animals of families fleeing from violence. None of them indicated that any abusers had tracked down where the animals were being kept, but all had concerns about that possibility. One program was planning a joint fundraiser with the animal shelter to raise money for food and other expenses when it dawned on them the publicity would also let abusers know exactly where the family pets might be located. Putting more people and animals at risk was not worth the potential financial gain. In fact, they are contemplating using this as a marketing tool, soliciting a select group of known benefactors and explaining this unique service and the need for private donations.

All the domestic violence programs I talked with indicated a real concern about how the welfare of family pets affects their clientele and an eagerness to join forces to find solutions and options. All programs, whether for people or animals, are hampered by financial and time constraints, but all it takes, in most cases, is one person willing to make the effort to bring people together. It can be energizing to find others in related fields who share these concerns. Joining forces with other programs gives a broader base of power and support. Most grants these days are looking for collaborative efforts. Building a coalition means new opportunities for funding, publicity, education, and providing better, more comprehensive services. It means saving lives.

WHAT CAN DOMESTIC VIOLENCE PROGRAMS DO?

There are several things that domestic violence programs can do to address this issue. One of the simplest is to incorporate questions regarding client concerns about any animals into the screening process. Even if the program provides no assistance regarding animals, trained staff should be able to brainstorm some possibilities for the client. Even acknowledging her concern as legitimate can be beneficial. But if concern about the welfare of her pets is keeping a woman from leaving a dangerous situation, domestic violence programs need to have some answers for her. The staff should know if there is a humane society or animal shelter in their community. My experience has been that if approached as part of a community response to ending all forms of violence, the animal program staff has been very helpful. Many have offered to provide boarding of pets while the human family is in shelter. If that is not an option, often brainstorming will provide the name of a veterinary clinic or a concerned individual animal lover who is willing and able to provide temporary shelter. Exotic animals and livestock are more challenging and demand creative solutions. Because of these unique concerns, as well as the more ordinary ones, the best idea is to develop a community coalition to address them.

What worked in La Crosse, Wisconsin (the population of La Crosse County is only 100,000, but our domestic violence shelter serves the surrounding seven rural counties) was to identify someone from each of several disciplines able to see the large picture. Bringing several of these people together resulted in sharing of information and concerns, which lead to the formation of the Community Coalition Against Violence (CCAV).

We started by looking at how local cases involving both human and animal abuse were handled. New policies and procedures followed that incorporated joint efforts and cross-reporting. Although we met with some resistance, as is common with all new ideas and changes, it was quite easy to get cooperation and make the kinds of small changes in procedures that can have significant effects.

We got so excited about how well things worked out that we have since had two extremely well received and well attended conferences entitled "The Tangled Web: The Link between Domestic Violence, Child Abuse, and Animal Cruelty." The CCAV also received a United Way Venture Grant to buy the video and workbooks *Breaking the Cycles of Violence* by Phil Arkow that are published by the Latham Foundation. This allowed the CCAV to do training around the area for over 20 agencies and organizations. The CCAV has also given presentations at various conferences and workshops in Wisconsin and Minnesota. The core committee of the CCAV has never numbered more than 10, although we have numerous auxiliary members who contribute according to their ability. We firmly believe in being that small group of individuals who can change the world—at least in our little corner.

SCREENING CLIENTS

Suggested Screening Questions

Note: It is important to refrain from seeming judgmental if she indicates a need to leave animals behind. It may be her only choice and it may be causing her guilt and anguish.

Do you have any pets or other animals at home?
Are you concerned about their health or welfare?
Can we help you contact someone to care for them?
Are you aware that we can arrange for the local animal shelter, vet clinic, or other entity to temporarily board pets?
Although we can't have animals in the shelter due to allergies and state regula-

tions, we can help to place your pet in free temporary boarding. We will also work with you to find housing that allows pets when you are ready to leave the shelter.

Suggestions for Staff Training

It is important to educate staff (especially nonanimal lovers) that although the welfare of the animals may not seem all that important to the staff or be a priority when the family has so many other needs, the welfare of the animal may be very important to the client or her kids. Their ability to function, let alone make good decisions, may be impaired if they are anxious about the animal. The family's survival has depended on the ability to "read" the abuser. They are often afraid to tell the truth about what has happened in the home (e.g., killing an animal to protect it from further abuse). Families also see staff as authority figures and will take cues from them. If it seems that staff is unreceptive to hearing about concerns regarding the animal, they often will not mention it. They may believe it is not worth mentioning, but in fact it causes them a great deal of anxiety and may even precipitate their returning home.

SUGGESTED READINGS

Davis, Diane. 1985. *Something is wrong at my house: A book about parents fighting,* illustrated by Marina Megale. Seattle: Parenting Press. This is a very useful book for almost any age group, recommended by the National Coalition Against Domestic Violence.

Martin, Del. 1981. *Battered wives.* San Francisco: Volcano Press; first published by Glide Publications, 1976. This is the first, and still first-rate, analysis of wife abuse, its history, and the response of social and legal institutions.

NiCarthy, Ginny. 1986. *Getting free: A handbook for women in abusive relationships.* Seattle: Seal Press. This is the first book written for the abused woman, explaining why abuse happens, what she can do about it, and where she can go.

Schechter, Susan. 1982. *Women and male violence: The visions and struggles of the battered women's movement.* Boston: South End Press. This book details the history and politics of the movement to shelter abused women, to make laws, and to change social policy.

Walker, Lenore E. 1979. *The battered woman.* New York: Harper & Row. This book contains an early theory of battering, its psychological effects, and some of the ways women cope.

First-Person Account
Life and Death inside the Cycles of Violence
Marsha Millikin

I GET UP every morning about 5 A.M., drink coffee, and watch the news. I wake my 16-year-old daughter, Christine, about 7 A.M. to get ready for school. By this time, I've fed our two dogs, three cats, and the hedgehog. I'm done with the bathroom and she can have it all to herself. There is no sharing the one bath in our house. We get dressed, me for my job as interim director and production editor of the Family Violence & Sexual Assault Institute, and she for school. After lunch, Christine joins me at work, where she is also employed as clearinghouse coordinator and staff assistant. Looks pretty normal from the outside.

But about five years ago, my seemingly family-valued and family-oriented world of myself, fiancé, and daughter went to pure hell upon my daughter's disclosure of the most horrible of secrets. The man she called "Daddy," Jamie Duane O'Farrell, now identified by Texas Department of Criminal Justice number TDCJ-720602, currently serves 40 years for the aggravated sexual assault of my daughter—abuse that started almost at the beginning of our relationship and only stopped when Christine told of O'Farrell's abuse. He is eligible for parole November 14, 2003. O'Farrell has credit for almost 15 years after serving less than 3 years of his sentence.

Our lives, a composite of startings and finishings, beginnings and endings, all overlap one another. Adrienne Rich, essayist and poet, believes for one to have a sense of self, one must study history—the history of men, women, and particularly the history of one's self. We did not just get here from nowhere. We are all a composite of our diverse upbringings and our experiences—those experiences we control and those experiences over which we have no control.

Any aspect of family violence cannot be told from any one aspect or point of view. Although this text is a testimony of how animals were used to control certain aspects of my daughter's behavior, this is also a story of how animals were used to bribe and console her—not by just the perpetrator, but by me, too. Therefore, this account of animal abuse in conjunction with child sexual abuse serves the primary purpose of how one particular perpetrator used animals; however, his abuse of pets was but one of the many ways he controlled Christine and me. He used brutal physical cruelty to animals in order to control her, but his use of animals to control me was much more subtle.

Perhaps this account started about 10 years ago, when Christine found a stray kitten in the parking lot of the apartment building where we previously lived. I said she could keep him. His foot pads were burnt from walking on the sunbaked blacktopped parking lot, hunks of fur were missing from his skinny body, and his nose was bloody and scabbed. We took this pathetic little thing to the veterinarian. Whiskers was dewormed, immunized, and given an excellent prognosis for full recovery from his ordeal with homelessness. Christine rubbed salve on his feet and nose three times a day like the vet instructed. Whiskers grew up to be a beautiful, long-haired, black cat who weighed about 20 pounds—the perfect model for Halloween. He soon adjusted to his role as Lord of the Manor. Whiskers was not our cat, we were his family.

A few years later, Christine wanted a dog. I told her she would get a puppy when we no longer lived in an apartment, trying to explain the problems of having a dog tear up the place while we were at work and school. Of course, her concept of puppy was much different than mine. All she could see were the cute, fuzzy creatures on dog food commercials—not the animals who messed up the house, chewed on furniture, and needed care and training to become productive pet citizens. Keeping my promise, one of my first orders of business as soon as we moved into the house was to get her a puppy.

One day, before I picked Christine up at the sitter's, I went to a pet store where the owner sold mutt puppies for a few dollars. I picked out a German shepherd mix with a black-tipped tail. He looked like a golden German shepherd and I believed this dog would grow up to weigh about 70 pounds and be a good companion for Christine and guardian of our home. I paid for the dog and asked the owner to hold it until I brought Christine because I didn't want to take her to the pet store to find a dog and there not be any for her to choose. When we returned to the store, I told Christine, "Go with the gentleman and get your dog." She said, "But I don't have a dog." "You do now," I replied. While I paid for dog food and a dog toy, Christine went to get her puppy.

There are no words to describe the feeling of a mother who fulfills a dream of her child. Christine held the puppy and he licked her face, just like in the movies and sit-coms. We left and went home. While in the car, the puppy kept licking her face; I thought to myself, "Yech." Christine giggled, snuggled, and petted the little guy. She named him Dusty. He was an inside-outside dog, spending nights in the house and days tied up to his doghouse. Little did I know this dog would someday be the glue that held my daughter's life together, emotionally and literally.

One day, I noticed Christine coming out of the house of the man next door. I asked her what she was doing in there and she said, "Playing video games with this man and Kyle" (a boy about her age who lived in the neighborhood). To say I didn't like this one bit is a gross understatement, but I was faced with what do I tell my child, how much do I tell my child, and how do I do this without alarming her? I told her to never go into his house again. We talked about good touches and bad touches again—my brain overloaded with blaring alarms and red flags strewn throughout my being.

I had not met this man, did not know his name, and did not know anything about him. My daughter did not belong in his house for any reason. She went over there again and this time, I became quite angry because she disobeyed me. The third time, I went over to his house and told him my daughter was not allowed to play in his house. He assured me they only were playing video games, he was lonely and liked kids. This is when he introduced himself as Jamie O'Farrell, and said he understood my concerns, and that he would never deliberately have Christine disobey me and would not have her into the house unless she had my permission. As this conversation took place, I stood on the porch and noticed the interior of his house was very clean and well-kept. As I walked back to my house, I thought he seemed like a nice enough guy and maybe I was overreacting to the situation and overprotecting Christine. After all, he sure didn't look like a child molester.

He owned a dog named Princess. She was an outside dog, living in a fenced area with a doghouse. When the winter temperatures dropped below freezing, O'Farrell left the dog in his house while he went to work. When he returned home, O'Farrell discovered Princess had chewed his telephone, the mini-blinds, and his collection of pornographic magazines hidden under the bed. In front of Christine, he beat Princess, punching her in the face and kicking her across the room. Christine had never witnessed this kind of anger and rage. He explained, "This is what you do to dogs or kids who don't do what they are supposed to." When she said, "My mom never does that to me or Dusty," he replied, "Then your mom is wrong and doesn't know what she's doing."

Not too long after this incident, Christine remembers that Princess disappeared. I once asked O'Farrell what happened to the brown dog he used to have and he said, "I was keeping her for a friend and he came and got her." I accepted this reason, unaware of the lie. Why not? I had no reason to disbelieve him. But I never learned of Princess's beating or the pornographic magazines until recently, when Christine and I began work on this narrative.

As time passed, O'Farrell and I, usually with Christine accompanying us, went out to dinner, walked around the mall and fell in love. This was my dream family. I thought I had found a man who worked, did not drink alcohol or take drugs, and a man who loved my daughter. I did not realize how he chose and groomed us to satisfy his needs of power and control over a mother and her daughter. He would babysit periodically so I did not have the added expense, supported my plans to go back to school, and did little favors for Christine and me. For example, once she missed the bus because I slept in. He offered to take her to school on his way to work because he knew how tired I must be working all night, so I was to go back to bed and not worry about a thing. "I can handle this," I thought, as I went back to bed; maybe having a man around wasn't so bad after all. About six or seven months later, Christine and I moved into his trailer with Whiskers and Dusty. I still paid rent on my house for three months, thinking if this did not work out I would have a place to live if I needed it.

About three months later, I came home from work and Whiskers was outside. I let him back into the house, wondering how he got out. The next morning, I mentioned this to O'Farrell and he told me, "He got up on the counter and peed. That goddamned cat ruined a loaf of bread so I threw him out." I did not quite believe this story, for Whiskers was not a counter cat and never missed his box, yet I accepted this. To say this was not true was to call him a liar, and since I was not home during the alleged incident I did not think I was in a position to question it. O'Farrell never lied to me that I was aware of. Besides, maybe the cat did mess on the counter due to the stress of the move. A few weeks later, Whiskers was found under a neighbor's shed, dead. I guessed he had eaten something and got food poisoning. Now I suspect O'Farrell was somehow responsible for Whiskers' death. He was responsible for letting the cat outside, knowing Whiskers was declawed and could not protect himself.

And then there was Rocko, a collie–German shepherd mix dumped off at our house by his owner, Scott. We were going to take care of the dog while Scott found a place to live. No one asked me if this was all right with me. O'Farrell decided Scott took too long to come back for his dog so O'Farrell took Rocko and Christine out to a country road for a demonstration of what O'Farrell would do to Dusty if Christine ever told of her abuse. O'Farrell beat up Rocko, punching and kicking him in the face and throwing bottles at him, glass shattering and cutting the dog's face and body. Christine remembers Rocko's bloody eyes and O'Farrell telling her, "If you ever tell, I'll do this to Dusty." When I asked where Rocko was, O'Farrell told me Scott came back and picked him up. But there is another version of this story, according to Christine, and I suspect O'Farrell tortured, killed, and butchered that poor dog.

Time passed. The relationship between me and O'Farrell changed and so did Christine. I attributed these changes to the magic going out of the relationship and the changes in my daughter due to adolescence and puberty. She was also jealous of the relationship between me and O'Farrell—she never had to share her mother before, or so I rationalized. I lost my job and took three part-time jobs so I would not put a financial strain on the family. I still went to school, driving about a hundred miles round trip. Then came the day I was called out of class because Christine took a knife to school. I drove that hour with my mind racing as fast as the engine in my car, hoping I wouldn't get stopped. I got to school and the principal told me she would not call the police because Christine had never been in any trouble before and made good grades, but she would be suspended for three days. I thanked her and left with Christine.

Dumbfounded, I couldn't speak. I finally asked her, "Why?" and she said, "It was my friend's birthday and I wanted to give him something nice." I found out she had gotten the knife from O'Farrell. When I confronted him and asked why and how my daughter had access to a hunting knife, he said, "She knows to leave my things alone. I'm going to beat her ass." I told him I would not allow this. I did not believe in spanking or beating kids, no matter what they did, and there were to be no exceptions. We argued. I never gave in on this because my father would often use me as a punching bag and that was never going to happen to any of my children. Little did I know, he regularly beat Christine when I was at work, school, or shopping for groceries. He even beat her when she began menstruating because now she might get pregnant, but his abuse of her did not stop. In fact, she tells me it escalated. I later learned she took the knife to school, planned to ask her teacher for a bathroom pass during class in order to kill herself when there was no chance of anyone walking in on her.

That summer, Dusty somehow wrapped his chain around his neck and almost choked to death. When Christine and I drove up into the driveway he did not come and jump around like he always did when we came home. We found him prostrate on the ground. We ran over to him, looking into his glassy eyes. We could not get the chain off him. A neighbor came over and helped us, saying he could not believe the dog "accidentally" wrapped the chain around his neck. Once we took the chain off, Dusty started having seizures every few minutes. Christine and I watched him try to walk around. We brought him into the house, and during each seizure, he urinated uncontrollably. I felt so sorry for this poor dog, who I believed would spend the rest of his life a vegetable. When O'Farrell came home, I said, "This isn't right. Maybe we should put him to sleep." But O'Farrell said no, he might be okay and it would break Christine's heart. I agreed with him but thought we should also consider more humane treatment for this poor dog. We watched Dusty for several hours. By the next day, he seemed to be all right but disoriented. I let him stay in the house and Christine took care of him, let him sleep in her bed, and watched him like her sick child. I later learned O'Farrell hoped the dog would die in front of Christine. Sometimes I wondered if he wrapped the chain around the dog's neck with a slip knot. Dusty certainly did not do this himself.

About three years into our relationship, O'Farrell quit his job. He was going into business for himself building and maintaining computers. He came to me and asked for support for his decision. I said something to the effect that I didn't really care what he did as long as I had help paying the bills. I also told him I was tired of being the sole financial support of the family. We did not have enough money for necessities let alone any discretionary income. Therefore, if he was going to chase a dream, he better have some money behind it. He said something about having plenty of money in the checking account, as if $400 was "plenty of money." I reminded him that my car insurance was due, my inspection sticker expired at the end of the month, and I needed new tires to pass inspection. He twisted my concerns to mean I did not support his decision. I reminded him I was chasing my dreams by going to school while working and taking care of this family. I only expected him to do what I did myself, no more and no less. I reminded him this was only fair and I did not feel in the past few months he was being entirely fair or sharing financial responsibilities. He ignored me after this exchange for a day or two, which was customary.

A few days later, under the guise of needing a few groceries, O'Farrell and Christine took a trip to the pet store to "look around" while I studied for a test. He took the checkbook. When they came home about an hour later, Christine held a purebred husky puppy. O'Farrell came into the house with a huge bag of high-dollar puppy food and I learned that the bank account had been depleted by more than $300. "Look what Daddy bought me." I looked at O'Farrell and said, "I can't afford to feed the people around here, let alone another pet." "But she wanted it and I just can't tell her 'no'. What did you expect me to do?" he asked with his sweetest smile. But this time, I did not melt. Remembering the pile of utility bills we probably could not pay and my car expenses, I told him, "Don't you ever override another one of my decisions again. Now you can figure out how to pay the bills. Maybe the dog can do it." I walked back into the bedroom, trying not to make Christine feel bad because I knew he manipulated me through my daughter and none of this was her fault. He named the dog Sheba.

I knew this relationship was on the rocks. Driving a wedge between my daughter and me, O'Farrell made me out to be the witch who tells Christine to clean her room and he tells her not to. I came home from work and school, sometimes as late as midnight, to a pile of dirty laundry and dishes while both of them watched television. I know these mind games. But she loved him, called him Daddy, and I did not know how to leave him without it having a devastating effect on her, I naively thought to myself. O'Farrell found a job as a copy machine technician and he spent a lot of time at work, not coming home in the evenings, and trying to pick a fight when he did. I refused to argue with him. He never beat me. It could be worse. Besides, I had no money, my car was illegal to drive, and the tread was coming off the rear tire on the driver's side.

For the first time, I felt trapped. I didn't want to leave when he was at work and leave my furniture and other belongings because I knew there would be no furniture when I returned. I remember how he cleaned out his shed—making a huge bonfire out of old boards, pieces of broken furniture, and other things he did not want anymore. I remembered my grandmother's antique bowls set out on the porch to feed dogs and cats—bowls Grandma used to make bread and cookies, now broken and thrown away. The same with antique quilts and a satin blanket of my grandfather's—all used for dog beds or to lay under the car and change the oil. I remembered the times I told both Christine and O'Farrell to use plastic butter dishes or an old pan to feed the animals but I always came home to find my good dishes on the porch, knocked into the dirt, or broken. And O'Farrell always used the same excuse, "I had to use something to feed the dog. Do you want the dog to starve?"

After a while, I quit trying to explain that the dog would not starve if it was fed from a plastic bowl and how the disrespect of my dishes symbolized the disrespect for me, but O'Farrell pretended not to understand and Christine thought I was an old witch and did not want anyone to feed the dog. In my absence, he twisted my words. I became the stranger in the house, the isolated one, and I started to doubt myself. The smart, strong, tough one, why can't I handle this? After a while, I couldn't define "this" or whatever it was I was supposed to be handling so I went through the motions—working, going to school, paying all the bills, and trying to take care of Christine.

I befriended a professor at school. One day, he asked me how my daughter was doing and I said something like, "Sometimes, she doesn't act like my daughter." He replied, "I know what you mean, they grow up so fast." And as I ducked into the restroom, his polite voice and remarks brought no comfort as I soundlessly cried in the stall. I realized I was in way over my head and had no idea what I was drowning in. The professor and I became good friends—I guess it was because were just a couple of old hippies who loved literature.

Not too long after this, O'Farrell picked a fight with Christine, knowing I would interfere and set up the confrontation. He told her to get off the telephone and jerked the cord out of the wall. She yelled and called him nasty names and I came down the hall and into the bedroom, asking what all the noise was about. She ran toward the kitchen and he pushed me against the wall in the hall. Christine yelled, "I ought to kill you for that." O'Farrell ran down the hall after Christine, who was looking for the gun on top of the refrigerator in the kitchen. He wrapped his hands around her throat and threw her down on the kitchen floor. I saw this and yelled for Christine to get into the car, knowing this situation would only get worse before it got better. (I had seen my parents do this many times.) Christine scrambled from him and ran out the door to a neighbor's. I found her, made sure she was safe, went back to the house for our school books, clothes, her stuffed "Snow Bunny," and retrieved the little bit of money I had hidden. He followed, apologizing, begging, telling me "we can work it out," "I know I never told you I love you," and I realized he was reciting lines from various rock songs as I left. Depersonalized into a rock song, I left and picked up Christine. She insisted I go back and get the dog. As I untied Dusty, O'Farrell watched me as he leaned over the porch railing. I wondered, what am I going to do with no place to go, no money, a kid, and a dog? But I have to do this. There is no going back to live in that house.

We left and stayed with a friend of mine from school (Elizabeth, a nurse) but could not take Dusty. By this time, O'Farrell and I had discussed our problems; he cried and vowed to change and I accepted this. Everyone deserved a second chance. We took Dusty back to O'Farrell's trailer, but Christine was cold and distant. I attributed this to the incident when O'Farrell grabbed her by the neck and threw her to the kitchen floor. She did not want to leave Dusty and I attributed this to her love for her dog and her loneliness. I found a full-time job working evenings and continued school.

It was at Elizabeth's that I was first told of the signs of sexual abuse. Elizabeth believed she observed behaviors in Christine that led her to this conclusion. She gave me a litany of reasons and signs—specifically behavioral and physical manifestations of abuse, such as uncontrollable anger, uncontrollable eating, and discharge from her vagina. I attributed these changes to the upheaval in our lives, changes in school, residence, and our standard of living. I knew we had problems but still refused to acknowledge sexual abuse. O'Farrell might have problems and be a jerk, but a child molester? Never. I would not, nor could not, believe it. It was when I woke Christine to go to school and she went into convulsions that I knew Elizabeth was right. As I watched my child during this flashback, arms rigid by her sides and eyes rolled back into her head, I noticed Christine sleeping in three layers of clothing. Why hadn't I ever seen this before?

As O'Farrell and I tried to re-establish our previous relationship and work out our differences, the story of Spencer was born. There was a boy living in the neighborhood who broke into cars and garages, stealing, who also got the blame for carrying "you show me yours and I'll show you mine" too far. I once asked Christine if Spencer made her do things she didn't want to and when she nodded her head "yes," I accepted this. Case closed. It was too painful to her for me to ask any more questions. I later asked a friend of mine, a policeman, what I could do about this and he said, "Forget it. She's not hurt and it's his word against hers. You can ask for a police report, but the DA will never prosecute because they're so close in age." Even though I was angry with his response, this made sense to me, so I thought as long as we were no longer living in that neighborhood, there would be no more problems from Spencer. O'Farrell corroborated this story, adding minute details to deflect any attention away from him, and I dropped the Spencer matter. Dusty continued to stay at O'Farrell's.

In the meantime, Christine and I moved into an apartment next to the university. O'Farrell drove the hundred miles and visited on weekends. I was not quite ready to pursue our former relationship because I still stung from his emotional, financial, and physical abuse. One day, he showed up on our doorstep with his clothes, some personal belongings, and Sheba. I asked him what he thought he was doing and he replied, "I'm selling the trailer and all the utilities are shut off. I just can't afford it by myself. Is it okay if I stay here for a while?" I reluctantly let him in because I still could not be cruel to Christine's "Daddy." He seemed to be glad to be with us again, but on the first of the month I asked for some help with expenses. Of course, he didn't have any money. The honeymoon period did not last very long, but I really did not expect it to.

That night, I laid down the law. My house, my rules, and the first rule was that he pay the pet deposit. I would not be evicted because of a dog. He said he would, but of course he never did. I lived in constant fear of eviction, but I would not pay $300 to live with his dog. As he traveled back and forth from our apartment to his home, he never mentioned Dusty. I asked him how the dog got food and water and he said a neighbor was feeding him. I told O'Farrell to bring Dusty to the apartment because it was not fair to the dog or Christine to make him live alone in the summer heat. O'Farrell complied, but this was just another facet of his abuse. I wondered how I was going to hide two dogs in an apartment. I believed the best solution was to give both of them away. But now, Sheba was pregnant and eventually had six puppies in our little apartment. I just knew the eviction notice was coming any day now.

Dusty did not adjust to apartment life, but he sure adjusted to life with Christine. It was evident that he had missed her, even following her to the bathroom. He never let Christine out of his sight. Dusty urinated on O'Farrell's stereo speakers and messed on the rug regularly. O'Farrell severely beat him. He also made Dusty eat feces as part of his punishment and always made sure Christine witnessed this discipline. The implication was clear—if I can do this to a dog, a living creature, what makes you think I won't do this to you if I have a reason? And disclosure of sexual abuse was one such reason. I later learned O'Farrell fed Dusty horse feed, knowing he wouldn't eat it, and hoped the dog would starve while chained up at O'Farrell's trailer.

Each morning, about four or five, I would awake to the smell of dog diarrhea. Sheba would have messed all over the living room rug—a mess that could not be ignored. I would get up and clean it up while O'Farrell pretended to sleep. If he cleaned up the mess, he used a good bath towel, pillowcase, or an item of my clothing, never his. After a few weeks of this, the apartment smelled and I was forced to rent a steam cleaner. I asked O'Farrell if he thought my only function on this earth was to clean dog manure and he said he was so sorry the dog had a problem. I told him I would take her to the Humane Society if I ever woke up again in the middle of the night to the smell of dog manure all over my apartment. Sheba never had another accident and I learned later he had fed her laxatives. One morning, as I retrieved the morning paper from the porch, Sheba got out of the apartment and ran off. I can honestly say I was never sorry, nor that I cared. I called the Humane Society to see if she had been picked up or turned in as a lost dog. I was told "no." Having done my duty to a dog I didn't particularly care for, I gave up on Sheba.

We still had Dusty and he was slowly adjusting to apartment life when O'Farrell discovered Dusty urinating on his stereo speakers. Maybe the dog was getting even. O'Farrell told Christine to get her dog and get into the car. They were going for a ride. About a hundred miles down the interstate, O'Farrell opened the car door and ordered Christine to kick Dusty out. When she refused, he told her he would do to Dusty what he did to Rocko, only he would do it right this time, and she could watch while he tortured and killed Dusty and dumped her off on the side of the road, too. Then O'Farrell said he would come home and kill me and Christine would be left alone with him.

As Christine slowly nudged Dusty out of the car, she remembers watching him marking the stop sign as his territory as O'Farrell drove away. On the way home, he told her Dusty was now free and would have a good life, someone would adopt him, give him a good home, and he wouldn't have to live in an apartment anymore. Then O'Farrell told her how much he loved her in his own way and other things she chooses not to remember aloud. But Dusty marking a stop sign was the symbol Christine needed—a symbol the abuse must stop.

When they returned, Christine ran to her room and cried uncontrollably. Then I found out what happened to Dusty. I later asked O'Farrell if he cared that he just broke a little girl's heart. His response was, "If the damned dog hadn't peed on my speakers, he would still be here." That's when I told him to be out by the first of the year; it was a few weeks before Thanksgiving and I would not give him an excuse to tell his family and friends I was the witch who threw him out for a Christmas present. It was a few weeks after Christmas that I was called by Child Protective Services (CPS) and Christine's abuse was disclosed. I was given a choice—throw him out or she would become a ward of the court and placed into foster care.

No problem. I took O'Farrell's dirty clothes to where he worked, told him of the complaint and that he should find somewhere else to live. He said it must be because of a dirty joke he had told Christine, to which I replied that he had no business telling dirty jokes and CPS did not investigate dirty jokes. It all fit into place. The late nights he worked, except when I worked or went to class, Christine's behavior, quitting his job, me supporting the family, the wedge he attempted to drive between me and Christine, and all the other unexplainables.

O'Farrell raped Christine her first night alone in our new home while I was at work, telling her this is what dads do and he was making a woman out of her. She had just turned eight. As time went on, he told her how pretty and grown up she was, and that I knew of the abuse or I would never leave the house. He also told her no one would believe her if she ever told, and used money and presents to bribe her. Christine learned from DARE, a drug intervention program at school, what to do if someone touches you in private places. Christine realized O'Farrell was abusing her and she must tell someone or his abuse would not stop. When she confronted him and said she would tell a counselor at school, he told her no one would believe her because she let it happen, she came on to him, and she liked it more than he did. I learned this during Christine's deposition at the District Attorney's office. In a few days, I learned a lot of other things too, like how he and his father had abused his two younger sisters. O'Farrell's first offense took place when he was eight years old. Quickly, I was becoming an unwilling and unwitting "expert" in child sexual abuse, the mind of the child molester, and mother blame. All I wanted was to put this guy in prison and forget about the whole stinking mess.

Christine and I stumbled through the legal system. We learned a whole new language. The criminal justice system is just that—justice for the criminal. (How many phone calls to a detective do you have to make to have one returned? As many as you want. Detectives do not return phone calls.) A couple of days after her disclosure, O'Farrell went to the police department and confessed on video tape so "he would not get in trouble." I have requested numerous times to view this tape, but am told this is not procedure, this would be a violation of his right to privacy, and I don't really want to see it anyway, as if I cannot make that decision myself. While O'Farrell waited 10 months for his trial, he sought out two other single mothers, one with three children and one with two, as girlfriends. Just before his trial, he was arrested in another county on a marijuana charge and detained because of the warrant in Smith County, Texas.

As his trial date drew closer, he asked for a lesser charge, to which both the District Attorney and I said a vehement "no." Then he asked for a jury trial and his attorney advised him to plead guilty and throw himself on the mercy of the court. According to his attorney, he would probably receive a maximum sentence, 99 years, if a jury examined the physical evidence coupled with Christine's testimony. This county historically does not approve of drug dealers or child molesters, and not necessarily in that order. O'Farrell followed his attorney's advice and was sentenced to 40 years in prison because this was his first offense—something quite different from the truth. Who knows which offense it actually was; it was just the first time he got caught. After he moved out of my apartment, I found a shoe box full of pictures of small children. These were assorted school pictures, studio pictures, and pictures from instant cameras. Most of the children were girls, pictured with their mothers. There were no pictures of fathers. This must have been his trophy case or filing cabinet of his victims. I wish I would have saved the pictures instead of throwing them away.

During this time, Christine ran away from home countless times. Sometimes she was gone a few hours, other times a month or two. She never called and I never knew where she was. No longer under her abuser's physical control, Christine dealt with her abuse the only way she knew how. We moved to another city, obtained a post office box and unlisted phone number, and got rid of the furniture, piece by piece, so there would be no physical reminders of O'Farrell. I went to work, went to school, went to the grocery store, and tried to have a normal life, whatever that meant. I wasn't sure anymore. Counseling did not help. She ran away either before appointments or after. When Christine was home, she constantly threatened to kill herself. I believed she placed herself in a position where someone would do the job for her, and explained this theory to the local police chief. He explained to me the dynamics of many runaway adolescents. They don't want to be found. We became good friends and now, I don't know what I would have done without him or my favorite professor. A survivor of child sexual abuse himself, he helped me keep my head on straight and put in the proper perspective so many issues I wrestled with.

About a year after O'Farrell went to prison, Christine asked for a puppy for Christmas. I talked to her about responsibility and her running away from home and not taking care of a puppy. She promised to quit running away. I had heard this many times and wanted to believe it, so amid her promises we went to a pet store that sold Humane Society puppies and bought her one. This little thing, a black German shepherd mix, was so chubby her belly almost scraped the floor. I named her Tazmanian Doggie because she chased her tail and ran in circles like the cartoon character. A few days later, Christine ran away from home. This time, she was gone almost two months and I spent Christmas Day alone, snuggling Taz and crying.

About a week after Christmas, I came home from work and noticed Taz was weak and shaking. I picked her up and she felt cold. I noticed bloody vomit or diarrhea in her bed and immediately took her to the vet. Diagnosed with parvo, often terminal in puppies, Taz stayed at the vet's a few days for observation and treatment. I could not let this puppy die. When Christine came home she would think I did to her dog what O'Farrell had done to her pets. I feared her trust in me, what little she might have left, would be violated. Saving that little dog became a mission and symbol of so much more than the life of a puppy, but I never could tell the vet just what that sick little dog meant to me. Taz survived.

I went to school, went to work, and went to the store. Grocery shopping was the worst. I never knew what to buy. I either binged or starved. I went home every night and waited for Christine, reminding myself not to go crazy because she would need her mother together when she came home. That little dog and I became quite attached, spending long hours in front of the fireplace watching the flames. Taking care of everyone and everything except myself, I caught a cold, which developed into bronchitis and eventually pneumonia. But I still went to school, work, and the store. I was making good grades, doing my job, and taking care of business, wasn't I? One Saturday afternoon, I awoke from a codeine-induced stupor and answered the phone. It was Christine asking me if she could come home. As I took Taz to the car and drove about five miles to pick Christine up, I wondered if she would remember her young owner. As I watched the reunion a few minutes later, there was no doubt in my mind. Taz remembered.

This chapter in our lives ended about two years ago. Christine never ran away again and settled into school. I earned my bachelor's degree about the same time O'Farrell was sentenced. I continue working toward my master's. I've also testified before a Senate subcommittee about the effects of child sexual abuse on the nonoffending mother and child victim, advocating for more state money to be set aside for counseling victims and adolescent perpetrators, tougher sentencing for offenders to protect our communities, and stricter sex offender notification laws. Ashley's Laws, a set of laws dealing with sex offender notification and the removal of good time accrued by prisoners convicted of certain offenses including aggravated sexual abuse of a child, were passed by the Texas Legislature in 1994.

Christine and I work at the Family Violence & Sexual Assault Institute with Dr. Robert Geffner and two other staff members. We love our jobs and sometimes wonder if fate, if there is such a thing, or circumstances would have brought us here if we had not shared this experience. We are both changed and stronger people than we were eight years ago. When someone calls and tells me about disclosure of their child's abuse, I tell them I understand because I do. I also tell them with love, the right counselor, time, and support, their children will laugh and play again. I almost never hear from them again, and as I drive home from work, I wonder if they made it, because I know they can.

We still have Taz and she still chases her tail, and plays fetch, sings, and snuggles kitties. Seven, our mutt with six toes on one foot and seven toes on the other, looks like a Rottweiler with a long tail. He's not too smart and loves to chase cats. Shadow, a free-to-a-good-home Russian blue-Manx, weighs about 20 pounds and is a cat with a bad-cat attitude. He and Taz like to snuggle together and take naps. Smokey and Craig, our two outside cats, spend most of their time trying to sneak into the house every time the door opens. And Cedric, the hedgehog, sleeps all day under a bowl and wrestles with his water bottle at night.

First-Person Account
A Survivor Remembers
Annette W.

I AM A 30-year-old female, married mother of two young children, and an incest survivor. My mother's boyfriend sexually abused me around the age of 4 until I was 12. When I was 12, I finally realized he was always lying to me when he told me no one would believe me if I told them what he was doing. He was wrong. Someone believed me. A school teacher.

I remember him always kicking our dogs. I mean, really kicking them very very hard in their stomachs because they were barking. He was always mean to our animals. The worst of it all is remembering when he brought home a dead horse to slaughter it in our back yard, and we (there were five of us children) all watched and listened to him go on and on about slaughtering this animal. He laughed and thought it was very funny. He thought it was funny that it made my mom vomit. This man was very mean and cruel to all of us kids, all of our animals, and very demanding on our mother.

This man never had to pay for what he did to me, my sister, or any of our friends ... but we will pay for this the rest of our lives.

First-Person Account
Out of the Ashes . . . A Program of Hope
Tamara Barnes

FROM THE FIRM foothold I have these days in recovery from my codependency, along with what I have progressively learned about my disease, I can see how I managed to find myself in an abusive marriage. In my family of origin, there was no physical violence or chemical abuse, but alcoholism runs rampant on both sides of my family. My mother was and is extremely controlling and psychologically and emotionally abusive. She was to my sister and me as well as to my father. For example, on my eighteenth birthday, I was living in West Virginia with my father and my grand-mother and I remember my mother called me from Oregon and told me that if I would not take my dog, she would have her "put to sleep." My mother knew it was not possible for me to have my dog. I was hysterical for hours. She never carried out her threat, but the damage was done and has still not been repaired. For the past several years, I have practiced total abstinence from my mother. My father got tired of living in 1980, and decided not to have life-saving surgery. I know now he died from codependent burn-out.

I had been involved in therapy off and on for years to try to resolve issues that revolved around my mother. At the time of my marriage in 1993, I hadn't a clue how I had managed to get myself into this mess. I understand now.

Awareness began to take hold of me six weeks into my marriage to my abuser. He had been displaying fits of anger, stomping around, and yelling for no reason that I could fathom. It took me a while to understand what was going on with him. He had changed into something that I did not recognize.

At the time, I had had several pets for many years. I consider my pets my chil-dren. They are precious members of my family, and an important part of my support group. I had a wonderful elderly golden retriever named Jasmine, a mixed breed lab-shepherd named Jack, and three cats—Tom-tom, Jeepers, and Miranda. In addition, I had a bird named Albert. Out of the bunch, I still have all but Jasmine, whose old age and arthritis forced me to have her put to sleep. My abuser's need to dominate and control extended to them as well. I believe now that he saw them as direct com-petition for him and definitely a way to get to me.

The first abuse of my pets that I witnessed involved my bird, Albert. I came home from work and found Albert sitting on my abuser's hand (this was unusual because Albert likes no one but me) and he had no tail feathers. I confronted my abuser about the lack of feathering, and he said that he hadn't done anything, they had just "fallen out." Albert had been a member of my family for a couple of years, and his feathers had never just "fallen out" on their own.

The next injury was to my cat Tom-tom. I found him on my porch, in obvious pain. I looked him over and realized that his back feet and his tail were severely burned and swollen. I immediately took him to the vet for treatment. It did not occur to me that my abuser had done this. I kept wondering, who of my neighbors would do such a thing to my cat? We had lived in the neighborhood for several years and nothing like this had ever happened to any of my pets. Hindsight is 20-20; I wish I would have figured it out sooner.

My abuser began drinking enough that the fuel for his fire was apparent even to me. As his drinking escalated, so did his anger, need to control, and resentment. I was at a complete loss about what to do. I knew I was in way over my head, but didn't have a clue how to get myself out of the insane asylum my life had become.

One evening, I became so frightened that I took my dogs and went to the nearest phone booth to call his parents for help. His mother came over. I watched, horrified, as my abuser pushed her up against the wall, slapped her, then pushed her down to the floor and dragged her from the hall into the living room. I remember feeling like I was watching a very bad movie. Everything was in slow motion as I picked up the phone and dialed 911 for the first of about 15 times.

The police responded and my abuser left at their request. I remember his mother wanted to press assault charges; I could not believe that they wouldn't let her! They said that he hadn't "done enough" injury to her for them to take her complaint. Up until then, I had thought that assault was assault—confusing new rules for me to find out about.

We had just purchased a new home together and were preparing to move. While we were moving the contents of the garage, I found his stash of empties—I had never seen so many cans! There was a 33-gallon garbage bag *stuffed* with 16-oz. beer cans.

After witnessing my abuser assault his mother, I went to his employer to ask for assistance in intervening to get my abuser into treatment. Not knowing much about addiction diseases, I naively thought that everything would be "fixed" once he got into treatment. All I did was create another source of resentment.

My pets and I were very traumatized by his behaviors. I still did not suspect that he had hurt my cat and bird or that I might be in any danger at all. After all, he said he loved me!

He used the move into our new home (which never felt like my home until three years later, when he was finally gone for good) as an excuse to impose new rules on my cats. Although they had been inside-outside and were used to sleeping on my bed at night, they were now committed to mainly outside, and locked in the garage at night. "After all," he told me, "you could never tell what those damn cats did sneaking around at night without supervision." I missed not having them around me.

I was without a job and had no savings to speak of and a new house that had no equity. I remember this was when I began to feel trapped and I started wishing he would go away or die. Whenever I was with him, I found that I was mentally "checking out" for longer periods of time just so I could stand to get through the day. I had found Al-Anon by then, but was afraid to leave him alone in the house with my pets. He had begun to threaten to take one or all of my cats out to dump them somewhere. I lived in terror that he would.

When I could not find my cats at night, I remember checking the wood stove and the garbage cans for their bodies. I was also afraid he would let my bird outside. My abuser seemed to like the dogs, so they weren't as big a concern as the rest of my "kids" were.

One afternoon, I could not find Miranda, my calico. I looked and looked, in the wood stove, in the fireplace, in the garbage can. I found her in the backyard hiding under the deck. She would not come to me. I could see that she was injured. Her right eye was swollen shut and one of her teeth was broken off at the tip. I knew in my heart that my abuser had done this to her—but since I had not caught him in the act, I felt like I couldn't confront him about her injuries. At the same moment, my denial kicked in and I wondered if she had been hit by a car.

Shortly after that, in August of 1993, I discovered my abuser in the garage with my orange cat Tom-tom. He had completely wrapped Tom-tom up with duct tape. Tom-tom's legs, feet and tail were taped to his little body. Tape was also wrapped around his head and neck. He had been laid, all trussed up, in the litter box.

I remember feeling, for the first time, what it was like to want to beat another person senseless with a board or tire iron. I had to physically clasp my hands behind my back so that I would not strike out at him. I was completely freaked out. I could not comprehend what I was seeing! I grabbed my cat from the litter box and ran to the phone to call the police. With a really smug look on his face, my abuser told me that he could kill Tom-tom if he wanted to, and he would kill me too. The police responded—but did nothing except request that he leave. I wanted them to *do something* to my abuser for hurting my cat. They said I had not been hurt and they had no recourse to prosecute him for anything. After all, it was just a cat.

I held Tom-tom and cut the tape into small sections. His eyes were huge, his little paws soaking wet. He remained perfectly still as I removed all the tape from his body, taking lots of fur with it. After what he had been through, he still trusted me. I felt so guilty that I had been unable to protect him.

Denial and financial fear are the great motivators of very bad decisions. After a few days, my abuser was again back at home, promising to be a good boy and promising to do better in his treatment. Hope does spring eternal, especially in a new marriage. I could not believe that my abuser would not get well and be the person I had married and I cared about. This person appeared just often enough to feed my hope and to keep me hooked.

I had taken Tom-tom to my vet, who kept him for a couple of weeks. I was so afraid for him at home. I also feared for my bird, not because he had been recently threatened, but because he was so vulnerable. My abuser's parents kept him at their house for a couple of weeks. I missed having them around. I could hardly stand it.

Christmas of 1993. A couple of days before, Tom-tom turned up with a broken leg, and Miranda had another puffed-up eye and would not come in the house, even if I were there. She ran and hid if she heard his voice or footsteps. I knew that my abuser was somehow responsible, but denial kicked in. I wondered about that car that kept hitting my cats.

All my friends, people I knew at the treatment center and other Al-Anon members, kept telling me that I was in danger and that they were worried about my safety. Even after I had witnessed all the animal abuse and the assault on his mother, I did not understand that I was probably next. After all, he said he loved me!

My abuser drank heavily from very early Christmas day to well into the evening. At 8:30 P.M. he assaulted me, enraged because I had told his mother he had been drinking all day. He pinned me down on the bed and, as I was trying to call 911 for help, he got the phone from me, smacked me just below my right eye, and began to come toward me with the cord stretched out like he was going to use it to choke me. I remember screaming and screaming—I looked to the end of the bed, and my dogs, Jasmine and Jack, were there. I remember they looked very confused and upset. They did not leave me, but did not know how to intervene. I pushed my abuser off me and ran down the hall screaming and shoving my dogs in front of me, terrified that he would hurt them.

I opened the front door and propelled my dogs outside. My abuser came up behind me, grabbed me, and threw me to the floor. I remember seeing the front door open, my dogs still there for me, looking through the screen door. I continued to scream, kicking at my abuser. I was finally able to get to the door and run outside. I ran to the neighbors and found they had already called 911 and the police were on the way.

My abuser took off when he found that the police were coming. I was thankful he left because I was worried about my other pets that were left behind in the house. with him. My eye began to swell, and I realized that I was also bleeding.

The police came and took a report, a picture, and left me with information on what I needed to do to follow through with my complaint and prosecute him for *misdemeanor* Assault IV. It sure did not feel like a misdemeanor to me. Misdemeanors are like traffic tickets, aren't they? He picked up garbage for six weekends as punishment for hitting me in the face with a telephone. It hardly seemed worth all the effort it took for me to have him prosecuted.

Depression really set in then. I found that I could hardly rouse myself off the couch. I felt hopeless and worthless. I began to think that one of us had to die, because I could not conceive that anything else would release me from this relationship. He obviously was not going to oblige me by dying. I was hospitalized for depression. The entire time there, all I wanted was to be able to go home and be with my dogs. I can't remember ever being so tired in all my life. I called Womenspace, the local woman's shelter, to see if they could help me. They could help me, but not my pets. I would not leave them behind. I felt really stuck.

My abuser's disease escalated rapidly. Another DUI on top of the assault was enough at the time to push him into in-house treatment. In retrospect, I believe he was going for "look-goods" for the judges. His going into treatment was the best thing that could have happened to me. The biggest key to my comprehension of my codependency was that the deeper my abuser fell into his disease of alcoholism, the more like my mother he behaved. I began my difficult road of recovery from codependency while my abuser was in treatment.

Things were better for a couple of months after he was released. My abuser amended with me and with my pets. Things seemed to at least be heading in the right direction. It was during this time that I lost Jasmine. I was devastated to have lost my friend of 15 years.

Eventually, my abuser stopped his self-care and stopped going to meetings. He had not begun to drink again that I could confirm, but I knew it was not *if* as much as *when*. I was afraid all over again. I had a job, but not one that would support me. We still had very little equity in our house. The house payment far exceeded my income.

My abuser's work day ended at 3:30 in the afternoon. I worked until 5. Every day at 3:30 I would begin to worry about my animals. It would make me ill. I knew I would find a drunk when I got home—I just didn't ever know what else I might find. The insanity returned. I began looking again in the garbage and wood stove when I could not find my cats, crying when I found them safe. Some days I could not make myself stay at work and I came home early because I was so afraid. I was so freaked out that I didn't have the time to grieve for Jasmine. I missed her. Jack missed her.

We had purchased vacation property in the mountains. My abuser spent time alone there and when I went up one weekend I caught him drinking again, confirming my earlier fears. My level of anxiety really increased. It was difficult for me to function, wondering when he would start in again with the cats, or my bird, or me. I hated him. I was now between jobs, working for several temporary agencies, and still was not making enough to support myself.

I was under constant pressure from him to go to the mountains. He had lost his driver's license and considered me his chauffeur. I did not like to go with him as he took off for hours at a time to drink and the trailer was isolated—very few neighbors and no telephone. I slept with my truck keys. I was afraid he would leave me there, or worse kill me and dump me in the surrounding forest.

With help from my therapist and family group at the treatment center, I was able to stick to a decision one weekend of not taking him to our vacation home. He got really angry and decided that he would drive himself. While he was gone, I had the locks changed on the house and put his belongings outside. Again, with help from my support group, for the first time I was able to stick to my decision and not let him back in. I also had gotten a job that would allow me to support myself. This was the beginning of the end of our marriage and of my abuser being in my life. I got to be the miracle instead of him.

The fear did not stop there, and I had to face my own demons in my disease of codependency. I don't want to make that journey again. The pain would often bring me to my knees. Sometimes I longed to return to the familiar insanity of my life with my abuser rather than face my painful journey. I was afraid I would not survive. But I have. The telling of my story is part of my recovery; it's about facing the fear and walking through it anyway.

My abuser had assaulted me again and had left the state to avoid prosecution. Overwhelmed by anger, I spent a few months writing letters to anyone I could think of to protest the inadequacies of the system. Although they knew where he had gone, they would not extradite him because the assault was another misdemeanor. I had to find a way to find some justice and equity, knowing that the system would not help me and he would get away with what he had done to me.

I decided to try to find a way for other battered women to leave their abusers without sacrificing their pets too. The opportunity arose in September of 1996 when the Centers for Disease Control and Prevention in Atlanta, Georgia, chose Eugene, Oregon, as one of three communities to receive a large multi-year grant to finance resources for victims of domestic violence and to fund community education projects. (The two other cities were Boston, Massachusetts, and Spokane, Washington.) Programs developed in these three communities were to be used as models for the rest of the country. I knew that this was the perfect opportunity to see if the emergency pet care that I had needed so badly could be made a part of this model. I called the director of the Greenhill Humane Society in Eugene, Kimball Lewis, to see if he could help.

Lewis has seen how abusers use animals to control their partners. Some of the abuses he investigated while working for the state Bureau of Animal Protection in southwestern Colorado included a litter of puppies stuffed into a coffee can and set on fire, and dogs, cats, and horses stabbed, slashed, or mutilated.

In February 1997, Greenhill announced its Domestic Violence Assistance Program (DVAP). A press conference held at the Humane Society shelter was attended by Oregon Congressman Peter DeFazio, Lane County District Attorney Doug Harcleroad, Captain Roy Brown and Lieutenant Becky Hansen of the Eugene Police Department, and Jennifer Inman, Project Coordinator of the Sacred Heart Medical Center Domestic Violence Project. DVAP offers emergency shelter for the pets of at-risk women who want to leave their abusive environments.

I was able to contact other agencies and form a community coalition that supports the Greenhill program. The DVAP is in community partnership with Womenspace, Lane County Domestic Violence Council, Lane County Victim Services, and Sacred Heart Medical Center Domestic Violence Project. Short- and long-term goals of this program are not only to establish a pet foster-care network, but also to coordinate community education by tapping into the network of other CDC coalition members; to form a referral system with resources such as Womenspace, Lane County District Attorney Victim Services, law enforcement and veterinarians; and ultimately to lay the foundation for training and implementing a cross-reporting system of agencies to protect all who are vulnerable to violence.

Prior to DVAP, victims in Lane County had the unacceptable choices of either leaving their animals behind or surrendering them to county animal control. In that situation, animals with known owners that were surrendered to animal control were euthanized and not offered for adoption. Now, DVAP's network of foster homes will take any companion animal from gerbils to horses and extends care until victims can accommodate their pets' safety, either on their own or by placing their pets with friends.

The opportunity to take control away from abusers by offering shelter for their victims' companion animals pleases Lewis. "I hope I am very unpopular with them. If we have a woman whose daughter or son had a steer as a 4-H project, we'd find a home for it. The idea is to give victims maximum mobility," he said.

Community leaders need to recognize that animal welfare and health and human service issues are both important parts of our social and economic health. Now that DVAP is a viable program, the direct benefit to health and human services can be accurately gauged. At this writing, the program has housed 18 to 20 animals, immediately impacting the lives of approximately 10 families. Greenhill has a roster of some 65 potential foster homes waiting for inspection.

I have been invited to tell my story at several meetings to put a face on the statistics. I have discovered there is not yet general awareness that *all* members of a household are at risk of violence, or awareness that victims often will not leave their abusive environment if they have to leave their pets behind. I am on the pathway to founding an organization that will raise consciousness about family violence and animal abuse and that will advocate solutions.

All victims are entitled to protection and should not be forced to sacrifice something they love in order to be safe. I am available to assist anyone interested in starting a similar emergency animal foster care program.

Connections—Animal Abuse

Animal shelters are the institutional centers for the ethic of compassion. Unfortunately, humane societies and SPCAs have not succeeded in putting themselves out of business.

—Elaine Sichel, *Circles of Compassion*

Men will be just toward men when they are charitable toward animals.

—Henry Bergh

The custom of tormenting and killing of beasts will, by degrees, harden their minds even towards men; and they who delight in the suffering and destruction of inferior creatures, will not be apt to be very compassionate or benign to those of their own kind.

—John Locke, *Some Thoughts Concerning Education,* 1705

The Battered Pet
Signs and Symptoms
Helen M. C. Munro

THE TERM *abuse* includes physical abuse, neglect, sexual abuse, and emotional abuse. This essay is about *physical abuse,* also known as *non-accidental injury* or *NAI.* The aim of this essay is to raise awareness of such abuse and to give veterinarians and other animal health personnel some overall guidelines on its diagnosis, within the current knowledge, which, it must be emphasized, is very limited. It is also hoped that by bringing the abuse to the profession's attention, we can begin to tap the wealth of experience that already exists but has never been quantified and analyzed.

SCENE-SETTING

In 1962, the physician Henry Kempe and his colleagues published a paper with the deliberately emotive title "The Battered Child Syndrome," and at long last the world and the medical profession began to pay attention to what Dr. Kempe had been saying for years—that parents could quite deliberately injure their children and then present them for medical examination (Lynch 1985). Since then, child physical abuse has been extensively researched and a wealth of information is now readily available to help health professionals differentiate between genuine accidental injuries and those which have been caused deliberately. In other words, the history, clinical signs, and pathology of child physical abuse are well documented.

It doesn't take much imagination to see that babies/young children and animals share one particular characteristic: *they cannot speak for themselves.* Yet, although "cruelty" to animals is universally acknowledged to occur, and a " typology" of cruelty has been postulated (Vermeulen & Odendaal 1993), there has been no attempt to describe the clinical signs and pathology of animal physical abuse. This means that the present situation for veterinarians and other animal health personnel parallels the one in which physicians and human health personnel operated before Kempe.

The author gratefully acknowledges the support of the Royal Society for the Prevention of Cruelty to Animals of England and Wales and the Scottish Society for Prevention of Cruelty to Animals.

DIFFICULTY OF DIAGNOSIS

Not only does the lack of information make the actual diagnosis of NAI very difficult, but the veterinarian, in particular, may find it hard even to *think* that deliberate physical abuse may be occurring—a phenomenon known to occur among physicians and described by Kempe so elegantly and tactfully as "emotional unwillingness" to "recognize abuse as the cause of the child's difficulty." Modern textbooks on child abuse all warn of the same phenomenon. For example, in the *ABC of Child Abuse,* Nigel Speight (1993) cautions that "The most important step in diagnosing injury is to force yourself to think of it in the first place." Veterinarians need to remember that this may also apply to them. They may find it will help if they can learn to "forgive themselves" for having missed cases in the past.

Some veterinarians may feel that the diagnosis of "battered pet" poses a dilemma, because they consider that not only do they have an animal welfare responsibility to their patient, they also have a responsibility of confidentiality to the patient's owner, their client. But in view of the increasingly large volume of evidence that animal abuse may indicate more generalized abuse in the family and may also predict future antisocial behavior, it is time for veterinarians to consider, in addition to their animal welfare responsibilities, their more general social responsibilities. Before Kempe, the medical profession collectively buried its head in the sand and denied that child physical abuse existed. First impressions may be that the veterinary profession has acted along similar lines but recent research by the author indicates that this is not so. Many veterinarians, independent of one another, have recognized that deliberate abuse occurs.

The new American Veterinary Medical Association (AVMA) (1996) position on cruelty to animals, animal abuse, and animal neglect and an amendment to the Model Veterinary Practices Act calls for veterinarians to take responsibility for reporting such cases to the appropriate authorities:

> The AVMA recognizes that veterinarians may have occasion to observe cases of cruelty to animals, animal abuse, or animal neglect as defined by state law or local ordinances. When these observations occur, the AVMA considers it the responsibility of the veterinarian to report such cases to the appropriate authorities. Such disclosures may be necessary to protect the health and welfare of animals and people.

In the United Kingdom, the Code of Conduct of the Royal College of Veterinary Surgeons (1996) states in the section on confidentiality that veterinarians may divulge information to a third party "where in an exceptional case they are clearly of the opinion that animal welfare or the public interest is so endangered as to outweigh any obligation to the owner."

SOCIAL BACKGROUND

Physical abuse seems to be reported more often from homes where there is poverty and deprivation. Veterinarians working at clinics run by animal welfare organizations for owners who cannot afford veterinary fees are often uneasily aware that they see, or suspect, more than their fair share of cases. As with children, however, abuse also occurs in more affluent homes, where it may remain unsuspected and undiagnosed. DeViney, Dickert, and Lockwood (1983) found high prevalence of physical animal abuse among families where physical child abuse was present, and also found that these families made visits to veterinarians at rates consistent with cultural norms.

One of the aims of this essay is to promote discussion of how to deal with a client (including the more affluent one) who brings a possible abuse case to the surgery. It is neither an easy nor comfortable situation but the medical profession has shown that the problem can be tackled. Clearly, as in child abuse, multidisciplinary investigations may be needed.

PERPETRATORS

In distinct contrast to child physical abuse, where parents of both sexes may batter their children, present knowledge indicates that, in the vast majority of cases, it is men who batter animals (Watt and Waran 1993). (Both sexes neglect or abandon them.) This apparent difference is interesting but it is always possible the picture will alter with more research.

PREVALENCE AND INCIDENCE

Prevalence refers to the number of cases in the population at any one time. *Incidence* refers to the number of new cases over a period of time (usually, one year).

Reliable estimates of prevalence and incidence of animal abuse are not available; without guidelines for the recognition and diagnosis of NAI, nor clear definitions as to what exactly constitutes "animal abuse," neither has been accurately recorded or researched. It should be remembered that in the 35 years post-Kempe, researchers have found it very difficult to come up with consistent research data on the true prevalence and incidence of physical abuse in children (Gillham 1994). This does not constitute a warning against conducting similar research regarding animal abuse; it is merely a caveat that to carry out this research may not be as simple as it first appears. Much can be gained by studying the development of child abuse research methodology and by using accepted child abuse terminology. This approach facilitates understanding between veterinarians and other health professionals.

RANGE AND NATURE OF PHYSICAL ABUSE

As with children, physical abuse to animals is wide and varied. The most common type, in the United Kingdom, is kicking, followed by punching, beating with an instrument, and throwing across the room, upstairs, downstairs, and out of the window. Other types include administration of drugs and poisons, asphyxiation, burning and scalding, drowning, shooting and stabbing.

DIAGNOSTIC FEATURES

Having established that any research in this difficult area is in its infancy, what do we know so far that can begin to help us identify the battered pet? It will not come as a surprise that the diagnostic pointers that follow will be very familiar to those with a knowledge of the signs and symptoms of child physical abuse. None is absolutely diagnostic, but neither does the absence of any of them exclude NAI. It goes without saying that it is essential to take a careful history and be meticulous both with the clinical examination and any necropsy.

The cases in the following sections illustrate these pointers. The sections cover the history given by the owner, behavioral signs, clinical signs and pathology, and also include special forms of abuse.

History

The account of the accident does not fit with the injury observed.

Case 1. A kitten was presented with the claws missing from all his feet. The owner's explanation was that the kitten had been dropped into a hot bath but there was no evidence of scalding. The veterinarian suspected that the claws had been forcibly removed, the owner's behavior reinforcing this suspicion.

The owner refuses to comment on how the injury came about.

Case 2. A thin Rottweiler dog had a four-inch-long wound on his right flank. The wound penetrated to the ribs. Two smaller cuts were present on the left elbow. The veterinarian considered that the wounds were caused by a blunt instrument but the owner refused to comment on how the dog was injured.

The owner shows a lack of concern for the animal's injures.

Case 3. A working collie was seen to have a fractured fore-leg while being used to drive sheep. She was in considerable pain and the veterinarian found that the fracture was not recent. The owner stated, "I think she was hit by a car or had been in a fight about two weeks ago. I though that she would get better as it had happened before."

There is a delay in seeking veterinary treatment.

Case 4. A concerned neighbor reported a severely lame twelve-week-old collie puppy to an animal welfare society. The puppy was found to have a fractured foreleg. The owner claimed that the puppy had "fallen off the sofa" two days before. No veterinary treatment had been sought.

Behavioral Signs

The animal may be subdued or openly frightened in the owner's presence but becomes open, happy, and affectionate when the owner goes away or when the animal is hospitalized. Some may even appear desperate to please any person who takes an interest in them. Others take a long time to regain their trust in humans. However, it is important to realize that a maltreated pet will by no means always appear frightened of an abusive owner. Many an abused animal has given a remarkable welcome to a returning owner who is known to have been abusive.

Case 5. A Labrador was finally rescued from his owner, an abusive man who, over many months, had beaten and burned him. He was extremely friendly, well-behaved, and quiet with the animal welfare officers but his demeanor immediately and totally changed when he saw his owner again. He appeared terrified and made desperate efforts to get away. The welfare officers commented that they found his behavior really pitiful.

Clinical Signs and Pathology

Fractures. Fractures are important indicators. Multiple fractures in various bones, in different stages of healing, should give cause for concern, particularly when the history offered does not fit.

Case 6. A four-month-old puppy was presented with multiple fractures. She had fractures of the femur, pelvis, and ribs, all estimated to be about two to three weeks old, and a fracture of the tibia, approximately five to six weeks old. In addition, there were two large open wounds on the skin overlying the broken ribs. Her owner claimed that the pup had "fallen down some steps and she was limping but I thought it was getting better." Later she changed her story and said that she did not know how the puppy had been hurt.

Case 7. Neighbors were suspicious when they saw a husband and wife carrying something heavy, wrapped in a blanket, into the garden. The two then dug a hole and buried what they had been carrying. Police and animal welfare officers were called to the scene and dug up the body of a large dog wrapped in a blanket. At necropsy, the dog was found to have hemorrhaged from the right ear and had extensive subcutaneous and muscle hemorrhage over her neck, shoulders, and thoracic verte-brae. In addition, she had multiple healed fractures to both sides of her ribs.

Bruising. In abused children, the pattern and appearance of bruising is well docu-mented (Kessler & Hyden 1991). These stereotypical patterns include forceful slaps that leave the outline of individual fingers, finger, or thumb prints; linear marks that indicate beating with a belt or strap; thin, circumferential bruises around ankles and wrists indicative of binding with cords or rope; thicker marks indicating friction burns from sheeting material; similar marks in the corners of the mouth suggest-ing that the child was gagged; bizarre-shaped marks with sharp borders generally caused by blunt instruments such as a hairbrush, comb, or fork; and paired, crescent-shaped bruises associated with teeth marks.

In farm animals, bruising associated with transportation or beating is well rec-ognized but the situation of domestic pets is much less certain. The differentiation of bruising arising from accidental trauma from that caused by deliberate injury is under investigation. Tenderness over the injured area may well be a sensitive in-dicator of what is present subcutaneously, even in the stoic patient. Where it is fea-sible, shaving or clipping suspected areas may be rewarding in both light- and dark-skinned animals.

Experience has shown that clinically detectable bruises around, say, the head and face are generally found to be much more extensive when examined at necropsy. Where there is a suspicion of abuse and a necropsy is indicated, it is essential that reflection of the skin over the head, thorax, limbs, and pelvis is carried out, so that bruising that is inapparent on clinical examination will not be missed. In addition, in animals subjected to repetitive abuse, old healing bruises will come to light. It is not uncommon for injuries to be repeated to the same area (e.g., over the spine of the shoulder blade) and for new bruising to be superimposed on areas of previous hemorrhage.

As mentioned before, the pattern of bruising in abused pets is still being inves-tigated. Nevertheless, some bruises are sufficiently unusual for deliberate injury to be suspected. For example, single or multiple bruising over the mid-rib area behind the shoulder blade, in the absence of *clear* evidence such as a motor vehicle accident, might be regarded with some concern.

Bruising caused by whips on horses and sticks on cattle at markets are often linear and approximate to the shape of the instrument causing the injury. In small animals, the angle of striking is usually downwards and the length of the stick, broom handle, or other implement may not hit the skin. Consequently, the bruise that results may be round rather than linear and may give a false impression of the object used. Flexible instruments such as a chain lead may be more liable to cause linear bruising.

Case 8. A man admitted beating his nine-month-old bitch to death. Externally, findings on the body were limited: general pallor, a small bruise on the abdomen, a small skin tear at the medial canthus of one eye, skin abrasions on the nose and chin, and tears in the upper gums near the canine teeth. Internally, however, there was subcutaneous bruising over the head, bruising on the medial aspect of the right stifle and elbow, and hemorrhage extending over the thorax to the abdomen. In addition, there were multiple bilateral rib fractures, which had caused a pneumothorax, and the liver was ruptured in several places.

Eye Injuries. There is a large amount of knowledge with regard to eye injuries and their association with child abuse (for example, retinal hemorrhages are one of the cardinal signs in the "shaken baby syndrome") but there are no firm data with regard to animals. Suspicions sometimes have been aroused by eye injuries, such as scleral hemorrhages, for which the owner's explanation is unsatisfactory. This is an area that needs more research, both by clinicians and pathologists.

Case 9. Intraocular hemorrhages were found in a small dog. The veterinarian was told in confidence by the owner that the injury had been caused by violence from her husband. The owner also said that her husband beat her.

Burns and Scalds. In children, although certain burn and scald patterns are recognized (for example, cigarette burns, immersion burns, splash burns, or "stocking" burns on the feet) (Barnard et al. 1995), the actual separation of the purely accidental from the non-accidental injury may still be difficult, particularly when the child is too young to speak.

In domestic animals, little is presently known about the pattern of injuries caused by deliberate actions. However, pouring or splashing scalds are liable to be on the back or head. Careful questioning of the owner may reveal a history that may not match the injury.

Case 10. A very depressed golden retriever was brought to the surgery with extensive and severe burns over her back. The young veterinarian realized that the owners were uneasy but accepted their story that the dog had been burned when she jumped up to the stove and upset a pan of very hot soup over herself. They also said that they hadn't realized just how bad the burn was and that was why they had delayed coming to the surgery—hence their guilt feeling, the vet thought. Only afterwards she did wonder why the burns hadn't been over the front part of the dog's body.

Case 11. A witness saw a 15-year-old boy burning a 10-month-old kitten in a large garbage can. The boy claimed that the kitten had already been dead. At necropsy, it was found that the body was burned on all surfaces, but the internal organs were still fresh. Soot and burns were present in the airways, indicating that the kitten had been breathing at the time of burning.

Special Forms of Abuse

Munchausen syndrome by proxy. In the veterinary context, Munchausen syndrome by proxy refers to circumstances where physical signs are faked or deliberately caused to an animal by the owner, who then, to satisfy his or her own need for attention, takes the animal for treatment. Repetitive injury to the animal may occur.

Case 12. An adult old English sheepdog arrived at the surgery with a fracture of the femur. Her owner said that the dog had "slipped on ice." Two weeks later, the dog was back at the surgery, this time having "fallen downstairs." She now had a second fracture of the same leg, one inch below the first fracture. Some weeks later, her owner called the surgery to report that her dog had "fallen down a drain" but the person taking the call did note that she seemed unconcerned about any injuries. Two weeks later, the owner called the surgery again and two veterinary nurses went to her home. The dog was wrapped in a sweater and lying on a urine-soaked blanket, her face caked with blood from a seeping wound. Both her forelegs were fractured, one of the fractures being compound. Both breaks had occurred some days before. The owner was in tears and claimed that her dog had been attacked by a neighbor's dog.

Drowning. Deliberate drowning of an animal occurs more commonly than is appreciated. Animals of all ages can be drowned—in the bathtub, a container, a river, pond, or sea. If drowned in the home, the body is often buried in the garden, usually wrapped in a piece of material, such as a towel. It may seem an obvious point but because the coat retains water, the body is usually wet.

Drowning requires effort and, sometimes, planning. Inevitably an animal being drowned needs to be restrained or held down by some weight. Restraint may consist of a rope, bag, box, or weight or the animal may merely be held under water. Attempted drownings do occur and may even be presented at the veterinarian's office.

Externally, there may be very little to see, although small amounts of blood may issue from the nose. But the history given by the owner may be less than convincing.

It should be appreciated that, unfortunately, necropsy of suspected drownings may not provide clear evidence of drowning. Froth, sometimes blood-stained, may be found in the trachea and larger airways but many cases show very little. Bruises may give an indication if the limbs have been held or tied together or where the body has been pressed to the bottom of the bath or container.

Case 13. A mongrel puppy was taken to the veterinarian's office, unable to stand and in shock. The owner said she had "fallen downstairs." Three months later she was brought in again, collapsed and dying. She was dripping blood-stained fluid from her mouth and nose and she was wet. There were no other obvious external findings. She died shortly afterwards. The owner's story this time was that while he was bathing her she jumped out of the tub but was unable to keep her balance and fell over. At necropsy, the pathologists found extensive internal bruising on the left side of her face, right side of her neck, over her left shoulder, inside and outside the right side of the chest wall and over her back in the lumbar region and pelvis. It was considered that she had received a blow of considerable force to the right side of her chest and that the pattern of the bruising was consistent with her having been held down against a hard surface. Both lungs showed only congestion. The trachea was clear. Histopathology of the lungs showed only congestion and hemorrhage. The bruising over the left shoulder showed recent hemorrhage but, significantly, had an older injury that was healing in the center.

Asphyxiation. Asphyxiation covers a variety of conditions that result in interference with oxygen uptake and utilization, together with failure to eliminate carbon dioxide. Causes include inadequate oxygen in inspired air, obstruction to air passages, and restriction of chest movements. Of these, strangulation by ligature or by hanging may represent the most common forms of non-accidental asphyxiation.

Case 14. A well-nourished collie was found hanged by a piece of rope in a stairwell. Her owner was very distressed and claimed that some youths had wrestled his dog away from him, tied the rope around the dog's neck, and dropped her over the bannisters. The pathologist noted that there were no external marks on the body, but dissection revealed hemorrhage on the ventral and left lateral larynx, over the angles of the jaw and around the glosso-epiglottic fold.

Administration of drugs and poisons. The compounds administered are frequently those which are used by the owner. They include, for example, alcohol, cannabis, heroin, cocaine, amphetamines, and paracetamol.

Case 15. A dog belonging to a self-confessed drug addict was presented with a temperature of 108F, hyperaesthesia, dilated pupils, repetitive movements, hypersalivation, tachycardia, and tachypnea. It was believed that amphetamines had been administered to this dog.

A FINAL WORD

The key to preventing the abuses described in the case examples just presented is the establishment of diagnostic criteria that separate accidental from deliberate injury. We are in a veterinary "pre-Kempe era"; research and a sharing of information are urgently required. We must tap the experience of veterinarians and other health professionals, both human and animal, and collate their information. Only then will the salient diagnostic features be identified more quickly and the lot of abused animals—and the animals' "families"—improved.

REFERENCES

American Veterinary Medical Association. 1996. *Animal Welfare: Position statements and background information*, 2. Schaumburg, Ill.: American Veterinary Medical Association.

Barnard, S., C. Parry, M. Edwards, E. Muslim, and M. Kaufmann. 1995. *A training guide for recognizing and reporting child abuse for animal control officers and humane investigators.* Englewood, Colo.: American Humane Association.

DeViney, E., J. Dickert, and R. Lockwood. 1983. The care of pets within child abusing families. *International Journal for the Study of Animal Problems* 4:321–29.

Gillham, B. 1994. *The facts about child physical abuse.* London: Cassell.

Kempe, C. H, F. N. Silverman, B. F. Steele, W. Droegemuller, and H. K. Silver. 1962. The battered child syndrome. *Journal of the American Medical Association* 181:17–24.

Kessler, D. B., and P. Hyden. 1991. Physical, sexual, and emotional abuse of children. *Clinical Symposia* 43(1). Summit, N.J.: Ciba-Geigy.

Lynch, M. A. 1985. Child Abuse before Kempe: An Historical Review. *Child Abuse and Neglect* 9:7–15.

Royal College of Veterinary Surgeons. 1996. *Guide to professional conduct*, 21. London: Royal College of Veterinary Surgeons.

Speight, N. 1993. Non-Accidental Injury. In R. Meadow, ed., *ABC of child abuse.* London: BMJ Publishing Group.

Vermeulen, H, and J. S.J Odendaal. 1993. Proposed typology of animal abuse. *Anthrozoös* 6:248–57.

Watt, S. L., and N. K. Waran. 1993. Companion animal cruelty: Who are the offenders? *Applied Animal Behavior Science* 35:295–96 (abstract).

Why The Link Is Important to Animal Care, Animal Control, and Veterinary Personnel

Laurel Lagoni, Carolyn Butler, and Patricia Olson

> The devaluing of animal life is a kind of training ground for devaluing all life.
> —Gloria Steinem

MORE PEOPLE IN the United States today have pets than children. One study (Voith 1985) shows that 99 percent of dog and cat owners consider their pets full-fledged members of their families. The status and positive regard that most companion animals enjoy is based on strong, healthy bonds or attachments that form between animals and their human owners. When attachments remain strong, animals are loved, cared for, and protected.

Unfortunately, in our increasingly violent society, there are more and more people and animals who share a home, but do not share the deep attachments that offer animals a high quality of life. Without feelings of attachment, many animals are neglected, subjected to cruelty, and even abused.

The same premise can be applied to parents and their children, as well as to husbands and wives. The majority of children benefit from healthy bonds that form between them and their parents and thus are loved, cared for, and protected. Likewise, many married couples enjoy healthy, loving relationships. But when the various members of families do not attach in healthy ways, they can be in danger of becoming victims of some form of domestic violence.

Attachment was first investigated by studying the relationships between mothers and infants in humans, nonhuman primates, and other species of animals. In those studies, when mothers failed to form attachments to their infants, the infants often exhibited symptoms collectively termed "failure to thrive" and some were further deemed to be "at risk" in terms of their potential to be neglected, treated cruelly, and even abused.

The parallels between how animal and human family members are treated in terms of attachment theory leads to the assumption that other parallels exist as well. In support of this hypothesis, numerous studies demonstrate that there is a significant link between animal neglect, cruelty, and abuse and other forms of domestic violence like child and spousal abuse. Examples of this link drawn from research and clinical experience include

1. the strong association between childhood cruelty toward animals and later adult criminal behavior;
2. violence toward animals as a form of punishing children, perpetrated by parents;
3. animal abuse used as a threat to maintain the silence of abused children;
4. forced sexual interaction of children with animals;
5. the ritual mutilation or killing of animals as reported by children who have been victimized by pornographers or ritualistic abusers; and
6. animal abuse as a prelude to child or spouse abuse.

MULTIDISCIPLINARY OBSERVATION

Ten years ago, while employed as a social worker on a nationally renowned Department of Social Services' Child Protection Team, one of the authors of this article investigated a case of third-party sexual assault on a child. The case involved an eight-year-old girl who had been sexually assaulted by her schizophrenic mother's male roommate. Along with other forms of abuse, the man had intercourse with the child and infected her with gonorrhea. After a very difficult court process that ultimately resulted in a plea bargain, the man was sentenced to eight years in prison with the expectation he would be released in four. For her protection, the child was placed in foster care. This move forced the child to leave behind her cat that she loved very deeply. Because at that time the links between animal abuse and child abuse were not known to the author or to the other members of the child protection team, no one acknowledged the bond the young girl had with her pet or the possibility that the cat also had been abused and could be at risk for abuse in the future.

Several months ago, a veterinarian with whom the authors work received a call from a colleague who was treating a dog who had been severely abused. In this case, the animal's owner had hanged the dog, beat him until he became unconscious, and then buried him alive. A neighbor witnessed the incident, rescued the dog after the deranged owner left the scene, and rushed the dog to a nearby veterinary clinic. This veterinarian dealt with the medical needs of the dog, but now needed to know how to relieve the animal's and the neighbor's emotional distress. The dog whined and cried constantly and was unable to sleep. The neighbor also showed signs of trauma in that she seemed overly protective of the dog and mistrusting of the veterinarian and his staff. In addition, the neighbor confided that two children lived in the house and may also have been abused.

In another incident, one of the authors was asked to consult, as a veterinary specialist in reproduction, to identify the type of spermatozoa present in the vagina of a sexually abused toddler. The attending physicians and pathologists recognized that the sperm were not of human origin, and believed the father had somehow forced the family dog to participate in the sexual assault, or had collected the dog's sperm to cover his own abuse of the girl. According to the district attorney, the father had told the attending physician that he knew dogs could rape little girls as he had observed it many times in the adult videos he watched.

Abuse cases involving animals, children, or adults do not always come to the attention of the appropriate authorities. In fact, they rarely do. Families prone to domestic violence and children and animals who are at risk of abuse may be observed by people who work in a variety of professions. Because the cycle of abuse often starts with the abuse of animals, animal care, animal control, and veterinary medical personnel are often asked to respond to adults, children, and animals in need, even when they feel that what is called for is out of their realm of expertise and clearly outside their comfort zone.

The case of Tammie (not her real name) is a prime example. Five years ago, 12-year-old Tammie was present when her injured horse was euthanized at Colorado State University's Veterinary Teaching Hospital. The child was distraught about the animal's death because the horse was injured while she was riding him during a barrel-racing competition. The child's mother asked one of the counselors with Changes: The Support for People and Pets Program to provide grief support to the child, adding that the child's father was an alcoholic and that the child seemed to be afraid of him. Over the course of four grief counseling sessions, the child revealed that her father had had sexually inappropriate contact with her. Subsequently, a court case ensued and the father was ordered to have no unsupervised contact with his daughter. In this case, the primary witness in a child abuse case was not a social worker, but a grief counselor affiliated with the professional veterinary medical community.

All three of the authors of this article have encountered situations where the link between animal and child abuse is evident. Many of these situations have involved veterinary medical students who experience severe anxiety and distress when memories of childhood abuse resurface. These memories are often triggered by the overwhelming nature of the professional veterinary medical curriculum, which can restimulate feelings of "helplessness" or of "being out of control." In addition, some students' feelings are stirred when they witness the suffering or death of an animal they can not protect or save.

As these examples demonstrate, animals and humans affected by domestic violence can be identified in a myriad of settings. Professionals who serve animal populations occasionally observe incidents of human abuse and vice versa. Thus, there is a need for information regarding the links between animal abuse and child or spouse abuse to become more common knowledge within all disciplines of the helping professions. There is also a need for more multidisciplinary, cross-professional training programs regarding abuse assessment and reporting.

In this essay we address the reasons that the link between animal abuse and child or spouse abuse is important to animal care, animal control, and veterinary personnel. For the purpose of this essay, these professionals are collectively referred to as "animal caregivers."

FIVE REASONS WHY THE LINK IS IMPORTANT TO ANIMAL CAREGIVERS

A helping profession is one that provides direct services to people in order to fulfill one or more of those persons' needs. This definition encompasses a wide range of services, from physicians who treat ill or injured human patients to mental health professionals who provide crisis intervention to child care providers who nurture and protect the children of working parents. Because animal caregivers also provide valuable services in order to meet one or more of the needs of people and animals, they are by definition part of the helping profession. Animal caregivers, like all other members of the helping professions, must accept that animal abuse, spouse abuse, and child abuse and neglect are realities of life. Abuse and neglect cut across all cultural, educational, and socioeconomic lines. Incidents happen in large cities and in small, rural communities.

There are five main reasons why the link between animal abuse and child or spousal abuse are important to animal caregivers. These are

1. All animal caregivers *will* encounter incidences of abuse at some point in their careers.
2. Animal caregivers are well-equipped to assess both human and animal neglect, cruelty, and abuse.
3. Animal caregivers are in a position to break the cycle of abuse by reporting it and, in some cases, are morally and ethically bound to do so.
4. Animal caregivers are part of the community of helping professionals.
5. Animal caregivers can help victims begin the healing process by supporting grief.

Let's examine each of these reasons in more depth.

All animal caregivers will *encounter incidences of abuse at some point in their careers.* Animal, child, and spouse abuses are prevalent and inseparable. Potent statistics support this statement. For example, family violence is the leading cause of injury for U.S. women 15 to 44 years of age and, according to the results of one study of families being treated for occurrences of the physical abuse of children, 88 percent of the families had animals in the home who had also been abused (DeViney, Dickert, & Lockwood 1983).

There are several possible explanations for the prevalence of animal abuse in families where domestic violence occurs. For example, some abusers view animals as symbolic of someone or something else in their lives and use animals as avenues of retaliation. Still other abusers take out their frustrations on pets rather than hurting or abusing their children. Children in violent homes frequently participate in "pecking order battering," which results in the killing or maiming of animals or the battering of siblings. Being on the receiving end of abuse may leave children feeling powerless, thus they attempt to manage their feelings of helplessness by abusing their family's pets.

Animal caregivers are well-equipped to assess human and animal neglect, cruelty, and abuse. The formal training animal caregivers receive allows them to understand normal animal behavior as well as plausible explanations of an animal's physical injuries. For instance, animal caregivers have a clear understanding of how healthy, well-adjusted animals behave and understand the emotional and psychological needs of animals. They know, then, that a dog who cringes when his owner approaches or a cat whose ribs have been repeatedly broken, supposedly due to "clumsiness and several falls off the fence," are the most likely victims of abuse.

In most cases, animal caregivers have face-to-face contact with their human clientele. These daily interactions allow animal caregivers to observe suspicious human behavior or physical injuries, overhear comments that may indicate abuse has occurred, serve as confidantes for human victims of abuse, and even witness abusive acts as they occur.

As part of assessment, animal caregivers are in a position to document injuries, suspicious behavior, and inconsistent medical findings. They can also ask questions in order to determine whether or not a person's or an animal's injuries are consistent with the cause that is given. This foundation can help animal caregivers identify neglect or abuse. It can also help build viable legal cases against abusers.

Animal caregivers are in a position to break the cycle of abuse by reporting it and, in some cases, are morally and ethically bound to do so. Animal caregivers who identify animal abuse may be seeing just the "tip of the iceberg." Because patterns of domestic violence often begin with animal abuse, injured pets may be the first indicator that other forms of abuse are occurring in the home. Therefore, in some cases, animal caregivers may be able to actually prevent abuse from escalating and to break the cycle of family violence simply by reporting it. As one veterinarian says, "As far as I'm concerned, it's my job as a veterinarian to report. We're the first line of defense for these animals." Animal caregivers are often the first line of defense for children and abused spouses as well, because reporting animal abuse to appropriate authorities may also bring human victims of abuse into the view of appropriate professionals who can thoroughly assess whether or not they are at risk.

When it comes to abuse, some animal caregivers resist taking on roles resembling those of "counselors" or "social workers." They adamantly declare that, because their missions involve serving animals, the protection and care of animals are their *first and only* priorities. But many other animal caregivers disagree. They have no problem with also being helpers and advocates for people. In fact, many of them believe that both the Veterinarian's Oath and the Principles of Veterinary Medical Ethics by which many animal caregivers abide are human-oriented as well as animal-oriented, as each charges members of the veterinary medical field with promoting and safeguarding the public health and with contributing to the communities in which they live. Therefore, they feel they are just as obligated to prioritize and attend to human needs. As William McCulloch (1985, 423) says:

> In addition to caring for animal patients, today's veterinarian is responsible, directly or indirectly, for maintaining and improving the physical, mental, and emotional well-being of his or her clients. Society has only recently begun to realize that veterinarians in companion animal practice are more than "luxury" practitioners serving those who can afford pets. They are increasingly applying their veterinary skills, knowledge, and resources to the protection and improvement of human health.

In reality, though, most animal caregivers and veterinary medical professionals do not carry out the duties of their jobs with an exclusive focus on meeting either animal or human needs. In fact, in a survey conducted at Tufts University, veterinary students were asked, "Do you see yourself first serving clients or animals?" On a 10-point scale, with 1 representing clients and 10 representing animals, the students placed themselves, on average, at 7 on the scale. It can be concluded that animal caregivers attempt to strike a balance between the care they provide for animals and the emotional support they provide for humans.

Veterinarians take an oath to use their scientific knowledge and skills for, among other things, "the benefit of society" and the "promotion of public health." According to the terms of the oath, they also promise to accept as their "lifelong obligation" the continual improvement of their "professional knowledge and competence." Veterinarians also agree to abide by the Principles of Veterinary Medical Ethics (LaFrana 1993, 43). Within the principles, one of the stated Guidelines for Professional Behavior is: "Veterinarians should seek for themselves and their profession the respect of their colleagues, their clients, and the public through courteous verbal interchange, considerate treatment, professional appearances, professionally acceptable procedures, and the utilization of current professional and scientific knowledge. Veterinarians should be concerned with the affairs and welfare of their communities, including the public health."

Research suggests that there is a correlation between social support and the quality of people's physical and mental health (Lynch 1977). Thus, if people's mental and emotional well-being are included in the definition of public health, it becomes the veterinarian's responsibility to assess and report suspected abuse so that its adverse affects can be minimized or prevented altogether. Although animal caregivers other than veterinarians may not be legally required or ethically bound by oath to report abuse, they are morally bound to do so. As professionals, animal caregivers have responsibilities to each other and to society to act when they see something that is wrong. If abuse is ignored or condoned, those observing it become part of the problem.

It is more likely that victims will share information about neglectful or abusive treatment with a person such as an animal caregiver who is seen as less threatening and not considered to be in a position of legal authority. This kind of disclosure (one that is not solicited or coerced) has more strength in the legal system because it was expressed openly and willingly. Thus, information of this nature should always be passed on to the appropriate authorities for further investigation. In the states of California and Colorado, animal control officers and veterinarians, respectively, are mandated by law to report child abuse (Arkow 1994).

Animal-caregivers are part of the community of helping professionals. Because animal caregivers provide valuable services in order to meet one or more of the physical, psychological, emotional, social, or spiritual needs of people and animals, they are by definition part of the helping profession community.

Like other members of the helping professions, animal caregivers are often asked to respond to complex situations that call for sophisticated helping techniques. They are thrust into the middle of private family matters and asked to handle disputes, resolve conflicts, report abuse, and at times, confront potentially dangerous individuals. Regardless of the situation, it is assumed that animal caregivers just naturally know how to handle these situations, even though little training has been provided, financial resources are often limited, and back-up support is often nonexistent.

Because most animal caregivers are trained to assist animals, but not formally taught how to help humans, most do not have a great deal of knowledge in the area of helping. A survey conducted by Fogle and Abrahamson (1990) reports on this deficiency in training. The example they cite states that 96 percent of veterinarians surveyed had received no training on how to explain terminal illness to clients and 72 percent thought this training would be helpful. It can be assumed that an even higher percentage of animal caregivers would claim to have received no training regarding identifying and reporting incidents of abuse.

When incidents of abuse come to light, animal caregivers often witness the manifestations of the victims' fears and anxieties. Like others who witness emotional crises, many want to reach out to victims, but are unsure about the kind of help they can appropriately provide. When people are in the midst of emotional crises, it is hard to know what to say or to do that will comfort, rather than offend them. This feeling of helplessness is supported by a research study which showed that 80 percent of women and 74 percent of men reported feeling sympathetic and indicated they would like to respond in a supportive manner when someone else cries. Yet the majority of subjects said they typically did not respond because they simply did not know what to say or what to do.

It is every animal caregiver's responsibility to move beyond the feelings of awkwardness and self-consciousness and learn to deal with people who have experienced incidents of neglect, cruelty, and abuse. As valuable, contributing members of the helping profession community, animal caregivers are in prime positions to act as educators, sources of support, facilitators, and resource and referral guides.

As educators, animal caregivers can take advantage of the informal opportunities they have to teach people about proper and humane ways to treat animals and people. They can also take steps to better educate themselves, their staffs, and their clients about family violence.

As sources of support, animal caregivers can listen to peoples' feelings of fear, anger, and shame without trying to "fix" their problems with advice, rationalizations, or heroic rescues as these techniques are not helpful or appropriate when dealing with another person's emotions. Rather, supportive animal caregivers can normalize their clients' feelings, give them permission to express their thoughts and emotions, and listen attentively to their painful stories. Listening is an overlooked skill in many professions and animal caregiving is no exception. Animal caregivers sometimes think they cannot be of help unless they know the "right" thing to say or the "right" thing to do. Yet people in distress often find that it is infinitely more comforting to simply sit with someone who understands and can openly listen to what is being said.

As facilitators, animal caregivers can help people decide what to do next. This can be done by asking questions, making suggestions, and reviewing pertinent facts about each situation. Facilitators never "take charge" of another person's life, but rather provide enough structure to prevent emotions from interfering with the goals to be accomplished. For example, in incidents of abuse, the first task that often must be accomplished is connecting the victim of abuse or neglect with appropriate community resources. Community resources are agencies, programs, organizations, or groups that can be drawn on during times of need. In cases of abuse and neglect, the people and programs offering expertise in particular areas of human-related and animal-related services certainly qualify as resources. These resources exist so facilitators can direct and refer those in need to them.

Referring people to community resources means leading them or showing them the way. When animal caregivers act as referral guides they inform people about available resources and sometimes make recommendations about which are most appropriate for them to contact. In order to do this, animal caregivers must know in advance who and what are available in their community. The general rule about

making referrals is to give people information about how to contact community resources, but then to let individuals who are in need do the "leg work" themselves. In
reality, the more people do for themselves, the more control they feel over their situations.

In most areas there are numerous resources that troubled individuals and families can use. This being the case, it can be viewed as neglectful to not report suspected abuse or neglect and let the appropriate authorities handle the case.

Animal caregivers can help victims begin the healing process by supporting grief.
Unfortunately, many abused animals either die or need to be euthanized due to severe injuries. Because most animal caregivers are well-acquainted with animal
death, they are also familiar with the grief that accompanies loss.

Even under the best of circumstances, grief can be difficult to support. When
animal death has occurred due to abuse, people's grief responses can become extremely complicated. When humans have survived abuse and their companion animals have not, their grief is often complicated by guilt and unfinished business. Animal caregivers are in a position to help victims deal with both these conditions.

Guilt. Guilt is the inner voice that judges thoughts, actions, behaviors, decisions,
and feelings. Sometimes guilt is justified and other times it is not. For instance, some
people create the circumstances that either directly or indirectly "cause" their pets'
deaths. They may be negligent in how they care for their companion animals or they
may knowingly abuse an animal. When injury or death occurs in these cases, feelings of guilt may be justified.

When guilt is present in people who have themselves been victims of abuse or
who have witnessed the abuse of an animal, the guilt probably results from the belief that they have breached a "contract" they made with their pet to keep the pet
alive, safe, and healthy. Animal caregivers can be effective helpers in this situation
by simply acknowledging the guilt and by creating opportunities for victims to talk
about their feelings.

Helpers cannot change or "fix" guilty feelings. They can only listen without
judgment. For example, instead of saying, "Don't feel so bad," or "It wasn't really
your fault," animal caregivers can say something like, "I hear how guilty you feel
about Samson's death, Mary, and I know you would give anything to go back in time
and remove him from your ex-husband's house."

Most clients who feel guilty also feel embarrassed because they know they may
have harmed their pets by making bad decisions or by allowing the pet to participate in a dangerous activity (e.g., allowing the pet to attempt to protect the person
from the abuse). Animal caregivers can soothe victims' anxiety by separating the
person from their questionable behavior and saying something like, "Mary, I can see
that this mistake is making you feel terribly guilty. However, I believe you are a con-
scientious pet owner who never intended to bring any harm to Samson. I know
you've learned a lesson from this experience."

Occasionally, animal caregivers have contact with abusers themselves. In these cases, the animal caregiver's goal is not to alleviate the abuser's guilt, but to act as an advocate for the animal. In most instances, these are the people animal caregivers want to report to appropriate authorities in order to prevent them from abusing other animals.

Unfinished Business. Sometimes victims or other family members who were not present when an abused pet died or was euthanized may want to view the animal's body before it is buried or cremated. Animal caregivers can encourage this. Grief experts agree that seeing a dead body helps people accept the reality of death. It also allows people to say a final good-bye to their pets.

Creating opportunities to view a pet's body is an extremely effective aspect of an animal caregiver's helping role. Even though anticipating a viewing often creates anxiety, the actual viewing of a body usually provides relief.

It is beneficial for grievers to view a loved one's body, but it is up to helpers to make the experience a positive one (Lagoni, Butler, & Hetts 1994). Therefore, when people wish to view an animal's body, the body should be cleaned of any blood or waste material and positioned so it will be pleasing to see. In other words, the body should be curled slightly, with the head and limbs tucked into a "sleep-like" position. (This is most easily accomplished by placing the body in a container of some sort.) The body should also be placed on a blanket, fleece, or a soft pad and covered from the neck down, leaving the face and head exposed so people can see and talk to the pet.

If a pet's body is going to be viewed after death, people also need to be prepared for what they will see and feel and be offered guidance regarding what will be acceptable for them to do. Animal caregivers can accomplish both of these tasks as well as accompany people while they view their pet's body. In addition, animal caregivers can make the first move toward touching, petting, and talking to the animal. They can act as role models and demonstrate the helpful actions people can take in order to finish business with a pet. This is often as simple as encouraging them to say a last, heartfelt good-bye.

CONCLUSION

It is not unusual for animal caregivers who take their role in the human service profession seriously to become emotionally involved with some of the abuse cases they encounter. These are the cases where, for one reason or another, animal caregivers get emotionally "hooked" by the human or animal victims, the circumstances surrounding the incident, or even the abusers themselves. These cases can be especially painful for animal caregivers as they may stir up old losses and hurts from the past. Experienced animal caregivers know when these cases arise because they are the ones that get everyone agitated, upset, and are the ones that become extremely difficult to terminate or to detach from emotionally. It is always difficult to learn of a person's or animal's mistreatment. It may be doubly difficult to acknowledge that intervention temporarily interrupts the abuse cycle, but often does not change the ingrained behaviors that are inherent in families experiencing domestic violence.

When animal caregivers are stirred by the cases in which they intervene, they often need to debrief. Debriefing refers to a specific form of crisis intervention that is often effective when applied to personal crises. The goal of debriefing is to eliminate or at least minimize delayed stress reactions and the toll they can take on people's physical and psychological health.

Debriefing is usually not effective in the hours immediately following an incident of abuse, but can be used in the days or even weeks following. It is effective when used one-on-one or in a group. Anyone accustomed to assuming a helping role can facilitate the debriefing process. All that needs to be done is to:

1. Ask about the facts.
2. Inquire about thoughts.
3. Acknowledge and validate feelings.
4. Reassure and support.

Debriefing is often enhanced by an understanding of the underlying causes of abuse. For instance, it can be helpful for animal caregivers to remind themselves (or be reminded by a debriefer) that perpetrators' abusive and neglectful behaviors stem from deep-seated emotional problems and histories of personal maltreatment. In addition, mental health experts believe that abuse and neglect result from high levels of personal frustration, poor impulse control, a lack of resources, and ignorance of how to properly care for children and animals. Most abusers have been victimized during their own lives. Their abusive behaviors, then, are rooted in low self-esteem and are reinforced by poor role models. Children and animals are often safe targets for abusers because most cannot or do not retaliate and cannot or will not report the abusive behavior. When their actions are reported, however, abusers themselves *can* get help. Therefore, reporting abuse may ultimately be the most kind and helpful step anyone can take on an abuser's behalf.

REFERENCES

Arkow, P. 1994. Child abuse, animal abuse and the veterinarian. *Journal of the American Veterinary Medical Association* 204(7):1004–7.

DeViney, E., J. Dickert, and R. Lockwood. 1983. The care of pets within child-abusing families. *International Journal for the Study of Animal Problems* 4(4):321–29.

Fogle, B., and D. Abrahamson. 1990. Pet loss: A survey of the attitudes and feelings of practicing veterinarians. *Anthrozoös* 3(3):143–50.

LaFrana, J., ed. 1993. *AVMA Directory.* Schaumburg, Ill.: American Veterinary Medical Association.

Lagoni, L., C. Butler, and S. Hetts. 1994. *The human-animal bond and grief.* Philadelphia: W. B. Saunders.

Lynch, J. J. 1977. *The broken heart: The medical consequences of loneliness.* New York: Basic Books.

McCulloch, W. F. 1985. The veterinarian's education about the human-animal bond and animal-facilitated therapy. *Veterinary Clinics of North America: Small Animal Practice* 15(2):423–29.

Voith, V. L. 1985. Attachment of people to companion animals. *Veterinary Clinics of North America: Small Animal Practice* 15(2):289–95.

Should Veterinarians Tell?

Robert Reisman and Cindy A. Adams

GINGER HAD BEEN brought to her veterinarian repeatedly after being mutilated and tortured by her well-to-do, sadistic owner. Astro, a severely neglected Doberman pinscher, was deliberately starved and soon would have died had he not been rescued. Ceci, a pregnant dog, was kicked and stabbed by her owner's enraged, drunken boyfriend.

Fortunately, these animals are now success stories, due to expert veterinary care and intervention into the violence they had experienced. Ginger, who continued to be an affectionate and trusting cat, healed and is now living in a bucolic setting with the gentlest of human caretakers. Astro also was rehabilitated at the Bergh Memorial Animal Hospital of the American Society for the Prevention of Cruelty to Animals (ASPCA) and went to an adoptive home in which he receives love and attention from adults and children. Ceci's owner relinquished her to ASPCA Humane Law Enforcement after the attack was reported. She received extensive treatment and foster care; later, she and the eight puppies she delivered were placed in new homes.

The effect of Ceci's abuse upon the two young children in the household remains unclear. Unfortunately, at the time, ASPCA attempts to involve child welfare authorities were unsuccessful. But these children, very likely, also were victims of emotional, if not physical, abuse from this live-in household member. Whenever there are multiple individuals—animals, children, spouses, or the elderly—in a household where violence is present, each is susceptible to harm. And only heightened awareness among officials able to intervene can rescue these individuals.

Judges, prosecutors, social workers, educators, law enforcement personnel, and health professionals are the workers on the front lines, identifying and intervening for the human victims of abuse. For that reason, they commonly are mandated to report suspected or observed child abuse to the proper authorities. And because intervention in the syndrome of family violence is so important, mandated reporters virtually always are protected from civil or criminal liability as a result of their reporting.

Except for a few states (like Colorado, where reporting is mandatory), veterinarians are excluded from the ranks of mandated health caregivers who must report child maltreatment or animal abuse. This would seem to ignore the veterinarian's

221

role in benefiting the welfare of animals and people. Frequently, the time a veterinarian spends educating and helping the person responsible for an animal's welfare is significantly greater than the time spent providing medical care for the animal.

Veterinarians treat puppies or kittens who have been stepped on, cats who have fallen from windows, dogs who have fallen off roofs or been hit by cars, and animals who have been attacked by other animals. Veterinarians are trained to recognize trauma, and to take immediate action to staunch the bleeding, salve the wound, and do whatever it takes to stop the immediate suffering of an animal. On another level, they are disturbed by all the trauma they see. The more they learn about family violence, the more they are forced to think about trauma differently, to at least consider that an injury to an animal may have been intentionally inflicted. Once they establish this possibility, they must have a course of action available to them.

Much thought is being given today to the need for veterinarians to become more involved in identifying abuse, to formulate plans to address it, and to become mandated reporters. Though it doesn't carry the force of law, the American Veterinary Medical Association (AVMA) issued a policy statement two years ago calling for veterinarians to take responsibility for reporting cases of cruelty, abuse, and neglect. Further, the AVMA approved an amendment to the association's Model Veterinary Practice Act requiring veterinarians to report abuse cases within the dictates of state law, recognizing that "Such disclosures may be necessary to protect the health and welfare of animals and people." (This amendment was removed in 1997, however, by AVMA officials, because, by defining the reporting of animal abuse as a component of veterinary medicine, it in effect precluded the reporting of animal abuse by nonveterinarians.)

SEEING IS BELIEVING

The first step in identifying abuse is recognizing that it is possible. A veterinarian's primary focus is medicine. She or he agonizes over the accuracy of diagnoses, choice of treatments, and the result of these decisions. But what happens when a veterinarian suspects family violence through child abuse or animal abuse? And how is abuse defined? The basic tenets of state animal cruelty laws are a good place to start. Usually, these outline minimum standards of care regarding such factors as food, water, shelter, and the absence of intentional harm.

Ironically, the need to intervene is clearest when intent is impossible to ignore. By 1995, Ginger had been brought three times to one of New York City's largest veterinary practices with various injuries to her jaw, back legs, and ribs. The last time, she came in with severe chemical burns to her eyes, nose, and ears and a hole in one ear from a cigarette burn or hole puncher. At that point, her medical providers could no longer ignore the cat's plight and called ASPCA Humane Law Enforcement. Faced with certain prosecution due to Ginger's medical history and testimony from other household members, her abuser fled our jurisdiction.

DOCTOR AS TEACHER

Astro's neglect was intentionally inflicted; to his owner, starvation was an acceptable means to end the dog's life. Many cases seen by veterinarians are more subtle—a lack of attention to shelter or nutrition, for example. In these instances, where one has to ask if the neglect is due to ignorance or carelessness, most veterinarians opt to educate, rather than report, their clients.

John Aldridge, D.V.M., Chief of Staff of the Hospital Department of the San Francisco SPCA (SF/SPCA), reports that education is key at that practice, which sees between 25,000 and 30,000 clients a year, 35 to 50 percent of whom need some amount of financial assistance. "The only set policy that guides us [in abuse cases] has to do with the fighting dog law, which California requires us to report. Other than that, what happens on a regular basis is a constant assessment of neglect and abuse issues. Certainly we recognize abuse and terribly neglectful situations, but we also recognize 'the ignorance rule,' " comments the 21-year SF/SPCA veteran. "[Clients] are allowed to make one mistake. If an owner seems concerned and upset about a neglectful situation, we'll tend to give them the benefit of the doubt. In our day-to-day work we don't see that much of what I'd call deliberate, versus ignorant, abuse."

Such cases warrant a stern lecture about proper care. Likewise, the Massachusetts SPCA has designed a unique way to educate neglectful owners. Three years ago, the agency's enforcement arm, set up as a special division of the state police

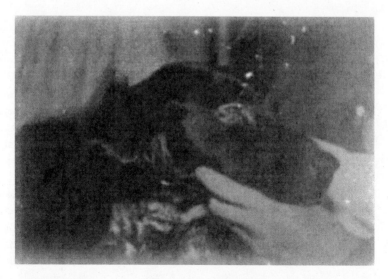

Animal abuse can be intentional or due to neglect. Signs of intentional abuse, such as this dog's wound, call for immediate intervention. (photo by Amber Alliger, ASPCA)

with search and seizure powers, created a Veterinary Compliance Officer position. As staff nutritionist at the MSPCA's Angell Memorial Hospital in Boston, Rebecca Remillard, Ph.D., D.V.M., sees clients who walk in. She also devotes roughly 20 percent of her time to assisting enforcement officers. While this can entail documenting findings so that a court warrant may be obtained, Remillard also is called to the scene when officers are unsure of whether a situation in a home is medically serious enough to intervene. In such cases, says Remillard, "The officers have done a very good job of clearing the way, saying to the client, 'Can we bring in a vet to help you?'" Often, this kind of help allows owners to learn how to care for their animals properly and avoid prosecution. Comments Remillard, "Some of the problem is cultural. Other societies don't view animals in the same way we do."

TEACHING THE DOCTOR

Comparison of violence toward animals and children is made because of both groups' vulnerability, but identification of each form of violence is quite dissimilar. There is a wealth of information about child behavioral and physical development that is helpful in verifying or disputing an adult's account of a child's injuries. For example, a fall from a bed is not possible before the child can roll over; a fall down the stairs cannot happen until a child can crawl. In addition, depending on the individual, by the age of three or so children have a capacity to speak about their problems and can communicate through drawings or other outlets at school and with other families. This kind of information is never available in the evaluation of an animal's trauma injuries.

By and large, animal health care practitioners who graduated a decade ago or more from veterinary school emphatically agree that they were not formally trained to recognize and address the issue of violence. Dr. Patricia Olson, Director of Training Operations for Guide Dogs for the Blind, says, "Part of the problem is that [the subject of abuse] does need to be added to veterinary education. Veterinarians are well aware of horrific cases, but don't have the expertise to recognize more subtle ones. Forensic pathology, for example, toxicology screening, is not as far along in the veterinary arena. Poisoning is a huge cause of animal suffering, but we don't routinely have screens. We are a long way from where we need to be," Olson says.

Fortunately, veterinary schools appear to be picking up the gauntlet. At the University of Pennsylvania's School of Veterinary Medicine, the subject of abuse comes up constantly as students review cases during instruction. The students, who spend their last 12 months of schooling in clinical settings on- and off-campus, also learn about abuse and neglect from guest lecturers and discussions among clinicians and interns at the university's bustling hospital, which recently instituted an abuse reporting policy (see Arkow, "Initiating an Animal Abuse Reporting Policy at a Veterinary Teaching Hospital," this volume). The hospital handles a caseload of 22,000

Veterinarians are trained to recognize and treat trauma. They are also disturbed by all the trauma they see. When they are educated about abuse, they are able to recognize it and take action. (photo by Amber Alliger, ASPCA)

to 24,000 per year, about 10,000 of which come in as emergencies to the 24-hour, seven-days-a-week facility.

Dan Mitchell, Academic Programs Manager at the School of Veterinary Medicine at the University of California at Davis, says a mandatory, two-term Ethics and Issues class was introduced there in 1991. Guest speakers from a variety of disciplines, including animal welfare and science, involve students in discussions about important issues throughout the term, including animal abuse and how to handle it (see Landau, "The Veterinarian's Role in Recognizing and Reporting Abuse," and Sharpe, "A Survey of Veterinarians and a Proposal for Intervention," this volume, for veterinary student reports on the abuse issue from Purdue and Ohio State Universities).

THE LATEST REPORT CARD

With regard to mandated reporting, "Veterinary medicine is probably where human medicine was 20 years ago and dentistry was 10 years ago," says Roland Olson, D.V.M., executive director of the Minnesota Board of Veterinary Medicine, the state's licensing board. But Olson, who worked for the Humane Society of Ramsey County for years, and who regularly addresses junior classes at the University of Minnesota's College of Veterinary Medicine on ethics and statutes, agrees that change is under way.

Since 1993, veterinarians practicing in Minnesota can be charged with nonprofessional conduct for "failing to report to law enforcement or humane officers inhumane treatment to animals, including staged animal fights or training for fights, of which the veterinarian has direct knowledge" (Minnesota Board of Veterinary Medicine rule book, section 9100.0708, "Unprofessional Conduct").

Charles Newton, Associate Dean at the University of Pennsylvania's School of Veterinary Medicine, voices frustration with a system that doesn't take animal abuse as seriously as it takes child abuse. "If [authorities] would look for associations, they would take animal abuse much more seriously as a way to intervene before a child becomes involved," he says.

Even veterinarians who are well aware of the implications of animal abuse are discouraged from intervening because the system just doesn't support them. According to the office of the ASPCA General Counsel, "Currently, only three states encourage or require veterinarians to report animal abuse cases, and only two of the three states grant vets immunity from liability. State laws should not only mandate that veterinarians report animal cruelty, but also should insulate them from civil liability and criminal prosecution so that they may carry out their ethical and legal responsibilities without the fear of being dragged into court."

West Virginia law reads, "It is the duty of any licensed veterinarian and the right of any other person to report to a humane officer any animal found, reasonably known or believed to be abandoned, neglected or cruelly treated as set forth in this article, and such veterinarians or other persons may not be subject to any civil or criminal liability as a result of such reporting" (West Virginia Code 7-10-4a [1994]).

In March 1996, Idaho's governor approved a bill mandating that "Any Idaho licensed veterinarian shall be held harmless from either criminal or civil liability . . . for his part in an investigation of cruelty to animals, provided, however, that a veterinarian who participates or reports in bad faith or with malice shall not be protected under the provisions of this section" (1996 Ida. ALS 229, ch. 229, section 11, 25-3514A, "Immunity").

SF/SPCA's Aldridge points out that mandated reporting would simplify the decision-making process a veterinarian naturally goes through when confronting abuse. "Having mandated rules and regulations sometimes offers a very handy technique that allows vets to be able to report because they're forced to. . . . It allows you to tell the client that it's the law. It's an easier and cleaner decision."

Other concerns are having to take time away from a practice for court appearances and possible retribution from a violent individual. This points to the need for more support from "the system"—meaningful prosecution of, and rehabilitation programs for, animal abusers.

Meanwhile, veterinarians can take steps toward formalizing a plan to handle the issue of family violence when it presents itself in their clinical practice. For example, they can seek training in family violence from a variety of sources, including humane societies and local and state veterinary associations. Clearly, they should know the cruelty laws in their state, i.e. what constitutes abuse and neglect. They also can try to create an atmosphere in their practice that allows clients to feel safe in discussing abuse.

Veterinarians also can create or become part of a network within the community that can help combat abuse. At the ASPCA, for example, an initiative called Family Vision (Violence Information Sharing, Intervention and Observation Network) includes the active participation of both authors of this essay, other members of ASPCA staff, and representatives of social service, legal, and law enforcement agencies in the metropolitan area.

There is no question that the veterinary profession is adopting a broader perspective about family violence, and such community networks are a crucial element in the continuing education and evolution of a profession filled with dedicated individuals. The veterinary contribution is an important inclusion in the United States' collective effort toward the prevention of family violence.

Animal Abuse and Family Violence in a Rural Environment

Lisa Lembke

UNLIKE OTHER MEDICAL professionals and social workers, veterinarians are not mandated reporters of either animal abuse (except animal fighting, which is a felony crime) or child abuse in the state of Wisconsin. This is a moral oversight. As medical professionals, veterinarians generally have the basic training to recognize when a story recounting an accident is a confabulation that cannot account for the injuries observed. We expect clients to be truthful: the first obstacle to reporting animal abuse is failing to realize the client is lying.

Many of my veterinary colleagues are uncomfortable with the idea of becoming mandated reporters of abuse. My colleagues protest, "We know nothing about children, we only know animals." But we *do* know something about children, as parents and grandparents, as aunts and uncles; we *do* know how to detect signs of distress and pain in another living thing that has no power of language, whether animal or human child. Because veterinarians, especially rural farm call practitioners, often know their clients socially as well as professionally, they have insights into client farm family sociodynamic interactions that others like the grocer, the banker, and the meter reader lack. Yet social intimacy may increase the reluctance to report abuse in a tightly knit rural farming community.

Rural veterinarians rightly fear that reporting a client's abuse of animals to the local law enforcement agency will cost them dearly by eroding their client bases. An abuser is, with very few exceptions, a relative or close friend of other clients in the practice. Those other clients, upset that the veterinarian broke rank and made a complaint to law enforcement officials, cease to call for veterinary services out of anger at the apparent betrayal of the client-veterinarian relationship and out of fear that *they too* might become the subject of a similar report.

An animal abuse case may take more than a year to wend its way through the court system before a verdict is returned. The veterinarian may have to testify on behalf of the prosecution and against his own client. A solo rural practitioner can be run out of business through client attrition and forced to leave the community in the aftermath of an abuse report. The courtroom solution is to bring in a neutral third-party veterinarian, who is not a local practitioner, as the animal expert in such cases. Doing so, however, begs the question of how the complaint comes to the attention of the court in the first place.

Rural animal abuse is not limited to the species used for meat or milk production, fiber, traction, or locomotion. Companion animals as well are commonly found in rural surroundings: family pets, barn cats, and farm dogs, as well as in commercial enterprises such as kennels and turnkey puppy brokerage operations.

Some animal collectors move to the country to escape scrutiny by urban zoning and animal control officials. The *Posted: No Trespassing* rural fortress of an animal collector is an archetype for animal suffering and mental illness. Some animal abusers disguise their lethal acts under cover of legitimate sport hunting. The hunter whose vicarious target includes anything that moves is a lawless thief of private and public property.

The abuse of a family pet is well recognized as a companion behavior to child and/or spousal abuse. The abuse of a herd of Hampshire pigs or a milking string of Holstein cows engenders a new dimension of economic self-destruction exacerbating the cycle of family violence.

ECONOMIC IMPLICATIONS OF ANIMAL ABUSE

The beneficial economic implications of state-of-the-art animal husbandry and nutrition have been well documented in the scientific agricultural and veterinary medical literature. The better cared for, tended, and fed an animal is, the more efficient that animal becomes at growth, production, and reproduction. Expert, observant, consistent husbandry translates as good health and welfare for the animals under care. Some animal rights activists have protested that technology-intensive practices such as bovine growth hormones are not in the cow's best interest, alleging that just because we can use drugs to increase milk production does not mean it is ethical or right to do so. There are complex animal welfare issues on the cutting edge of agricultural production, but these are ethical debates about technology versus humane treatment, not about the absolute benchmarks of life and death.

The adverse economic impacts of substandard animal husbandry and nutrition are less well studied. In fact, we know very little about the physiology of starvation in livestock species. It is clear that chronic pneumonia, intestinal parasitism, poor sanitation, lack of adequate feed or water, and a host of other management related, preventable, or treatable conditions all adversely affect health. Quantitative health and economic data exist for quite a few conditions such as Johne's disease in cattle and atrophic rhinitis in pigs. Certain diseases such as brucellosis, tuberculosis, and pseudorabies, because of their tremendous negative economic impact to the livestock industry or zoonotic potential, are subject to ongoing federal and state regulatory efforts.

But the microeconomics of a particular management style on a single working farm can be difficult to model. When farm management becomes so awful that animals are dying of neglect there is an obvious animal welfare problem with significant, negative economic consequences. Dead cows don't give milk. If there is no milk check, there is no farm family income. Economic stress can be a contributing factor to domestic violence.

Wisconsin statutes prohibit the imposition of requirements for farm animals more stringent than normally accepted husbandry practices in the particular county where the animal is located. "Normal husbandry practices in the county" may be established by the courtroom testimony of a veterinarian. The local interpretation of the adequacy of animal husbandry varies widely across the state. Practices that are sufficient to obtain a conviction for animal cruelty in the relatively more urban southeastern region may continue without comment or intercession in the northern tier of counties. The differences in interpretation are minimized in cases where animal mortality is greatly excessive and cannot be accounted for by accident (e.g., a lightning strike or livestock trailer rollover) or by underlying, mitigating pathologic mechanisms (e.g., Johne's disease, a chronic, contagious, progressive, incurable, and ultimately fatal intestinal infection estimated to affect more than a quarter of Wisconsin's dairy herds).

The worst-case scenario in livestock cruelty investigations is mass starvation from lack of available feed. In these cases, there may be feedstuffs present on the premises, but grain and forage may not be within reach of the animals. There are four principal causes of mass starvation:

Economic disaster. The farmer is too poor or debt-ridden to continue and too proud to sell the herd. Selling out means admitting failure, abandoning farming as a way of life, not just as an occupation. It may mean losing the family farm and all the history and sense of self it contains.

Physical frailty. This may be a product of the farmer's advancing age, disability, or injury. Without physical strength, the work of feeding and caring for the animals is simply overwhelming. Often, physical frailty is accompanied by poverty and an absence of younger family members to carry on the farming tradition.

Lack of knowledge. This is a particularly pernicious etiology. It may be demonstrated by a person who bought a hobby farm with a herd of animals, of whose behavior, physiology, reproduction, and nutritional needs he has only vague or rudimentary knowledge. It may also be a farmer operating with 1930s-era husbandry standards that have long since been made obsolete by advances in management, nutrition, pharmacology, and technology. Ignorance of modern husbandry practices is no defense for starvation and excessive mortality.

Intent. Intent as the etiology of starvation or dehydration has the most significant link to domestic abuse. It is based on an act of omission—not feeding the animals—rather than an act of commission. It is not a nominal neglect of a day's chores because it must consistently recur over time. Animals that are starving will be noisy at first, barking, squealing, braying, lowing, bleating, complaining in their hunger. As they weaken, they fall silent. Dehydration kills an animal in days; protein-energy malnutrition (the 20-dollar term for starvation) takes longer. Animals (except, perhaps, for cats) do not suffer from anorexia nervosa. They will not generally voluntarily starve or dehydrate themselves to death. And they do not suffer peacefully.

In every animal cruelty case I have investigated, one or more of the human principals were socially dysfunctional, violent, sociopathic, mentally challenged, or mentally ill. The departure from normal may be subtle or flagrant; whatever its manifestation, it is clear that the perpetrators of abuse are not functioning according to social and societal norms. The ruinous nature of their human-animal relationships is consistent with and illustrative of the perpetrators' interactions with other human family members. The conscious, chosen pattern of behavior may become generalized to all living things, not just animals. There is virtually certain to be something else going on in addition to the animal-related problem. Animal abuse cannot happen in a vacuum—it *must* have a human component. There will be, now or in the future, a human target if the abuser's behavior remains unchecked.

In a rural setting, abuse in any of its various incarnations is likely to be an open community secret. Everybody knows about it, but nobody does anything about it. Nothing is done because of

- a reluctance to interfere in another's affairs;
- fear of personal consequences, including retribution;
- lack of specialized knowledge of the laws pertaining to abuse; and/or
- absence of shelters for battered spouses, abused children, and maltreated animals.

TWO EXAMPLES

One starvation case came to the attention of law enforcement officials when the milk hauler reported there were less than 300 pounds of milk in the bulk tank after eight days of milking, and that the water to the barn had been turned off but the animals were still in the barn. The owner was a "sundowner," doing barn chores in the early morning and late evening while working full-time in a day job because the family farm had not made a profit in more than 10 years. A search warrant was issued based on the milk hauler's complaint.

On this farm, the calves were born healthy but typically failed to thrive. There was less than one week's supply of calf milk replacer on the premises. One young calf was running loose among the stanchions, surviving on what she could steal from the mother cows in the milking string. Another seven-month-old heifer calf weighed just 10 pounds more than she had at birth (she died the day after the search warrant was served). The farmer attributed her poor condition to the lice she had.

A horribly stunted, 14-month-old Holstein bull found inside the dairy barn weighed just 300 pounds. In the milking string, there were dead cows lying in the barn with their heads still in the stanchions—he was milking the live ones and walking over and around the dead ones. The corn cribs and hay mow were full. He just did not seem to be able to find the time, what with a full-time day job, for shelling the corn, throwing hay down to the cows, or bottle-feeding the baby calves. Oddly for a dairy farm where artificial insemination is practiced, there were no reproductive records kept in the barn—except for one animal: the man's 15-year-old stepdaughter.

Because he had a previous conviction for sexual assault of a minor, this man was highly averse to being jailed again for animal abuse. A deferred prosecution agreement was quickly made in exchange for a permanent retirement from farming and the sale of the remains of the herd for salvage. Within four days of serving the search warrant, the cows had all been sold and shipped off the farm.

Another starvation case came to the attention of sheriff's deputies through repeated reports by tourists of dead animals in the barnyard adjacent to the county highway that was the primary route into a rural Wisconsin vacation getaway. Livestock carcasses, according to passers-by, would remain bloated and putrefying in the sun for days, sometimes for weeks at a time. The front yard was littered with the skulls and rotting hides of butchered rabbits.

The farmer, who also worked as a long-haul trucker, had instructed his wife to not enter the barn, even in his absence, no matter what. She had disobeyed him once, in response to the bellowing of cattle and the bleating of hungry sheep. Upon discovering this, he beat her bloody and threatened to knife her if she ever entered the barn again. She obeyed in fear for her life. The man was known for his violent temper and penchant for weapons. Many in the community feared him.

Over time, the perimeter fences enclosing the livestock and horses on this farm fell to the persistent push of grazing animals trying to reach the grass that literally was greener on the other side. As the fences failed, the animals began to forage on public rights-of-way and feast on the neighbors' shrubbery. The sheep were habitually upon the highway, causing a hazard to passing traffic. From the air, cowpaths worn by the farmer's livestock into the public landscape and neighboring fields could be seen stretching for several miles. Being free to range at will, the animals ceased to starve. The fences were boundaries in common between the farmer and the municipality, and both parties are liable for the cost of fence repair. Forcing repair of the fences would have cost the township a substantial sum of money. They elected to not fix the fences.

The sheriff's deputies began issuing $200 tickets for livestock on the highway. The wife, during one of the farmer's absences, fled with her children to a safehouse and never returned. Over time the animals disappeared or died variously from predator coyotes and dogs and the neighbors' rifles—hardly an ideal end to a thorny, intractable problem in a very small tourist town.

JUDICIAL RELUCTANCE

Wisconsin statutes allow a sentencing judge to prohibit a person convicted of animal abuse from owning or having any contact with animals. The court is reluctant, however, to deprive a farmer convicted of animal abuse of his or her economic means of support, and so it is rare for a judge to order a farmer to divest him- or herself of the livestock. Recidivism is high among certain classes of animal abusers, and appropriate monitoring by probation and parole agents is essential in abuse cases.

In one such case, a swine producer was convicted of starving his herd and was placed on probation; the judge was sympathetic to the man's tearful pleas that without his hogs he had no means to support his family. There were recurrent complaints for some months afterwards from the neighbors about fences in shabby repair and swine escaping to run at large, rooting up heifer pastures, and causing significant property damage.

Accompanying the probation agent and a social worker, I made an unannounced visit to evaluate the health and husbandry of the swine. Razor-thin, dead, and dying pigs were found in both barns, and some of the dead showed evidence of cannibalism. The only nutritionally fit swine were the ones that had escaped to run at large. Given evidence of recidivist animal cruelty, a complaint was made, a new search warrant was generated, and sheriff's deputies were dispatched to the farm. The man's terrified, mentally challenged 18-year-old son fled on foot from the house when he saw the squad car pull into the farm yard, howling that Daddy was going to kill him. Officers secured the scene and confiscated a rifle from the defendant. The father, an alcoholic, had delegated animal care to the son, who did what he could to the best of his limited ability. The man was convicted a second time of starving his livestock, and the judge ordered him to have no contact with swine. It was whispered, common knowledge that the farmer regularly beat both his wife and retarded man-child. The domestic violence was not brought to the attention of the court.

AGGRESSION AND ASSAULT

The economic devastation of poor husbandry practices leading to death losses is apparent. Insidious economic harm can also arise from physical mistreatment of the animals through acts of aggression or assault.

I once consulted on a case for a local practitioner who was stumped by the lack of reproductive efficiency in a small dairy herd. A farm visit was made and records were analyzed for calving interval and the ratio of inseminations per conception and days open and so on, technical measures of reproductive efficiency. Samples of the ration were taken for nutritional analysis. The farmer was interviewed at length about management and husbandry practices. The barn was checked for stray voltage. Analysis of the reproductive parameters showed that there was a problem with apparent infertility and early embryonic death losses. The ration was somewhat deficient for some micronutrients, but not sufficient to account for the reproductive difficulties.

During the farm visit, the cows in the barn seemed restless. Cows will sometimes be edgy when someone they don't know is in the barn. The cows in this herd were also head shy in the extreme. Looking at them closely, many of them had facial deformities of apparent traumatic origin. Every single one of the cows in the milking string had a broken tail—some recent, others old and healed fractures. Having associated pain with someone behind them, artificial insemination must have been difficult in these cows.

Later, privately, the farm wife said to me that he would take his anger out on the cows, twisting their tails until the bones snapped and they hung limp and bleeding, bashing them on their faces with a three-foot length of heavy pipe. Then he would come back to the kitchen and tell her, "See? I didn't hurt you *this* time."

She had no place to go, and no money to leave. I had no diplomatic way to note in the case report my belief that the stress and pain of physical abuse suffered by these animals was significant to the herd's reproductive difficulty. Nor did I want to make my concern for the woman's safety part of a public record on a herd of cows.

Antisocial acts of animal cruelty may be directed at the community at large rather than concentrated within the family unit. A cancer patient in a remote northern Wisconsin village, whose dearest companion was his dog, lost his animal to such a neighbor. The trapper, who was never charged criminally, cut a two-by-two-foot opening into the bottom of his garage door. Inside the garage, he placed a large conibear trap baited with deer carcass parts. The trap set was illegal, even on private property, because Wisconsin law allows conibear traps of that size to be used only in baitless, underwater sets for furbearing species such as beaver.

The dog, attracted by the deer meat, was caught and squeezed to death in the trap. The dog's owner found the frozen, ritually mutilated body of his dog, still in the trap, after trespassing on his neighbor's land and peering through the window of the garage door. The neighbor, asked several times by the dog's owner whether he had seen the missing dog, had repeatedly denied all knowledge of the animal's whereabouts.

Although the dog's owner requested assistance from both the sheriff's department and the game warden, he was unable to recover the dog's body and equally unable to influence the officers to pursue the matter as a criminal act of animal cruelty. Careful retrospective investigation by the dog's owner revealed that more than 100 dogs had disappeared from the small rural community of some 400 people in the preceding seven years, far too many missing animals to be accounted for solely by accident and old age. The trapper had evidently been systematically luring and killing his neighbors' dogs over time. The dog owner filed a civil suit against the

trapper but was unable to pursue the claim due to limitations imposed by his terminal illness.

LINKS WITH PUBLIC HEALTH

On occasion, an investigation of nuisance violations or public health complaints
opens up a cesspool of domestic violence. What begins as an animal problem may
quickly grow into a complex set of animal and human welfare issues.

As an example, one such case began as a rat infestation complaint lodged by a
rural downtown business with the local department of public health. Upon investigation of the rat complaint, it was discovered in rapid succession that a rented single-
family dwelling was the source of the rat problem; from it emanated a foul odor
detectable from the street; the smell was a nauseating combination of accumulated
putrescent garbage and human and animal waste; there was no gas or electric service to the premises and therefore no refrigeration or hot water; the four children
inside were hungry and filthy; and the dog and cats inside the residence were malnourished and flea-infested. The children's mother, who earned only $2.70 an hour
plus tips working part-time as a waitress, was feeding her children on what she could
glean from the restaurant trash. The mother had chosen the biological father of the
youngest child as their babysitter—ordinarily a fine choice, but this father was a
convicted pedophile with a no-contact-with-children order as a condition of his probation.

The residence was placarded by the building inspector as unfit for human habi-
tation. The animals were removed by the animal shelter. The children were removed
by the human services department and placed in foster care. The health department
wrote abatement orders for the human health hazards and vermin infestation problems. The mother, herself the victim of domestic violence, was arrested and charged
with child neglect and animal abuse. The pedophile fled from justice and as of this
writing is wanted on a bench warrant.

COMPLICATIONS IN THE RURAL ENVIRONMENT

Victims of domestic violence in rural environments may face barriers that are not
present in more urban settings. The culture of farming communities, among families
who have known each other for three or four generations and intermarried for good
measure, is that one goes along to get along. Neighbors do not like to be tattling on
their own. There is a certain tolerance of eccentricity, a deep respect for personal
privacy, a high sense of autonomy, and a weighty reluctance to interfere in the business of another, especially in social matters. Perhaps in the Upper Midwest this is
partly a cultural product of middle European and Scandinavian ancestral roots.
This cultural privacy metamorphoses into stark isolation for a victim of domestic
violence. Other people are reluctant to, or just plain refuse to, intercede on behalf

of the battered woman, because doing so would splinter the veneer of communal peace through confrontation.

Physical isolation in a rural environment is the rule rather than the exception. It may be a half-mile or more to the next farmhouse (and in the Great Plains states, it may be many miles to the next ranch). More than half of rural battered women have no access to transportation, according to Wisconsin state survey data. They may be deprived of access to the family vehicle, rather than lacking a vehicle altogether. There is no public transportation of any sort available in many rural areas. Without access to transportation, especially in the depth of winter, it may not be possible to reach the next house. When the violence begins, the victim cannot slip out to the neighbor's home to get help.

Lack of telephone service exacerbates rural isolation. Among Wisconsin's rural families, about 31 percent do not have working phone service. For many, the solitude is complete. There is no way to call for help, and no way to get out.

In the last decade, there has been considerable emphasis placed on educating law enforcement officers to help them recognize domestic violence and understand its implications and consequences. The same is not true of animal abuse, which commonly continues to be unrecognized and unaddressed by law enforcement officers. Officers are often unfamiliar with the highly specialized body of laws that pertain to animal cruelty. The tangled web of child abuse, animal abuse, and spousal abuse is not understood widely or well enough in rural settings. Animal abuse is not explored as an indicator of other family violence.

In contrast, failure to arrest the abuser is a declining obstacle to intervention in spousal and child abuse cases. Wisconsin recently enacted mandatory arrest laws for perpetrators of domestic violence, and it is even possible for both parties to be arrested under certain circumstances. Before any arrest can be made, officers must arrive on the scene. The ability to intervene quickly in a violent encounter is critical to a victim of domestic abuse. Because of large geographic territories, however, the response time by rural law enforcement authorities to a call for help can be slow.

For domestic violence to be prosecuted, it must be reported. Often this is a self-report, an abused woman asking for help. The greatest functional obstacles faced by women who want to leave a battering partner in Wisconsin are the family court system, the lack of available beds in shelters, and the lack of affordable housing. In a certain subset of cases, the lack of available alternative housing for beloved pets may also be an obstacle. for women leaving.

The human services system in Wisconsin is mandated to keep families together whatever the cost, which may very well be great to the well-being of the woman and her children. This is true of the family court system as well. The abuser may take particular advantage of the court system by drawing out the legal process into a protracted series of battles over separation, child custody, child support, and visitation. The victim of domestic violence is controlled and punished, worn away to exhaustion, through this process.

In a similar vein, it has become a standard tool for accused animal abusers to delay court proceedings as long as possible, increasing the costs of caring for animals seized as evidence and impounded for their welfare. Faced with budget-breaking bills for custodial care, some prosecutors elect to not take animal abuse cases to trial in front of a jury.

A 1993 Wisconsin needs assessment survey undertaken by the Coalition Against Domestic Violence showed that for every 660 battered women, there is only one bed in a safe shelter. In addition, there is the concurrent need to house the children of women seeking safety, which triples the number of victims in search of refuge. Access to help is location-dependent. Just over half of the 72 counties in the state have safehouse facilities for battered women, making access to help location dependent. Almost half of the state's domestic abuse programs serving battered women reported that they were forced to turn away or place on waiting lists women and children who needed help. As is true across the country, the number of safehouse beds for women and children displaced by domestic violence is too small to meet the need. The fact that animal shelters and animal protection groups outnumber domestic abuse programs is a telling social criticism.

For the woman who succeeds in leaving, her income and standard of living are likely to be sharply reduced. She may have great difficulty finding affordable housing, particularly if the housing market is tight or if distances are great and she lacks transportation. If she has children and especially if she has pets, she will have greater trouble still, fair housing laws notwithstanding. She may literally have nowhere to go.

REPORTING CONSTRAINTS

Reporting animal abuse is derivative of its identification. The number of abused animals subsequently presented by the abuser to a veterinarian for treatment is probably small. It is ironic that once having hurt an animal, failing to obtain treatment to relieve the animal's suffering is itself a form of animal cruelty. Presenting an animal for treatment that has been intentionally harmed could conceivably lead to self-incrimination.

Among private practitioners, the index of suspicion that an animal's condition is the result of abuse or neglect tends to be low. Veterinarians naturally and understandably want to believe their clients are nice people who depend upon and dearly care for their animals. Veterinarians confronted with clients who are habitually mistreating livestock or animal collectors who own more animals than they are capable of competently caring for may elect to discontinue serving the client, thereby terminating the veterinarian-client-patient relationship. It is rare that a veterinarian takes the affirmative step of making a formal complaint to the authorities alleging animal maltreatment. It is almost unheard of for a veterinarian to report any other type of domestic abuse.

But some clinical presentations beg for answers, however. For one veterinarian, suspicions were raised by a new client who presented a sturdy, four-month-old mongrel puppy for treatment of a matched pair of transverse, midshaft femoral fractures. Recounting the history, the man claimed he had tripped over the dog on the stairs. The client appeared late on a Friday afternoon without an appointment. Given his place of residence, he had driven past two other, more convenient, veterinary practices. Accompanying the man was a preteen child with one arm in a cast well past the elbow. The child remained silently passive throughout the visit, offering up no details of the dog's life, habits, or condition. The explanation of the dog's injury was inconsistent with the severe trauma observed. In exchange for asking no more questions, the veterinarian convinced the man to surrender ownership of the dog, which eventually recovered. How the child came to have a broken arm was not determined. The veterinarian, reasonably certain he would never see the client again, was concerned enough (and felt safe enough) to refer an account of the matter to law enforcement.

HUMANE SOCIETY INVOLVEMENT

I have seen and treated more injuries and disabilities resulting from cruel maltreatment and neglect in companion animals surrendered to humane societies than I have seen presented for treatment in private practice. The person surrendering an injured or mistreated animal may fail to acknowledge the injury at the time the animal is relinquished, or will give an explanation of the animal's condition that is inconsistent with the findings upon physical examination. Gross malnutrition, blunt trauma, and gunshot wounds are common in this category. It is not uncommon for the owner to deny ownership, insisting the animal (whose behavior gives away the lie) is a stray.

The act of surrendering the animal may itself be an instance of cruelty directed at another person. The animal may be surrendered as a means of inflicting emotional harm on the child or spouse who dearly loves the animal. (In some states, spouses going through bitter divorce proceedings have been known to put family pets up for adoption so the other party would not get custody of them.) Most often, the person surrendering the animal is an angry man, although women have also surrendered household pets as a means of punishing their children.

Conversely, local humane societies are sometimes able to provide a safehouse for companion animals that are not allowed in shelters for battered women. Protecting the animal property of battered women who flee domestic abuse is problematic. In some cases, love and concern for the animals prevent the woman from leaving in the first place, because she knows that if she leaves the animals behind he will hurt or kill them in retribution for her flight. As with battered women's shelters, animal shelters' cages and kennels are often full and pets in need are turned away for lack of space.

Our humane society's practice has been to accept the animals without question and find space. Due to security concerns, we sequester animals belonging to battered women, often housing them at remote locations or in foster homes. We give these animals thorough physical examinations; about half of them have nutritional problems or suspicious injuries requiring veterinary attention and nursing care. Holding animals for battered women entails social and legal risk. Wisconsin is a community property state. If the batterer discovers where the woman has housed her animals, he may legally demand and regain custody of the animals because they are marital property held in common.

THE VETERINARY RESPONSIBILITY

As medical professionals, veterinarians have a moral and social obligation, if not a legal one, to report suspected abuse. The elements of the tangled web of spousal abuse, child abuse, and animal abuse share an etiology of conscious behavior and are all permutations of the same social ill, the same crime. The social status and value of the victims differ greatly, but the root cause does not.

Failing to report abuse enables the abuse to continue. Terminating a veterinarian-client-patient relationship as a response to animal mistreatment is a half-hearted gesture that stops short of intervention and cure. Yet the cost to the veterinarian who reports animal abuse or neglect may lead to the crippling or failure of the practice in a rural environment. In this way, the moral victory of reporting abuse is also a Pyrrhic one tantamount to economic self-destruction.

Veterinarians are awkwardly positioned, given this equation of social benefit versus personal cost. Until the balance is shifted toward social benefit and away from direct personal cost, it will remain a difficult decision for a veterinarian to report suspected animal abuse.

Mandating the reporting of animal abuse may not significantly improve the situation in all cases, but it should substantially improve the current state of affairs. Animal fighting is currently reportable, but undoubtedly reporting happens far less frequently than it could. This is partly due to the sociodynamics of the people attracted to blood sports. Animal fighting is known to be associated with high-stakes gambling, prostitution, and drugs. The owners of fighting animals are unlikely to seek veterinary care from the average practice.

Presented with such a client, it may seem to be the better part of valor, if not survival, to treat the injured animal quietly and be done with it rather than report the animal fighting and risk assault by the animal's owner in retribution. Removing any fear associated with acts of reprisal should increase compliance with mandatory reporting. For categories other than fighting, mandating reporting and indemnifying the veterinarian who reports in good faith should be productive in those instances where abused animals are seen in private practice. It will do nothing for the hidden population of animals that are not seen or treated by veterinarians.

Voluntary reporting of other types of domestic violence in any of its various manifestations should be easier for veterinarians, because there is no direct economic stake in the matter. The social relationship is no different from that of any other intimate member of a community. All of the trappings of social intimacy serve as powerful factors in weighing whether to report domestic abuse: having commitments to the well-being of the community, knowing the abuser as neighbor and friend, allowing for eccentricities, and honoring the customs of independence and privacy. The difference is that the veterinarian has general medical knowledge and, therefore, a duty.

Any report of suspected abuse is born of a thoughtful, painful introspective process about what is the greater good for all concerned. Making the reporting process mandatory and permitting indemnification for reports made in good faith makes it easier because the report is then in compliance with a neutral legal requirement. The responsibility is dictated by the law, not voluntarily assumed. It becomes much less feasible to construe the report as a personal persecution and less likely there will be adverse personal consequences for the reporting veterinarian.

SELECTED READINGS

Hannah, H. 1993. The impact of animal welfare and animal anti-cruelty laws on veterinarians. *Veterinary Clinics of North America, Small Animal Practice* 23(5).

Wisconsin Department of Corrections. July 1996. *Domestic violence: A handbook for agents.* Madison, Wis.: Department of Corrections, Division of Community Corrections.

The Veterinarian's Role in Recognizing and Reporting Abuse

Ruth Landau

THE ROLE OF the veterinarian as a health care provider in recognizing and reporting suspected animal abuse, child abuse and domestic violence is a highly contentious issue. To help determine the extent to which today's practicing veterinarians and tomorrow's future veterinarians currently studying in colleges of veterinary medicine are sensitized and trained regarding this issue, a survey was conducted in the summer of 1997 under the auspices of a grant from the Geraldine R. Dodge Foundation.

It was hypothesized that, first, practicing veterinarians are reluctant to report suspicions of domestic family violence directed against animals, children, or spouses for a variety of reasons. These reasons include lack of adequate training, fear of litigation, that the practitioner is too busy, fear that the violence will escalate and the veterinarian may become a target, a feeling that it is not the veterinarian's place to intervene, lack of knowledge about whom to contact, and fear of losing the client's business.

Second, practicing veterinarians, in both large and small animal practices, may not be aware that animal patients and human clients may have been abused; and being unfamiliar with this diagnosis, they are unfamiliar with the mechanism for reporting the suspected abuse, especially human abuse.

And third, veterinary school curricula could be modified to improve the exposure and training of veterinary students with regard to the interrelationship of human and animal violence. These curriculum changes could shape the veterinarians of the twenty-first century to be more sensitive to and skilled at recognizing animal and human abuse, thereby reducing the risks to animal patients, other animals in the household, and human clients, and helping to fulfill veterinary responsibilities to the protection of animal health, the relief of animal suffering, and the promotion of public health.

This project surveyed all 31 colleges of veterinary medicine in the United States (27 schools) and Canada (4 schools) and a small sample of large and small animal practitioners in Indiana in order to understand the degree to which the current veterinary curricula prepare students to recognize abuse of animal patients and human clients, and the extent to which practitioners recognize and report their suspicions of abuse to appropriate authorities. The data gathered clearly indicate a discrepancy between belief about the occurrence of abuse and the amount of time spent educating veterinary students to recognize and report such abuse.

A NEW ERA

The American Veterinary Medical Association (AVMA) estimates there are approximately 50,000 veterinarians in private practice in the United States today (see www.avma.org). It is conservatively estimated that two million U.S. women are assaulted by their partners each year (Browne 1993). Of these two million battered women, half may have pets (Ascione 1992). If Ascione is correct, half of these families may have pets that have been hurt or killed by the batterer. Conservatively, this means that the veterinary community treats hundreds of thousands of abused animals annually.

As a student of veterinary medicine and a member of our global community, I am very concerned about the training we, as veterinarians of the twenty-first century, are receiving with regard to our role as community leaders in breaking the cycles of violence and abuse. The purpose of this study was to understand what sort of curriculum changes need to occur so that the future veterinarians will be empowered to help stop the pervasive violence that occurs against the most vulnerable members of our society: animals, children, and women. A veterinarian may suspect that either an animal patient or human client is being maltreated, but often has had no formal training in how to identify abuse and no formal mechanism by which to report that suspicion of abuse. The current curricula offered to veterinary students could be vastly improved with regard to the training about how to handle suspicions of abuse. Much as the identification of the "battered child" syndrome (Kempe et al. 1962) initiated an era whereby physicians began to recognize consistent pathologies as indicative of suspected child abuse, and to report these findings to appropriate Child Protection Services, veterinary medicine stands poised at the threshold of a new era to do likewise regarding "battered pets" (Munro 1996).

OVERVIEW

In April 1996, the Executive Board of the American Veterinary Medical Association approved a position statement presented by the AVMA Animal Welfare Committee, which stated:

> The AVMA recognizes that veterinarians may have occasion to observe cases of cruelty to animals, animal abuse, or animal neglect as defined by state law or local ordinances. When these observations occur, the AVMA considers it the responsi-

bility of the veterinarian to report such cases to the appropriate authorities. Such disclosures may be necessary to protect the health and welfare of animals and people. (American Veterinary Medical Association 1997, 3)

This resolution is a harbinger of a new era for veterinary medicine, one for which current veterinary school curricula may not be fully prepared. Research in New Jersey suggests a significant likelihood that veterinary practitioners may encounter clients and patients who have been abused (DeViney, Dickert, & Lockwood 1983). Researchers in Wisconsin, Colorado, and Scotland are beginning to identify the symptoms of suspected animal abuse, which are similar to pathologies of child abuse that have been defined and presented to human medical professionals for 35 years. Currently, only four states have enacted legislation addressing the issue of requiring veterinarians to report suspected animal abuse, and only two states include veterinarians among the health professionals mandated to report various forms of family violence to appropriate authorities (Patronek 1998).[1] Approximately 90 percent of all U.S. veterinary practitioners are currently *not* required to report their suspicions of abuse.

METHODOLOGY AND DESIGN

A questionnaire was used to survey curriculum content of the 31 veterinary medical schools in Canada and the United States regarding the inclusion of training on how to recognize animal abuse and client abuse and what to do about suspicions of abuse. For the purpose of this study, the term "human abuse" is used to describe clients who themselves are victims of maltreatment; "client abuse" encompasses child abuse, spouse abuse or domestic violence, and elder abuse; and "animal abuse" encompasses animal cruelty, abuse, and neglect. The original structure of the questionnaire was modeled after that created by Wiebers et al. (1994) with permission of the authors.

Using this questionnaire, we surveyed the deans' designees (most often the associate dean of academic or student affairs, or the professor of veterinary ethics and jurisprudence) of the veterinary schools on the nature and extent of the curriculum dealing with this issue. The survey was faxed to the designee, and then follow-up phone calls were made until the respondent was reached and able to review his or her responses by phone with the author. We achieved a 100 percent response rate to this questionnaire.

We designed a second questionnaire that was used to survey a small, random sample of small and large animal veterinary practitioners in Indiana regarding their experiences and beliefs about recognizing and reporting suspicions of both animal and human abuse. Using a list generated by the Indiana State Board of Animal Health of the 1,358 veterinarians licensed to practice in the State of Indiana, 15 randomly selected veterinarians (determined by a random number generator) were contacted and participated in a 15-minute telephone interview. The respondents varied by number of years in practice, as well as by type, size, and location of practice.

RESULTS AND DISCUSSION

Curriculum Survey: Key Findings

The emphasis placed on teaching veterinary students how to recognize and report suspected animal abuse and human abuse varied greatly among the 31 North American veterinary schools. With regard to the animal patient, nearly all schools (97%) agreed or strongly agreed that veterinarians will encounter incidents of severe animal abuse some time in their career; 75 percent of the schools address the topic of recognizing and reporting animal abuse in their curricula. Less than one-third of the schools (31%) have a hospital policy for reporting suspected severe animal abuse; only 17 percent of the schools explicitly make their students aware of that policy.

With regard to the human client, almost two-thirds (63%) of the respondents agreed or strongly agreed that veterinarians will encounter incidents of human abuse at some time in their career; less than a quarter of the schools (21%) address the topic of recognizing and reporting human abuse. Furthermore, only two schools have a hospital policy for reporting suspected severe human abuse; both of those schools make students explicitly aware of that policy.

Finally, although 80 percent of the respondents believe that there is a link between animal abuse and human abuse, the idea of mandating the reporting of abuse for veterinarians evoked heated debate on both sides of the issue. Two-thirds of the respondents agreed that veterinarians should be mandated reporters of suspected animal abuse (63%), but less than a third (30%) thought that veterinarians should be mandated reporters of suspected human abuse. Clearly there is a discrepancy between belief about occurrence of and exposure to abuse, and instruction and policy related to reporting that abuse.

Practitioner Survey: Key Findings

The 15 veterinarians interviewed for this study varied widely in terms of years, type, setting, and size of practice (see table 1 below). The majority of practitioners surveyed (87%) indicated that during their years in practice they have treated mildly abused animal patients, most commonly (50%) treating one to three such patients per year. Most respondents said they handled suspicions of mild abuse by treating the animal and educating the owner. Only one respondent reported such suspicions to a local humane society; the other 92 percent of practitioners indicated that education and discussion with the owner was adequate in these cases. Nearly two-thirds (60%) of the veterinarians interviewed indicated that they had treated an animal which they suspected had been severely or intentionally abused or neglected, over half of these incidents (53%) occurring one to three times per practice. In these cases of severe abuse, 89 percent of the veterinarians stated that they reported their suspicions to an outside agency, most frequently law enforcement officials, humane societies, newspapers, or referring veterinarians. Finally, 20 percent of those surveyed stated that they had worked with clients whom they suspected were themselves being abused, but none of these veterinarians reported their suspicions to an outside agency. During their veterinary school training, less than 7 percent of the veterinarians surveyed had received any training on how to handle suspicions of animal abuse; none had received training on how to handle suspicions of client abuse.

Belief about the likelihood of encountering abuse and instruction on how to handle such an encounter are not congruent. During a student's entire professional training, she or he receives an average of 76 minutes of training on the topic of animal abuse and 8 minutes on the topic of client abuse. Only half of all veterinary schools see a need to increase the time allocated to the study of these two topics. The reasons most often cited to not include more training in these areas are "already have adequate coverage" or "lack of time in the curriculum." Finally, only one-third of all schools provide cross-training and dialogue with humane and animal control workers, while 70 percent utilize social workers in their training. Clearly

Table 1. Characteristics of Veterinarians Participating in the Survey

Male : Female practitioners	Male = 11 Female = 4
Average number of years in practice	19.4 years (Range: 5 to 40 years)
Type of practice = % respondents (number)	Small animal = 60% (9) Large animal or mixed = 33% (5) Research = 7% (1)
Type of practice = overall % Indiana veterinarians	Small animal = 46% Large animal or mixed = 38% Other = 8%
Practice setting	Urban = 2 Suburban = 7 Rural = 5 Other = 1
Average number of veterinarians, veterinary technicians, other employees	Veterinarians = 2.5 Veterinary technicians = 1.5 Other = 5.2

there is room to develop programs and experiences that encourage cross-training and interaction with other helping professionals.

CONCLUSIONS

The interrelatedness of human abuse and animal abuse is a complex and perplexing issue (Ascione 1991, 1992, 1993; Fucini 1978; Kellert & Felthous 1985; Lockwood 1987; Lockwood & Hodge 1986; ten Bensel 1984), and numerous initiatives are underway to encourage cross-training and cross-reporting among various disciplines (Ascione, Weber, & Wood 1997; Boatfield 1996; Ehrhardt 1995; Humane Society of the United States 1997; *Irish Veterinary Journal* 1996; Lockwood 1989). Several years ago, the Latham Foundation established a Child and Animal Abuse Prevention Project to identify key issues and to coordinate community coalitions in response to violence. The first stage of this initiative was a national needs assessment survey. Of the 582 respondents surveyed nationally in the fields of child protection, domestic violence, animal welfare, animal control, and veterinary medicine, 90 percent thought there is a connection between cruelty to animals and family violence, and 88 percent thought that learning more about this link would benefit their work (Arkow 1995).

The results of the current study suggest similar ideas: 80 percent of the veterinary schools surveyed and 90 percent of the practitioners interviewed also thought there is a link between the two forms of cruelty. The data clearly indicate a discrepancy between thoughts about occurrence of abuse and amount of time spent educating veterinary students to recognize and report such abuse. In the future, it would be interesting to survey a sample of individuals from each state who potentially have a vested interest in the curriculum of the veterinary school serving their state. These persons might include other veterinary school personnel, representatives of state Veterinary Medical Associations, state veterinarians, public health veterinarians, humane society veterinarians, veterinary school alumni, legislators, district attorneys, judges, private practitioners, and AVMA representatives.

The idea of legally mandating veterinarians to report suspicions of abuse, both animal and human, evokes heated debate both in favor of and opposed to such a mandate (Arkow 1994). Those opposed warned that we do not yet have a clear definition of and criteria for what constitutes abuse; we do not use precise enough language to distinguish between "abuse," "cruelty," and "neglect"; veterinarians do not have immunity from civil and criminal liability in the event that they are erroneous in their reported suspicion; and there is often little consequence or penalty for those prosecuted on animal abuse charges. "This is a matter of citizenship rather than professionalism," replied one respondent opposed to the concept of targeting a profession as a mandated reporter. "It's dangerous to go off reporting assumptions. We need to distinguish between legal, ethical, and moral mandates," wrote another.

Those in favor of reporting suggest that we as veterinarians should get involved in the legislative process, writing in safeguards and codifying immunity for ourselves. "If veterinarians and the AVMA don't legislate and codify reporting, other interest groups will do it for us," wrote one respondent. Others argued that mandatory reporting would protect the veterinarian: "A client could get angry and sue. Mandatory reporting would protect the vet by law; they must report not because they're the bad guys but because it's legally required of them," wrote a respondent. "Vets deal with *people;* veterinary medicine is a people business," wrote another.

Although it is beyond the scope of this study to draw any conclusion about the mandating of reporting, this author strongly believes that veterinary students need to be brought into this discussion, to become aware of the issues around mandated reporting, and, most importantly, to receive information about the interrelatedness of violence toward animals and humans.

Thanks to the participation of several local practitioners and all veterinary schools in the United States and Canada, we are now in a better position to understand the veterinarian's reluctance to get involved in these issues, and to develop appropriate veterinary curricula that will not only create competent medical practitioners but also encourage empathic professionals who actively help reduce violence and abuse directed at all members of our communities. This can only serve to enhance our ability to provide humane care for both our animal patients and our human clients, and to position veterinary medicine as family practice in the changing economy of the twenty-first century. Such an interdisciplinary approach to veterinary education will reach far beyond the walls of the veterinary schools or even of veterinary practices; it will reach into the cores of our communities, helping to break the cycle of violence against all beings.

NOTE

1. California and Colorado include veterinarians among health professionals mandated to report suspected child abuse. Arizona, Idaho, and West Virginia exempt veterinarians from civil or criminal liability if they make good-faith reporting of suspected animal abuse; Minnesota requires veterinarians to report suspected animal abuse. Legislation is proposed in Pennsylvania to include veterinarians among reporters of suspected animal abuse.

REFERENCES

Adams, C. J. 1995. Woman-battering and harm to animals. *Animals & women: Feminist theoretical explorations,* edited by C. J. Adams and J. Donovan, 55–84. Durham: Duke University Press.

American Veterinary Medical Association. 1997. The veterinarian's role in animal welfare. January 3. Available at <http://www.avma.org/care4pets/morewelf.htm#rights>.

Arkow, P. 1994. Child abuse, animal abuse and the veterinarian. *Journal of the American Veterinary Medical Association* 204:1004–7.

Arkow, P. 1995. *Breaking the cycles of violence: A practical guide.* Alameda, Calif.: Latham Foundation.

Ascione, F. R. 1991. *Childhood animal maltreatment: Research issues.* Englewood, Colo.: American Humane Association.

Ascione, F. R. 1992. Enhancing children's attitudes about the humane treatment of animals: Generalization to human-directed empathy. *Anthrozoös* 5:176–91.

Ascione, F. R. 1993. Children who are cruel to animals: A review of research and implications for developmental psychopathology. *Anthrozoös* 6:226–47.

Ascione, F. R., C. V. Weber, and D. S. Wood. 1997. The abuse of animals and domestic violence: A national survey of shelters for women who are battered. *Society and Animals* 5(3):205-18.

Boatfield, M. P. 1996. *Guidelines for implementing a program for animal/child abuse prevention.* Maumee, Ohio: Toledo Humane Society.

Browne, A. 1993. Violence against women by male partners: Prevalence, outcomes, and policy implications. *American Psychologist* 48:1077–87.

DeViney, E., J. Dickert, and R. Lockwood. 1983. The care of pets within child abusing families. *International Journal for the Study of Animal Problems* 4:321–29.

Ehrhardt, J. 1995. *A training guide for recognizing and reporting child abuse.* Englewood, Colo.: American Humane Association.

Fucini, S. 1978. The abuser: First a dog, then a child? *American Humane Magazine* (May), 14–15.

Humane Society of the United States. 1997. "First strike: The role of the community in reducing violence," booklet from First Strike Campaign. Washington, D.C.: Humane Society of the United States.

Irish Veterinary Journal. 1996. Animal abuse and the veterinary surgeon. *Irish Veterinary Journal* 49 (December):692.

Kellert, S., and A. Felthous. 1985. Childhood cruelty toward animals among criminals and noncriminals. *Human Relations* 38:1113–29.

Kempe, C. H., F. N. Silverman, B. F. Steele, W. Droegemuller, and H. K. Silver. 1962. The battered-child syndrome. *Journal of the American Medical Association* 181:17–24.

Lockwood, R. 1987. Two-legged animals: Is there a link between antisocial behavior and animal abuse? *Social Issues and Health Review* (February), 146–47.

Lockwood, R. 1989. Cruelty to animals and human violence. *Training Key,* no. 392. Arlington, Va.: International Association of Chiefs of Police.

Lockwood, R., and G. Hodge. 1986. The tangled web of animal abuse: The links between cruelty to animals and human violence. *The Humane Society of the United States News* (Summer), 10–15.

Munro, H. 1996. Battered pets. *Irish Veterinary Journal* 49:712–13.

Patronek, G. 1998. Issues and guidelines for veterinarians in recognizing, reporting, and assessing animal neglect and abuse. In Patricia Olson, ed., *Recognizing and reporting animal abuse: A guide for veterinarians,* 25–39. Englewood, Colo.: American Humane Association.

ten Bensel, R. 1984. Historical perspectives of human values for animals and vulnerable people. In R. K. Anderson et al., eds., *The pet connection: Its influence on our health and quality of life,* 2–14. Minneapolis: University of Minnesota, CENSHARE.

Wiebers, D. O., R. A. Barron, J. Leaning, and F. R. Ascione. 1994. Ethics and animal issues in U.S. medical education. *Medical Education* 28:517–23.

A Survey of Veterinarians and a Proposal for Intervention

Melanie S. Sharpe

THE VETERINARIAN'S ROLE in protecting public health is critical. Historically, veterinarians have accomplished this mainly through the prevention and treatment of zoonotic diseases and maintaining food safety. But veterinarians may have a new role to play in protecting public health: violence prevention and intervention (Arkow 1994). Anecdotal evidence dating back to the thirteenth century has led to the widespread belief that a person who abuses animals may be more likely to engage in violence against humans (Regan & Singer 1976, 59).

Recent empirical evidence supports this belief. The relationship between child abuse and animal abuse was reported by DeViney, Dickert, and Lockwood (1983). In a study of pet-owning families who were documented for child abuse or neglect, 88 percent of these families also abused their animals. Ascione, Weber, and Wood (1997) linked spouse abuse and animal abuse when 71 percent of pet-owning women entering domestic violence shelters reported that the abuser had hurt, killed, or threatened their pets. Several studies have linked child and adolescent involvement in animal cruelty to future violent acts against humans (Kellert & Felthous 1985; Ressler, Burgess, & Douglas 1988; Tingle et al. 1986). The American Psychiatric Association (1987, 53–56) included animal cruelty as a trait associated with Conduct Disorder in its *Diagnostic and Statistical Manual of Mental Disorders.*

Veterinarians may be in a unique position to recognize both animal abuse and family violence. DeViney, Dickert, and Lockwood (1983) showed that veterinary services were utilized at least once by a majority (55%) of families with documented child abuse and animal abuse. Involvement by veterinarians in abuse cases may improve public health and relieve animal suffering, both of which are professional responsibilities outlined in the Veterinary Oath.

But what role should a veterinarian play if animal abuse or human abuse is suspected? The results of the study described here may provide some insight into what small-animal practitioners feel their role should be. The goals of the study were (1) to summarize, via a mail survey, small-animal veterinarians' attitudes and related information with regard to human and animal abuse intervention, and (2) to develop a model resource list for small-animal practitioners to utilize in the event that abuse cases are encountered.

METHODS

Survey Methods

A national, random sample of 1,000 veterinarians who described their practice as limited to small animals received a two-page mail survey along with a letter describing the study and a stamped return envelope. The survey was anonymous, which prohibited individual follow-up. Two weeks after the initial mailing, all practitioners received a postcard outlining the importance of their participation and reminding them to return the surveys. Practitioners were asked to provide information regarding demographics (age, sex, race, graduation year, and highest level of veterinary education), practice characteristics (practice type, practice setting, number of patients seen per year) and animal abuse and family violence (number of animal abuse cases seen per year, definition of animal abuse, opinions about appropriate veterinarian responses to violence, and 13 Likert-scale questions regarding violence intervention).

All data were entered into a computerized database using Microsoft Access, and analyzed using SPSS for Windows. The Mann-Witney U test was used to determine if significant differences existed between demographic or practice groups for Likert scale questions. The student's t-test was used to determine if there were significant differences in mean animal abuse incidence reported between practice setting groups (urban, suburban, and rural).

Methods for Developing the Resource List

The resource list was developed to provide small-animal practitioners with information about animal abuse, child abuse, and spouse abuse prevention and intervention. Representatives from five county and five national organizations provided information for the resource list. In addition, two Franklin County, Ohio, attorneys with special interests in animal legal defense provided legal assistance.

RESULTS

Mail Survey Results

The response rate was 36.8 percent (N = 368) after six weeks. Table 1 describes the respondent and practice characteristics.

The mean number of animal abuse cases seen per year was 5.6 per 1,000

Table 1. Respondent and Practice Characteristics

Respondent Characteristics	Number (%)
Gender	
Male	182 (50)
Female	186
Age (mean = 41.2)	
40 years or younger	189 (50)
41 years or older	173 (48)
Highest Education	
Veterinary college	308 (85)
Internship or residency	38 (11)
Other	15 (4)
Race	
Caucasian	333 (94)
Asian	9 (3)
Mixed Race or other	7 (2)
Hispanic	4 (1)
African American	3 (<1)

Practice Characteristics	Number (%)
Type of practice	
Group	227 (62)
Solo	103 (28)
University	7 (2)
Other	30 (8)
Practice setting	
Suburban	185 (51)
Urban	125 (34)
Rural	42 (12)
Other	12 (3)

patients (range 0 to 250). The wide range may be attributable to the variation in veterinarians' definitions of abuse. Urban, rural, and suburban mean abuse incidence rates were not significantly different.

Figure 1 displays what veterinarians described as appropriate professional responses to suspected human and animal violence. In summary, only 2.4 percent thought that a veterinarian should do nothing if animal abuse is suspected and only

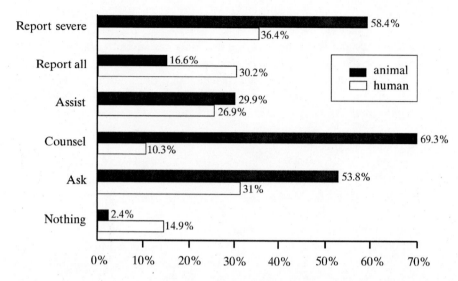

Figure 1. Responses to suspected animal and human abuse cases. Veterinarians were asked to choose the appropriate response to suspected animal and human abuse. The possible responses were "no intervention," "ask the client," "provide counseling to the client," "assist the client in getting help," "report all cases," and "report only severe cases." Only 2.4 percent and 14.9 percent checked "no intervention" and nothing else. The remaining categories were not mutually exclusive.

14.9 percent thought a veterinarian should do nothing if child or spouse abuse is suspected.

Answers to Likert scale questions summarize veterinarians' opinions and attitudes about human and animal abuse. The overwhelming majority (86%) agreed that clients who abuse their animals are more likely to abuse their children, while 77 percent agreed that clients who abuse their animals are more likely to abuse their spouses. Half of the sample agreed that veterinarians have a responsibility to intervene in situations where they suspect family violence. Most (85%) disagreed that veterinarians have the necessary resources to offer help to their clients in preventing family violence. A slightly higher percentage (86%) disagreed that veterinarians understand their legal rights and responsibilities if child or spouse abuse is suspected.

With regard to animal abuse, slightly over half (54.6%) thought they had the necessary resources to offer help in prevention, and only 43.8 percent agreed that veterinarians understand related legal rights and responsibilities. Only 8 percent thought that veterinary education provided adequate training in general abuse prevention.

Results of the Mann Witney U test revealed some differences between older

(41 or older) and younger veterinarians. In general, older veterinarians were less likely to agree that (1) there is a correlation between animal abuse and human (child or spouse) abuse, (2) they had the necessary resources to offer help in preventing animal abuse, or (3) abuse is a major companion animal health problem. Results of the Mann Witney U test also revealed that rural veterinarians were less likely than urban veterinarians to agree that they have the necessary resources to offer help to their clients in preventing family violence.

Resource List Results

The resource list was completed using a brochure format. The brochure provides information in four main areas instructing veterinarians about actions to take if (1) spouse abuse is suspected, (2) child abuse is suspected, (3) a child is abusing animals, or (4) animal abuse is suspected. Although state law determines the criminality and prosecution of abuse cases, there is significant county variation in how and where abuse is reported. Therefore, the resource list was developed for Franklin County, Ohio, but may be used as a prototype for other counties.

With regard to spouse abuse, veterinarians can provide information to clients about a local shelter, make written information available in office waiting areas, and help to determine what options are available for endangered pets. Experts warn against talking with the victim in the presence of the suspected abuser. With regard to child abuse, veterinarians are able to report child abuse anonymously to the local Children Services agency. Again, it was suggested that the veterinarian not confront the child or parent directly but to report to the appropriate agency. With regard to children who are abusing animals, the veterinarian may provide some information about child counseling services. With regard to animal abuse, it is suggested that the veterinarian contact the county humane officer. Many related legal issues and considerations as well as telephone numbers, addresses, and contact people are included in the resource list.

CONCLUSIONS

A majority of veterinarians surveyed thought that there is a correlation between family violence and animal abuse. Slightly over half indicated a professional responsibility to intervene if family violence is suspected. However, the overwhelming majority thought they were inappropriately trained and lacked knowledge regarding legal issues. Over a third thought that veterinarians lack the resources to help clients prevent animal abuse, and a greater percentage (43%) thought that veterinarians do not understand legal issues surrounding animal abuse. Despite the lack of preparedness, an overwhelming majority agreed that they should do something when they suspect human abuse or animal abuse (85.1% and 97.6%, respectively), but without proper resources and information, veterinarians may not be intervening effectively.

Rural small-animal practitioners may be in greater need of information on abuse intervention than their urban counterparts and older veterinarians may be less likely than younger veterinarians to recognize the connection between human and animal abuse.

RECOMMENDATIONS

Veterinarians need more information about how to recognize animal abuse and human abuse, appropriate agencies to contact in their respective areas to prevent abuse, what constitutes abuse, and what their legal responsibilities are. County, state, and national veterinary medical associations may provide this information through educational seminars. Education target groups should include all small-animal veterinarians, with an emphasis on rural and older veterinarians. Veterinary medical schools should include this information in their curricula.

The development of tools similar to the model resource list for Franklin County, Ohio, may provide veterinarians with accurate information about abuse intervention and empower them to act when they suspect abuse. The resource list may be provided in an educational setting to veterinarians along with information about recognizing signs of abuse.

The benefits of early intervention in animal abuse and human abuse cases are clear. Animal suffering and human violence may be prevented if proper information is provided to the clients and appropriate authorities. Although small-animal veterinarians may be in a situation to become involved, the study described provides evidence that they are lacking the necessary resources and training to do so.

REFERENCES

American Psychiatric Association. 1987. *Diagnostic and statistical manual of mental disorders,* 3rd edition, revised. Washington, D.C.: American Psychiatric Association.

Arkow, P. 1994. Child abuse, animal abuse, and the veterinarian. *Journal of the American Veterinary Medical Association* 204(7):1004–7.

Ascione, F. R., C. V. Weber, and D. S. Wood. 1997. The abuse of animals and domestic violence: A national survey of shelters for women who are battered. *Society and Animals* 5(3): 205–18.

DeViney, E., J. Dickert, and R. Lockwood. 1983. The care of pets within child abusing families. *International Journal for the Study of Animal Problems* 4:321–29.

Kellert, S. R., and A. R. Felthous. 1985. Childhood cruelty toward animals among criminals and noncriminals. *Human Relations* 38:1113–29.

Regan, T., and P. Singer, eds. 1976. *Animal rights and human obligations.* Englewood Cliffs, N.J.: Prentice Hall.

Ressler, R. K., A. W. Burgess, and J. E. Douglas. 1988. *Sexual homicide: Patterns and motives.* New York: Lexington Books.

Tingle, D., G. W. Barnard, L. Robbins, G. Newman, and D. Hutchinson. 1986. Childhood and adolescent characteristics of pedophiles and rapists. *International Journal of Law and Psychiatry* 9:103–16.

Initiating an Animal Abuse Reporting Policy at a Veterinary Teaching Hospital

Phil Arkow

In 1997, the Veterinary Hospital of the University of Pennsylvania (VHUP), recognizing the links between animal abuse and other forms of family violence, initiated a policy regarding the responsibility of hospital personnel to report suspected animal abuse and neglect. The policy, developed over a period of several months by the hospital's Ethics Committee, was presented at a meeting with all SPCAs in the Philadelphia region where the teaching hospital is located. The meeting was also believed to be the first time all area humane groups had met with VHUP officials. The meeting, and subsequent interactions, focused on the dual needs of establishing diagnostic criteria to assist veterinarians in recognizing abuse and collecting data on the incidence of abuse and neglect cases. Other issues under ongoing discussion include the legal and liability ramifications for veterinarians who report cases of suspected abuse and maintaining communications between veterinarians and humane groups.

The University of Pennsylvania policy addresses many of the concerns that have been raised by veterinary officials. For additional details, contact Dr. James Serpell at the Department of Clinical Studies, 3900 Delancey St., Philadelphia, Pennsylvania 19104, or call 215-898-1004, or e-mail serpell@pobox.upenn.edu.

THE VETERINARY HOSPITAL OF THE UNIVERSITY OF PENNSYLVANIA POLICY REGARDING SUSPECTED ANIMAL ABUSE AND NEGLECT

A Latham Foundation study* of nearly 600 individuals in the field of child protection, domestic violence, animal welfare, animal control, and veterinary medicine showed that 90% of the respondents believed there is a connection between animal

---

*The Latham Foundation conducted a national needs assessment in 1994 among animal protection, child protection, and domestic violence prevention personnel, to ascertain professional needs in the field. The publication of this book, the 1995 training manual and video *Breaking the Cycles of Violence,* and the findings that 90% of respondents felt the three forms of family violence were linked, were among the outcomes of this informal study.

cruelty and family violence. Because of that report and subsequent discussion by VHUP's Ethics Committee, the hospital has developed a policy covering clinicians' responsibilities when animal abuse is suspected.

Please understand that clinicians are not asked to be judges or juries sentencing clients to penalties for animal cruelty. Instead, they are medical investigators whose role is to represent the animals' and families' interests and request that appropriate agencies with knowledge of animal and/or child abuse review the facts and evaluate the environment into which their patients will be discharged after medical care has been provided.

It shall be Hospital policy that veterinarians and support staff who, in the context of a veterinarian-client-patient relationship, suspect animal abuse and/or neglect consult with their Section Chief or Service Head at the time the suspicion arises to determine whether such concerns should be communicated to appropriate humane agencies. If a Section Chief or Service Head is not on the premises, the senior person in the service should be notified. In instances when clinicians are on duty with other clinicians of equal status, documented consultations between them should occur. Clinicians who are on duty alone may call humane agencies without any consultations based on their own judgment.

Often a determination of suspected animal abuse or neglect is an educated guess and may be based on a pattern of activity over time involving specific clients. Furthermore, the law does not require absolute assurance of abuse to provoke a response to authorities, merely suspicions. It is important to understand that VHUP and its personnel have no legal jurisdiction to intervene on behalf of an animal's welfare. That role is the responsibility of the SPCA officers who have the police power to investigate reports of alleged animal abuse and take custody of such animals during the investigations and/or after they have made determinations of abuse or neglect. Signs suggestive of abuse and/or neglect include:

1. Lameness or other injuries without histories supporting the severity of the clinical signs, injuries to pets where owners describe ongoing toilet training "accidents."
2. Multiple bite wounds in patients with numerous scars around the head and legs from previous injuries. (NOTE: Suspected dog fighting is not addressed by this policy statement.)
3. Severely matted animals where the animal's condition is not consistent with its pleasant disposition and/or temperament.
4. Severe malnutrition from underfeeding.
5. Chronic, infected, untreated wounds, often present in pets where grooming has been neglected (maggots may or may not be present).
6. Chains and collars that have cut through the skin and into the musculature of the neck; often related to rapidly-growing, medium- to large-breed dogs with inadequate owner attention.

7. Aggressive, defensive or other abnormal animal behavior with the caveat that reports shall be made only in situations where other evidence of abuse is also present.
8. Unexplained chemical or thermal skin burns.
9. Stupor from possible drug or alcohol ingestion.

Abuse or neglect can occur in the form of a) omissions; b) commissions; and/or c) apparent use of animals in staged fights. Because the reporting of suspected staged animal fighting produces concerns for staff security, a Hospital policy on that issue is not addressed in this statement. Instead, clinicians are advised to report their suspicions to the Director's office on the next business day to enable personnel there to pursue further investigations through local police and/or humane organizations.

Clinicians are asked NOT to inform clients that they are reporting the suspected abuse or neglect to local SPCAs. If SPCA officers instruct clinicians to detain animals until they can investigate, SPCA officers must notify clients of such action. When concerns about owner violence exist, campus police should be present at the time of any SPCA-owner or doctor-client interactions. In situations where owners request that animals be discharged before SPCA officers have time to investigate, such animals should be released and SPCA officers will be expected to pursue home investigations. Clinicians should document information regarding the suspected abuse or neglect using histories, photographs, examination notes, and all other avenues in gathering information.

(Legislation is being proposed in Pennsylvania that allows veterinarians who report suspected abuse or neglect to be immune from criminal or civil action. Until that proposal is law, however, the University will defend any veterinarians and/or staff person who reports suspected animal abuse and/or neglect to proper authorities based on well-documented histories, thorough physical examination, and supporting diagnostic workups.)

In the event of suspected child or spousal abuse, clinicians and support staff are to inform the hospital's social worker, Ms. Kathleen Dunn, of such information.

To assist staff with an understanding of terminology, "abuse" means every act, omission or neglect which causes or unreasonably permits unnecessary or unjustifiable pain, suffering or death to animals. "Neglect" is a flexible concept embracing matters such as failure to provide food, water, protection from the elements, or veterinary and/or other care generally considered to be normal, usual and accepted for an animal's health and well-being consistent with the species, breed, condition, use and type of animal. "Pain" is the experience of stress from injury, disease or neglect. "Suffering" is the condition of enduring the pain or distress.

The policy concludes with a list of eight area SPCAs and contact names and phone numbers.

The Relevance of Cultural Competence to the Link between Violence to Animals and People

Michael E. Kaufmann

CULTURALLY DEFINED ATTITUDES toward animals challenge animal care and control agencies on a daily basis. For example, a Hispanic community is involved in cock fighting, or a group of rural children train pit bull terriers by throwing live kittens to the dogs. It is not productive or effective to simply deem these acts as wrong and label the people who participate in them as immoral. But groups like the Amish communities who contribute to the pet overpopulation crisis by operating puppy mills present a challenge to the animal shelter trying to curb euthanasia of unwanted pets. And the Asian markets that keep live turtles stacked for days in orange crates in order to provide fresh food for their customers are in direct opposition to a belief system that all animals deserve respectful and humane treatment free of suffering. Even the U.S. Supreme Court has been asked to address cultural issues related to the treatment of animals in a case involving animal sacrifice during Santeria religious rituals.

In recent years, a special focus of many animal care and control agencies has been on the correlation between child abuse and animal cruelty, and on how domestic violence often involves women, children, the elderly, and family pets as victims. This topic, perhaps more than any other animal welfare issue, has forced the animal protection community to look outside of its ranks for information and guidance. Collaborative relationships are being established with social workers, psychologists, the legal system, and law enforcement officials. Many of those agencies, realizing the diverse nature of their communities, long ago made a commitment to culturally competent service delivery. This has not been the case in most animal care and control agencies.

Rarely has animal protection in general, and the violence link specifically, been discussed in the context of a multicultural society. Social service agencies dealing with substance abuse, domestic violence, and child abuse have considered cultural competence an important component of their service delivery for many years. Because animal care and control services are increasingly being viewed as a human social service, a move toward culturally competent service delivery is relevant. In order to develop an effective community response to animal cruelty and specifically to cases of animal abuse that correlate with other forms of community violence, animal care and control agencies must comprehend the importance of familiarity and comfort with the multicultural milieu.

A culturally competent response is indispensable in all facets of animal care and control. Infusing such proficiency into the mission of all animal care and control agencies will be especially useful when dealing with cases where cultural values clash.

WHAT IS CULTURAL COMPETENCE?

Cultural competence is a set of congruent behaviors, attitudes, and policies that come together in a system, agency, or among professionals that enables that system, agency, or those professionals to work effectively in cross-cultural situations. The word "culture" is used because it implies the integrated pattern of human behavior that includes thoughts, communications, actions, customs, beliefs, values, and institutions of a racial, ethnic, religious, or social group. The word "competence" is used because it implies having the capacity to function effectively. A culturally competent system of care acknowledges and incorporates—at all levels—the importance of culture, the assessment of cross-cultural relations, vigilance toward the dynamics that result from cultural differences, the expansion of cultural knowledge, and the adaptation of services to meet culturally unique needs (Cross et al. 1989).

THE CULTURAL COMPETENCE CONTINUUM

Cross and his colleagues, Bazron, Dennis, & Isaacs (1989), have defined a continuum of attitudes prevalent in multicultural understandings. These may be summarized as follows:

Cultural Destructiveness. The negative end of the continuum; the dehumanization and intentional destruction of a culture. Example: Genocide.

Cultural Incapacity. A biased approach to cultural communities based on fear and ignorance. This approach fosters discrimination in hiring practices and devalues other, non-mainstream cultures. Example: Segregation under the law.

Cultural Blindness. The belief that culture and ethnicity do not matter, that everyone is the same. This well-intentioned approach leads to the belief that everyone thinks, acts, and believes the same. Example: An agency that claims to be unbiased, but does not have any diversity in its large staff.

Cultural Precompetence. This term implies movement toward integrating cultural issues. Questions are asked on how better to serve a multicultural clientele. Although this level can lead to a false sense of accomplishment and "tokenism," it is the start of cultural competence. Example: Asking minority clients, "What do you need from us?" and then meeting those needs.

Cultural Competence. The stage of viewing minority groups as distinctly different yet equal. Agencies seek staff diversity to meet the needs of a multicultural world. Cross-cultural situations are comfortable both philosophically and in practice. Example: The United Nations.

Cultural Proficiency. The most positive end of the scale. Culture is held in high esteem. Agencies hire a multicultural staff proficient in culturally competent practices. Cultural competence is valued in every aspect of policy and practice. All levels of an agency, individual, administration, board, policy makers, and clients participate in the process. Example: CNN.

A FLUID PROCESS

Today, cultural diversity encompasses not only ethnicity, but also gender, age, individuals with disabilities, socioeconomic background, and sexual orientation. Rural and urban cultures also can be of significance. Cultural values are fluid and constantly evolve and change. Therefore no cultural group can be rigidly stereotyped as to behaviors, attitudes, or customs. Although there can be commonalities of beliefs or customs in certain ethnic groups, individual members will always represent considerable variation. Cultural competence within an agency should never rely on a simplistic and static set of rules that dictate policy or behavior. For example, it would be deplorable if an agency, in an attempt to become culturally competent, falls into a pattern of treating all Asians in a certain way based on one or two cultural criteria. This approach leads to stereotyping and is prejudicial.

Cultural proficiency within an agency is not "us" working with or for "them." Inclusion and sensitivity are keys to cultural competence. It is an approach that acknowledges differences and is inclusive of diverse views and interests. A welcome by-product of cultural competence is that an agency ideally strikes a democratic balance between the needs and desires of culturally diverse employees and clients. This inclusiveness requires participation of both staff and clients in the creation of programs, policies, and procedures throughout an animal care and control agency.

COMING TO TERMS WITH DIFFERENCES

The practical significance of cultural diversity to animal care and control agencies can be seen in the interpretation of what a "pet" is. Today, mainstream American culture would dictate that a pet is a beloved dog or cat or other commonly kept companion animal that lives in the home and shares life with a family. Yet that relationship is not universal even within the United States. Dogs are viewed as pets by many Americans, yet other cultures view them as filthy animals to be kept outdoors or even as an animal to be eaten. The rural American who keeps pigs for utility purposes in the barn is appalled at the urban dweller who shares his or her bed with a pet potbellied pig.

This disparity in attitudes leads directly to an inability to find culturally shared values regarding the treatment or alleged maltreatment of animals. Although one individual may be horrified by a litter of kittens being drowned, another might interpret this as a negligible act of low significance or even something beneficial to the community.

This disparity is further exacerbated by great inconsistency in what constitutes cruelty to animals in the United States (American Humane Association 1996). Even the anticruelty laws in each state do not clearly define abuse to animals. To cut the tail off a cat without anesthesia would constitute cruelty in most states, yet doing the same to a lamb would be considered standard agricultural practice. It therefore is not the pain caused an animal that determines if the act is cruel, but rather culturally defined criteria. Such disparity based on random classification (farm animal, pet, reptile) makes the enforcement of anticruelty laws on the state level very difficult. Humane law enforcement agencies are frustrated by the arbitrariness of anticruelty laws and the lack of a shared cultural value regarding their enforcement. Heated arguments occur regularly between rural people and urbanites as well as between various cultural groups when it comes to the appropriate or inappropriate treatment of animals.

In an extensive national survey of adult Americans, Kellert (1980) identified 10 basic human attitudes toward animals, ranging from strong affection for individual animals to hatred of all animals:

Aesthetic: primary interest in the physical attractiveness and symbolic appeal of animals
Humanistic: primary orientation one of strong emotional affection for individual animals
Moralistic: primary concern for the right and wrong treatment of animals, with strong ethical opposition to presumed cruelty
Naturalistic: primary interest in direct outdoor recreational contact and enjoyment of animals
Dominionistic: primary interest in the mastery and control of animals
Ecologistic: primary concern for interrelationships among species and natural habitats
Utilitarian: primary interest in the practical value of animals or the subordination of animals for the material benefit of humans
Scientistic: primary interest in the physical attributes, taxonomic classification, and biological functioning of animals

Negativistic: primary orientation a fear, or dislike of animals
Neutralistic: indifference toward animals.

Although cultural diversity was not a focus of the study, Kellert did discover that demographic factors, including whether the person was raised in an urban or rural environment, helped predict the attitudes people would have toward animals. Other factors influencing these attitudes included education level and gender, with women demonstrating a higher concern about animal cruelty issues. This study provides indirect evidence of the impact that cultural background has on the relationship between people and animals. It can therefore be proposed that cultural issues may also play a considerable role in the link between abuse to people and animals. Anyone seeking to understand violent acts against animals, or seeking to develop preventive programs to halt such abuse, ought to be culturally competent.

ANIMAL CARE AND CONTROL AGENCIES

The animal care and control agency is a "system of care" in much the same way as is a child welfare agency. Although animal care and control personnel may focus their energy on abused or neglected animals, the actual clients of their agencies are people in all their diversity. Every aspect of successful animal care and control begins with an effective approach to a diverse public. No studies have been conducted and published to assess the cultural competence level within animal care and control agencies.

Based on observation, it could be asserted that most animal care and control agencies fall somewhere between cultural blindness and cultural precompetence. The culturally blind animal care and control agency fosters the belief that color or culture makes no difference and that all people are the same and share a common mission when it comes to animals and their treatment. This leads to a belief that the worldview of a dominant culture is universal. Internally, such agencies often have low or no minority participation in their policy making or even within their staffs. Though a well-intentioned approach, this is totally inaccurate and results in the gross misunderstandings that one view of animals and their treatment is universal.

Culturally precompetent animal care and control agencies comprehend that issues of culture are relevant internally and in terms of community outreach. These agencies realize that there is significant variance among cultural groups in their approach to animals. At this stage, agencies seek staff diversity and attempt to address the needs of a multicultural clientele.

Deplorably, many animal care and control agencies have settled into cultural incapacity. These agencies lack diversity in their staffs and dwell on a belief that "those people" just don't care for animals. As a result, they treat diverse communities with disrespect and condescension. Policies and programs within this type of agency rarely serve the needs of the human members of the community. It can be presumed that the animals in the community also are not optimally served.

APPLYING CULTURAL COMPETENCE TO THE LINK

Because various cultural groups within the United States see animals differently and each individual defines the treatment of animals in a personal context, there is no clearly defined standard. The law is ambiguous and depends on the interpretations of individual judges and enforcement agencies to define cruel acts against animals. Even in cases where an animal was hurt or killed intentionally and maliciously, there often is a lackluster response. Only by proposing that violence to animals can have a direct connection to domestic violence, child abuse, abuse of the elderly, and other issues of broad societal concern has it been possible to motivate a wider discussion of the animal abuse issue.

The exact nature and extent of the link between animal abuse and violence to people continues to emerge, and there are still many unanswered questions. At the 1992 Summit on Violence to Children and Animals (American Humane Association 1992), an invited panel of experts identified four main areas of focus regarding the link between animal and human abuses: research, intervention strategies, programmatic change, and education and prevention. Reviewing them today with the added mandate to infuse cultural competence into each area can serve as a sound master plan when further developing approaches to the cycle of violence and other issues that relate to the human-animal relationship.

Research

A greater body of sociological and psychological research is needed to define the link between human abuses and animal cruelty. Whether the focus of a study is directed toward the animal victim, the perpetrator, or society's response to an incident of abuse, a culturally competent approach must become the standard. Researchers need to develop and evaluate their proposals in terms of cultural competence. Sample sizes must be representative of a community. Questions asked of perpetrators of animal cruelty should reflect culturally relevant information as well as the experience of the individuals surveyed. Is the hypothesis free of assumptions about a community and its diverse cultural groups? The validity of research increases as greater focus is placed on the cultural significance of the proposed project.

Example. A study focusing on children who are abusive to animals will naturally include a focus on the familial system of the young perpetrators. The question might be asked: Who in the family had influence over the child, and did the adult caregivers contribute, encourage, or even bring about the cruel act? Mainstream culture defines the nuclear family as the norm (father, mother, children), so significant information may be missed in cases where ethnicity defines the family differently.

In many Asian, Hispanic, or African American communities, parents, grandparents, cousins, and even nonblood relatives may be considered an integral part of the immediate family group and have significant influence over a child. In some settings, the grandparent might be considered the head of the household, with the mother or father playing a lesser role in the raising of children. A greater focus on such issues during interviews and observational studies of child perpetrators may reveal valuable information. At the same time, knowledge of cultural variations in familial relationships can prevent a researcher from interpreting results in a prejudicial or skewed fashion. (A child's moving frequently among the homes of cousins, aunts, and grandparents may seem chaotic and of concern when looking at the profile of a child perpetrator, yet in some cultural settings such moves would be considered the norm and might have little significance. Erroneous conclusions can be avoided by understanding the cultural setting in an unbiased way.)

Intervention Strategies

Because animal cruelty is a reality and animal care and control agencies increasingly encounter intentional maltreatment of animal victims, a greater focus must be placed on intervention strategies. Specific intervention programs must be developed and validated for such types of perpetrators as the youth who shoots arrows into dogs. A targeted law enforcement response and a more forceful legal response need to be identified for dealing with adult animal abusers. The most effective intervention responses include a culturally competent system of protocols that have been formulated and implemented by a culturally diverse agency for a diverse audience.

Example. A group of young Hispanic men have been apprehended while fighting pit bull terriers. A judge sentences the young men to community service at the local humane society. The young men arrive at the humane society, where they are treated like outcasts by the staff and volunteers. No one among the Anglo staff actually speaks to them. For several days they are supervised by an unfriendly young female kennel attendant while they scrub cages and paint the walls.

This is not an effective intervention strategy. Dog fighting may be illegal, but it also is sanctioned and promoted in some segments of the Hispanic culture. The young men likely will have great resistance to seeing their actions as wrong. The humane society may also be known to these individuals as a place where crazy "white" people think animals are better than humans. Once there, no one speaks to them, confirming that these "Anglos" are unfriendly and very strange. As teenagers, with a solid dose of Latino machismo, scrubbing kennels may seem demeaning, yet being supervised by a young woman may make the experience even more humiliating. This is a successful intervention only if the goal was to cause embarrassment to these young men. It would, however, be absurd to assume that this experience in any way would make them more humane to animals or see their dog fighting in a different light. Any chance of changing attitudes and behavior would rely on a respectful, culturally competent course of action. One of the most important components of such intervention might be to have peer counselors or adults conduct the intervention program who not only understand but actually are part of the community these young men represent.

Programmatic Change

The link between violence to people and animals must continue to be addressed by various professions in an interdisciplinary effort. Psychology, law enforcement, social services, community groups, and others must develop a more refined understanding of animal cruelty as it relates to other forms of interpersonal violence. Animal care and control agencies often are the driving force behind advocating for a new ethic against violence that includes the animal victim.

Cultural competence can be the catalyst to infuse the link between violence to people and animals into other professions such as social work, psychology, education, and law enforcement. Because many professionals outside animal protection seem to have resistance against viewing animal abuse as significant, the root causes for that resistance must be sought out and replaced with a new shared understanding of the issues. This process can best be accomplished through coalitions that include diverse participants who can recognize and reduce culturally based barriers with a resistant audience. Prior to changing any policy or procedure, that change must be created, reviewed, and then accepted by a culturally diverse audience in order to be relevant.

Example. A group of animal control officers is being trained in the recognition of child abuse. It is not enough to merely discuss the various categories of abuse (sexual, emotional, physical, and neglect) but some care must be taken to educate these professionals on cultural competence as it relates to social work. Although it may be obvious to recognize bruises on a child, much human interaction is based on subtle signals. Eye contact, for example, is very culturally influenced. In some settings eye contact is seen as a sign of trust, of honesty. In another context (some Asian groups) the same type of eye contact is seen as disrespectful and even aggressive. Therefore, when an officer notices a child who always averts her eyes, never directly speaks to him, and appears to be shy and withdrawn, incorrect conclusions might be drawn that the child is afraid, intimidated or possibly abused. In the absence of more concrete evidence of abuse, specific training in various cultural communication styles would provide more information to assess the situation more accurately. Cultural diversity training should therefore be part of the programmatic change of training animal control officers to recognize child abuse.

Education and Prevention

Humane education has long been advocated by animal care and control agencies as a long-term measure to prevent animal cruelty. This may be true, but more targeted research is needed to validate humane education critically. Further definition is also needed to define the goals and objectives of strategies to prevent violence and animal abuse. Because humane education focuses on the relationship between people and animals, it is vital to develop curricula and programs within a culturally competent context. When developing policy, selecting and training staff, and dealing with the public, animal care and control agencies must make cultural competence a prerequisite. Without critical evaluation of all goals, objectives, and procedures, and without regular and unbiased evaluation from a multicultural perspective, it will be difficult to develop an effective response to animal abuse and community violence.

Example. A humane educator has prepared a 50-minute informational lesson on the humane treatment of animals. This lesson is presented throughout the community. The audiences represent various ethnic groups and come from different socioeconomic groups. Therefore, this educator must be culturally competent to adapt the same lesson for these various audiences. Issues such as spaying and neutering, euthanasia, and humane vermin control need to be approached differently. For example, placing a pet in a boarding kennel while the family is away on vacation may be the humane choice for many suburbanites, but this scenario has no relevance to the inner-city child who has never been on a vacation and is always home with the pet. The child from the wealthiest part of the city, on the other hand, travels a lot yet would never utilize a boarding kennel because the maid watches the pets while that family is away. Some religious groups may take exception to the concept of spaying and neutering because they perceive it violates their prohibitions against birth control. If such seemingly simple choices and behaviors involving companion animals fluctuate dramatically in various cultural contexts, then far greater attention must be paid to this area when trying to develop and enhance the impact of humane education programs.

CONCLUSION

It has been projected that the U.S. society of the next millennium will be shaped by an increase in cultural diversity through immigration and shifts in demographics of existing minorities. This broadening of, up to now, a defined mainstream will impact all areas of daily life. It will significantly influence language, culture, commerce, education, law enforcement, and politics. Culturally competent service delivery will become ever more relevant to educators, social workers, the law, and commerce. Although there may well be moral and ethical reasons why such changes ought to be welcomed, there also is the issue of being effective and of not wasting financial resources on programs and policies that ultimately are unsuccessful. Corporate America has already discovered the financial rewards of a marketing strategy that takes demographic variations and culturally defined expectations, values, and needs of various cultural groups into consideration. One standardized approach simply cannot serve the multicultural society of today. In order to bring about the more humane treatment of animals and a more refined understanding of the connections of animal abuse to human violence, animal care and control agencies will need to make cultural competence a priority and prerequisite.

As the correlations between cruelty to people and animals are examined further and a wider number of professionals become aware of the cycle of violence against all vulnerable populations, animal care and control agencies will increasingly communicate with social service agencies, law enforcement officials, psychologists, and the courts. Their credibility and impact will increase dramatically with a systematic effort toward culturally competent service delivery.

APPLYING THE CONCEPTS

Why is cultural competence desirable in the animal care and control agency? What compelling reasons would dictate a call for cultural competence?

1. Cultivating a diverse staff ensures that an animal care and control agency truly reflects the community it serves. Negative messages are sent to a community surrounding an agency when no members of that community are visible on staff. The capacity to be inclusive and reach out to a wider clientele dramatically rises when a staff and board reflect the diversity of a community at every level.

Although staff diversity is to be welcomed, care must be taken by an agency that the needs and concerns of a diverse staff are respected and considered in practice. Many agencies do have a level of diversity, but also have issues of staff discontent due to the perception (or reality) that minority staff are not treated in an equitable fashion.

2. Training in cultural competence can make the culturally diverse staff and board more effective in their work. Be it in adoptions, cruelty investigations, or policy development, a culturally competent staff is ready to meet the demands a diverse public expects of a professional agency. This capacity directly benefits the animals in the community.

3. Animal care and control agencies rely on financial support from municipalities and private individuals. Cultural competence within the agency can lead to more compelling appeals for patronage. A culturally diverse and sensitive staff and board are in a good position to develop effective strategies that will reduce

objections and encourage the wider community to support the animal protection work.

4. Animal care and control work is controversial and often unpopular. A culturally competent agency can cultivate community relations that will result in better community relations. This can favorably affect the image of the agency and help solve pet overpopulation, increase adoptions, and so on.

5. The humane philosophy may be unfamiliar and suspect to individuals from certain cultural backgrounds. Because an animal care and control organization wants to advocate on behalf of animals, these suspicious individuals must be appealed to. A persuasive approach can only be based on open communication, mutual respect, a level of trust, and a sincere interest in communication.

6. By understanding and considering the needs of diverse members of a community, a culturally competent animal care and control agency can adjust its policies and procedures to meet the needs of the organization as well as the clients. Modifying the shelter's hours to serve people who work, hiring Spanish-speaking investigators, providing taxicab service for seniors needing to bring animals to the clinic, printing fliers in Vietnamese, and making free pet food available for homeless individuals with pets—all these are services that benefit people and animals in the diverse community.

7. A visible, unfeigned, and ongoing interest in attaining cultural competence in all areas is the ethical choice for an agency dedicated to the humane care and treatment of all animals.

REFERENCES

American Humane Association. 1992. *Report on the summit on violence to children and animals.* Englewood, Colo.: American Humane Association.
American Humane Association. 1996. *Cruelty statutes: United States and Canada.* Englewood, Colo.: American Humane Association.
Cross, T., B. Bazron, K. Dennis, and M. Isaacs. 1989. *Towards a culturally competent system of care: A monograph on effective services for minority children who are severely emotionally disturbed.* Washington, D.C.: Georgetown University Child Development Center.
Kellert, S. 1980. *Attitudes of the American public regarding animals.* No. 024-010-00-624-2. Washington, D.C.: U.S. Government Printing Office.

Legislative and Legal Contexts

No man shall exercise any Tirrany or Crueltie towards any bruite Creature which are usuallie kept for man's use.

—The Body of Liberties, Massachusetts Bay Colony, 1641

The Prosecutor's Role in Preventing Family Violence

Wm. Andrew Sharp

THE LAST THING that prosecutors feel like they are doing is preventing crime. No matter how many complaints are filed, no matter how many defendants are sentenced, no matter how much jail time is recommended, fresh police reports still come in and new cases are filed. More victims come to the office to relate new stories of abuse, which, to our ears, sound very old.

I am a prosecutor in a small rural community. Our local paper doesn't cover criminal cases, except for murders, and we haven't had a murder in over eight years. I once asked the local editor why he didn't cover criminal court. He told me he didn't want to destroy everybody's illusion that we were living in Mayberry.

Yet, even in Mayberry, we are not immune. The largest category of criminal offenses that my office files, aside from traffic matters, is domestic abuse charges for battery and disorderly conduct. The most unpleasant cases that I deal with on a regular basis are for child abuse, especially child sexual assault. The most expensive cases, with the most tenacious and unreasonable defendants, are cases charging animal abuse and neglect. These cases are no less difficult, complex, or horrific simply because they happened in a small town. Our court room has heard its tales of pathos, cruelty, and revenge. The state prison system holds erstwhile members of our community.

We have cases like that here in Mayberry? You betcha.

That is why judges and prosecutors everywhere are so interested in preventing domestic abuse, child abuse, and animal abuse. No matter where we are or how insulated we may seem, we see the effects of such crimes first hand. We meet the victims of these crimes. We read reports of how they were beaten and brutalized. We actually see the injuries, fresh and bleeding in the clinically graphic pictures taken at the scene or with bruises beginning to fade when we meet the victim to go to court. We listen to women describe how they lived for years in constant sweating anxiety, knowing that some unknown "wrong" word, look, or movement could result in a beating. We are there when a 12-year-old girl is asked on the witness stand why she didn't tell her teachers that her father was sexually abusing her, and we writhe inside when she breaks down and sobs out, "I was too ashamed." We help execute search warrants on houses that have four-inch carpets of dog feces and vomit and urine, and pat the heads of the dogs that come running up to us, wagging their tails.

Cases involving domestic abuse, child abuse, and animal abuse have many similarities, but one feature stands out. The victim. The victims dominate these cases. They are the focus. Actual harm has been done to their bodies and minds. They have reported the persons they love most in the world, and are trying to cope with the estrangement and displacement this "betrayal" has caused. Oftentimes, they have lost their homes, their cars, their clothing, their families. They are being pressured to recant by their children, by their parents, by their in-laws, by their friends. They look to us for help, while we stand by helpless, able only to redress the wrongs, not to undo them.

Little of the real work done by prosecutors and judges can be termed "prevention." Our jobs involve picking up the pieces after the harm has occurred. It is only at sentencing that any question of prevention comes into play. Obviously, by sentencing the defendant to jail or probation, we are trying to make his victims safe in the future. Thus, for that one victim, further harm by this perpetrator is prevented.

At the same time, it is recognized that sentencing has purposes other than simple punishment. One of these is rehabilitation of the defendant. In our county, that means counseling and possibly community service work. We have a well-established batterers' group that every domestic abuser must attend as a condition of his sentence.

In addition to rehabilitation, sentencing serves the purpose of sending a message to the community that criminal behavior will not be tolerated. The father who was sexually abusing the 12-year-old girl I mentioned above was sentenced to 60 years in prison. I do not know whether that sentence deterred any other potential abusers or not. All I know is that it could not have encouraged them.

Thus, for a prosecutor, prevention boils down to an effective prosecution that results in a sentencing opportunity. The cases will never stop. But perhaps the numbers can be reduced by effective and timely prosecutions.

INITIATING THE PROCESS

Most domestic abuse and child abuse cases begin with a report by the victim. Either an abuse victim finally feels she can no longer stand the abuse or she becomes so fearful during a beating that she calls the police. With child abuse, some third party usually sees bruises on the child or the child blithely makes some remark to a teacher or relative that raises suspicions.

Animal abuse is different. Most of these cases have their genesis with neighbors who witness abuse or complain about unbelievable odors coming from a residence. A significant number are also reported by some service provider, such as a milk truck driver reporting a barn full of manure and starved cattle.

But a significant number of these cases are reported by total strangers. A man takes some misdelivered mail over to his neighbor and notices that she has a black eye. A shopper sees a small child shaken and screamed at in a parking lot. A couple out for a Sunday walk sees a dog thrown bodily out a door.

What should the person do? Ignore it? Intervene? Report it to the police? What will happen if they do?

Almost everyone has been in this situation at some point in his or her life. Most of the time, the incidents seem minor. No one wants to appear to be a busybody or to be snooping into the lives of those around them. Besides, the police are busy chasing muggers and drug dealers. They don't want to be bothered with something like that.

Right? Not necessarily. Oftentimes, whether the police will be interested depends more on how well the information is reported rather than on how serious the incident seems to be. Vague and unspecific information will get a noncommittal response from officers, while specific and direct information may lead to results.

As a prosecutor, I have read literally thousands of police reports. On average, I file charges on only about 40 percent of the reports I read. Some are sent over by the police "for information only." Some are rejected because the police did a poor investigation that can no longer be corrected. But most of the reports that hit the proverbial wastebasket are closed because the person who reported the suspected crime never gave the police enough information to go on.

The most difficult types of crime to report are domestic abuse, child abuse, and animal abuse. Reporting these types of crimes is seen as impinging on the privacy of the family, the most protected institution in our society. How other people choose to live their lives is considered to be their own business. Interference by strangers is strongly resented. After all, how would you like someone else telling you how to live?

But the truth is that people in society are not free to live any which way they choose. When they engage in criminal conduct, they have to expect to be interfered with. If a man breaks his wife's nose during the course of an argument, why should he expect to be left alone?

Of major concern for the person who witnesses such crimes and wishes to report them is how to report them. The easiest way to make a report is to call an organization like Crimestoppers. Anonymity is guaranteed. Callers are never asked who they are and the Crimestoppers organization will pass the information on to the police as "a Crimestoppers' tip." Alternatively, a person can call the police and give the information anonymously. There is no possibility of a reward and anonymity cannot always be guaranteed. Police lines are recorded and courts can, in limited circumstances, order that the identity of the confidential informant be released.

The police are often not very receptive to anonymous calls. One reason is that such calls are often made by persons with a grudge and the information is therefore suspect. But the biggest problem is that such information is often simply more frustrating than helpful.

Why? Because police will often end up with information such as, "I think Bob Jones is beating his wife." That type of information is useless.

REASONABLE SUSPICION

Police officers are bound by very rigid rules, which have been developed by state legislatures, state courts, and the U.S. Supreme Court. One rule is that the police are not allowed to detain a person for investigation unless they have a reasonable suspicion that criminal activity is going on. This rule began in the U.S. Supreme Court case of *Terry v. Ohio.* In that case, the Supreme Court described a "reasonable suspicion" by stating the following:

> The police officer must be able to point to specific and articulable facts which, taken together with rational inferences from those facts, reasonably warrant that intrusion. . . . And in making that assessment it is imperative that the facts be judged against an objective standard: would the facts available to the officer at the moment of the seizure or search "warrant a man of reasonable caution in the belief" that the action taken was appropriate? . . . Anything less would invite intrusions upon constitutionally guaranteed rights based on nothing more substantial than inarticulate hunches, a result this Court has consistently refused to sanction. . . . And simple good faith on the part of the arresting officer is not enough.

One part of having a reasonable suspicion is having reliable information upon which to base it. The problem with anonymous information is that it is usually not considered reliable. No one knows who gave the information, why they gave it or if it is accurate.

So a police officer who is informed that "Bob Jones beats his wife" really has no grounds to begin an active investigation. An "active investigation" means speaking with Bob Jones or his wife and asking them whether Mr. Jones has beat Mrs. Jones. Proof of such a charge would require the testimony of someone who witnessed the beating or was in it. In fact, the officer would look foolish if he did confront the Joneses on the basis of such sparse information. They could simply deny the allegations. Without information about when it happened or how it happened, the officer could not challenge their statements.

The problem of the unreliability of anonymous information can be avoided if the anonymous informant gives the officer enough information to establish the informant's reliability. This rule comes from the United States Supreme Court case of *Illinois v. Gates.* In that case, an anonymous person wrote an unsigned letter to the police alleging that Sue and Lance Gates were bringing drugs into Bloomingdale, Illinois, from Florida. The informant stated that Sue Gates would drive down to Florida, leave the car "to be loaded up with drugs," and fly back. Lance Gates would then fly to Florida, pick up the car and drive it back. The informant named the next date they would make a trip. The police checked the information and found it to be accurate. Upon arriving back from Florida, the Gates' vehicle was searched. Three hundred and fifty pounds of marijuana were seized. The Gateses argued that the police did not have probable cause to search their car and home because the information came from an anonymous source, which was therefore not reliable. The Supreme Court ruled that the anonymous information was reliable because the police had verified everything the informant said was true before they sought a search warrant.

The situation with the call concerning the Joneses would be different if the call had included enough information to permit the officer to verify the caller's statements. An example would be:

Hello. I'm calling because last night there was a big argument between Bob and Mary Jones. They live at 123 West Side Drive. They have two children, Justin and Jennifer. Bob came home from his job as a foreman at the Acme Corporation at 6:30 P.M. He may have been out drinking after work at the Happy Tap on Front Street. Bob drives a big, blue Chevy pickup truck. The argument went on for half an hour or so. A mirror was broken during the argument. Later that night, Mary went to the emergency room at Memorial Hospital. Her nose was broken. She may have told them that she fell down the stairs.

Please note that none of this information in any way identifies the informant. It could be a neighbor. It could be a friend of Mary Jones who heard the story from her or pieced together enough information to guess what had happened. It could be a relative. It could be someone from down the street who got their information from various sources.

Given this information, an astute officer can do a background investigation to attempt to verify the accuracy of the anonymous informant. The phone book will tell the officer if the Joneses live at the address given. The officer can drive by the residence to see if they own a blue Chevy pickup truck or could check that information with the Department of Motor Vehicles. The officer can call the Acme Corporation to inquire if Bob Jones works there. The officer can call the Happy Tap to see if Bob Jones goes there and was there on the evening in question. The officer can check with the emergency room at the hospital and see if Mary Jones was there. A truly dedicated officer could even intercept the Jones' garbage on trash pickup day to see if there are pieces of a broken mirror in it.

If the information substantially checks out, the anonymous informant becomes "reliable." The officer then has a reasonable suspicion that Bob Jones broke Mary Jones' nose on the day in question. He can now speak with Mary Jones to see what she will say. If she says nothing happened, the officer can ask about her injuries. If she says she fell down the stairs, the officer can ask about the argument on the day in question that began after Bob came home from the Happy Tap after work. If she denies that an argument took place, the officer can ask about the broken mirror. If she denies the broken mirror, the officer can tell her about finding the pieces of glass in her garbage. It may well be that she will refuse to admit anything. If so, there will probably be no case. But at least the officer has made contact with her. If the officer is kind, perhaps she may call to speak to the officer at some point in the future when she has had enough. But without the cooperation of Mary Jones, or a confession from Bob Jones, their denial will almost certainly end the matter.

A person who calls the police, gives a name, and is willing to testify has vastly improved the chances of being taken seriously by the police: anonymous persons are treated with some suspicion because they are often persons with grudges trying to make trouble. Additionally, an unknown or unwilling witness makes a "hole" in the officer's investigation because the officer cannot use information from that witness in court. That means the officer must go out and repair the hole by getting the same evidence over again from some willing source.

But how does one get the police to take an interest in a case? The answer is simple: you have to show them you have a real case. How do you do that? By being specific.

Specificity is what everything boils down to in a criminal case. Just as with an anonymous informant, a named citizen who calls in and tells the police, "I think Bob Jones is beating his wife" has told them next to nothing. To charge Mr. Jones, the police will have to be able to say when the beating took place, where it took place, what the extent of Mrs. Jones' injuries were, and why Mr. Jones decided to beat her up. Charging someone with a crime cannot be done on a lark or a guess. It requires specific and exact proof.

DUE PROCESS

This specificity is required by the legal concept of due process, which is guaranteed by the Fifth and Fourteenth Amendments of the U.S. Constitution. A discussion of what due process is could fill several books. It has application in both criminal and civil law. But in simple terms, it means giving accused persons enough facts to know what they are charged with, enough time to prepare a defense, and a meaningful opportunity to tell their side of the story.

A prosecutor cannot file a criminal complaint that simply says "Bob Jones beat up his wife." How could Mr. Jones defend against that? When did this occur? As he does not know, he would have to be prepared to potentially defend what he did on every single day of his married life. Where did this occur? As he does not know, he cannot defend himself by saying he was somewhere else, if he was. What is he supposed to have done? As he does not know, he must try to recall each and every time he ever touched his wife. Who saw this? As he does not know, he is prey to any and every person who might have seen him and his wife together while they were married. Nor could he possibly secure witnesses on his own behalf, as he cannot bring every person he has ever had contact with into court.

A criminal complaint therefore starts out by stating the specific day the offense occurred. If the date cannot be fixed with certainty, it is permissible to say it occurred "on or about" a certain day, although this usually only gives leeway of one day either way.

The complaint then states the location of the event, which is more important than many people realize. First, a defendant must be told almost exactly where the crime is alleged to have taken place in order to provide him with the opportunity of an alibi defense. Lee Harvey Oswald never denied he was at the Texas Book Depository when Kennedy was shot, but he did claim he was in the lunch room downstairs rather than on the sixth floor. Second, the location of the crime affixes the venue of the case. Each court is assigned its own venue, which is usually either a municipality or a county. If a charge is brought in the wrong venue, it must be dismissed and started over in the correct venue.

The complaint then names the specific crime the defendant is alleged to have violated. This is obviously a very important bit of information. First, crimes are very specific laws. Proof of one crime is almost never proof of another. A defendant will sometimes tailor his entire defense to disprove the charged crime. Often this involves admitting to some other crime, usually of a lesser degree. The best-known example is admitting to accidentally killing someone by manslaughter in order to defeat a charge of intentionally killing the person by murder.

Second, different crimes have different penalties attached to them. For instance, there are usually several levels of battery offenses in state law. Striking someone and causing them pain has less potential penalty than striking someone and breaking a bone, which again has a lesser penalty than beating someone until they are almost dead.

Third, only a very small portion of negative human conduct is covered by laws with criminal penalties. I constantly run into people who seem to believe that I as a prosecutor can charge people for anything I don't like the sound of. I sometimes wish I actually had the power some people think I do. In truth, the legislature decides what is criminal and makes a law against it. I then am presented with police reports detailing specific conduct and I must decide whether a criminal law has been broken.

My favorite anecdote on this particular subject occurred one winter when we had been having a string of 30-degree-below-zero days. A woman called me up because she wanted the local school bus company charged with a crime. When I asked her why, she explained that the bus driver made her son walk to the end of their driveway to get picked up, rather than driving right up to their house to get him. She said she lived in the country and had a long driveway. Her son was in danger of freezing to death. I told her that it was an unfortunate situation, but there was nothing criminal about it. When I finally convinced her that I could not issue a charge, she requested that I simply call the bus company and order them to pick up her son at the house! I regretfully informed her that I had no such power and bid her goodbye.

Does this mean that you should read the statutes in your state to be sure what you are reporting is actually against the law? No. Just be aware that what you might think is criminal conduct may not actually be criminally chargeable. If there is no statute against it, it cannot be charged. It should be mentioned that statutes are written in relatively general terms, so that many types of specific acts of the same nature can be covered with one law. A resourceful and intelligent prosecutor can sometimes come up with a statute that, at first glance, does not seem to fit, but with a liberal reading actually does apply.

Finally, a criminal complaint then goes on to give details concerning how the crime was committed. This narrative section relates the facts and circumstances of the actual commission of the crime. It names the witnesses to the events and describes or quotes the statements they gave to the police. It may refer to physical evidence taken or to the results of scientific tests.

JUST THE FACTS, MA'AM . . .

All of this explains why the person who calls the police and says, "I think Bob Jones is beating his wife" may not get much of a response. General suspicions get the police nowhere. They need hard facts.

To get a response from the police, you should follow the same rule in telling your story that every newspaper reporter is taught: use the "five Ws": who, what, when, where, and why. Every recruit school teaches police officers to use the "five Ws" when interviewing witnesses or writing reports. If you take the same approach with the police, you are making their job easier for them.

Does this mean that a person must go out and investigate before calling the police? No. Police officers investigate crimes. Citizens are merely witnesses. Doing investigations could be dangerous and could spoil the investigation. Just be careful and specific in making your observations. Write down dates and times of occurrences. Make sure you have identified the persons involved correctly. Finally, let the facts speak for themselves. If you embellish the story with too many opinions or suppositions, you are only going to lessen your credibility. You should take the attitude of a neutral but concerned citizen who believes he or she has information about a crime and would like to have the matter investigated.

Once the police have begun their investigation, what does a prosecutor want? Every police officer knows the answer to that question: perfection! If the police officer does his job perfectly, the prosecutor will probably say nothing, or simply offer a laconic "good job." But if the officer misses one little thing . . . watch out!

A better question is: what evidence does a prosecutor need to pursue a case adequately? That answer depends on the type of case and the particular facts and circumstances surrounding it. But, in a general sense, the type of proof needed for domestic abuse cases, child abuse cases, and animal abuse cases is very similar.

Most domestic abuse and child abuse cases will be generated by a person calling the police while the evidence is fresh. The police respond and, in short order, will be talking directly to the persons involved, including the victim and the perpetrator.

First and foremost, to prosecute there must be statements taken from a witness or witnesses who either observed the abuse or who heard the defendant describe how it happened. This is because a mark or a bruise or a broken nose can be received by means other than physical abuse. The fact that the victim went into a house where she was alone with the defendant and came out with a broken nose does not mean the defendant punched her. It is possible that she fell down the stairs.

In domestic abuse cases especially, and in child abuse cases, it is imperative that a detailed statement be taken from the victim. This must be done immediately. The greatest problem with domestic abuse cases is recantation by the victims due to pressure from the defendant. If she is locked into a detailed statement, her recantation will be much less credible. The statement should be taped and the tape preserved. Statements should be as detailed as possible and as lengthy as necessary. All of this makes her recantation less credible, as it will be hard for the jury to believe she could make up such details and relate the story with such emotion if she were supposedly lying. The tape of the initial call by the victim requesting an officer should be saved for the same reason. One hears the frantic victim calling in, pleading for an officer to come to the scene to protect her from the defendant. Sometimes one can even hear the defendant in the background screaming and yelling abuse.

Likewise, the officer should always attempt to take a statement from the defendant. If he refuses to talk, fine; at least we tried. Sometimes the defendant will confess. Even if he tells some story contradicting the victim's version of the events, at least he is locked in to that statement. The rationality of the stories defendants come up with is directly proportional to the amount of time they are given to think up the story. A story with five minutes of mental preparation is usually almost incredible, but after five days the defendant will have a carefully crafted lie.

Finally, a statement must be taken from all who were present at the altercation, even if their statements are that they didn't see anything. There is nothing worse at a jury trial than having some unquestioned witness come forward and corroborate the defendant's lying tale after careful rehearsal. Most times, the witness could not have come up with this tale if he had been asked what he knew the night of the occurrence, as he could not have communicated with the defendant to get the story straight.

Second, pictures are all-important in cases like these. Juries like hard evidence. Pictures are important because they can help determine the time of the offense. Bruises develop and fade along time lines that are roughly similar from person to person. The statements of witnesses are subject to memory lapses and will probably be radically disputed by the statements of other witnesses or the defendant. But, to the jury, pictures cannot lie. Obviously, pictures also describe the abuse in a way words simply cannot match.

All of this means the officer should always take photographs if any injury can be seen. Generally, a Polaroid camera should not be used unless there is no other camera available. Polaroids have a tendency to wash out marks and bruises to such an extent that it ruins the case. The social worker describes dark marks and bruises, but the camera, which cannot "lie," shows almost nothing. Thirty-five-millimeter cameras are better, especially if they are taken with a flash. The flash often reveals marks the naked eye cannot see. Additional photos should be taken two or three days after the initial injury or contact, when the bruises are at their peak color.

If there was an altercation in the house, photographs should be taken of the mess. This also may corroborate details concerning the course of the argument. If the victim says the defendant kicked the bathroom door open, and the bathroom door jamb shows damage, the case is one step closer to a conviction.

Medical records and a doctor's testimony are also important, especially in child abuse and animal abuse cases. Doctors are trained in observing the differences between accidental and intentional injuries on children. Factors such as the location of the marks on the body, the number of marks, and the shape and severity of the marks are all-important. Because the doctor did not witness the abuse, the doctor will never be able to say that the marks are the result of abuse. But a doctor's testimony that "the marks are not consistent with accidental injury and are probably the result of abuse" is devastating to the defendant's case.

Seeing a doctor should be considered mandatory in a child abuse case. Children usually will not be good witnesses concerning their own injuries. Often, children do not have the vocabulary or the sophistication necessary to describe their own injuries adequately. There are often memory problems, where the child cannot differentiate between various injuries and when they were received. Also, as noted previously, the testimony of the doctor can sometimes make the case.

Even if the doctor cannot give an opinion about the probable cause of the injuries, the fact that the victim sought medical attention is significant. The date of the visit to the hospital or emergency room can help ascertain the date of the abuse. In addition, seeking medical attention shows that the victim considered the injuries to be significant at the time they were received. If there is an issue as to whether the abuse actually happened or is being fabricated, such a visit can also help dispel those concerns.

Officers should always ask victims if they have seen a doctor. If not, and they are agreeable, they should be taken to a doctor. This also means a medical records release form should be signed by the victim with a duration of at least one year. When there are no visible injuries, this will avert the standard defense attorney question of, "Well, if you were hurt so bad, why didn't you go see a doctor?"

These are the essential building blocks of a good case. This does not mean, however, that if all of these things are done, one will have a good case. That depends on the facts of the case, the ability of the witnesses to relate their observations, and the victim's mental fortitude in holding up during the entire process.

PROBABLE CAUSE

Investigations in cases of suspected child or animal neglect are often more problematic. The police usually have to develop enough information to obtain a search warrant. This means they must develop the legal degree of suspicion known as probable cause, which is required by the Fourth Amendment of the U.S. Constitution. The U.S. Supreme Court has described "probable cause" by stating:

> "The substance of all the definitions" of probable cause "is a reasonable ground for the belief of guilt." And this "means less than evidence which would justify condemnation" or conviction, as Marshall, Ch. J., said for the Court more than a century ago in *Locke v. United States.*" . . . Since Marshall's time, at any rate, it has come to mean more than bare suspicion: Probable cause exists where "the facts and circumstances within their [the officers'] knowledge, and of which they had reasonably trustworthy information, [are] sufficient in themselves to warrant a man of reasonable caution in the belief that" an offense has been or is being committed.

This level of suspicion is greater than "reasonable suspicion." In simple terms, it is the difference between "something may have happened" and "something probably happened." Although reasonable suspicion is enough cause to stop a person in some public place and ask him questions, our Constitution requires a greater level of certainty before the police forcibly go on someone's premises.

Developing this level of suspicion can be a long task. As a search warrant is often necessary in suspected animal neglect cases, and because these types of cases are too often ignored or given short shrift by police, I will discuss search warrants in the context of a suspected animal neglect case.

Law enforcement officers usually become aware of these types of situations on the basis of reports by private citizens. Neighbors are the most frequent source. The overwhelming smell from a house, along with the yapping of dozens of dogs, prompts the person to complain. Farm animals constantly straying into the road through neglected fences of a farm where the farmer is seldom seen is another common situation. Reporting persons may also develop information based on their employment. Perhaps the milk inspector at a dairy farm can no longer keep silent about the conditions he sees when he goes to the farm for inspection. Perhaps an animal shelter worker converses with the owner of a strayed dog who is thin and ungroomed and learns that the owner has 20 other dogs in the apartment.

Once officers have a reasonable suspicion that animal neglect is occurring, the officers need to gather enough information to get the probable cause needed for a search warrant. The question becomes how to discover what is going on in a house without actually having gone into it. To the uninitiated, the answer may seem simple: send some private citizen in to check. This cannot be done. If the police request a private party do something for the police, that person becomes an agent of the police and is subject to the same limitations as the police. Were it otherwise, the police could evade their constitutional limitations by hiring or requesting private citizens to do what they cannot. Nor is it advisable for a private citizen to try to do more on his own, such as peer through windows or enter the house under false pretenses. Not only are such actions dangerous, they will also look bad in front of a jury.

The answer is usually to check with persons who have a right or permission to go in or near the residence. Neighbors are a primary source of information. Postal workers are also excellent, as they often come right up to the door, visit the residence on a daily basis, and have knowledge of who occupies the dwelling.

Local veterinarians can be checked with, assuming the local jurisdiction has no confidentiality laws prohibiting veterinarians from discussing the health care records of their charges. States with such laws should have an exception in the law when police are investigating suspected animal abuse. Veterinarians may have recently seen the animal or animals owned by the suspected person and will have records as to the condition of the animal. Although it is suspicious if no health care provider can be found, especially in the cases where numerous animals are involved, such noninformation is meaningless. The animals may not have required veterinary care or the owner may receive veterinary services out of the local area.

If dogs are involved, a check can be made with the local dog licensing entity to see how many dogs are currently vaccinated and have tags. Some forward-thinking municipalities also require shots and licenses for cats. A lack of records may in and of itself be sufficient evidence for a search warrant, as some jurisdictions make it a crime to fail to license pets.

If the suspected residence is a farm, the scope of possible persons with knowledge becomes wider. Milk haulers make regular visits to farms in my state and are good sources of information. State inspectors for milk, meat, or produce can also sometimes provide information. Although one might think that, if the situation is truly critical, they should have reported the farm to local authorities themselves, some states prevent them from doing so. Oftentimes, the state statutes prohibit inspectors from contacting the police, but they do not prohibit them from answering questions by the police, if asked.

Local feed stores can sometimes provide information, as can implement salesmen, seed dealers, breeding services, and dead animal removers. Because animal neglect suspects are often animal collectors, amassing huge numbers of animals they cannot care for, animal auctioneers can be a source of information. I can recall a case where we were executing a search warrant on a farm full of neglected animals. The farm house was the one I mentioned earlier, with the four-inch carpet of dog excreta everywhere. When we arrived, the owner wasn't home. We finally located him at a farm auction—buying more animals!

If it is possible to see the residence from a highway or public property, the investigator can do so without a search warrant. Sometimes enough information can be obtained in this manner to get a warrant. For instance, many states require dead animals to be removed in a certain period of time. An unremoved dead animal might be visible on the farm. The investigator should also drive by the residence to get a description of the property to be searched. This is necessary for the search warrant, which must describe the area to be searched with specificity. Oftentimes, the lack of a description is the big delay in preparing the search warrant, as the officer has not thought to get a description. Long-range pictures are also very helpful in getting a good description.

Once the search warrant is ready to be executed, the assistance of a veterinarian is absolutely essential. This is especially true in neglect cases, where it must be proven that the animal's condition is due to neglect rather than disease. But even in cases of animal abuse, a veterinarian should be present to describe the animal's condition. Obviously, the animal is even less able to testify on this subject than a child, and no one else will have the credentials to describe the injury exactly.

A word of warning: veterinarians may be unwilling to testify against their clients or against local people. They fear hurting their business and that, if word spreads concerning their involvement, clients will be afraid that the vet will report them for animal abuse, even if the animal's condition is due to normal illness or injury.

A veterinarian will also be necessary to counter the testimony by the defendant's veterinarian witness that there was nothing wrong with the animal. Would another veterinarian really testify against the prosecution in an obvious animal abuse or neglect case? Yes. Several years ago, I charged two local men with cruelty to a horse. They were trying to break the horse to pull a harness racing cart. The horse repeatedly threw herself down. After the horse had done this about a dozen times, they became frustrated and dragged the horse back to its stall, 682 feet over frozen limestone gravel. The horse suffered numerous scrapes and abrasions, including a five-inch by eight-inch wound on the point of the horse's left shoulder. The wound was completely devoid of hair and skin and went deep into the muscle of the shoulder. A local veterinarian of 20 years' standing, well-known in the community, was called by the defendants. He testified that this wound probably did not cause the horse any pain! The jury, provided with 10-by-14-inch glossy photographs of the injury, found both defendants guilty of animal cruelty. As an ironic sidelight, one year later, the city elected one of the defendants mayor.

ON THE SCENE

Once inside the building, a team must swing into action. Ideally, there should be an officer in charge of the people in the residence, officers or animal care workers in charge of handling the animals, an officer in charge of taking photographs, an officer to sketch the residence and take evidence, and the veterinarian. I urge prosecutors to attend also. To understand a complicated scene such as you are likely to encounter in these types of cases, there is nothing like being there.

It is sometimes suggested that the scene be videotaped. I am neutral on this issue. While videotape takes one to the scene live and puts all the pieces together, it also creates difficulties. Defense attorneys are certain to object to the tape, claiming that the operator of the camera dwelt excessively on the bad aspects of the situation and avoided anything positive. The videotapes are usually long and full of dead spots. Jurors, accustomed to professional television, become bored. Additionally, videotapes simply do not have the frozen impact of a photograph.

But it is imperative to photograph the scene in detail. Each animal should be photographed. The best method is to have the animal care workers remove each animal one by one from the building and bring it to the vet. The animal should then be photographed twice as the veterinarian examines it. The animal is then put in a separate location from the unprocessed animals or is loaded for transport. This allows investigators to count the animals, to differentiate between the animals, and to have an assessment of each animal's condition at the time it was taken into custody. This will be useful in contrasting the animal's condition after it has received sufficient care.

Samples should be taken in an animal neglect situation. These should include skin scrapings if skin diseases are evident, stool samples, food samples, and possibly water samples. All animal medicines present on the premises should be catalogued or taken. This will probably either show that the defendant did not get needed medicine or had the needed medicine but did not administer it. All samples must be logged and maintained in a strict chain of custody.

Animal seizure should be decided upon in consultation with the veterinarian. From bitter experience, I have found that it is best not to seize animals on an initial search warrant. The better practice is to only seize the animals that need immediate medical treatment for injuries or that require intervention to stay alive. There are several reasons for this. First, storage of the animals is usually a very expensive proposition—just ask my county board. Second, when going out for the first time, one usually does not know exactly how many animals or what type of animals are present. This means that you do not know how many animals will need to be transported, treated, or placed.

Third, I have found we are in a much better position at trial if, on the initial contact, the veterinarian simply gives the owner specific advice on what must be done to bring the animal's living conditions up to reasonable standards. This includes sanitation, treating diseases, feeding, and living quarters. This advice is later repeated in a letter to the owner. The owner is given a specific period of time to come into compliance, such as two weeks. Getting back into the residence in two weeks is usually not a problem, as the information received during the first search warrant will provide a clear basis for the second.

It is at the second search warrant that the animals are all seized if sufficient progress has not been made, which is usually the case. By that time, one can be prepared for exactly the number and types of animals that were present on the first go-round. At trial, the prosecution can argue that the defendant was given an opportunity to comply and escape being charged, but failed to do so. This lessens the jury's fear that the state is overzealous and, if the jury votes guilty, they will be encouraging the state to come after people for failing to scoop out their cats' litter boxes.

Much the same formula can be used in executing search warrants in cases involving flagrant child neglect and unsanitary living conditions. The major difference is that the children are taken into custody immediately. This is because there are usually fewer children and social services departments have foster homes where children can be placed immediately, unlike the situation of having to find room for 27 dogs. Again, the children would be photographed at the scene, but then taken to an emergency room for evaluation. The condition of the entire house should be photographed, good and bad. The refrigerator should be photographed. The bathroom should be photographed. An inventory of food and other items in the house should be made. Samples should be taken, if applicable.

CONCLUSION

In recent years, the scourge of domestic abuse and child abuse has received unprecedented news coverage. Prosecution of these cases has been increased by police training and new laws. All of this is laudatory, but animal abuse still remains in the background. There are many reasons for this. Animals are animals and do not have the same rights as people. Officers are often unfamiliar with animal abuse statutes and shy away from such cases out of ignorance. The most likely animal abusers, in the sense of abuse rather than neglect, are batterers and child abusers. But because their crimes against people are more serious, the animal abuse is never asked about or even mentioned by the victims. Finally, these cases are generally enormously expensive, and all usually for the sake of dogs or cats that have no commercial value. All of this adds up to a system with laws in place but little active enforcement.

There is no reason why this should be so. Animals can be the most helpless of victims and probably have a greater incidence of having outrageous cruelty inflicted on them. After all, if some boys were to hang a baby on a tree and throw darts at it until it was dead, the story would sweep across the nation. If they did the same to a kitten, they probably would not even be charged. It is hoped that the future will see greater interest in protecting the animal world from the human world.

Finally, it must be remembered that a prosecutor cannot win a case. A prosecutor can only lose a case. If the case is won, it is because the police and witnesses won it with their investigation and testimony. It is because the jury agreed that the criminal statute violated was one that should be enforced. Prosecutors only get their chance at prevention when all the parts in the system do their job, too.

The Legislator's Perspective on Preventing Family Violence

Patrick Dougherty

IF YOU ARE reading this book, presumably you have an idea or two about how you would like to improve your state's laws regarding abuse—child abuse, animal abuse, adult abuse—all forms of domestic violence. There are undoubtedly others who share your concerns. One of the keys to success in your efforts will be how well you can define your goal(s) and then build coalitions to convince the representatives and senators in your state that a change is needed and why it is in their best interest to support such a change and support it now.

Our challenge is to change both the attitudes and the laws of our country. Our attitudes play an important role in determining what we do and how we see things. When we are able to change attitudes about abuse, we are well on the way toward reaching our goal of changing the public policies that govern our states and cities.

One way to begin to change attitudes is to showcase successful programs that demonstrate to elected officials how abuse—in any of its destructive forms—negatively impacts the lives of us all, not just the child, the adult, or the animal who is the victim of the violence. In addition, programs that positively show our interrelatedness as people and animals can go a long way in getting minds to change old ways of thinking.

Attitudes are effectively changed when we reach out and involve the community we serve. Creative and innovative programs frequently help people think about animals differently, and seeing things from a new perspective can help bring about change. Citing effective programs where humans and animals interact with one another and support each other can show those who make public policy how important animals are in our lives. And it is not so far a jump from this to the realization of being so interrelated, that violence to one group is really violence to us all.

CHANGING LAWS

Laws and attitudes can be changed in the legislative arena if we go about it in the right way. In tackling the political realm we challenge established practices, and, it is hoped, cause people, both legislators and citizens, to look at the care and protection of animals differently than they have before. Going about it in the right way means constantly driving home the interconnectedness of humans and animals. It means telling our stories in ways that bring home to each policy maker and elected official why it is important—important in their home district. It means developing and fostering groups of individuals in each legislator's home district who constantly work with their legislator. And it means committing oneself for the long haul.

Try to get a team of legislators to work on your bill. Every attempt should be made to get bipartisan support as well as support from rural and urban areas. It is usually best to have the majority party member(s) be the main sponsors of the bill. But always strive to get strong interparty backing.

Going about it in the right way also involves doing your homework. Research past history of related legislation and know why it either passed or failed. Call on those who have been around, both legislators and advocates, to find out the background. Glean what you can from these individuals to help you build a good foundation and strategy.

Check the political climate too. If the legislation is presented by someone who is not well liked, who has a reputation for being too controversial or combative, you may be doing yourself more harm than good. If the bill is presented in the "wrong" way or by the "wrong" political party, or if it requires raising taxes, if it is perceived to impose state control over local government, if it interferes with dozens of political footballs that are out there, then it has a very good chance of being defeated. Good research will help you avoid many of these pitfalls.

What are sometimes called state "bluebooks" are good sources of information. These are printed by many state governments and give you overviews and biographies on all elected officials, describing where they go to church, the schools they attended, and which organizations and boards they belong to. Although initially you are focusing on the committee members, this method of research needs to be done on all legislators as time allows. This information will help you and your coalition members to develop contacts.

In short, if you approach the legislative process with a coherent agenda and well thought-out strategies, and make good contacts in the legislature and the community at large, you not only enhance your image but you may get the laws passed as well.

PREPARATION

Effectiveness demands planning and coordination. Your first efforts should start long before a session of the legislature begins. This is the time to do the basics.

First, decide exactly what goal you are trying to achieve—what law or policy you want to change or enact. Research what other states have done in this area. Make contacts to see what they have found successful, and what did not work. Then develop a draft and circulate it among your friends and supporters. Ask for concrete

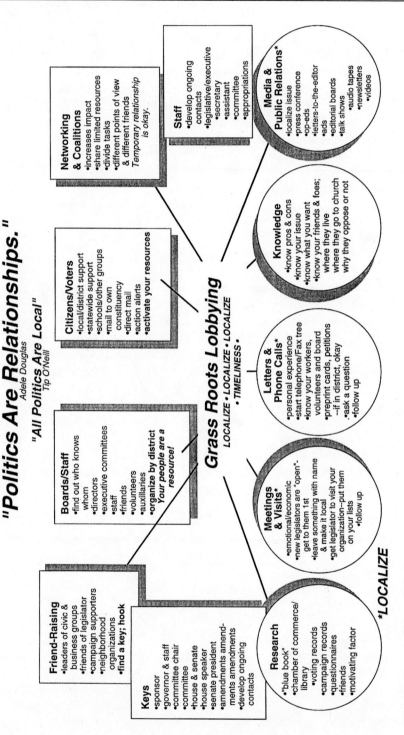

"Politics Are Relationships."
Adele Douglas

"All Politics Are Local"
Tip O'Neill

Grass Roots Lobbying
LOCALIZE • LOCALIZE • LOCALIZE • TIMELINESS •

*LOCALIZE

Networking & Coalitions
•increases impact
•share limited resources
•divide tasks
•different points of view & different friends
Temporary relationship is okay.

Staff
•develop ongoing contacts
•legislative/executive
 •secretary
 •assistant
 •committee
 •appropriations

Media & Public Relations*
•localize issue
•press conference
•op-eds
•letters-to-the-editor
•ads
•editorial boards
•talk shows
 •audio tapes
 •newsletters
 •videos

Citizens/Voters
•local/district support
•statewide support
•schools/other groups
•mail to own constituency
•direct mail
•action alerts
•**activate your resources**

Knowledge
•know pros & cons
•know your issue
•know what you want
•know your friends & foes; where they live where they go to church why they oppose or not

Boards/Staff
•find out who knows whom
•directors
•executive committees
•staff
•friends
•volunteers
•auxiliaries
•**organize by district**
Your people are a resource!

Letters & Phone Calls*
•personal experience
•start telephone/Fax tree
•know your workers, volunteers and board
•preprint cards, petitions --if in district, okay
•ask a question
•follow up

Friend-Raising
•leaders of civic & business groups
•friends of legislator
•campaign supporters
•neighborhood organizations
•**find a key; hook**

Meetings & Visits*
•emotional/economic
•new legislators are "open"-- get to them 1st
•leave something with name & make it local
•get legislator to visit your organization--put them on your lists
 •follow up

Keys
•sponsor
•governor & staff
•committee chair
•committee
•house & senate
•house speaker
•senate president
•amendments amendments amendments
•develop ongoing contacts

Research
•"blue book"
•chamber of commerce/ library
•voting records
•campaign records
•questionnaires
•friends
•motivating factor

The Key Issues in Citizen Lobbying

feedback—pros and cons. Write and rewrite it until you feel it is ready to go. Don't be afraid to be innovative, but your idea has a much better chance of passage if it is also realistic. The best idea will not make it through the legislature if it is unconstitutional, unenforceable, or carries an unacceptable fiscal or political price tag.

While you are working on your draft, find a sympathetic legislator in both the House and the Senate who will put his or her heart and soul into working on your bill, one who will put the time and effort into understanding its pros and cons, and who has the ability to convince other legislators of its merit. It is not necessary to find someone who has previously worked on similar legislation.

A word of caution! Just because you have found a legislator who will work with you, don't assume the biggest hurdle has been crossed. Although an important and indispensable part of your effort, he or she cannot do it all alone.

"NO MAN IS AN ISLAND"

Your efforts are vital, but do not try to do it all by yourself! It is not easy to work effectively on a statewide basis, so building a coalition is a necessity. Organize groups that will be supportive. Search your friends, boards, staffs, and business contacts to find out who knows which legislator. Coalitions can rally around one topic, even though they may be far apart on other issues. Don't let the fact that you cannot agree on all things prevent you from working together. But keep in mind, it takes cooperation and teamwork to bring results. Analyze your coalition for its strengths and capitalize on them. Identify your weaknesses and address them. If your coalition has differences, iron them out before you go to the legislature. If you cannot solve them, at least set them aside until your legislative work is completed.

However, think carefully about combining groups that are far apart in their ideologies. They may bring more baggage to the table than assets.

You need a united front! Build the broadest base of citizen support that you can.

TARGETING AND RESEARCH

Because you can't be everywhere at once or do everything at the same time, you must break down your efforts into manageable pieces (if there is such a thing in the legislative arena).

Effective action demands that you target legislators when it comes time for a vote. Find out who knows whom. Break down your membership lists according to legislative districts so you can use your members wisely. Have people visit, write, and call their legislator and set up a plan to have them make contacts to legislators when the timing is right.

In many state legislatures, any bill that involves animals is routinely assigned to an agriculture committee. Even though the issue of animal abuse and domestic violence may be of more interest to a committee dealing with family-type issues or judicial concerns, it may be routed to a committee representing rural and farm interests. It is normally up to the head of the legislature and sometimes the sponsor of the bill as to which committee it is assigned. Be aware that you may have to be creative in asking that your bill be assigned to a committee that you perceive to be more favorably attuned to your concerns. Work with your sponsor for this.

When the bill is assigned to a committee, a real push should be made to try to have the bill be made a priority of that committee. This can be accomplished in a number of ways. Although you have no direct control over this, one of the best ways to increase your chances is to have your sponsor be the chair or a member of the committee that will be hearing the bill. If you know which committee your bill will be sent to, work to get members of that committee to co-sponsor and support the bill even before it sets a hearing on the bill.

When you know which committee your bill is going to, it is never too early to begin making contacts and building support. This is particularly vital if your legislature only deals with a limited number of bills in any session. Yours will only get to the top if you make a lot of friends and a lot of polite noise. Concentrate on contacting and visiting the committee members and convincing them how important this bill is before they have to vote on it. Remember, make your presentations focus on the individual legislator and where he or she lives. It is true that "all politics are local." Use good stories to get your points across.

How you conduct yourself is so very important. Some watchwords are *credible, factual, compassionate,* and *persistent.*

MAKING YOUR CASE

When you present your bill to legislators, be factual. State your case simply, with the best facts available. Never make up answers. Often you are the only link a legislator has and if you provide false or misleading information, you could easily turn him or her against your bill.

Do not overstate your case, but bring out the magnitude of the problem—how many people and animals are affected. Relate how the need for this legislation will help people and society. Show how it will impact the entire state as well as local areas, especially the legislator's own district. Be sensitive to the possibility that the concerns of one region may not be universally accepted statewide. Legislators from rural areas may not be attuned to what they perceive to be "big city" issues, and legislators representing urban districts may not think that a farm issue affects their constituencies. Stress the positive points; be ready with sound answers when legislators raise questions. If you don't know the answer, tell them so and get back to them immediately.

Be persistent. If you cannot get in to see your representative or senator, keep trying. If you telephone and don't receive a return call, keep calling. If you write and no letter is forthcoming, keep writing until you receive a letter in return. Persistence, not pestering, is the key word. Restrain yourself from going overboard, and try to restrain the fanatics and zealots in your group. It is possible to make important gains toward your goal and have them dashed because of overzealous supporters.

Legislators, especially part-time ones, have very little time during short sessions. Always be concise. Do not waste your elected official's time. If you can say it in five minutes, don't take a half-hour.

Do not be afraid to make some compromises to reach your legislative goals. You must determine exactly what you need and what you may need to give up. At some point you will be able to determine the point at which you will not want to compromise any further. There is nothing wrong with negotiating. It is the art of how all of us interact every day of our lives. Remember, you can compromise without compromising your own values and principles.

Find out the process used by your state legislature to keep track of when bills are scheduled for hearing. In most cases, everything is keyed to the number of the bill. You may have access to this schedule via on-line services or by seeing a weekly calendar. Don't count on the media or the legislator calling you. It is your responsibility to know what is happening to the bill at each step.

Once the hearing date is set, seek a number of articulate individuals who can provide expert testimony and will be able to field questions, including negative ones. Be ready for the unexpected. Make careful use of audio-visuals. Try to get presenters from the districts of the chairman and the committee members.

You will not always be able to meet with legislators individually, so it is vitally important to work closely with their staff, secretaries, and aides. Administrative assistants will be your best friends: take time to develop a good working relationship. If you work well with them, you have reached the legislator, and that is part of your goal.

VOTE

You are now at the stage where your bill will be voted upon. Get supporters to the hearing and try to visit and reinforce your votes. Assuming you get your bill out of committee, intensify your campaign to contact and convince other legislators of the merits of your bill. This needs to be done with visits, letters, and phone calls.

You do not need to dump dozens of letters all at once; space them out and then intensify the campaign when you see your bill will be up for a vote. Do not use form letters and petitions. Nothing beats a letter that is short, to the point, and clearly written by hand. Make your point and ask a question to the legislator to increase your chances that it will be read and answered.

Sometimes you will not be able to get a bill out of committee. Be ready to work with your sponsor and others to turn your bill into an amendment that may be attached to another bill.

In developing your membership lists and those of your coalition, set up a membership telephone, fax, or e-mail tree to contact legislators at a moment's notice. Begin this tree focusing on the committee that will hear your bill, then expand it until it covers all legislators.

TIMELY PUBLICITY

While you are working the committee and the legislative process, do everything possible to work the media to publicize your bill. Professionals can help you immensely. If you have a professional public relations person or firm who will donate expertise, all the better. However, most of the time you'll be on your own.

Try to use the media to your best advantage to reach all those you need in order to build stronger bases of support in the community. The more the support, the better your chances are of making an impact on the policy makers. Use all the media you can—print, radio, broadcast and cable TV, and a web site.

If you can, you should be setting up news conferences, especially in the "big" media markets. But don't forget the media markets of the big decision makers too—like the chair of the committee, the heads of the House and Senate.

Have charts, pictures, audio and video tapes, and a press kit for your press conferences and for follow-up to the press who did not attend. Don't forget the talk shows. Try to get on a variety of stations. Guest columns are often available. Don't forget letters to the editor. Meet with the individuals who write editorials.

You do not have to do it all at once. Sometimes it's better to space these presentations over a period of time that best suits your strategies. Working with the media is not a one-shot approach—it begins when you introduce the bill and continues until it is passed.

WORKING BOTH HOUSES

When your bill clears its committee, if you can get the support of the speaker or president of your assembly, now is the time to have them push their colleagues to pass the bill. Work closely with the floor leader too.

Once you pass the bill in one house of the general assembly, the work begins all over again in the second. Basically you follow the same procedures. Although you are starting over in the next chamber, you have all the experience and groundwork under your belt.

Introducing your bill in each house enhances the chances of getting a bill passed. It's more work, but it can be well worth it. If you introduce your bill in both and one gets sidetracked, you will be able to work on it in the other house. If you get the bill passed in each house but there are differences, you will need to work with the committee that is named to iron out the differences.

When all is said and done, efforts will likely pay off. But if fate does put you back a year or two from your goal, realize that if your work has been credible and factual, you have laid a strong basis for coming back the following year and reaching your goal. You will have gained a lot of experience from the process and will have learned what worked and what didn't and why.

THE CHALLENGE

Many legislatures have a difficult time addressing violence issues, particularly involving animals. Part of this may stem from how and where we grew up. Many from the farming communities have a deep love and respect for the land and have raised farm animals all their lives. Their domestic pets are loved and cared for, their livestock are raised for sale. But many in rural areas don't see anything wrong with the traditions of violence against some animals. Cockfighting is a perfect example. While they care for their domestic pets like family, many see nothing wrong with the tradition of fighting the killing chickens. Yet these same communities often support bans against pit-bull and other dog fights. When city legislators push animal abuse laws, they are often rebuffed by rural legislators who do not want to upset the traditions of their constituencies.

This duality of attitudes on animals and violence exists in many legislatures that have large rural-urban mixes. This duality must cause advocates to use different approaches to gaining support, especially for animal violence issues. Strategies should include gaining the backing of important members of the local rural communities such as the clergy, chambers of commerce, and local business leaders. Getting broad-based bipartisan support from legislators to help push your bill is essential to avoid a hostile reception by many members of the legislature.

Constantly remember to make your approaches local—make it fit the district where the official is from. Theology, philosophy, and ideology are fine, but unless you make your case on a personal, local level, you won't have the best chance to really reach your public officials and change policies and laws.

The more you can establish the link between abuse and violence of any kind and the destruction of our families—the core value of our society—the more success you will have in changing negative attitudes, challenging apathy, and positively influencing legislators' votes to improve our communities. Show your elected officials how violence in one section of our lives often begets violence in others. The more you can show concrete examples, especially from their own areas, the better the chance you can reach their minds as well as their hearts.

We are all victims of family and community violence. Getting those who run our governments to learn this truth is a challenge. This issue of abuse and violence is but one of hundreds about which legislators must learn. Convincing policy makers that this issue will make a difference in the lives of their constituents is a great challenge.

Violence is an insidious evil, no matter where and to whom or what it occurs. The more we are able to help legislators make the connection that all forms of violence tear apart the very fabric of our society, the better we will be able to reach our goals of less violence to all. The more we are able to challenge legislators to really see that violence to spouses, adults, seniors, children, and animals are all inextricably linked to the destruction of our families and our very society, the better we can increase our chances of making a difference through legislation.

Zero Tolerance for Cruelty

An Approach to Enhancing Enforcement of State Anticruelty Laws

Joyce Tischler

In THEORY, state anticruelty laws provide some of the most broad-reaching protections available to animals. With certain exceptions (most anticruelty laws exclude "game" animals, some laws exempt animals used in research or raised for food), anticruelty laws acknowledge that animals should be provided with the basics of food, water, shelter, and veterinary care and protected from negligent or intentional acts that cause them pain and suffering. Violations of the cruelty laws can be punished by criminal convictions and the sentence may include fines, forfeiture of animals, jail time, and community service. Anticruelty laws vary from state to state; some cover a wide variety of topics, others are minimal (American Humane Association 1996; Soehnel 1992; Leavitt & Halverson 1990).

In practice, anticruelty laws are severely underutilized by law enforcement officials. Local sheriff and police departments do not train their staffs to investigate animal cruelty cases, leaving the problem to the local humane or animal control agency or simply ignoring it. Prosecutors (a term used to designate governmental officials such as district attorneys, state's attorneys, or county attorneys who prosecute criminal actions) often do not prosecute cruelty cases because they think that their limited resources should not be wasted on animals.

For years, we at the Animal Legal Defense Fund (ALDF) received phone calls from members of the public who complained about acts of cruelty they had witnessed and wondered what we, as lawyers, could do. Our response was disappointing to them and to us. As lawyers in private practice, we have no legal authority to prosecute animal abusers; that right is exclusive to the state (Chambers 1996).

Yet, out of that frustration grew a campaign that we call "Zero Tolerance for Cruelty." It is a combined effort of ALDF's staff and volunteer attorney members to provide direct legal assistance to prosecutors handling cruelty cases and thereby make the enforcement of state anticruelty laws more effective.

At the core of the program is outreach to local prosecutors handling cruelty cases. We locate these cases from several sources, including humane officers, concerned citizens, and Internet searches. Then, we contact the prosecutors and offer free legal assistance: ALDF attorneys will perform research on legal issues that the prosecutor must deal with in handling the case, but may not have time to research himself or herself. We will submit *amicus curiae* (friend of the court) briefs in support of the prosecution's case. We will locate expert witnesses and provide information about other cruelty cases that may prove helpful in the current case.

MAKING THE CONNECTION

A major component of the campaign is outreach to judges and prosecutors to educate them about the connection between violence to humans and violence to animals. We find a lot of resistance to enforcement of cruelty laws from both groups. Prosecutors have complained to us that they have rapes and murders to handle and do not have time to deal with cruelty. Many have expressed their dismay that they receive more calls and mail about cruelty cases than about child abuse. Cruelty cases, if handled at all, are assigned to the newest deputy on the staff or to the "dog lover." Handling cruelty cases is not a positive career move and is largely frowned upon.

Judges are equally resistant. One prosecutor told us of a judge who was enraged that she dared to take up his court time with such trivia as a cruelty case. Too often, judges hand out unreasonably light sentences for crimes that caused terrible pain and suffering. For example, in North East, Maryland, a man beat an older collie and left her for dead. Upon conviction, he was sentenced to a $140 fine and probation. In East Greenwich, New Jersey, a man who hanged his dog from a tree by a lead wire, causing a slow and painful death, was convicted and sentenced to 30 days in jail (later suspended; he spent one day in jail), $250 fine, and $30 court costs. Albany, Wyoming, appears to be a good place for animal abusers: one man shot and killed his neighbor's dog. He pled guilty and was fined $20; another man beat his own puppy with his fists, dragged the dog, and threw her over a fence where she was attacked by another dog. The defendant pled guilty and was sentenced to a $30 fine and court costs. Initially, the defendant remained in possession of the puppy, who received no medical treatment. Later, the dog, a wolf hybrid, was rescued and sent to a sanctuary.

There is no single or simple reason why we see a systematic refusal to prosecute and punish animal abusers aggressively. Perhaps it is because our society as a whole has mixed feelings about animals. When surveyed, the overwhelming majority of people favor strengthening the enforcement of cruelty laws (*U.S. Newswire* 1997). When a particularly vicious act of cruelty occurs, the public is up in arms to bring the animal abuser to justice. On the other hand, most people were taught to consider animals less important than humans, and the message sent to a criminal law system overwhelmed by crime and violence is that animal cases are to be given a very low priority.

We think that animals should be protected because their pain matters. But to reach those law enforcement officials who view animals as unimportant, we stress the close connection between violence to animals and violence to humans. Consider the following example: a San Francisco man was prosecuted for cruelty after he slit his cat's throat and tossed the dead cat on the doorstep of his ex-wife. Too often, animals are used as a psychological weapon to control spouses and children. In a recent study, Ascione (1996) noted this phenomenon, stating: "The results of this study suggest that a significant proportion of a sample of women seeking safety at a shelter for battered partners have experienced their partners' threatened and/or actual maltreatment of pets." Focusing on the connection between violence to animals and violence to humans provides benefits to both groups of victims. The ex-wife in the preceding example got a clear and chilling message from her ex-husband. By prosecuting the man for cruelty, the district attorney sent a clear message back.

There is much to be gained from educating judges and prosecutors about the human-animal violence connection. If we can sensitize judges and prosecutors to the statistically significant chance that a violent animal abuser may move on to violence directed at humans or may already be harming humans (Lockwood & Church 1996), we not only protect animals. We also enable our peers in the domestic violence and child abuse communities to protect their constituents more effectively. An example of this symbiosis was the amendment of California Penal Code Section 11166, The Child Abuse and Neglect Reporting Act, which added animal control officers and humane society officers to the list of professionals who are mandated to report suspected cases of child abuse and neglect. Juvenile authorities get some much-needed assistance in detecting child abuse, and the animal cruelty case that may grow out of the same home environment gets more serious attention from the legal system.

Our message to judges and prosecutors is: don't focus on the victim, focus on the course of conduct. If the perpetrator appears to "enjoy" causing pain to sentient beings, let's consider that person to be dangerous and work to punish or rehabilitate the defendant and protect the public from further violent acts.

BOYS WILL BE BOYS?

One of the most dangerous things that can happen to a child is to kill or torture an animal and get away with it.

—Anthropologist Margaret Mead

ALDF regularly receives reports of teenagers mutilating and torturing animals. Recently, we have responded to the following:

- In McClain, Oklahoma, three male teenagers fractured a cat's skull and ribs, beat her, bound her legs and set her on fire.

- In Albemarle, Virginia, three male teenagers mutilated two cows, stabbing one and gouging out the eye of the other, killing both cows by using a rope and rocks.
- In Oswego, New York, two male teenagers tortured a six-month old kitten for three hours, including burning his genitals with a curling iron, and putting him in a freezer and in an oven set at 200 degrees. The kitten belonged to the girlfriend of one of the teens.

These images haunt us and we see ourselves on the "tail" end of a legal system that is unable to deal effectively with large numbers of teenagers acting out years of physical, sexual, or emotional abuse. Mirroring the legal system, we are overwhelmed by the size and complexity of the problem.

To make matters worse, the adults who interact with these teenagers often downplay the significance of the violent acts toward animals. Teachers, football coaches, principals, and parents defend the youths, making excuses and accusing those who would prosecute for cruelty as fueling a tempest in a teapot. We repeatedly hear such rationalizations as "don't ruin his (or in some cases her) whole life for a silly prank," and "it was only a cat." In response, we stress to law enforcement authorities that the community and the teenagers involved will be better served if the legal system views this behavior as an important indicator of serious underlying problems. We urge them to intervene; provide counseling and help now while we ponder how we can work cooperatively with child abuse agencies to reach out to these troubled individuals before the violence erupts.

A NATIONAL DATABASE OF CRUELTY CASES

What lawyers call "case law" are court decisions by judges at the appellate level. Most cruelty cases are resolved at the trial level and are not appealed. Thus, it is extremely difficult to find the "written decision" and most law enforcement officials rely on local anecdotal information about such crucial issues as available sentencing options and jury instructions. There has been no central repository for case law on cruelty cases and this absence has been debilitating to law enforcement efforts.

To remedy this, ALDF created a database with information about each case that we are following. Each file includes the name of the defendant(s), the charges filed, the name and location of the prosecutor, a short description of the facts and the species of the animals who were the victims, jury instructions, disposition (guilty or not guilty), and sentences imposed. The database is available to anyone working to protect animals.

For example, in a recent case prosecuted near Seattle, Washington, the defendant shot his neighbor's puppy with a pellet gun. During the sentencing phase, the prosecutor planned to recommend only 20 hours of community service, perhaps because the defendant was a wealthy and prominent member of the community. Our database revealed that other jurisdictions had imposed much stronger sentences for similar crimes and we provided this information to the dog's owner, who urged the court not to accept the prosecutor's recommendation. We also wrote to the judge and urged a stronger sentence. The database gave us the ammunition we needed to argue that the sentence was too weak.

CAN YOU LOCATE AN IGUANA EXPERT?

One of the most frequent requests we receive is for expert witnesses. In one case, a Christmas tree lot owner was keeping reindeer (actually fallow deer) in inhumane conditions on the premises. We located a zoo veterinarian who could testify about the standards for humane treatment of fallow deer. A turtle soup manufacturer was housing live turtles (who were going to be killed and made into soup) in such poor conditions that some were found dead or dying; many had cracked shells and were suffering. We were asked to find an expert on the standards for humane transport of turtles. Because of our long-term involvement with animal protection, we are able to follow a lead, and although it may take many hours and many tries, we find the expert.

A problem area has been where the prosecutor needs a veterinarian who can testify about the cause of death, for example, starvation as opposed to disease. It has been disappointing to us that many of the veterinary pathologists we have contacted are unwilling to get involved and to testify in court. Individual private practitioners, although sometimes intimidated about testifying, have been more willing to work with prosecutors. We would like to encourage a consciousness among veterinary pathologists that they have an obligation to utilize their valuable expertise to enhance the enforcement of anticruelty laws.

BRIEF BANKS FOR CRUELTY CASES

One afternoon, a former law clerk stopped in. He was working for a local district attorney's office and after only three days, he was frustrated. He slumped into a chair and said: "It's overwhelming; these lawyers are so busy that they don't even have time to do original legal research for their pleadings. Every time I ask a question, they tell me to look in the brief bank" (a library of documents containing legal arguments used in prior cases on a similar issue). "And you know," he added, "there's no brief bank for cruelty cases."

That pointed to a major problem: cruelty cases are different from other criminal cases and in most prosecutors' offices the cruelty cases are assigned to the newest deputy, the one with the least training and experience. The lack of a brief bank could mean that essential legal arguments never get made.

We formulated a plan to develop cruelty brief banks. Because of variances in state anticruelty laws, a cruelty brief bank will have to be separately researched and written for each state. At this writing, the first one has been written for the State of Arizona and was distributed in hard copy and on disk to every local prosecutorial office.

121 ANIMALS CRAMMED ON A BUS

The prosecution of animal "collectors" can be a nightmare. An animal collector is usually defined as a person who amasses more animals than he or she can properly care for (New York State Humane Association undated). The collector fails or refuses to acknowledge that these animals are suffering from gross neglect.

Meet Sheila Boyd (due to the nature of this type of personality, all names and locations have been changed), a classic example of an animal collector. With at least two known aliases and a criminal record dating back to the late 1960s, Boyd surfaced in the early 1980s when neighbors complained about dozens of dogs and two horses kept in her mother's suburban home. She claimed that she was a victim of a massive government conspiracy. She was eventually run out of that community and surfaced again in another state, where she "saved" scores of dogs and convinced some well-meaning folks that she would take them to a shelter out west.

Her trail of animal collecting moved to three other states. She was arrested in April 1993, after 115 dogs, 4 cats, and 2 chickens were found crammed into her dirty, dilapidated school bus without food and water. The animals were filthy, diseased, and malnourished. One dog, who died soon afterwards, was autopsied: there was no food in his system and no body fat, a sign of long and painful starvation. The bus was so badly caked with feces and urine that officers had to wear gas masks to go inside. She boasted that she had not let any of the dogs off the bus for weeks, to avoid their getting fleas. But the dogs were suffering from almost every other parasite, including hookworm, whipworm, and in 16 cases, deadly heartworm.

Animal collectors are tenacious and clever and she manipulated the legal system masterfully for the next two years. She was given nine different court-appointed defense lawyers, none of whom met her satisfaction. She went through six judges, all of whom, she claimed, were prejudiced against her. She filed dozens of self-styled legal motions and had the system tied up in knots.

Animal collectors exist in many places in the United States, but most law enforcement officials allow them to slip through the cracks—it is simply too hard to fight them. But she finally met her match, first in the animal control supervisor who discovered the animals on the bus, and then in the newly appointed district attorney. Both worked against incredible odds to bring her to justice. Her trial began in January 1995 and went on for almost a month; she acted as her own attorney and badgered the district attorney, the judge, the witnesses, and even the jury. The jury convicted her of 42 counts of first- and second-degree animal neglect. She ultimately spent most of a year in jail.

About 80 percent of the dogs could be rehabilitated and adopted. The others had to be euthanized or died while Boyd was awaiting trial (she actually convinced a judge to issue an order that medical care could be given only with her permission and she refused to allow them medical care). The rest of the story is predictable: in March 1997, she was arrested while driving a car containing 5 dogs, 40 cats and 1 rabbit. She had just been evicted from a trailer home in which about 100 dogs and cats were found.

As this example illustrates, dealing with animal collectors requires more resources than most counties are willing to commit. We have only just begun to identify this syndrome. Whenever we suspect that a defendant is a collector, we send the prosecutor a packet of information specifically designed to assist in identifying the animal collector and some of the problems that one can expect.

Randall Lockwood (1994; Lockwood & Cassidy 1988) and his colleagues at the Humane Society of the United States have studied this syndrome and written and lectured extensively about it. Educating the public and law enforcement community is a massive undertaking and to date we are only scratching the surface. Those who have studied the collector syndrome still do not know whether it is an obsessive-compulsive disorder or an addiction, and no course of treatment has been suggested. Without treatment, the recidivism rate for animal collectors is 100 percent. Clearly, research and study are needed to deal effectively with this problem, which causes long-term suffering for large numbers of animals and can impact mental health and social service agencies.

UPDATING ANTICRUELTY LAWS

Anticruelty laws exist in all 50 states, some dating back to the 1820s (American Humane Association 1996; Favre 1993). Some provide strong protections for animals, others only minimal protections. ALDF encourages efforts to strengthen cruelty laws. The following is a summary of improvements that we recommend:

Add felony provisions. In most states, all forms of animal cruelty are misdemeanors. In some instances, such as where there is an intent to harm animals, charging a defendant with a felony should be an option available to the prosecutor.

Forfeiture provisions. If the individual has been convicted of cruelty, the abused animals should not be returned. Additionally, during the probation period, the animal abuser should not be allowed to own any animal.

Removal of abused animals. If an animal is being harmed, law enforcement officials should be given the authority to take the animal into custody immediately and provide medical and other care as needed. It is important to provide for seizure prior to conviction.

Psychological counseling. Effective treatment of mental health disorders may prevent future animal abuse and other violent acts.

Reimbursement of costs, posting bond. Convicted animal abusers should incur the costs of caring for the animals during the prosecution and trial stages (a cost that is currently borne by animal control agencies and humane societies).

Increase penalties. Penalties for animal cruelty violations in most states are unreasonably low and should be increased to a level that will deter crime.

Exemptions. Exemptions should be eliminated. Many states' statutes specifically exempt certain classes of animals, such as game animals and those in research laboratories. Such blanket exemptions are overly broad and create unnecessary loopholes. ALDF has drafted and disseminates a model anticruelty law. The Humane Society of the United States disseminates examples of preferable anticruelty provisions taken from existing state laws. Both of these resources can be used to strengthen and improve state anticruelty laws. We have witnessed some progress: as of this writing, 20 states have classified deliberate (intentional) cruelty as a felony, but we have also noted some pitfalls: agricultural lobbyists have tried to bargain in exemptions for farm animals in return for the addition of felony provisions, a dangerous precedent.

CONCLUSION

It's a matter of taking the side of the weak against the strong, something the best people have always done.
—Harriet Beecher Stowe

In the last 20 years, we, as a society, have come to recognize the sad fact that violence is generalized and the weakest members of our society are easily victimized. Sometimes, it feels as though we are powerless and overwhelmed in our efforts to protect those "weakest members." Thus, it is gratifying to see law enforcement and human care professionals begin to view nonhuman animals as part of the family.

Those of us working toward Zero Tolerance for Cruelty do not see ourselves as being in competition with child abuse and domestic violence professionals. Rather, we view ourselves as on a path toward protection of all members of the family: the companion animal along with the spouse and the child. It is a depressingly long path, filled with potholes, but we do see some signs of progress. The approach we have taken, offering free assistance to prosecutors, has come as a welcome surprise to many of the prosecutors we contact. We have garnered a lot of good will and support for our efforts. More importantly, we have seen prosecutions begun and successfully handled, convictions obtained and sentences getting stronger—a subtle ripple of change that we hope and pray will grow and continue.

REFERENCES

American Humane Association. 1996. *Cruelty statutes: United States and Canada.* Englewood, Colo.: American Humane Association.

Ascione, F. 1996. Domestic violence and cruelty to animals. *Latham Letter* 17(1) (winter):1–16.

Chambers, S. A. 1996. Animal cruelty legislation: The Pasado law and its legacy. *Animal Law* 2 (spring):193–95.

Favre, D. 1993. The development of anti-cruelty laws during the 1800s. *Detroit College of Law Review* 1(1) (spring):1–35.

Leavitt, E., and D. Halverson. 1990. The evolution of anti-cruelty laws in the U.S. In *Animals and their legal rights*. Washington, D.C.: Animal Welfare Institute.

Lockwood, R. 1994. The psychology of animal collectors. *American Animal Hospital Association Trends* 9(6):18–21.

Lockwood, R., and B. Cassidy. 1988. Killing with kindness? *The Humane Society News* 33(3):14–18.

Lockwood, R., and A. Church. 1996. Deadly Serious: An FBI Perspective on Animal Cruelty. *HSUS News* (fall).

New York State Humane Association. undated. *Fact Sheet*. New York State Humane Association.

Soehnel, S. 1992. *What constitutes offense of cruelty to animals-modern cases*. 6 ALR 5th 733.

U.S. Newswire. 1997. HSUS: Public wants tougher laws, enforcement, tracking of animal abuse. *U.S. Newswire* March 11.

Treating Serious Animal Abuse as a Serious Crime

Mitchell Fox

WHEN A CAT left footprints on Randy Roth's newly waxed car, he caught the cat and bound her with duct tape to the drive shaft of her owner's car. When the owner started his car, the cat was quickly dismembered, her screams muffled by the sounds of the engine. Roth later murdered his wife by drowning her in Lake Sammamish, near Bellevue, Washington.

Richard Davis, convicted of murdering 12-year-old Polly Klaas after kidnapping her from her home in Petaluma, California, reportedly set fire to cats and used dogs for target practice as a child. Jeffrey Dahmer had an early childhood fascination with dismembering animals before he tortured and cannibalized 18 people.

David Berkowitz shot his neighbor's dog. He confessed to six murders as the "Son of Sam." And Albert DeSalvo put dogs and cats in crates and then shot them with arrows. We know him better as the Boston Strangler.

A history of practicing on animals before moving on to human victims is not limited to the nation's most notorious criminals. In June 1992 Wayne Wooten, a 17-year-old resident of Tacoma, Washington, killed a cat by bashing her head against a newspaper vending machine. A year later he bombed the NAACP office in Tacoma.

Faced with scores of recent scientific papers that have examined the links between animal abuse and other violent antisocial behavior, and convinced that animal abuse is no trivial matter, a group of animal advocates in Washington State spent several years attempting to upgrade our antiquated cruelty-to-animals statutes, which had been on the books since 1901, an era when most animals were regarded as beasts of burden. We were not making much progress, given traditional legislative reluctance to enter this arena.

And then came the Pasado case.

PASADO

On the evening of April 15, 1992, three young men, aged 16, 18, and 20, broke into Kelsey Creek Park, a children's park operated by the City of Bellevue. According to a witness familiar with one of the young men, the three had, on several past occasions, gone into the unguarded park after hours to harass the animals. On this particular night the 20-year-old (who is the son of a Bellevue police major) had in mind that he wanted to ride Pasado, a popular donkey who had entertained children at the park for 21 years. They had brought two ropes with them.

The three tried repeatedly to get on the donkey, but Pasado kept running away; Pasado was caught once, but broke free. Court records say Pasado ran to the shelter of his small shed, where the three tried to frighten him again by banging sticks on the ground. When the donkey would not go back out, the three then dragged him to a tree in the corral about 50 feet away.

He was tied to the tree with the rope tied in a hangman's noose, and all three proceeded to chase the terrified donkey in a circle around the trunk. The rope wound tighter and tighter around the tree and Pasado's neck. When he grew exhausted from the chase, he stopped running and began to pull desperately against the rope, cutting a half-inch gouge into his neck. Pasado began to choke and cough up blood.

The eldest of the three argued that he did not want to see the donkey suffer and was trying to put Pasado out of his misery. Regardless of the veracity of this argument, Pasado took a savage beating as the three took turns hitting him on the head with branches and a two-foot-long iron bar found among the rustic farm equipment. Police estimated the attack lasted 45 minutes.

The young men decided to go, leaving Pasado tied to the tree, still alive. At 8 A.M. the following morning, a maintenance worker found Pasado dead. The bones in his face were chipped, his nose was lacerated, and he had hemorrhaged through his nasal passages. He had several open wounds on his head and legs. At least one of the blows broke his skull. He had strangled to death during the night.

In the days after the killing, police said the viciousness of the attack had them especially concerned about Pasado's assailants. The act, they said, appeared to have been premeditated and was an example of sociopathic behavior. "Why would anybody kill a defenseless, innocent beast?" asked Bellevue police Lieutenant Bill Quinn. "This wasn't something the animal provoked. This was blatant torture. It was planned. They came in to kill the animal."

Six days later, after two rewards were offered and an enormous outpouring of public concern, police arrested the three after receiving a tip. King County Prosecutor Norm Maleng was faced with an immediate challenge: the most serious charge he could file against the suspects was a felony charge for burglary. The animal cruelty charge, which was also filed, was only a misdemeanor.

"This was a brutal and senseless crime," said Maleng at a press conference. "In my 14 years as prosecutor, few crimes have incensed the public more than the killing of Pasado."

DEFICIENCIES IN THE LAW

The Pasado case illustrated the shortcomings of our existing laws, under which the brutal beating of a donkey and leaving him to strangle in a noose was a misdemeanor, equivalent with attempting to shoplift a pack of gum. As a misdemeanor, law enforcement agencies and the courts could not give the case the attention many felt it deserved, nor impose sentences many in the community felt fit the crime. "What we need in these cases is the ability to intervene early," said Maleng. "We're not just talking about cruelty to animals, we're talking about violence perpetrated disproportionately by kids."

The idea that serious, intentional animal abuse should be treated as a serious crime seemed patently obvious. Felony classification would allow police and prosecutors to allocate more resources and attention, as well as give judges more flexibility in imposing stiffer penalties and requiring treatment for offenders. There was tremendous public support for this idea: Maleng received an unprecedented 1,200 letters and phone calls from people angered by Pasado's killing. He attributed the level of outrage to the public's belief that the criminal justice system does not take crimes against animals seriously.

There was considerable reason for public skepticism. The anticruelty laws were vague, antiquated, and unenforceable; the prohibitions against "overdriving" and "overworking" plow animals no longer seemed relevant. In the century since the law was enacted, there has been a dramatic shift in society's views of animals, many of whom are considered beloved family members; indeed, many people rank their love for animals as higher than their affection for some human relatives. For any compassionate person, the thought of having a loved one bludgeoned, used for target practice, tortured, or suffocated is too horrific to imagine, whether the loved one has two or four legs. Animals give us their loyalty, their affection, and their trust. In return, we must give them protection.

Strengthening the animal cruelty laws was not necessary just to intervene on behalf of children in abusive situations and head off future antisocial behavior. It was also essential for the animals' sake.

A LIGHTNING ROD FOR COMMUNITY ACTION

The Pasado case stirred something deep in the conscience of individuals throughout western Washington. Ancient debates were revived in which people began to examine again the questionable protection under the law which dogs, cats, and other animals supposedly enjoy. An instant movement drew together sundry voices and powers hoping to find both common and comprehensive ground upon which to fight back against wanton, malicious behavior toward animals. Pasado gave the animal protection community, so to speak, a poster donkey. The common ground seemed to be to increase the penalty for serious, intentional animal abuse from a misdemeanor to a felony. It took more than two years for this legislation to be enacted.

In a letter to the state representatives and senators considering the felonization bill, Bruce Moran, Washington State Superior Court Juvenile Services Administrator in Okanogan, noted, "As a person who has spent over 20 years in working with juvenile delinquents and dependents, I can attest to the fact that the current laws and punitive sanctions simply do not allow the important accountability, logical consequences, and treatment that are almost always necessary in cases where juveniles have mistreated, tortured or maliciously killed animals. This situation almost always leaves us with a seriously disturbed individual and little or no authority or discretion to deal with [him or her] effectively."

"It is more serious for a youth to steal candy from a store than it is to cruelly and maliciously torture an animal," said Moran. "The logic behind this discrepancy is almost incomprehensible and certainly gives youth (and, I believe, the majority of the general public) the wrong message in terms of how our state values animal life and its protection.

"All too often, our department has been involved in cases where youth have cruelly and maliciously mutilated, tortured or murdered animals (quite often someone's treasured pet) only to find themselves hamstrung in dealing with holding the youth accountable and providing an appropriate message to our community, by a law which makes it a minor offense, which severely restricts our ability to impose longer terms of probation to address offender treatment needs, and virtually negates our ability to incarcerate the offender, who in many cases desperately needs just such accountability. Virtually without exception we have found that those youths who are involved in this type of behavior are extremely disturbed and their behavior towards animals is often found to be related to other serious problems such as assaults against persons, fire setting, sexual offenses, and substance abuse."

Moran's sentiments were echoed by others in humane and human services. "We want people to understand that deliberate crimes against animals are a sign of future violence against people," said Bob Walters, education director for the Pierce County Humane Society in Tacoma. "Some may say that the public is not yet ready to make it a felony for cruelty to animals, but how many children have to be tortured and killed by past animal torturers? This is a cruelty issue."

Karil Klingbeil, associate professor of social work at the University of Washington and director of social work at Harborview Medical Center, a level-1 trauma hospital, testified before the Senate Law and Justice Committee about how 25 years ago she did clinical work-ups and assessments on children brought in by parents for behavioral disturbances. "Without question, every week I saw a child who hit, maimed, often killed a pet in the family or a neighbor's family. Oftentimes an adult would also abuse the animal," she said. What became clear to her were three themes:

1. that pets were being physically abused and killed by family members;
2. that children mimicked adult behaviors in abusing the pets; and
3. that these were families who solved their problems or handled their stress by acting it out against their pets, striking out in anger.

"Unfortunately, 25 years later this continues to be true except the practice of pet abuse has increased in both severity and numbers. Such heinous pet wounds as breaking a leg, pulling off a tail, stabbing an eye, shaving off fur, and mutilating genitals, either purposefully or in seeking sexual gratification, are not unusual sequelae. Clearly pets share the limelight with children when it comes to the need for protection as vulnerable species," she testified.

"Pets are even more vulnerable for obvious reasons, but like abused children they often return to the side of the offender hoping for love, attention, and nurture, even in the face of adversity."

Klingbeil also cited some of the less obvious avenues of animal abuse:

- parents who psychologically torture children by threatening to abuse the animal;
- parents who threaten to, or actually do, sell or abandon the animal in another neighborhood, thereby destroying the only positive bond the child knows; and
- parents who use pets as pawns during separation and divorce.

"Whenever we find a pet who is injured and who has 'unexplained injuries,' we usually have a family that practices abusing its members in one form or another," Klingbeil said. "Pets may be the first to come to the attention of authorities or veterinarians."

UNEXPECTED BACKLASH

Unfortunately, public reaction to Pasado's killing was not uniform. There was criticism by some who felt our moral priorities were completely out of whack: though nobody thought slaughtering donkeys was a good thing, why was there no similar outrage about the beating murders of children or random killings of innocent humans? Some were opposed to what they called "felony creep"—the escalation of too many crimes into felony status, thereby clogging already overburdened courtrooms and prisons. Some accused animal advocates of caring more about animals than about people. Others balked at the idea of giving unbridled authority to humane society investigators. Some opposed the idea of "knee-jerk" legislation; others thought we wanted to outlaw all animal husbandry practices. Even the *Seattle Times* editorialized that public outrage should not drive the courtroom process and that salvaging three young lives ought to take precedence over vengeful punishments.

The judge in the Pasado case, King County Superior Court Judge Michael J. Fox (no relation to the author), imposed sentences on the three young men. The eldest received nine months in jail and 240 hours of community service. The second received 30 days in jail and 240 hours of community service. The juvenile received 30 days and community service. Fox's rulings came less than an hour after he had sentenced a 20-year-old man to 17 years in prison for the abduction and assault of a 16-year-old girl, who escaped with her life only by playing dead in the dumpster in which he threw her. Fox issued a stern tongue-lashing to the public, criticizing them for expressing outrage at the death of a donkey while remaining silent about a teenager stripped naked and left for dead in a dumpster with her throat slashed.

"People have a right to feel outraged by this [Pasado] crime," said Fox. "It was depraved, cruel, and senseless. But we must have a sense of proportion in the expression of our outrage. I would hope the public could demonstrate the same level of community indignation and sorrow for that 16-year-old girl as it has for Pasado."

THE NEED FOR TOUGHER LEGISLATION

Lest anyone think that Pasado's case was an isolated incident, some other graphic examples are instructive. Marc Mayo, deputy prosecuting attorney for the City of Seattle, writing in support of the felonization bill, said, "As a public defender, I had clients who were accused of assault, kidnapping, and sexual assault, many of whom had a history of abusing animals. They had done such things as tie the family dog to a tree and throw rocks, eggs, and other debris at the dog for target practice, and catching squirrels and wrapping them in duct tape. One man threw the family dog out of a third floor window to intimidate his wife. As a prosecutor our office has reviewed or filed cases of persons who poisoned the neighborhood cats, shot at cats, skinned raccoons alive, and used dogs to menace and intimidate girlfriends and children."

It is not that there is more animal abuse occurring today, but there is an increase in public awareness and concern for animals. Imposing felony penalties for severe animal abuse would give city and county prosecutors more resources and enthusiasm in approaching cases. Prosecutors and law enforcement agencies often report having less time and staff than is needed. So they have to ask, are we going to spend five or six hours to develop a case where the perpetrator may get 20 hours of community service, or one in which he may get five years in prison? The notion that perpetrators can also be sentenced to counseling or treatment is also compelling to prosecutors. They like the possibility that they can turn these kids around before they commit heinous and felonious assaults against people. Prosecutors see the felony law as an investment in the future.

As examples, since the felony law went into effect in Washington, there have been a number of high-profile cruelty-to-animals prosecutions with decisions now consistent with the gravity of the crime. The Progressive Animal Welfare Society (PAWS) monitors cases throughout the state, such as individuals who have shot dogs with pellet guns and clubbed geese with tire irons, who have stomped cats to death and skinned dogs alive. We have incidents in which people starve herds of horses and keep hundreds of dogs in unimaginable filth and squalor. Here are some cases that have had cruelty convictions handed down since the felony law was enacted:

Beise Blake, 41, King County, pled guilty to first-degree animal cruelty for killing a stray cat by hitting the animal across the back with a shovel to paralyze her, then chopping off her head with a hatchet. Then the dead cat's legs were all sawed off. Sentence: 12 months minus time served, cannot possess firearms, financial penalty waived.

Two 16-year-olds in Kelso who were "looking for something to shoot before school" cornered a neighbor's dog on the patio. The dog was shot with a bow and arrow and died instantly. They then took the dog's body to another location and ran over it to make it look as if the animal had been killed by a car. One boy pled guilty to first-degree animal cruelty and second-degree burglary. Sentence: 20 days detention, 96 hours community service, one year probation, hunting privileges suspended for a year, $1,500 restitution to victim, and $100 to the state victim's fund. The second boy was convicted of second-degree burglary and sentenced to 10 days detention and 80 hours community service.

Jabari Sanders approached Jeffrey Mitchell and his dog, Sheena, near a Seattle high school and offered to sell him cocaine. When Mitchell declined the offer, Sanders became angry; Mitchell commanded Sheena to keep Sanders at bay. Sheena took hold of Sanders' leg then returned to Mitchell's side. Sanders left and returned with a gun and shot Sheena, who died an hour later. Sanders was found guilty of first-degree animal cruelty and sentenced to four years and five months plus fines.

John Paul Andree, 31, was accused of stabbing to death the kitten of his girlfriend with whom he had recently broken up. The cat had been stabbed at least eight times with a 9-inch knife, and there was evidence of numerous superficial wounds inflicted prior to the fatal chest and neck injuries. He was convicted of first-degree animal cruelty and sentenced to one year in jail and one year of community supervision.

Two juveniles threw several lit firecrackers into an Auburn street where Kelsie, an eight-year-old Chesapeake Bay retriever, tried to retrieve them. The dog died when she picked up an M-80, which exploded in her mouth. One boy was sentenced to 48 hours of community service (only 16 of which were for animal cruelty; the rest were for convictions for shoplifting and giving a false name to police), court supervision for nine months, counseling, and financial restitution to the owner. The second boy received 90 days in jail with 30 converted to community service and 60 converted to work release, $329 in fines, $320 in restitution, and $100 to the victim assistance fund.

Michael Scott Siddons, 18, of Kent, stabbed a friend's cat 22 times after becoming angry at the cat's defecating in his house and biting him. He threw the cat's carcass into a schoolyard. He had an extensive conviction record as a juvenile, including robbery, theft, taking a motor vehicle without permission, and possession of a dangerous weapon. He was convicted of first-degree animal cruelty and sentenced to nine months in jail plus probation, costs, and assessments.

Clayton Butsch, 29, was charged with first-degree animal cruelty for burning an eight-month-old kitten in an oven in a dispute with the cat's owner, who had put Butsch's boots outdoors. The kitten survived, but was thrown out of the house by Butsch; the cat was euthanized the following day. The incident was reported to PAWS by Butsch's mother. He pled guilty and was sentenced to one year in prison for animal cruelty with an additional four years for intimidating a witness. He was also charged with raping the female witness he intimidated, but under a plea bargain the rape charge was dropped.

REVISING THE LAW

The original 1901 Washington animal cruelty statute, as in many states, was clearly antiquated and unsuitable for animals in today's environment. To accomplish the passage of the bill required considerable give-and-take, critical compromises, and shuttle diplomacy that reached fruition in the closing days of the legislative session. After more than two years, 10 drafts, and 30 amendments, House Bill 1652 became law on June 9, 1994.

The new law (Title 16, RCW: Chap. 16.52, Prevention of Cruelty to Animals) created a new category of animal cruelty in the first degree, a class-C felony, which can now be charged for

Anyone who intentionally inflicts substantial pain on, causes physical injury to or kills an animal by a means causing undue suffering, or forces a minor to inflict unnecessary pain, injury or death of an animal.

Animal cruelty in the second degree, a misdemeanor, may be charged for:

Anyone who knowingly, recklessly, or with criminal negligence inflicts unnecessary suffering or pain upon an animal under circumstances not amounting to first degree animal cruelty;

An owner of an animal who knowingly, recklessly or with criminal negligence:

Fails to provide the animal with necessary food, water, shelter, rest, sanitation, ventilation, space or medical attention and the animal suffers unnecessary or unjustifiable physical pain;

Abandons the animals.

A civil penalty of $1,000 shall be paid to the county to prevent cruelty to animals. A convicted person shall also be liable for reasonable costs incurred by law enforcement, animal care, and animal control agencies. A court may also order a defendant to participate in an animal cruelty prevention or education program or to obtain psychological counseling, at his or her own expense, for treatment of mental health problems contributing to the crime.

The law also declares that when a domestic animal has been confined without necessary food and water for more than 36 hours, anyone may enter the premises and supply the animal with food and water. This person shall not be liable to action for entry and may collect from the animal's owner the reasonable cost of the food and water. If an investigating officer finds it extremely difficult to supply the confined animal with food or water, the animal may be removed to protective custody, in which case the owner will be given written notice of the circumstances of the removal and the legal remedies available. The agency with custody of the animal may euthanize it or place it up for adoption not less than 15 business days after it is taken into custody.

What does all this mean from a sentencing standpoint? Misdemeanors carry 0 to 90 days jail time and up to a $1,000 fine, while class-C felons can be imprisoned for up to five years and fined up to $10,000. (By comparison, class-B felonies include first-degree manslaughter; class-A felonies include kidnapping and premeditated murder or arson.)

A BEGINNING

Writing to the Senate Law and Justice Committee in support of the felonization bill, Heather Chambers, coordinator of the Sex Offender Treatment Program for the Snohomish County Juvenile Court and a therapist in private practice specializing in treating survivors of sexual and other kinds of childhood abuse, urged the legislators to consider the human health implications of animal abuse.

"I have had more than ample opportunity to observe that very often animal abuse is also present in families where other types of physical and emotional violence are present," she wrote. "Frequently in these situations the abusive family member will not only maltreat, injure and/or kill family pets, but often does this deliberately in front of other family members as a way to intimidate them, thus further traumatizing the human victims. In turn, victims (primarily children) begin abusing family pets or wildlife as a result of their own victimization, the pet frequently being the only living being in the home over whom the child feels any power.

"If society is to make any significant dent in the enormous problem of family violence of all types, which I am certain is the original cause of all the street and gang violence, preoccupation with guns, myriad serial murders, etc., that occur today, we must approach this issue from every direction possible. *As long as we as a society condone, allow or excuse any type of violence, we give the perpetrators leeway to justify all types of violence.*"

The Pasado case, the outpouring of support in its wake, and the legislative legacy that resulted with the enactment of the new law, brought Washington's animal cruelty laws into the twenty-first century. We presumed that by making serious animal abuse a more serious offense, judges and law enforcement officials would take it more seriously, and in the years since enactment this has turned out to be absolutely true. With the upgrade has come an increase in court activity. This has led to more newspaper coverage as well. And we do not have a cavalier dismissal of cases any more.

The felony law sends a powerful message and helps the law enforcement and criminal justice communities recognize animal cruelty as having serious implications not only for animal protection, but also for society's welfare.

So many people were involved in the struggle to secure passage of the law that if I were to take my hat off to each of them it would look like an Air Force Academy graduation ceremony. We were also very lucky in that the bill was directed initially to the Law and Justice Committee, where we found a far more receptive audience because these committee members did not have an animal usage agenda. State legislatures' Agriculture Committees, where animal bills usually go, typically see animals in terms of food and fiber production and they tend to fight the encroaching of any laws into animal husbandry. They see animal rights in terms of conspiracies and hidden agendas. The Law and Justice Committee did not; they just saw an inequity in the law and they did not question our motives.

It was doubly tragic that it took the death of a donkey to achieve the critical mass needed to galvanize the public, the press, and the legislature into updating a law that was a century behind the times. We are pleased, however, that the experience raised the consciousness level of animal welfare in our legislature and our state. The case, and the new law, told everyone that animal protection is an issue worthy of debate, and that animal abuse is a serious crime worthy of serious sanctions.

Animal Abuse and Law Enforcement
Sherry Schlueter

To RECOGNIZE ANIMAL abuse or neglect, one need not be an expert in any field related to animals or their care. Good common sense, an acquaintance with applicable laws, and a basic familiarity with the species' healthy, normal state of being usually suffice.

Evaluating the appearance and circumstances of most mammals is not difficult, as the human mammal has more in common with other (nonhuman) mammals than not. Avians, reptiles, amphibians, and certain wild or exotic species, whose physiology and needs pose greater challenges to the novice, still offer clues to their states of contentment or distress that can be recognized by the amateur.

Objective, compassionate instincts are far more valuable than rigid, dispassionate assessments of "legal" circumstances. The self-posed questions, "What would I do if I found a child in this predicament?" or, "Would I want my own companion animal to be in this environment?" can go a long way toward guiding one to make reasonable judgments. If the act, omission, or neglect causes or is likely to cause unnecessary, unjustifiable pain, suffering, or death where there is reasonable remedy or relief, report it.

STANDARD SIGNS OF ABUSE

Though state laws and local ordinances vary widely across the country, there are generally some standard, telltale signs of animal abuse that anyone can recognize and for which caseworkers, in particular, should be looking.

Animals in poor physical condition. The animals may have poor body weight; they may be skinny, malnourished, or starving. They may be dirty or have dull coats or feathers; sores or a loss of hair or feathers; matter in the eyes or nose; or a foul odor. They may exhibit excessive head shaking or scratching or they may be weak or lethargic. They may have long hooves, nails, beaks, or teeth; or cracked shells or hooves or loose, broken, decaying or missing teeth.

Animals that are excessively aggressive. Animals may lunge, snap, or growl; lay back their ears; kick, or squawk and act overly agitated or hyper-aggressive toward people or other animals.

Animals that are excessively submissive. Behaviors include poor eye contact, head-shyness, cowering, crawling or slinking, urinating, hiding, and backing away.

Poor general sanitation. Excessive feces or urine may be present. The house or yard may be filthy. The animals' stall, cage, tank, or general environment may be unclean or inappropriate. Debris such as broken glass, protruding or broken boards, slack or barbed fencing, wire or nails on the ground or about the area, are likely to pose potential danger to animals or persons present. The animals may have marginal or no access to potable water, nourishing food, or shelter appropriate for the species, breed, and weather. Odor, flies, maggots, and other so-called vermin may be present. The adults or children in the household may likewise be dirty, malodorous, un-bathed, ungroomed.

Space, light, and ventilation deficiencies. The animals' space may be too confining, such that the animals cannot get wholesome exercise or have an adequate exchange of air. The facilities may be over- or under-ventilated. Animals may be subjected to long hours of darkness without light or long hours of light without quiet and darkness.

Excessive numbers of animals for the space and other resources. Investigators frequently find these conditions among private animal "collectors," typically a person with 10 to hundreds of animals inside a house. These animals may be caged, tied, or otherwise inhumanely confined in bedrooms, bathrooms, garages, sheds, ware-houses, basements, and other inappropriate locations in order to reduce detection by neighbors, authorities, or disapproving family. They are often identified as "strays rescued" by the collector. Overcrowded housing conditions may also be found in pet shops, farms, kennels, ranches, private breeders, or other businesses where animals are considered commodities and individual needs are not met. The animals' environment is usually marked by filth and odor; the animals consequently experience a variety of illnesses. Many "collectors" are also responsible for the welfare of children or elders in their homes. Animal "collectors," surprisingly, are often connected to the professional human caring fields: nursing, teaching, home health care, and so on. Overcrowded circumstances in their own homes should send up a red flag regarding their other contacts with the vulnerable.

Cruel confinement. Animals may be confined on a short tether; they may be housed in a cage, stall, or tank too small for them. They may be left tied on self-tightening collars. Investigators may find incompatible animals that are confined together or in close proximity. Animals may be confined in hot motor vehicles.

Lack of necessary medical care. Investigators may find sick, injured, or dying animals that are deprived of basic medical care and pain-reducing measures. Another aspect of this is failure to euthanize an animal when medically indicated.

Evidence of dead animals, buried or unburied, on the property. Investigators should be alert to the possibility of dead animals or body parts concealed in freezers, sheds or other storage containers, to avoid detection.

Species not permitted by zoning regulations. Although the presence of exotics, wildlife, farm mammals, or fowl in urban settings may be more of a concern for zoning violations than for abuse, humane investigators may nevertheless become involved for enforcement reasons. Often, persons who acquire unusual animals do so for the novelty and may not know the proper care of these animals, leading to abusive and neglectful situations. Urban settings rarely provide the space and other circumstances necessary for optimal comfort of such species.

Excessive fascination and enjoyment by people of live-feedings of mammals or small birds to reptiles or exotics.

Financial inability to afford animal food, veterinary care, or self-care.

Evidence of ritualistic sacrifice. These may include Santeria, Voodoo, Satanism, and other ritualistic religions and cults. Investigators should be alert to signs or evidence of inhumane transport, cruel confinement and brutal killing methods. Animals obtained for rituals are often immobilized with twine, rope, wire, or duct tape and transported in vehicle trunks, floors, backseats or beds of trucks. They may be left thus bound to await their fate, deprived of food, water, freedom of movement or other reasonable necessities or comforts. They then may endure an agonizing death preceded by prolonged protracted suffering, as evidenced by the volumes of blood, dull killing instruments, and severed body parts commonly found at such rituals.

Law enforcement officials are often confused about the legality of these live sacrifices. Although the pursuit of religious freedom is a right guaranteed to Americans, generally one cannot violate state law in the pursuit of that right. Therefore, if state laws are broken (i.e., polygamy, illegal substance abuse, neglect, inhumane transport) officers can and should vigorously prosecute offenders. This should be done objectively and without prejudice, comment, or disrespect concerning the religious beliefs of the practitioners.

Evidence of animal baiting and fighting. There should be cause for concern if you observe pit bull terriers confined separately from one another that bear scars, short-cropped ears, or bite wounds; male game fowl caged separately from one another, often denuded of feathers on the chest, back, stomach, and leg areas; apparent fighting paraphernalia, such as cockfighting spurs or dogfighting treadmills and training apparatus; and fighting pits or arenas.

Absence of appropriate food for species. Or, in the case of "collectors," an abundance of animal food but inadequate food for human members of the household.

Evidence of bestiality. Bestiality, just as sexual battery upon a person, may take many forms. However, unlike these crimes against humans, many states do not specifically outlaw sexual acts upon or with animals. In the absence of bestiality laws, investigators may still be able to prosecute under available anti-cruelty laws if actual injury or suffering to the animal victim can be proved.

The most common injuries include vaginal and rectal tears and internal trauma, especially when implements are used to penetrate. Recurring vaginal and rectal discharges or bleeding, as well as a depressed or fearful demeanor can be clues that the precious bond of trust between human and animal has been grotesquely violated.

Humans with pets living in a state of social isolation.

Abandonment of animals.

Excessive matting of hair coat. Tangles found close to the skin may cause pulling of the skin. Investigators may observe evidence of a previous year's winter coat present during later seasons, or an animal that has not been brushed or groomed for many months.

Collars, harnesses, halters, bridles and bits, or saddle cinches that are too tight or ill-fitting. It is not unusual for investigators to encounter a collar, rope, or chain that has been allowed to grow into the musculature of the neck of a dog as the dog grew up. Horses, cattle and other farm animals are similarly vulnerable when a halter or other controlling device is left on the animal continuously. Conditions like these may cause acute and chronic pain or injury and produce open necrotic flesh wounds accompanied by foul odor and maggot infestation.

Inhumane transport. Inappropriate transport of animals on or within cars, trucks, trailers, and so on.

Parasite infestation. External infestation of fleas, ticks, flies or other insects, or internal infestation with bots or worms usually indicate neglect and contribute to needless, preventable suffering.

DEFINITIONS

When reporting suspected acts of abuse or neglect involving animals, it is helpful to be familiar with the laws that may be applicable. But to investigate these reports one needs to be thoroughly acquainted with not only the laws themselves, but also with the legal definitions of important terms contained therein.

For example, how is the term "animal" defined? Is it all-encompassing ("The term 'animal' is held to include every living dumb creature")? Or is it more restrictive ("The term 'animal' is held to include all domesticated mammals")? A necessary component for successful application of the law is that the species meets the definitive criteria of the ordinance or statute. Some ordinances specifically exclude some animals: pigeons, starlings, or rats may be defined as pests that can legally be poisoned; cocks may be excluded from prohibitions against animal fighting.

How are such terms as "torture," "torment," or "cruelty" defined? Are they generous in their scope ("The words 'torture,' 'torment,' and 'cruelty' shall be held to include every act, omission, or neglect whereby unnecessary, unjustifiable pain or suffering is caused, permitted, or allowed to continue where there is reasonable remedy and relief")? Or are they more modestly applied ("'Cruelty' is the intentional maiming or killing of another person's livestock or pet without just cause")?

The investigator must also be aware of the jurisdictional restrictions of various laws. Federal and state statutes and county and city ordinances may be criminal or civil in nature. Most abuse investigators will deal mainly with criminal state statutes, applicable anywhere within the state of origin, and with county and city ordinances. Ordinances enacted by cities or counties, not by the state legislature, may be applied only within those restrictive boundaries. Investigators should be aware that local ordinances often track the language of state statutes, but the provisions for punishment, penalty or fines may have been significantly altered (usually downgraded). Ordinances of this type may virtually decriminalize the same acts (making them civil infractions), which would have been arrestable offenses had the charge been filed under the state criminal statute.

Abuse investigators should also be alert to laws that appear to be protective of animals but whose focus is actually upon protecting the property rights of the animal's (i.e., the property's) owner. Careful attention must be paid to choose the most effective and appropriate avenue of enforcement.

GOALS OF PROSECUTION

If prosecution of an offender is the goal, it is important to be aware of specific legal definitions of terms and of statutory criteria to determine if a law has indeed been violated. Bear in mind, however, that matters involving animal suffering need not always reach the criminal realm before intervention can begin. Alert citizens and caring professionals should react to disturbing tendencies as soon as they are recognized. The real goal should always be elimination (or at least reduction) of victim pain and suffering. Prosecution of perpetrators often does little to assist the victim. Removal (permanently) of the victim is far more important to the victim than is punishment of its abuser. Ideally, both should occur.

Reporters of these crimes, witnesses, and legally obtained evidence such as photos or recordings become extremely important to the successful prosecution of a case. Members of other social service and investigatory agencies will likely be viewed by the courts as witnesses with professional credibility and more than average knowledge of abuse or neglect, regardless of the species of the victim. In jurisdictions where animal abuse is not handled progressively, this professional involvement may be crucial to a successful outcome. For these reasons and others, including the need of the law enforcement agency to contact the reporter at a later date, anonymity in reporting is discouraged.

PROTECTIVE CUSTODY

What determines whether animal victims are removed into protective custody is varied. It may be the seriousness of the abuse or neglect, the satisfaction of the elements of the crime occurring, the competence, fortitude and courage of the investigating agency, the economics of the action, the continuing nature of the jeopardy, or other factors. It would not be an exaggeration to say that most animal abuse investigators err on the side of caution far too often, probably in response to the abundantly litigious nature of today's society. This is a tragic mistake. One should not wait until a situation is sufficiently "serious" before taking action. Early intervention is preferable. Waiting until the animal is severely debilitated may enhance prosecution, but does the animal victim little good. Look for a solution that best serves the victim.

Some laws and ordinances grant humane or law enforcement officers specific powers to rescue or confiscate abused animals (mindful of such constitutional procedures as obtaining court orders or search-and-seizure warrants) under exigency conditions when the animals' safety or welfare is in grave and immediate danger. Even when such powers are not specified, however, all law enforcement officers have the power to confiscate abused animals when laws are being violated. They may do so under their granted powers to seize evidence of a crime, as most abused animals' bodies yield information of evidentiary value. Also, the premise of protecting the victim is a powerful and historically accepted one.

A key distinction between animal abuse and other forms of family violence is that the ultimate goal of animal abuse prosecutions is to remove the animal permanently from the abuser. The ultimate disposition of the confiscated animal depends largely upon the legal procedure by which it was impounded, the outcome of the investigation or prosecution, the community's standards, and the wisdom of the authority presiding over the case. It is unfortunate that the "property" rights of the abuser are often considered more important than the secure future of the victim. This must be guarded against with diligent vigor.

WHO HANDLES ANIMAL ABUSE CASES?

The responsibility for investigation of reports of animal abuse varies according to jurisdiction. In some communities, elaborate programs exist within animal caring organizations, such as humane societies, SPCAs, or animal control agencies, which credibly and vigorously address these complaints. Conversely, there are many places, especially in the rural United States, where no animal care, regulation, or control organizations can be found—no shelters, no investigators, and no local ordinances to deal with esoteric issues effectively.

Law enforcement agencies, on the other hand, exist everywhere in the United States and enjoy responsibility for enforcement of all laws pertinent to their jurisdictions, including animal protection laws. Few such agencies, however, fulfill this obligation or accept this responsibility.

Investigators of child abuse and other family violence cases may wish to remind law enforcers of the "indicator crime" status of animal abuse when trying to rouse interest in the investigation of these matters. Conclusive studies demonstrating the "cycle" of violence prove powerful motivators for authorities otherwise indifferent to animal concerns.

HOW TO BUILD A CASE

Regardless of which discipline the initial information comes from or the type of victim involved, all law enforcement agencies require similar information to initiate an investigation. To get the agency to take an initial report, the complainant should convey as much of the following relevant information as possible to the intake person, dispatcher, or operator.

Exact addresses. These are preferable to vague approximations or a rambling set of directions to the site.

Identification of the offender(s) by name, date of birth or age, sex, and physical description, is important. The time of day the suspect is usually home, and location where the suspect works, are also helpful.

An accurate, objective explanation of the nature of the suspected abuse. Was the matter a singular act of violence or was it part of a chronic pattern? Was there prolonged intentional deprivation or was it more likely a passive, borderline neglect based upon ignorance or lack of finances?

Time frame of occurrence. Exact dates and times are best. Saying, "My neighbor always beats his dog" is not usually sufficient to file charges unless a specific date and time of a particular beating incident can be established.

Other potential witnesses and information on how to contact them are extremely helpful.

Evidence present at the scene or in someone's possession, which investigators should recover, is very useful. *Note:* If someone other than the investigator has lawfully obtained evidence or items of evidentiary value, such as audiotape recordings, videotape recordings, photographs, witness statements, suspect admissions, and so forth, this information should be conveyed to the investigator. Child abuse investigators especially may find themselves privy to information child victims may present during investigatory interviews that implicates suspects in animal abuse as well: "Here is the club my dad beat Sparky with after he had used it on me and my mom," or "My mom's boyfriend killed my kitty when he thought I was gonna tell. He buried her over there in the yard by that bush."

Persons reporting suspected abuse should also ask questions of the agency while imparting information regarding a complaint, such as:

When will you be sending someone out to investigate?
Will this complaint be addressed if I report it anonymously?

Is a signed complaint or sworn statement required before you will initiate this inquiry?

May I be kept apprised of the progress and results?

Without the child's testimony about what she or he witnessed, will you have a case?

How can the impact upon the rest of the family be minimized?

What likely will happen to the animal victims?

How can I help?

To prepare to file a complaint, it is a good practice to begin to log all pertinent information in chronological order once you are aware of suspected abuse or neglect. Document dates, times, places, names, confidential sources, vehicle tag numbers, descriptions, and conversations as they are encountered.

Mark any evidence that you have, such as photographs, by date, location obtained, and subject matter contained. Sign or initial and date the backs of the photographs. Carefully store and mark the negatives or turn them over to investigators after obtaining a receipt for them. Be careful not to alter or destroy evidence, such as fingerprints, blood, or hair, by improper handling or storage practices. Try to leave these matters of evidence identification and collection to the experts, if at all possible.

Note when and to whom the report was given. Provide complete information if possible of how the agency can contact you if they have questions, including times you are available, and different phone or pager numbers. Request timely progress updates on the case. Document each contact, whether initiated or received, with the investigating agency. Update the investigator with any new leads or information without delay.

If the situation is urgent, convey this. Remain professional. Relate the information without hyperbole; do not exaggerate the facts.

Contact the supervisors of reluctant or ineffective agency members when reasonable expectations have not been met. Try to respect the organization's structure by using the "chain of command" to successively reach the level of hierarchy sympathetic, or at least sensitive, to your concerns. Be fair, firm, objective, courteous, and not overly emotional. Credibility is crucial.

When conventional methods fail, judicious use of the media to illuminate a problem can be quite effective. Done responsibly, the results are usually overwhelmingly favorable, with few negative repercussions. Never exaggerate information to the media. The truth is all you need.

Bear in mind that one of the most challenging aspects of reporting animal cruelty is achieving the acceptance of the complaint by the intake operator or dispatcher. When a report is directed to an animal protection or sheltering organization, one is unlikely to meet with much resistance, unless the agency has no cruelty investigator of its own. In such cases, the shelter may simply refer the complaint to another resource, such as a sheriff's office or police department, without questioning the need for the alleged crime to be investigated.

Some law enforcement agencies, however, are as yet unfamiliar with the important role they should play in the investigation of these crimes—crimes with victims who suffer fear, pain, deprivation, and death. This perceived indifference by law enforcement agencies does not usually reflect an absence of actual concern or compassion for animals on the part of individual officers or dispatchers. It is more likely a result of a long-held belief, often manifested in a long-standing policy, that animal welfare matters are not as serious as other crimes, or that handling of animal abuse cases is within the purview of animal protection agencies rather than law enforcement agencies. These attitudes are both unfortunate and erroneous.

STRATEGIES FOR SUCCESS

Once one becomes alert to a potentially abusive situation, the suspicions should be reported without delay to encourage timely assistance to the victim. It is not unusual for a reported complaint to take days or weeks to receive its first attention by an understaffed agency. Nor would it be unusual for initial complaints to be disregarded entirely by investigatory bodies burdened by cases assigned a higher priority status due to their greater perceived seriousness.

To make matters worse, some law enforcement agencies fail to respond in person to many misdemeanor-level issues, opting instead to document the complainant's concerns by telephone only. Others use nonsworn service aides to handle lower priority or noncriminal matters, and unfortunately, animal complaints often inaccurately fall into this classification. This approach is particularly troublesome when the report is about criminal abuse or neglect of animals. Offenders sometimes exhibit unpredictable, violent, or sadistic tendencies as evidenced by the very nature of their crimes. It is inappropriate to send unarmed civilian investigators to these scenes, as they are likely ill-equipped and undertrained for such, thus needlessly imperiling their safety.

A frequent concern of those contemplating filing a report is determining whether the matter is indeed criminal, whether it meets the criteria for a formal complaint. Rather than agonize over this question, it is best to just report it and let the agency determine the legitimacy of the information.

Even situations that fall short of criminal status or the ability to prosecute often cry out for intervention of some sort—warnings, education, or suggestions for improvement. Each investigatory visit by an agency allows for evaluation and possible correction before actual tragedy occurs.

The decision about whether to report a concern should not rest upon the perceived seriousness of the offense, nor upon the degree of suffering the victim endures. Although it is certainly true that more egregious cases generate more interest, any suffering is too much suffering. A community's standards, although a factor for consideration, should not necessarily dictate what qualifies as abuse or neglect.

Challenge of the status quo is necessary for progress to be attained. Where laws are antiquated, ineffective, or absent in a jurisdiction, concerns should be reported and investigated anyway to at least arouse public attention that may rectify the immediate situation and eventually lead to beneficial ordinance revision.

One can help persuade authorities to improve the circumstances of animals by offering respectful encouragement and assistance, and by being mindful of differing priorities. Everywhere, investigators and law enforcers exert influence over people daily in matters in which no crime or breach of the peace has actually occurred.

The handling of noise disturbance complaints illustrates this reality easily. Many noise control ordinances are in effect (enforceable) only during the late evening through early morning hours, that is, 10:00 P.M. to 8:00 A.M. or 11:00 P.M. to 7:00 A.M. But if an excessively loud stereo or chronically barking dog is causing neighborhood discord at any hour, responding officers are likely to "direct" the responsible party to stop or reduce the offending noise. Few citizens would fail to comply with an officer's request or order, even though the ordinance at that time may be technically unenforceable as no violation is technically occurring. The same principle, logical and resolution-oriented, can and should be applied to any reasonable issue a responsible citizen poses to authorities—including animal issues.

There is a promising philosophy of "policing" spreading across the nation that has been embraced by many progressive, service-oriented law enforcement officers and agencies for years. It is called "community oriented" or "community-based policing" and it incorporates, as one of its most basic tenets, the concept of early response to a community's concerns in an effort to reduce crime occurrence. The concerns do not necessarily have to be criminal in nature.

When law enforcement officers get back in touch with the people they serve, learning which issues really trouble them, effective remedies can be put into place before tempers flare, property is damaged, and violence escalates. Concerns about animal well-being easily qualify for this kind of corrective intervention.

Innovative community policing approaches include coordination of efforts in matters generally considered the purview of others, that is, zoning, code enforcement, and fire inspections. These agencies and others can address the animal issues, as well as the junk cars, overgrown yards, and dangerous structures the neighborhood is complaining about. Even if no one addresses the complaints about a neglected animal, someone may respond to a report of foul odors, flies, putrid water, or excessive waste matter from the purview of a public health problem. This strategy at least initiates an investigative response that gets the animal and its circumstances looked at. Rectification of some degree should follow.

Community policing, with its focus upon policing (proactive, preventive, victim-oriented) rather than law enforcement (reactive, arrest or offender-oriented) bodes well for citizens and officers interested in reducing or eliminating the suffering of others.

ANIMAL ABUSE AND OTHER FORMS OF FAMILY VIOLENCE

Animal abuse investigations are similar to child abuse and other abuse or neglect investigations in many ways. Each deals with an essentially powerless victim who has little voice or choice in controlling its circumstances or directing its life. Although these victims are protected by laws, their inherent rights are rarely acknowledged, recognized, or considered except through the assertions of interested adult persons.

The most notable legal distinction between the child victim and the animal victim is the obvious status of personhood the child enjoys. The animal, unfortunately, is presently still universally considered "property." In most cases it would lack legal standing of its own and could not assert its "rights" were it granted any.

The protections afforded children and animals vary from jurisdiction to jurisdiction. Undoubtedly, investigators will find it easier to remove animal victims from jeopardy and retain permanent custody of them than they will child victims.

Most human service agencies dealing with family violence and related issues have, by virtue of federal mandate, the responsibility to try to keep the family united. This is attempted by offering or ordering attendance of parenting classes, anger management classes, marriage or family counseling, and by placing some other needed services into the home. Usually, no such expectation of "reunification" of an abusive owner with animal victims burdens animal protectors. Indeed, protectors should strive to achieve the converse—permanent removal of the animal victim from the offender.

Child victim advocates confront numerous delicate issues, including questions of parental rights (including the abuser demanding visitation with the abused) and obtaining the victim's cooperation in the investigation without causing further psychological distress or other harm to the victim.

The human elderly, suffering from the infirmities of aging, and significantly disabled adults, any of whom may be victims of abuse, neglect, or exploitation, may find themselves in similar predicaments as child victims: with "advocates," "guardians," or persons appointed as "powers of attorney" representing their interests and directing their futures. They may find that their abilities to cooperate in the investigations and prosecutions of their offenders are influenced by their lapses in lucidity; their lack of orientation to date, time, and location; and by their physical abilities to even survive until trial or to participate in the rigors of court cases.

The advantages of victim cooperation cannot be negated. Realistically, however, in abuse cases involving nonhuman animals or the very young, the very old, the very disabled, and the very traumatized, this ability to cooperate cannot be expected or relied upon. Those victims of abuse, neglect and exploitation who are able to provide assistance to authorities enhance the chances of successful prosecution of their offenders. This can have the added benefit of providing a sort of cathartic relief, easing the victim toward recovery. Animal victims, however, can assist only by exhibiting certain behaviors, injuries, or pathologies that are indicative of abuse, provided that these can be documented.

In the best of circumstances, some human victims are able to voice their case outcome preferences. A conversant child victim may say, "I want to live with Daddy!" The infirm, aged person may say, "I don't want to go to a nursing home; I want to go stay with my daughter!" The domestic violence victim may seek a restraining order and begin divorce proceedings. But the animal victim's fate is always dictated by another—a human other. Also, no human members of this sphere of violence and neglect need fear euthanasia as a final solution to their victimization. Advocates for animals must always strive to insure that the resolution to the case, whether it be adoption, euthanasia, or some other disposition, is mindful of the victim's best interests.

In dealing with abuse, neglect, and exploitation of animals, children, disabled adults or the elderly, one must recognize that these are the most powerless, most oppressed, most disenfranchised, and most vulnerable of all of society's members. It is up to those of us who are fortunate to not count ourselves among their ranks to report, to advocate for, to investigate, and to defend them. Through awareness, vision, courage, and tenacity, the insidious cycle of violence may finally be broken.

Cruelty and Abuse to Animals
A Typology
Andrew N. Rowan

In 1987, Alan Felthous and Stephen Kellert published an important but little-cited review article on the available research linking cruelty to animals with aggression toward humans. They found 13 reports that examined the link, 9 of which concluded that there was little or no basis to this link, contrary to folk wisdom. When they examined the 13 analyses more carefully, however, they found that the 9 reports that found no link tended to define both cruelty to animals and aggression to fellow humans very broadly. Thus, in these studies, almost any mistreatment of or harm to animals (including tormenting flies) was classified as cruelty while an occasional outburst of aggression toward fellow humans was sufficient to categorize individuals as aggressive.

The four reports that did find an association between cruelty to animals and aggression toward humans defined cruelty and aggression much more narrowly. One had to display repeated violent behavior toward humans to be included in the aggressive group and only those performing premeditated and deliberate abuse of vertebrate animals were categorized as displaying cruelty to animals. Under these circumstances, cruelty to animals and aggression to humans were correlated, although the studies could not determine whether they were causally related.

This anecdote illustrates not only the care that investigators of cruelty need to take in defining terms but also the tendency to overuse certain terms, thereby diminishing their impact. Unfortunately, the term "cruelty" is subject to such overuse and debasement of meaning. It is ingrained in American culture via the centuries-old "cruelty to animals" laws and is widely used in everyday language to describe a broad range of human behaviors and motivational states. Thus, although people still condemn cruelty to animals, the term has lost some of its power.[1]

DEFINITIONS

The *Shorter Oxford English Dictionary* (3rd edition) defines "cruel" as "disposed to inflict suffering; indifferent to or taking pleasure in another's pain; merciless, pitiless, hard-hearted." This definition incorporates at least two different motivational states that should be more carefully distinguished in any detailed consideration of animal cruelty and abuse. Someone who takes pleasure in the deliberate and premeditated infliction of suffering on another being is engaged in behavior (an act of commission) that can be distinguished from someone who is simply indifferent to the same suffering (an act of omission).

Webster's Third New International Dictionary (1993) is more particular, defining "cruel" as

(1a) "disposed to inflict pain, especially in a wanton, insensate, or vindictive manner: pleased by hurting others";

(1c) "arising from or indicative of an inclination to enjoy another's pain or misfortune"; 2b) "stern, rigorous and grim: unrelieved by leniency or softness"; and (3) "severe, distressing: extremely painful."

This definition is significantly weighted toward the notion of the actor enjoying another's pain or suffering. Abuse is defined by Webster as "to use or treat so as to injure, hurt or damage."

In a recent survey (Penn & Schoen Associates 1997), 1,005 American adults were asked about animal and human abuse. Although the respondents found human abuse to be much more serious than animal abuse (79% considered human abuse to be serious or very serious compared to 42% for animal abuse), they tended not to distinguish between cruelty and neglect. In response to the following question:

There are two types of cruelty to household pets. Animal abuse is the intent to cause harm and includes torture or malicious killing of animals. Animal neglect is the withholding of food, water, shelter, medical care, or care because of ignorance. Speaking generally, do you think animal neglect is as bad as animal abuse or not?

70 percent said neglect is as bad as abuse;

18 percent said neglect is not as bad;

5 percent said neglect is worse than abuse;

1 percent said that neither are bad; and

6 percent did not know.

I would argue that we should be much more careful in our use of terms that refer to animal abuse for reasons of justice, criminology, public policy, and public debate. The typology that I would propose divides behavior that causes animals pain, suffering, or harm into one of four categories: cruelty, abuse, neglect, and use (see table 1 below).

TYPOLOGY

Cruelty

The term "cruelty" should be restricted to a relatively small subset of cases of animal abuse. This group is so small that in order to qualify as cruel, an act must not

Table 1. Categories of Human Behavior and Motivation Associated with Animal Use
That Sometimes Causes Distress

Term	Actor's Motivation	Animal Suffering	Societal Attitude
I. Cruel	Takes satisfaction from suffering	Always	Condemnation
II(a). Abuse	Satisfaction derived from dominance or behavioral response	Usually	Condemnation
II(b). Neglect	No satisfaction derived	Usually	Condemnation
III. Use	Justified by claims to personal or societal gains	Sometimes	Approval when are attempts to minimize suffering

only involve the deliberate causing of (or intent to cause) some harm to an animal, it must also include the actor's desire to gain satisfaction from the infliction of suffering, pain, or some other harm. Setting a cat's tail on fire so that one might enjoy the sight of the animal fleeing in pain is an example of cruel behavior. This type of behavior would, by definition, then be different from behavior in which force is used to control or discipline an animal or from the adolescent curiosity (mostly male) that causes animal distress and suffering. Thus, one needs to distinguish between motivations of power and control, curiosity and knowledge, and sadism and other psychopathic behavior. Lumping all three motivations together will waste law enforcement resources. Clearly, individuals displaying psychopathic behavior need to be dealt with very differently from the adolescent boy who is simply curious. The abusive use of power also needs a different set of social interventions.

Another form of animal abuse that might be included under the definition of cruelty are those cases represented by individuals who do not view animals as capable of suffering. Arnold Arluke (personal communication, 1997) indicates that some of the individuals he interviewed simply did not consider their animal victims to be worthy of any concern whatsoever. Insofar as this attitude might spread to their relationships with humans, or certain minority groups of humans, it is clearly a concern for the agents charged with maintaining a civil and humane society.

Abuse

Some (but still a minority of) cases of animal mistreatment are caused by the abuse of power and physical force. Modern society has begun to frown on the use of corporal punishment to discipline children and there is much debate in the animal training world over the appropriate use of reward and punishment in training an animal to do what one wants. In fact, the links between reward, punishment (which can vary from the use of the word "no" to vicious beating), and effective behavior shaping are complex and frequently misunderstood. Nonetheless, although the abusive use of force and power may be difficult to define, it is usually not difficult to recognize (like obscenity). Abuse of an animal may result from the use of inappropriate levels of force, from an inappropriate response to what is a natural behavior (e.g., kicking a cat that rubs against one's leg), to inappropriate restrictions on an animal's normal behavior.

Neglect

The majority of cases of nonsanctioned animal suffering and harm are caused by people who are either careless or neglectful (see Vermeulen & Odendaal 1993). Such instances should not qualify as cruelty or the abuse of force or power but as "neglect." From a law enforcement perspective, willful neglect should probably still be classified as abuse but there are many cases where the animal suffers as a result of a lack of thought or a lack of competence and these cases need to be treated differently by law enforcement authorities. An extreme example of animal suffering caused by a lack of competence or knowledge is the animal collector.

Every experienced shelter worker will have at least one "war story" of an animal collector where scores or hundreds of animals are crammed into a house, apartment, or small property and living in filth, disease, and squalor. Typically, collectors share the same living conditions with the animals and are often brought to the attention of the authorities because of their own body odors or the stench from their homes. Collectors usually start off by trying to help animals and save them from some real or imagined danger or death, such as euthanasia by a local shelter or veterinarian. In one case, a woman kept a dog with a broken back, which dragged itself around her yard. She would not take it to a veterinarian because she knew it would promptly be euthanized. Although we would regard such behavior as horrible, Jain animal hospitals in India also refuse to euthanize injured animals and keep them as comfortable as they can until they die.

Animal collectors, who often distrust institutions and authority and deny death— either their own or their animals (Worth & Beck 1981)—sooner or later lose control of their animal rescue activities and end up sharing conditions of incredible squalor with the animals they are trying to save. Collectors usually know all or most of their animals and, hard though it may be to understand, are just as concerned about each animal as the Humane Society inspector who wants to rescue them. Animal collectors who are criminalized and prosecuted for cruelty usually revert to their collecting ways as soon as they are free of the legal system again. These individuals represent one subset of individuals known to the psychiatric profession as hoarders. They need treatment and care, and their behaviors can, in some cases, be dramatically changed by the use of some of the new psychiatric drugs (such as Prozac).

Use

Finally, the vast majority of animals that are caused either distress or harm are under the control or reach of humans who are performing some socially sanctioned activity—such as animal research, raising animals for food, animal transport and slaughter, hunting, and the like. People may obtain satisfaction and pleasure from these activities but the presence of animal distress is not only an unnecessary part of gaining such satisfaction, it is regarded as an unfortunate consequence of the activity. When defending such activities, people usually express the wish to eliminate all animal pain and distress. This is where the use of terms such as "cruelty" interfere with the progress of a constructive public debate and the development of public policy that can advance the aim of developing a humane society.

Scientists who use animals in research that sometimes causes suffering take strong (and appropriate) exception to being called cruel. The implicit or explicit accusation of cruelty by critics (and hence the categorization of their motives as evil or malign) is one of the barriers to establishing a reasoned public dialogue about animal distress and suffering and its alleviation in research. People who work in slaughter plants similarly do not view their activities as being cruel (Grandin 1988). They use what are well-recognized psychological devices to deal with their very stressful jobs such as blaming societal demands for what they do and by desensitizing themselves (behaving as though they are simply stapling boxes, in Grandin's words). In some societies and cultures, slaughter is conducted by men of special character who are considered to be better able to bear the burden and associated guilt of the animal killing.

CONCLUSION

It is quite common to find evidence of prior animal torture in the early lives of serial killers like Ted Bundy or the Boston Strangler. There are also disturbing signs that young murderers may practice their trade by killing animals (Lockwood & Hodge 1986). And yet, there is a tendency for the courts to deal relatively leniently with even fairly graphic examples of deliberate animal abuse. If we defined cruelty more narrowly (and more accurately) and distinguished it from abuse based on the motivational state of the actor, we might then pick up more psychopaths before they turn their attentions from animals to humans.

Nonetheless, drawing such distinctions is likely to be difficult because of the widespread use of the term "cruelty" and also because establishing motivation and intent is never easy. For example, one of the few books to address the concept of cruelty in a systematic and detailed fashion uses examples drawn from cases of sadistic psychopathology as well as abuse sanctioned by society (Hallie 1969). Also, we have to deal with the tendency, especially among young males, to tease and torment animals. We need to identify what might be happening in such instances and to determine if we can distinguish between such youthful curiosity and indiscretions and incipient psychopathology.

Ascione (1993) has produced an extensive review of the literature on the links between childhood abuse and abusive behavior toward animals and he cites data that show that victims of sexual abuse in childhood are much more likely to demonstrate abusive behavior toward animals. This notion of humans progressing from animal abuse to later criminal behavior is a fundamental facet of anticruelty statutes and societal support for humane education. There is, however, very little evidence to support the idea that teaching children to be kind to animals will have beneficial effects on their character as adults. Just as we need to be more careful in defining human behaviors that lead to animal suffering, so we must also be more careful in examining human nurturing behaviors and the development of empathy toward both humans and animals.

One interesting study of a small sample of survivors (those who did not show later abusive behavior) and nonsurvivors (those who did show later abusive behavior) of childhood abuse found that the survivors were more likely than nonsurvivors to have had responsibility for the care and nurture of either a sibling or an animal (Zimrin 1986). It is generally acknowledged that child protection services have many survivors of abusive upbringing among their ranks (more than would be expected simply from chance) and I have anecdotal knowledge that there are survivors of childhood abuse also active in animal training and in the animal protection movement. It may be that those subjected to abuse in childhood might include not only one subset who are more likely to continue the cycle of child abuse as adults but also another subset who become what might be called "supernurturers." Determining the factors that predispose an individual to proceed along one path or the other could have important consequences for both intervention and treatment strategies as well as for public health and social order.

Cruelty to animals is a disturbing event that can elicit a tremendous outpouring of emotion from the public. When three youths tied a dog to train tracks in Boston and watched it being run down (Anonymous 1992), the public was outraged, even more so than by equally disturbing cases of child killing. Such cases of malicious abuse of animals appear to be relatively rare but it is not a well-studied issue. Public health authorities should take the issue more seriously and begin to use such cases as important predictors of sociopathology.

NOTE

1. Editorial note: Criminologist Piers Beirne of the University of Southern Maine argues in a similar vein that the term "bestiality" should be recast as "interspecies sexual assault" to be more

consistent with contemporary criminal justice systems and because the victimization of animals parallels that of women and, to some extent, of infants and children. Interspecies sexual assault invariably involves coercion, causes pain and even death, and animals are unable to communicate consent to us or speak out about their abuse (Beirne 1997).

REFERENCES

Ascione, F. R. 1993. Children who are cruel to animals: A review of research and implications for developmental psychopathology. *Anthrozoös* 6:226–47.

Anonymous. 1992. On public expressions of sympathy for animals and people. *Anthrozoös* 5:257–58.

Beirne, P. 1997. Rethinking bestiality: Towards a concept of interspecies sexual assault. *Theoretical Criminology* 1(3):317–40.

Felthous, A. R., and S. R. Kellert. 1987. Childhood cruelty to animals and later aggression against people: A review. *American Journal of Psychiatry* 144:710–17.

Grandin, T. 1988. Behavior of slaughter plant and auction employees towards the animals. *Anthrozoös* 1:205–13.

Hallie, P. P. 1969. *The paradox of cruelty.* Middletown, Conn.: Wesleyan University Press.

Lockwood, R., and G. Hodge. 1986. The tangled web of animal abuse: The links between cruelty to animals and human violence. *Humane Society News* (summer), 10–15.

Penn & Schoen Associates. 1997. *December, 1996 survey on public opinion and animal abuse.* Washington, D.C.: Humane Society of the United States.

Vermeulen, H., and J. Odendaal. 1993. Proposed typology of companion animal abuse. *Anthrozoös* 6:248–57.

Worth, D., and A. M. Beck. 1981. Multiple ownership of animals in New York City. *Transactions and Studies of the College of Physicians* (Philadelphia) 3:280–300.

Zimrin, H. 1986. A profile of survival. *Child Abuse and Neglect* 10:339–49.

A Congressional View of the Cycle of Violence

William S. Cohen

MR. PRESIDENT, Derrick Robie's tiny, battered body was discovered in the afternoon of August 2, 1993. The small town was shocked to find that 13-year-old Eric Smith had murdered this 4-year-old child.

Investigators found an indicator of violent crime in Eric Smith's behavioral pattern: one year prior to killing Derrick Robie, Eric had strangled his neighbor's cat with a hose clamp. At the time, no one paid much attention to this so-called prank.

Mr. President, it is time that we took a serious look at animal abuse and its link to crimes against people. Perpetrators of serious animal abuse often lack empathy and respect for life in general. The absence of empathy is often manifested by striking, torturing, and abusing an innocent animal. Abusing animals is a despicable act, and psychologists and criminologists tell us those who lack empathy for animals may also lack empathy for humans. As a result they may be predisposed to other violent behavior.

Violence begets violence. Child, spousal, and elder abuse are unfortunately too commonplace in our society. Often physical abuse is coupled with sexual abuse against a family member. Aggression is passed from one generation to another. In a hostile home environment, children often mimic their parents' abusive behavior. They become abusive to others, including the family pet, and they learn that violence and cruelty are a way of life. Unless intervention occurs, such children are likely to continue violent acts to others, perhaps become abusive spouses, and possibly commit other criminal acts.

The National Research Council and the Federal Bureau of Investigation agree that cruelty to animals is one childhood behavior that is a powerful indicator of violence elsewhere in the perpetrator's life. There is a strong probability that youths who abuse animals are themselves victims and perpetrators of violence.

On May 2, 1996, William S. Cohen, then the senior Republican Senator from Maine, introduced the following testimony into the Congressional Record ("Cycle of Violence," Congressional Record, May 2, 1996, pp. 54630–31).

Dr. Frank Ascione of Utah State University has been conducting research on the animal-people abuse phenomenon for more than 15 years. He has studied the common roots of violence toward people and animals and has found a strong correlation between animal abuse and people abuse. He is a leader among many researchers who have been scientifically studying this phenomenon since the 1970s. One study of 38 abuse victims at a crisis shelter found nearly 75 percent of women with pets reported their partner had threatened, hurt, or killed the animal. Researchers in child abuse cases found that in 88 percent of these family situations, the pet was also abused.

Violence is not an isolated event and animal abuse is often part of a larger cycle of violence. For this reason, violence toward animals must be taken much more seriously. Cruelty to animals can be a predictor of future violence and an indicator of the violence already in the perpetrator's life.

Experts in the family violence field instruct us to treat a single act of violence as an indicator of past and future violence. Our public support systems must be coordinated so when an adult or child abuses an animal, the animal control officer will notify other public health officials to determine whether there is evidence of child, spousal, or elder abuse. The perpetrator of animal or people abuse may, himself, be a victim of sexual or other abuse. Further, the Federal Bureau of Investigation has identified animal abuse as one of a cluster of juvenile behaviors that could suggest serious violent behavior later in life.

The good news is that experts are finding that compassion and empathy can be taught. Various schools across the country have recognized the linkage of animal and people violence. They have added specialized humane education to their curriculum in order to teach compassion and empathy.

In 1994 the National Research Council released a comprehensive study on understanding and preventing violence, showing that childhood behavior is more important than teenage behavior in predicting future violent behavior. The report suggests that early prevention efforts have a greater potential for reducing adult crime than criminal sanctions applied later in life.

Cities and towns across the country are beginning to recognize the potential for further violence in the link between animal abuses and other abuses. Last year the city of San Diego enacted an unprecedented interagency agreement, requiring its children's services agencies to report to animal control officials suspected instances of animal abuse within 24 hours of becoming aware of it. Further, the animal control officers must report suspected child abuse to the proper authorities. These workers are cross-trained to recognize signs of abuse in animals and people.

Other cities and states are strengthening penalties for animal abuse as well as requiring mental health care to be administered to the perpetrators of animal abuse. There is much to be done, and progress begins when those of authority become educated on the significance of animal cruelty.

It is the responsibility of our private and public support systems to recognize signs that a child is in trouble and intervene in an effective manner. The FBI has identified clusters of traits indicating problems: firesetting, cruelty to animals, truancy, and so on. When there is fire setting, there could be sexual abuse. When there is truancy, there could be drug problems. When there is fighting and cruelty to people or animals, the perpetrator could be responding to abuses he is suffering or has suffered. Most importantly these signals should not be treated as isolated events, but rather trigger responses from the educators, criminal justice professionals, public health officials, and animal control specialists, working in concert.

I believe that this cycle of violence merits further investigation. We must recognize that there is continuity between animal abuse and people abuse. Further research is needed on the predictable influences of violence. Meanwhile, we must take action on the known data. Individuals, the public health system, the criminal justice professionals, and the educators must coordinate their efforts in recognizing, intervening, and preventing future violent acts.

In order to encourage more in-depth analyses of this link between people and animal violence, I have asked Attorney General Janet Reno to accelerate the Department of Justice's research in this area and to take appropriate action based upon what we already know. One particular area of interest to me is the education of prosecuting attorneys and judges regarding the correlation of animal cruelty to other crimes. Although experts agree the penalties for such abuse should be stiffened, they are also in agreement that a mental health analysis of the entire family involved in an abusive case may be necessary.

I intend to continue my examination of violence prevention and I intend to continue investigating where the public support systems may be further strengthened in breaking this cycle of violence. The professionals in criminal behavior are reporting to us that violence has warning signals. It is our responsibility to recognize these signals and intervene swiftly and effectively.

Admittedly this is not an exact science. Every child that abuses an animal will not necessarily become a violent offender or become a victim of violence himself, but it would be a mistake to dismiss the strong correlation between animal and people violence. As a society, we must realize that violent behavior rarely exists in a vacuum. We must recognize at-risk youths who lack empathy and compassion for animals and other human beings. It is our responsibility to do all that we can to teach these personality attributes to our youth so that today's animal abusers do not continue these despicable actions and become tomorrow's dangerous felons, thereby perpetuating the cycle of violence that has taken such a devastating toll on our society.

Statewide Commission Created for Cross-Reporting Legislation

Phil Arkow

WITH ANECDOTAL AND research data continuing to indicate linkages between various forms of family violence, a number of communities and states are enacting legislation requiring officials in child protection, animal protection, and domestic violence prevention to report suspected abuse to each other. The State of Rhode Island created a statewide commission to research the issue and draft appropriate legislation.

In the spring of 1997, the Rhode Island General Assembly created a bipartisan Special Legislative Commission to study the associations between domestic violence, child abuse, and animal abuse with a goal of producing statewide legislation that would require the Department for Children, Youth and Families (DCYF) and animal protection officers to cross-report incidents of abuse.

The special commission, believed to be the first of its kind in the nation, is comprised of 15 individuals. State agencies on the commission include the State Senate, the State Veterinarian, DCYF, and the State Department of Health. Community groups include the Windwalker Humane Coalition, the Rhode Island Animal Legislative Coalition, the state Veterinary Medical Society, the Rhode Island Animal Control Officers Association, the Coalition Against Domestic Violence, and Volunteers in Service to Animals. Other members include a mental health professional, a veterinarian, and the general public.

"The purpose of said commission shall be to study the association between and amongst domestic violence, child abuse, and animal abuse to produce legislation to require cross reporting between DCYF and Animal Control Officers (SPCA)," says the Resolution. The commission was charged with reporting back to the legislature by January 22, 1998.

The resolution, 97-S 0462, was spearheaded by Rhoda E. Perry, State Senator from Providence and Deputy President Pro Tempore, and the Windwalker Humane Coalition. Excerpts of the resolution follow:

WHEREAS, Members of most societies have long believed that a person's treatment of animals reflects his or her treatment of other human beings; and

WHEREAS, Scientific, social service, medical, judicial, and law enforcement communities are beginning to recognize violent behavior often first reveals itself in the form of cruelty to animals; and

WHEREAS, Some of this recognition has come about through detailed profiles of violent criminals. There exists compelling circumstantial evidence linking serial and mass murderers with earlier acts of cruelty to animals; and

WHEREAS, Acts of animal cruelty are very likely predictors of both domestic and societal violence; now therefore be it

RESOLVED, That a special legislative commission be created consisting of 15 members: two of whom shall be from the Senate, not more than one from the same political party, to be appointed by the Majority Leader; one shall be a member of the Windwalker Humane Coalition; one shall be the State Veterinarian or designee; one shall be the director of the Department for Children, Youth and Families or designee; one shall be the director of the Department of Health or designee; one shall be a member of the Rhode Island Animal Legislative Coalition; one shall be a veterinarian; one shall be a mental health professional; one shall be a member of the Animal Control Officers Association; one shall be a member of the Rhode Island Veterinary Medical Society; one shall be a member of the Volunteers Services for Animals Society; and three shall be members of the general public to be appointed by the Majority Leader.

The purpose of said Commission shall be to study the association between and amongst domestic violence, child abuse and animal abuse to produce legislation to require cross-reporting between DCYF and Animal Control Officers (SPCA).

The members of the Commission shall meet at the call of the Senate Majority Leader and organize and shall select from among the legislators a chairperson. Vacancies in said Commission shall be filled in like manner as the original appointment.

The membership of said Commission shall receive no compensation for their services.

All departments and agencies of the state shall furnish such advice and information, documentary and otherwise, to said Commission and its agents as is deemed necessary or desirable by the Commission to facilitate the purposes of this Resolution.

The Joint Committee on Legislative Services is hereby authorized and directed to provide suitable quarters for Said Commission; and be it further

RESOLVED, That the Commission shall report its findings and recommendations to the General Assembly on or before January 22, 1998 and said Commission shall expire on March 22, 1998.

For further information, contact Sen. Rhoda E. Perry, Room 312 State House, Providence, RI 02906.

Applications

Tell me if you can find a better way under heaven for making children merciful than by teaching them to be constantly doing kind acts and saying kind words to God's lower creatures, by whom they are surrounded, and which they are meeting on the streets and elsewhere a hundred times a day.

—George T. Angell, president, Massachusetts SPCA, 1868–1909

The Challenge of Trying to Promote Kindness to Animals in a Violent Society

Debbie Duel

D.C. TEEN PLEADS Guilty to Murder in Rampage. A typical *Washington Post* headline. I am addicted to such headlines. I read them all. Every day. I spent nearly a decade in the D.C. public schools promoting kindness as the Washington Humane Society's Director of Humane Education; yet not a day goes by that I don't scan the local pages to read the gory details of the murder or murders of the day. Usually I know the neighborhood. I know the crime scene's proximity to *my* schools. The "rampage" article was the first account where I actually knew more than the place—I knew the perpetrator, a cold-blooded killer who, seven years earlier, had regularly attended my after-school Kindness Club.

Sixteen-year-old Curtis Pixley, Jr., shot Patricia Ann Davis twice in the face, then once in the back as she tried to escape an attempted robbery in her home on Thanksgiving Day. Curtis pleaded guilty to Davis's murder and four other robbery-shootings. This brutal rampage was not surprising. Two months earlier, Curtis had stomped the leg of a neighbor's puppy, then kicked the injured animal with such force it flew five feet before landing on the sidewalk. He did this to get even with a boy he didn't like. Even as a fifth grader Curtis was scary. Kids feared him. Adults called him "trouble." The system failed. It would have taken much more than a Kindness Club to save his victim's life.

I was asked to write about how educators can teach humane education in a crumbling urban environment where poverty and lack of family support predominate. I don't know that they can. Certainly not in isolation. The much quoted African proverb, "It takes a village to raise a child," says the entire community is responsible for the moral development of its citizenry. Humane education must be a team effort—Humane Society representatives, teachers, social workers, law enforcement agents, and, most importantly, parents.

Humane education is far from a cure-all, but it can and does make a difference. The majority of kids in our school district are not ruthless murderers with a laundry list of troubles. Most are good kids living in bad situations—drugs and violence are woven into their daily lives. Their view of companion animal care is often skewed by the kinds of animals in the neighborhood. Pit bulls and Rottweilers are fought or used as weapons. Akitas, German shepherds, and Dobermans are favorite backyard guard dogs. Most urban dogs live on short chains or roam the streets. Cats are often stray, feral, or "owned" for a very short period of time. Animals are not revered companions; they are, for the most part, objects of utility or fleeting amusement. And, quite often, they are victims.

STARTING AN INTERVENTION

The Washington Humane Society's (WHS) education program began in 1987. It was created to cover the very basics of companion animal care. The department was a staff of one—me.

In a school system of nearly 80,000 kids, how many could I see in a day, week, month, or school year? My goal was to reach as many kids as possible. Five classes a day, five days a week—the same presentation over and over to different kids. "The Washington Humane Society is there to help; spay and neuter your companion animals; report animal cruelty; take care of your animals." Forty-five minutes later they were all kind, caring kids who couldn't wait to spay or neuter their companion animals, report cruelty, and provide proper care for their companion animals for all the rest of their days!

Wrong.

Time to regroup.

By 1989 my program had changed. Instead of visiting lots of different schools with hundreds of nameless faces, I focused on 10 schools in areas with the highest incidence of animal cruelty. My audience consisted of a couple of hundred fourth, fifth, and sixth graders. I visited the same classes every other week from September to June. I knew each kid by name, and sometimes I knew their animals' names or met their families. The messages were basically the same, but they were said over and over in hundreds of ways.

Kids wrote letters to the mayor asking for city funds to run a spay and neuter program and letters to the editor validating such support. They used role-plays to discuss dangerous dog legislation. They became chained, ignored yard-dogs when they stood in the corner while their peers played games. Kids developed advertising plans, wrote stories, raps, poems, and songs about animal suffering. They recorded videos. They read books and watched videos about animals. They collected animal current events. They even went to the U.S. Capitol and protested against Ringling Brothers' 125th anniversary congressional performance on the Hill. We partied together and did serious work. Kids looked forward to my visits as well as presentations by WHS-sponsored guests. Our spay and neuter veterinarian and her dog demonstrated basic vet care. A local radio personality and her dogs performed obedience demonstrations. An animal control officer showed tools of the trade and recounted stories about actual cases, using photographs that sometimes shocked.

Some teachers used the humane education lessons as building blocks to other lessons. A sixth grade teacher created an "animals in the news" current events board. Another sixth grade teacher helped her children organize a food drive for the shelter animals. A fourth grade class made ornate gingerbread houses complete with pictures of happy companion animals looking out the windows of comfortable graham cracker homes. The team teachers who supervised the Ringling Brothers protest developed a thematic unit around the plight of the circus animals—letters, journal entries, and poems were written, banners and posters were drawn and displayed.

The Washington Humane Society's education program was free to all schools, but it didn't come cheap! We spent money. We had to. City teachers had no classroom stipend and were already spending hundreds of dollars out-of-pocket to cover classroom materials. We purchased 100 *KIND News* subscriptions a year from the Humane Society of the United States for D.C. elementary school teachers. We bought materials from the American Humane Education Society (AHES) and Animalearn. In 1992 we obtained a $5,000 grant from the Edith Goode Residuary Trust to purchase library books for 10 schools. We compiled a companion animal reading list and partnered with a local bookstore to get the books at cost. Special bookplates were inserted into each gift book and teachers were introduced to the new selections during staff development days. We bought trinkets for the students—pencils, rulers, magnets, Frisbees—all bearing the WHS logo and phone number. Kids love things. The teachers liked them too.

The program boasted more than a few successes. Kids were deputized as junior humane officers and pledged to prevent cruelty and treat all living creatures with kindness. Junior humane officers had an obligation to report animal abuse to the Washington Humane Society. And, as card-carrying WHS representatives, they took their jobs very seriously—especially when the media took notice.

In January 1994, *Washington Post* columnist Courtland Milloy praised three junior humane officers for their animal rescue efforts. William, Daiquon, and Dawn received additional attention from U.S. Attorney Eric Holder, Fox Morning News, and a national pet food company. The positive reinforcement spawned a huge increase in the number of student-generated cruelty reports. By the end of the next school year, WHS threw a pizza party for more than 20 junior humane officers at Ferebee-Hope Elementary School—all had either rescued animals or reported acts of animal cruelty. A story highlighting the party aired on a local all-news radio station. Ferebee-Hope is located in the heart of one of the most violent areas of the district. Boarded-up buildings, smashed windows, clay dirt lawns, hypodermic needles, equipmentless playgrounds, and trash mar the community. Baby birds, kittens, and stray dogs managed to escape the area thanks to Ferebee-Hope Elementary School junior humane officers.

Kids living east of Washington's beautiful Rock Creek Park are used to getting attention. Attention for poor test scores. Attention for high dropout rates and high teenage birth rates. Attention for violent crime. Good behavior is usually not news. But a little effort and encouragement proved that not all is bad with our kids—the increase in their involvement demonstrated how well children can rise to the occasion when given the tools and choices. We spent a good deal of time contacting the media, asking them to highlight local kids doing right by the animals. In spite of that, the murders of the day prevailed on the evening news and in the newspapers. As junior humane officers continued to perform rescues, their heroic deeds were generally featured not on TV, but in our newsletters.

During that year, nearly 60 kids were praised as exemplary junior humane officers. Though most did not receive media attention, all were awarded a WHS tee-shirt and a certificate of merit in classroom ceremonies across the district.

A CENTURY LATER... HAVE WE MADE PROGRESS?

George Angell said it best more than 100 years ago.

> I am sometimes asked, "Why do you spend so much of your time and money in talking about kindness to animals, when there is so much cruelty to men?" And I answer, "I am working at the roots." Every humane publication, every lecture, every step, in doing or teaching kindness to them, is a step to prevent crime—a step in promoting growth of those qualities of heart which will elevate human souls, even in the dens of sin and shame, and prepare the way for the coming of peace on earth and good will to men.

Humane education works at its most basic level, when you get to the kids one by one. Through individual attention we made sure that animals were spayed or neutered and vaccinated. Shelter staff tried to make an extra effort to find homes for animals found or surrendered by caring kids.

I gave out my office phone number left and right. When we went to an automated answering system I would explain the system over and over again. Kids called. Like Marquis. He was a sixth grader the summer we met through a library program. He kept my number and used it several times over the years. Shortly after our first meeting he called to arrange for his cat to be spayed. Marquis had no money and no transportation, but he loved his cat and remembered that I said that spay surgery was important for the cat's health and prevented unwanted kittens. So, his cat was spayed. A humane officer picked up the cat, brought her to the clinic, and took her home after surgery. WHS absorbed the costs, and Marquis continued to love and care for his cat. A couple of years later he called again. His uncle had been cited for keeping his dogs outside without proper shelter. Marquis wanted information on building an adequate dog house. He told me he helped take care of the dogs and wanted his uncle to be able to keep them. He and his uncle made the houses and a humane officer brought hay for bedding at the time of the inspection. The last time I talked to Marquis he was in high school. He sheepishly asked if I could arrange for his cat to be picked up and if I could please find her a good home. He could not keep her. A humane officer picked up the cat, we placed her in a new home, and I never heard from Marquis again.

There were other kids. Cherie was in the fifth grade when we met at Shaed Elementary School. She was a quiet, mature kid who carried the weight of the world on her shoulders. Not only did I see her regularly in her class, but she assisted me with a class of younger children. Her dog, Oreo, needed to be vaccinated and neutered. Cherie's mom did not want the dog neutered so Cherie asked if I could talk to her. I went to her home and explained the benefits of neutering. It didn't help. Cherie's mother gave permission for shots, but not neutering! So, I drove Cherie, her stepsister, and Oreo to the shelter for vaccinations. Cherie's mom died two years later. The shelter was called to pick up the dog. The family moved. I lost touch.

Welton didn't have an animal but he loved them all. He won second place in our annual Be Kind to Animals Week essay contest during his sixth grade year. After that we became pen pals. Welton wrote often. I brought him to the shelter once. Every letter after that asked about each staff person he met during his visit. We continued to write through his junior high years. The year I left WHS, Welton was being considered for a summer kennel staff position.

There were others. The kids who called just to talk, the kids with questions about the essay contest or animal care, the ones who wanted to know if we had any pit bulls, and a couple who apologized for the behavior of their classmates. My accessibility made me a useful resource.

INTERDISCIPLINARY RESPONSES

The kids' calls were the highs and the humane officers' reports were the definite lows. Humane officers routinely investigate cases that involve kids who are perpetrators of crimes against animals as well as animal cruelty cases where kids in the home are also victims of gross neglect or abuse.

I am not a psychologist, nor do I pretend to be. When I got the first report of a child involved in an animal cruelty case I sought out some professional advice and then tried to go it alone. The seven-year-old boy had gouged the eyes out of a stray kitten because older kids told him to do it. He later told me that he was surprised that blood came out of the animal's eyes. I went to his summer school program and conducted three programs. The principal and teacher were supportive. Through the help of the humane officer, I arranged to pick the boy up two or three times a week for several weeks and bring him to the shelter. I became totally engrossed with "saving" this kid. I picked him up from a house that had little furniture, but two VCRs. There were always lots of people around. He said he wished his mother didn't do drugs. I felt sorry for him—that doesn't help. I took him to museums via the subway (he had never been on the train system); I took him to the movies; and I took him out for pizza. I bought *KIND News* for his class. I visited his third grade class a couple of times. The teacher shook her head when I talked to her privately about his situation. Then he moved. I don't know where.

There were dozens more kids who needed "saving" but I wised up and realized that there wasn't a lot I, alone, could do. When I got Marlin's case on my desk and read that he had been breaking bottles and using them to slice the necks of neighborhood cats I felt angry. When I read that he did it because he wanted to die, I knew that I needed to find help.

It only took a few phone calls before I hooked up with Dr. Frances Raphael-Howell, a school psychologist and director of the mental health branch of the federally funded Title One program. Dr. Raphael-Howell immediately set the gears in motion. She, too, was working on Marlin's case. She said that his family had been known to the system for at least three generations. WHS's testimony was needed. Marlin was assigned institutional care less than a year after I met Dr. Raphael-Howell.

Dr. Raphael-Howell and I began to collaborate more formally on cases. I realized immediately that collaboration with mental health and other agencies is paramount for long-term success in violence prevention. It became routine for all cases involving children as either perpetrators or victims of abuse to be referred to Dr. Raphael-Howell. We tried desperately to expand our network by involving representatives from Human Services, the Metropolitan Police Department, and the judicial system in a cross-training, cross-reporting effort that would better serve the children—and the animals. Unfortunately, D.C. social service agencies—most in receivership—lacked the funds and people power to do anything more than tread water. When we were able to assemble group discussions we hit major roadblocks. Confidentiality laws prohibited agencies from sharing information on the children everyone knew were in trouble. Although we sporadically provided cross-training for social workers and had several round table meetings, the goal of an interagency coalition set up to insure a holistic approach to case management never materialized. I left the Washington Humane Society, and Dr. Raphael-Howell's entire department was eliminated through budget cuts.

Not long after I had left the classroom, I read a follow-up article about Curtis Pixley, Jr. It detailed the gruesome letters and graphic photographs Curtis had sent, from his jail cell, to Patricia Davis's husband. Earlier, Curtis had mailed a threatening letter to one of his surviving victims. Both letters were signed "Devil's Son-in-Law."

The *Washington Post* reported that Curtis expressed no remorse at his sentencing in D.C. Superior Court on one count of first-degree murder while armed and two counts of assault with the intent to kill. The judge handed down the maximum sentence—60 years to life. Judge Reggie B. Walton described Curtis as a "monster who has no redeeming value to society."

HOPE FOR THE FUTURE?

Halfway into the 1996–97 school year the tragedies continue to mount. Two sisters were murdered during their walk home from elementary school by their mother's estranged husband. A 12-year-old boy was beaten and abducted in front of his junior high school by gang members. He was found dead several days later. A junior high student was knifed in school in the middle of the day; the school's metal-detectors had gone on the blink that morning. Three teens dragged a trusting spaniel-mix to the roof of a three-story apartment building and tossed her off; witnesses identified the boys as neighborhood bullies but were too frightened to testify.

When the nation's capital's neighborhoods look and sound like war zones, does a humane society's education program make a difference? We have to believe it does. Like her counterparts across the country Lisa Moore, the Washington Humane Society's education director and a veteran D.C. public schools teacher, believes that the simple concepts of kindness and reverence must become a part of every teacher's behavior and daily lesson plans. She is reaching out to them with her own new ideas and planning for the future of the program. Ideally, Lisa says she would like to offer prospective new teachers enrolled at the local universities a curriculum that fosters respect for our fellow beings, both two- and four-legged. She wishes that there were funds for an education center and for field trips to wildlife rehabilitation centers and sanctuaries for rescued animals. While wishes do come true, Lisa can't wait— she is busy visiting classrooms often and reminding children and their teachers that she, and the animal shelter, are only a phone call away.

FOR MORE INFORMATION AND HUMANE EDUCATION RESOURCES

American Humane Education Society (AHES) 350 South Huntington Ave., Boston, Mass. 02130; phone number (617) 522-7400. Operation Outreach, a humane literacy program.
Animalearn, 801 Old York Rd., Jenkintown, Penn. 19046; phone number (215) 887-0816. Animalearn Kid Kits, Animal Issues Teen Kits, and Teacher Resource Kits; teacher training.
Free Spirit Publishing Inc., 400 First Ave. North, Suite 616, Minneapolis, Minn. 55401; phone number (800) 735-7323. Publishes *The Kid's Guide to Social Action* by Barbara A. Lewis, provides a catalog of other Self-Help for Kids materials.
National Association for Humane and Environmental Education *(KIND News)* P. O. Box 362, East Haddam, Conn. 06423-0362; phone number (860) 434-8666. *KIND News,* KIND Workshop Leader's Guide.
The Shiloh Project, 11278 James Swart Circle #170, Fairfax, Va. 22030; phone number (703) 502-7098. A model hands-on dog training program for at-risk youth.

Teaching Tolerance, 400 Washington Ave., Montgomery Ala. 36104; Fax number (205) 264-0629. Twice yearly magazine, *Teaching Tolerance,* is made available free to educators.

The Washington Humane Society, 7319 Georgia Ave., N.W., Washington, D.C. 20012; phone number (202) 723-2071. Companion animal fiction reading list, junior humane officer information, child abuse–human violence link posters.

How to Build a Successful Community Coalition

Mary Pat Boatfield and Sally Vallongo

IN TOLEDO, Ohio, public and private agencies addressing animal welfare or child safety issues traditionally have been so intent on carrying out their individual missions that they have had little to no awareness of the common ground they tread. Then, in 1989, a call to the Toledo Humane Society to investigate a battered kitten began a process that would draw the human and animal sectors closer, finally yielding a ground-breaking coalition among major community service agencies.

That the first step was made by the Humane Society, a 113-year-old private nonprofit organized to relieve suffering, prevent cruelty, and provide for humane treatment of animals, makes the achievement even more unusual, for in the unwritten hierarchy of community agencies, those serving human needs typically rank higher than animal welfare groups. Certainly the Humane Society had paid little attention to places where its service overlapped child and adult safety agency turf. Like those agencies, its own heavy caseload, including as many as 1,600 investigations each year, challenged staff and volunteers bent on achieving a vision of an educated and caring community free of animal neglect and cruelty. The idea of connecting with other agencies did not loom large in our day-to-day operation.

Yet coalitions are increasingly being seen as improving community effectiveness in responding to overarching problems. "A coalition is an organization of diverse interest groups that combines their human and material resources to effect a specific change the members are unable to bring about independently," writes Cherie Brown (1984:45) in *The Art of Coalition Building*. "In a pluralistic society such as ours, community leaders increasingly have become aware of their limited ability to bring about social change when they work alone. The need to become more effective in a time of proliferating single-interest groups and decreasing resources has led many to recognize the potential utility of coalition building."

Some specific benefits of coalitions include:

the chance to significantly improve each participating group's effectiveness in achieving its primary mission;

prevention of duplication of effort, allowing more efficient utilization of resources;
encouragement of sharing resources and ideas;
the extension of the service area;
the capability of addressing even larger concerns on many levels simultaneously,
increasing the potential of bringing about major systemic change;
creation of a sense of trust and community among coalition members by offering
all participants nurturance, encouragement, recognition, and feedback, and the
chance to share effective methods;
the opportunity to brainstorm solutions and approaches in a larger context, to
generate more innovation, and to allow for shared experimentation; and
reducing unnecessary competition.

Although many social service agencies recognize the advantages of coalitions
to address temporary crises and ongoing concerns, the idea of bringing together
groups with differing ethnic, cultural, philosophical, and organizational purposes
seems overwhelming. This essay describes how our agency worked with other community groups and individuals to create a successful coalition uniting all major aspects of the service community. We achieved cooperation among child protection,
physical health, mental health, education, judiciary, law enforcement, residential
care, and community and social service systems as well as animal control and welfare protection.

INITIAL EFFORTS

A one-day community workshop, "Violence Is Preventable," organized by representatives of many of these disciplines, was the initial effort. From that event grew the
Peace Connection, a coalition that, over the next year, fostered mutual trust and cooperation within the community. It also paved the way for sustained relationships
for future efforts. The accumulation of experience from the coalition-building process proved beneficial in working with other agencies on common concerns.

In the process of building the coalition, we overcame many of the barriers that
commonly present themselves: inability to formulate a common vision; territorial-
ity; fears about loss of financial support, time, and human resources; inertia; perceived threats to individual and agency autonomy; conflicts over style and method;
and unrealistic expectations.

Our approach is described in a five-stage matrix created by Teresa Hogue of the
Oregon Center for Community Leadership (table 1). It works through each stage
or level, from initial networking through collaboration, by addressing key issues of
purpose, structure, and process. The matrix is very useful in helping track our progress and identify issues throughout the development. The story of how the Humane Society participated in a community coalition can be told within the context

Table 1. Community Linkages-Choices and Decisions. The structures of community relationships are described in this matrix. This matrix will assist organizations to determine where they presently are in a working interactive structure, and can be used to assist in the decision to move to a different level of collaboration as the purpose, structure, and process permit.

Levels	Purpose	Structure	Process
Networking	Dialog and common understanding Clearinghouse for information Create base of support	Nonhierarchical— loose or flexible link Roles loosely defined Community action is primary link among members	Low-key leadership Minimal decision making Little conflict Informal communication
Cooperation or Alliance	Match needs and provide coordination Limit duplication of services Ensure tasks are done	Central body of people as communication hub Semiformal links Roles somewhat defined Links are advisory Group leverages or raises money	Facilitative leaders Complex decision making Some conflict Formal communications within the central group
Coordination or Partnership	Share resources to address common issues Merge resource base to create something new	Central body of people consists of decision makers Roles defined Links formalized Group develops new resources and joint budget	Autonomous leadership but focus in on issue Group decision making in central and subgroups Communication is frequent and clear
Coalition	Share ideas and be willing to pull resources from existing systems Develop commitment for a minimum of three years	All members involved in decision making Roles and time defined Links formal with written agreement Group develops new resources and joint budget	Shared leadership Decision making formal with all members Communication is common and prioritized

Continued on next page

Table 1. *Continued*

Levels	Purpose	Structure	Process
Collaboration	Accomplish shared vision and impact benchmarks	Consensus used in shared decision making	Leadership high, trust level high, productivity high
	Build interdependent system to address issues and opportunities	Roles, time, and evaluation formalized Links are formal and written in work assignments	Ideas and decisions equally shared Highly developed communication

Source: Teresa Hogue, *Community Based Collaborations-Wellness Multiplied* (Oregon Center for Community Leadership, 1994). Reprinted with permission.

of those five stages. For other guides to building coalitions, see the list of suggested readings at the end of this chapter.

NETWORKING

Generally, getting the attention of many and diverse agencies to start the cooperative process requires a disturbing or dramatic event. That trigger was case no. 5887, opened after an incident reported on the evening of September 19, 1989. The Humane Society investigator found a 10-year-old girl standing outside her home in a working-class neighborhood, holding a kitten that was paralyzed and in shock. Her younger sister, her mother, and a neighbor were nearby. The girl told the investigator that their stepfather had wrung the kitten's neck and thrown the animal to the ground. Before storming off to a tavern, he had threatened similar treatment to any other cat the girls brought home. The girls' mother had unsuccessfully attempted to intervene.

The investigator also learned that the stepfather was being investigated by Lucas County Children Services for abusing the older sister. After removing the injured kitten (it had to be euthanized), the Humane Society investigator contacted the child service agency. The clear parallel between abuse of human and animal made us aware of a gap in our operation that had not been visible before. We realized that by ignoring the human perspective in our training we were providing less than thorough service.

For example, during an earlier animal abuse investigation, our field agent had radioed back to the office reporting a tiny baby in a crib. Flies swarmed through a dirty house in which there seemed to be no food. At first, we were not sure where to turn. Yes, we were aware of child and adult welfare agencies in the area. No, we had never forged direct and official contact with those groups. Nor had those agencies ever contacted us, although there had been other instances where overlaps of service were apparent. We called First Call for Help, a local hotline, which referred us to Children Services.

On other occasions, our investigators walked into family situations where emotional fuses were burning quickly. In such incendiary circumstances, one false move or wrong word might well trigger violence against our staff.

From our animal welfare position we began to see a far more complex picture. We began to understand how little we knew about the larger safety issues in our community: human needs, family dynamics, the effects of alcohol and drug dependency on families, how adults learn, and how we could deal with explosive emotional situations more effectively.

It became clear that action was needed. The question was, how should we go about it most effectively, given our already stretched resources? The first level of community linkages is networking, to open a dialogue, create a base of support, and become a clearinghouse for information.

We began in-house. Our first objective was to convince our own staff to expand their service viewpoint and to prepare and adapt new procedures. Field investigators, some of whom had worked in human service fields before joining the Humane Society, affirmed our approach and helped move us through this initial stage. To maintain a nonhierarchical approach, we held staff brainstorming sessions in which new and innovative approaches were encouraged. We favored information and idea-seeking rather than decision-making at this stage, but tried to emphasize how our agency shared components of community service such as violence involving children and animals.

COOPERATION OR ALLIANCE

At this point we realized that we needed more training and began to look beyond the agency. We contacted the Family and Child Abuse Prevention Center, a local, private organization funded by the United Way, which provides training, but our initial approaches were rebuffed by center staff who could not understand why we thought such training was necessary. This reaction is often typical of community groups when first approached to build a coalition.

Finding a common goal is a primary step to pulling agencies together. We told the Abuse Prevention Center staff that often our agency receives the first call regarding an abusive home. Our investigators have entered houses where a woman had been viciously beaten, yet called for help for a dead kitten or puppy. We have been called to homes of the elderly who also did not seek help for themselves but would take action on behalf of a beloved pet.

After we convinced staff at the Abuse Prevention Center to provide cross-training, we sought and obtained seed money from the United Way. Again, our actions raised questions among other agencies vying for the grant. We are not United Way members. Because many agencies focus only on their own priorities, they may see their issues as more important than those of others. Isolation can generate fears that, though unfounded, may hinder efforts to make connections across many service agencies. The idea of a coalition was not yet formed, but the sparks of interest we were generating seemed to be raising awareness of common ground. We found, for example, that we could continue cross-training through the Criminal Justice Training Center for the cost of a year's membership. And we began to participate in seminars and other activities, raising our visibility and spreading the coalition idea among the social service community.

During this time we attended a memorable training program presented by a coalition of local agencies. "Through the Eyes of the Child: Abused and Neglected Children and Their Families," a three-day conference at the Medical College of Ohio, resulted from a collaboration by the Medical College, Children Services, and the Toledo Bar Association. It synthesized multidisciplinary perspectives on child abuse affecting special populations; reviewed legal issues of reporting, protecting, and litigating child abuse cases; and applied principles of interviewing and intervention to the best interests of the child. A discussion of opportunities for a multidisciplinary team approach to child abuse and neglect inspired us to start networking in earnest with other agencies.

COORDINATION OR PARTNERSHIP

Despite our greater visibility at community service events, it remained clear that other agencies' staffs were surprised to find animal welfare workers taking training, asking questions, and becoming involved in issues of human care. Yet we believed, then and now, that the leadership of animal welfare and protection organizations is critical to the success of coalition building. Out in the field our agents were beginning to recognize and be recognized by investigators from other agencies. One might be following up on a reported case of pet abuse, for instance, coming up to the front door from the backyard and meet a child or adult protective services worker leaving the house. Furthermore, heads of several key agencies who had quickly grasped the common quality of our agencies' goals began reviewing old cases. There they found many instances of abuse that also involved pets. Often, these executives admitted, their field workers had not known what to do with animals they discovered injured or neglected. Thus the potential for sharing resources and merging resource bases, level 3 in the community linkage matrix, seemed to develop naturally out of a rising awareness of our intersecting work. We further advanced cooperation by identifying community leaders with expertise in areas we felt needed development and recruiting them for our board of directors.

The links between abuse of humans and animals has been well documented and that body of evidence also shored up our efforts to forge new alliances in the service community. In Toledo, for example, a man charged with two brutal 1992

murders also was charged with animal cruelty for an incident that preceded his human attacks by a mere two weeks. Another man convicted of a bizarre live burial
murder in 1993 had a long history of killing and torturing dogs, cats, and birds—including burying some of them alive.

The American Humane Association has cited commonalties between animal
abusers and child abusers, qualities that include

distancing from the social world;
ranking low in social and familial hierarchies;
low self-esteem;
being targeted for aggression by others, including family members;
having been a victim of abuse in childhood
passivity;
anxiety about human relationships; and
feelings of incompetence and lack of control over life.

Reinforced by positive feedback and recent studies, Humane Society staff began to speak up at training conferences and seminars. We felt it was necessary to
take a leadership role in creating a coalition, yet it was vital to keep all potential
participants on equal footing. One major obstacle to building coalitions is the fear
potential participants share that they may lose something important in the process.
It is important that each agency maintain its unique identity and autonomy, and
keep sight of individual goals and projects.

Building trust among groups entering into an alliance happens more readily
when three qualities are maintained: a climate of cooperation, a group network, and
a coordinating group. Cooperation reinforces the sense of shared concerns and allows agencies to overlook divisive factors in pursuit of common goals. Networking
helps spread the work and prevents early burnout. Networks also allow participants
to be visible and participatory in ways that benefit each agency without forcing
agreement on delicate issues.

COALITION

Level 4 of the community linkages matrix calls for sharing of ideas and pulling resources from existing systems, as well as development of a long-term commitment.
By 1994 the Humane Society had become part of a growing network of service
agencies working together to explore alternatives to violence. With Nancy Maylath,
then coordinator from the University of Toledo, and administrative support from
the American Red Cross, a new cooperative venture began taking shape (table 2).
The resulting one-day workshop, "Violence Is Preventable," had five objectives:

1. to direct public attention to the need for training in alternatives to violence
   and conflict mediation;

Table 2. A Model for Coalition Building: Using a Workshop to Get Started. Nancy Maylath developed this model during the creation of the coalition, in Toledo, Ohio, which was called the Peace Connection. The coalition met for one year following the one-day conference "Violence Is Preventable." Dr. Maylath is currently in the health promotion program at Purdue University.

Getting Started →	Keep Moving →	Expand Horizons →	Take It Home

• Grant proposal
• Workshop planning
• Coalition exploration
• Coalition formation
  & continuity
	• Participant
	  recruitment
	• Leadership &
	  participant roles
	• Funding & agency
	  support
	• Mission statement
	• Networking
	• Logistics
		• Education
		  committee
		• Public policy &
		  advocacy committee
		• Communications
		  committee
		• Roles, activities, &
		  interaction
			• Potential for a coalition in
			  your locality
			• Brainstorming
			• Action plan

Source: Peace Connection, Nancy Maylath, Purdue University. Adapted and reproduced with permission.

2. to provide information on local and national resources available in the area of violence prevention, conflict mediation, and related topics;

3. to identify successful local initiatives on violence prevention and conflict mediation;

4. to provide opportunities for local agencies, churches, schools, and individuals to network with each other to maximize resources and minimize duplication of effort; and

5. to focus a community coalition that will meet regularly to share existing resources and seek new methods to work toward violence prevention in a unified fashion.

After the one-day conference, members of the coalition agreed to meet regularly for the next year to continue to explore matters of common concern and potential. Mutual trust and cooperation continued to blossom in these meetings and the process paved the way for sustained future relationships. The coalition took the name the Peace Connection.

COLLABORATION

When the coalition organizer moved out of town and leadership at the Red Cross changed, the coalition dissolved after one year of meetings. Despite its relatively short life, many changes brought about during the period of creation and development will not be undone. The process paved the way for sustained relationships for other efforts in the future. Accumulated experience that resulted from working with this coalition has been beneficial in working with other agencies on common concerns.

At the Humane Society, changes resulting from the coalition are more philosophical than structural, with one big exception: we moved to a case management system modeled after that in the human services field. I believe we are the only humane society to do this. Now we want to go a step further, developing a resource directory that will help workers stay in touch with other community agencies. We also now make more referrals to other agencies.

According to the community linkages matrix, the fifth level is one of collaboration, setting the stage for continued growth by all participants. This has happened in many and surprising ways at the Humane Society. For example, today, when investigators from our agency and human service groups get together, they have a common language to use talking about issues of placement, behavior, foster care, and other situations in which we have common concerns.

Another benefit accruing from this year of collaboration has been the knowledge that we are not alone when public misunderstanding of our mission casts us in unfavorable light. Much as we would love to address every issue that comes to our attention, our job is not to save animals—or to kill them, as some charge—but to prevent cruelty, and to show the public how to work toward that goal.

The approach we take and the amount of change we can bring about in each case is shaped by that basic philosophy, a reality not at all dissimilar from that of human services. We are in the community to help people take care of their animals, but we must respect each family's level of behavior and development. We must start with people where they are and attempt to raise their standards from that point. Comparing notes with human service groups helps remind us that we are not alone.

An interesting benefit noticed by the human service agency staff members was that our workers seemed able to help lift their spirits. They often get depressed under the burden of complex details that direct every move. When animal protection people come in, we are optimistic and somewhat idealistic. We give them an infusion of hope. We have found that, whether you are working with dogs and cats or boys and girls, violence prevention is a tough, emotional business. The whole principle behind case management is that our clients do not become dependent on us.

We hope the example of what we've been able to accomplish so far in Toledo will be useful in other communities' service sectors looking to build greater cooperation and increase effectiveness. Other action strategies that have emerged from the process we undertook at the start of this decade include

holding staff meetings on topics of child abuse and community violence with a recognized leader as special guest;
volunteering for the boards of community nonprofit agencies working in homeless, domestic violence, and child abuse programs;

sharing ideas and approaches on a day-to-day basis with colleagues;
staying in touch with current literature on the topic;
holding staff brainstorming sessions to update procedures and contacts;
placing articles in agency newsletters to keep the coalition progress in their minds; and
monitoring Humane Society personnel's involvement with other agencies to obtain feedback and improve evaluation methods.

SUGGESTED READINGS

Bercher, J. and Costello, T., eds. 1990. *Building bridges: The emerging grassroots coalition of labor and community.* New York.
Bergstrom, A., et al. 1996. *Collaboration frame work: Addressing community capacity.* Fargo, N. D.: The National Network for Collaboration.
Brown, C. R., 1984. *The art of coalition building: A guide for community leaders.* New York: American Jewish Committee.
Dluhy, M. J., 1990. *Building coalitions in the human services.* Newbury Park, Calif.: Sage Publications.

FOR MORE INFORMATION

The National Network for Collaboration, 219 FLC. Box 5016, Fargo, N.D. 58105-5016; phone number: (701)231-7259; fax number: (701)231-8568; e-mail address: nncoinfo@mes.umn.edu; web site: http://www.cyfernet.mes.umn.edu:2400.
Lynn M. Borden, The Ohio State University, Department of Agricultural Education, 2120 Fyffe Road, Columbus, Ohio 43210-1067; phone number: (614)292-6321; fax number: (614)292-7007; e-mail address: borden.23@osu.edu.
Nancy S. Maylath, Purdue University, Health Promotion Programs, 1826 Student Health Center, West Lafayette, Ind. 47907-1826; phone number: (765)494-9559; fax number: (765)496-1227; e-mail address: nsmaylath@push.purdue.edu.

Starting and Sustaining Effective Community Coalitions

Gary Tiscornia, Hedy Nuriel, and Michele Mitchell

DOMESTIC VIOLENCE PROGRAMS, child protective services, and animal protection agencies have, for the most part, not crossed programmatic paths for over 70 years. In the early years of the animal protection movement, some animal welfare agencies, such as the Michigan Humane Society (MHS), found themselves caring not only for *animals* at risk, but also for children, women, and the elderly who were victims of abuse. In the 1920s, when government agencies were established to address the specific needs of these various groups, and in an effort to avoid duplication of services, organizations like the MHS began to focus entirely on serving animals.

Now, after decades of working in isolation from each other, we are realizing a need for professionals on all sides of the equation to be educated regarding the cycle of violence, which victimizes both animals and people. This pivotal step is the beginning of a common language, which is critical to the successful operation of a community coalition against violence.

THE FIRST CONFERENCE

In 1995 and 1997, the Michigan Humane Society held two conferences on the connection between animal abuse and family violence. Both conferences targeted professionals, both featured expert speakers and presenters, and both were well attended. Yet the first conference accomplished little, if any, real change. The second one became a springboard for real enlightenment, action, and commitment to lasting collaboration on the part of human service professionals.

The initial "Protect Our Future" conference, cohosted by the MHS and one of the area's leading child protection agencies, targeted key groups including social workers, educators, law enforcement, clergy, medical and legal professionals, veterinarians, and animal protection workers. We utilized credentialed professionals of national prominence as presenters and mailed informative invitations to hundreds of individuals. A nominal fee was charged. Attendance at this conference was respectable and participants went home with a feeling of accomplishment. The end result was good feelings but little demonstrable change in our community. In retrospect, we realized that attendance was made up predominantly of the converted, rather than the uninformed. The majority of the audience was involved in some sort of animal care, and was already relatively well-informed on the issue. Those leaders in the *human* service fields, however, who were in positions to facilitate change in the community, were not there and therefore did not receive the message. We had seriously underestimated the challenge of attracting the attention of very busy, overburdened decision makers, most of whom had never considered the problem of animal abuse as a critical indicator of other types of domestic violence.

Two years later, after assessing the obstacles that had limited the first "Protect Our Future Conference," and after conferring with Michael Kaufmann and Suzanne Barnard of the American Humane Association, we developed a plan for what we hoped would be a harder-hitting session involving a smaller, but more empowered, group of attendees. In planning a conference of this sort, we recognized that the key role of the chief executive of the sponsoring agency is to identify and secure the attendance of a broad spectrum of leaders who have the capacity to be "agents of change." These individuals may vary from community to community, but should include prosecutors, attorneys training others or practicing in the areas of child abuse and domestic violence, domestic violence shelter directors, youth services professionals, juvenile and adult corrections officials, sheriffs and chiefs of police, school superintendents, medical professionals responsible for pediatric and emergency room care, humane society and animal control directors, veterinarians, and clergy. Because these people are, by nature of their roles, extremely busy, securing their participation requires personal contact by the chief executive(s) of the sponsoring organization(s), giving the cause importance and credibility. It is also important to share with each invitee a succinct statement of the mission and goals of the conference. For example, the following was developed for the Michigan Humane Society Protect Our Future conference:

> The Protect Our Future conference on the link between animal abuse, child abuse, and violence in our communities is the beginning of an ongoing process of collaboration that will allow agencies to effectively address issues of community violence in a more holistic manner than is currently practiced.
>
> A small, hand-picked group of individuals who are leaders in their agencies and professions will engage nationally recognized presenters and each other in a series of dialogs. The dialogs will focus on broadening the participants' perspectives on violence and allowing them to become agents of beneficial change in their agencies and communities.
>
> Participants will be asked to continue the efforts of the group by setting an agenda for future actions, activities, and information sharing that will increase the level of beneficial collaboration between agencies and individuals.
>
> The outcomes anticipated from the conference are
> — increased knowledge about violence, the issues surrounding it, and the disciplines involved in combating it;

— through knowledge, an ability to collaborate more effectively with other agencies and disciplines against violence; and

— through a holistic approach, meaningful progress toward reducing violence in our communities.

THE SECOND CONFERENCE

We intentionally formatted "Protect Our Future II" differently. The first conference in 1995 featured an entire morning of presenters, speaking for 45 to 90 minutes each, in a large, theater-style auditorium, followed by an afternoon of separate break-out sessions. This time, we utilized a smaller, more informal set up, with tables grouped around the room, encouraging conversation among attendees. The conference, led by a facilitator, allowed the speakers to interact with the audience. Later in the day, brainstorming in breakout groups among 5 to 10 persons representing different disciplines helped participants internalize the concept of the relationship between various forms of violence. This also allowed attendees to begin the process of understanding each other's missions and identifying common interests, as well as the more subtle function of assessing each other as potential partners for future collaborative efforts. Before adjourning, we asked each participant to put in writing his or her ideas and commitments to future joint action.

Attendees left the conference educated, enlightened, and energized. We knew it was critical that the seed planted that day be nurtured, however, and that attention be given to sustaining the post-conference excitement and momentum.

Two weeks after the conference, we distributed an audiocassette package of the entire conference so attendees would be able to share the experience with colleagues. We also made follow-up calls soliciting feedback on what actions had taken place within their agencies as a result of Protect Our Future. Here are some of those responses.

Richard S. Bearup, Children's Ombudsman, State of Michigan: "Based on the conference sponsored by the Michigan Humane Society, my office changed our case management software to include animal abuse as a trackable item in our child abuse and neglect investigations."

Lynda Baker, Director, Wayne County Coordinating Council to Prevent Domestic Violence: "We are presently working on the third edition (of the Wayne County Case Management Protocol for Child Abuse), and our committee would like to include the role of the Humane Society in the response to suspected child abuse in Wayne County. As you will see, the responses by all the disciplines are interactive. The expansion of our protocol to include the Humane Society would mean: agencies that respond to a report of child abuse would also look for indications of animal abuse or neglect and, if necessary, make a report to the Humane Society; animal control personnel when responding to a report of animal cruelty or neglect will also look for indications of child abuse and neglect and, if found, take the appropriate steps in reporting."

Carol Siemon, Esq., Child Abuse Training Attorney for the Prosecuting Attorneys' Association of Michigan: "We are now including animal control officers as one of the resources we encourage child protective services workers and police officers to interview in the course of investigating a case. We are also excited about having invited Dr. Barbara Boat to speak on this issue at an upcoming conference the Prosecuting Attorneys' Association will be sponsoring for child protective services, law enforcement and prosecutors."

Joseph Maniaci, President, Michigan Association of Animal Control Officers: "Our Association had become aware of the connection between animal abuse and family violence about three years ago. Following the MHS conference, we invited Suzanne Barnard from the American Humane Association to address animal control officers at our statewide annual meeting. The program was a continuation of our efforts to educate the officers out in the field about what to look for when they investigate cases of animal abuse. Suzanne gave an excellent 4-hour training session on how to spot signs of child or spousal abuse, what to look for in the home environment, and how to go about reporting these cases to social services."

In addition, as a result of his involvement with the Protect Our Future Conference, Dr. Frank Ascione was invited back to Michigan to speak at the October 1997 "Summit III," a statewide conference sponsored by the Michigan Domestic Violence Prevention and Treatment Board. Dr. Ascione addressed over 300 domestic violence workers and professionals from related fields about the issues of animal abuse and interpersonal violence. The inclusion of Dr. Ascione as one of only two featured presenters at this important conference was a major step forward in educating the human services community and planting the seeds for collaborative relationships.

BUILDING A RELATIONSHIP

Perhaps one of the most exciting developments to date is the initiation of a very promising relationship with HAVEN, an organization that provides services to victims of domestic violence, sexual assault, and child abuse throughout Michigan's Oakland County. Asked to summarize the cooperative program between her agency and the Michigan Humane Society, forged as a direct result of the 1997 conference, HAVEN's Executive Director Hedy Nuriel writes:

> On a regular basis, our 24-Hour Crisis and Support Line program receives calls from women who would like to come to the shelter but are unable to for fear that their batterer will either kill or abuse their pets. In many cases, the abuser has

harmed the pet in the past and the victim is afraid the pet will be harmed again in an attempt to retaliate or threaten her so that she will come back to him, or to punish her for leaving him. For years, we have also heard stories of women who have been forced to have sexual relations with animals in their households or other households and saw this as an awful form of sexual assault and women abuse. We have heard stories over the years of children who have been raised in violent homes, seeing their pets destroyed and punished as a way of punishing a child. And we have seen children who have been abused sexually by using the family pet. We did not, until recently, however, see the connection between child abuse or domestic violence and cruelty to animals.

In March 1997, I was invited to a conference put on by the Michigan Humane Society. I decided to go to that conference with the expressed intent of finding a way to make a connection with the Humane Society and our domestic violence shelter, in hopes that we could find lodging for the animals of women who needed to come to the shelter because they were in danger. I came away with so much more. That conference was a starting ground for the collaborative that has since been formed between the Michigan Humane Society and HAVEN.

Both the Michigan Humane Society and HAVEN have high hopes for the success of this newly formed alliance. The MHS is already providing foster homes for the pets of HAVEN clients who might not otherwise seek shelter for fear of leaving their animals. HAVEN is developing plans for a new facility, which now include a kennel and boarding area for pets. The Michigan Humane Society will also be conducting training and recruitment among HAVEN staff and volunteers who are interested in becoming foster families for the pets of domestic violence victims.

HAVEN plans to incorporate sessions on animal cruelty into its counseling curriculum for batterers and perpetrators of child sexual assault and abuse, along with sessions on grief and loss for clients whose pets have died. And for the first time, the care and protection of household pets will be part of the safety planning the agency does with women and children.

As we proceed further with strategic team planning, our primary goals include the development of a cross-training program for employees of both agencies, teaching them to understand the connection between various forms of violence, and to recognize the signs of both animal abuse and human abuse. From here we must formulate a system for data collection, reporting, referrals, and response. We must begin asking the right questions, both at the time HAVEN staff does an intake and when the MHS makes a call investigating reports of animal cruelty. We must have in place a mechanism by which information is reported and referrals are made promptly to the correct person or department. And finally, we must be equipped and prepared to respond quickly and appropriately, depending upon the severity of the situation.

The Michigan Humane Society and HAVEN are in the process of identifying and recruiting staff members to form a strong, committed team who will make the achievement of our mutual goals a reality. We believe that a collaboration such as this cannot succeed if merely handed down as a mandate by heads of the respective organizations. Although the commitment of leadership is essential, the mission must be embraced by individuals who truly have a passion for the issues and will keep that passion alive on a daily basis as they work together. It is this team who will not only sustain our coalition but will ensure that it becomes an effective model for other agencies.

Green Chimneys
We Give Troubled Children
the Gift of Giving

Samuel B. Ross, Jr.

WHEN GREEN CHIMNEYS was started in 1948, it offered boys and girls a year-round home school and farm, a place to grow and learn, free from harm and under careful supervision. Back then, the 74-acre farm raised its own meat, poultry, and vegetables. Every opportunity was made to bring the resources of a farm and country atmosphere into the curriculum. Daily contacts with the many pets and farm animals provided an excellent chance for the child to learn.

Animals and nature have always been key components of the therapeutic environment at Green Chimneys. Back then, the children had a wide selection of pets from which to choose. The older boys helped raise calves. They all harnessed ponies and cared for them. They went through the motions of farming. They learned to love flowers and to respect them. These farm chores helped the children become independent as well as develop the feeling of belonging to a group.

The program is a lot different today. We do not raise food other than vegetables for the table; we do not eat our therapists. We have many more children and animals around at all times. Hundreds of thousands of visitors come to our campus or enjoy our Farm on the MOO-ve mobile educational animal awareness program. Many camps and schools have animals on loan for their use. But as much as the types of people we serve has expanded, there has been one constant: animals are present in all of our programs.

Our staff has discovered scores of ways in which the animals improve life for the children. It is no secret that animals heal the children in our care. In our setting we can add that children heal animals in their care. We have all heard, read, and seen animals with children. Thank goodness the majority of times the relationship has been positive, but we must not overlook that it is not always that way. My friend Steve Zawistowski of the ASPCA has pointed out to me that to speak of unconditional love assumes that the caregiver has given freely, gently, and with complete kindness, love to the animal. The young caregiver needs to have received a wholesome, loving upbringing in order to understand what we mean. We therefore strive

Springtime at the farm means new arrivals.

to create nurturers of our children. What they learn may well be the way we will develop adults who do not abuse humans or animals. At Green Chimneys we work hard to interrupt the cycle of abuse.

The people at Green Chimneys believe that you cannot learn in isolation from the world around you. We have been able to make the community a part of us and we have become a part of the community. That community includes animals. On any given day, local residents and visiting professionals often join Green Chimneys' 102 young residents and 35 day students for classes in nature, horticulture, and horse care as well as riding lessons.

DAILY MIRACLES WITH ANIMALS

It may be hard to imagine a tough, troubled young person from what has been called the mean streets of New York patiently soothing a frightened pheasant or gingerly setting a ferret's broken foot. These are just some of the many small daily miracles at Green Chimneys, where animals help troubled youngsters heal and blossom. We have been one of the pioneers of the use of the healing power of human-animal interaction. For 50 years this has been the cornerstone of our work.

Many of the children come here with histories of neglect or sexual, physical, or

Grooming a sheep for the 4-H fair is just one of many animal activities at Green Chimneys.

emotional abuse, as recipients or perpetrators. Most are reported to be school failures, others are learning disabled, and most have never experienced success at school. Some have been truant for more time than they have attended school. They come defeated because they have failed in those things by which children get judged, but we have never had an animal ask a child his achievement test score.

Certified by the state and federal governments as a disabled wildlife rehabilitation center, the barn and pens shelter mending turkeys, geese, owls, hawks, and falcons. According to Paul Kupchok, director of the farm and wildlife program, "In the disabled wildlife program the students appreciate the opportunity to help something disabled. It gives them a feeling of self-worth and self-pride."

Rare breeds of sheep, goats, cattle, and pigs graze together. Green Chimneys residents and local visitors learn to care for these and the hundreds of other animals on the grounds, in classrooms, and in the living units. Often, on weekends, Green Chimneys' youngsters gently help children from the community out of their wheelchairs onto horses. In the summer, they serve as aides to the children who attend our Ability Camp for children and adolescents with very special needs. They also provide daily animal and horseback riding experiences for the ongrounds community preschool.

Taking care of animals teaches children responsibility and lets them know they count. Caring for animals can be the first step in developing the humane ethic: a concern for other people that comes from the opportunity to love and be loved. I constantly emphasize that we do not use children and we do not use animals. We encourage the opportunity to help something disabled. The protection of both is vitally important.

WHO ARE THE CHILDREN WE SERVE AT GREEN CHIMNEYS?

A recent report from New York State indicated that 6,526 emotionally disturbed young people from New York City were placed in congregate care placements. Green Chimneys admits 102 youngsters on its campus with the majority coming from New York City. One might state that 1 out of every 65 children placed from New York City arrives at Green Chimneys. We operate at 99+ percent capacity at all times.

During our 1995–1996 year, 34 young people were admitted. Over 80 percent who went to our residential treatment center were admitted from psychiatric hospitals or diagnostic centers. The level of care in our 14-bed residential treatment facility is higher and 67 percent have had in-patient care in a psychiatric hospital or a residential treatment center. The average length of stay is around 28 months. The majority of our children are placed on a voluntary petition but 32 percent have been placed on a neglect petition. At the time of discharge 60 percent return to their family, which makes work with family of primary importance. We continue to see young people, 20 percent of whom require a more intensive level of care than we offer.

A study was conducted of 18 children who were admitted to our Residential Treatment Center from July 1 through November 1, 1996. A number of key indicators were selected and the results are summarized in table 1.

These statistics are noteworthy and should be interpreted as understating the problems that bring young people into residential care. In many cases, the abuse has been mentioned but unfounded with strong suspicion that the case should have been founded. Sexualized behavior is not always highlighted and animal abuse is generally not documented unless it is of a serious nature. Most significant is that 15 of the 18 children came directly from psychiatric hospitals and diagnostic centers where they had extensive work-ups, which indicated that residential care in a treatment center was absolutely necessary. Also significant is that 10 of the 18 were below age 10.

WHAT HAPPENS TO THEM WHILE THEY ARE
AT GREEN CHIMNEYS?

When a child is referred for admission, assessments are made to help determine his or her suitability for treatment. Periodic assessments determine progress and monitor and guide the treatment process. At the time of discharge, assessments provide

Table 1. Characteristics of 18 Children in Green Chimneys' Residential Treatment Center

Age upon admission	
under 10 years	10
10 to 12 plus	8
Legal Status	
voluntary placement	7
neglect or abuse placement	11
Physically abused	11
Physically and sexually abused	4
Family alcohol and drug use	12
Family affected by AIDS	2
Significant medical problems	5
Education deficits	18
Hospitalized at least once prior to admission	15
Placed in diagnostic center prior to admission	3
History of animal abuse	1
History of physically assaultive or abusive behaviors	14
History of sexualized behaviors	3
Documented history of known firesetting; suspicion of others	4

information to agencies and professionals who will provide aftercare. The data collected at admission and discharge provide an index of the change that occurs during residency.

In June 1996 a preliminary study evaluated changes in the functioning and performance of children during their residence. Forty children were randomly selected from those who had been discharged between July 1993 and June 1995. The study compared the evaluations, assessments, and ratings made upon admission and discharge.

These children had been in residence for an average of 31 months. Some of the more dramatic changes that occurred during that time included

an increase in psychiatric Global Assessment of Functioning (GAF) ratings from 45.0 to 60.3 on a scale of 0 to 100;
an increase of 2.6 years in reading comprehension; and
an increase for 9.5 points in Full Scale IQ.

Although a number of factors are responsible for these changes, we believe that

There's nothing like a smooch from a pooch to brighten your whole day!

many of the improvements are the result of our animal programs. Perhaps some vignettes best describe the animal connection for our young people.

N.U., 18, has been at Green Chimneys Gramercy Residence for one and a half years. Passed from house to house as a small child, he had become defiant and hyperactive. His growing attachment to a rare white ferret named Fergie tempers his ups and downs. He is working on his high school equivalency. He can still flare up, but recently landed a construction job. He took pains to arrange for and train another resident to take care of Fergie during the day—and checks to make sure the care is "A-1 quality." N. U. enjoys walking Fergie on a leash. For the first time, he meets and greets people with ease, including members of the opposite sex who show an interest in Fergie.

N.R., an energetic, bright-eyed, 10-year-old boy, has been at Green Chimneys for one year. His depression, anxiety, and self-destructive behavior made a traditional group home impossible. His learning disability led to failure in public school. N.R. is now thriving socially and academically. Still impulsive and easily distracted, he has become an affable, well-motivated child, who easily engages other children and particularly the staff. A sponge for adult supervision, N.R. is enthusiastic and tries hard at everything he does. N.R. is fond of all the animals and can be counted on to work with anyone assigned to him. Somewhat awkward with his peers, he gets along famously with the four-legged creatures (the rabbits are his favorites). The satisfaction he gains is starting to rub off in his budding friendships with other children.

A.T. is bright, bubbly, and talkative. But as a toddler her tantrums turned to such deep depression and self-destructive behavior she had to leave home, then later school. Soon after a stormy adjustment to Green Chimneys, Rosie the rabbit, horseback riding, and visual arts gave her confidence. She now comes out of bouts of distress and interacts with other youngsters. An exceptional rider and hard worker, she is beginning to show signs of trust. Now a caring, concerned child, A.T. feeds, grooms, and handles Rosie with considerable skill. She likes to talk about her to any interested listener. A.T. has told the staff that being with Rosie relaxes her so that she can do her school work better.

N.N. is a heavy-set, robust 12-year-old who has been here for almost two years. Before that, he had spent four years in special education classes due to disruptive behavior and lack of academic progress. A pattern of acting-out in class and truancy landed him at Green Chimneys. Not only have his grades gone up, N.N. is on Green Chimneys' athletic team. He no longer overreacts to teasing about his weight. He has shown his rabbit, Tiger, at the 4-H County Fair and won the blue ribbon for best buck rabbit, which gained his friends' respect—and made him quite proud of himself.

O.Z. is nearly 11. A small, sensitive-looking boy, he has been at Green Chimneys for eight months. His learning disabilities and severe behavior problems were more than his parents could control. Indeed, before Green Chimneys, O.Z. had both in- and out-patient psychiatric care for seriously aggressive, reckless, and self-destructive behavior. O.Z. loves his job at the farm and often lingers after hours. The staff describe him as very nurturing and personable with all the animals, treating each as his personal project and responsibility. He works closely with a rabbit named Crystal and the concern he shows is touching. With the animals, O.Z. expresses his tender side without fear of rejection, criticism, or scorn.

THE FAMILY CONNECTION

At Green Chimneys, families—natural, adoptive, and foster ones—become an integral part of the treatment plan. Many of our children come from an intense urban background of what has been called "ghetto-related behavior and attitudes." These include out-of-wedlock pregnancies, elevated school dropout rates, gang warfare, and other social disorders. Joblessness has contributed to the decline in marriage and the rise in the single-parent family. Many of our students face the challenge of no role model.

But many of our families came from an agrarian background. They seemingly relate better to their children as they visit the farm and wildlife center. In fact, one finds that it is perhaps the first time they can have a pleasurable conversation with their child, a conversation that can be positive and upbeat.

Our farm environment helps bring families together. America has been described as having become two societies, one of arms and backs, one of suits and laptops. Many parents would unquestioningly send their children to computer camps to learn how to gain access to information, but few would give their children a shovel and gloves and send them to dig weeds for a month to develop a sense of what it means to get dirty and tired for someone else. Many families of Green Chimneys children cannot send them to computer camps, nor can they give them a chance to plant, grow, weed, and harvest.

We try to get both the child and family "rooted" through our We Are Family weekends. These weekends allow children to work side by side with their families, staff, and key personnel on chores related to daily living and the maintenance of the farm. We try to establish rituals and ceremonies they can all share as a means of creating an extended family—a support group. We want the group to come together.

Surveys of teenagers have cited the overwhelming problems that have resulted from having two parents at work; in the single-parent family it can be even harder to keep things in order. Parents have been described as being the real dropouts. The disappearance of the parents and the disarray in the family, plus, in many cases, the overwhelming, consuming problem of holding their lives together leaves no time for the children. We consider that a major part of our work. We want to strengthen and support the family so that our children can return home. (We recognize, however, that family preservation will not work in all cases; we see many damaged, disturbed children whose problems are so severe that removal is the only way the remaining members of the family can survive. We also believe that adjusting the times when professionals provide help can do much to improve the families' situations; giving help is not a nine-to-five-weekdays-only way of working.)

Work with families is not something that can be best left to others, avoided, or worked on only if time permits. It is of major concern to all of us. Green Chimneys' We Are Family weekends at the Outdoor Education Center provide a family-centered approach to out-of-home child welfare service. Associate Executive Director Gary Mallon notes that families and their children participate in a variety of activities, including group sessions to discuss issues of separation and placement; communal cooking of various cultural and ethnic foods by parents, children and staff; recreation that builds team spirit and cooperation such as horseback riding, swimming, canoeing, high ropes, and campfire sing-alongs; and educational sessions geared toward helping children, families, and staff to work effectively together. Families, family workers, and the child's social workers spend the weekend with child care staff and recreation staff, getting to know and trust one another, and beginning to break down the many barriers that can exist between child welfare agencies and families. In an effort to empower families, parents are encouraged to assist in the planning process and in helping to set goals during these weekends. Like many traditional child welfare agencies, Green Chimneys has struggled toward developing a family-centered approach. The camp has proven effective, is relatively low in cost, is easy to replicate, and is beneficial for all involved.

THE STATUS OF CHILD ABUSE AND NEGLECT

The Child Welfare League of America (1998) reported the following:

In 1996, an estimated 3,126,000 children were reported abused or neglected. From 1987 to 1996, the total number of children reported abused or neglected increased 45 percent (National Committee to Prevent Child Abuse 1997).

Every day more than three children die as a result of abuse and neglect. In 1996, an estimated 1,046 children died of abuse and neglect; 82 percent of the children were under five years old and 43 percent never reached their first birthday. From 1985 to 1996, the rate of child fatalities due to abuse and neglect increased 20 percent (National Committee to Prevent Child Abuse 1997).

Violence occurs against both women and children in the same family. Various studies indicate that between 50 and 70 percent of men who assaulted their wives also abused their children (McKibben, De Vos, & Newberger 1989; Stark & Flitcraft 1988).

WHAT ABOUT THE ANIMALS, PLANTS, AND THE ENVIRONMENT?

There are living things in all Green Chimneys places. We believe very strongly that Edward O. Wilson's writings on biophilia, which he describes as humans' innate interest in nature, can be seen in the daily life at Green Chimneys. It exists on our campus, in our group homes, in our residence for adolescents, in our apartment program, and in our runaway program.

You will find animals and plants in offices, classrooms, bedrooms, and carefully maintained outdoors. You will be surrounded by many animals. You will see plants indoors and, when the weather permits, flower gardens, trees, and vegetables. You will see children and adults enjoying their contacts with living things.

The wildlife center provides evidence of animals' struggle to survive. Children and adults learn first-hand how animals are able to exist despite disabling conditions. As long as the quality of life for the animal is always in mind, then the life of the animal should be preserved. As the children observe the care and attention given to the animals, they are able to verbalize that they know that they, too, will be well cared for because they see the animals receiving excellent care.

The study of wildlife is as important as working with domesticated animals.

We have chosen to have pets in the living units. We want the children to learn what it means to have to give care on a daily basis around the clock every day of the year. We have animals in our classrooms and children learn that they have to be concerned not only during the week but on weekends too. We have animals at the farm and even when the snow makes things difficult, the animals must receive care.

Our children know that there are many people who know nothing about animals. Some people think Jersey calves are deer, Scotch Highland cattle are yaks, goats seen kneeling down are animals with shorter front legs, Muscovy ducks are turkeys, and any cow with horns is a bull. Is there any wonder why we need a Farm Animal Awareness Week? We have developed our Farm on the MOO-ve to educate the public. We are very careful to see that the animals are rotated and not stressed from these visits. A veterinarian checks on the health of each animal before each visit.

We decided to concentrate on rare-breed domestic animals. They are sometimes referred to as the animals of antiquity. They are very interesting to see. They provide an opportunity to talk about endangered species. You get the feeling that you are making a contribution to the preservation of livestock that are in danger of disappearing.

Each week, animal control officers from New York City bring animals that need care to our campus. Many animals remain, but others are adopted by families. At our group home in Bedford, New York, we have established a wildlife rescue substation so that people can drop off animals without coming up to the campus, which is about a half-hour further north.

As animals are ready for release, you can be sure there is a child ready to move on and so we allow the child to release the animal back into the wild. It's a ceremony to which everyone is invited.

Our yearly Blessing of the Animals is another ceremony that allows us to recognize the value the animals have to us all. It helps us recognize our role as stewards and awakens us to the importance of the work we are doing.

FINAL THOUGHTS

At Green Chimneys we make the connection between children and animals, children and children, and children and adults. It has become apparent that animals play a much more important role than was once recognized. To ignore this phenomenon is to lose a chance to improve learning, increase socialization, and ameliorate problems through activities that are fun, long-lasting, and healing. Animal-based programs can be useful in speeding up the child's participation and involvement in the treatment. For the nonverbal child, much can be revealed from observation of the child's behavior in the presence of an animal. The humane education model at Green Chimneys provides such important contributions as:

improvement of self-esteem: recognition, gaining confidence, performing service to others, making a contribution;
willingness to try: developing trust, creating calmness out of chaos, reconnecting with family;
establishing new relationships including intergenerational relationships;
learning responsibility, cooperation, and the value of help from others;
noting that time with the animal provides a means of inclusion;
gaining practical hands-on experience: an experiential way to learn, being realistic, increasing scholastic ability and willingness to accept scholastic help;
seeing growth in social integration: understanding the value of community acceptance, learning the value of community service;
meeting educational and behavioral requirements; and
understanding the value of the involvement and how long-lasting it can be in terms of life skills;
seeing the involvement as a possible career goal or as a lifetime interest.

The animals are the catalyst that attracts the interest of the children. The animals speed up the process of communication between the child and peers and the child and adults. Staff are alert to take advantage of the desire to communicate. Breakthroughs with children and their families are very important. Families are crying out for help. Children are exhibiting more and more serious problems. Soci-

An equation for success: kids + animals = self-confidence.

ety wants to invest less and less time in making things better. Animals, like children, have become throwaways. Putting children and animals together with proper supervision and care can prove to be a wonderful means of helping both. Although animal programs are no panacea for all the ills we see around us, they work well with many children. They are worthy of attention. They should be tried. Above all else, they should be taken seriously. They can also be a lot of fun.

This, then, becomes the meaningful purpose of our work. We give troubled children the gift of giving. It is hoped that we create better humans, better caregivers for the world of tomorrow.

SUGGESTED READINGS

Child Welfare League of America. 1998. *Children '98: America's promise fact sheet.* Washington, D.C.: Child Welfare League.

Levinson, B. 1997. *Pet-oriented child psychotherapy,* 2nd edition, revised. Springfield, Ill.: Charles Thomas.

Mallon, G. 1992. *Utilization of animals as therapeutic adjuncts with children and youth. Child & youth care forum*

McKibben, L., E. De Vos, and E. Newberger. 1989. Victimization of mothers of abused children: A controlled study. *Pediatrics* 84:531.

National Committee to Prevent Child Abuse. 1997. *Current trends in child abuse reporting and fatalities: The results of the 1996 annual fifty state survey.* Chicago: National Committee to Prevent Child Abuse.

Senter, S. 1993. *People and animals: A therapeutic animal-assisted activities manual for schools, agencies and recreational centers.* Brewster, N.Y.: Green Chimneys.

Stark, E., and A. Flitcraft. 1988. Women and children at risk: A feminist perspective on child abuse. *International Journal of Health Services* 18:97.

The Role of Animals in the Emotional and Moral Development of Children

Mother Hildegard George

THE USE OF animals can be a highly efficient tool in the treatment of children and teens with emotional problems, as well as with normally developing children who experience stress along the continuum of growth. Literature (Arkow 1998; George 1988; Levinson 1969) indicates that the introduction of animals into the lives of children is highly successful, especially in developing self-esteem, self-control, and responsibility. Through case studies and personal observations, I illustrate in this essay how animal-assisted interventions can help children problem-solve such emotions as anger, aggression, frustration, and hate. Animals can also help children develop relationships with their peers as well as with adults.

Gandhi once wrote that the greatness of a nation and its moral progress can be judged by the way its animals are treated. It can also be judged by the way its children are treated.

Programs that incorporate animals help build self-esteem and give children and teens a chance to show that they can do something well. Such programs give them a place to develop relationships safely by beginning with a relationship with the animal. Often, children and teens have not had good relationships with the adults in their lives. To start with an animal and those who relate to the animal is an honest and safe way to begin.

Many years of incorporating animals into therapy sessions with children and teens have demonstrated that animals are appropriate for therapy with emotionally disturbed, learning-disabled, and normally developing children experiencing stress (Arkow 1998; George 1988; Katcher 1981, 1983, 1985).

CHILDHOOD STRESSES

Childhood is not the carefree, lighthearted playful time remembered nostalgically by many adults. It involves a series of physical, emotional, cognitive, and social changes that most normal children will, at least once in their development, experience as difficult. The accompanying stress or conflict can possibly lead to behavior

Animal-based interventions can help create healthy environments to assist children in coping with stresses while deepening their sensitivities.

or learning problems. Normal childhood requires undergoing difficult processes of developing self-esteem, achieving independence, learning to relate to others, peers in particular, coping with a changing body, and forming basic values. Added to these are the stresses of modern society and problems such as divorce and drugs that were not prevalent to the same extent in generations past.

Children's reactions to stressful experiences are dependent upon their perceptions of self and of the experiences. These perceptions can be accurate or inaccurate. Children who view themselves as vulnerable or unable to control their lives may perceive themselves as helpless. Few children, even those who are competent, are able to handle stress easily. The majority of children have to work at dealing with stressful events. Even if they are unable to integrate an experience into their lives in a positive way, they frequently do manage to cope with the stressful experiences and get on with their lives. If they are successful their self-esteem grows.

Other children, however, become extremely disorganized by a stressful experience. They struggle hard to overcome the experience but are unable to integrate it into their lives. Most children, even the best copers, are at one time or another in need of help in dealing with stress. When children are overwhelmed by stressful events and not helped to integrate them, developmental personality problems and maladaptive behaviors can occur that could prevent children from attaining their fullest potentials.

Because the physical, mental, and emotional development of children is often interwoven with disagreeable events, children experience, on the one hand, confidence, acceptance, and success and on the other, doubt, rejection, and failure. Even though negative experiences develop inner resources, tension is also produced that can cause a slowdown or delay in development. What is considered by adults a normal event in a child's life, such as entering school or the birth of a sibling, can be seen as a trauma by the child. Who is to say that every major trauma in the life of a child does not add a scar to his or her psyche? Who is to say if these scars ever totally heal? In some children we know they do not. The more help the child has in coming to grips with the traumas of his or her life, the less scarring there will be and the healthier the growing child will be.

Childhood should be a time for healthy growth, establishing warm relationships, exploring the world, and developing confidence in self and significant others. It should contain fun and carefree times as well as provide a foundation for the growing child. It is up to all who work with children—teachers, parents, and therapists—to see that children receive guidance in becoming all that they have the potential to become. Parents and professionals need to look more for the strengths and gifts of the child and not so much for the problems. If we capitalize on the strengths, children can be better served and better help themselves.

AN ERIKSONIAN MODEL

Erik Erikson's (1950) stages of man for the first 12 years of life provide a framework that helps us see how children develop; from this we can learn how moral development fits into growth and how animals may be used to help children in that process.

In the first year and a half, infants learn trust, that they are valued beings and can have hope that they will always be taken care of. In the first three years children learn about autonomy and that they have a will to assert. In the preschool years children learn to explore, create, and act on their world, and they discover that there is a purpose to their lives. In the school years, ages 6 through 12, children learn industry and that they can master many things.

The values that most of us would like to see inculcated into children as they head toward adulthood are: self-esteem, or an ability to like and believe in oneself; integrity, or being true to one's moral and ethical beliefs; honesty; respect for others; courage; self-discipline; compassion; patience; courtesy; responsibility; cooperation; and a work ethic.

At what ages can we expect children to develop these values? Infants who are cared for, held, and loved are developing trust, the cornerstone of all moral development. Preschool children tend to operate egocentrically but they can still begin to apply their developing intellectual abilities to moral and social issues. Between the ages of four to six, children should have a sense of the principles of generosity, courtesy, kindness, and helpfulness. By the age of six or seven they should know the difference between generosity and selfishness, what constitutes fair and unfair behavior, and honesty versus dishonesty. They should be learning a variety of ways to help others and to be kind to others. They should also be developing a sense of rules for home and school.

By the age of eight or nine children should develop a sense of the rights of others as well as valuing the differences in others. They should likewise be overcoming childhood fears and developing courage and a conviction in what they believe.

Between the ages of 10 and 12, children should develop a sense of the feelings of others, especially those less fortunate than themselves. They should be able to work with others who are different from themselves and respect the ideas of another. They should have a sense of perseverance in tasks. This is the beginning of the stage where negative peer influence can be the most harmful to children who have not developed a sense of who they are. By the age of 12 children should be able to consider the consequences of their actions and have a positive attitude about themselves as well as others if they are to flourish during the teen years.

ANIMALS AND CHILDREN

Because of the growing need for ways to help children, I have looked for alternate means to help them on the course of normative growth. Utilizing animals in therapies, programs and classrooms with normally developing and at-risk children and teens has proven to be a successful way to help prevent seemingly small problems from turning into nightmares. Animal-based interventions can be methods for creating a healthy environment to assist children in coping with stress as well as deepening their sensitivities.

Not only do animals bring out the personalities of children and improve their receptiveness to the environment and to other people, they often teach children how to relax and be themselves. Play is one of the most important health-related aspects of the human-animal bond relationship. Animals are often better playmates for children than toys because animals constantly bring the child back to the reality of the relationship. An animal can also contribute to the development of children as an animal is an active playmate helping to release energy and tensions in the child.

The play of children with emotional problems often differs from the play of normally developing children. The former often display an inability to relate to peers and enjoy games. Because these children have not matured to age-appropriate play, they often crave sensory stimulation that is more appropriate to younger

Direct contact with animals helps children develop
empathy with other living creatures and with the
environment.

children. The touch and response of an animal can have a positive effect on these
children.

One of the most important virtues we are not instilling in young children today
is empathy. Direct contact with animals is one way of helping children develop empathy with other creatures, other humans, and with the environment. I once worked
with a 10-year-old boy from the inner city who was in a residential farm school for
children with emotional problems. He often said that when he grew up he wanted
to be an architect so he could design cities that people would want to live in and
take care of. His daily contact with and care of the farm animals had helped develop
an empathy that enabled him to care about others in the environment.

Because children often learn best by example, they can develop an awareness
of the needs and feelings of others by seeing how adults care for and relate to animals. Children can practice a variety of interactions with animals that can later be
incorporated into relationships with others. Animals can teach children behaviors
not easily acquired by usual learning techniques, such as a capacity to communicate
nonverbally, and social behaviors such as sharing and responsibility for others. Animals also help children to develop self-esteem, a sense of achievement, nurturing,
cooperation, and socialization, all of which contribute to the building of empathy.

Part of building self-esteem is learning discipline and responsibility, learning to work with and get along with others, and learning to trust another and to love. By learning to respect animals through proper handling, children learn that there are limits and mutual respect in a relationship. By learning to nurture and care for animals, children are being nurtured themselves and learning skills for future relationships. Animals also help children and teens incorporate an understanding of suffering and death into their worldview because they can see that other beings can have pain, illness, and even die, and that they need to be cared for and loved by others.

Programs incorporating animals create an environment, physically as well as emotionally, in which wounded children and teens can discover the part of themselves that was lost or never discovered in the chaos of the environment from which they came. Such programs are not only treatment for present and past problems but also prevention for future problems. By stressing the concepts of humaneness, these programs can help children to see how animals should be treated, concepts that can be translated into other relationships. Humane education is more than learning responsibility; it is the place where we create proper attitudes for children about right actions toward all life. Children who have animal interactions as a component of therapy can solve problems of aggression, anger, frustration, and hate. Animals can help at-risk children develop relationships with their peers as well as with adults. My experience has shown that animals should be introduced to at-risk children not as a reward for good behavior, but rather as a catalyst for creating good behavior. Too often, the opposite is seen in animal-related programs.

THE ABUSED CHILD

Abused children may exhibit a wide range of characteristics such as low self-esteem, stubbornness, unresponsiveness, negativism, depression, fear, apathy, physical aggression, and self-destructive behavior. These children may also demonstrate severe deficits in a wide variety of ego controls such as reality testing, body image, impulse control, and overall ego competency (Green 1978).

One aspect of the pathology of these children is the impairment of ego functioning they display. These children are often found to be hyperactive, impulsive, have little tolerance for frustration, and many are verbally limited. There is often an absence of the defenses that enable the normal child to cope with stress and conflict. Thus, the child is abnormally preoccupied with external danger and with an overstimulated drive activity that impairs learning. I have found that the typical play of these children is characterized by inappropriate aggression and anger and a lack of ability to enjoy play, as well as anxiety and difficulty in interpersonal relations.

A reasonable goal to set for these children would be strengthening of the ego function, which would include such objectives as encouraging verbalization, controlling impulsive action, and increasing frustration tolerance.

Example

Jimmy (real names of children have not been used in these examples) was a nine-year-old boy who was brought to me after having been in foster care since age three. He was frequently abused physically by his mother and as a result had temper tantrums and was sullen and depressed. He was fearful of adults and obviously trusted no one. He was unable to relate to peers and saw all interactions with them as assaults on his person. He had a poor image of himself and little self-control. A goal for Jimmy was to increase frustration tolerance and to encourage positive relationships with peers and adults that included verbalization of his feelings.

When I first saw Jimmy at a residential farm treatment center, we went for a walk up to the barn. Jimmy made it obvious that he did not want to be with me, another intrusive adult. I told him that it was his time and he was free to do what he wanted. On the way to the barn he found a large cat. Jimmy spent the entire time playing with the cat and ignoring me. When I came to get him the next week, he was willing to go with me though he did not say anything. Within a few weeks he was laughing in sessions as he played with various animals. It was noted that he was extremely gentle with all the animals and even the most fearful of the animals took to him. I tried to encourage Jimmy in front of others and soon it was obvious that he knew he had a special gift with animals. Although he continued to do poorly in school, he was an "ace" in handling even the most difficult animals. At one point he was introduced into a class with other children and large dogs and was asked if he would like to help the younger children learn to interact with the dogs. He seemed to look forward to each session. His performance in school, especially math, began to improve over several months. Although he continued to have problems he was a far happier child after a year. The steady work with the dogs increased his frustration tolerance in school and he was interacting with peers and adults and seemed to seek positive attention from them.

THE ABANDONED OR NEGLECTED CHILD

Abandoned or neglected children exhibit many of the characteristics of abused children. They have a typical pattern of depressive affect with low self-esteem that is often accompanied by self-destructive behavior. These abnormalities are attributed to the physical and emotional trauma on the normal development of the child's adaptive ego functions as a consequence of deviant parenting. The play of these children is characterized by unusual anxiety, inappropriate aggression, flat affect, inability to play with one object for long periods, permeable boundaries (easily distracted), and lack of ability to enjoy play.

For these children the focus would be on developing nurturing skills and would include experiences where they could be nurtured as well as learn to nurture another living being. Petting, grooming, and feeding an animal as well as watching interactions between mother animals and their babies would be important. Reality orientation could be improved by learning to interact appropriately with an animal.

Example

Davie, age seven, came from a broken, neglecting home. He often appeared to be confused and fearful of his surroundings. He was often aggressive toward peers and acted out in class. It was very difficult to talk to him even though he appeared to be cooperative in sessions. A major goal set for Davie was better interaction with his peers. The method used was nurturing the animal he chose for himself.

Initially, Davie was asked what kind of animal he wanted to work with and he chose a baby goat. Goats, it should be noted, are very social creatures and extremely responsive to children. From the beginning, Davie was told that he had to talk to his goat to let her know what he expected from her. If she was good he was to tell her so, and if she was bad he had to correct her. Davie learned to groom, feed, and lead the goat on a leash. After three weeks (one hour per week) Davie was not only talking to his goat but to me as well. He was also reported as being more vocal in class and interacting better with peers. He rarely lost an opportunity to show off his relationship with his animal.

ATTENTION DEFICIT DISORDER WITH HYPERACTIVITY

Attention Deficit Disorder with Hyperactivity (ADHD) impairs a child's psychological, cognitive, motor, and social development. Children with this disorder are characterized by impulsive, inattentive and hyperactive behavior. They often have learning difficulties and show signs of depression and separation anxiety. There is also an increased risk for developing Conduct Disorder as their impulsive behavior often leads to trouble in the classroom and at home due to their inability to relate to peers and family members.

The play of these children is characterized by boredom, lack of ability to play with one object for more than a few minutes, a lot of running or roaming around the room, and often an inability to even choose a toy.

Because many children with ADHD also have learning disorders, special education is the primary treatment. The children benefit from small classes with fewer distractions and extra tutoring is often recommended.

For many of these children the primary task is to change their self-concept from being inadequate underachievers to a sense of themselves as competent individuals. The therapist's role with these children is often educational as well as interpretive. It is the therapist's task to help these children recognize the symptoms of their problems and develop internal controls. These children often experience low self-esteem due to poor academic performance, so it is necessary to find ways in which they can achieve and feel good about themselves in some aspect of their lives.

Examples

Steve was a nine-year-old who came to the treatment center with a diagnosis of ADHD and Conduct Disorder. He had a history of chronic antisocial and self-destructive behaviors. He had a stormy beginning at the center but appeared to make good, though erratic, progress in overall behavior and academic programs.

Steve was recommended to me for work with my Newfoundland puppy, Pooh Bear. A goal set for Steve was development of internal control that was expected to improve his negative self-image. As he played with and worked on training Pooh Bear, Steve learned to gain control over his impulses while watching the puppy learn to control his own impulses. It was noted that as Steve was better able to control his behavior, depression surfaced that had previously been masked by his clownish behavior. It appeared that because Steve felt he was able to do something worthwhile (help in training the dog) and have a relationship with the dog and therapist, he was better able to relate consistently with peers.

Henry, age eight, came from a neglecting home and was diagnosed with ADHD. Initially he was very hyperactive and distracted, darting from one animal to another. It was thought that animal puppets in a quiet room would be a good introduction for him to the real animals in the barn. After four weeks (two one-half hour sessions per week) during which he focused on the cow and rabbit puppets, Henry was taken to the barn, where he chose a miniature rabbit to work with. He was able to hold the rabbit and comb it for about 10 minutes during the first session. With each session we focused on the rabbit for longer periods of time. One day he said, "I wish I could sit this still in class so I would not always be in trouble." After several months he was able to come daily for an hour and care for his rabbit. He was more focused, less distracted, and calmer in his movements. In the time with the rabbit, Henry learned to relax and be himself.

One of the most successful ways to work in group therapy with older children and teens is weekly dog training classes. Each child is assigned to his or her own dog while the owner of the dogs, who is a specialist in dog training, puts the children through the paces with their dogs. For younger children it is best if the dogs are already trained and obey the children with ease.

Many of the ADHD children who cannot stay on-task for 10 minutes in academic programs are able to work for an hour with the dogs. There is a rule in the dog training groups that each child must teach his or her dog to sit quietly and patiently while other children go through the exercise paces with their dogs. As the child tries to control his own dog, he is controlling himself. The children learn to focus not only on their own dogs but on their peers as well.

It is the role of the therapist to watch the child's interactions with the trainer, dog, and peers and to note any problems that can be addressed in individual therapy sessions. It is also the therapist's task to call the child's attention to problems that can be dealt with immediately within the group.

THE DEPRESSED CHILD

Until recently it was generally believed by clinicians that depression simply did not occur in children. Today there is general agreement that depression does occur, even in infants. The DSM-IV (American Psychiatric Association 1987) does not list separate diagnostic characteristics for affective disorders in children but does recognize the existence of cognitive, social, and developmental differences.

Depressed children have feelings of worthlessness, self-reproach, and excessive guilt. There is evidence of an inability to concentrate, loss of energy, and fatigue. There is also a loss of interest or pleasure in usual activities. Often there are recurrent themes of death and suicidal ideation or attempts. I have found that the play of these children is often characterized by their just sitting, merely looking at toys but not engaging in play, and by a sad expression.

Example

Benji was an eight-year-old who was overwhelmed by sad and angry feelings. He was diagnosed as a depressed child with reactive anger. By the age of seven he had attempted suicide twice. His father had deserted his mother when Benji was three. Benji was the oldest of seven children, four of whom have different fathers. He was unable to admit to family problems, often had nightmares, and screamed in his sleep. Although he was an emotionally fragile child, he put on a "street tough" front. He had low frustration tolerance and often had temper tantrums and angry outbursts with peers. Major goals set for Benji were to try to help him enjoy activities, decrease anxiety, and increase self-esteem through training of a dog.

After only two months of therapy there was a noted change in his behavior. During group work with the dogs, Benji knew that if he was to work with his dog, he must keep certain rules set by the trainer. This meant he must try to get along with peers and control his language and angry behavior.

In individual work with Benji, he was free to play and work with the dog and thus was more able to act out his feelings, especially about his mother who never came to see him. He realized that Pooh Bear was abandoned too, had been found by someone who cared, and then "adopted" by the therapist. The puppy helped him to address questions about his mother which he was not able to in the beginning.

NORMALLY DEVELOPING CHILDREN

One of the most important roles animals have in the lives of children is prevention of problems within normal development. Over the years I have been struck by how many adults confess that an animal helped them come through what could have been major crises. In some cases the animal was there for them when no one else was; in other cases the animal helped to soften the pain of trauma. Within Erikson's development model we need to see where animals fit into the schema of the child's growth. The presence of a well-cared-for animal in the family may help develop the infant's own developing trust as he or she experiences another creature's being loved. Children who have animals in the family tend to develop autonomy quicker as they feel safer in exploration outside the family. Children who have family pets are often more able to get along with peers.

Examples

Lacey, an only child, was seven when her upper-middle-class, well-educated parents decided to divorce. Her mother, who had never had a pet, took my advice and got Lacey a kitten. Within weeks that small cat became a member of the family, so much so that hundreds of dollars were spent on it when he was hit by a car. Today, Lacey is in college and looks back on that kitten as the savior in her times of doubt, loneliness, and pain. Although she probably would have survived the family crises, the kitten certainly gave her an emotional boost with its unconditional love at that time.

Peter was nine when his mother died from cancer. Although there were loving grandparents and an aunt present to help the family, Peter suddenly took to carrying the family pet everywhere he went. It was as if his caring for the cat filled in some of his own need to be cared for by the mother who was no longer present. Animals may act as transitional objects for children, much like the favorite ragged blanket or much-loved teddy bear. When children, especially boys, get older, our society frowns upon their reverting to such baby objects. No one objects, however, when the child takes up with an animal. In fact, we see it as wholesome.

Animals can help children during periods of bewilderment and anxiety by providing a gentle presence. Sometimes they provide reorientation for those temporarily lost.

ANIMAL ABUSE

I am often asked if there is animal abuse by children who have been abused themselves. In the various programs I have encountered, animals are rarely hurt deliberately. Animals may accidentally get stepped on or brushed or embraced too hard but there is rarely real damage and the animal is the first to come back for more attention and affection.

CONCLUSION

When children are taught empathy from the beginning by watching the adults around them and from interaction with their peers, they learn the proper way to behave around animals. It all has to do with supervision and good education, which involves more than demonstrations. It involves care and love. By teaching children

The author with one of her llama friends.

to care we can change their attitudes about violence. We do this by healing them and healing the wounds within, whether emotional, physical or spiritual. Then we change children's vision for the future by helping them to recognize negative behavior and its consequences.

Too often, we professionals think that we cannot do much because there is neither the time nor money nor staff nor whatever. We need to see things as the child does—in simplicity. There are many ways to teach children about animals that cost little but time: nature walks, a visit to a dairy or farm, local AKC trainers, a blessing of the animals in the community, tours of humane societies, animal-assisted therapy visits to hospitals and nursing homes, and riding programs for the handicapped.

It is up to those who treat and work with children to see that they receive all the help they can in order to become their richest selves. What greater gift can we give children—who are our future—than a sense of their own self-worth and the knowledge that life is precious no matter how difficult. The development of empathy for all of God's creation, no matter how great or how small, is how we teach children to care for and protect their future. The development of values, truly a part of the child's developing personality, should be one of our top priorities in education, both at home and in the classroom. To paraphrase Albert Schweitzer, children must be taught that all life is valuable and that we are united to all life. From this knowledge comes our spiritual relationship with the universe.

REFERENCES

American Psychiatric Association. 1987. *Diagnostic and statistical manual of mental disorders,* 3rd ed., rev. Washington, D.C.: American Psychiatric Association.

Arkow, P. 1998. *"Pet therapy": A study and resource guide to the use of companion animals in selected therapies,* 8th ed. Stratford, N.J.: self-published.

Erikson, E. H. 1950. *Childhood and society.* New York: Norton.

George, M. H. 1988. Children and animals: A new way for an old relationship. In C. Schaefer, ed., *Innovative interventions in child and adolescent therapy.* New York: Wiley-Interscience.

Green, A. 1978. Child abuse. In B. Wolman, ed., *Handbook of treatment of mental disorders in childhood and adolescence.* Englewood Cliffs, N.J.: Prentice-Hall.

Katcher, A. 1981. Interactions between people and their pets: Form and function. In B. Fogel, ed., *Interactions between people and pets.* Springfield, Ill.: Charles C. Thomas.

Katcher, A. 1983. Man and the living environment: An excursion into cyclical time. In A. Katcher and A. Beck, eds., *Perspectives on our lives with companion animals.* Philadelphia: University of Pennsylvania Press.

Katcher, A. 1985. Physiologic and behavioral responses to companion animals. In J. Quackenbush and V. Voith, eds., *The Human-Companion Animal Bond, The Veterinary Clinics of North America: Small Animal Practice,* 15(2):403–10.

Levinson, B. 1969. *Pet-oriented child psychotherapy.* Springfield, Ill.: Charles C. Thomas.

Forget Me Not Farm

Teaching Gentleness with Gardens and Animals to Children from Violent Homes and Communities

Carol Rathmann

FORGET ME NOT FARM is infinitely more than a place, it is a happening. It is an event. And to the children who have experienced the programs and the lessons that are taught there it is an unforgettable part of their lives that will have an enduring and positive effect on them as they move toward and into adulthood.

In March 1992, a program about child abuse and animal abuse was presented by the San Francisco Child Abuse Council and the Humane Coalition Against Violence. After attending this moving and provocative presentation, staff members of the Humane Society of Sonoma County in Santa Rosa, California, decided to expand their services by developing an education program for abused and neglected children in their community, in an effort to break the cycle of animal abuse. Founded in 1931, the mission of this Humane Society has been the development of a "Society for the Prevention of Cruelty to Animals and Children" by encouraging a truly "humane society."

The shelter manager of the Humane Society contacted the local YWCA, a nonprofit community agency that operates the Domestic Violence Services Program, which includes the Women's Emergency Shelter, and A Special Place, which is a therapeutic child care services program, to see if they would be interested in participating in the development of this new program. They were definitely interested.

A few months later, with no budget, more than an acre of tall weeds, some decrepit unused animal corrals, a handful of enthusiastic volunteers, and a project coordinator, development of Forget Me Not Farm began. Out of a shared commitment to do something to break the intergenerational cycle of abuse and neglect, the Humane Society of Sonoma County, the San Francisco Child Abuse Council, and the YWCA of Sonoma County established a collaboration to design and implement a model program that would teach gentleness and nonviolence to at-risk children and families through gardening and animal care in a totally nonthreatening environment. Following careful and thoughtful development, the Forget Me Not Farm program emerged and has grown. It now accommodates children of all ages and, when safe, their parents. The children and parents work with staff and volunteers to bring forth the undeveloped ability to nurture, care for, and respect all living things.

THE CHILDREN IN THE PROGRAM

When this program began, two groups of four or five children from the YWCA participated each week. Volunteers were limited to one master gardener, the project coordinator, and staff from the participating agency. Over the next five years, eight additional agencies serving "at-risk" children requested participation and began to attend on a regular basis. Our volunteers now number 30 and there is a waiting list of agencies and individuals wishing to participate.

The following agencies and the program we have established for each illustrate the variations in the backgrounds of the children and the programs. These variations are designed to fulfill the needs of each group maximally and allow us to optimize the results that will be of benefit to each child.

YWCA-WOMEN'S EMERGENCY SHELTER

Families residing in the Women's Emergency Shelter for battered women are limited to a brief stay with minimal involvement in outside activities. For the children, their visit to the farm is the only time they spend away from their shelter in a totally safe environment. Our focus at Forget Me Not Farm is in giving the children something normal to look forward to after having had their lives disrupted so abruptly.

The children from the Women's Emergency Shelter are usually between 3 and 12 years of age; occasionally there will be teenagers. These children visit the farm site once each week for one hour, and they typically approach the farm with the exuberance one would expect of children who have not been anywhere or had any positive diversion for a week. Therefore, we allow them time to "blow off steam" by running, jumping, and being free to play in a safe setting. Because we have such a high turnover in participating children, we begin by introducing ourselves and then we explain some very simple rules: all living things—plants, animals, insects, and equally important, each other—need to be treated with kindness and gentleness at the farm. We then break into groups for our gardening activities.

After a half-hour, the animal experience begins by having a pet-assisted therapy volunteer arrive with her dog. Then sequentially, volunteers bring out one or more of the resident animals and the children have some time to interact with each animal. The farm animals include a lamb, two pigs, a small horse, a very gentle yearling cow, two llamas, two dwarf goats, a goose, and several rabbits. Other animals visiting the children may include cats, kittens, puppies, and our pet opossum.

A brief lesson, which varies with the children's ages, is given about the animal

Participants learn how to approach a gentle
lamb and experience how much the lamb loves
the soft touch.

they are visiting. At the end of animal visiting time a snack is served and the children prepare to leave. We thank them for visiting and tell them how much we have
enjoyed our time together. It is important that we say our good-byes, for we do not
know which of the children might or might not be returning the following week. The
maximum stay for women at the emergency shelter is six to eight weeks, so children
arrive and leave in an irregular manner.

WOMEN'S RECOVERY SERVICE—A UNIQUE PLACE

Women's Recovery Service is a residential treatment facility for women with chemical dependencies. The children from this agency are living with a mother who has
completed certain requirements before she is reunited with them; these children
may have been living with a member of their extended family, in the county dependent unit, or in foster care prior to moving back with their recovering mother.

A very special part of the program is that each week a mother is assigned to
accompany the children to the farm. She may or may not be the mother of a child

Children harvest peppers to take back to their
shelter at Women's Recovery Service.

present; in fact, she may not even have custody of her own children if she is in the
early stages of recovery.

We usually see five children and one adult from this agency. When they arrive
they are greeted by smiling, caring volunteers anxious to spend the next hour providing a normal environment in which to learn and have fun. These children come
directly from school, so we often begin the hour with our snack. We offer the children two or three activities involving gardening as well as care or feeding of certain
animals. Sometimes there will be craft projects related to the gardens. After their
snack, the children select their preferred activity and off we go. Often, one activity
will lead to another related activity and the staff is constantly alert to ascertain that
the day's activities go forward in an orderly and productive manner. It is not unusual for the children, after having their own snack, to pick some greens so the animals can have something to eat. Then they get involved in their other garden projects.

We try to have some large-motor skill activities such as digging, raking, moving
the irrigation hoses, and sometimes some weeding. Small-motor skill activities such
as seeding, transplanting, and pruning old growth and flowers are done in the qui-
eter times and often follow the more active jobs.

When vegetables are available for harvest, the children gather some to take home. At A Unique Place, meals are prepared in a community dining room by the women in recovery and it gives the children a great sense of accomplishment to be able to contribute food to be shared by everyone.

The presence of a "mom" allows the volunteers an opportunity to model good interactive skills with the children. We "chat"; we always share with our new friends how much we enjoy them and how good it makes us feel to be in their company. We want to maximize their feeling of acceptance and self-worth. It is important that they feel a sense of belonging with this group and that we are not just baby-sitters.

We maintain a very casual and open environment. We will stop everything to admire someone's good work or interesting discovery. We always endeavor to use good garden vocabulary and as a result we find that the children enjoy adding new terms to their own storehouse of garden words.

The mothers see people who are welcoming, friendly, and not pre-judging. They often arrive uncertain or even angry; they are involved in a battle against themselves just to survive. The farm offers them an hour to relax and work their hands in the soil, brush an animal's hair, or watch a hot pig take a mud bath to cool off. The mothers seem to enjoy the interaction with the volunteers and animals as much as the children do.

These children and their mothers stay with the recovery program for three to six months. This long time frame gives the volunteers an opportunity to develop special bonds with the children and we expect that these bonds will be of lasting value for the children as well as for the volunteers.

SONOMA COUNTY DEPENDENT UNIT—VALLEY OF THE MOON SCHOOL

The children who come from this county emergency shelter have been removed from their homes and placed in a protected environment, and are awaiting foster care or possible reunification with their families. Each week we see 12 to 32 children ranging in age from 5 to 18. The duration of their participation is varied, depending on the timing of their successful placement. They may join us only once or they may be with us for as long as two years. Confidentiality is important, so the volunteers' knowledge of their background and future is limited to what the children choose to confide in them.

The Sonoma County Board of Education has approved this program and it has been a part of the Valley of The Moon School's regular curriculum since 1994. The wide range of children's ages and abilities, coupled with the lack of attendance continuity, makes it more challenging to plan activities for this group than for other groups; this also makes it more important to have structure. The needs for increased structure have been met with a consistent program. We start our weekly program by gathering in a circle. Volunteers discuss their thoughts on what projects should be worked on that day and they present a brief overview of the activities that will be offered. While the children are still in a circle an animal is introduced and a lesson is given; the depth of the lesson will be dependent on that particular group. When an animal is being introduced and talked about, the children are usually fascinated and very attentive. The same animal may be a regular guest in this circle for several weeks as the children learn about it and interact with it.

Following the animal lesson, the children are given choices of several activities. These could be gardening, helping with the animals, or food preparation such as making salsa from the garden. They have the opportunity to be involved in all of the various activities. Volunteers provide a snack that the children help to prepare; the snack is often from the garden or is something related to the garden and is usually made from fresh fruits and vegetables. Older children have voiced enthusiastic acceptance of our snacks, having had a diet of institutional food most of the time.

This group needs a high level of structure and the volunteers meet every four to six weeks to plan activities. With a group of this size and with the age variations of the children, we need a minimum of one volunteer for every two children. The more volunteers, the better the experience is for everyone.

The teacher accompanying the children communicates with the volunteers about disciplinary rules at the Dependent Unit and supports the volunteers in their dealing with the children. If a volunteer or staff person sees a need for discipline it is handled by Dependent Unit staff; volunteers are not asked to discipline the children.

We have a new policy in place. The trip to the farm was once a right for all of the children; now it is a privilege they must earn with good behavior during the week, and they must agree to participate in our program when they arrive. When a new child is admitted to the Dependent Unit, it is not long before he or she hears, "Don't do that or you won't be able to go to the Humane Society on Tuesday," or a new student will be told, "If you don't come to class every day you won't go to the farm next Tuesday." As a result of the children looking forward to the farm, there has been a definite improvement in their behavior between weekly visits. Teachers have reported noticeable improvement in students' school work.

NORTH VALLEY SCHOOL

This is a certified private special education school with approximately 42 students. It is operated by Willow Creek Treatment Center, which specializes in serving youth who have a history of abuse, neglect, or multiple placement failures. The school's mission is to provide a successful, comprehensive, and therapeutic educational program for its severely emotionally disturbed students. The students are between the ages of 12 and 18 and are referred through the contracting counties' departments of mental health, social services, and probation. Referrals are children who are behaviorally or emotionally disturbed to the point that they cannot be maintained in a less restrictive environment. The only other choice for these children would be state hospitals.

These children have been removed from their families and are now living in group homes with six to eight children in each house. At these residential facilities they are taught living skills that develop independence and self-sufficiency to prepare them for a less restrictive setting. The residential program is based on a strong emphasis and protocol for behavior modification. Consequently, the students are always being evaluated by their teachers or other staff members. Although it is difficult to maintain a high level of good behavior in the school setting, this has not been an issue at the farm. During the three years they have participated in our program, we have not encountered any major problems with these students.

Forget Me Not Farm is an elective class offered every nine weeks, year-round. The average class size is usually nine students. The students may repeat the class during any subsequent nine-week period that they are in school. Everyone that signs up for this class has an opportunity to come to the farm, but preference is given to first-time attendees in cases of scheduling conflicts due to staffing limitations.

The children arrive at the farm and put on name tags (everyone wears one). An opening circle is formed, plans for the day are outlined, and the children are introduced to an animal before breaking into groups to work in the garden. Some 20 percent of the students are hearing-impaired or deaf so a translator, provided by the school, may join in the circle as we discuss an animal and its characteristics, needs, diet, and so on. This is a time for the students to interact with the animal and bombard the presenter with questions. Hands-on may be required for the hearing-impaired to "listen" to a cat purr or feel the vibrations of a pig grunting.

After visiting with the animal(s), the children break into groups to go into the gardens to weed, mulch, plant, harvest, or touch and learn about the different characteristics of the plants. As with the other groups, the children will choose food for the farm animals, and when the garden work is complete they will feed the farm animals some of the food they have grown. At this time the children are usually ready for a snack and they reflect on the good time they have had during their visit. It may be the animals they petted, the weeds they pulled, just enjoying the fresh air and sunshine, or the interaction with a certain volunteer that makes their visit special that day. This is a time cherished by all of the children because they are given an opportunity to say what they liked about their day or, in some cases, what they didn't like.

SONOMA COUNTY MENTAL HEALTH SERVICES

The children in this group come from three different cities and are brought together at the farm by their case management specialists. These children are in the public

This boy just realized he had actually grown something. Even though he had never tasted a pepper, he was anxious to pick one and bring it home.

school system but are receiving special services. Their ages range from 8 to 14 years and the group size never exceeds 10 children.

New challenges are presented by this group. These children are living at home with a parent or guardian and are picked up at their house by their caseworker. It can be frustrating relying on an undependable parent to make sure the child is available when the car arrives to transport the child. It is not unusual for a parent to forget the child needed to be there, or for no one to be at home; this can delay the arrival of the children and it ultimately shortens the time they will spend at the farm. Another challenge was that the children were often strangers to each other. They would meet for the first time when their caseworker would pick them up without any introductory interaction between the children. This resulted in excess anxiety and stress for the children. The case workers now set up a picnic in a central area and bring all of the children together for an informal "get to know you" gathering before their first trip to the farm. This has proven to be an effective way to ease some of the fears the children have about being with a group of strangers. Like all of the children, after their first visit any anxiety is quickly dispelled and subsequent trips are anticipated eagerly.

Visually impaired students take a closer look at recently planted seeds.

The children participate once a week for nine weeks. If the caseworker feels it will benefit the child and the child wants to, the child may come out for more than one nine-week session.

Volunteers usually meet before a nine-week session to plan projects that can be completed within this time period. Fast-growing flowers and vegetables are planted so the children can see the whole cycle of life. Toad houses and other habitat projects will be worked on and some type of animal lesson and interaction is planned for each week. Greens are always available to feed the farm animals. After snacks, food scraps are fed to the farm animals or placed in the worm bin or the compost pile. A circle is formed before the session ends and each person is allowed time to talk and share thoughts and feelings about the visit. This is a most valuable time for the children, as they are not asked very often about their likes and dislikes.

SONOMA COUNTY OFFICE OF EDUCATION

The children in this group are from the public school system's special program for the visually impaired. As with all the other groups, this group is comprised of children with a history of abuse and neglect. This group is a fairly new addition to our program and the children require some special attention. Most of these children have limited distance vision, so on their first visit a great deal of time is spent walking the entire garden and animal compound in detail so they are able to "see" everything. Much time is spent in the sensory gardens and there is a lot of hands-on with the animals. The Department of Education has also approved this weekly visit to be incorporated into the students' regular school curriculum.

Teachers accompany the children and the Office of Education provides transportation. This is also a group that meets for the first time at the farm site, with teachers coming from three different locations. The participants from this group range in age from 11 to 17. The structure and activities of this group during their nine weekly sessions are much the same as for the group from Sonoma County Mental Health Services.

OUTREACH LOCATIONS: A SPECIAL PLACE AND A CHILDREN'S PLACE

These are two therapeutic preschools operated by the YWCA for children who have experienced violence and victimization. Because of transportation limitations we now have volunteers who visit the children at their location each week, taking an animal to each school and introducing the children to the animal. The interaction and educational protocol between all animals and children is similar to those at the farm site.

In 1996 we trained high school seniors to visit the children's schools each week. These students went through the same orientation and training process as all other volunteers, and in addition received special training for their particular program. The program has proven to be very successful. This project was recognized by the high school as a community service program and the students are allowed to leave their school for four hours each week to participate. They drive to the Humane Society, pick up a preselected animal and proceed with their visit. The students provide their own transportation and take the animal with them. They take a wide variety of animals including pigs, goats, lambs, and opossums. Occasionally, they take bottle-fed orphan kittens and puppies, talking birds, or unusual animals housed at the Humane Society.

This project not only educates the children in the preschool but has proven to be of great value for the high school students. As a part of this community service project the students must do research, oral reports, and make a final presentation. This presentation is judged by a panel of peers, mentors, counselors, and parents; it also represents 20 percent of their semester grade in three classes.

This program is structured the same at both schools. There is a covered area outside where the animal is taken and the children are brought out in groups of four to learn about that particular animal. There is plenty of time for each child to interact with the animal and for questions to be answered. The high school students have noted that even at three years of age, some of the children have already developed abusive habits toward animals.

LA TACERA ELEMENTARY SCHOOL

This is a public school 15 miles from the Humane Society. Again, senior high school students, carefully selected and screened, volunteer to visit a special class of high-risk children. The class is a combination of first-, second-, and third-graders with only about eight students.

Once a week, two high-school students will visit a classroom with an animal. With such a small class size, it is not necessary to break into groups and presentations are done for the whole group for the entire hour. This allows plenty of time for presentation, questions and answers, and interaction time. It also allows the children plenty of time to tell their own animal stories. Many of these children have already witnessed animal abuse in their homes and this gives them a chance to share their stories in a safe environment with someone who cares about animals.

VOLUNTEERS

The volunteers for this program include master gardeners from the University of California Extension Service; members of the California Landscape Contractors Association; public school teachers; veterinarians; therapists; graduate students in psychology serving internships from nearby state, private, and community colleges; retired physicians; pet-assisted therapy volunteers with their dogs; and members of the community at large. Each volunteer is meticulously screened, interviewed, fingerprinted, and educated about the special needs and concerns of abused and neglected children. Ongoing training and workshops are provided on a regular basis.

Because many of the volunteers are retirees, they are like grandparents to the children, a fortunate relationship in two aspects. First, most of these children come from fragmented homes and may not have contact with grandparents. Second, parents do not see these older volunteers as rivals for the affection of their children and do not begrudge their children an afternoon of gardening and caring for animals with surrogate grandparents.

The best place to recruit volunteers is from areas where people are already working as volunteers; for instance, if your agency is a humane society or other animal care or nonprofit organization, you will probably have an existing pool of volunteers working in various capacities. They will already be familiar with your agency and its philosophy; they will have demonstrated a willingness to provide community service and will have a track record of attendance, attitude, commitment, and so on.

Public advertising for volunteers is discouraged for a number of reasons. Programs like this may attract people with inappropriate reasons for wanting to be around these high-risk children and the location of the farm should be kept as confidential as possible to insure the safety of the children and volunteers. An important question to include on your volunteer application would be, "Were you a victim of abuse and neglect as a child?" If the answer to that question is yes, you will need to find out what measures that person has taken in his or her own recovery process. This is not a program to heal adult victims; this is a program for healthy adults who want to teach children some basic animal husbandry and gardening with the hope that they will learn nurturing skills and a love for gardening, animals, and all living things to be used in their everyday lives. Forget Me Not Farm is a place where children are comfortable and safe.

Because instability is the hallmark of the lives of these children, every effort is made in the program to provide stability. Therefore, the same volunteers and pet-assisted therapy assistants come each week, and the farm animals live at the site as permanent residents. Volunteers must agree to at least a one-year commitment. The children develop specific attachments to favorite animals and adults, and these are encouraged with the aim of making the children feel successful in initiating and cultivating relationships. The children are prized and valued, and their specific charms and accomplishments are celebrated.

THE FUNDING

All funding for the program is from donations and grants. With the exception of the project coordinator, almost all of the project's needs, including time and supplies, are donated. The Humane Society made its facilities available and allowed the shelter manager to adjust her schedule to include the program. She, in turn, recruited and screened the volunteers, and persuaded local business people, service clubs, and nursery owners to donate goods and supplies; the National Guard was the first to clear and plow the field. The San Francisco Child Abuse Council donates training and consultation. A local, licensed counselor donates one evening a month to assist volunteers with problems or concerns regarding the children. Veterinarians from the community donate their services for the farm animals.

In 1995 the California Landscape Contractors Association developed a small park with a grassy knoll, six separate sensory gardens, a redwood grove, fruit trees, and an irrigation system for new and existing gardens. Small grants and individual donations have provided supplies for the garden and for the care of the farm animals beyond what was donated by local businesses. The shelter manager and executive director speak at local service clubs, resulting in financial and community support. One Rotary Club was so impressed by the program that they donated the money for a much-needed tractor. Several other service clubs continue to donate annually and invite the program coordinator back for updates.

The Forget Me Not Farm program is recognized by the Board of Education as a valuable class. With this recognition, grants are applied for and received from local businesses that might normally issue grants for educational programs in a more traditional school setting.

THE BENEFITS OF THE PROGRAM

The purpose of the Forget Me Not Farm program is to provide children from violent homes the opportunity to become a part of a nurturing series of relationships in which seeds grow into vegetables and flowers, animals grow into companions to be cared for and played with, and adults grow into trusted and protective guides to the life cycle.

Children who have been abused or witnessed abuse are often frightened of touch—worried if it will hurt or if they will get by safely. Thus, they lose a whole world of sensory information at their fingertips. At Forget Me Not Farm, the children dig in the dirt, sow seeds, separate roots for transplanting, feel the difference in the textures of the roots and leaves, smell the differences in their scents, and discover through transplanting that much goes on below ground as well as above. The children prepare the soil to be a welcoming new home for their plants, water and weed them, and watch them grow. They learn to handle these small seedlings with gentleness and respect for their fragility.

They learn about habitats and how to create a safe nurturing environment for wildlife, including caterpillars, ladybugs, butterflies, and wide assortment of frogs, insects, snakes, moles, and gophers. After looking through binoculars and identifying different birds, the children are taught which of the flowers will have nutrients for the birds and which of the birds will need food set out for them. When necessary, bird feeders are made by spreading peanut butter on pine cones and corn cobs and dipping them into wild bird seed. Children are taught that everyone has the right to be safe and cared for and they make every effort to see that all living things at the farm are cared for properly. For the first time, they are able to touch horses, pigs, goats, and opossums and show their surprise at the wiry hair of a pot bellied pig or the soft, warm fur of an opossum's pouch or the velvet ears and twitching nose of the resident bunny. The children learn that when approached gently, a llama does not spit and horses do not kick.

Compassion and empathy are learned through human interaction with and tending of the animals. A special opportunity arose when an orphan cow fell off a truck on the way to the auction yard. She was only about seven days old and needed someone to take care of her wounds from the fall, then to bottle-feed her for several months. The children gave her lots of attention and were given the opportunity to help with the feedings. For children whose homes have been disrupted and who live in a shelter, taking care of an orphaned and injured animal shows them that such problems are not insurmountable and can be overcome with affection and caring rather than with anger and rejection. The children named this gentle cow Daisy Mae; many thought she should be named Lucky, having escaped not only the horror of the auction yard but to end up in a place where she will be safe her entire life and surrounded by the love of many kind children and adults. Now, at 600 pounds, she

A visitor to Forget Me Not Farm meets and touches Daisy Mae for the first time.

likes nothing more than to lie in the shade and have the children stroke her neck or rest their heads on her side.

Another opportunity arose when a resident bunny, Petal Paws, was struck with a severe infection and, as a result of her illness, lost her appetite. The children were worried about her and were digging up the carrots they had planted to see if they could entice her to eat. She barely nibbled at the greens, until one six-year-old girl broke a carrot in half to show the bunny how sweet it was inside. There were smiles on all of their faces when the bunny started munching on the carrot, and the little girl knew she had helped nurture this animal back to health.

Because of the length of time the volunteers commit to the program, the children get to know them very well and feel safe in this environment. These children are often shifted from agency to agency within social services; often, coming to the farm is the only constant in their lives.

A sister and brother who first came to the farm as three- and four-year-olds are examples of what can happen. They were in a special therapeutic preschool and their mother was receiving mandatory counseling; the mother relapsed with her drinking and was incarcerated, not for the first time. The children were then sent to the county emergency shelter; however, amid the chaos and fear of being with strangers they still came to the farm once a week, not with the same group but they were with the same volunteers. These children then went into a recovery program when the mother had been released from jail and given an opportunity for rehabilitation and reunification with her children. At that time, the children had been visiting the farm for three years. When they arrived at the farm for the first time with their mother, the boy ran anxiously to the strawberry bed to pick a sweet berry for her. He was very proud to show her plants he had planted and cared for and animals he was feeding. She was able to meet the people who had been a constant in her children's tumultuous lives. She was not threatened by what they had taught her children; instead, she was anxious to work in the garden herself.

Recently, a student from our visually impaired class was removed from an abusive stepfather during the middle of the night. He is legally blind, and as he was whisked away from his home to the county emergency shelter he left his glasses in his bedroom. When he met the project coordinator eight days later, he was delighted to "see" a familiar face. Stunned to see him without his glasses, the coordinator spoke with his teacher, who did not know about his vision impairment. A business card was given to the teacher with his previous teacher's name and phone number and the slow process began to have his glasses returned. This process took almost 21 days. During that time, he continued to come to the farm and relax with trusted volunteers in a familiar environment.

Students have commented on how different their teachers are when removed from the classroom context. Teachers have noted the changes they see as the students interact with the animals. One teacher said, "I usually just see them in a classroom environment where we are not as free as we are here and I really enjoy what happens here with the kids and the animals and the gardens." Another commented, "I always enjoy watching different young people come and enjoy the flowers and planting things, and the wonderful volunteers that spend their time with the children. I really look forward to this visit every week because almost every single time we come, somebody has a real positive, happy experience."

Many of these children are rarely exposed to a "normal" world. They are in alternative schools; they live in group homes or shelters; their view of the world is somewhat tainted by years of abuse. Because of that abuse, they have no trust, no sense of the goodness of life, and no reverence for life; the places they live in and the people they live with are good until something bad happens. When the children arrive at the farm, they are exposed for the first time to "normal conditions." The children are treated with the kindness, love, and respect that all creatures deserve. They work side-by-side with mature adults, with no expectations other than to be kind while at the farm. They are exposed to normal relationships for the first time. It takes them a while to learn that nothing bad is going to happen. When they realize that, they can begin to build their own healthy relationships. They learn about reciprocal touch as they get acquainted with the farm animals and learn their likes and dislikes. It is an exciting moment for a child to realize he or she has made an animal happy simply by petting it or by taking the time to select the animal's favorite food. To have an aloof llama come up to the fence to greet you is quite an accomplishment; but this type of relationship takes time and patience. It is a lesson to the children that it is okay to take time to develop their own relationships, you do not have to trust someone the first time you meet them, and it is okay to be sure the relationship is going to be safe.

Children from abusive homes are resilient, and just one significant caring adult can make a difference in a child's life. The children visiting the farm are aware that the volunteers are different than many of the people in their chaotic lives. One 16-year-old student said, "What I like most about this place is that there are people willing to come here and work with us kids from group homes." What she did not say, but is certainly aware of, is that these are the only adults in her life who are not being paid to be with her. She lives in a group home where the staff receives a salary for their around-the-clock jobs, attends a school where teachers and counselors are being paid, and receives therapy or medical care where those caretakers are also paid. Often, the question is asked of our volunteers, "Do you get paid to be here with us?" When the response to that question is no, the students often inquire, "Why would you be willing to spend time with us if you aren't getting paid?" The answer is always the same: "Because we like you and like spending time with you, teaching you great things about gardens and animals." Just knowing that someone finally values them for who they are is very empowering for these children. One young girl, after working in the garden with one of the volunteers, said she did not know men could be so kind. We hope this experience will help her make healthy choices when entering into future relationships.

HOPES AND DREAMS

Humane societies are ideal sponsors of programs designed to intervene in the cycle of abuse. By teaching mastery of skills and empathy for other living things, they can instill in children and their parents the value of nurturance and gentleness. Through gardening and tending to animals in the company of capable and appropriate volunteers in a safe and relaxed setting, children learn that they are both worthy of care and capable of caring. When possible, including parents in the program should be encouraged. Because abuse and neglect is cyclical, oftentimes the parents are lacking these skills. Volunteers are discouraged when they think that children leaving the farm may be returning to an abusive or neglectful situation. The lessons learned at Forget Me Not Farm are not specific to children, but to persons of any age; a visiting mother learning how to comb and braid the pony's mane was able to go home and braid her daughter's hair for the first time without causing tears. She learned to be patient and to untangle the pony's hair gently, an experience that was easily transferred to her daughter.

Animal abuse may precede child abuse. If this cycle is not broken there will be another generation of abusers, victimizers and possibly serial killers. We have the potential to reduce the risk factors by intervening and teaching skills neglected by their parents. By offering programs like this around the country we have the opportunity to make and see changes.

The Humane Society of Sonoma County, in conjunction with the San Francisco Child Abuse Council and the San Francisco Department of Animal Care and Control, has hosted conferences entitled "Teaching Gentleness With Gardens And Animals To Children From Violent Homes And Communities." Participants have come from all over this country as well as from England. This gentleness program is being modeled in several states with a strong interest from England, Australia, Switzerland, and Germany.

In 1994, the Forget Me Not Farm program received the California Consortium to Prevent Child Abuse's Henry Bergh Award, honoring the organization exemplifying the spirit of innovation in promoting child abuse prevention, intervention, and treatment. That same year, volunteers were honored by the J. C. Penney Foundation for their commitment to a valuable community program. In 1995, the program coordinator received the Outstanding Technician of the Year award from the California Veterinary Medical Association. In 1996 the American Veterinary Medical Association awarded us their Humane Award in recognition of humane efforts on behalf of animals and exceptional compassion for the welfare of animals. The program has been recognized by the Chamber of Commerce as exemplifying the Spirit of Santa Rosa.

This is a community-based program funded by local businesses, organizations, and service clubs and staffed with caring volunteers. This program can be replicated in any community at very little cost to the administering organization.

People and Animals Learning
The PAL Program
Jill De Grave

SPANKY, THE one-year-old spaniel mix, was in trouble. The beautiful black and white dog was a bundle of undisciplined energy, she did not know the meaning of "sit," "stay," or "come." She was a stray, which may have been a final, intentional act by her previous owner. A concerned citizen brought her to the Wisconsin Humane Society and she was never claimed.

Otis, a fifth-grader attending a central-city school in Milwaukee, lacked motivation and maturity. Living in a neighborhood where drug deals, gang skirmishes, and human and animal abuse are not uncommon, Otis spent most of his time indoors. He had little choice; violence surrounded him. His teacher described him as quiet and sensitive but lacking in self-esteem. He loved animals, but his dog, Cherry, had been stolen from his backyard.

When Spanky and Otis met that summer six years ago, a friendship began that made a big difference in both of their lives. They met at the Wisconsin Humane Society while participating in the pilot program called PAL—People and Animals Learning. The program links central-city children, who may be involved in behaviors that would classify them as at-risk, with unwanted dogs and orphaned wild animals in a three-week training session. The experience gave Spanky the obedience training and socialization she needed to successfully adapt to a new home in upcoming months. Otis gained a sense of responsibility and self-respect. A letter from his teacher arrived at the Wisconsin Humane Society later that year. The teacher wrote, "You and Otis made my day, month, season, and school year. I'm sure that the program made this young man's self-concept and forthcoming year at Grand Avenue Middle School full of hope!"

Spanky was adopted into a loving home. Her new owner was so impressed with the fine job Otis did working with Spanky, she continued with training in a more advanced obedience class.

Since its start in 1993, the PAL Program continues to build self-esteem in young people and provide well-behaved, highly adoptable dogs for suitable, caring homes. During a three-week session of PAL, the youths are paired with formerly unwanted dogs at the Wisconsin Humane Society. Under the guidance of a professional trainer,

Dog training teaches the value of patience and hard work.

they train their dogs to respond to basic obedience commands. The children also are responsible for feeding and caring for orphaned and injured wildlife. Most importantly, they are taught to be neighborhood ambassadors of kindness toward animals.

WHY PAL?

In recent years, the Milwaukee area has seen an increase in the number of violent acts that children commit against animals. In 1993, several youths attacked a puppy named Hank, doused him with gasoline, threw him into a trash bin, and set him on fire. In another case, a kitten was placed on a lit barbecue grill. Yet another incident involved a golden retriever that was shot to death in his own fenced yard. Most recently, a group of children ages 8 to 11 were playing in the parking lot of a fast food restaurant while on their way to school. Witnesses inside the restaurant thought the children were kicking and tossing a toy. What appeared to be a toy was, in fact, a five-week-old kitten. The restaurant patrons were able to get the kitten away from the children, but it was too late. The kitten died on the way to the Wisconsin Humane Society.

Spurred by these incidences, my colleague Lynn Derr and I decided to do some-

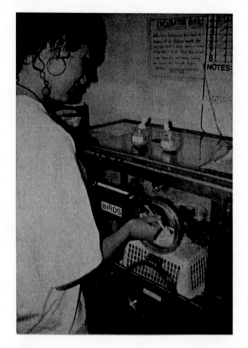

The PAL Program teaches central-city youth a
sense of responsibility and respect for life.

thing to curb the rise of violent acts committed by children against animals. We
formed an advisory board comprised of central-city teachers, a leader in sensitive
crime and child abuse, and a businessman heavily involved in community youth activities. Together, we laid the foundation of what was to become the PAL Program,
which was implemented in June 1993.

OUR GOALS

The PAL Program's mission is to teach at-risk youth about responsibility, accountability for actions, self-respect, respect for others, and respect for animals. It gives
children an opportunity to participate in positive, rewarding experiences where respect for themselves, other people, and animals is enforced. Through the program,
we promote trust and nurture friendships between children and animals.

By creating an environment that is both educational and fun, the PAL Program:

teaches children the importance and benefits of being kind to animals;
gives them the opportunity to learn the positive benefits of being responsible;
builds empathy for animals and people;
affirms the belief that each child has the power to succeed;

Young people develop self-esteem when they can
make a positive contribution.

develops a passion for excellence by focusing the children's energies on goal
achievement;
gives the children an opportunity to believe in themselves and develop self-esteem;
teaches respect by modeling and creating a reciprocal system of respect;
makes the children believe that they are valued for their contributions, and that
their achievements in the program are special and unique;
develops self-confidence, and gives the children consistent opportunities to take
control of a variety of situations in a responsible manner; and
places children in the role of nurturers and gives them the positive experience of
being needed.

The PAL Program also helps to create more adoptable dogs through obedience
training. Most of the dogs surrendered to the Wisconsin Humane Society lack obedience. The PAL Program provides the training necessary to create well-mannered
dogs that adapt well into their new adoptive homes upon completion of the program. PAL has become popular among potential adopters. Many of the dogs are
spoken for prior to completion of their training by the children. Nearly all of the
dogs are adopted on graduation day. In fact, interested adopters begin calling months
in advance of the summer program, inquiring about the canine PAL graduates.

PAL participants train the dogs to respond to basic obedience commands.

Furthermore, the PAL Program helps to fill the need for volunteer assistance in the Wisconsin Humane Society's wildlife rehabilitation program. Each year, 5,000 orphaned or injured urban wild animals require care. The PAL youth provide much-needed assistance in caring for hundreds of these animals each summer.

WHO IS ELIGIBLE FOR PAL?

The PAL program is designed for central-city children ages 10 to 13. Many of these children have been identified by their teacher or social worker as being at-risk. Those involved in PAL are living in neighborhoods challenged by single-parent homes, drugs, poverty, and glorified violence. Some are from stable family units, but the parents have little control over what activities take place in their neighborhoods. The challenges facing these families are immense.

Milwaukee area teachers are encouraged to nominate qualified students for the PAL Program. To promote interest, the Wisconsin Humane Society's Education Department schedules presentations during the school year in central-city schools for students in the upper elementary grades. These programs include PAL Program information and interactive dog training demonstrations. Throughout the presentations, students are encouraged to become animal advocates, spreading the kindness-

PALs are taught to be ambassadors of kindness toward animals.

to-animals message in their neighborhoods. These neighborhoods are not always a kind place for animals, as one PAL graduate, Lamar, explained: "Sometimes kids in my neighborhood are bad with animals; I don't know why. They take cats and swing them against walls. The other day a friend of mine found a bird and killed it with a stone. I said 'Man, why did you do that?' They don't know any better." The PAL Program aims at teaching the kids to know better, to help rather than hurt animals.

Each year, the Wisconsin Humane Society receives over 100 PAL nominations representing at least 20 schools in the Milwaukee area. Because program participation is limited to 20 children each summer, the selection process is difficult. We communicate closely with the nominating teachers to gain as much insight as possible into each child's personal situation. Also considered in the selection process is a short application form from each nominee. The program costs nothing to the children and bus transportation is provided.

Although PAL students represent a variety of neighborhoods across the greater Milwaukee area, they have a common thread: they are at an age where they are targets for gang recruiters and are determining their life's path. Low self-esteem, poverty, family problems, and glorified violence on the streets are common. But an interest in animals also abounds.

Erica, a PAL graduate, is an excellent example. Erica's fifth-grade teacher wrote

PALs present a demonstration about dog training to children at a
central-city day care facility.

on the nomination form, "Erica's mother has 'given her away.' Presently she is living
in a shelter. When I first got her as a student, she was loud and violent. I have discovered, however, that she's a very intelligent, funny, and sensitive child. This program was designed for her. She needs it." Erica wrote, "I am a person in need of care
and love, and I would care and love someone even if no one can care for or love me.
I am a nice person and I like for things to go the good way and not the bad way. I
want to be in PAL because I am missing something in my life and I need to fill it up
as full as I can with the love of animals. I think that my participation in PAL could
help others learn to respect animals as well as they respect people." Erica and her
canine, Molly the German shepherd mix, graduated from the PAL Program with a
new sense of hope for the future. A more self-confident Erica now lives with her
grandmother, and Molly was adopted into a caring family.

A HELPING HAND

The Wisconsin Humane Society conducts two sessions of the PAL Program each
summer. Each session lasts three weeks and meets Monday to Friday for three

hours. Ten children are accepted into each session of PAL. PAL participants are involved in a hands-on experience from day one.

The children meet the dogs they will be working with on the first day of the PAL Program. Each child works in partnership with another child for dog training. The dogs are preselected several weeks earlier. They are chosen on the basis of temperament and capacity to learn quickly. Each dog is inoculated, sterilized, and kept separate from the rest of the dog population at the shelter. Volunteers walk and socialize the dogs during the few weeks leading up to the start of the session. No dog is too large or small for the PAL Program. Dog breeds have ranged in size from a petite Pomeranian to a giant schnauzer.

Obedience training begins the moment the PAL students meet their dogs. After the initial introduction, which usually involves a combination of excitement and apprehension, the children begin calming techniques and attention-getting exercises. They learn how dogs think and why they act as they do. Over the next three weeks, they see a transformation in the dogs—from out-of-control to obedient. They look forward to seeing their dogs each day, and the dogs reciprocate that excitement by bounding straight to their junior handlers when they enter the training room. The dogs learn basic manners, like heeling on leash at their handler's left side. Under the guidance of a professional dog trainer, the children also teach their dogs to sit and stay on command, and come when called. These behaviors will help these companion animals find a permanent home in the weeks that lie ahead.

But the dogs are not the only ones who are learning. From working with the dogs and modeling the adults' behavior, the children are learning as well, which is the key to the success of the PAL Program. They are learning patience, perseverance, self-control, cooperation, how to deal with frustration, and the positive benefits of acting responsibly. They learn that kind actions obtain better results than harsh ones. The children are not simply taking care of these dogs, they assume teaching responsibilities. They experience the joy of achievement every step of the way. There is a mutual respect between dog and child, and as the days pass, the bond becomes even stronger.

At the end of the three-week training program, PAL students and their canines visit a local, central-city day care facility. There, the PALs present a talk and demonstration about dog training to the day care children. After the formal presentations, the day care children are invited to pet the dogs and talk with PAL students. It is an impressive day. The PAL children realize just how important and successful their hard work has been. It is a day of pride and high self-esteem.

Each day during the three weeks of PAL, the children spend time in the Wisconsin Humane Society's wildlife rehabilitation department. Here, they help the staff care for injured and orphaned birds and ducks. Food preparation, feeding, weighing, and cage cleaning are all important duties in caring for wildlife. The time spent in the wildlife rehabilitation center are hours of nurturing and caring for small, helpless creatures. Children must carefully heat a special blend of food and gently feed each tiny bird with a coffee stir stick. When the bird is reluctant to eat, the child must softly tap the side of the bird's beak, just like the mother bird would do, and encourage the little one to open wide for the next mouthful. It can be a tedious process that transforms even the toughest of kids into gentle beings. All feedings and cleanings are noted on charts to keep track of each creature's health and growth progress. The birds and ducks grow quickly and many are released back to the wild throughout the three weeks of PAL. It is a rewarding experience for PAL participants to see a bird they have cared for take its flight to freedom at last.

At the close of each day, PAL children are encouraged to write in their journals. It is a time for them to record their day's activities and accomplishments, and for most, a time to share their innermost feelings about their dogs and their personal successes with the PAL Program. Examples:

> "It was a great day in training. Jake sat when I told him!"
>
> "Today Barney looked sad. I don't know why, but he just didn't look right. I hope there isn't nothing wrong with him. I can't wait till my mom sees him because I want her to adopt him because he's sweet and I love him very, very, very, very much."
>
> "Today was the first day at PAL. I had the time of my life!"
>
> "These weeks have been very hard lately. This program is one of the best things that can happen. I have never had anything as wonderful as this."

A formal PAL graduation is held on the last day of each session. It is an exciting time for the PAL graduates, but also a time of sadness. This is the day when each child will say farewell to the dog that has become a close companion for the past few weeks. It also is the last time that each child will run out to catch the bus headed for the Humane Society. Many people attend the formal graduation ceremony, including Wisconsin Humane Society staff and volunteers, parents and siblings of the graduates, teachers, and even the families that are adopting the canine graduates. At the ceremony, the graduates present a demonstration with their dogs. They also receive an official certificate of graduation. Now it is time for the children to say a final good-bye to the dogs. Hugs, kisses, tears, and the words "I'll never forget you" are flowing. Afterwards, the group enjoys a feast of special treats that are provided by the children and the staff and volunteers of the PAL Program. After the celebration, the graduates must board the bus for the trip back home. As the bus leaves the Humane Society parking lot one last time, we are all left with a sense of hope for the future of the children and the animals in our community thanks to the PAL Program.

OUR SUCCESS

The cornerstone of the pyramid to success is expectations. The expectations for PAL children are high. We expect each child to become outstanding. We provide the tools and training to reach their goals. We focus on success and guide the children every step of the way to personal achievement.

Regular attendance is vital to the success of PAL. Absenteeism is kept to a minimum because of the provided transportation and our very strict attendance rules. Children are allowed only three absences before dismissal from the program. A lengthy waiting list allows us to quickly replace a child who does not comply with the expectations. The PAL students look forward to working with their dogs and caring for the wildlife and make every effort to attend the program each day. In fact, most are disappointed that they cannot attend on weekends.

In addition to regular attendance, the expectations for PAL are based on the philosophy that a successful PAL

will remember that my word is my bond (a commitment to the animals, program, and peers);
will be attentive when others are speaking;
will respect peers and activity leaders; and
will treat animals with respect.

These expectations are recited each morning.

Another ingredient to the success of the PAL Program is the continued involvement of the Milwaukee-area teachers. We keep in close contact with the teachers throughout the program. Some of the teachers have begun volunteering for PAL and others make periodic visits to check on their students during the session. Many attend the graduation ceremony. Teacher support is extremely meaningful for the children. They are very excited each time their teachers visit; it is another vote of confidence in them.

In PAL, we focus on making the experience a fun and rewarding one for the children. We teach respect rather than obedience. And we expect that everyone involved in the program treat both animals and people with respect. So often, kids hear things like, "If you are going to behave that way, you don't belong here." The PAL Program provides an environment where children belong, where they achieve, are given the independence to act responsibly, and are recognized for their success. This environment gives even the most apprehensive and hard- to-reach child the opportunity to experience the joy of achievement.

A DOG OBEDIENCE INSTRUCTOR'S PERSPECTIVE

Kathryn Haydon is a dog obedience instructor and trainer for the PAL Program. She helped to develop the training curriculum.

"The mechanics of teaching obedience training is easy enough; the real challenges and opportunities lie in relating the training and subsequent interaction between children and dogs to constructive attitudes toward life and toward other living beings.

"At the beginning of each PAL session I tell the children that the dogs they will be training are unwanted and unloved. Instead of teaching the dogs good behaviors, the owners have abandoned them. Since many of these children come from families whose severe problems preclude giving love and attention to one another, the children understand this all too well. They are immediately empathetic to the dogs. In addition, I tell them that they have the power to change things for the dogs and give them a chance to live happily ever after. I point out that these dogs may not have another chance unless we cure their problems with training. Therefore, the children's clear mission is to work very hard to teach these dogs well so that they will become pleasant companions for those who adopt them.

"Training dogs teaches the value of patience and careful repetition. The children can see the changes in the dogs as the weeks go by and know that they created those changes. The dogs quickly become attached to their trainers, reinforcing for the children the positive effects of discipline and hard work. Training also provides wonderful opportunities for teaching positive attitudes and constructive ways of thinking. For instance, half way through each session, I tell the children that all dogs are different; some are beautiful, some are not and some are appealing and some are not. But each dog has something good about him, just as people do. I ask the children to think hard about the dog each is training between now and the next day and to be ready to tell me what things they like best about the dog. The next day when each child has told what he most likes about his dog, I ask them if they would like to have other people look for the good in them. Not all people can be smart or athletic or thin or good-looking or tall, but each person (like every dog) has good qualities if we just look for them.

"One morning two boys were whispering together during their break. As I approached, one asked me if I could answer a question for them. The question was: 'Do dogs rape one another?' One youngster said they did; the other said they didn't. Thinking that they were trying to get a reaction from me, I quickly answered, 'No, they don't,' and moved away. That night I thought long and hard about the question and the hasty answer I had given. Since rape is a very real part of the harsh and violent world in which these children live, I concluded that they deserved more of an answer than I had given. As I faced the children the following day, this is what I said: 'Yesterday I was asked a question and gave a quick answer. The question was: Do dogs rape? My answer was: No. Although that is the right answer, I want to say more about it. Male dogs are interested in sex only when they smell the scent of a female who is in season. The female will only accept a male when she is in the most fertile time of her season. All other times, she will reject his attempt to mount her by sitting down. The male will accept this unwillingness. He will not force himself on her. Rape is an ugly act that is peculiar to human beings. Dogs are better than that. They have more respect for one another than to do anything like that.'

"The affection these children show toward those of us who work with them is profoundly touching. One day I was at the local festival grounds waiting with my dogs for a program in which they were to perform, when suddenly I heard someone excitedly calling my name. Out of the crowd, a boy hurled himself at me. He threw his arms around me and it was only then that I recognized Hector, who had been in the PAL Program the previous summer.

"The children are so proud of their accomplishments in PAL—even learning-disabled children can be successful. Antoine is one. He could hardly wait until his group presented their program with their dogs to a day care center and to an audience at graduation. After his first fine demonstration, which impressed the group of day care workers and children, he excitedly ran to me and said, 'I did a good job, didn't I?!' His joyful, sparkling eyes said it all.

"Children need to understand that they have something significant to contribute and they need to learn to be focused on a specific goal. PAL provides this understanding and it allows them to be recognized as important individuals. It also shows them that they can set goals and reach them. Yes, one person *can* make a difference. I know that these children will never forget me and many of the things I've taught them. Their important experiences in PAL will stay with them for life."

A TEACHER'S PERSPECTIVE

Robin Denison Squier is a fifth-grade teacher at Westside Academy II School in Milwaukee. She is a member of the PAL Advisory Board:

"My interest in the PAL Program began with a student. She had been in my class for two months, and I had yet to see her smile, talk to her classmates, or show any interest in her class work. She was totally passive and cut off from her classmates. I had not been able to contact any parent and when I talked to her, trying to establish some connection, she was polite but revealed nothing. She seemed to have learned at a very early age not to trust anyone.

"The beginning of a change came when I brought my black Labrador retriever, Shady, to school for the day. I told my students they could come up one by one to pet her when they had finished their work. I was at my desk when the student came up. She turned in her paper and then knelt down to sit next to Shady. I froze and watched out of the corner of my eye. Shady sat up and licked the student's hand, and then her face. The student leaned in and hugged Shady and began to talk. I sat there quietly and learned a great deal about the student that day; Shady gave me a doorway to the girl's life.

"When the Humane Society talked to me about their idea of the PAL Program I thought of that experience and marveled at how the PAL Program could magnify that experience one hundred times. All children would benefit from the program, for it gives children a chance to see the mark they can make on the world. They become empowered and responsible, perhaps for the first time in their life. They see their caring, patience, and determination change a wild and undisciplined dog to a well-trained companion. They watch as the wild animals they have cared for thrive and are finally returned to the wild.

"The program has the biggest impact, however, on children who have always presented an aggressive or passive face to the world . . . the children who tense up or wall off when an adult speaks to them. The children who think that there is nothing you can do, and nothing you can say that will truly make a difference in their life. The children who have already given up on the adult world—feeling that they have seen it all and heard it all before and nothing ever changes, or the child who has not found something to care about or believe in. The dog's love and trust, and the young nestling's constant and loud needs slip right through a child's defenses. The child finds a connection with the world, a chance to truly love and trust without risk, and feel the love and trust reciprocated. In short, the PAL Program takes the moment Shady provided, and expands it into a three-week program where children learn to love their animal, learn the discipline and patience needed to truly care for the animal. They learn that with effort and caring, they can bring about positive change, that with work, dreams can come true. As a teacher, this program is irreplaceable. My wish is that all children had the opportunity to experience it."

A PAL GRADUATE'S PERSPECTIVE

Ermamarie is 16 years old and is a PAL graduate:

"*Cruelty:* Once I saw a girl call her dog, and the dog was young. The dog didn't come when she called so she hit the dog with her leather jacket; I heard the dog cry out and I wanted to get the dog but I know she could call the police on me for trespassing. People have kicked their pets as though they had no feelings. Children throw rocks at birds and other small animals. People lock up animals and leave them in the cold all day and night. I've seen adults brag about their dogs, and yet not feed them enough, and when they feed them, it's food that sits in the dish until it's hard, dried up, or frozen, and yet they say they care. There have been times when I've seen people push their dogs into fighting one another and laugh about whose dog is the toughest. The dogs try to avoid each other but their owners keep pulling them and cursing them until they fight. They don't want them to stop until one can't get up and is bloody.

"*Pets Give You:* Pets give you a feeling of comfort. It's easy for you to communicate with them; it's like they feel what you feel. They make you smile even when you don't feel like smiling; they calm you when you're angry. Pets give you a good feeling about yourself, you can do it, you're not too little, you matter, and you can be good at caring for them, and be responsible, a real feeling of accomplishment.

"*You Can Give Pets:* We can all give pets a warm place in our hearts and show them love. You can give them a feeling that they belong and that they matter to us.

"*PAL:* I've always liked animals but I never knew how important it is to think of how an animal feels. PAL has helped me to appreciate animals more. From the things I did and saw I know you can train just about any dog to be obedient without yelling and hitting. I've learned that having a pet is a responsibility, you must care for it. I've learned to discipline in a loving way. When I see how people treat animals it can sometimes make you want to give up, but I know that these animals need my help and I don't want to let them down. Ever since my experience in PAL I am determined to become a veterinarian and I am working toward that goal. I try to be kind to all animals.

"As I was growing up I always wanted to kick a dog or throw things at animals because people used to tell me that animals don't have feelings, but I know that wasn't true. This PAL Program has helped me see that I don't have to be like everyone else. When I was in PAL I remember holding and feeding a little helpless bird and it made me want to do all I could to help him survive and get strong enough to make it on his own. I feel this way about all animals today."

Since its inception in 1993, the PAL Program has graduated 150 students and 65 dogs. The summer program has a solid future and the Wisconsin Humane Society is currently developing a similar program to be conducted within the schools during the school year.

Kids and Critters
An Intervention to Violence
Dick Dillman

IT IS APPARENT that violence is escalating at an alarming rate in our society. One only has to observe the trends in movies, television, children's toys, and sports to understand why our children are so negatively influenced. All these facets of children's lives greatly influence the development of their personalities, moral values, and personal success. The violent scenes in movies and television, marketing of toy guns and "tough guy" dolls, and the fighting among sport "heroes" in a game sends the message that violence is appropriate. By allowing this behavior to continue, the moral standards of our youth are jeopardized. Add the fact that the wholesome family unit is not as common as it was in past generations, and we can readily see why children are having a hard time maturing.

I have been working with inner-city disadvantaged elementary school children in Miami, Florida, for the past 12 years. The programs that we developed in the schools use companion animals and nature to encourage active participation. Although academics are important, the main idea of the programs is to emphasize values such as respect, responsibility, trust, and sensitivity. It has become increasingly clear to me that pleasant interactions between children, animals, and compassionate adults are a magnificent way to impress young children that violence is not acceptable.

In this essay, I emphasize three main points in working with children:

1. Let them be children!
2. Children's needs are basic.
3. Programs and concepts involving animals can teach children compassion.

By understanding what children need and how animals can greatly influence their lives, we can initiate school programs and curricula that will intervene in any tendency for a child to become a violent person.

THE ENERGY OF CHILDHOOD

It has been said that the average child laughs aloud about 300 times a day—an adult approximately 15. Why then do adults too often try to structure children's lives so

424

they may accelerate into adulthood at the fastest rate possible? As a society, we probably do not do this on purpose, but it is all too common. The natural and instinctive behavioral patterns of children are often sacrificed for disciplines that are more convenient for the adults. Children laughing and screaming with glee in a playground are asked to be quiet because it disturbs us. Two boys wrestling in fun are told to quit because it may dirty their clothes. Human play is analogous to a litter of wild wolf pups wrestling, playing, growling, and making dirt fly. Such behavior is as essential to the socialization and physical development of the wolf pups as is it for children.

Just watch normal children of elementary school age in a playground or recreational setting and it is apparent that their energy level is enormous. They don't walk when they can run. Screaming and yelling are preferred over speaking softly. That is all good—it is normal and absolutely necessary for healthy childhood development. Children vigorously participating in play are exercising and toning their bodies for the physical demands of life. Play is the dominant social activity for children as they mature from infancy to puberty. At puberty, a child's physical and mental development gets all out of whack when the hormones take over, and play becomes secondary to personal and sexual identity. It is very important that we, as adults, be responsible for our children's early development and use creative ways to incorporate play into education, teaching of social values, and promoting positive self-esteem.

It has been said that nothing is certain except death and taxes. The fascination children have for animals is also a certainty. Children may show their fascination in different ways. Generally, there is a strong desire to interact with animals in a way that is stimulating and fulfilling. Usually, we know what to expect when a child can play with a puppy, kitten, baby duck, or any other cuddly creature; joy, laughter, and curiosity will prevail. Granted, some interactions with animals may elicit fear, intimidation, or anxiety in a child, but these learned attitudes can readily be overcome by appealing to the intrinsic fascination of animals within each person. Opportunities for the child to interact with animals in a pleasant, nonthreatening manner can convert the feelings of fear or intimidation into respect and love. This simple concept allows us to develop programs that can be tremendously educational and therapeutic.

LEARNING ABOUT ANIMALS

The variety of responses that children exhibit in regard to animals is largely due to learned experiences in childhood and to instinctive fascination. The child who naturally loves to cuddle a bunny or a puppy may also believe that all snakes are horrible and should be feared. He learned about snakes as a child from his parents who hate them, from movies that depict their aggressive attitude, from "old wives' tales," or from all of the above. Persons raised in the city who have never visited a farm would likely be intimidated by a horse, bull, or even a goat. This was the case for inner-city, elementary school children participating in a Miami-Dade County, Florida, Public Schools farm program. But almost without exception, the students would ultimately succumb to their natural fascination when they were allowed to interact with the animals in a relaxed manner.

Bumper is a Brahma-mix steer who was orphaned and bottle fed as a calf by school children. He became bonded to children and is as sweet a kitten. Bumper weighs 1,880 pounds. This alone might be intimidating to a 70-pound fourth grader. Students who would not even approach him at the start of the school year eventually competed for the opportunity to brush him, comb his tail, pick sand-burrs from his feet, and wash away tears that occasionally stain his face.

A small child must learn that little critters like lizards, toads, frogs, butterflies, and beetles are significant in our lives. Teaching this in the classroom or on nature walks can provide an exercise in personal compassion. By linking this with other lessons in human-animal interactions, children will ultimately develop a respect and sensitivity for living creatures that reflect to their associations with people.

The use of animals in the classroom, in the outdoors, or in farm programs has proven to be a great tool in developing motivation. Most of these programs have originated through innovative private organizations or individual teachers. The beauty of these programs is that all students may benefit—from the gifted to the learning-disabled.

In 1986, the Miami-Dade County Public School System initiated a farm program to address the personal and academic needs of elementary school children who were identified as potential dropouts. The Animal Companion Science Program utilized a beautiful farm maintained by the county Parks and Recreation Department. Two hundred and seventy children from eighteen elementary schools were bused to the farm each week. Each student remained in the program for the full school year and was exposed to hands-on, personal experiences with farm animals such as horses, cows, sheep, goats, chickens, and pigs. In the classroom, the children would interact with resident rabbits, gerbils, turtles, frogs, doves, and snakes. All animals were selected for their ability to interact with the students in a relaxed and trustworthy way.

Simple is best! Although serious efforts went into program organization, there was a strong attempt to avoid a too rigid academic structure. This philosophy proved to be great for the youngsters. It also demanded that teachers and volunteers be very creative in the way they used the concept as an educational and motivational program.

THE VALUE OF ANIMALS

What is it that animals can provide that is so special? First, we must recognize what is necessary in children's lives that will allow them to develop positive self-concepts and reach their potential. All children need unconditional love. This is the love that is shown to a child for who they are and not for what they do. When children are judged only by their accomplishments, they feel they have to earn love. A frisky dog, a playful kitten, or a cuddly rabbit can provide unconditional attention and love when allowed to interact. Even a horse that allows a child to ride and control his movements is unconditionally accepting the association. The animals will show a regard for the child that does not differentiate between physical appearance, race, religion, or even personal accomplishments.

Very important in all children's development is to have achievements they experience themselves—real accomplishments. When a youngster learns to ride a bicycle or swim, it is not necessary to tell the child that he or she did well. The accomplishment is obvious when the child reaches the goal. Using animals to help children set realistic goals is a pleasant and effective way to bolster their ability to feel good about their achievements. The child who learns to love a pet, train a dog, ride a horse, or even overcome a fear of an animal will experience a personal real accomplishment.

Psychologists are striving to understand and guide children into all the benefits of being an adult. But if children laugh 300 times a day and adults just 15, maybe we may need to appreciate what a joy it could be if we were more like the children. The kitten that plays repeatedly with a child who offers a wiggly string is in line with what that child really needs to appreciate the joy of life. A dog that playfully retrieves a ball thrown by a youngster is endorsing the mutual need to frolic and be happy. That's what children need to do—frolic and be happy!

Too often, children receive messages from adults that are negative or directive. "You're too lazy," or "Sit in your seat and don't talk." Much of what children hear at home or in school is either correcting or instructing. It is not realistic to think that all feedback can be positive, but positive reinforcement should be a constant factor in a child's life. Simple remarks such as, "Good job," or "That's a great answer," can have a profound positive effect on a youngster if repeated enough with compassion. In working with children, the results of positive reinforcement can readily be monitored by the smiles on their faces and the glee in their actions. A tail-wagging dog that wants to play with a child says, "You're nice and lots of fun." A thousand-pound horse that allows a child to ride and control him says, "You are in control and let's have some fun." All of this adds to the positive reinforcement that is so essential in the development of an individual needing positive self-esteem.

POSITIVE REINFORCEMENT

Positive reinforcement is more a sensitivity than a technique. It is the feeling and understanding of how a certain action can elicit a favorable response from a youngster. These actions do not always have to be profound. Subtle remarks in the classroom like, "I like your thinking," or, "You've been doing well lately," can really boost a child's attitude and lead to enthusiastic participation.

Sometimes positive reinforcement can come in the form of not saying or doing anything about a situation. On a class nature walk a student can easily get his sneakers soaked by slipping into the pond while chasing a frog. Now, what really did the child do wrong? One response by the teacher may be to verbally reprimand the youngster. If nothing is said, the child will know that he didn't do anything really badly. After all, it was the school activity that set up the possibility for this to happen.

Another form of positive reinforcement can be in the form of physical contact. It is a shame, but in this day and age a person must be careful of the circumstances in which physical contact may be utilized as reinforcement. A most natural thing to do in our society is to shake hands, pat on the back, hug, or kiss. I feel if any of this display of affection is done with discretion and in the witness of colleagues or others, it is appropriate. Personal contact with a child, in the child's eyes, individualizes your interest or concern for him or her.

Children can be devils sometimes, and they may be hard to understand. But if we realize that basically the child wants to be loved and respected, it gives us the basis for providing positive reinforcement. It is often too easy to yell at some youngsters when they get out of line. Of course, sometimes this is necessary. If this is blended with a pat on the back, hug, or even a smile, the child will make the distinction between being "bad" or just making a mistake. Simply allowing children to do kid things rather than do it the "adult" way will reinforce their confidence. Let a child play and get dirty. Little girls can play ball or go fishing, and it is alright for little boys to play with dolls or cry when they get hurt.

A child can spot a phony quite easily. Praises given haphazardly will not have the same impact as those that come from the heart. We may not deliberately want to act insincere, but we may do so out of improper experience or training. It is imperative that we understand children's needs and nurture a sincere compassion for them.

Unfortunately, all too many of our youths are deprived of adequate love and nurturing by the time they reach kindergarten. These children I term "disadvantaged," because the basic needs of unconditional love and respect are often not present in their young lives. These youngsters fall into a number of categories: physically or sexually abused, neglected, academically low, low self-esteem, or a feeling of hopelessness. As these children progress through elementary school, their personal handicaps challenge the school teachers to provide guidance and an education. With classroom overcrowding and budgets for education inadequate, it makes the challenge overwhelming. School systems stubbornly adhering to outdated concepts of education further complicate this dilemma. Too often the new and innovative programs only reach a small number of students and are not incorporated into the general curriculum.

From the beginning of children's first elementary school days, they are tested, evaluated, and graded. Unfortunately, at this point, they are also often labeled. Academically they are classified as smart, fairly smart, average, or dumb. Personally they may be classified as nice, normal, bad, or disturbed. If certain academic criteria are met, the child can progress to the next level of achievement. Ultimate achievements for the high school graduate would be to have become very knowledgeable in science, proficient in algebra and geometry, able to speak a foreign language, and be very articulate. But what if a first or second grader is not considered "smart" or not even "average?" What if that youngster's personal stress, low self-esteem or delayed maturity—not the fact that he or she is not smart—is preventing the accepted academic achievement? At this point, failing the student, repeating the grade level, and classifying him or her as academically low would be the worst thing that could be done for that child's personal development. These acts will reinforce a child's low self-esteem and feeling of hopelessness. Children who are convinced that they are dumb will have no confidence in their further commitment to academics.

Once teachers judge students incapable of learning complex facts, they are not motivated to teach the children what is essential for their development. This sends messages to the youngsters that teaches them to view themselves as dumb. Such a self-concept will devastate their self-esteem and discourage their commitment to learning. This syndrome often shows up early in the primary grades.

"Smart" is not something children are born with, or have it or they don't, or something that they just are. Smart is simply something that a child can learn! Jeff Howard, in a paper presented for the National Urban League, offers an opinion that he believes is critical to children's academic success: "If you believe in yourself, if you think you can, then you will be able to work hard at what you are trying to learn. And if you work hard . . . you will learn." Is this concept divorced from classroom reality? No, it is the key to all successful teaching and learning. Make children feel good about themselves, provide a stimulating and fun curriculum, eliminate the feeling of hopelessness with positive reinforcement, and the student will "learn to be smart."

I have the greatest respect for the teaching profession, and there is no question that a good teacher is a true professional. As a school volunteer and a program consultant for public schools, I realized what a challenge it is to address the many individual needs of the students. The teachers whom I have worked with in new and innovative companion animal programs demonstrated a great amount of enthusiasm and creativity. When their administrators allowed them the freedom to create, I saw professionalism at its best. Very few children are congenitally deficient in intellectual ability; most are more than intelligent enough to learn if we learn to teach them.

Nancy Gilbert is a good friend of mine and a trainer in the Exotic Animal Show at Miami Metro Zoo. The animals in the show are raised and handled much the way a child would be raised in a loving family. This is done so that the critters will not be stressed when presented to the audience. Nancy had three clouded leopards at her house going through the bonding process. My wife and I were invited to come over and visit with the kittens. I did not know what to expect when the bathroom door was opened to allow the little guys to come into the bedroom. It immediately became evident that four-month-old baby leopards do not have a serious thought in their heads. They jumped on the bed, climbed up on the dresser top, scaled up to the handlebars of an exercise bike, and proceeded to do flying leaps all around the room. The human torso was not exempt from their playful attacks. A wadded sock tied to a string on the end of a fishing pole was used as a lure to get these characters to play "predator." Even a fuzzy teddy bear was not safe from the kittens' claws and teeth. After the better part of an hour of uninhibited play, the kittens stopped playing, laid down, and fell asleep in our laps.

Nancy explained that clouded leopards are arboreal and nocturnal. As adults they hunt in trees at night for other predators and mammals. They will jump on their prey and knock it to the ground. Everything these youngsters did that evening was a lesson in survival and socialization. They were playing hard to learn!

In some respects our children's needs are analogous to those of the leopard kittens to play and learn. It is generally accepted that pre-kindergarten and kindergarten youngsters need much play in their school curriculum; however, as the students progress in elementary school levels, play is rapidly replaced by structured disciplines. Too often, the teaching process deviates from the normal tendencies of child behavior to the stress of personal restraint. It is not natural for small children to sit still and rigidly adhere to rules that inhibit their normal impulses for a whole school day. I am a firm believer of discipline, but rules of conduct can easily be enforced even if the youngsters are allowed to act just like kids.

THE COMPANION ANIMAL FARM PROGRAM

The children involved in our Companion Animal Farm Program exhibit their most basic impulses when they interact with the animals on the farm. All of them laugh and giggle. Most of them pet and cuddle. Some are reluctant to handle the animals. Occasionally a child may be aggressive or mean to an animal, and this is not tolerated. Moral values of respect, responsibility, trust, and sensitivity are continuously emphasized and any deviation from these values elicits discipline. However, two things must be considered when taking disciplinary action. One is that reference to the incident must be directed toward the reasons why such action was bad rather than that the child was a bad person. The other is that the incident be viewed as an opportunity to teach rather than belittle. A change in facial and voice mannerisms, expression of concern for the animal, and an appeal to the child's intrinsic sensitivity almost always changes an aggressive act into a learned lesson in respect.

The Animal Companion Science Program is a magnificent example of incorporating play into classroom lessons for fourth and fifth graders. This starts when the students are escorted by the teachers and aide from the bus into the classroom. This is a time for adult-child interaction. Pleasant greetings, conversation, "high fives," and the occasional hug are exchanged. In the classroom, the children engage in activities that teach about science and animals, and associate with the resident rabbit, gerbils, cockatiel, or snake. They are then oriented to the rules and values that are expected of them as they participate in the outdoor activities. The children proceed to the barnyard for people-pet bonding with an assortment of farm animals. Structured academics are put on hold while we tap their enthusiasm as they feed, groom, pet, or converse with the animals. When the students get the chance to witness a calf, lamb, or baby goat being born, a lesson in reproduction and birth is initiated right there in the barn. A mother hen and her chicks represents a great lesson in responsible parenting. Overcoming the fear of a horse or bull will provide a personal real accomplishment for a child, and that opens the door for the adults to congratulate and offer positive reinforcement.

After the barnyard experience, the children may be taken on a nature walk in the nearby woods. Rolling over a dead log to expose beetles, centipedes, scorpions, and ants elicits a basic course in entomology. The enthusiasm and appreciation by the adults of these natural things soon generate similar enthusiasm in the youngsters. The children are not allowed to hurt any living creatures or damage any plant life. These valuable lessons in respect and sensitivity will carry over in their association with each other.

A child who comes to school after being abused or humiliated will not be ready to learn. Classroom tension may further depress the youngster. Providing special attention for this child may reverse a feeling of despair into happiness. One way this can be accomplished is to let the child interact with an animal that will give unconditional love. Allow the youngster to cuddle a rabbit, or help clean and care for the gerbils, or attempt to teach the parrot some new words and you will have a child who forgets her or his problems. When the mood changes, it is the ideal time to provide as much positive reinforcement as possible.

One good way for a school to provide these opportunities would be to have a well-organized animal room with specially selected animals that will enjoy the interaction. The care and cleaning of the animals can be delegated to the students. They will love it. A comfortable lounge area will allow a child to relax with an animal, and the area would also be a great place for counseling. Selection of special animals and veterinary care can readily be solicited from local veterinarians who would be pleased to help the kids out.

Over the years, I have had the privilege of working with children in need of special attention, and my enthusiasm continues to increase as I see what a beautiful effect this concept of education has on the children. All of society be must be involved in the welfare of our children. The concern utmost in my mind is that the basic natural needs of children should be the greatest influences in determining educational reform. All children are born with the same innocence and basic needs. As they grow, their lives are changed by parental attention, cultural differences, prejudices, health, economic status, and other social influences. For those children who do not have the love and respect that they need, other people must compassionately assume the responsibility of nurturing them very early in their development.

These basic needs are not complicated and are easily identifiable—unconditional love, respect, and guidance. If kids have these factors in their lives, they will mature into compassionate adults. As adults, we must remember what it was like to be a child and realize that children act the way they do for good reasons. It is absolutely necessary for us to realize that children must be children first before they can become functioning adults. We must love the children, teach the children, guide the children, and always remember: First, let them be children!

Animal-Assisted Therapy for Sexually Abused Adolescent Females
The Program at Crossroads

Kelly B. Roseberry and Laurie Morstein Rovin

THE RELATIONSHIP BETWEEN children and animals has its origins deep in history. Adults often reminisce about childhood pets that they once dearly loved. Animals facilitate the expression of feelings, and animals aid human healing (Arkow 1998). Healing offers abused children the power to grow emotionally and to face life's daily stressors.

The use of animals during therapeutic interventions assists clinicians in teaching clients how to cope with their feelings. Development of coping strategies enables recognition of problem behaviors, and in turn, allows development of insight necessary to correct maladaptive behaviors. Animal-assisted therapy (AAT) and animal-assisted activities (AAA) are key interventions implemented at Crossroads Group Homes, in Greenville, South Carolina, to aid in the facilitation of recovery from childhood sexual abuse.

In 1995, over 1,000,000 children were victims of substantiated or indicated child abuse and neglect; 2,000,000 reports were filed alleging the maltreatment of almost 3,000,000 children. Some 25 percent of these victims suffered physical abuse, and 13 percent experienced sexual abuse. More than 21,000 cases of child abuse are reported, and more than 6,400 are substantiated, annually in South Carolina (U.S. Department of Health and Human Services 1997). Many of these children and adolescents are placed into alternate care facilities such as foster homes, residential treatment facilities, or group care centers.

Crossroads' treatment for this special-needs population of abuse victims includes AAT and AAA. Animal-assisted activities are conducted by specially trained professionals, paraprofessionals, and volunteer staff who use trained animals that meet specific criteria. These activities give clients an opportunity to interact spontaneously with the therapy animals and other group members. The activities do not necessarily meet specific treatment goals outlined in clients' treatment plans, nor do they require extensive documentation. But they serve to enhance the treatment milieu, create catalysts for communication, and provide numerous opportunities for socialization, reminiscence, group interaction, and nonjudgmental affection.

Animal-assisted therapy, on the other hand, is a goal-directed intervention in which an animal that meets specific criteria is an integral part of a client's treatment process. AAT is directed and delivered by a health or human service professional with specialized expertise, within the scope of his or her profession. AAT is designed to promote improvement in human physical, social, emotional, and cognitive functioning. AAT is provided in a variety of settings and may be group or individual in nature (Arkow 1998). AAT groups at Crossroads are provided by specialized human service providers supervised by licensed clinicians who have been trained to work with animals. Licensed clinicians utilize AAT during individual therapy and are responsible for documentation and evaluation of AAT throughout treatment.

ABOUT CROSSROADS

Crossroads is the first residential group facility in South Carolina to serve uniquely the female population, addressing sexual, physical, and emotional abuse through a multimodality approach utilizing animals. The treatment team offers ongoing assessment and services to adolescents ranging in age from 10 to 21 with the goal of reuniting each child with her family or helping her move into alternate, less restrictive care or to independent living.

Crossroads invests in children. Because abuse is often dealt with years after its occurrence, quality and effective intervention is paramount. Treatment must interrupt the cycle of abuse in order to combat problems that lead to deterioration of the individual, requiring further societal support and subsequent costly adult mental health services.

Several therapeutically intense programs were developed to help each resident move from the status of victim to that of a survivor and integrate the catastrophe into her life history and use it as a source of strength. Residents participate in expressive therapies, recreational therapy, a comprehensive educational component, and AAT and AAA.

The intensive therapy program initiates crucial steps in addressing abuse issues. The more intensive high management program helps the child attain a sense of accomplishment in behavioral, cognitive, and emotional development and learn necessary life skills. Abuse-related issues are addressed through individual and group therapy sessions conducted on such topics as establishing adequate social skills, anger management, relaxation techniques, developing trust, and identifying and decreasing cognitive distortions. The supervised independent living program involves a range of rehabilitation services that help young women assume responsibility over their lives, strengthen vocational skills, develop environmental supports, and function actively and independently. Staff invoke and foster self-worth, motivation, responsibility, and creativity as they guide clients through treatment. Aftercare is available following discharge.

Clinically, the programs focus upon trauma recovery issues and psychological tasks of recovery, taught via Crossroads' Maladaptive Behavior/Inter-Relational Cycle and the Post-Traumatic Stress Disorder model. Programs are cognitive and solution-focused. Residents are actively involved in developing treatment plans that address specific needs. Weekly reviews address issues, life options and transitional and discharge planning. Symptoms, behavioral and psychological indicators, obsessions and repulsions, fear and phobias are addressed, often utilizing AAT.

PROGRAM MODEL

The staff at Crossroads think it is critical to talk with clients about their experiences with animals. Early in treatment, clients' experiences with animals are assessed in a questionnaire, which assists the treatment team in identifying the types of experiences the child has had with animals and serves as a tool to prompt the child to disclose any animal abuse experiences.

AAT and AAA are implemented in conjunction with the maladaptive behavior/inter-relational cycle of abuse and cognitive-behavior treatment. This model was developed to help at-risk individuals break an abusive cycle that is pervasive among our clientele and is utilized as an interactive therapeutic intervention to educate clients on how to stop misbehavior leading to abusive behavior toward themselves, others, and animals.

The animal-assisted work motivates the client to try new experiences and begin to address unresolved treatment issues. The relationship between the cycle and AAT is critical, as the dynamics of the human-animal bond are often ignored when addressing trauma-related issues. The therapist uses the model to guide clients through positive and negative experiences that may have involved animals. The model is often taught during AAT because animals assist clinicians in reducing clients' fears of addressing emotionally laden experiences. Examples include the client who works through identity issues by gaining improved confidence while working with animals, or by interacting with others while grooming, feeding, or caring for the animals. The first example aids the client in becoming more aware of her abilities, and the latter helps develop trust, enabling her to decrease withdrawal symptoms while increasing positive social interactions.

AAT, in conjunction with the Maladaptive Behavior/Inter-Relational Cycle Treatment (figs. 1 & 2), is a cognitive intervention plan that educates clients in strategies to achieve a healthy lifestyle and leave problems behind. This is done by exploring eight unhealthy survival skills that are replaced with healthy psychological constructs. These unhealthy skills and their healthy constructs are:

1. a false sense of self, which is replaced by a positive self identity (awareness);
2. withdrawal or isolation, which is replaced by positive social interaction (trust);
3. cognitive distortions, replaced by rational thinking (understanding);

False Sense of Self →	Withdrawal & Isolation →	Cognitive Distortions →	Work/School Dilemma →	Lack of Self-control →	Verbal Aggression →	Physical Aggression →	Power and Control
• Fear of success • Attention-seeking • Impressing others, "being cool" • Minimizing actions	• Fear of others • Fear of intimacy • Poor self-esteem • Loner	• Believes behavior is acceptable • Unable to recognize problems • Distorted perceptions ("I'm different ... it won't happen to me") • Jealousy	• Poor grades/work habits • Frequent suspensions & absences • Learning difficulties • Poor productivity	• Lacks understanding of cause and effect • Impulsive • Denies responsibility of actions • Unable to wait turn	• Threatens others • Loud talking • Screaming & yelling • Bullying others	• Physical interactions • Use of body posture to frighten others • Destruction of property	• Physical, emotional, and/or sexual violence against others or animals • Firesetting

Figure 1. The Maladaptive Behavior Cycle

Awareness →	Trust →	Understanding →	Accountability →	Responsibility→	Tolerance →	Compassion →	Empathy
• Successful Self-actualization • Believes in self	• Positive social interaction • Improved self-esteem • Shares ideas with others	• Rational thinking • Recognizes & owns the problem • Helpful to others	• Improved work/study habits • Improved attendance & productivity • Focused	• Respects others' boundaries • Completes tasks • Understands cause and effect	• Even-tempered • Positive communication • Works well with others	• Healthy interaction with others • Good listener • Able to be a friend	• Assertive leader • Reliable • Protective and forgiving

Figure 2. The Inter-relational Cycle

Table 1. The Relationship of Animal-Assisted Activities and Therapy to the Maladaptive Behavior/Inter-Relational Cycle

Animal Characteristic	Helps to Reduce	Helps to Develop
Responds positively to pleasurable stimuli	Withdrawal and avoidance	Awareness
Unconditional love and acceptance	Distrust of others and feelings of rejection	Trust
Gentle interaction	Low self-esteem and cruelty	Understanding
Instinctive	Manipulation of others	Accountability
Dependent upon caretaker	Minimization of actions and dishonesty	Responsibility
Protective	Intrusiveness	Tolerance
Forgiving	Guilt and shame	Compassion
Vulnerability	Submissive behavior and self-mutilation	Empathy

4. a work or school dilemma, which is replaced by work or school achievement (accountability);
5. lack of self control, which is replaced by respect for boundaries (responsibility);
6. verbal aggression, which is replaced by positive communication (tolerance);
7. physical aggression, which is replaced by healthy interaction (compassion); and
8. power and control, which is replaced by assertive leadership (empathy).

AAT and AAA help victims of sexual trauma work through underlying reasons for acting-out and negative behaviors. Crossroads typically works with children diagnosed with oppositional or conduct disorders. Often, an assessment will indicate the child also suffers from Post-Traumatic Stress Disorder (PTSD). The staff at Crossroads thinks that when left untreated, PTSD produces a host of misbehaviors characterized through the maladaptive component of the above model. Through AAT and AAA, clients learn how characteristics of animals can teach strategies to reduce maladaptive behaviors and facilitate a healthy inter-relational lifestyle. The model utilizes Cognitive-Behavior Treatment by structuring a client's environment toward understanding how animal characteristics can reduce post-traumatic stress symptoms and facilitate healthy psychological constructs as illustrated in the inter-relational component of this model shown in table 1.

ANIMAL THERAPY COMPONENT

Interaction with animals is of particular value when encouraging clients to test and modify maladaptive behaviors and inaccurate cognitions. Companion animals operate largely in the here- and-now and are able to "let go" of past negative experiences. They openly express their feelings through candid, nonjudgmental means. They are tolerant and accepting, and will not harm others unless trained to do so or maliciously provoked. Animals have an innate ability to nurture humans who are feeling down or depressed, and in turn, to stimulate humans' nurturing qualities. The simple act of petting an animal reduces heart and pulse rates and anxiety levels and sets the tone for immediate relaxation.

Many people's fondest memories include family pets. Animals can be invaluable to teach us acceptance, responsibility, empathy, bonding, love and compassion, acceptance, understanding, accountability, awareness, and trust.

The Crossroads animal therapy programs began in 1993 with only a dachshund and a vision for helping children heal. Today we include therapeutic horseback riding, certified Pet Partners of visiting animals, and a working farm that includes various breeds of horses, cows, sheep, rabbits, dogs, cats, ducks, chickens, peacocks, a donkey, and a mule.

The inclusion of animals during therapy sessions provides clients with a conduit for information regarding past experiences frequently repressed. The following case studies (names have been changed to ensure confidentiality) are illustrative.

Julie

Julie was a 15-year-old referred for high management care after receiving treatment, including three hospitalizations, at four previous placements. Her diagnosis history included extensive emotional disturbance, including PTSD and major depression. Julie had experienced severe physical and sexual abuse from both her father and grandfather. Her mother's mildly impaired cognitive ability affected Julie's early development. After her parents' divorce, both Julie and her mother lived with a known perpetrator. Julie's sister was married and pregnant by age 15. Julie presented with low self-esteem, oppositional behavior, self-mutilation, encopresis, enuresis, physical aggression, auditory hallucinations, drastic mood swings, refusal to eat, and self-induced vomiting. Her rehabilitation prognosis was poor.

The primary goal of therapy was to address the trauma-related issues that she dramatized through control-oriented means and distorted body images. Julie entered treatment exhibiting significant anger, often refusing to cooperate with simple staff directives or to participate in therapeutic groups. Though individual therapy was conducted weekly, her ability to engage varied from week to week. Julie entered the sessions unable to focus or commit to goals, preferring the therapist to drive the session and teach her the skills necessary for functional living. Throughout the course of treatment she frequently struggled through discussions about family experiences. Her attempts to gain control over her anger appeared futile as she repeatedly abused her body by bingeing and purging, self-mutilation, and bouts of encopresis and enuresis.

Julie's experiences with animals during therapy were extremely revealing. Julie had the opportunity to bond with newborn kittens, one of which she became fond of and named Hungry. The therapist carefully guided Julie through alternate strategies to release anger by utilizing the Maladaptive Behavior/Inter-Relational Cycle to educate Julie about her maladaptive behaviors. Hungry was brought into the therapy session initially to assist Julie in accepting more specialized treatment for anorexia nervosa. In this instance, Hungry merely served as a source of comfort. As young Hungry sat on Julie's lap, Julie was taught to gently pet Hungry. It was beautiful to watch both bond and relax. Julie began to feel accepted, to become aware of her body, and to trust her therapist and express feelings about past trauma.

Facing anorexia was disturbing for Julie. She disliked restrictions placed on bathroom time and abhorred being closely monitored by a dietician. Subsequently, enuresis and encopresis episodes worsened. Julie became resistant in verbalizing feelings resulting from her anorexia. She again attempted to re-establish control over her life and began exhibiting maladaptive defense mechanisms through bodily excretions. Julie began to have fecal incontinence during the day and night. In her anger, she refused to take responsibility to clean herself, and was not disturbed by her peers' repulsion or anger with her. After multiple interventions were unsuccessful, the treatment team again reached a consensus to implement AAT during individual therapy. A grown Hungry, now with seven-week-old kittens, participated in Julie's therapy. The therapist carefully worked with Julie to train the kittens to use the litter box, subsequently freeing Julie to relate her own experiences to the process. Julie and her therapist cleaned the litter box weekly while discussing the care and guidance the kittens needed in their training. She was able to relate the kittens' experience to her own and began taking responsibility for her own encopresis and enuresis. She later was able to verbalize positive "I statements" clearly indicating progress with control and body image issues. Animal-assisted therapy bolstered Julie's ability to verbalize feelings and better manage her anger. Julie began to exhibit psychotherapeutic change.

Leigh

Leigh was a 15-year-old admitted for treatment of sexual abuse, family abandonment, and impulse control disorder. She had previously received treatment in three hospitals and three foster homes.

Leigh responded most to animal-assisted activities and worked diligently during individual and group therapy to understand her own maladaptive abuse patterns. Leigh worked hard identifying her own "red flags" or triggers of misbehavior and then worked with her therapist and animal-assisted specialist to replace maladaptive behaviors with healthier living styles. An incentive for Leigh was to earn, as a part of her therapy, weekly horseback riding lessons. Leigh was always eager to participate in all animal-assisted activities, often taking on extra responsibilities which were related to the horses in particular. The following structured therapeutic journal activity response describes the human-animal bond that Leigh developed:

Journal Question: How do the animals help you achieve your treatment goals? Leigh's Response: "My favorite animal is Fluffanella (donkey) because she listens to me when I talk to her. She comes to me and she knows how I feel, and I know how she feels. We have a lot in common, like sometimes she is very stubborn, like me!"

The therapist was able to engage Leigh in treatment through the therapeutic interventions of animals. Each time she would begin to address a difficult issue, her bond with and support of Fluffanella grew stronger.

During therapy, Leigh talked about her past and current relationships with animals. On one occasion she was eager to share her experiences of loss as a young child. She began by expressing her sadness of losing a cat, and progressed to verbalizing her feelings of abandonment when she lost her mother's support. Leigh described her cat being abruptly taken from her, then her mother disappearing from her life, and learning of her mother's death shortly thereafter. She was able to describe the loss and anger she felt when a foster mother took the cat, "just because I was spending too much time with her." No one had ever helped her to verbalize or label the correlation between losing her mother and cat. Educating Leigh about the Maladaptive Behavior Cycle and teaching her strategies to achieve a healthy living style helped her recognize she could re-establish healthy relationships with new people and animals in her life. Prior to this type of therapy, Leigh thought she could never survive the loss of both her mother and cat. Leigh was later able to form positive relationships with her grandmother, peers and group home staff. In this case, the combination of cognitive-behavior treatment, AAT and AAA became the integrated interventions to allow Leigh to experience success.

MANAGEMENT OF AN ANIMAL-ASSISTED THERAPY PROGRAM

Careful consideration should be given when considering the integration of animals into the treatment process. First, decide whether the client is amenable to interacting with therapy animals, then determine if the therapeutic goal can be attained through the use of animals. The availability, care, safety, and maintenance of animals must also be evaluated on a regular basis. An animal behavioral specialist should continuously monitor the stress level of the animals to ensure their well-being.

When working with any animals, it is important to assess the animals' strengths, weaknesses, and limitations to ensure proper alignment with therapeutic goals. Animals must be docile, even-tempered, and must meet established risk management criteria. It is advisable for two staff to work with larger animals: an animal handler who is familiar with animal behavior and feels comfortable in manipulating the activity with the animal; and a therapist who can focus strictly on the interaction between the animal and client. The age and physical condition of the animals must be thoroughly assessed by a veterinarian prior to using animals in therapy to ensure controllability, reliability, predictability, and suitability.

When planning activities, keep sessions brief, lasting no longer than one half-hour. This allows adequate interaction between the client and animal without inflicting undue stress on either. Ensure sessions are carefully planned and prepare an alternate activity in case of inclement weather, or in the event that the client is too disruptive to interact with an animal. The client's level of functioning should always be considered. It is advisable to include both short-term and long-term goals to enable the client to experience a sense of accomplishment. Written incident reports should be kept in the client chart to assure comprehensive documentation. Finally, frequent written evaluations noting positive and negative observations and client progress including resolutions and follow-up should be included in client records. Individual treatment plans should always identify animal-assisted activities or therapy to strengthen the efficacy of using animals in therapy.

CONCLUSION

Crossroads Group Homes began treating children in May 1993 after many years of attempting to convince state licensing agencies that children could benefit from the inclusion of animals in their treatment. Skeptics initially referred to Crossroads as the "farm." Clients, too, were skeptical; most had never been in a treatment facility that included animals. Never did the children believe they could begin to have a life of normalcy that included playing with animals.

Today, prospective clients are amazed when they walk on the property and see all the animals and old friends whom they knew as "problem children" in previous facilities doing so well. There are still many unanswered questions about the implementation of animal-assisted therapy. Research to validate the effectiveness of AAT and AAA remains in its infancy (Arkow 1998). Until more data are available, all one needs to do is ask those who matter—the children: without a doubt, every client at Crossroads will tell you that animal-assisted therapy works.

REFERENCES

Arkow, P. 1998. *"Pet therapy": A study and resource guide to the use of companion animals in selected therapies,* 8th ed. Stratford, N.J.: self-published.

U.S. Department of Health and Human Services. 1997. *Child maltreatment 1995: Reports from the states to the national child abuse and neglect data system.* Washington, D.C.: U.S. Government Printing Office.

Making Respect Part of the Curriculum

Pearl Salotto

COULD IT BE that teaching respect as part of the school day could make the difference between a violent and a peaceful world? In today's world, where many, if not most, families are very stressed, where dysfunction and abuse too frequently replace quality family time, where substance abuse, early pregnancy, and domestic violence all too often interfere with healthy communication and caring, how can we expect that children will come to school "ready to learn?" And all too often, schools are not "caring communities" but rather environments filled with metal detectors, guns, violence, and emotional abuse from classmates. Is it any wonder that many children find solace in drugs, teen pregnancy, and even suicide?

Numerous school districts are incorporating character education programs. On a recent CNN program, *Both Sides,* which focused on "Fixing Education," Acting Deputy Secretary of Education Marshall Smith stated that teaching respect is among the critical needs that our schools must address, and noted author Jonathan Kozol stated that young people need to go into a school where they feel respected. Smith added that the notion of respect is one thing he has heard over and over as he talks to schoolchildren around the country: respect from each other and respect from teachers. He feels children cannot work very hard without respect. So the question becomes: What is the most effective way to teach respect?

PET-INSPIRED HUMANE EDUCATION

In 1933 the National PTA Congress said:

> Children trained to extend justice, kindness, and mercy to animals become more just, kind, and considerate in their relations with each other. Character training along these lines will result in men and women of broader sympathies, more humane, more law abiding—in every respect more valuable citizens. Humane education is teaching in the schools and colleges of the nations, the principles of justice, good will, and humanity toward all life. The cultivation of the spirit of kindness to animals is but the starting point toward that larger humanity which include one's fellow of every race and clime. A generation of people trained in these principles will solve their international difficulties as neighbors and not as enemies.

443

Similar statements were made by Edith Latham, George Angell, and other early proponents of humane education (Arkow 1985). In addition, therapy pets are now being recognized for their abilities to comfort the elderly in nursing homes, motivate persons in need of rehabilitation, and change angry and depressed prisoners into cooperative and responsible individuals (Arkow 1998).

Perhaps the time is right to integrate the teaching of respect in our schools with the concept of the therapeutic benefits of pets. One such model is the "D.J. Respect for Living Things" program, where a loving therapy animal, working with a professional pet-assisted therapy facilitator who cares deeply about the children as well as the animal, can have a significant and life-changing impact on children. These hour-long sessions can be powerful in reaching the whole child, helping him or her discover a new sense of identity and a new view of the world in which he or she feels responsible for choices and behaviors toward all living things. The sessions reach children's minds, hearts, and bodies through a multi-sensory approach combining interactions with the dog, essay writing, reading, singing, drawing, and discussions about respect for other people, ourselves, animals, and the environment.

As an eight-year-old girl in the program said, "I felt good when I petted D.J. She made me and my whole class feel good and she gave us feelings for other people. So if we have feelings, we can make our world a better place to live in."

D.J. is an 11-year-old Samoyed and the centerpiece of this program, which I teach to third-graders in Central Falls and Woonsocket, Rhode Island. D.J. also visits nursing homes and hospitals. Her impact on the elderly and on individuals with handicaps inspires and empowers children to seek meaningful roles for themselves in which they can make a difference for people and animals. Another girl in the program expressed this idea: "We can learn to be gentle to living things. We can also learn to not be discriminators. D.J. does not go around and only play with white or black people. She's always happy, smiling, and calm. We could learn from her example. We can be kind to people that have disabilities. We can learn to be kind and gentle. These are all things we can do to help. That's what we can learn from D.J."

Providing children opportunities to relate to animals, so simple and yet so meaningful, helps them develop an enduring understanding of and respect for the wonder of it all. When you teach a child about animals, he or she learns facts about animals. But when a child develops a strong connection with animals, he or she learns to care. Perhaps this powerful emotional experience of gentleness and intimacy with a living creature, combined with an intellectual understanding of our responsibilities to all living things, can pave the way for children's future choices to

respect themselves and their families, teachers, friends, pets, and other animals; advocate for those in need;
help them bloom into caring and compassionate persons who make a difference in the world by helping others.

Listen to the words of a child: "D.J. made me feel good about myself and for some reason she made me feel beautiful unlike I really am. She didn't turn away when I told her my problems."

BRINGING ABOUT CHANGE

What brings about these behavioral and cognitive changes? Children's overflowing need to express themselves within a validating and empowering environment along with their deep appreciation and amazement at the opportunity to give and receive love from a companion animal friend within the school environment mesh together to allow the children to develop a new view of the world and their potential roles and responsibilities in it.

D.J., who has been described as a magnet, not only draws people to her, but allows people to get in touch with the best in themselves as well. In the "joy of the moment" when a child's mind, body, and heart are in perfect harmony, real learning takes place. D.J.'s gentleness allows children to get in control immediately of their own behavior. Her trust encourages them to share, and her needs allow them to be respectful. D.J. has invited us into her world of gentleness with all our senses.

Debbie Fahrenholtz, a student in my university course on pet-assisted therapy, expressed the impact of the program. "I know from personal experience what an animal can bring to a life, but I was still impressed and awed by what I saw on two field trips. In a visit to St. Joseph's Hospital I saw a beautiful Akita, working with her pet-assisted therapy intern, bring smiles and life to many faces. I saw people confined to wheelchairs reaching to touch a soft trusting face. I heard memories and conversation between people of all ages. I saw a dog bring moments of happiness to an otherwise unhappy experience. Being confined to a hospital, away from family and alone for most of the day, can make any of us lonely and depressed. To bring small moments of joy and fun into lives which are pained and frightened is so special.

"As we walked into the hall of Social Street School for the Respect for Living Things program, small faces lit up in amazement and excitement. One little boy was surprised, saying, 'I didn't know they would let pets into our school.' When we walked into the classroom, more faces lit up, smiles spread from ear to ear, and little bodies could hardly be controlled, as D.J., tail wagging, entered the room. Every child gave Pearl and D.J. immediate attention. D.J. slowly walked down the first row of desks, as small hands reached out and caressed and touched this soft white dog. One little girl with a smile so wide said, 'She looks like a big white bear. I just want to hug her.' As D.J. continued her stroll, small groups of children asked and were allowed to surround D.J., petting, kissing, and just being close.

"D.J.'s gentleness and love began to shine. Each child got to participate. The message of respect for animals, ourselves, and others seemed to reach each child as they all related what they felt and knew about respect and love. When they heard that D.J. would be returning in a week, the smiles spread wider in anticipation. This was a part of school and learning that was fun! How can these children not take this memory with them for the rest of their lives?"

A similar program is offered by Denise and John DeSanty with their therapy dog, Jessie, a four-year-old springer spaniel. Karen Pagano, a teacher of an inclusive special-needs class at Plunkett Elementary School in Adams, Massachusetts, participated in that program.

"I originally signed up with the hopes that the activity would afford my special-needs class the opportunity to have an up-close and personal experience with a trained animal. That has happened and more. The changes that I have seen in my group since we have begun the program are wide-ranging and truly therapeutic," Pagano said.

"The kids now can find a way to open up, communicate, and trust their own perceptions and ideas as well as those of the therapeutic team. Because of that trust and the honoring of truthfulness and respect, we can begin to change our perceptions and beliefs.

"We are learning how to be empathetic, to step into another's shoes (or paws) and try to understand the feelings and experiences of another. We are practicing self-control in order to be more like Jessie in her ability to recognize temptation and trouble. We can now talk about and practice patience because of the way that Jessie shows us it can be done. We are learning about safety and personal space and we try to reflect on the behaviors that Jessie demonstrates to show her needs and abilities in nonthreatening ways. It is so wonderful to watch the process of change as it happens naturally and productively.

"My students demonstrate severe social and behavioral difficulties. They need to be helped and taught how to get along in the world in as many ways possible. Because of their relationships with Jessie, they can start to expand and practice what they are learning," she said.

Pagano asked her students about the lessons they are learning from Jessie. These are a few of their comments:

Talking about our problems helps us learn.
Jessie is teaching me to be gentle.
It's okay to cry in front of Jessie.
Because Jessie barked and protected us when someone came to the door—that means she cares about us.
I don't want to hurt her feelings and she won't hurt mine. I think she loves me.

"I know of no way as powerful as listening to the honest thoughts of the children to describe and determine the magnitude and importance of our experience with Jessie. I hope that we can continue to work together with Jessie to become safer, gentler, more understanding and successful in our relationships with family, teachers, and friends," Pagano said.

In Israel, a similar program is enabling Jewish and Arab children to cooperate with each other as they care for animals at a shelter. Jewish and Arab children in Tel Aviv are bused after school to an SPCA where they learn to care for animals in a hands-on interactive environment. This Living Together program, developed and coordinated by Nina Natelson of Concern for Helping Animals in Israel (CHAI), teaches children about the web of connectedness of all living things and to respect and appreciate individuals of other species and other ethnic backgrounds.

With a child's enthusiasm, it is easy for a pet therapy facilitator or teacher to direct that passion and energy for animals toward kindness and compassion for all living things. Couldn't this keep children from joining gangs, from discrimination, from cruelty?

DOGS AS ROLE MODELS

Dogs as role models? Why not? Perhaps Pet-Inspired Values Development programs such as these can give children a new sense of self-respect and help them not only to realize their responsibilities to all living things, but also allow them to recognize appropriate and inappropriate behavior on the part of others toward them. I have heard comments such as the young girl who told me that her older sister, who takes care of her when her mother is working, hits the dog and hits her, too. As the teacher and I exchanged glances and the teacher quietly informed me that she would make a referral, the child also realized, in that instant, following our 30-minute discussion of respect, that all of our talk about respect applied to her as well, that she is a special person who does not deserve abusive treatment. In that moment of internalization she realized that something was wrong with what she and her pet had been experiencing. Perhaps at some point in her life she would have realized that anyway, but somehow a program that tied it all together allowed her to realize that she did not need to keep her awful secret any more. Not only children who have been abused, but also those who have lost their trust in people through divorce or abandonment can perhaps take the first step toward finding their way back to trusting people within a program of caring and sharing.

In a children's book that I wrote entitled "D.J. A Member of Our Family" (Salotto 1998), I explain how D.J. has been a beloved member of our family for many years and how she works as a pet therapy dog giving unconditional love to one and all, how she loves making people happy and how she gets love and respect from me even if I'm tired, busy or sick. The children love this book and read it again and again. It seems to strike a responsive chord deep within.

I do not tell children to respect animals and people. I ask them questions that allow their minds and hearts to recognize and acknowledge their responsibilities. I ask them how they show respect to their pets at home, what they think I would do if D.J. has to go out in the middle of the night, what they should do if they see children throwing rocks at an animal, or how they can show respect to parents, siblings, a new friend in the neighborhood, or a new classmate who is physically challenged.

KEY MOMENTS

From such moments of closeness and caring comes our vision of our own role in the world. My daughter's vision of her world and her place in it was shaped by an unforgettable few minutes she had when she was 11 years old, when she accompanied me to my substitute teaching job at a school for children with cerebral palsy. During music therapy, she lifted an eager youngster from his wheelchair, cradled him in her arms and danced with him. The emotional impact of this brief moment in time set Ruthie on a course so clear, so strong, that despite many obstacles she is today, 20 years later, a teacher, an advocate, and a leader in the movement for inclusion of children with special needs in regular classrooms.

Perhaps the power of a moment in time with a beloved animal will also set children on a course of caring and compassion, help assure their roles in relationships based on respect and commitment, and help assure their life's work that will make a positive difference to others.

One fourth-grader wrote an essay a year after the D.J. program was presented in her class. She expressed powerful memories, just like it was yesterday. "The program built up character in me—my esteem and respect for others. Last year, the second D.J. walked through the classroom door, I loved her. I will always remember that day, when D.J. came to school, to teach us to be nice."

Perhaps relating to our best friends as part of the school curriculum can help make the world a safer place for us all to relate to each other. Today's leading educators, social scientists, child advocates, counselors, ethicists, and writers are desperately searching for solutions to end the violence in our streets, communities, schools, and homes. They are open to creative and effective programs to build empathy and self-discipline. Teaching respect and care for animals and translating that caring to all living things may be one such strategy.

Community violence is a serious public health issue. Any significant reduction in the level of violence in this country requires the creative energy, commitment and perseverance of all Americans. Teaching children to love and care for animals also teaches them the necessary skills to develop and sustain loving relationships with people.

So it appears not only possible but likely that our canine friends, long known as man's best friends, are children's best friends as well. They can help to lead the next generation to "step in another's paws," thus helping to pave the way for a more civilized, peaceable and respectful world.

REFERENCES

Arkow, P. 1985. Humane education. In *Operational guidelines.* Englewood, Colo.: American Humane Association.

Arkow, P. 1998. *"Pet therapy": A study and resource guide to the use of companion animals in selected therapies,* 8th ed. Stratford, N.J.: self-published.

Salotto, P. 1998. *Loving intervention: Pet-assisted therapy as an emerging profession leading to a friendlier, healthier and more peaceful society.* (In press).

Conclusions

It may well be that the survival of the species will depend on the ability to foster a boundless capacity for compassion. Compassion alone stands apart from the continuous traffic between good and evil proceeding within us. Compassion is the antitoxin of the soul. Where there is compassion, even the most poisonous impulses remain relatively harmless. It is our last great hope.

—Eric Hoffer, *The Human Factor in Science, Technology and the Human Prospect*

How to Heal the Sickness?

Cherish Women, Children, and Animals

Scott McVay

DURING THE EARLY years of her studies of the chimpanzee—then thought to be our closest cousin in the animal kingdom—Jane Goodall was seeing a scrubbed-up version of us. She reported on benign and cooperative social behavior, mother-infant care and bonding, even the use of a tool—a reed for probing a nest of termites to fish out some delectable morsels. But she acknowledged at the 20-year mark evidence of occasional negative behavior—premeditated assault, males choking females, and infanticide—and she felt obliged to report it.

Nearly four decades of study of the chimpanzee, which has DNA that is 98.4 percent identical to ours, may help us to understand the nature of violence in our own species, especially as perpetrated by males. I am talking here about the shallow undercurrent of violence, sometimes seemingly idiosyncratic and isolated, sometimes broadly sanctioned and collectively pursued, that seems woven through human societies even though a strong cooperative nature must permeate most societies for them to function.

As we consider the nature of our abuse of children, animals, and women, and how to prevent it, we must try to understand the origin of violence and manage it through moral sanctions, behavior modification, laws, and the exposure of youth to the wonder and joy of all forms of animal life from the antics of a pet dog or cat to acrobatic mating of dragonflies to the awesome architecture of the bowerbird of Papua New Guinea.

The horrors of human violence, recorded repeatedly in chilling stories in this book, are mimicked and amplified at the societal and transnational level throughout this century by violence of a scale not possible earlier. The single greatest atrocity was the death of some 53 million people through actions by Joseph Stalin, building on and extending patterns of brutal repression begun by Vladimir Lenin. This reign of terror may or may not have to do with communism, but it did have to do with belief systems and the nature of power and desire for control.

Because the nature of violence and aggression and abuse is still only dimly understood, few scholars have attempted to advance the prospect of a "nonkilling society." Professor Glenn Paige of the University of Hawaii has pursued this quest for three decades, finding the Indian subcontinent more open than ours to wholly peaceful solutions to human conflict because of a profound shift in perception down the years exemplified by Mahatma Gandhi's lifework.

As we scan the animal kingdom, the recent work of Frans de Waal and others reveals that another ape, the little bonobo found only in the Democratic Republic of the Congo, with DNA as oddly close to ours as the chimpanzee's (only 1.6 percent divergence), offers quite a different strategy for resolving conflict in an essentially peaceful and egalitarian society. Instead of violence, the bonobos are highly tactile and seem to use sex to calm things down, to resolve a quarrel, to maintain relationships across generations and gender. At first blush, this does not seem to be the solution for us.

In the recent past, new insights about our behavior have been revealed through such landmark works as *Against Our Will: Men, Women, and Rape* by Susan Brownmiller (1975). Through papers published 10 years later in 1985, Stephen Kellert and Alan Felthous showed the inextricable connections between boyhood cruelty to animals and men's heinous crimes. The book you hold in your hands is a fresh compilation of findings by scholars, humane workers, even the Secretary of Defense, suggesting that we can create a more humane and just society if those working to mitigate and eliminate abuse of animals, children, and women could pool their talents and experience—and bring society along.

It was only seven years ago (September 1992) that the American Humane Association convened a conference on "Protecting Children and Animals," the first to address formally the connected nature of the problem. Since offering the keynote remarks, "The Continuum of Violence: A Counsel of Hope (From Biophobia to Biophilia)," and particularly after reading the contributions to this book, often courageous and hard-won, one thought recurs. As we contemplate the big-ticket issues that may foreshorten the human experiment—soaring human numbers, voracious consumption patterns, loss of primary habitat with a wondrous array of species, global warming, life-altering chemicals that now reside in every living organism, mounting energy needs from nonsustainable sources—our response to violence toward the defenseless, the voiceless, and the vulnerable may well be the issue that will determine the longevity and lilt of our tenure here and beyond the bounds of earth's gravity.

Rather than simply preventing abuse, and dealing with the ugly manifestation of human frustration brought on by lack of work, scant resources, desire for control, or whatever as it pops up, we need to foster human inquiry, whether in the tiniest tot or the lackadaisical teenager, about our place in the natural world and the diverse forms of life who share this seascape with us.

A PERSONAL CONVICTION

I confess to an abiding interest in bright, motivated people who make the world a better place. I confess, too, a fascination with empathetic children and their evolutionary potential for our species as stewards of the natural world and problem-solvers of the first magnitude. They need to be adequately stimulated, nourished, and nurtured as children. We need to know what works in the family and in the community.

A marvelous book, *The Children on the Hill: The Story of an Extraordinary Family*, by Michael Deakin (1972), revealed a family in Wales with four children, all of whom were precocious in different ways, from music to mathematics. My copy of this glorious little book, dog-eared and replete with underlining and notes in the margin, was lost in a fire that destroyed our home in February 1981. I had forgotten the title and author until reminded recently, but I had not forgotten the spirit of joy and discovery and mutual support in that family. In a society obsessed by dysfunction, such a family's life is happily instructive.

This comes to mind now because of another amazing family, living not 20 minutes from our office, who has overcome some formidable obstacles to evoke high performance among four children in a home where a sense of wonder and awe, diligence, integrity, grace, laughter, and harmony prevail. The family first came to my attention two years ago when the third child won the National Geographic spelling bee at a record-young age.

The older daughter, talented in all subjects and valedictorian of her class, a sprinter and soccer star, and a musician, has just entered Harvard. Her younger brother is following in her footsteps as editor-in-chief of the school newspaper. Number three, as noted, gained national attention through the spelling bee in 1996. The youngest, Dayo, age six, is in the first grade.

I asked Dayo when he had learned to read. He said, "Two." His siblings smiled, "We believe you had turned three." The lad then listed his first half-dozen books and then jumped to this past summer when he read several novels. He is apparently able to recall, word for word, what he reads. He recites whole pages with the understanding and conviction of an accomplished actor. He puts a dramatic flair in his renditions until he is thanked by his parents.

Why bring up this splendid family here? Because the harmony and spirit of adventure within the family are worthy of broad emulation. Indeed, a fascination with the natural world seems to be part of the connective glue—as is the children's good fortune to do well on tests offered by the Center for Talented Youth at Johns Hopkins and then as middle-schoolers to take three-week summer courses that cover an entire high school year.

George Santayana wrote, "The family is one of nature's masterpieces." Because we tend to fasten on dysfunction—and make it the lead on the evening news—we can learn from and honor families that hum with life and love. That, too, can lead us out of the darkness and draw us closer to the light. If we could but "feel the dignity of the child," in Robert Henri's words ("do not feel superior to him, for you are not"), we could discover our own callings and carry the spirit of childhood into maturity.

One of the four reasons that Jane Goodall carries hope in her heart as she quietly crusades for an intact planet is "the energy of youth." That energy carries far greater power than the atom for affirming our ultimate destiny.

I believe that the authors and readers of this book, through their networks and organizations, can begin to turn the tide of local violence against the physically "weaker" animals, children, and women, to a discovery of the boundless light and lift they possess. I sense that animals, and little children, and women contain the mystery and awe of life in all its fecundity. As our collective consciousness comes to treasure each one more and more, our inability to hurt or defile or degrade will grow, and behaviors even now tolerated as "acceptable under the circumstances" will be beyond the pale of possibility in a healthy society.

A GENTLER ETHIC

But how do we heal the sickness when it seems rampant and omnipresent? By cherishing animals, children, and women as vessels of a gentler ethic, compassion, consciousness, empathy, light, and laughter.

One of the hopeful places to look for the transformation that must occur within our society is the Frontiers for Veterinary Medicine initiative. Backed by five funders, this program invites veterinary students in the United States, Mexico, and Canada to submit applications for research over a summer on a topic of humane consequence. The winning students and the projects they have chosen to pursue point the way. Two winners from the 1997 cohort, Melanie Sharpe and Ruth Landau, address the precise subject of this book, and summaries of their work are included.

The others are as amazing as they are far-ranging along the continuum of our relationships with animals, whether companion animals, livestock, or wildlife. Patricia Olson, DVM, Ph.D., caught the intention of this initiative in saying that each student inevitably carries a big dream of what she or he can do to enhance the welfare of animals and these initial projects set them on an unmistakable course.

And with three-fourths of the places in veterinary schools occupied now by women, a palpable gentling of the profession is occurring. The push for noninvasive strategies for healing is being accelerated. Eighty-three percent of the initiative's 1997 applicants were women and 31 of 37 students chosen were women.

In study after study, old patterns were brought under fresh scrutiny and new solutions were offered.

In Julie Arsenault and Anne Desrochers' study of the catching and transportation of poultry, a huge issue with numbers and trauma staggering our imagination, they found that the practices impelled by humane legislation in the United Kingdom are leagues ahead of ours.

In examining the welfare of pack animals in three Mexican states (Mexico, Oaxaca, and Puebla), Mariza Martinez and Claudia Herrera noted that animal power produces 67 percent of agriculture products—horses, donkeys, and mules are of invaluable help to peasant farmers. They carry people or loads like wood and water; they pull carts and plow the fields. Often they are the only means of transportation. Yet these animals are often neglected, undernourished, overworked, heavily parasitized, and suffer from lesions caused primarily by bad tack. The absence of knowledge and training are the culprits. The authors aim to introduce educational programs that will improve the well-being of both the pack animals and their owners.

In a parallel and complementary study in the Peten region of Guatemala, Cynthia Duerr noted, "Some people will cut a hole in the padding to accommodate an ulcer or a sore on the animal's back."

Lisa Lund, a farrier with 10 years' experience, noticed that more horses cast off their shoes and suffer deteriorating hoofs in the summer months. Why? Apparently due to much stomping and stamping in response to flies and other biting insects. Lund devised a fly wrap for the front legs of 70 horses in central Pennsylvania to test the hypothesis. She found that fly wraps are effective in reducing stomping due to insect irritation. (What man would have thought up and pursued such a study?)

Picking up on the immense threat to endocrine disruption of the immune systems in living organisms, described in *Our Stolen Future* by Theo Coburn et al. (1996), Cynthia Smith and Stephanie Presti of Tufts University's School of Veterinary Medicine chose their subjects with care: the surf clam and sea turtle, especially the severely endangered Kemp's Ridley. Their results contribute to a fuller picture of the terrifying results of persisting toxins in our midst.

TO CHERISH OR TO PERISH?

To understand the nature of our domineering behavior in recent times, one needs only look at a letter Christopher Columbus wrote on March 14, 1493, after visiting several islands in the Caribbean: "None of them [the "Indians," since he believed he had reached the eastern shores of Asia] are possessed of any iron, neither have they weapons . . . they are very simple and honest and exceedingly liberal with all they have, none of them refusing anything he may possess . . . they exhibit great love toward all others in preference to themselves." Columbus was deeply touched by the gentleness and generosity of these people, so welcoming and trusting, in contrast to some aspects of European culture where "might makes right," which led to "conquests" worldwide and the imposition of a "dominant" culture over other diverse and sometimes gentler cultures.

Although I have not visited the fabled Galapagos Islands, which were a crucible in Charles Darwin's five-year voyage aboard the *Beagle,* I have read Darwin's journal, recalling especially the two pages devoted to the 13 species of finches, whose beaks suggested their adaptability to available food sources. Playwright Tom Stoppard, in a mere three sentences, conveyed the nature of our responsibility to the creatures there (and elsewhere): "What, then, puts one in mind of paradise? Simply this, and nothing in countryside or garden, safari park or rainforest, prepares one for it: the animals are in a state of innocence. They have no idea that you and I are, as the biologists put it, the most successful of species, and that we could choose to wipe them out, if we did not choose to cherish them."

We have no choice really but to cherish them—or to perish ourselves. One also recalls the caution from Antoine de Saint-Exupéry's *The Little Prince*, which rings hourly in my head: "The fox said to the little prince: Men have forgotten this truth, but you must not forget it. You remain responsible, forever, for what you have tamed."

We know very little about the planet we are despoiling, except for a few phenomenal forward observers whose consciousness has been enfolded by close study of an animal or family of organisms, creating pockets of luminosity, such as

- Dian Fossey's affiliation with the mountain gorilla;
- Birute Galdikas's pursuit of the often solitary orangutan;
- Ed Wilson's fastidious scrutiny of ants;
- Roman Vishniac's voyeuristic travels in the microcosmos;
- Archie Carr's devotion to the green turtle's migrations and nesting;
- George Archibald's long flights with all 15 species of cranes;
- Merlin Tuttle's emergence in the fabulous world of bats whose feeding habits secure and restore habitat;
- Ted Parker's knowledge of the calls of 4,000 species of birds;
- Sylvia Earle's rapture at the eye of the grouper;
- Don Griffin's discovery of sonar in the bat, a leap because we lack that sense;
- Charles Darwin's lifelong fascination with the earthworm, the topic of his last book;
- Jared Diamond's wide-eyed accounts of the bowerbird's aesthetic design capabilities;
- John Terborgh's discovery of a tamarin with a family group consisting of two males who tend the young and one female who does the foraging;
- Cynthia Moss's careful work on elephants revealing the deep bonding of these maternal societies; and
- David Nickles's glorious inventory of over 400 species of katydid in Amazonian Peru, which reflects incredibly diverse strategies for survival.

We are a little like the blind men trying to visualize the elephant, as described by John Godfrey Saxe:

It was six men of Indostan
To learning much inclined,
Who went to see the elephant,
Though all of them were blind,
That each by observation
Might satisfy his mind.

The first approached the elephant
And happening to fall
Against his broad and sturdy side
At once began to bawl.
"God bless me! but the elephant
Is very like a wall."

The second, feeling of the tusk,
Cried, "Ho! What have we here?
So very round and smooth and sharp?
To me 'tis mighty clear:
This wonder of an elephant
Is very like a spear!"

The third approached the animal
And happening to take
The squirming trunk within his hand
Thus boldly up and spake:
"I see the elephant
Is very like a snake!"

The fourth reached out his eager hand
And felt about the knee:
"What most this wondrous beast is like
Is mighty plain," quoth he.
"'Tis clear enough the elephant
Is very like a tree!"

The fifth who chanced to touch the ear
Said, "E'en the blindest man
Can tell what this resembles most:
Deny the fact who can.
This marvel of an elephant
Is very like a fan!"

The sixth no sooner had begun
About the beast to grope,
Then seizing on the swinging tail
That fell within his scope.
"I see the elephant
Is very like a rope!"

And so these men of Indostan
Disputed loud and long.
Each in his own opinion
Exceeding stiff and strong.

Though each was partly in the right,
And all were in the wrong!"

A NEW VISION

We are like the men of Indostan, having parts of the picture of a land blessed with enchantment and great fertility, but we are dismembering and disfiguring what we emerged from the day before yesterday and upon which we utterly and inextricably depend. It is late in the day, and the forces we have unleashed through technology and weaponry seem to have a life of their own. And yet, the young and the old, the poets and artists, the musicians and dancers, are hearing and transmitting a new vision that respects and builds on many human tribes' deep affiliation with the idiosyncrasies of the places where they have lived.

That emancipating vision hears the voices and laughter of children, notes the differing beaks of the finches of the Galapagos (a key to Darwin's interpretation of evolution), and sees the astonishing gifts of women celebrated in Ashley Montagu's book, *The Natural Superiority of Women* (1953). In that unambiguous and tightly reasoned book, Montagu noted, "Woman is the creator and fosterer of life; man has been the mechanizer and destroyer of life."

Montagu points out, "The fact that men cannot have babies and suckle them, nor remain in association with their children as closely as the mother, has an enormous effect upon their subsequent psychological development." Well, a new generation of fathers is emerging who are taking a more active role in the rearing of their children, and even grandfathers are discovering a magic in the flood of sunlight that children bring. May the enchantment continue into their teens.

If we can move past patterns of domination, command, and control, to a profound and grateful respect for the world in which we breathe, walk, sing, and imbibe, if we can truly cherish animals, children, and women, we may well be able to halt destructive trends from the family to the world stage by saluting the grace of every critter that stirs, the learning of children, and the boundless nurturing of women. As with a play, we have to suspend judgment and allow ourselves to enter the world the cosmic playwright has shaped.

The playwright for the larger script of which we are a tiny part is unknowable at close range except through the creation all about us. Our roles can be rescripted, rewritten, and freshly sung if we are able to pause and receive signals for the affirmation of life, not its brutish and unfeeling destruction.

Poets, including many men, reflect our ineffable, innate affiliation with the natural world. *Animals and People: The Human Heart in Conflict with Itself,* an astonishing work by Pattiann Rogers, a poet of meticulous observation who catches the animate all about, captured the essence of our long interconnected set of relationships with the other animals (*Orion,* Winter 1997):

We name mountains and rivers and cities and streets and organizations and gangs and causes after them. We name years and time and constellations of stars after them. We make mascots of them, naming our athletic teams after them. Sometimes we name ourselves after them. . . .

We will never, we cannot, leave them alone, even the tiniest one, ever, because we know we are one with them. Their blood is our blood. Their breath is our breath, their beginning our beginning, their fate our fate.

Thus we deny them. Thus we yearn for them. They are among us and within us and of us, inextricably woven with the form and manner of our being, with our understanding and our imaginations. They are the grit and the salt and the lullaby of our language.

Recall, too, Wendell Berry's words:

When despair for the world grows in me
and I wake in the night at the least sound
in fear of what my life and my children's lives may be,
I go and lie down where the wood drake
rests in his beauty on the water, and the great heron feeds.

Or Mark Doty:

Only animals
make me believe in God now
so little between spirit and skin,
any gesture so entirely themselves.

Storyteller Joseph Bruchac, part Abenaki, part Czech, caught this spirit in a poem called "Prayer":

Let my words
be bright with animals,
images the flash of a gull's wing.
If we pretend
that we are at the center
the moles and kingfishers,
eels and coyotes
are at the edge of grace,
then we circle, dead moons
about a cold sun.
This morning I ask only
the blessing of the crayfish,
the beatitudes of the birds.

We can get our priorities right and do so with modest resources. We can begin to pay attention to children as if the future of the world depends upon them. We can honor creatures, vast and tiny, for their place in the great scheme is no more nor less than ours. And we must salute women for all they have endured and made possible and allow their aims for their families and the larger community of humankind to have greater sway in reconnecting us with all life. To continue as we are will cause immense travail and stifle the human experiment just when we are on the verge of flight.

Recommendations

Phil Arkow and Frank R. Ascione

FOR DOMESTIC VIOLENCE

1. Systematically include questions on intake forms, both in the shelter and for crisis calls, that capture data regarding the number of animals in the household, histories of abusive incidents involving the batterer, the current status and welfare concerns of the animals, and whether there are provisions for the animals' care while the woman is residing in the safe house.

2. Revise women's safety plans to routinely include provisions for transport, housing, and care of animals in the event a woman is forced to leave home.

3. Initiate discussions with local humane societies, SPCAs, animal control agencies, veterinarians, and breed rescue clubs to establish short-term foster care programs for animals belonging to sheltered women. These programs should include provisions for care of companion animals, horses, livestock, and unusual pets.

4. Make modifications, if feasible, to the shelter to allow kennel and cage space for a limited number of dogs, cats, and small household pets belonging to sheltered women.

5. Be sensitive to the emotional attachments that women who are battered and their children may have to their animal companions and to pet loss they may have experienced. We know little about battering victims' reactions to and interpretations of violence directed against their animals: for example, under what circumstances does such abuse further immobilize her and heighten her fear of leaving, and when does it prompt her to escape an abusive situation?

FOR ANIMAL PROTECTION

1. Establish a care plan to provide short-term emergency housing for pets belonging to women who are battered. This plan may involve housing at the animal shelter, or in foster care homes or other off-site locations. Guidelines and concerns regarding such programs are described in a guidebook published by the American Humane Association (1997) and by Ascione, Weber, & Wood (1997).

2. Initiate therapeutic and rehabilitative programs that offer victims of child

abuse and domestic violence opportunities to nurture and work with animals in structured, controlled, supervised settings (Arkow 1998).

3. Invite representatives from community child protective services agencies to conduct in-service training for shelter, kennel and field officer staffs in the recognition and reporting of suspected child abuse and neglect. The Latham Foundation's *Breaking the Cycle of Violence* video and training guide (Arkow 1995), and two American Humane Association publications (1996, 1995) will help effect this training.

4. Establish protocols whereby animal protection personnel who observe suspected child abuse and neglect can report such findings to appropriate child welfare authorities.

5. As incidents of animal abuse frequently suggest that other human and nonhuman family members may be at risk with a wide range of accompanying public health implications, veterinarians should receive training in the recognition and reporting of abuse. Veterinarians should support professional and legislative initiatives that would encourage their involvement and guarantee their immunity from civil and criminal liability in this arena. Diagnostic criteria to identify the pathologies of suspected animal abuse and to assess the risk factors of maltreated animals have been published by the American Humane Association (1998). Further training should be implemented as part of the regular curricula of colleges of veterinary medicine.

FOR CHILD PROTECTION

1. Invite representatives from local and state humane societies, SPCAs, and animal control organizations to conduct in-service training to explain the legal and operational definitions of animal abuse and neglect in your jurisdiction. The Latham Foundation's training manual and video, *Breaking the Cycles of Violence* (1995), will be helpful in initiating this cross-training.

2. Establish protocols whereby caseworkers who observe suspected animal abuse and neglect can report such findings to appropriate humane and animal control authorities.

3. Systematically include questions relating to family histories of animal abuse and neglect on intake and risk assessment questionnaires. Reports of frequent turnover or loss of pets, or of incidents of animal abuse, frequently describe a chaotic household where the safety of human members of the family are compromised, and may generate information that could be helpful in the child's treatment plan and in prosecutions. Clinicians should be sensitive to the separation, loss, and grief issues of children who have lost contact with their companion animals or who have seen them destroyed, and to the impacts that witnessing and perpetrating animal abuse may have upon children.

FOR LEGISLATORS AND THE CRIMINAL JUSTICE SYSTEM

1. Introduce and support legislation that elevates the commission of serious animal abuse into the status of felony crimes or higher-level misdemeanors, where appropriate.

2. Introduce and support legislation that includes animal protection personnel among those already mandated to report suspected child abuse and neglect.

3. Consider legislation modeled after child protection laws that redefines "cruelty to animals" and "bestiality" into a less emotionally charged and more objective nomenclature of "abuse," "physical abuse," "emotional abuse," "sexual abuse," and "neglect."

4. Initiate systems whereby cases of animal abuse are documented and tracked systematically through the criminal justice process.

FOR ALL

1. Closer cooperation, coordination, and collaboration should be effected among the three disciplines. Failure by one profession to recognize and report suspected abuse in another domain only serves to condone and perpetuate the maltreatment. Explore synergistic arrangements that can augment the resources of notoriously understaffed and underfunded community service agencies.

2. Create interdisciplinary teams of community social service agencies that will meet regularly to identify cases in which a high risk of lethality is indicated, and to initiate appropriate responses.

REFERENCES

American Humane Association. 1995. *A training guide for recognizing and reporting child abuse for animal control officers and humane investigators.* Englewood, Colo.: American Humane Association.

———. 1996. *The visual assessment of physical child abuse.* Englewood, Colo.: American Humane Association.

———. 1997. *Handling the pets of domestic violence victims.* Englewood, Colo.: American Humane Association.

———. 1998. *Recognizing & reporting animal abuse: A veterinarian's guide.* Englewood, Colo.: American Humane Association.

Arkow, P. 1995. *Breaking the cycles of violence: A practical guide.* Alameda, Calif.: Latham Foundation.

———. 1998. *"Pet therapy": A study and resource guide for the use of companion animals in selected therapies.* 8th ed. Stratford, N.J.: Self-published.

Ascione, F. R., C. V. Weber, and D. S. Wood. 1997. The abuse of animals and domestic violence: a national survey for women who are battered. *Society & Animals* 5(3):205–18.

Contributors

Cindy A. Adams has worked at the American Society for the Prevention of Cruelty to Animals for eight years. She is currently Senior Director of Publications at the ASPCA and Editor-in-Chief of *Animal Watch*, the quarterly magazine of the American Society for the Prevention of Cruelty to Animals, and *Animaland*. She is a graduate of Hunter College.

Phil Arkow chairs the Latham Foundation's Child and Animal Abuse Prevention Project and authored *Breaking the Cycles of Violence*. He has written eight books on the human-animal bond and animal-assisted therapy and previously worked as humane educator and administrator for Humane Societies in Colorado, Florida, and New Jersey. He teaches two courses on animal-assisted therapy and writes a weekly newspaper column on pet care.

Frank R. Ascione is Professor of Psychology at Utah State University. He has written numerous articles on children's development of empathy, childhood and adolescent cruelty to animals, and the value of humane education. He lectures internationally, has testified before several state legislatures, and is active in many child protection and human-animal bond organizations. He is co-editor, with Randall Lockwood, of *Cruelty to Animals and Interpersonal Violence: Readings in Research and Application*.

Suzanne Barnard is Acting Director of the Children's Division of the American Humane Association. She previously worked in child protection with the Denver Department of Social Services and has served as Executive Director of the Denver Family Crisis Center and of Families First, a crisis shelter for abused and neglected children. She holds a master's degree and has presented papers and conducted seminars on community involvement in child maltreatment issues.

Tamara Barnes volunteers at the Greenhill Humane Society and speaks to audiences about her experiences with domestic violence and animal abuse.

Barbara W. Boat is an associate professor at the University of Cincinnati College of Medicine, where she directs the Program on Childhood Trauma and Maltreatment. She holds a Ph.D. in psychology from Case Western Reserve University. Her special clinical interests are the diagnosis and treatment of dissociative disorders in traumatized children and working with families where children have witnessed domestic violence.

Mary Pat Boatfield is Executive Director of the Toledo Humane Society, where she oversees staff operations, field operations, and the direction of community programs and services. She has a bachelor's degree in public health education and a master's degree in education and is registered with the Ohio Veterinary Medical Board as a veterinary technician.

Carolyn Butler is Director of the Changes Program at the Colorado State University Veterinary Teaching Hospital, an internationally known pioneer in the field of pet loss support, grief counseling, and grief advocacy in veterinary medicine. She holds a master's degree in human development and family studies and lectures internationally on issues related to the human-animal bond. She is the co-author, with Laurel Lagoni, of *The Human-Animal Bond and Grief.*

William S. Cohen is the U.S. Secretary of Defense. He previously served three terms in the U.S. Senate for the State of Maine and three terms in the House of Representatives from Maine's Second Congressional District. He is the co-author of eight books.

Jill De Grave holds a bachelor's degree in social welfare and a master's degree in management. She has been the Education Manager at the Wisconsin Humane Society since 1985, and under her direction the Education Department has developed a variety of innovative, nationally recognized educational programs. Previously she headed the society's Hearing Dog Program.

Dick Dillman was a practicing veterinarian in south Florida for more than 25 years. He has won awards as volunteer of the year for numerous groups, including the Dade County Public Schools and the Florida Department of Education. He directed a W. K. Kellogg Foundation grant project and wrote its accompanying photo-essay, *First, Let Them Be Children.*

Patrick Dougherty is a state representative from the 67th district of Missouri, representing parts of St. Louis. He chairs the House Children, Youth and Families Committee and has sponsored several bills which have become law regarding animal care facilities and stalking. He was formerly a caseworker at the Department of

Family Services and has worked with the American Humane Association and the National Conference of State Legislatures.

Debbie Duel is a former humane educator for the Washington Humane Society and currently works part-time for the Humane Society of the United States on First Strike™, an anti-violence campaign designed to increase public awareness of the animal cruelty-human violence connection and to provide guidance to individuals and organizations striving to identify the origins of violence and prevent its escalation. She holds a master's degree in education.

Mitchell Fox is Director of Animal Advocacy for the Progressive Animal Welfare Society, an animal protection organization outside Seattle that combines programs in animal advocacy, wildlife rehabilitation, and companion animal sheltering. In his position at PAWS, he helped coordinate efforts to pass the felony animal cruelty bill in Washington State.

James Garbarino is Director of the Family Development Center and Professor of Human Development and Family Studies at Cornell University. His research focuses on the impact of family and community violence and trauma on child development and interventions to deal with these effects. He is the author of *Raising Children in a Socially Toxic Environment* and *Lost Boys: Why Our Sons Turn Violent and How We Can Save Them.*

Mother Hildegard George is a Benedictine nun with a doctorate in child and adolescent psychology. The emphasis of her work, which includes consulting and workshops, is the incorporation of animals into treatment. Her work has been published in various journals and newsletters, and she teaches courses on the human-animal bond at Washington State University. She also tends the flock of rare Cotswold sheep, llamas, and alpacas at Our Lady of the Rock.

Anne Grant has worked a teacher, writer, producer, and parish minister. She has spent the past decade focusing on battered women and their children, including eight years as Executive Director of an emergency shelter, hotline, and transitional service. She is Pastor of Trinity United Methodist Church in Providence, Rhode Island.

Robert P. Hall is Executive Director of the Delaware Ecumenical Council on Children and Families, an organization that involves the religious community in issues ranging from health care reform to the prevention of interpersonal violence. He has written educators' guides and curricula to prevent child abuse and sexual abuse and was named Humanitarian of the Year by the International Cat Association in 1990.

Star Jorgensen works with victims of crime and on public enlightenment on the issues of animal protection and care. She developed the animal abuse protocol for the Center for Prevention of Domestic Violence when she was an advocacy case manager there. She has also served as a victim advocate at the District Attorney's Office in Colorado Springs, Colorado. She holds a master's degree.

Michael E. Kaufmann is Coordinator of Education for the American Humane Association, where he supervises the development of training programs for animal care and control professionals. He was previously Director of Education for the ASPCA and has an extensive background in zoos, circuses, and interactive horse and nature programs for children. He chairs the Latham Foundation's Humane Education Advisory Council.

Charlotte A. Lacroix holds doctorates in veterinary medicine from the University of California at Davis and in law from the University of Pennsylvania Law School. She is a solo practitioner with Priority Veterinary Legal Consultants in Yardley, Pennsylvania, where she focuses on veterinary and animal law. She has written articles and chapters on animal abuse and is an active participant in the American Humane Association's Dog Training Task Force, a coalition that promotes humane dog training.

Laurel Lagoni is co-founder and former co-director of the Changes Program, an internationally known pioneer in the field of pet loss support, grief counseling, and grief advocacy in veterinary medicine, at the Colorado State University Veterinary Teaching Hospital. She is currently Managing Director of the Argus Center at Colorado State University. She holds a master's degree in human development and family studies and is co-author, with Carolyn Butler, of *The Human-Animal Bond and Grief.*

Ruth Landau is a third-year veterinary student at the Purdue University School of Veterinary Medicine. She holds a master's degree and received training as a family therapist at the Philadelphia Child Guidance Center. Her research was conducted under a grant from the Geraldine R. Dodge Foundation to explore the frontiers of veterinary medicine.

Lisa Lembke has 15 years of experience assisting law enforcement and human services agencies with the investigation and prosecution of animal and child abuse. She was the staff veterinarian for the Watertown Humane Society and Director of the Wisconsin Center for the Study of Animal Welfare. She formerly served as the State Humane Agent with the Wisconsin Department of Agriculture, Trade and Consumer Protection.

Lynn Loar holds a doctorate from Duke University and works as a licensed clinical social worker with the San Francisco Child Abuse Council. She co-founded the San Francisco Humane Coalition against Violence, an advocacy and training program devoted to increasing awareness about the roles animals play in human violence. She co-sponsored California Senate Bill 665, which concerns mandated reporting of child abuse.

Randall Lockwood is Director of Higher Education Programs at the Humane Society of the United States, where he also served as vice president of field services. He was formerly an assistant professor of psychology, and his articles have appeared in a wide variety of publications. He is co-editor, with Frank R. Ascione, of *Cruelty to Animals and Interpersonal Violence: Readings in Research and Application*. He holds a doctorate in psychology from Washington University.

Lisa Maloney is an advocacy program coordinator at the Center for Prevention of Domestic Violence in Colorado Springs, Colorado. She facilitates a psycho-educational group for victims, Domestic Violence Education, and serves as an expert witness in the court system. She works closely with the DVERT team as a victim advocate and responds to the scene as part of the DVERT team.

Scott McVay is the past Executive Director of the Geraldine R. Dodge Foundation. He has published 25 papers and articles and has focused his conservation efforts on the preservation of biological systems and the reduction of violence. He serves on the board of directors of several organizations, including the World Wildlife Fund, the W. Alton Jones Foundation, and Bat Conservation International.

Marsha Millikin is a master's degree candidate at the University of Texas at Tyler. She was the interim director and production editor of the Family Violence and Sexual Assault Institute in Tyler, Texas.

Michele Mitchell is Director of Community Relations for the Michigan Humane Society. She helped coordinate the 1995 and 1997 conferences on the link between animal abuse and interpersonal violence and is actively involved in developing community coalitions to address violence.

Helen M. C. Munro is a veterinary pathologist. She is an Honorary Fellow attached jointly to the Departments of Clinical Studies and Pathology at the Royal (Dick) School of Veterinary Studies at the University of Edinburgh. She is undertaking a research program on the clinical features and pathology of non-accidental injury in companion animals.

Hedy Nuriel is Executive Director of HAVEN, an organization that provides services to victims of domestic violence, sexual assault, and child abuse in Oakland County, Michigan. She previously was Executive Director of the Michigan Coalition Against Domestic Violence. She is co-author of *Families of Abuse: The Connection between Substance Abuse and Violence.*

Patricia Olson is Director of Training Operations for Guide Dogs for the Blind. She previously was Director of Veterinary Affairs and Studies for the American Humane Association. She was a founding member of the National Council on Pet Population Study and Policy and served as a congressional science fellow to Sen. John D. Rockefeller IV, where she authored legislation for research to investigate the causes of Gulf War illness.

Jane Ann Quinlisk is the Executive Director of the Domestic Violence Intervention Project and of the Cuan Foundation. She holds a master's degree in counseling and is a licensed independent clinical social worker. She has coordinated counseling services at a shelter for battered women and children and has served on many state and local committees involved with domestic violence.

Carol Rathmann is a registered veterinary technician and shelter manager for the Humane Society of Sonoma County. She is the founder and coordinator of Forget Me Not Farm and coordinates other community outreach programs. She offers training for agencies that are interested in developing similar programs and sits on the board of directors of the Sonoma County Child Abuse Prevention Council.

Robert Reisman is a clinician at the American Society for the Prevention of Cruelty to Animals' Bergh Memorial Hospital and a contributing editor to the ASPCA's magazine, *Animal Watch.* He graduated from the New York State College of Veterinary Medicine at Cornell University and spent seven years in private practice before joining the ASPCA in 1988.

Kelly B. Roseberry is co-founder and program director of Crossroads Group Homes. She works with severely emotionally disturbed adolescents, specializing in sexual victimization and perpetration and has implemented animal-assisted therapy in a residential setting. She is a certified criminal justice specialist and a certified instructor of crisis prevention intervention.

Samuel B. Ross, Jr. is the founder of Green Chimneys School and Green Chimneys Children's Services. He served as executive director from the program's inception in 1948 until 1996, when he assumed the position of managing director of the Friends of Green Chimneys.

Laurie Morstein Rovin is Clinical Director of Crossroads Group Homes. She holds a master's degree in deafness rehabilitation counseling from New York University and has worked with abused children and adults for 15 years. She uses animal-assisted therapy throughout her clinical interventions and lectures internationally on animal-assisted therapy programs in mental health practices.

Andrew N. Rowan is Senior Vice President of the Humane Society of the United States. He was formerly Director of the Center for Animals and Public Policy at the College of Veterinary Medicine at Tufts University, where he initiated the nation's only master's degree program in human-animal relationships.

Pearl Salotto teaches certificate programs in pet-assisted therapy, and her D. J. Respect for Living Things Program is listed in the Harvard School of Public Health's manual *Peace by Peace.* In 1995 she organized a statewide conference which led to the formation of the Windwalker Humane Coalition, a group that educates Rhode Islanders about the links among the abuse of animals, women, and children.

Sherry Schlueter is a detective sergeant with the Broward County Sheriff's Office in Ft. Lauderdale, Florida, where she heads the only police unit in the country focusing on the abuse of animals, children, disabled adults, and elders. She has authored successful local and state legislation and has founded several programs to benefit animals, including one that assists human victims of domestic violence who fear for their animals' safety.

James A. Serpell is the Marie A. Moore Professor of Humane Ethics and Animal Welfare at the School of Veterinary Medicine of the University of Pennsylvania. He was formerly Director of the Companion Animal Research Group at the University of Cambridge. He has published numerous scientific articles on dogs, cats, animal welfare, and human-animal interactions. He is the author of *In the Company of Animals* and *Research on Human-Animal Relationships: An Annotated Bibliography.*

Wm. Andrew Sharp has been District Attorney for Richland County, Wisconsin, since 1992. He has successfully prosecuted numerous animal abuse cases. He has served on the Wisconsin Department of Agriculture's Animal Welfare Committee and provides training to the department's field veterinarians concerning legal procedures. He is a graduate of the University of Wisconsin.

Melanie S. Sharpe is a third-year veterinary student at the Ohio State University College of Veterinary Medicine, where she is enrolled in the dual-degree program (D.V.M./Ph.D.) in veterinary epidemiology. She is interested in applying the principles of epidemiology to study animal abuse and overpopulation. Her research was conducted under a grant from the Geraldine R. Dodge Foundation to explore the frontiers of veterinary medicine.

Hugh H. Tebault, Sr., is President Emeritus of the Latham Foundation for the Promotion of Humane Education. He has been associated with the foundation since 1944 and was instrumental in the concept and development of this book.

Joyce Tischler is Executive Director of the Animal Legal Defense Fund, a national nonprofit organization of lawyers and law students dedicated to the protection of animals and the establishment of their legal rights. She co-founded the organization in 1979 and throughout the 1980s served as its chief litigator, representing such clients as feral burros, captive elephants, and genetically altered mice. She is a graduate of the University of San Diego School of Law.

Gary Tiscornia is the Executive Director of the Michigan Humane Society. He has been active in educating law enforcement agencies on animal fighting and the link between animal abuse and other forms of violence.

Sally Vallongo is Senior Writer at the *Toledo Blade,* where she has written about the arts and culture since 1980. She has a bachelor's degree in education and graduate training in community information. She is the co-author of *Parenting through the College Years* and writes about health, consciousness, and culture for national publications.

Annette W. works in the violence-prevention field but has requested that her name and address be kept confidential.

Index